The Young Child

Development from Prebirth Through Age Eight

SIXTH EDITION

Donna S. Wittmer
University of Colorado Denver, Emerita

Sandra H. Petersen
Early Head Start National Resource Center

Margaret B. Puckett
Texas Wesleyan University, Emerita

PEARSON

Boston   Columbus   Indianapolis   New York   San Francisco   Upper Saddle River
Amsterdam   Cape Town   Dubai   London   Madrid   Milan   Munich   Paris   Montréal   Toronto
Delhi   Mexico City   São Paulo   Sydney   Hong Kong   Seoul   Singapore   Taipei   Tokyo

W9-BLP-581

Vice President and Editorial Director: Jeffery W. Johnston
Vice President and Publisher: Kevin Davis
Editorial Assistant: Lauren Carlson
Vice President, Director of Marketing: Margaret Waples
Marketing Manager: Joanna Sabella
Senior Managing Editor: Pamela D. Bennett
Senior Project Manager: Mary M. Irvin
Senior Operations Supervisor: Matt Ottenweller

Senior Art Director: Diane Lorenzo
Cover Designer: Diane Lorenzo
Cover Art: © Mark Evans/iStockphoto
Project Coordination and Composition: Integra
Printer/Binder: Edwards Brothers Malloy
Cover Printer: Lehigh-Phoenix Color/Hagerstown
Text Font: 10.5/12.5 Times LT Std

Credits and acknowledgments for materials borrowed from other sources and reproduced, with permission, in this textbook appear on the appropriate page within the text.

Every effort has been made to provide accurate and current Internet information in this book. However, the Internet and information posted on it are constantly changing, so it is inevitable that some of the Internet addresses listed in this textbook will change.

Photo Credits: Natalia Olejarnik, pp. 2, 24, 34, 50, 144, 201, 216, 222, 241, 282, 314, 340, 374, 393; Dawn Brackpool, pp. 6, 183; Donna Wittmer, pp. 9, 124, 162, 258, 343; © Diego Cervo/Fotolia, p. 42; Blend Images/Shutterstock.com, p. 48; © Monart Design/Fotolia, pp. 62, 298; © Alexander Raths/Fotolia, p. 68; Laurence Dutton/Stone/Getty Images, p. 69; © Kim Ruoff/Fotolia, p. 77; Golden Pixels/SuperFusion/SuperStock, p. 98; © Vojtech Vik/Fotolia, p. 102; John Clauson, p. 110; © Kablonk Micro/Fotolia, p. 120; Tony Wear/Shutterstock.com, p. 135; Iofoto/Shutterstock.com, p. 136; Nyul/Fotolia, p. 137; © AVAVA/Fotolia, p. 148; © Joanna Zielinska/Fotolia, pp. 156, 276; © Nadezda Postolit/Fotolia, p. 171; © St-fotograf/Fotolia, p. 176; © Niderlander/Shutterstock.com, p. 180; © Iofoto/Fotolia, p. 184; © Joanna/Fotolia, p. 196; Privilege/Shutterstock.com, p. 199; Vanessa Davies/Dorling Kindersley, p. 207; Deanna Wittmer, p. 212; © Deber73/Fotolia, p. 231; © JG Photography/Alamy, p. 233; © Tomas Sereda/Fotolia, p. 236; © Jeff Greenberg/Alamy, p. 248; CROX/Shutterstock.com, p. 251; © Luana Rigolli/Fotolia, p. 266; © Darya Prokapalo/Fotolia, p. 267; © Igor Yaruta/Fotolia, p. 277; © Thomas Perkins/Fotolia, p. 279; Anatoliy Samara/Shutterstock.com, p. 285; Hanna Derecka/Fotolia, p. 291; © Yanlev/Fotolia, p. 297; © Hallgerd/Fotolia, pp. 303, 408; © Raywoo/Fotolia, p. 317; © Mitgirl/Fotolia, p. 318; Elaine Clauson, pp. 320 (top), 404; Nina Vaclavova/Shutterstock.com, p. 320 (bottom); © Knopsik/Fotolia, p. 330; © Matka_Wariatka/Fotolia, p. 344; © Melanie DeFazio/Fotolia, p. 347; © Harry HU/Fotolia, p. 350; © Jaimie Duplass/Fotolia, p. 355; © Janine Wiedel Photolibrary/Alamy, p. 363; © Jane September/Fotolia, p. 370; © Saksoni/Fotolia, p. 377; © Lurii Sokolov/Fotolia, p. 382; © Fancy/Alamy, p. 387; Emese/Shutterstock.com, p. 409; Shane Trotter/Shutterstock.com, p. 415; © Jim West/Alamy, p. 417; © Monkey Business/Fotolia, p. 421; © Pressmaster/Fotolia, p. 429; © Christian Schwier/Fotolia, p. 432; © Prod. Numérik/Fotolia, p. 441; Golden Pixels LLC/Shutterstock.com, p. 445; © Forestpath/Fotolia, p. 448; © Tom Wang/Fotolia, p. 462; © Image100/Alamy, p. 468; © Eléonore H/Fotolia, p. 471; © Micromonkey/Fotolia, p. 476.

Library of Congress Cataloging-in-Publication Data
Wittmer, Donna Sasse.
    The young child: development from prebirth through age eight / Donna S. Wittmer, Sandra H. Petersen, Margaret B. Puckett.—6th ed.
      p. cm.
    Includes bibliographical references and index.
    ISBN 978-0-13-294401-4
  1. Child development.   2. Infants—Development.   3. Child psychology.   I. Petersen, Sandra H.   II. Puckett, Margaret B.   III. Title.
    HQ767.9.B56 2013
    649'.1—dc23

2012022311

10 9 8 7 6 5 4 3 2

ISBN 10:   0-13-294401-4
ISBN 13: 978-0-13-294401-4

To Our Children and Their Children
and
To Their Teachers

Preface

Welcome to the sixth edition of *The Young Child: Development from Prebirth Through Age Eight*. This text is written to provide you, the student of child development, with the most current information concerning the resiliency and vulnerabilities of young children and the importance of the prenatal through age 8 years. This tool is a knowledge base of current theory and research in the field of early growth, development, and learning and its translation into practice in the daily lives of very young children. Indeed, optimal child development depends on families, caregivers, and educators who provide for and interact with children from a knowledgable and growth-promoting perspective.

You may find it fascinating that today's scholars have views of how best to support human growth and development that differ from those of many scholars of the past. You may even experience challenges to your long-held assumptions and views on childhood and perhaps your childhood experiences. You may also find comfort in learning about the "tried and true," theories and research studies now considered classic, that continue to guide and support the study of child development and inspire continued research. As you study and follow growth and development from prenatal development through the early school-age years, you will be introduced to contemporary insights on such topics as the following:

- The effect and long-term consequences of early biological and psychological experiences on brain growth and neurological development
- The importance of, and potential impediments to, optimal prenatal development
- Increasing scholarly interest in the mental health of infants and young children
- Cultural diversity and the positive potential of varying developmental pathways
- How growth and development of children with challenges are supported
- Contemporary health, safety, and well-being issues of children and families
- How children learn and become literate
- The evolution of childhood social and moral competence
- The changing American family and the ecological systems surrounding and influencing families and children
- The changing dynamics and structures in child care and early education and their effect on childhood and individual child well-being

New to This Edition

There are many new and innovative features in the sixth edition of this text:

- Time-honored theories such as Skinner's Behaviorist Theory, Piaget's Constructivist Theory, Maslow's and Roger's Humanistic Theory, and Freud and Erikson's Psychosocial Theories are discussed and applied to current knowledge about how children develop and learn. Contemporary theories, such as Cognitive (Core Systems and Neoconstructivist) and Contextual (Dynamic Systems and Relationship-Based) theories are added to this edition to further aid understanding of the early childhood years, birth through age 8. Furthermore, Vygotsky's Sociocultural and

Bronfenbrenner's Bioecological theories, and the supporting research based on these theories, are applied to early childhood education practices in the classroom and with families.

- More information on *brain* and *neurological development* as well as the implications of research on these topics to educational and policy practices is included. New insights into brain development emphasize the importance of the early childhood years and early childhood education for young children's optimal language, cognitive, motor, social, and emotional learning. The detrimental effects of stress on young children's physical and mental health as well as the structure of the brain are emphasized.

- Culture sections have been added to many chapters to reflect current research and thinking about how children from different ethnic and culture groups develop and learn within cultural norms and context. Readers will consider how their practices contribute to or inhibit the growth and development of children from families and communities with a variety of cultural beliefs.

- In the sixth edition, information has been updated for all topics, and new references, additional readings, and resources have been added. The latest research on topics such as prenatal development; family structure; cognitive, language, literacy, social-emotional, and motor development; growth and physical development; and health and safety are highlighted to enable readers to consider how current research methods and knowledge impact our understanding of how young children learn and also how they impact our interactions with children and families.

- New features include text boxes on milestones in development in all domains, and the role of the early childhood educator. This information supports the reader's ability to apply the latest thinking about young children's learning and development to optimal practices in early childhood education.

- *MyEducationLab™* provides both instructors and students with video clips, application exercises, and multiple choice/true false questions. A detailed *Instructor's Manual* supplies instructors with a multitude of resources and ideas for facilitating active student learning. Instructors can use a bank of multiple choice, true/false, and essay questions for student exams or knowledge checks during class time.

Organization of the Text

This text is divided into six parts. Part One, *An Overview of Early Childhood Development*, outlines historical viewpoints and the evolution of the study of early childhood. It presents both classic and contemporary theories of early childhood development and emphasizes the importance of this information to our understanding of growth, development, and learning and to the practices of parents and early childhood education professionals. Through this discussion, the reader is introduced to contemporary issues associated with childhood and family life today and emerging research areas in the early childhood care and education profession.

Part Two, *The Child's Life Begins*, discusses the family before birth, with attention to educational, sociocultural, and economic considerations in the decision to parent.

It describes prenatal development with an emphasis on health, nutrition, and medical supervision of pregnancy. Childbirth and family dynamics surrounding the newborn are also examined.

Parts Three through Six trace perceptual, motor, physical, emotional and social, and cognitive, language, and literacy development during the following stages: infancy, ages 1 through 3, ages 4 through 5, and ages 6 through 8. This organization facilitates either chronological or topical discussion and study.

The chapters include charts and boxed material to amplify concepts and to give prominence to specific issues. Margin notes are provided to define new or unfamiliar terms. At the end of each chapter are Review Strategies and Activities, which include relevant, hands-on suggestions, field experiences, and reflective exercises. In addition, Further Readings are suggested along with relevant Web sites and other print or electronic resources. A full Glossary is included at the end of the text along with a helpful Appendix.

Angela and Jeremy

Two young children, Angela and Jeremy, are introduced in Chapter 2, and subsequent chapters follow their development and relationships. These vignettes illustrate the uniqueness of children's experiences and their growth and developmental pathways. Angela and Jeremy are composites of many children the authors have known. We caution the reader to avoid viewing these children in a stereotypical or prejudicial manner. Although both children and their families experience adversity to varying degrees, the vignettes attempt to illustrate the power of resiliency and potential for learning and development in all individuals and in all types of family contexts.

Instructor Supplements

The following supplements are available:

- *Online Instructor's Manual and Test Bank*, which is available to instructors on www.pearsonhighered.com, contains chapter summaries and objectives, suggested class activities, additional resources, and a test bank for every chapter.

- *TestGen*, also available to instructors on www.pearsonhighered.com, is a computerized replication of the online test bank that allows instructors to create and customize exams.

New! CourseSmart® eTextbook Available

CourseSmart® is an exciting new choice for students looking to save money. As an alternative to purchasing the printed textbook, students can purchase an electronic version of the same content. With a CourseSmart® eTextbook, students can search the text, make notes online, print out reading assignments that incorporate lecture notes, and bookmark important passages for later review. For more information, or to purchase access to the CourseSmart® eTextbook, visit www.coursesmart.com.

Acknowledgments

As with previous editions of this text, we are especially grateful to our many colleagues in universities, teacher training programs, and advocacy groups whose research and writing provide inspiration and content suggestions. To our many friends and colleagues around the country whose support and interest have always exemplified the caring of the early childhood professional, we say a hearty thank you.

We also thank the reviewers of the sixth edition: Brigid Beaubien, Eastern Michigan University; Maria Victoria Calderon, University at Buffalo, State University of New York; Sharon Engh, Western Technical College; and Pamela Giberti, University of Oklahoma.

To our colleagues at Pearson—Kevin Davis, Mary Irvin, and Lauren Carlson—whose expertise in preparing a manuscript for publication is without equal, and whose skill and patience deftly guided this sixth edition of *The Young Child* to its final form, we extend genuine appreciation.

And, to our families, who tolerated our long and tedious hours of book and online time, we extend profound appreciation. It is hard to imagine pursuing this type of task without the support and encouragement of family and friends.

Donna S. Wittmer, Ph.D.
Sandra H. Petersen, M.A.
Margaret B. Puckett, Ed.D.

Brief Contents

Contents

Contents

PART THREE   INFANCY

chapter 9   Emotional and Social Development: Ages
One Through Three   258

chapter 10   Cognitive, Language, and Literacy Development:
Ages One Through Three   282

chapter 1

The What and Why of Early Childhood Development

There are two lasting bequests we can hope to give our children—one is roots; the other is wings.

—Hodding Carter

After studying this chapter, you will demonstrate comprehension by:

▶ describing how the study of child growth and development gives families and practitioners necessary information

- ▶ reflecting on personal goals as a developing early childhood professional;
- ▶ defining early childhood development;
- ▶ describing the importance of understanding early childhood development;
- ▶ outlining historical perspectives on childhood;
- ▶ describing the evolution of the study of early childhood development;
- ▶ identifying current theories and research emphases in the study of early childhood development; and
- ▶ listing emerging issues in the field of early childhood development.

Have you ever found yourself wondering about the types of childhood experiences people have had—the famous, the infamous, the notorious, the obscure? Do you find yourself observing children in various contexts and marveling at their robust energy, outgoing personalities, or unbridled curiosity?...or contemplating their reticence, timidity, or apparent discomfort, maybe sadness? Are people just born the way they are? Do children come into the world with personalities and behaviors over which they or those around them will have little influence?

When childhood segues into adulthood, what could—should—might—growth, development, and learning outcomes be? These are important reflections for the student of child growth and development and for parents and early childhood educators, who play important roles in the lives of children. We all benefit from knowledge of child growth and development. Such knowledge enhances self-understanding and acceptance, informs relationships with others, lays the most important foundation for parenting, and establishes informed rationale for the types of child care and education policies and programs provided for children and their families. Importantly, **professionals** who work with children and families have an ethical responsibility to make the study of child growth and development a career-long pursuit.

Child Study in Contemporary Contexts

The study of child growth and development throughout history has provided both stable and evolving perspectives on the biological characteristics of human beings, the origins of human behavior, and the outcomes of human experience. However, few eras have demanded a greater need for knowledge about child growth and development than the current one. Read a newspaper or magazine, notice the contents of "infotainment" programs on television, surf the Internet, and scan the tables of contents of a variety of professional journals, and you will soon notice an array of reports about the status, concerns, and accomplishments of contemporary families and the needs of children. Each day you may read exciting new information about scientists who are making discoveries about young children's remarkable capacities for learning and yet also read about the increases in children who have learning challenges, such as autism and Attention Deficit Hyperactivity Disorder (ADHD). Accurate knowledge about how children grow and develop, how they learn, and the long-term consequences of early experiences is as critical to a healthy society as it has ever been. Who needs knowledge about child growth and development, and what should they do with that information? Think about the following questions:

1. As young adults become parents, frequently without the benefit of extended family support systems, what do they need to know to ensure the best possible outcomes for their children?

professionals individuals who have internalized the evolving knowledge base of their particular fields and use this knowledge to improve practices that affect the lives of children and families

2. With greater numbers of children at younger ages attending child care, what concerns should we have about childhood health, safety, personality development, and early learning? What are the benefits of child care and education programs for young children?

3. What changes must public schools make to meet the unique needs of their youngest students?...of young children with special needs?...of young children of different cultures and who speak multiple languages?

4. What are the effects and long-term consequences of violence and other asocial events experienced either firsthand or vicariously through toys, movies, television, video and computer games, and the Internet?

5. How can early childhood professionals help children and families meet the challenges posed by stress, violence, and threats of terrorism?

6. Politicians who have made child care, education, and welfare issues part of their platforms exert considerable power over the types of home and out-of-home experiences that children have. How can early childhood professionals help families access quality resources to enhance life for themselves and their children? How can early childhood professionals protect infants and young children from policies that may be harmful?

7. Various interest groups frequently exert influence on policy makers, educators, directors of child care programs, and other professionals to enforce schooling, child care, and family life agendas that may not be appropriately generalized to all children and families. How will these decision makers know how to respond to requests that do not serve the best interests of all children? In short, how might individual families make distinctions between what is best for their children and what is clearly not in their children's best growth and development interests or the best interests of their families? Many children in the United States and the world are thriving; however, there is still work to be done to improve the lives of all children. In the United States, for example, the Children's Defense Fund organization (2011) reports that each day 949 babies are born at low birth weight, 2,573 babies are born into poverty, 2,058 children are confirmed as abused or neglected, and 2,163 babies are born without health insurance. As demonstrated by these figures, policies, laws, and systems can make a difference in the lives of young children.

Yes, knowledge of child growth and development is important in numerous aspects of our lives and in many sectors of society, for every minute of every day, children are affected by whether parents, educators, policy makers, the media, and all who interact with them can make sound judgments based on their best understanding about how children grow and develop. How do we determine what serves their best long-term developmental interests? Again, as in no time before, all of us must become students of child development.

Information abounds. Some of it is reliable, some is not. Hence, scholars and practitioners in the field of early childhood development take a discerning look at both classic and emerging research within the field and from a number of allied disciplines. The study of early childhood development draws knowledge from research and practice in many fields: the biological and neurological sciences, medicine, psychology, sociology, anthropology, education, and political science. Thus, the study of child growth and development is an interdisciplinary one, as is illustrated in Figure 1.1.

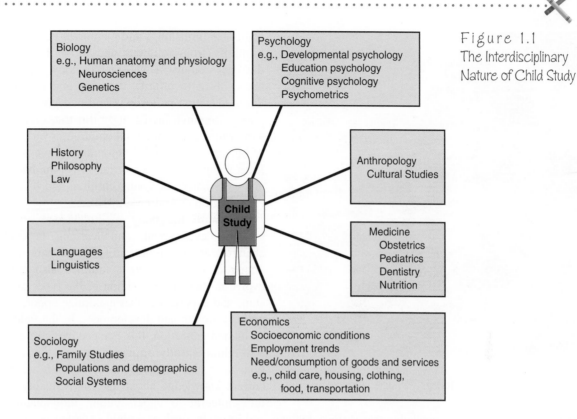

Figure 1.1
The Interdisciplinary
Nature of Child Study

Research from many disciplines is bringing about new perspectives on growth and development and the human experience. As you read this text, you will see that childhood is quite different today from what you experienced. Contemporary researchers are interested in learning more about not just the sequences and patterns of growth, development, and learning, but also how various and numerous influences in many different contexts (home, school, neighborhood, social networks, and other contexts) affect individual developmental pathways and outcomes. Our knowledge base is expanding rapidly and altering many long-held assumptions about children, for example, that they are resilient, when in fact they are both resilient and vulnerable (Shonkoff & Phillips, 2000). It isn't always true that what worked in the past (even the recent past) is appropriate or best for today's child. Hence, the study of child growth and development gives families and practitioners necessary information to make wise decisions about what children need and how to relate to them.

The Early Childhood Development Profession

Professionals learn the knowledge base of their particular field. This knowledge base, coupled with practice in the field, facilitates the development of competent practitioners. Becoming a competent early childhood professional begins with learning about growth and development of young children. Professionalism entails continuously learning about young children and their families throughout one's career.

The study of children had its beginnings in the late 1700s during a period when children as young as 3 years of age could be found working in factories and formal schooling was reserved for well-to-do boys, who were expected to sit quietly in

"We worry about what a child will become tomorrow, yet we forget that he is someone today." —Stacia Tauscher

developmentally appropriate

pertains to (1) age appropriateness, the universal and predictable patterns of growth and development that occur in children from birth through age 8, and (2) individual appropriateness, the individual rates and patterns of physical/motor, social, emotional, cognitive, language and literacy development, personality and learning style, and family and cultural background of each child

adult-size furnishings and memorize curricula derived primarily from religious and moral beliefs. Within the past century, a substantial body of knowledge has evolved to inform parenting and teaching practices, education philosophy and pedagogy, and public policy. Research increasingly illustrates that although similarities exist among all children in various aspects of human growth and development, there is a need to learn about and respect variations in the backgrounds and experiences of young children and their families (Washington & Andrews, 2010).

Because the body of knowledge about child growth, development, and learning is continually changing and enlarging, professionals who work with young children and their families also continually evolve in their understanding of the types of relationships and experiences that maximize opportunities for optimal growth and development. In the field of early childhood education, this perspective is referred to as a **developmentally appropriate** one; that is, interactions with and expectations of children are based on current knowledge about age, individuality, and culture. Integral to understanding individuality is the knowledge that various contexts and interrelationships a child experiences as he or she grows, develops, and learns are often particular to the child's cultural heritage and milieu (Copple & Bredekamp, 2009).

Today, most of the 50 states require teachers of young children to have specialized training in early childhood development and related areas. Saracho and Spodek (2007), in an analysis of 40 research studies on how teacher preparation affects the quality of Early Childhood Education and Development (ECED) programs, found that teacher education is a significant influence on both the quality of ECED programs and children's developmental outcomes.

The National Association for the Education of Young Children (NAEYC, www.naeyc.org) has a strong history of creating standards for professional development. In 1982, NAEYC developed standards for training professionals who work with young children. In 1992 NAEYC's National Institute for Early Childhood Professional Development launched a nationwide review process seeking professional input. From this effort, a national professional consensus was established, and the 1982 guidelines were revised and published in 1996 as the *NAEYC Guidelines for Preparation of Early Childhood Professionals* (National Association for the Education of Young Children, 1996). These standards were revised again in 2009 for associate, initial licensure (baccalaureate and five-year), and advanced (master's or doctoral) programs. (See Box 1.1 for a list of the six core standards.) Box 1.2 provides an example of the key elements of standard 1 that specifically address knowledge of child development and learning. To become accredited by NAEYC, training programs at universities and colleges are required to demonstrate that future Early Childhood Education and Development (ECED) teachers have developed the knowledge, skills, and dispositions defined in the standards during their educational experience.

Box 1.1   Six Core Standards

Standard 1:   Promoting Child Development and Learning

Standard 2:   Building Family and Community Relationships

Standard 3:   Observing, Documenting, and Assessing to Support Young Children and Families

Standard 4:   Using Developmentally Effective Approaches to Connect with Children and Families

Standard 5:   Using Content Knowledge to Build Meaningful Curriculum

Standard 6:   Becoming a Professional

Excerpt from the National Association for the Education of Young Children (2011) Web site: www.naeyc.org

These efforts to define standards for professional development reflect two important federal laws: the Individuals with Disabilities Education Act, passed in 1991 and revised in 2004 (idea.ed.gov), and the Americans with Disabilities Act, passed in 1992 (www.ada.gov). These laws mandate that individuals with disabilities are entitled to equal rights in (1) public accommodations such as child care centers, family child care homes, preschools, and public schools; (2) state and local services; and (3) employment. Specifically, all early childhood programs must provide services to young children with developmental delays or disabilities and to those who are at risk for developmental delays.

Implicit in these laws is the concept of **inclusion.** Inclusion refers to procedures and curricular means for ensuring that all children are fully accepted members of the ECDE programs and communities in which they participate. The practice of inclusion benefits all children and families. Inclusion helps children to appreciate and accept individual differences while developing caring attitudes and a recognition of our human interdependence. The Division for Early Childhood (DEC) of the Council for Exceptional Children

inclusion
the education model that includes children with developmental challenges in general education settings

Box 1.2   Key Elements of Standard 1

Tomorrow's teachers should know and be able to promote child development and learning, which includes:

- knowing and understanding young children's characteristics and needs, from birth through age 8;

- knowing and understanding the multiple influences on development and learning; and

- using developmental knowledge to create healthy, respectful, supportive, and challenging learning environments.

Excerpt from National Association for the Education of Young Children Web site: www.naeyc.org

(CEC) also created standards for the personnel development of Early Childhood Special Education/Early Intervention (ECSE/EI) (birth to age 8) professionals. Colleges and universities that educate teacher candidates in ECSE/EI strive to demonstrate that their teacher candidates acquire the knowledge and skills to become accredited by CEC; for example, they use strategies to facilitate integration into various settings and plan, implement, and evaluate developmentally appropriate curriculum, instruction, and adaptations. See www.dec-sped.org for a detailed list of the 10 core standards.

The ever-changing perspectives on human growth and development and, most recently, the growing emphasis on the genesis of many anomalies that can be traced to early brain and neurological growth and development and the types of pre- and postnatal experiences that promote or impede optimal development in children have quickened the profession's desire for knowledgeable and well-prepared early childhood care and education personnel. Contemporary studies offer hope for continuing revelations, preventive measures, and potential treatments for children with special needs.

Another effort to provide training and credentialing for those who work with young children is the Child Development Associate (CDA) National Credentialing Program (www.cdacouncil.org). This program was initiated in 1971 for the purpose of enhancing "the quality of child care by defining, evaluating and recognizing the competence of child care providers and home visitors" (Council for Early Childhood Professional Recognition, 2008, p. 1). A person who is awarded a CDA credential has demonstrated competency in working with young children and their families by successfully completing the CDA training and assessment process in one of four areas: (1) preschool, (2) infant/toddler, (3) family child care, or (4) home visitor. Child care providers often use the CDA credential to advance in their careers.

There are also increased educational requirements in Head Start (HS) and Early Head Start (EHS) programs. HS and EHS are federally funded programs designed to provide early childhood education along with comprehensive services (developmental health and well-being screening, monitoring, and intervention; psychological services; and others), family involvement, and support for children living in poverty. In recognition of the importance of professional development and education, Congress mandated, in the Head Start Act of 2007, that "by September 30, 2010, all EHS teachers must have, at a minimum, a CDA credential, and have been trained (or have equivalent coursework) in early childhood development" and "by September 30, 2012, all EHS teachers must be trained (or have equivalent coursework) in early childhood development with a focus on infant and toddler development" (Early Head Start, 2010). There definitely has been an increased recognition and demand for professionally educated teachers in child care and education programs.

The recognition of the importance of training for those who work with young children also arises from the results of longitudinal studies on early childhood programs for both **at-risk** and **low-risk** children that traced long-term outcomes for school performance and life adjustments (Camilli, Vargas, Ryan, & Barnett, 2010; Chambers, Cheung, Slavin, Smith, & Laurenzano, 2010; High/Scope, 2007; Schweinhart et al., 2005). Emphasis on the professional development of early childhood educators also emerged from studies that revealed the effects of various types of parenting practices and early care and education programs on children's physical/motor development; social and emotional development; and cognitive, language, and literacy outcomes (Booth-LaForce & Oxford, 2008; Lubell, Lofton, & Singer, 2008; NICHD Early Child Care Research Network, 2009).

at-risk
infants and children who are subject to any of a number of risk factors (such as poverty, drug exposure, genetic and/or developmental anomalies, and family dynamics) that make them vulnerable to compromised growth and development

low-risk
infants and children whose risk factors are minimal or absent

Hence, it is appropriate that professional development guidelines emphasize that early childhood and elementary education personnel:

- have knowledge of and respect for wide variations in children and the uniqueness of each;
- understand the importance of full inclusion of children with special needs and developmental challenges;
- relate appropriately to individuals and their families;
- provide developmentally appropriate experiences and set challenging yet achievable goals for individual children;
- apply sound and ethical principles in screening, diagnosis, and ongoing assessments of all children; and
- learn about and access appropriate resources to facilitate and enhance the developmental outcomes for each child (NAEYC, 2011).

Increasing emphasis on the importance of the early years in growth and development and a concurrent trend of mounting need for nonparental child care for infants, toddlers, preschool-age children, and before- and after-school care for school-age children have evoked concerns and prompted studies of the quality, accessibility, and affordability of child care (Helburn & Bergmann, 2002; National Institute of Child Health and Human Development, 2010; Stebbins & Langford, 2006). As evidence of this growing recognition of the impor-

developmentally inappropriate expectations or practices that fail to acknowledge age and individual characteristics and needs

tance of the early years, professionals in different states in the United States have developed early learning guidelines that describe the learning outcomes for children who live in that state. In addition, program accreditation guidelines that define quality in ECED and family child care homes have also been created. These guidelines are discussed in later chapters.

Unfortunately, at times, young children are in settings that are **developmentally inappropriate** because the adults who are working with them are unaware of information about how children grow, develop, and learn or of the nuances of developmental, socioeconomic, and cultural diversity. Often concurrent with this lack of knowledge is the failure to recognize the effects that one's own interactions with and expectations of children can have on behaviors and development.

The growing recognition of the unique nature of early growth, development, and learning and of the importance of the early years for lifelong well-being and productivity has created a demand for professionally trained and knowledgeable early childhood educators. The goal of this text is to provide students with the background information needed to develop into competent early childhood professionals. Such competency requires the perspective that learning about young children and their families is an ongoing, career-long process.

The student of child development is both a scholar and a practitioner who gains knowledge and skills from professional literature and observation and interactions with children.

The What and Why of Early Childhood Development

Definition of Early Childhood Development

The study of early childhood development is about how children from prebirth through age 8 grow and develop in the physical/motor, social, emotional, cognitive, language, and literacy domains. For convenience, this text discusses the various domains separately. Nevertheless, it should be noted that all development is interrelated, interactive, and mutually dependent; development in one domain influences or is dependent on development or behavior in another domain. For example, children's sense of trust (emotional development) influences the extent to which they will explore their surroundings for new information (cognitive development), and hearing acuity (physical development) influences the development of speech and language (cognitive, language, and literacy development). The uniqueness of the individual child is emphasized throughout this text, as are the many forms of diversity, including developmental, cultural, gender, and socioeconomic diversity, and the interdependence and interplay among various contexts in which children live, play, and are educated.

The Importance of Understanding Early Childhood Development

It is important to know about early childhood development for several reasons. First, knowledge of early childhood development helps parents and professionals to facilitate optimal growth and learning in young children. Second, a knowledge of growth and development in the early years can facilitate self-understanding. Knowledgeable parents and educators relate and interact appropriately with children and conscientiously provide the **essential experiences** that are now associated with earliest brain growth and neurological development and are linked to optimal long-term developmental and behavioral outcomes (Cozolino, 2006; Schiller, 2010; Shonkoff & Phillips, 2000; Thompson, 2008). Early childhood educators who understand child development are better prepared to interface individual developmental characteristics with appropriately challenging expectations and education practices and to provide the emotional support and social interactions that lead to optimal development.

essential experiences experiences deemed critical at certain times during early growth and development, which have growth-inducing influence on the brain's neurological structures

Evolution of Child Study

John Locke (1632–1704) was one of the earliest scholars or philosophers to advocate humane treatment of young children. He also was one of the first to suggest that the child's environmental experience may influence the development of the child's knowledge. Locke described the newborn's mind as a *tabula rasa,* an "empty slate," on which knowledge is written that is based on the child's sensory experiences in his or her environment.

Jean Jacques Rousseau (1712–1778) was instrumental in dispelling the prevalent view of his era that children were simply miniature adults. He believed that children are born innately good and that growth and development follow the laws of nature. He suggested that there are distinct stages in growth and development: birth to age 5, age 5 to 12, age 12 to 15, age 15 to 20, and age 20 and older. He believed that development unfolds according to this set schedule. He published his beliefs about child development and education in his book *Émile* (1762), a story of a fictional child who was reared with special motherly care complemented by a tutor. Rousseau stressed that education must begin at birth.

In 1774, Johann Pestalozzi (1746–1827) published a study of his son that also gave serious attention to the nature of development during the early years of growth and development. He emphasized that children's development physically, mentally, and morally depends on experience, which must include sensory stimulation.

Nearly a century later, Charles Darwin (1809–1882) published a day-to-day record of the development of his young son. Furthermore, Darwin's publication of *On the Origin of Species* (1859) had far-reaching effects on many aspects of scientific knowledge, including the study of children. As a biologist, Darwin took a trip to the Galapagos Islands in the South Pacific, where he collected birds and other animals that were virtually unknown and, therefore, had not been classified according to any designated species. Darwin used these birds and animals to disprove the idea of a fixed nature of species. His conceptualization that the world is dynamic, not static, set the stage for the scientific study of children.

Darwin's theory that animals adapt to their particular environments over time led biologists, psychologists, and others to begin studying the adaptive characteristics of humans. One of these psychologists, G. Stanley Hall (1846–1924), was instrumental in implementing the scientific method to study change and development in children. In 1893, Hall published *The Contents of Children's Minds*. This book was one of the first texts to be used in universities for training students who wanted to learn about young children. Another of Hall's important contributions to the study of child development was the establishment of the first child development research journal, the *Journal of Genetic Psychology*. Some of Hall's more illustrious students included Arnold Gesell, who later developed **norms** regarding the physical maturation of children; John Dewey, whose democratic ideas about the learning process created major educational reform; and Lewis Terman, who developed the idea of the intelligence quotient (IQ).

norms
the average ages of the emergence of certain behaviors or average scores on tests that are based on large representative samples of a population

After World War I, Lawrence K. Frank (1890–1968) was influential in obtaining foundation monies to establish various institutes to study child development. The Society for Research in Child Development was founded in 1933. During World War II, child development research and study declined. However, the conclusion of World War II brought a substantial increase in the number of investigations into the nature of children. This intense interest in learning about young children continues today on many fronts, as is illustrated in Figure 1.1.

The Nature of a Theory

Every theory presented as a scientific concept is just that; it's a theory that tries to explain more about the world than previous theories have done. It is open to being challenged and to being proven incorrect. (Marvin Harris)

Scholars have proposed ideas or **theories** that attempt to explain in an organized or systematic manner how young children develop and learn. The backgrounds of these theorists, as well as political and sociological events, often influence the development of ideas and the nature of research. At times, radical thinkers propose such new ideas that they change previously accepted theories. Thus, as knowledge evolves, a theory may change. If research and practice continue to support a theory, it will continue to be instructive, but if new information does not support it, the theory will be modified or discounted.

theories
bodies of principles used to interpret a set of circumstances or facts

Theories of Early Childhood Development and Learning

As can be seen in Table 1.1 a number of theories attempt to explain early childhood development and learning. Theories such as Freud's psychoanalytic, Erikson's psychosocial, Maslow's and Roger's Humanistic, Gesell's maturational, Piaget's cognitive, and

Table 1.1 Master Table of Theorists and Theories Discussed in This Text

Specific Theory	Primary Theory and Theorists	Primary Focus	Educational Focus
Psychoanalytic & Psychosocial			
Psychoanalytic	Sigmund Freud (1856–1939)	Early emotional and social experiences influence the quality of each stage of development and children's later lives.	Emphasize the importance of healthy parent-child interactions and relationships. Understand the unconscious motivations that drive behavior.
Psychosocial	Erik Erikson (1902–1994)	Stages of social and emotional development and the effects of early relationships are emphasized.	Meet children's psychological needs for trust, autonomy, and independence.
Maturational			
	Arnold Gesell (1880–1961)	All areas of development are important with an emphasis on physical growth and abilities. A child learns at his or her own pace.	Allow children to mature. Observe and provide an environment with many learning opportunities.
Behaviorism and Learning			
	Ivan Pavlov (1849–1936) John B. Watson (1878–1958) B. F. Skinner (1904–1990)	Behavior is influenced by external rewards and punishments.	Create objectives for child learning. Reward and punish children to ensure desired behavior. Use behavior modification strategies for behavior problems.
Humanistic			
Humanistic	Carl Rogers (1902–1987)	People are innately good. The self exists in a constantly changing world of experience, and the child knows the most about his or her own experience.	Have compassion and respect for the child's needs, abilities, interests, and learning styles. Promote children's self-efficacy, self-actualization and self-direction.
Hierarchy of Needs	Abraham Maslow (1908–1970)	Human beings have basic needs that are graduated to self-actualization. Needs must be met in order for child to achieve self-actualization.	Meet young children's needs for safety and belonging during the early years.

chapter 1

Table 1.1 continued

Specific Theory	Primary Theory and Theorists	Primary Focus	Educational Focus
Cognitive Developmental/Constructivist			
	Jean Piaget (1896–1980)	There is a focus on the invariance of cognitive stages of development and how each stage is qualitatively different from other stages. Children learn through assimilation, accommodation, and equilibration.	Observe children's stages of development and interact accordingly. Encourage children to explore the environment and discover and construct knowledge through activity and mental operations.
	Jerome Bruner (1915)	There is a focus on discovery learning and how culture shapes the mind.	Scaffold children's learning to build on previous knowledge. Promote discovery learning. Understand that learning is always within a cultural context
Cognitive			
Social Cognitive Theory	Albert Bandura (1925)	Individuals are self-organizing and reflective. They can self-regulate their thoughts and actions. Self-efficacy is important.	Children learn by observing and imitating others. Modeling for children is crucial. Promote children's self-efficacy as learners through problem-solving and reflection.
Information Processing	George A. Miller (1920)	There is a focus on cognitive processing, including attention and memory.	Devise methods to enhance children's attention and memory. Tie new information to child's existing knowledge. Chunk information to enhance learning.
Multiple Intelligences	Howard Gardner (1943)	Nine qualitatively different kinds of intelligence exist.	Learning experiences should match the child's intelligence style; however, Gardner recommends that teachers help children expand on all of the types of intelligences.
Core Systems Theory	Elizabeth Spelke (1949)	Evolution produced core systems of knowledge or heightened abilities to learn concepts most tied to survival. Infants have surprising capabilities, e.g. understanding that others have goals and an ability to orient themselves in space.	Respect the infant's ability to learn. Recognize that knowledge builds over time and through experience.

(continued)

The What and Why of Early Childhood Development

Table 1.1 continued

Specific Theory	Primary Theory and Theorists	Primary Focus	Educational Focus
Neo-constructivism	Nora S. Newcombe	The biologically prepared mind acts in evolved ways with an ever-changing environment.	Brain is ready to learn, and experiences provide information. Teachers who use guided discovery methods rather than pure discovery strategies enhance children's learning.
Contextual			
Sociocultural Theory	Lev Vygotsky (1896–1934)	The emphasis is on the ability to think. Learning is a result of human interaction, culture, and social experiences.	Adults and more skilled peers scaffold new information to make it accessible. Use the concept of zone of proximal development to enhance learning.
Bioecological Systems Theory	Urie Bronfenbrenner (1917–2005)	There are interactions among biological factors, the child's immediate family and community, and societal and cultural factors.	Every level of influence affects children's learning, growth, and development. Adults pay attention to all of the systems of influence, including family life and support for families in a society.
Relationship-Based Theory	Robert (1923) & Joan (1933) Hinde	The focus is on how the child exists within a system of relationships and the dimensions of those relationships.	Adults focus on the role of meaningful, ongoing relationships in learning.
Dynamic Systems Theory	Esther Thelen (1941–2004) Karen Adolph	There is a focus on how brain structures change with use and the challenges posed in context.	Learning experiences may challenge the child in ways that cause fundamental brain and behavior change.
Transactional			
Transactional Theory	Arnold Sameroff	Parents' child-rearing beliefs and behavior, children's characteristics and behavior, and the quality of the environment have effects on each other and on the child's development. Both children and contexts influence each other.	Notice the inter-relationships of child, teacher, and environment. Consider both risk and resiliency factors and that an accumulation of risk factors has consequences for children's developmental outcomes.
Developmental Attachment			
	John Bowlby (1907–1990) Mary Ainsworth (1913–1999)	Early attachment experiences influence children's present and later lives. There are different attachment patterns that occur.	Support healthy attachments among parents/teachers and children.

Skinner's behavioral are theories that continue to influence our thinking about children. In this text, we will integrate their influence with newer theories and the current explosion of research on how children develop and learn.

More recent theories that attempt to explain the multiple physical and social systems that influence the whole child and family include cognitive theories that emphasize mental activities. They include core systems theory, information processing theory, social learning/cognitive theory (Bandura), and neoconstructivist theory. The contextual theories place an emphasis on the interplay between individuals and their present and historical environments and include dynamic systems, sociocultural, and bioecological theory. These theories contribute to our current understanding of growth, development, and learning.

The following sections provide a brief overview of development/learning theories. In the following chapters, we discuss these theories in detail, apply them to our understanding of children's development and learning, and highlight the implications of these theories for early childhood development and education. Additional domain-specific theories are introduced in later chapters; for example, Relationship-Based Theory is discussed in the chapters on social and emotional development while Bruner's Discovery Theory and Social Interaction Theory are discussed in the chapters on children's cognitive and language development and learning. Transactional theory (Sameroff, 1995; Sameroff & Fiese, 2000) is also introduced in later chapters.

All theories provide information about *how* children develop and learn as well as *what* is important for them to learn. It is essential for us to reflect on the meaning of these theories because they guide *how* we think about children's learning, *how* adults interact with children, and *how* professionals set up systems that serve children. Here we take you through a brief summary of the theories, the primary theorists, and the influence they have had on early childhood care and education. We can begin to understand how a theory was often created to expand on or reject previous theories as new information about how children develop and learn was discovered. These theories tell a story of a sequence of thinking about young children's development but also present contrary opinions about what aspects of development and the environment are important to emphasize.

Psychoanalytic Theory

The first one, psychoanalytic theory, described biological stages of development that corresponded with ages of children and the conflicts that they felt at those ages. **Psychoanalytic theory** attempts to explain the inner thoughts and feelings, at both the conscious and subconscious levels, that influence behavior (Freud, 1938). Sigmund Freud (1856–1939) laid the foundations for psychoanalysis through his **psychosexual theory.** (See Table 1.2.) As a physician in Vienna specializing in nervous or mental conditions, he became intrigued with adults' problems that seemed to have begun in childhood. Freud developed a stage theory that suggested that certain drives and instincts emerge at various periods of development through biological systems, primarily the mouth, the anus, and the sex organs. Theorists and researchers currently think that this theory is simplistic and overly focused on sexual feelings and erogenous zones. It is also discounted because it was not based on empirical research—research that is based on experimentation and/or observation. However, Freud's basic premise that children's early experiences can influence their later lives has persisted through the years and into present-day perspectives.

psychoanalytic theory
a theory that attempts to explain the inner thoughts and feelings, at both the conscious and subconscious levels, that influence behavior

psychosexual theory
a theory that suggests that sexual drives play an important role in personality development

The What and Why of Early Childhood Development

Psychosocial Theory

In **psychosocial theory,** Erik Erikson, also a stage theorist, described how children developed characteristics such as trust or mistrust, autonomy or self-doubt, and initiative or guilt during their first five years of life. Erik Erikson (1902–1994), who studied with Freud's daughter, Anna, built on Freud's theories and believed that Freud's exploration of sexuality as the main explanation for behavior was too limiting. He focused on the broader social contexts of the child and family, theorizing that relationships within these contexts influence behavior in positive and/or negative ways. Thus, he proposed a psychosocial theory of personality development (Erikson, 1963). (See Table 1.2.) Erikson's theory was characterized by stages that extended from birth to later adulthood.

Maturational Theory

The maturational theory, described next, differs greatly from behaviorist theory in how it characterizes children's development and behavior. **Maturational theory** asserts that an "unfolding" or maturing of genetically preprogrammed traits and abilities characterizes children's growth and development. Development is thought to be a progressive reconstructing of old behaviors into new behaviors that results from physiological maturational changes. Growth and development are thought to proceed according to predetermined orderly and predictable patterns, but it is recognized that not all children proceed through these sequences at the same rate.

This perspective evolved from the early scientific studies in embryology. With the development of the microscope, scientists were able to microscopically examine the sperm and the ovum; they discovered that there was no fully formed organism in either, but the embryo developed in a series of predictable stages. This discovery led to an interest in the way the organism evolved not only prenatally, but also from birth onward. Arnold Gesell (1880–1961), a Yale University professor, is best known for his studies of this progression in infants and young children. Gesell's studies set forth a number of principles of development and sequences for the unfolding of characteristics and capabilities that in the maturationist view is only slightly influenced by the environment. Recent scientific discoveries, however, emphasize how both the environment and the genetic make-up of the child influence development.

Behavioral Theories

Proponents of **behavioral theory** concentrate on attending to observable, overt behavior rather than examining and explaining the internal processes of behavior. They do not classify behavior into stages but suggest that learning is a gradual and continuous process. Experience is considered most important. Behavioral theory is generally classified into three types: (1) classical conditioning, (2) operant conditioning, and (3) social learning theory. A technique for changing behaviors called **behavior modification** comes from this school of thought.

Classical Conditioning. The principles of **classical conditioning theory** were developed by Russian Ivan P. Pavlov (1849–1936). Pavlov paired two events, the placing of meat

Table 1.2 A Comparison of Freud's Psychosexual and Erikson's Psychosocial Stages of Development

Freud's Five Stages and Related Conflicts		Approximate Ages	Erikson's Eight Stages and Tasks
Oral	The primary focus of stimulation is the mouth and the oral cavity, and the primary sources of gratification are eating, sucking, and biting. Attachment to the mother is vital for the child's development, and weaning is a source of anxiety for the child.	Birth–1½ years	Basic trust versus mistrust The main task is to gain more trust than mistrust. "The first demonstration of social trust in the baby is the ease of his feeding, the depth of his sleep, the relaxation of his bowels" (Erikson, 1963, p. 247). Adults help the child gain a sense of trust through their responsive interactions with the child.
Anal	The primary focus of stimulation is the anal cavity. Toilet training is a source of anxiety and thus should not be harsh or premature.	1½–3 to 4 years	Autonomy versus shame/doubt The main task is to develop more of a sense of autonomy—a sense of "I can do it"—than a sense of shame/doubt. "From a sense of self-control without loss of self-esteem comes a lasting sense of good will and pride; from a sense of loss of self-control and foreign overcontrol comes a lasting propensity for doubt and shame" (Erikson, 1963, p. 254).
Phallic	The primary focus is on the genital area. Identification with the parent of the same sex occurs and causes anxiety but results in identification with the same-sex parent.	3–5 years	Initiative versus guilt The main task is to develop more of a sense of initiative than guilt. "Initiative adds to autonomy the quality of undertaking, planning, and 'attaching' as task for the sake of being active and on the move..." (Erikson, 1963, p. 255). Guilt can occur "over the goals contemplated and the acts initiated in one's exuberant enjoyment of new locomotor and mental powers" (p. 255)
Latency	Sexual drives are repressed in this stage as children's worlds expand to schools, clubs, and sports.	5½–12 years	Industry versus inferiority
Genital	There is a focus on sexual interest in the opposite sex. Adolescence tries to balance individual needs with the needs of others.	Adolescence	Identity versus role confusion
—	—	Young adulthood	Intimacy versus isolation
—	—	Middle adulthood	Generativity versus stagnation
—	—	Late adulthood	Ego integrity versus despair

Source: Erikson (1963) and Freud (1933, 1938).

The What and Why of Early Childhood Development

powder on a dog's tongue and the ringing of a bell, to create a conditioned stimulus. Over a period of time, these repeated events produced a conditioned response of salivation. The stimulus of the bell's sound alone caused the dog to salivate even if no meat powder was present. The dog's association of the meat powder with the sound of the bell stimulated a response.

In the United States, E. L. Thorndike conducted numerous animal experiments and is considered the father of behaviorism. However, John B. Watson (1878–1958) was responsible for implementing the ideas of classical conditioning:

> Give me a dozen healthy infants, well-formed, and my own specified world to bring them up in and I'll guarantee to take any one at random and train him to become any type of specialist I might select—doctor, lawyer, artist, merchant-chief, and, yes, even beggarman and thief, regardless of his talents, penchants, tendencies, abilities, vocations, and race of his ancestors. I am going beyond my facts and I admit it, but so have the advocates of the contrary and they have been doing it for many thousands of years. (John B. Watson, *Behaviorism,* 1930, p. 82)

Watson's famous experiment with an 11-month-old infant, Albert, was used to justify the notion that certain behavioral responses can be created through conditioning. In Watson's experiment (Watson & Rayner, 1920), Albert was shown a white rat at the same time a loud noise was made. Initially, Albert was not afraid of the rat but was distressed at the loud noise. Eventually, Albert's association of the loud noise with the rat produced a fear of many white furry objects, such as his mother's muff, rabbits, and Santa's beard. Unfortunately, Albert left the hospital where this experiment was conducted before Watson could **extinguish** the child's fear.

extinguish
stopping a behavior or response by not reinforcing it over a period of time

Watson's notions on child rearing were widespread and are still evident in some parenting practices today. Watson suggested that showing affection for young children would spoil them. He advocated feeding infants every four hours, advised parents against rocking their children, and suggested that a handshake was more appropriate than a goodnight hug and kiss (Watson, 1928).

Operant Conditioning. A later proponent of behaviorism was Harvard psychologist B. F. Skinner. Skinner explained Watson's views in a well-known book, *Walden Two* (1948). Skinner's philosophy and experiments expanded on classical conditioning theory and evolved into the **operant conditioning theory,** in which the operant is the action on the part of an individual as a response to environmental stimuli. Individuals ensure others' desired behavior by using positive or negative reinforcers. Positive reinforcement involves providing pleasant or satisfying consequences such as praise, food, a special privilege, a good grade, or other types of rewards after the appropriate behavior has occurred. Negative reinforcement occurs when behaviors are encouraged by the removal of a threatening or an aversive stimulus; for example, a child who is scolded for eating with his or her fingers may remove the aversive stimulus (scolding) by attempting to use a spoon.

operant conditioning theory
a theory in which behavior is changed or modified through the positive or negative consequences that follow the behavior

Both positive and negative reinforcement result in learning new behaviors or in strengthening existing behaviors. Punishment is used to decrease the frequency of undesirable behavior. However, sometimes punishment results in reinforcement. For example, a child who is frequently blamed for mishaps may learn to lie (deny complicity) if it helps to escape the unpleasantness of being punished when the child does cause a mishap. Skinner believed that punishment is generally an ineffective way to control undesirable behavior. Instead, he suggested extinguishing behavior or ceasing to reinforce the behavior until it stops. Skinner and his wife decided to try this technique on their 5-year-old daughter Julie (Skinner, 1979). Skinner reported that it took a month or two to accomplish. At first, Julie behaved in ways that in the past would have brought her punishment, and she watched her parents closely for their reactions. In time, the desired behaviors emerged. Skinner indicated that he and his wife found various reinforcement techniques more effective than punishment (p. 279).

Early childhood professionals who adopt a behavioral approach "generally follow more teacher-directed instructional practices, including didactic instruction with emphasis on acquisition of basic skills" (Grisham-Brown, n.d.).

Humanistic Theory

Two theorists whose ideas are rooted in the theories of Freud and Erikson are Carl Rogers (1902–1987) and Abraham Maslow (1908–1970), who, contrary to behaviorists, believed that the inner personal factors were important. However, unlike Freud, these scholars did not view growth and development as determined by negative early events, but they believed that individuals could change or be influenced by the choices that they make. The theories of Rogers and Maslow are classified as **humanistic** theories. The humanistic perspective is an outgrowth of clinical and counseling psychology. The primary focus of humanistic theories is on inner feelings, thoughts, perceptions, and the emotional and social needs of individuals. Much of the emphasis in humanistic perspectives is on the development of communication and problem-solving abilities.

humanistic
a theory that believes in the fundamental goodness of human beings

Rogers's theory suggests that individuals have the capacity for openness to their experiences and are capable of becoming fully functioning individuals, relatively free of ego defense mechanisms (Rogers, 1962). Such individuals are "unified" within themselves, where distinctions are made between the "role self" and the "real self," between a defensive facade and real feelings (p. 29). Such individuals are psychologically free to be themselves, be creative, and express themselves in unique ways. Rogers uses Einstein to illustrate this theory:

> Einstein seems to have been unusually oblivious to the fact that good physicists did not think his kind of thoughts. Rather than drawing back because of his inadequate academic preparation in physics, he simply moved toward being Einstein, toward thinking his own thoughts, toward being as truly and deeply himself as he could. This is not a phenomenon which occurs only in the artist or the genius. Time and again in my clients, I have seen simple people become significant and creative in their own spheres, as they have developed more trust of the processes going on within themselves, and have dared to feel their own feelings, live by values which they discover within, and express themselves in their own unique ways. (p. 30)

Rogers, in his later years, wrote about the goal of education, which he said was the facilitation of change and learning. "The only man who is educated is the man who has learned how to adapt and change; the man who has realized that no knowledge is secure, that only the process of seeking knowledge gives a basis for security. Changingness, reliance on process rather than static knowledge, is the only thing that makes any sense as a goal for education in the modern world" (Rogers, 1983, p. 104). Several of his 10 principles about learning (Rogers, 1969) apply especially to early childhood education:

- Human beings have a natural potential for learning.
- Much significant learning is acquired through doing.
- Self-initiated learning, which involves the whole person of the learner and feeling as well as intellect, is the most lasting and pervasive.

self-actualization
the process of having basic physical and social/emotional needs met so that the individual develops positive self-regard and becomes a creative, contributing member of society

Maslow proposed a concept of **self-actualization,** the process of growing toward self-acceptance and authentic relationships that lead ultimately to a sense of personal fulfillment. Maslow suggested that feelings and aspirations must be considered if one is to understand behavior (Maslow, 1962, 1968, 1970). Self-actualized individuals are continually in the process of becoming, are in touch with and accepting of reality, are confident yet aware of their limitations, and have a commitment to a meaningful project or goal. Maslow suggested that for self-actualization to occur, certain needs must be met. These needs appear in hierarchical order, beginning with very basic physiological needs for food, hydration, rest, and freedom from disease, moving upward as needs are consistently and adequately met, through safety needs, the need to be loved and to belong, the need for self-esteem, the desire for knowledge and aesthetic appreciation, and ultimately to self-actualizing behaviors. Recent research, however, questions the sequence of these needs as even children who are hungry still need and want to be loved and belong. Thoughtful early childhood education and care professionals, though, understand that it is difficult for children to focus on learning if their very basic physiological needs are not met first.

Piaget's Cognitive Developmental Theory

cognitive developmental theory
a theory that explains the development of learning in terms of how children think and process information

Piaget's **cognitive developmental theory** attempts to explain how young children think, process information, and generate meaning from their experiences. Jean Piaget (1896–1980) developed a major theory of cognition in child development. Piaget's theory achieved widespread recognition in the United States during the 1960s for several reasons. First, the insistence of the behaviorists on quantifiable research with large populations was beginning to be questioned. Second, Piaget's theory on the nature of how young children learn came into acceptance during a time of great interest in the development of cognitively oriented experiences for young children. Finally, Piaget's theory readily explained what perceptive parents and teachers of young children had already observed: The manner in which young children process information and relate to new knowledge differs distinctly from that of older children and adults.

Piaget worked in France to establish norms for Binet's Intelligence Test. In that process, he observed that many young children gave similar incorrect answers. Piaget began to wonder whether the development of cognition proceeded in stages. Using the clinical interview, Piaget questioned children to determine their thought processes. This approach, coupled with the detailed observations of his own three children, provided the basis for Piaget's theory (Piaget, 1952). Piaget suggested that thinking develops sequentially in four stages: sensorimotor, preoperational, concrete operations, and formal operations. (See Table 1.3.) The first three stages are discussed more thoroughly in later chapters on cognitive, language, and literacy development.

According to Piaget, all children proceed through a stage-related sequence of cognitive development, each stage building on the accomplishments of the previous one (a developmental view). Piaget viewed these stages as invariant; that is, one stage always follows another in a predictable sequence. Piaget proposed that all individuals proceed through the invariant sequence, but they do so at their own rates of development. Differences in rates of entering and exiting the stages are attributed to differences in individual genetic timetables and to cultural and environmental influences.

Piaget grew up around Lake Neuchâtel in Switzerland and became intrigued with the differences in behavior in mollusks at various locations around the lake. This fascination created a lifelong interest in the effects of the environment on living organisms' subsequent adaptations to the environment. He proposed that children order their interactions with the environment and then adapt to or change this order if they have new insights or information. See Table 1.3 for definitions of concepts proposed by Piaget. Ways of ordering thought were termed **schemata. Assimilation** represents the child's attempts to fit new ideas and concepts into existing schemata. **Accommodation** is the change in schemata that a child makes as a result of new information. As children grow older and have more experiences with their environment, their **equilibration,** or balance in thinking, is often disturbed. Piaget said that this dissatisfaction or **disequilibrium** with present ideas motivates the child to accommodate new information and change schemata.

schemata
mental concepts or categories; plural for schema

assimilation
the process of incorporating new motor or conceptual learning into existing schemata

accommodation
the cognitive process by which patterns of thought (schemata) and related behaviors are modified to conform to new information or experience

equilibration
the attempt to restore cognitive balance by modifying existing cognitive structures when confronted with new information

Table 1.3 Piaget's Constructivist Theory

Important Concepts	
Four Stages of Cognitive Development • Stages are invariant • Stages build on one another	1. Sensorimotor period *(Birth to 2 years)* • Direct sensory experiences and motor actions • Reflexes are base of later learning 2. Preoperational period *(2 to 7 years)* • Language, symbols • Fantasy 3. Concrete operations *(7 to 11 years)* • Think abstractly and make rational judgements about concrete or observable phenomena 4. Formal operations *(11 and beyond)* • Hypothetical and reflective thinking
Schemata	Mental representations of an associated set of objects, perceptions, ideas, and/or actions
Disequilibrium Assimilation Accommodation Adaptation	New experience brings new information that does not fit schemata New experience is modified in perception to fit existing schemata Existing concept is modified to include or adapt to new experience Restored sense of equilibrium between individual and environment with new schemata

The What and Why of Early Childhood Development

disequilibrium
an imbalance in thinking
that leads the thinker to
assimilate or accommodate

Although Piaget's theory is characterized by abstract language and ideas that are often hard to translate and to verify through research, his theory remains important to caregivers and educators for several reasons. Piaget's cognitive developmental theory:

- focuses attention on the sequential aspects of growth and development in the cognitive domain;
- emphasizes the fact that thinking processes in young children are significantly different than thinking processes in older children and adults;
- emphasizes the importance of firsthand, direct, interactional experiences with objects and people; and
- provides insight into numerous aspects of cognitive development, such as the development of cause-and-effect relationships; time, space, and number concepts; classification strategies; logic; morality; and language.

Piaget (1952) summarized the principle goal of education in the following way: "The principle goal of education is to create men who are capable of doing new things, not simply of repeating what other generations have done—men who are creative, inventive and discoverers."

While the term *constructivism* is a theory of knowledge, the term *constructionism* is the educational theory inspired by Piaget's theory. The term *constructionism* implies an educational approach in which children construct their own knowledge through exploration and investigation.

Other Cognitive Theories

The recent explosion of research provides us with insights on development as a complex interaction between nature (our genetic make-up) and nurture (the environment). Scientists are focusing on the remarkable capabilities of young children to learn as well as the influences of environmental experiences on their development. Many current cognitive theorists are interested in the remarkable capabilities of infants and other young children to process information, and they conduct research on the structural characteristics of the brain.

Cognitive theories focus on how children acquire, process, and store information. "Around 1970, in reaction to behaviorism's radical injunction against positing unobservable variables, cognitive psychology arose to return the focus of investigators to internal mechanisms of thought that may (or may not) result in a behavioral response but—more important—were of interest in their own right" (Camras & Witherington, 2005, p. 329). Exciting research highlights our current understanding of children's cognitive and language development.

Core Systems Theory. "How is the human mind organized, and how does it grow? Does all human development depend on a single, general-purpose learning system? At the opposite extreme, are humans endowed with a large collection of special-purpose cognitive systems and predispositions?" (Kinzler & Spelke, 2007, p. 257). These are questions asked by a new generation of researchers who believe that, instead of the two extremes highlighted in the questions, humans have "a small number of separable systems that stand at the foundation of all our beliefs and values. New, flexible skills, concepts, and

Table 1.4 Core Systems

Core System	Infants appear to be born with some knowledge of the following concepts:
Object Representation	Objects move as connected, bounded wholes; move on connected, unobstructed paths; and do not interact at a distance.
Agents	Agents are seen as directed by goals, achieving goals efficiently, acting contingently and reciprocally with each other, and using gaze direction.
Number	Numbers are imprecise and become increasingly imprecise as the cardinal value increases. Number representation is abstract and can apply to various entities, sounds and actions. Number representations can be compared through addition and subtraction.
Geometry	The geometry of a space (distance, angle, relation of extended spaces) helps an infant orient himself/herself.
Social Group Membership	Infants have an inborn preference for people of their own race and those who speak the child's home language; note that this idea is *not* established as a core knowledge but is acknowledged as a possibility.

Based on Spelke (2000, 2003); Kinzler and Spelke (2007).

systems of knowledge build on these core foundations." (p. 257). Spelke (2000, 2003) identified four core systems of the brain and Kinzler and Spelke (2007) discuss a fifth one that is emerging based on research findings in the past decade. The core systems of Object Representation, Agents, Number, Geometry, and Us versus Them are described in Table 1.4. Infants, according to this theory, are born with these structures that allow the child to understand, for example, how objects move, that when one object goes behind a screen only one object should come out from the other side, and how an object looks when only seeing part of it. This theory and the research have allowed us to see and understand the many capabilities of newborns and young children. You will find more information on these concepts and their educational implications in the cognitive and language chapters in this book.

Information Processing Theory. Information Processing Theory considers the mind as a computer that processes information, stores the information, and retrieves the information. The information processing theory (Case, 1992; Klahr & Wallace, 1976; Miller, 1956; Sternberg, 1985) likens cognitive development to the computer's *inputs, throughputs,* and *outputs.* Input refers to the individual's gathering of information from sensory stimuli: vision, hearing, tasting, smelling, tactile sensations, and sensorimotor activity. Input information is then acknowledged, compared to other data already stored in memory,

The What and Why of Early Childhood Development

Social cognitive/learning theory emphasizes that children learn through imitation.

categorized, and stored for future use. This process represents throughput. Subsequent verbal and/or nonverbal responses represent output. Information-processing theorists have been variously concerned about how the mind operates during memory, attention, and problem-solving activities. Findings from studies of these cognitive attributes suggest that information processing improves as individuals get older and can develop certain cognitive strategies that assist memory, attention, and problem solving. Nevertheless, information processing theory represents cognitive development as a continuous process in which there are age differences in children's cognitive abilities.

In an attempt to explain the adaptive nature of cognitive development, however, Siegler (1998) proposed, "All current theories recognize that people are biologically prepared to perceive the world in certain ways, that many important perceptual capabilities are present at birth, and that others emerge in the first few months of infancy given all but the most abnormal experience" (p. 92). Siegler further asserted that we all perceive the world through our senses, yet learning in infancy inevitably depends on three functions:

Attending: Determining what an object, event, or action will be mentally;

Identifying: Establishing what a perception is through relating a current perception to perceptions already held in memory;

Locating: Determining where the object of perception exists and in what location relative to the observer.

social learning theory
a theory that proposes that learning occurs through observing others, and emphasizes the influencing role of behavioral models

Social Learning Theory. **Social learning theory,** sometimes referred to as *social cognitive theory,* is an adaptation of both cognitive theory and behavioral theory merged into one. This theory was introduced in 1941 by Neil Miller and John Dollard in *Social Learning and Imitation.* Albert Bandura is a contemporary proponent of social learning theory. His research (1977, 1986, 1997, 2001) emphasizes the importance of role models, significant adults in children's lives, and learning. Social learning theorists propose that children learn and imitate behaviors from people who are important to them and that children do not always need reinforcement to learn. There is a cognitive component that influences who, where, when, and why a child may imitate adults, peers, or objects. Social cognition also helps children learn to understand others' needs and feelings.

Bandura proposed that learning does not depend solely on direct instruction. In his classic research, two different groups of children observed two versions of a film in which an adult hit a large plastic inflatable doll called a Bobo doll. In one version, an adult rewarded the model's behavior with praise, candy, and soft drinks. The second version concluded with another adult model hitting the first adult model with a rolled-up newspaper. After viewing the films, the children who saw the version with the reward were more likely to imitate aggressive behavior than were the children who viewed the version in which the model was punished. Bandura concluded that children learn from observing others, but also who children model and when they do the modeling is dependent on many factors including how much power the model has.

Neoconstructivism Neoconstructivism theorists use Piaget's constructivist theory as their foundation but have added concepts from information processing. Neoconstructivism embraces the following principles: (adapted from Newcombe, 2010, pp. vi–vii):

- "Experience expectancy is a key concept." Neural abilities allow the infant to develop expectancies based on experience. If an infant moves his feet and his mobile makes noise, he comes to expect the noise whenever he moves his feet and is surprised if the mobile doesn't make noise. The infant learns about his world by developing expectancies and testing them.

- "Action plays a key role in learning and development, just as Piaget thought, not only because it creates the occasion for experiment but also because it allows for situations that are full of more information than just observation."

- "The world is richly structured and well equipped with perceptual redundancies and correlations that support experience-expectant learning." This helps explain how infants and young children "pick up" knowledge. One event often follows another, so the young child is able to build knowledge based on these experiences and their expectations (Newcombe, 2010).

- Recent innovative research on how humans' brains process information demonstrates that young children, including infants, have an amazing ability to interpret patterns and make generalizations. For example, new research on how young children learn about language discovered that infants figure out by listening where a word begins and ends in a sentence spoken by an adult. They use their ability to perceive patterns to determine what sounds are likely to follow each other in a word (Kuhl, 2009).

The child's innate capacity to process information is important *and* experience or nurture is important because it defines, expands, and narrows the child's capacities. For example, young children before approximately 8 months of age can hear the differences between most sounds spoken in the world. However, between 6 and 12 months, infants focus on the language(s) being spoken to them (native languages) and they begin to lose the ability to hear the differences between sounds that they don't hear (nonnative languages). This narrowing of their capacity to process language is adaptive because it helps children focus and learn their primary language(s) more efficiently (Kuhl et al., 2006).

The results of research based on neoconstructivism is moving our understanding of young children's development and learning forward. Another example is research by Sommerville, Woodward, and Needham (2005), who gave 3-month-old infants, who generally have difficulty grasping objects, "training" in which they moved toys using Velcro mittens. These infants then touched toys more. With experience, the infants seemed to begin to understand goal-oriented actions in a different way.

Contextual Theories

Contextual theorists assert that we cannot consider the development and learning of individuals without also thinking about the influences of the environment, including the child's culture, family, community practices, and historical experiences. Contextual theorists focus on the immediate environment and historical context that influences how children develop within cultural settings that influence not only the pace of their development but also the types of knowledge they gain (Adolph & Berger, 2006). These theorists examine how the bioecological systems in which children and families live influence their **well-being** (Bronfenbrenner, 2004, 2005). Another contextual theory—Relationship-Based Theory—focuses on how children develop a sense of self-worth, language, and cognitive development within a circle of their key relationships (Hinde, 1992).

well-being
a state of feeling that all is well physically, mentally, and socially

Barbara Rogoff (2003, 2011) is a current theorist who studies contextual approaches that include ecological psychology and cultural psychology. Rogoff studies collaboration, learning through observation, children's interest and keen attention to ongoing events, roles of adults as guides or as instructors, and children's opportunities to participate in cultural activities or in age-specific child-focused settings. For example, Rogoff found that in the Mayan culture, young children learn through observing adults and participating at a young age in tasks such as weaving.

> "…people develop as participants in cultural communities. Their development can be understood only in light of the cultural practices and circumstances of their communities—which also change." (Barbara Rogoff, pp. 3–4)

Dynamic Systems Theory. While Piaget observed development as occuring in universal stages, dynamic systems theory views children as learning in culturally diverse settings that provide different opportunities and challenges for children as they develop, resulting in "instabilities, novelty, and variability" (Thelen & Smith, 1996, p. xvii). Dynamic systems theory describes children's development as a response to characteristics of their environment. Some children, for example, will need to learn to walk with shoes in the summer and boots in the winter. Each of these experiences requires that the children adapt their walking skills to master the environment, and only after watching children in context can we begin to see the range of responses and the capabilities of humans. Esther Thelen and Linda Smith, in their 1996 book *A Dynamic Systems Approach to the Development of Cognition and Action*, emphasize that development—the process of change—is dynamic. It "arises from a multitude of underlying contributing elements" (p. xviii). These authors:

> propose here a radical departure from current cognitive theory. Although behavior and development appear structured, there are no structures. Although behavior and development appear rule-driven, there are no rules. There is complexity. (p. xix)

Dynamic systems theory emphasizes that as new behaviors emerge (for example, walking), the child attempts to self-organize. Rather than in set stages, as Piaget believed, development occurs as the child attempts to make sense of different contexts. In fact, Fleer (2006a, 2006b), a dynamic systems researcher, emphasizes that many behaviors that we have thought to occur at set ages with all children, such as stranger anxiety, may actually be a result of cultural expectations for the child.

Dynamic systems theory affects how we educate young children. We need to take into consideration the multiple influences on children including both the environment and the biological systems with which children are born and how they interact and influence each other. For example, those who consider dynamic systems theory would not look for a simple, linear cause for why a child might be behaving in a certain way, but rather they would consider how the temperament of the child influences the parent and how the parent's stress level may be influencing the child as well as other influences within the system of the child's relationships, which is always changing (dynamic).

Sociocultural Theory. A view of the child in context has emerged with an understanding that children and adults give things, actions, people, and feelings meaning that is co-constructed with others (Taguchi, 2007). Learning is a social activity, and adults and peers have important roles to play as a child learns.

Recently, the work of Vygotsky has received considerable attention in the United States. Vygotsky produced some major works during a relatively short life. Two of his books, *Thought and Language* (1962) and *Mind in Society* (1978), have been translated into English. Many refer to Vygotsky's theory as a sociocultural approach to understanding child growth and development (Feldman, 2007). Vygotsky emphasized that cultures differ in the activities that they emphasize, stressing that child development takes place on both natural (biological/physiological) and cultural planes.

Vygotsky's sociocultural theory (1978) asserts that every child learns his or her culture first on the social level and then on the individual level. Think about how you may have learned how to behave in a religious setting as a young child because your culture modeled its expectations and primary caregivers talked about the appropriate behavior. As you became older, these behaviors became internalized, and you understood the reasons for why behavior in a religious setting is different than behavior at a party. As you can see in this example, Vygotsky believed that adults and peers influence learning and that society influences what is learned and how it is taught. His famous concepts are those of the **zone of proximal development,** the skills or knowledge a child does not yet have but could master with guidance, and **scaffolding.** These concepts will be discussed more in Chapters 6 and 7. Vygotsky believed that cognition is not just in the mind, but also in the social experiences in which the individual is engaged. Social experiences, then, are thought to shape the ways individuals perceive and interpret the world around them. Because language supports social interaction, and because language is a primary form of communication, it also serves as a critical tool for thinking. Vygotsky determined that when children are provided with words, they are better able to form concepts than when they are not provided with words. The relationships between language and thought are central to Vygotsky's theory. In his view, language is the cultural tool through which higher-order thinking and self-regulatory thought occur. Vygotsky's theory has had a profound influence on early childhood education practices that are discussed in later chapters on cognitive/language development and learning. An educator who considers Vygotsky's theory would think about how children gain knowledge, skills, and attitudes within their culture and with others.

zone of proximal development
the level of concept development that is too difficult for the child to accomplish alone but can be achieved with the help of adults or more skilled children through scaffolding

scaffolding
a process by which adults or more skilled children facilitate the acquisition of knowledge or skills in the learner through coaching or supplying needed information

The What and Why of Early Childhood Development

Bioecological Systems Theory. In the past, much of child development research focused on parent–child interactions or intrafamilial processes. Urie Bronfenbrenner (1979, 1986, 2005) argued that the factors influencing development are much more complex in that **intrafamilial** processes are affected by **extrafamilial** forces. The **bioecological systems theory** defines five interacting and interdependent systems, represented by concentric circles in Figure 1.2. The interactions between and among the systems influence the course of a child's growth, development, and learning over time. A bioecological systems theory emphasizes the multiplicity of relationships between and among the systems. When the linkages between the systems are characterized by harmony and positive interactions, healthy development can result. Conversely, when there is disharmony or conflict between or among the systems, child growth and development can be negatively affected.

The child is at the core of the five systems, typically depicted as a series of ever-widening circles of influence. The system closest to the child (the system containing the child) is called the *microsystem;* it includes all the settings where the child spends a significant amount of time (home, child care setting, school, neighborhood, and so on). The microsystem focuses on the roles, relationships, and experiences in the child's immediate environment. The *mesosystem* pertains to the linkages and relationships between and among the different *ecosystems* and is illustrated by the arrows pointing in either direction between the circles in Figure 1.2. The *exosystem* consists

intrafamilial
actions and behaviors occurring within the immediate family

extrafamilial
actions and behaviors occurring outside the immediate family

bioecological systems theory
a theory that argues that a variety of social systems influence the development of children

Figure 1.2
A Bioecological
Systems Perspective

Bronfenbrenner's bioecological systems theory reprinted with permission from Feldman (2007).

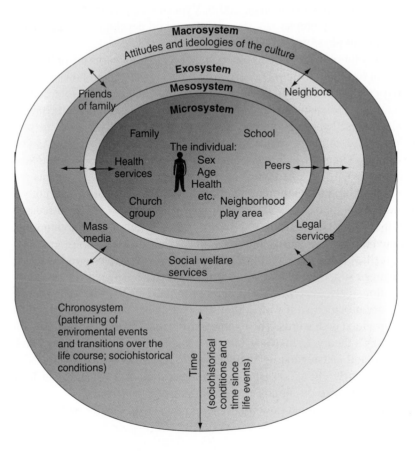

of three main interactive contexts: the parents' workplace, the parents' social networks, and the community influences on family functioning (Bronfenbrenner, 1986). Parental employment or unemployment characteristics, including the parents' education levels and the types of employment they can secure, along with their attitudes and feelings associated with work and employment, affect both the quantity and the quality of relationships and the types of child-rearing practices that take place within the family.

Similarly, social networks such as the presence or absence (and the characteristics of) kinship groups, faith-related affiliations, neighbors, and other friendships are believed to influence family processes and their developmental effects on children. Community characteristics are also influential. These include whether a child is living in a rural, urban, or suburban community and the types of opportunities and resources available to children and families. The fourth system, the *macrosystem*, involves the attitudes, values, customs, laws, regulations, and rules of the culture at large that influence all other systems and ultimately the family and the child. The chronosystem includes historical events, such as World War II, the Women's Movement, or more recently the Iraq War, that affect the lives of children. Over a child's life course, social historical events and conditions have an important influence on the other four systems. Bioecological theory is referred to as a *contextual theory* because of the influence of various contexts on a person's behavior.

Summary of Theories

The theories discussed in this chapter do influence our thinking about how children learn and develop. Theories relate to parenting and educational practice and practice relates to theories. What theory does a teacher have if she believes that if you comfort a crying baby that baby will cry more? What theory is a teacher following if she believes that if she responds to a baby's crying with words of comfort that as the baby develops he will learn new ways of expressing his discomfort? How do these teachers differ in their beliefs about how children learn new behaviors? The first teacher seems to believe that reward and punishment will change a child's behavior (behaviorist view) while the second teacher has a more developmental view of children's learning (cognitive developmental).

Theories help us "see with new eyes" how children develop and learn. From social learning/cognitive theory and research, for example, we begin to see how important observation and imitation are to children's learning. From dynamic systems theory, we see how children are active and forceful in their desire to learn and how cultures and context influence what and how children learn. It is obvious, based on the theories discussed above, that some theorists focus on different aspects of development, while other theorists try to explain how children learn. Theorists, such as Bronfenbrenner, focus on the systems that influence the lives of children. Reading about theories and observing children to test those theories will allow you to apply theory to practice and create your own theories about how children develop and learn. Children and parents create theories, too, about how the world of relationships and objects work, by constantly observing, experimenting, testing, and drawing conclusions.

While cognitive and contextual theories differ in their explanations of how children develop, they both propose that young children learn quickly and much earlier

The What and Why of Early Childhood Development

than we've previously thought, not by direct instruction, but rather by observing, imitating, and actively engaging with their environment to develop goals, strategies to achieve these goals, and tests of their own theories about how the world works. Children thrive within healthy relationships that support their emotional and social development, engagement, learning, and language. The emerging science on brain development and early learning (i.e., how infants begin to understand that others have intentions) has focused on how young children process information, how they enter the world with capabilities, and how important the early years are for young children's optimal development.

Each theory has an interesting perspective on not only how children learn, but also where, when, and why they develop and learn. Theories spark a body of research that supports or negates the theory. We will highlight that research in the chapters that follow. We hope that you will discover that early childhood development and theory is an interesting, important, and complex field of study.

Trends in Early Childhood Study

Topics of research about young children and their families continue to reflect society's concerns on a variety of issues. Some of these concerns are as follows:

- The translation of research from the fields of biology and the neurosciences about early brain growth and neurological development into appropriate and healthy experiences for infants and young children
- The translation of research from the biogenetics fields into appropriate education and counseling for families, and ethical and effective preventive or intervention measures to promote healthy child development outcomes
- Concern for the physical safety and mental health of children growing up in a society in which the threat of violence, terrorism, and homeland war are present and, concomitantly, the care and nurturing of children who have experienced atrocities
- The need for a well-trained, highly educated, eminently qualified early childhood workforce and the identification of the knowledge and skills essential for providing services to children and their families in many different contexts (e.g., schools, child care settings, social service agencies, foster care, health care services, and family counseling)
- The recognition that research must incorporate the influences of contexts (nationality, race, culture, region, family configuration, and socioeconomic factors) on the developmental trajectories (or pathways) of child growth and development
- The nature of contemporary family life, the multiple roles mothers and fathers play in sustaining family and child well-being, and how best to provide knowledge, skills, and support systems to families
- Continued study of the long-term benefits and/or consequences of varying types of child care and family services because of the growing number of infants and children in nonparental care for major portions of each day
- A need for continuing study on how to ensure that child care for infants and children is of highest quality and readily available to families who need it

- Exploration of developmentally appropriate, relevant, mind-engaging early child care and schooling experiences in the context of a changing society in which education and family services and support systems have become increasingly politicized, often circumventing the child development knowledge base and threatening efforts toward the best interests of children

Did you notice the quote at the beginning of this chapter? It says, "There are two lasting bequests we can hope to give our children—one is roots; the other is wings." A knowledge of how young children develop and learn helps parents and early childhood development professionals to provide the conditions in which young children can develop deep roots and strong wings—two prerequisites for leading happy, productive lives. We hope the following chapters help you learn how to provide both the roots and the wings to facilitate optimal development in young children.

Key Terms

accommodation
assimilation
at-risk
behavior modification
behavioral theory
bioecological systems
  theory
classical conditioning
  theory
cognitive developmental
  theory
developmentally
  appropriate

developmentally
  inappropriate
disequilibrium
equilibration
essential experiences
extinguish
extrafamilial
humanistic
inclusion
intrafamilial
low-risk
maturational theory
norms

operant conditioning theory
professionals
psychoanalytic theory
psychosexual theory
psychosocial theory
scaffolding
schemata
self-actualization
social learning theory
theories
well-being
zone of proximal
  development

Review Strategies and Activities

1. Review the key terms individually or with a classmate.
2. Begin a journal to record and track your supplementary readings for this course. Start your journal by jotting down your initial responses to the seven questions posed at the beginning of this chapter. When you have completed this text, return to these questions and consider whether you would change your initial answers and, if so, how.
3. Think back to your early childhood years through age 8. Try to recall your earliest memory. At what age did it occur? What other recollections do you have from your early childhood years?
   a. Chart a life line. State how old you were at the time of your earliest recollection. Describe that recollection and others that took place during that period of time. Continue this process up through age 8 or to your current age.

b. Discuss these recollections with other students in your early childhood development class. Your classmates have probably had similar experiences, or their recollections may help you to remember some events you have forgotten.

c. Relate events in your life to the various developmental theories.

d. Identify personal cultural influences within your life from childhood to the present.

4. What is your image of the child?

5. Why do you wish to become an early childhood professional?

a. List the people or events that have encouraged your interest in the profession.

b. What are your concerns about becoming an early childhood professional?

c. What are your short- and long-term professional goals?

d. Discuss your responses with students in your class.

Further Readings

Children's Defense Fund. *The state of America's children*. Washington, DC: Author. Retrieved from http://www.childrensdefense.org. [Updated editions of this report are published annually.]

Copple, C., & Bredekamp, S. (Eds.) (2009). *Developmentally appropriate practice in early childhood programs serving children from birth through age 8* (3rd ed.). Washington, DC: NAEYC.

DEC/NAEYC. (2009). *Early childhood inclusion: A joint position statement of the Division for Early Childhood (DEC) and the National Association for the Education of Young Children (NAEYC).* Chapel Hill: The University of North Carolina, FPG Child Development Institute.

National Association for the Education of Young Children. (2009). *NAEYC standards for early childhood professional preparation programs.* Retrieved from http://www.naeyc.org.

Washington, V., & Andrews, J. D. (Eds.). (2010). *Children of 2020: Creating a better tomorrow.* Washington, DC: Council for Professional Recognition and National Association for the Education of Young Children.

Other Resources

National Association for the Education of Young Children. (2011). *Improving Program Quality through Self-Study.* New video from the NAEYC Accreditation of Programs for Young Children promotes the value of programs enrolling in the NAEYC Self-Study process. Created for programs, affiliates, and accreditation facilitation projects to engage their families, community, and staff in the merits of the NAEYC Accreditation Self-Study process. www.naeyc.org/academy.

Children's Defense Fund. *Introduction to the Children's Defense Fund.* This video clip on YouTube introduces the important mission of The Children's Defense Fund Leave No Child Behind®, which is to ensure every child a Healthy Start, a Head Start, a Fair Start, a Safe Start, and a Moral Start in life and successful passage to adulthood with the help of caring families and communities. www.childrensdefense.org/about-us.

Kids Count Data Book: State Profiles of Child Well-Being. (2010). Baltimore: Annie E. Casey Foundation. Published annually. www.aecf.org.

National Center for Early Development and Learning, www.fpg.unc.edu/~ncedl. NCEDL is a national early childhood research project supported by the U.S. Department of Education's Institute for Educational Sciences (IES), formerly the Office of Educational Research and Improvement (OERI). Administratively based at the FPG Child Development Institute, NCEDL is a collaboration with the University of Virginia and UCLA. This site includes relevant information on research, products, and people related to early development and learning.

chapter 2
The Where, When, and How of Early Childhood Study and Assessment

More often teachers find as they study children, they themselves change. Thus (through child study), we often gain insight and understanding not only of the children but of ourselves as well.... But "understanding" alone, whether of the children or of ourselves, is not enough. The crucial question is whether such understanding improves the teacher's ability to help children learn, whether it facilitates provision of the experiences children need.

—Millie Almy and Celia Genishi

After studying this chapter, you will demonstrate comprehension by:

▶ describing the various types of child development research studies;

▶ stating the ethical considerations in conducting research on young children;

▶ discussing the importance of observing and studying children in a variety of contexts;

▶ describing the importance of developing reflecting-in-action and teacher-as-researcher perspectives in studying young children;

▶ outlining the various approaches the early childhood professional can use in studying young children;

▶ identifying resources that contribute to the study of young children; and

▶ describing how growth and development of young children are assessed and documented.

It is the first day of kindergarten, and Cathleen seems upset at having her mother leave her at the classroom door. Ms. Schwartz, Cathleen's teacher, invites her mother to stay awhile. This relieves Cathleen's anxiety, and she eventually begins to participate in the sociodramatic (pretend play) area of the classroom. She returns to her mother periodically but soon rejoins other children in the sociodramatic center. Eventually, Cathleen's mother tells Cathleen that she has some errands to run and will be back at 11:30 A.M. to pick her up. Cathleen seems to accept her mother's departure. This pattern is repeated for three days, with Cathleen's mother spending less and less time in the classroom. On the fourth day, Cathleen enters the classroom without hesitation and gives her mother a confident "goodbye." Later, Ms. Schwartz observes Cathleen in the sociodramatic area. Ms. Schwartz suggests that she "call" her mother on the toy phone and tell her what she is doing.

Juan is 18 months old. His mother plans to return to her job as a buyer for a large department store. She has enrolled Juan in a child care center. The director, Mr. Hubbard, has encouraged Juan's parents to visit the center with Juan several times a few days before Juan is to begin attending. Mr. Hubbard suggested that Juan's parents send Juan's favorite stuffed toy and blanket every day. A picture of Juan's mother and father was posted on a low-level bulletin board, along with pictures of the other toddlers' parents.

What would you have done had you been Cathleen's or Juan's teacher? Often, responses include telling Cathleen's mother to leave her and not allowing favorite blankets and stuffed animals to be brought into the child care center. Why did Ms. Schwartz and Mr. Hubbard act in the ways they did?

The Where, When, and How of Early Childhood Study and Assessment

The Contribution of Research Literature to the Development of the Early Childhood Professional

Ms. Schwartz and Mr. Hubbard acted on their knowledge of child growth and development research. Their training included many opportunities to read the professional early childhood development research and literature. Their training also provided them with opportunities to observe and study young children's behavior, as well as the responses and behavior of teachers of young children. In addition, their experience with children and families from diverse backgrounds helped them to become more appreciative and responsive to the uniqueness of all children and their families.

Through their reading and study of young children and observation of other early childhood professionals, Ms. Schwartz and Mr. Hubbard learned that a major developmental task of young children is to separate from parents and move into other social settings. Both Ms. Schwartz and Mr. Hubbard are familiar with the research on attachment (Chapters 6 and 9). They observed the techniques and strategies that early childhood professionals use to facilitate young children's adjustment to a new setting. Therefore, they make appropriate decisions about what to do to help children form additional attachments and assist them in separating from their parents.

Early childhood professionals learn about young children at both **preservice** and **inservice** levels by reading the studies and reports of researchers in the area of early childhood development. This is why you are reading this text. Early childhood professionals also learn about young children through observation and study of young children and their family backgrounds. Firsthand experiences with young children reinforce previously read child development information and facilitate further reading about the nature of behavior in young children. This chapter provides information about the study of children revealed through professional research literature on early childhood development.

Types of Child Development Research Studies

Scholars of child development may be affiliated with colleges or universities, research centers, public schools, other public agencies, or private research organizations. They often have hunches, or **hypotheses,** about the development of young children. They design research studies to determine whether their hunches are correct. The results of these studies may be published in theses, dissertations, professional journals, and scholarly books or presented in papers that are read at professional conferences and seminars. Often, research findings are reported in the media.

Professionals in all fields are discerning consumers of research information. Four criteria are used in evaluating the quality of a research study: objectivity, reliability, validity, and replicability. **Objectivity** refers to the researcher's ability to pursue and report the research in such a manner that personal feelings, values, assumptions, or other biases are avoided. **Reliability** refers to the accuracy of the study; that is, scholars must ask, "To what extent does the test or instrument used in the study provide the same or consistent, noncontradictory results when the same or different forms of the test are administered to the same subjects?" **Validity** refers to the soundness of the test or instrument used in the study. In assessing validity of a study, scholars ask the following: "What does the test or instrument measure?" "Does the test or instrument, in fact, measure exactly what it proposes to measure?" "How comprehensively and how accurately does the test measure

preservice
individuals who are in training to teach or serve young children

inservice
individuals who have completed professional training programs and are employed in the early childhood profession

hypothesis
a hunch or supposition that one wants to verify or prove

objectivity
the ability to observe and draw inferences about child development that are free of observer bias

reliability
the consistency with which various research methods produce the same or similar results for each individual from one assessment to the next

validity
the degree to which an instrument or a procedure measures what it is intended to measure

what it is supposed to measure?" There are statistical formulas that can be used to determine reliability and validity. **Replicability** refers to the likelihood that other researchers can, using the same research procedures, obtain the same results. When more than one researcher obtains the same findings, the credibility of the research is greater.

Assessing objectivity, reliability, validity, and replicability of studies prevents the dissemination of inaccurate or untrue information that can result from such research pitfalls as poor research design, researcher bias, inappropriate or inaccurate use of statistical methods, insufficient size of population studied, or inadequate or unclear instructions and procedures for research subjects.

A brief overview of some of the more common types of research in child development is instructive. Some of the common types of research in child development are descriptive, cross-sectional, longitudinal, correlational, experimental, and ethnographic research. Although these types are presented separately for purposes of discussion, many research projects employ combinations of research methods. For example, correlational techniques can be used with longitudinal, cross-sectional, and descriptive studies.

replicability
the likelihood that a research procedure can be followed by another person with the same or similar results

Descriptive Studies

Descriptive studies generally attempt to describe behavior without attempting to determine cause and effect. Many early studies in child development, particularly the maturational theory studies, were descriptive. During the 1920s through the 1940s, Arnold Gesell and his colleagues at the Yale University Child Study Clinic observed a number of children at various ages in selected areas of development—physical and motor development, adaptive behaviors, language development, and personal–social behavior—and described specific commonalities among children of the same age. This information about common characteristics was then converted into *norms*, or averages, whereby teachers, parents, and physicians could determine the extent to which a particular child was developing "normally," or in similar fashion as other children the same age. For example, research of this nature described the average age at which infants should sit, stand, walk, talk, and so on (Gesell & Amatruda, 1941). This maturational approach to studying child development later led to the development of readiness tests to determine a child's developmental age and readiness for specific new experiences, such as admission to kindergarten or readiness for reading instruction. Gesell's studies focused attention on the biological unfolding of growth and development characteristics and provided sets of benchmarks and principles of development that continue to influence child study today. However, today, researchers recognize that these early developmental studies were conducted primarily on children from Caucasian, middle-class families from Western cultures, and therefore the findings are not easily generalizable to all children.

descriptive study
research collected by observing and recording behavior and providing a description of the observed behavior

Cross-Sectional and Longitudinal Studies

A **cross-sectional study** looks at an aspect of development or behavior at various ages or stages at the same time. For example, a **representative sample** of children at ages 2 to 18 had their heights and weights recorded at the same time. This information was converted into charts that pediatricians use to predict young children's weight and height at later ages. Cross-sectional research can provide information about certain types of development, such as height and weight, within a relatively short time. However, this

cross-sectional study
research that studies subjects of different ages at the same time

representative sample
a sample of subjects who are representative of the larger population of individuals about whom the researcher wants to draw conclusions

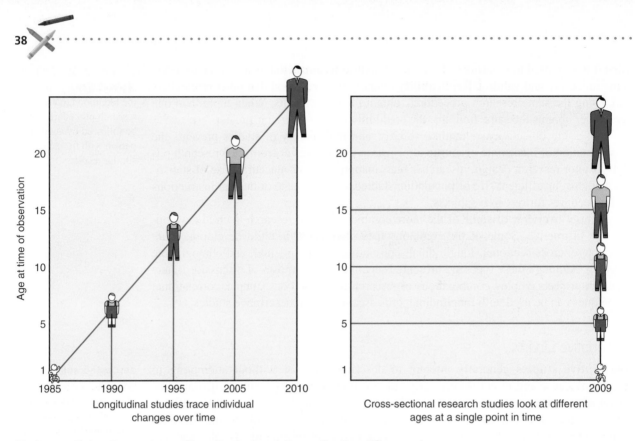

Figure 2.1   Comparison of Longitudinal and Cross-Sectional Research

(left graph x-axis label) Longitudinal studies trace individual changes over time

(right graph x-axis label) Cross-sectional research studies look at different ages at a single point in time

type of study cannot determine exactly when an individual changes. Figure 2.1 contrasts cross-sectional and longitudinal studies.

longitudinal study
research that collects information about the same subjects at different ages over a period of time

One way to study change in the development of individuals is the **longitudinal study.** This type of study looks at the same individuals over a period of time. An important example of this type of study is the research conducted on a number of young children in low-income families who were enrolled in early childhood education programs in the 1960s when the federal Head Start program was being launched (Barnett, 1995; Berrueta-Clement, Schweinhart, Barnett, Epstein, & Weikart, 1984; Lazar & Darlington, 1982; Schweinhart, Barnes, & Weikart, 1993; Schweinhart & Weikart, 1997). For example, in one of the programs studied, the High/Scope Perry Preschool Program at Ypsilanti, Michigan (Schweinhart et al., 1993; Schweinhart & Weikart, 1997; Schweinhart et al., 2005), 123 people from ages 4 through 40 were tested and interviewed over the years to determine whether their participation in high-quality preschool programs had long-term effects. They were then compared with children who had not attended a preschool program. Generally, these studies indicated that at-risk **preprimary** children who were in high-quality early childhood programs had higher educational performance as students in school; and as adults they had higher earnings, were more likely to hold a job, had committed fewer crimes, and were more socially responsible than were children of similar circumstance who were not enrolled in early childhood programs. Figure 2.2 illustrates the major findings of the High/Scope Perry Preschool Study when the program group and no-program group were 40 years old.

preprimary
the time in young children's lives before they enter the primary (first, second, and third) grades

chapter 2

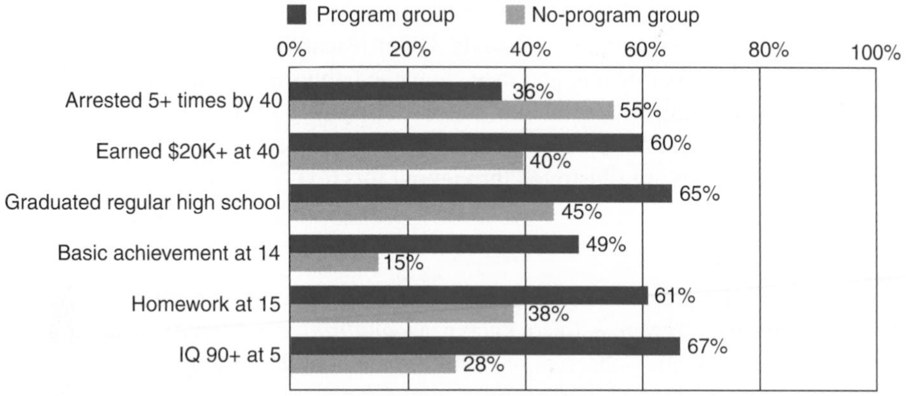

Figure 2.2 Major Findings: High/Scope Perry Preschool Study at 40

Source: Schweinhart, L. J., Montie, J., Xiang, Z., Barnett, W. S., Belfield, C. R., & Nores, M. (2005). *Lifetime effects: The High/Scope Perry Preschool study through age 40.* [Monographs of the High/Scope Educational Research Foundation, 14]. Ypsilanti, MI: High/Scope Press. Available at http://www.highscope.org

Correlational Studies

Correlational studies look at the nature of the relationship between two sets of measurements. For example, in a study of the effects of a training course on caregivers' behavior and children's development, Rhodes and Hennessy (2001) found a relationship between the resulting change in adult interactions with children and significant gains among the children in social and cognitive development.

Correlational studies indicate only relationships, not causes. Thus, it cannot be said that a specific type of caregiver training causes specific types of social or cognitive behaviors in children. It can be said only that there is a positive relationship between caregiver training and gains in social and cognitive development in children.

correlational study
research that attempts to determine a relationship between two or more sets of measurements

Experimental Studies

In an **experimental study,** the researcher usually divides the population under study into two groups by **random selection.** One group is designated as the *experimental group* and receives some special treatment, such as a particular type of teaching methodology or special coaching on a particular concept or skill; the second group is called the *control group* and usually does not receive this treatment. The control group is the baseline group to which changes in the experimental group are compared. Sometimes, the two groups receive two different types of treatment or experiences. In some experimental designs, subjects are given pretests and posttests to measure the influence of the treatment or experiences after the subjects have been exposed to it. The researcher then employs statistical analyses to determine if the differences between the groups (or within the same group after a particular treatment) were significant (that is, the differences were not simply by chance), and the same results would therefore likely occur with another similar group of subjects.

Another kind of experimental study takes place in university laboratories, especially with young children. Researchers set up experiments in which babies listen through earphones, for instance, to the sound "ah, ah, ah, ah," until they get bored; the researcher

experimental study
research that involves treating each of two or more groups in different ways to determine cause-and-effect relationships

random selection
a procedure for assigning subjects to an experimental or control group so that each person has the same chance of being selected for either group

then changes the sound to "oh" and the baby perks up with new interest. This tells the researcher that the baby can differentiate sounds. Other researchers let babies watch them put two items in a box, take one out, and then show the babies the empty box. The babies register their surprise with their facial expressions, appearing to do some form of addition and subtraction (Wynn, 1992).

Many of these studies are illustrated throughout this text.

Ethnographic Studies

More intimate than the previous types of research in child study is a form of research known as *ethnographic research* (also known as *qualitative research*). Ethnographic research entails systematic observation within the child's natural setting. Like Bronfenbrenner's bioecological perspective, ethnography requires the researcher to consider the relative and reciprocal influence of all aspects of the child's environment: biological, racial, ethnic, socioeconomic, sociocultural, psychological, and cognitive (Creswell, 2008). The researcher is interested in observing and assessing the individual child's responses and interactions within her or his natural environment.

participant–observer
a researcher who participates in the daily lives of the subjects of the study

This type of research is intensive and time consuming because it often requires the researcher to become a participant in the life and experiences of the research subject (child and/or family). As such, the researcher employs what are known as **participant–observer** techniques (Stringer, 2007). Because this type of research is open ended, research questions often evolve during the study. Unlike most studies where questions, assumptions, and hypotheses are framed at the outset and the study is designed to corroborate, prove, or disprove them, ethnographic studies can lead the researcher to unforeseen points of interest and inquiry. Thus, ethnography becomes a theory-generating rather than a theory-testing form of research (Stringer, 2007).

Interactions with the subjects of the study are generally unstructured and spontaneous, allowing participants to behave in context in their own unique and individualistic ways. The researcher may ask questions such as the following: "What do/did you think about that?" "What do/did you do when she said that to you?" "What did others do?" "What do you think happened when…?" "If it happens again, what will you do?" "Tell me how you learned to do that." Open-ended questions allow the research subjects to describe their thinking, behaviors, and intentions in their own words and from their own perspectives. Consider this account of a home visit given by an ethnographic scholar:

> The first time I visited one of our participants in her home, I noticed that her large apartment building looked almost deserted, even in comparison with the surrounding, equally shabby housing. The perception of abandonment deepened when I entered the building. I felt that the mother's apartment, up a winding flight of stairs and at the end of a long hall, was the only inhabited one. Once the videotaping began I heard squeals coming from somewhere in the small apartment. These were definitely animal sounds and were definitely not coming from a cat, dog, or mouse. I'm sure my attention was on the floor for much of that visit, looking out for rats. Later in the visit, when the mother and I had talked a bit and gotten to know each other a little, she told me that she had a crib for her baby but she preferred he sleep with her so she could keep watch over him. She was afraid that rats would bite her baby. I had an immediate, visceral understanding of this mother's fear and more empathy for her plight than I ever could have gained had she related her concern in a rat-free office. (Happily, by the time of the next visit six weeks later, the mother had moved to a building with no rats. I later learned that her former building had been condemned.) (Freel, 1996, p. 6)

Ethnographic studies use open-ended interviews-in-context, home visits, video and audio taping, and copious notes, which record verbatim and in strict chronological order the words, phrases, and sentences of the observed. Written narrative accounts are recorded immediately so as not to lose essential facts, impressions, or circumstantial data. The researcher is not focused just on the dramatic, but more importantly on the everyday, often mundane behaviors and events. Because this type of research project can yield an enormous amount of data, the researcher must analyze the data carefully for patterns, similarities, and discrepancies. The questions behind this process are as follows: "What are we seeing?" "What did it mean?" "How significant for child development were the behaviors that were observed?" (Freel, 1996).

Social Indicators

Social indicators are statistical markers that provide information on the well-being of specific populations. For example, the health care profession is very interested in tracking the evolution and spread of disease. The SARS epidemic in China in 2003 was followed through statistical tracking. Hence, policy makers could respond with intervention and prevention policies and scientists could focus their efforts on determining the cause, spread, treatment, and perhaps cure for the disease.

Social indicators do not determine cause and effect. Statistics can tell us that poverty is on the rise, or that more 2-year-olds in a certain year are fully immunized than 2-year-olds were in a previous year, or that there is an increase in stay-at-home fathers over previous accounts; but this information answers no questions about why these changes occurred. Social indicators often reveal a need to accelerate scientific efforts and often generate further research specifically focused on improving our lives.

Ethical use of social indicators can lead to socially responsible outcomes, such as identifying populations in need of supportive or health-promoting interventions, improving the conditions and experiences of children in public education, and improved quality of child care. State and local economic conditions can be projected and planning initiated for such needs as transportation, housing, food supplies, and employment opportunities. Unethical use of social indicators misleads by over- or underplaying selected findings (sometimes out of context) to arouse individual or public concern, to garner support for political issues, or to simply argue one's point of view. Professionals in early childhood education and family development learn to be discerning consumers of statistical information and to recognize its misapplication. Furthermore, professionals in all fields interpret and share valid statistical information in accurate and honest ways and use this information to serve the best interest of children and families.

Ethics of Child Development Research

Because of the increasing awareness regarding the rights and feelings of young children and their families, careful attention must be given to ensure that neither physiological nor psychological harm occurs to children during or as a result of a research process. Both the American Psychological Association (2002) and the Society for Research in Child Development, Committee on Ethical Standards for Research with Children (1990–1991) (Society for Research in Child Development, 2007) have developed procedures for conducting research with human subjects. These standards outline the rights of children and

Opportunities to interact with children in home and preschool settings provide students with important insights into child growth, development, and learning.

the responsibilities of researchers and stipulate that parental or guardian permission must be obtained before any research can begin.

Another area of ethics involves the honesty of the researcher in reporting the study. Most researchers plan well-designed studies. However, the unpredictable nature of children and other complications sometimes prevent the researcher from completing the study as originally intended. It is the responsibility of the researcher to acknowledge all limitations to the study when conducting or reporting the research and its findings. At times, pilot studies or smaller preliminary studies can help to identify potential problems with a research design before it is carried out on a full scale and its findings published or otherwise reported.

Sociocultural Perspectives in Studying Young Children

Often, early child development research information comes from studies conducted by researchers who have the same economic and sociocultural backgrounds as the children they have studied, as with the Gesell studies mentioned earlier. Therefore, the application of the research to other groups or to the general population of children is inappropriate. Researchers must include children from a variety of socioeconomic, cultural, and gender groups before attempts at universal application. If the group studied does not represent different populations (i.e., age, grade, socioeconomic level, race, ethnicity, gender, ability), then the researcher must accurately describe the population that made up the research sample population and generalize the findings to members of that particular population only. For instance, if the study included only low-income children, then its findings cannot be said to be true of children in families with higher incomes. Researchers acknowledge an array of diverse characteristics and influences among children associated with age, grade, socioeconomic background, race, ethnicity, gender, ability, and contexts in which the studies are conducted when attempting to design research or interpret findings. Sensitivity to cultural behaviors, values, beliefs, and expectations and to the effects of the research design on individuals prevents bias and accurately portrays the subjects of the study. Sensitivity to sociocultural perspectives facilitates accurate interpretation of findings.

Young Children with Special Needs and the Study of Child Development

The science of early childhood development has begun to take shape through recent studies and revelations about variations in developmental trajectories and the projection of developmental outcomes. Recognizing that there are wide ranges in what might be considered challenges or strengths in individuals, today's perspective on children with special needs is far more promising than historical perspectives. Historical perspectives tended to focus on children with disabilities as somehow deficient or as facing limitations in their potential developmental outcomes.

In this context, the most helpful and perhaps enlightened view of child growth and development is the one that states that:

> child development [is] a continuous process influenced by reciprocal transactions between children and their caregivers, caregivers and the caregiving environment, and an array of external systems. The cumulative effects of these transactions over time [are] seen to contribute to the complexity of human development and the poor predictability of individual developmental pathways. (Shonkoff, Phillips, & Keilty, 2000, p. 3)

This view acknowledges the difficulty of predicting developmental outcomes for both "typically" developing and "atypically" developing children. The influencing factors are many, and the degree of variation and levels of challenge are multiple. This requires that distinctions be made among concepts of persistent disabilities, maturational delays, and individual difference in development and behavior.

It is also important to recognize that for every child there are challenges and strengths, any of which can be met along the developmental pathway with obstacles and interference or with supports and buffers to optimal growth and development. Some children and families have greater knowledge and resources, whereas others may be limited in their information and support systems. Some children (and family members) are more resilient and adaptive and cope in more positive and constructive, growth-promoting ways than others.

The important thing for early childhood professionals to know, however, is that children with physical, cognitive, or social-emotional challenges are successfully included in every type of early childhood care and education program. Today, the early childhood professional learns how to work with families and early interventionists so they are able to assess the strengths of children and adapt materials and activities for children with disabilities. Both preservice and inservice training in inclusion of children with disabilities is now widely available. It is important for early childhood professionals to take a broad view of child development, particularly when engaging all children in inclusive ways in play groups, classrooms, and other groups.

Your Study and Observation of Young Children

Your study of young children can help you to develop a knowledge base regarding the unique nature of child development and behavior. This knowledge fosters an awareness of the enormous diversity in development and behavior among children. It can help you to select materials and instructional strategies for working with young children. Informed study can also help you to avoid bias and become more objective in looking at children. This study involves exploring topics of interest in the professional literature and observing children in many contexts. Studies have shown that teacher training relating to appropriate interactions and expectations resulted in more positive relationships and less detachment behaviors in their interactions with children, and their students exhibited significant gains in complex social and cognitive play (NICHD Early Child Care Research Network, 2002a; Rhodes & Hennessy, 2001).

However, it is important to acknowledge biases and to realize that early childhood professionals bring their own backgrounds, experiences, belief systems, and values to the interpretation of children's behavior. At times, it may be helpful to have other professionals use the same procedures and tools to verify your information and ensure objectivity.

Four behaviors are important for the developing early childhood professional to acquire: perspective-taking, reflecting-in-action, teacher-as-learner, and teacher-as-researcher.

Perspective-taking is the ability to view and understand a situation from another's point of view. This skill is a particularly important one for individuals who interact with children and their families on a day-to-day basis. The development of focused perspective-taking begins with reflecting on one's notions, assumptions, and perspectives of children, parents, culture, ability, teaching, and learning and how one thinks adults are "supposed" to interact with children, parents, and colleagues.

Generally, teachers' perspectives on children are influenced by the following factors (see Blosch, Tabachnick, & Espinosa-Dulanto, 1994, p. 225):

- The teacher's personal and professional experiences and beliefs
- The teacher's and the school's beliefs about assessment as it relates to children's age, developmental level, cultural and class background, and beliefs and policies promulgated at the national, state, school district, and individual school setting or campus levels
- The teacher's awareness or lack of awareness of children's competencies and broader social issues that relate to the teacher's attitudes toward children as being "different" with respect to ethnicity, gender, race, language, and class group identities or membership

A second behavior the developing early childhood professional must acquire is **reflecting-in-action.** From the outset of their field-based experiences, early childhood professionals need to reflect on their own behaviors and how those behaviors affect children and their families. Time can be set aside in both preservice and inservice settings for early childhood professionals to engage in reflection, both individually and in collaboration with colleagues.

Such opportunities assist the early childhood professional in developing habits of reflecting. These experiences cast the professional in the role of **teacher-as-learner,** one who learns continually from children, their families, and other professionals and from the changing professional research and literature. Reflection entails frequently revisiting one's image of the child, information gained about child growth, development, and learning obtained through observation, and one's image of self as a professional educator (Trepanier-Street, Hong, & Donegan, 2001). Teachers reflect on many aspects of their work, including the following:

- Their own perceptions, perspectives, and preferences
- Their observations of individual and group behaviors and developmental progress
- How best to facilitate growth, development, and learning
- Creative ways to problem solve
- How best to interact with challenging children, parents, or colleagues

perspective-taking
the ability to understand one's own or another's viewpoint and be aware of the coordinated and inter-related sets of ideas and actions that are reflected in behavior

reflecting-in-action
an ongoing process in which educators think about and critically analyze their own and their students' performance to review, assess, and modify interactions, expectations, and instructional strategies

teacher-as-learner
the process by which educators continue to learn from children, parents, other professionals, and the changing professional research and literature throughout their careers

- Ethical issues and sound decision making
- Their own continuing need to know

The process of acquiring new ideas, values, and practices leads teachers to enhance their personal and professional knowledge and skills.

Children, parents, and teachers learn from one another. In this process, new hypotheses about development and practice emerge. These hypotheses often lead to investigations into behaviors, teaching strategies, and approaches to assessment of learning and development. The result is often new understandings or perspectives about children, families, early childhood development behavior and learning, instructional methods, and oneself as a professional and as a person.

From this process emerges an expanded perspective: **teacher-as-researcher**. Early childhood professionals, through perspective-taking and reflecting-in-action, continuously learn about themselves and the children they teach, thereby acquiring and demonstrating the behaviors of a researcher. If this process is internalized, the early childhood professional becomes a skilled observer who views children and families from objective and empathic perspectives. For example, rather than viewing a child whose vocabulary is limited as having a language or an intellectual deficit, the teacher-as-researcher views the child from a developmental perspective that looks for causes and solutions. Awareness of the background experiences that may have deterred vocabulary development helps the educator to relate in appropriate and helpful ways to the child's parents or caregivers to further the child's vocabulary development. From this perspective, the early childhood professional assumes a proactive role in identifying and providing the types of experiences that help children progress.

As professionals adopt these behaviors, child study comes to focus on what children can do—their strengths and competencies—rather than on their differences from the so-called norm or their alleged deficiencies. This frame of mind and this level of professionalism are essential in child care and education settings because these programs are increasingly characterized by greater diversity among children in culture, socioeconomic backgrounds, ability, and knowledge and experience (Copple, 2003).

teacher-as-researcher
the process by which early childhood professionals, through their perspective-taking and reflecting-in-action, acquire and demonstrate the behaviors of a researcher

Ongoing Study of Children in Many Contexts

Competent early childhood professionals realize the importance of day-to-day observation and study of children in a variety of situations, including settings within the classroom, in outdoor learning areas, at mealtimes, and during rest and quiet times, as well as in the wider context of family and community. Complete understanding of young children involves study of their behavior in a variety of contexts over an extended period of time because children's behavior may vary from one setting to another. The nature of the setting, the people, the time of day, the child's personality, and many other factors influence the way children behave. In addition, contrived, unfamiliar, or laboratory-type environments can convey misleading information about children, their behaviors, and their competencies (Bronfenbrenner & Ceci, 1994).

When early childhood professionals study children in a variety of settings over a period of time, they see the common characteristics of young children as well as individual behaviors. The study of young children can also help the early childhood professional to provide specific examples of children's behavior when in conference with parents. The study of young children can also serve as a means of documenting that the program goals for facilitating young children's development and learning are being accomplished. Appropriate, reliable, and valid strategies for studying young children are becoming increasingly important because many early childhood programs depend on private, state, or federal funding and often require documentation of performance or achievement of goals and objectives.

Authentic Assessment of the Development of Young Children

Sociologists and psychologists emphasize that the competencies needed to function effectively in the 21st century include problem-solving skills; the ability to communicate orally, through writing, and through technology; the capacity to work with others in cooperative, collaborative ways; and the ability to view events from a changing and global perspective. The explosion of knowledge that characterizes the contemporary world suggests that children (and adults) need to know how to access information; develop skills in discerning, selecting, sorting, and classifying information; and develop skills in determining what information they need and can use.

These projections have been the impetus for the school reform movement that began in the 1980s and continues today. However, the school reform movement has been increasingly marked by greater emphasis on standards and required content in each of the subject matter disciplines. This has been coupled with accountability measures to ensure that the standards are being met and that curriculum content is adequately covered. Such emphasis has resulted in curricular designs that do not develop many of the skills and attributes citizens of the 21st century need. The reform movement thus has come to be characterized by more and more testing of children, mostly with standardized tests that employ paper-and-pencil tasks with multiple-choice questions. Many people in the field of child development and early education find this emphasis on testing and limited curricula to be deleterious. Increasing concern about excessive and inappropriate use of standardized tests in early childhood and elementary programs has precipitated the need to find new ways to evaluate learning.

authentic assessment
the ongoing, continuous, context-based observation and documentation of children's learning behaviors

One such approach is referred to as **authentic assessment.** Authentic assessment is the process of observing and documenting children's learning and behavior and using the information to make educational decisions that promote their learning and development. It is continuous, context bound, and qualitative in nature. Essentially, authentic assessment (Puckett & Black, 2008) is developmentally appropriate and performs the following functions:

- Celebrates development and learning
- Emphasizes emerging development
- Capitalizes on the strengths of the learner
- Is based on real-life events
- Is performance based
- Is related to instruction
- Focuses on purposeful learning
- Is ongoing in all contexts
- Provides a broad and general picture of student learning and capabilities
- Is collaborative among parents, teachers, students, and other professionals as needed

Clearly, skilled and focused observation is integral to authentic assessment. The student of child development employs a variety of techniques to record and assemble observational information. This information combined with more structural/formal approaches can provide an informative profile of a child or a group of children.

Approaches to Studying Young Children

A variety of tools and techniques are available to the early childhood professional in the study of young children. Generally, these tools and techniques are classified as formal or informal approaches to assessment (Table 2.1).

Formal Approaches to Assessment

Formal assessment generally includes the use of various types of **standardized tests,** including the following:

> **Achievement tests** measure *past* learning or what knowledge and/or skills a student has learned or achieved from instruction.
>
> **Intelligence tests** measure what an individual ostensibly *could* learn, establish an intelligence level rating (e.g., intelligence quotient [IQ]), and measure abilities associated with vocabulary and word meaning, concepts, and selected nonverbal tasks.
>
> **Readiness tests** assess skills that are thought to be prerequisites for success in formal instructional settings. Generally, these tests assess the following areas of development:
>
> 1. language development (e.g., speaking in complete sentences, number of words in vocabulary, listening to and recalling what was said or heard)
> 2. large and small motor coordination and development
> 3. visual–perceptual development (ability to distinguish size, shape, color, and other attributes)
> 4. reading readiness (recognizing and naming letters, attaching sounds to specific letters); number readiness (ability to count using one-to-one correspondence and understanding of a variety of mathematically related concepts such as "small" and "large," "more than" and "less than," "first" and "last," and so on)
> 5. social–emotional development (or adaptive behaviors), which can include, but is not limited to, how children interact with and relate to others, separate from their parents, and regard themselves and their own abilities

formal assessment
information gathered about young children, usually through standardized tests

standardized test
a test that is administered and scored according to set procedures and whose scores can be interpreted according to predetermined statistical measures

achievement test
a test that measures what children have learned as a result of instruction

intelligence test
a standardized measure used to establish an intelligence level rating (e.g., intelligence quotient [IQ]) by measuring a child's ability to perform various selected mental tasks

readiness test
a test that measures capabilities needed for certain new experiences or types of curriculum

Table 2.1 Formal and Informal Approaches to Studying Young Children

Formal	Informal
Achievement tests	Narrative observations; running records, specimen records, anecdotal records
Readiness tests	Checklists
Developmental screening tests	Rating scales
Diagnostic tests	Time sampling
Intelligence tests	Event sampling
	Interviews/conferences: child, parents, support staff, resource persons, peers
	Children's products: art, writings, class work, projects

**developmental
screening test**
an initial procedure for
identifying individuals
who may need formal
diagnostic tests

diagnostic test
a process of compiling
and assessing charac-
teristics and symptoms
(physiological, emotional,
or social) to identify needs
and establish treatment
and/or intervention
strategies

Developmental screening tests are used to identify heretofore unrecognized disease or disability. Results from these tests are used to determine whether a child needs more extensive evaluation and more precise diagnosis.

Diagnostic tests are individually administered by trained professionals for the purpose of determining the extent and identification of specific anomalies followed by intervention strategies and treatment.

As mentioned earlier, various professional disciplines have attempted to write sets of standards that state what children at each grade level should know and be able to do. The *standards movement,* as it has come to be called, has precipitated overreliance on scores from standardized tests to determine the extent to which children have "risen to the standard." This information is typically used to hold schools and school districts accountable. Unfortunately, young children do not do well on formal types of group-administered tests and have been shown to exhibit undue stress behaviors when taking them (Fleege, Charlesworth, Burts, & Hart, 1992). Consequently, the scores from such tests are of dubious value, and professionals have long decried subjecting young children to them.

Difficulties for young children in taking formal tests arise from the following:

- Discomfort, fear, or stress inherent in most formal testing situations
- Lack of familiarity and/or rapport with the person administering the test
- Insufficient fine motor control to manage the artifacts of formal tests (e.g., some types of manipulatives, pencils, test booklets, and bubble-in answer sheets)
- Insufficient language and vocabulary development to understand and follow oral instructions
- Limited listening skills
- Short attention span
- Distractibility

Further, early childhood development is rapid. Skills and knowledge are increasing at a pace that precludes the ability to draw conclusions or inferences that would remain stable over any appreciable length of time as descriptors or characterizations of a particular child's abilities or achievements.

Testing puts stress on young children, even those who perform well on tests. A study by Fleege et al. (1992) documented the stress behaviors of both able and less competent learners in a kindergarten classroom during the administration of a standardized test. This study indicates that kindergarten teachers may respond to the stress observed in their students by using a variety of techniques that violate standardized testing procedures, further rendering scores of dubious accuracy or usefulness.

Group standardized testing often causes stress in young children.

chapter 2

During the 1980s, when concern over the uses and misuses of standardized tests with young children was mounting among professionals in the early childhood development field, the National Association for the Education of Young Children published a widely disseminated position statement on testing. According to this statement, the increased use of standardized testing with young children is indicative of the escalating trend toward curricula that are inappropriate for children's ages and developmental levels (National Association for the Education of Young Children, 1988). Unfortunately, many contemporary kindergartens continue to mimic upper grades, with limited opportunities for appropriate developmental experiences, in spite of the fact that there is no research to indicate that this is the way young children learn or that their developmental needs have changed.

In 2006, there was a new emphasis from the George W. Bush administration on supporting early childhood educators. As part of the *No Child Left Behind Act,* the standards movement required all states to develop outcomes for their K–12 students. The *Good Start, Grow Smart* initiative asked the states to prepare early learning guidelines (ELG) for 4-year-olds describing what they should know about reading and mathematics before entering kindergarten. Most of the states developed ELGs that went beyond reading and math to include social-emotional growth, physical growth, and approaches to learning. Many states felt that it had been so beneficial to really study the current research and learn about how 4-year-olds learn that they continued the process and wrote ELGs for birth to age 3 (National Infant & Toddler Child Care Initiative and ZERO TO THREE Policy Center, 2010). These have been very meaningful in professional development in helping teachers, caregivers, and home visitors have the ability to recognize and anticipate learning. However, the very creation of these guidelines has raised considerable concern in the field as to whether they might be misused as assessments.

The preceding discussion indicates that formal methods of studying young children in educational settings need to be used judiciously and with caution. Some programs that use state or federal funds need to use standardized assessments to track children's learning and development. Formal standardized assessments help identify children who may have special developmental or educational needs and do provide information that, when combined with other types of assessment and sources of information, can provide a comprehensive profile of a particular child. However, informal approaches tend to be a more appropriate technique for general classroom use and professional development child study. Informal approaches provide more comprehensive and immediate information about current performance that can easily be translated into educational experiences for individual children.

Informal Approaches to Assessment

Informal assessments assess emerging development in all developmental domains and focus on what children do and how they do it. Informal assessments can focus on *performance* (what children do and how they demonstrate their capabilities), *processes* (what strategies children use to pursue information, acquire skills, or solve problems), and *products* (the types of constructions, such as blocks, clay, manipulatives, drawings, and writings, that children create and produce). As such, informal approaches, particularly in classroom settings, are said to be *performance based*.

informal assessment information gathered about young children through approaches other than standardized tests

The Where, When, and How of Early Childhood Study and Assessment

When teachers observe young children, they learn about many different aspects of their development.

Regardless of the techniques used, it is important to study and be aware of a child's total development and behavior. This study of the whole child includes focusing on the following:

- *physical/motor development* (health, hygiene, posture, movement, visual and hearing acuity, management of clothes and personal needs, coordination in using learning materials and play apparatus, and so on)
- *emotional/social development* (awareness and modulation of emotions, self-regulation and attention span, self-awareness, self-regard, self-confidence, interaction styles and social competence, prosocial behaviors, moral competence, and so on)
- *speech and language development* (ability to speak clearly, use of language, vocabulary, communication strategies, and so on)
- *cognitive development* (concepts, misconcepts, perceptions, reasoning, use of logic, perspective-taking ability, types of intelligences, and learning in the content areas, such as literacy, mathematics, science, social studies, and the arts)

The following are informal ways of studying young children.

narrative observation
a written observation of behavior

running record
a type of narrative observation that records all behaviors in sequential order as they occur

Narrative Observations. **Narrative observations** are records of behaviors as they occur. The period of time may vary from several minutes to hours at a time. Notepads, a pencil, and keen observational skills are all that is needed. Running records, specimen records, and anecdotal records are three techniques for obtaining and recording narrative information.

Running records are accounts of *all* behaviors as they occur during a specified time span. Figure 2.3 provides an example of a running record. These observations describe the sequence of behaviors as well as the setting and events surrounding the behavior. Running records provide a rich source of information. If there is only one teacher in the classroom with no assistant, running records may not be practical because they require focused attention on an individual for a sustained period of time. However, using parent volunteers or planning for a time when the children are involved in independent activity can give the classroom teacher some time to conduct running records. Procedures for using running records include the following:

1. Description of the setting, including the time the observation begins and the activity that is taking place
2. Recording information in a detailed, sequential, and unbiased manner. Information must be factual and objective, recording only what actually happened
3. Comments and analyses: drawing inferences and conclusions that evidence accurate child development descriptions

Figure 2.3
A Running Record

Child's Name: Daniel   Age: 3½   Date: 3/10
Observer: Veronica   Place: Lab   Time: 9:36 A.M.

Observations	Comments
Daniel is sitting at a table in the classroom rolling out clay. He is making primarily flat shapes with a rolling pin.	Daniel has excellent arm strength and good coordination of his movements.
He stands while rolling out the clay and sits to cut the shapes.	The table is evidently too high for Daniel because he had to stand while rolling out the clay.
After rolling out each piece of clay completely, he takes a cookie cutter and cuts circles out of the clay.	Daniel is cutting out circles exclusively because no other shapes are available. Other children working with clay are using other cutters.
Taking two of the cutout circles, he places them over his eyes and says, "I have new glasses, like my daddy."	Daniel has used the objects he created to move into fantasy and socialize with the other children.
Teacher asks, "What can you see with your new glasses?"	
Daniel: "Dark."	
Teacher: "No, what can you see?"	(Teacher is attempting to draw language from Daniel. His response indicates that he may not be certain of the teacher's intent or the actual meaning of the question.)
Daniel: "I can't see anything with my new glasses, it's just dark…they're just *pretend* glasses!"	

Specimen Records. **Specimen records** are narrative observations that are more detailed than running records. Specimen records usually focus on a particular time of day, setting, or child. Specimen records provide detailed information about such observations as the effects of scheduling, the influence of certain curricular or guidance techniques, and specific children and their behavior. The format used for running records can be used for specimen records. If needed and practical, recorders or video cameras may provide more complete and detailed information. Parental permission is required to tape or photograph children. Figure 2.4 provides an example of a specimen record.

specimen record
a type of narrative observation that provides detailed information about a particular event, child, or time of day

Anecdotal Records. **Anecdotal records** differ from running and specimen records in that they are usually written after the incident occurs. They are brief and describe only one incident at a time that the observer believes is significant. Anecdotal records are cumulative and describe in an objective and factual manner what happened, how it happened, when and where it happened, and what was said and done. The observer can write commentaries in the margin or at the conclusion of the anecdote. Anecdotal records can be particularly helpful to the busy classroom teacher who finds it somewhat difficult to do the more time-consuming running record and the more detailed specimen record, as

anecdotal record
a type of narrative observation that describes an incident in detail

Figure 2.4
A Specimen Record

A group of preschool-age boys were beginning an outdoor play activity. There was a disagreement about who was going to enact the more desirable characters. Their language characterizes the overt organizational behaviors of the fantasy theme among the frustrated subjects.

John (M1):	There will be three Lukes today.
All:	I want to be Luke today! (competing for the role)
Jim (M6):	I'll be Luke.
Bruce (M4):	There can't be all Lukes. (frustrated)
Kevin (M3):	I'll be Chewy.
Paul (M5):	Who else is Luke?
Chuck (M2):	He is. (points to Bruce)
Dan (M7):	What?
Bruce (M4):	We got our whole game mixed up!
Kevin (M3):	Right, I'm Chewy.
Bruce (M4):	Two people are Lukes, all right?
Jim (M6):	No, I'm Luke!
Chuck (M2):	I wanna…
Bruce (M4):	All right!
Jim (M6):	Let's have a converse (conference?), let's hold hands. Let's hold hands…we are having a converse, right? (looking for agreement among the play group members)
Paul (M5):	Right now?
Bruce (M4):	Hold onto my sleeve. (to Paul)
John (M1):	The game's mixed up. (directed to the adult observer)
Adult:	The game's mixed up? (responding to John's statement)
Bruce (M4):	Yeah, we get it mixed up all of the time.

The boys formed a circle and held hands during the "converse" (conference). The discussion developed out of frustration and lack of cooperation at the outset of the play activity. This specimen of linguistic behavior provides a source of information regarding play theme management and status hierarchies in play groups.

illustrated in Figure 2.5. Ms. Schwartz, a kindergarten teacher, became concerned about 5-year-old Ann's periodic aggressive behavior. Ms. Schwartz began to keep anecdotal records after these episodes occurred. These notes were then analyzed according to time, activity, and children involved. Ms. Schwartz was better able to determine what provoked Ann's aggressive behavior and then plan guidance strategies to assist Ann in managing her anger and frustrations.

Observation with Predefined Instruments. Predefined instruments used in studying young children include checklists, rating scales, time sampling, event sampling, and interviews. As with narrative observations, these techniques have advantages and disadvantages.

A **checklist** is a list of developmental behaviors that have been identified as important to look for in young children. They are helpful tools in studying children when many easily specified behaviors need to be observed and recorded. Checklists are usually used with one child at a time and are prepared in an objective manner that

checklist
a list of developmental behaviors that the observer identifies as being present or absent

Figure 2.5
An Anecdotal
Record

Date: February 19
Observer: Schwartz
Child: Ann S.
Time: 8:38 A.M. During center time this morning, Ann was playing in the dramatic play center with a rag doll. While sitting on the floor, Ann began to repeatedly beat the floor with the head and upper torso of the doll while holding on to the doll's legs and feet. At first she hit the floor lightly and sporadically. Then the intensity and frequency of the activity increased to the extent that the doll's arm began to tear away. I intervened at this point and redirected Ann to another activity with the teacher assistant.
Time: 9:20 A.M. During the transition from centers to story time, Ann walked past the block area and knocked down Daniel's tower of blocks, which he had built during today's center time. Daniel screamed as the tower fell, and Ann watched passively as he called for me. Ann was unable to verbalize what had happened but did manage to apologize to Daniel for this "accident."
Time: 10:30 A.M. On the playground, I observed Ann push her way past children on three separate occasions. Twice she pushed past children to gain access to the slide and once she pushed a child from behind to get a tricycle. The latter incident caused the child to skin her knee, requiring a trip to the school nurse. Ann was unable to verbalize what had happened and denied any responsibility for the incident.
Time: 11:15 A.M. As the children were washing their hands and getting drinks of water, I saw Ann purposefully tear her painting as it was hanging on the drying rack. Her expression was passive, a blank stare, as she tore the wet painting in two pieces. As both halves hung on the rack, she had no explanation for how the "accident" occurred.
Summary: While observing Ann throughout this morning, it was clear that something was bothering her. The aggressive incidents were uncharacteristic of Ann and appeared to occur without provocation. Despite efforts by the classroom teaching team to involve Ann in guided group activities this morning, she tended to lose interest and find solitary activities. Typically, when she was working or playing independently this morning, she had difficulty or acted aggressively. Further attention must be given to these behaviors for the next several days. A closer observation may be warranted. If this continues, I will contact Ann's parents to problem solve with them.

is cognizant of widely held expectations for age and individual differences. Figure 2.6 illustrates a checklist.

Rating scales are similar to checklists in that they include large numbers of traits or behaviors to observe. They provide more detailed information about the quality of traits or behaviors than checklists. However, the use of rating scales is dependent on the observer's judgment, so objectivity is critical. Figure 2.7 provides an example of a rating scale.

rating scale
a scale with various traits or categories that allows the observer to indicate the importance of the observed behaviors

Two other techniques that are used to observe and record behavior in young children are time sampling and event sampling. Time sampling and event sampling entail observing predetermined behaviors or categories of behavior at specific points in time or within a predetermined time interval. **Time sampling** is fairly simple and does not entail large amounts of time to do. However, time sampling does not provide information about the context or sequential nature of a behavior or event. Figure 2.8 illustrates time sampling.

time sampling
a procedure for recording selected observations on a predetermined schedule

In **event sampling** (Figure 2.9), the observer has a particular focus (event or behavior) in mind, such as a recurring problem of distraction or off-task behaviors. Event sampling

event sampling
a procedure in which the researcher notes the occurrences of particular behaviors or events

Figure 2.6
Checklist

Pretend Play Behaviors	Frequently	Sometimes	Seldom
Engages in imitative behaviors without props			
Engages in imitative behaviors using props			
Imitates actions and behaviors of adults			
Imitates actions and behaviors of playmates			
Verbally describes imitative actions			
Engages in sociodramatic play alone			
Engages in sociodramatic play with one or two playmates			
Engages in sociodramatic play with more than two playmates			
Communicates own perspectives and preferences			
Demonstrates ability to take the perspective of another			
Demonstrates willingness to cooperate			
Demonstrates a sense of fairness			
Uses language effectively to communicate during play			
Engages contextualized voice inflections, facial expressions, gestures, and other body language to convey meaning and intent			
Uses props effectively to support play themes			
Uses props creatively to support play themes			
Becomes actively engaged in the play theme			
Engages in prosocial play themes			
Accepts the gain or loss of players during a sociodramatic scenario without serious disruption			
Demonstrates ability to resolve conflicts			
Assumes leadership role			
Assumes follower role			
Appears to find satisfaction in sociodramatic play			

Figure 2.7
Rating Scale

Infant Language Behaviors

	Frequently	Sometimes	Never
1. Searches for and attends to another's voice			
2. Cues recognition of familiar voice			
3. Plays with voice: coos and makes gurgling and other mouth sounds			
4. Coos, smiles, makes eye contact with familiar person			
5. Cues a desire for interaction			
6. Cues a desire to cease interaction			
7. Responsive to singing voice			
8. Babbles			
9. Repeats one sound over and over (echolalia)			
10. Points and gestures			

Figure 2.8
Time Sampling

Behavior: Hitting other children
Subject(s): Jimmy (2 years, 6 months)
Observer: Ms. Gilliam
Observation Begins: 8:00 A.M.
Observation Ends: 4:00 P.M.
Date: 6/7

Hour of the Day	Time of Incident	Observer Notes
8:00		Observation begins
	8:09	
	8:35	
9:00		Morning snack
		Group time
10:00		Centers
	10:32	
11:00		Begin lunch routine
12:00		
1:00		Nap time begins: 12:30 P.M.
		Nap time
2:00		Nap time
		Child awake: 2:36 P.M.
3:00	3:02	Selected centers
	3:48	
4:00		Observation ends

Findings: 5 hitting incidents during observation period

Figure 2.9
Event Sampling

Behavior: Biting other children
Subject(s): Joaquin (1 year, 6 months)
Observer: Ms. Katz
Observation Begins: 8:00 A.M.
Observation Ends: 4:00 P.M.
Date: 6/7

Time	Observed Behavior	Observer Comments
9:10 A.M.	Joaquin and Josh are pulling on a large unit block. Both are kneeling facing each other. Each is using two hands to hold onto the block. Joaquin has lowered his head as a wedge between Josh's body and the block. After a brief pause, Josh screams, releases the block, and grasps his left forearm. Josh runs to the classroom teacher, still grasping his arm, crying, and unable to speak.	The physical behavior of biting appears to be Joaquin's strategy for gaining materials and objects that are held or claimed by other children. No audible language was observed during the confrontation.
11:15 A.M.	Joaquin repeats a similar conflict with Kenneth over a pair of headphones in listening center. Same physical posture and strategy to gain control of a disputed object.	Similar circumstances—no language observed, physical posture was similar, confrontation was brief with no amiable solution.

records how often these behaviors occur over a period of several days. Such observation techniques help to identify the causes of the problem. Information can be used to plan alternatives or to modify situations that cause the targeted behavior.

interview
engaging in a dialogue with a child that is either free-flowing or with predetermined questions to assess understandings and feelings

Other Methods of Gathering Information About Young Children. At times, **interviews** can be helpful in obtaining information about young children. During an interview, an adult enters into a one-to-one dialogue with the child, either free-flowing or using predetermined questions, depending on the intended focus of the interview. The purpose of an interview is usually to find out how and what children think and the way they are processing and using information. It is important for a successful interview that the interviewer spend time establishing rapport with the child. If the interview is to provide useful information, the following are essential:

1. The child must be able to express her- or himself verbally and feel psychologically safe in doing so.
2. The child must be physically comfortable, neither tired nor sleepy, hungry, thirsty, or in need of a rest room break.
3. The interview dialogue must in no way coax or probe for information that threatens the child or seeks information that should be held private or has no bearing on the assessment itself.
4. The child must trust and feel comfortable with the interviewer.

5. The interviewer must be sensitive to the child's psychological comfort level and to the child's receptive language and cognitive development because some responses may represent appropriate and effective thinking but provide an incorrect answer (e.g., "What color is an apple?" The child's answer could be "red," "yellow," or "green"; but the scoring instructions may require a "correct" answer of "red").

6. Interviews are best conducted in a familiar, child-friendly setting that is free of distractions.

Sometimes, teachers find that engaging in group dialogue sessions provides information about various group dynamics and their effects on individual children. Group dialogues provide an opportunity for teachers to observe how children are faring in a group context. During these dialogue sessions, the teacher may discover how one child's behavior affects another, how children interact in guided discussions, what kinds of perceptions or misperceptions seem to be common among many or all of the students, what kinds of behaviors are occurring that interfere with learning or positive social interactions among the children, and so on.

Other methods of gathering information about a young child include samples of the child's products, such as artistic creations, writings, and daily class work; informal and formal meetings, including conferences and home visits with the child's family; school records, if objective and factual; and other teachers, **support staff, resource persons, and peers.**

Technology can be helpful in recording various types of information. Audiotapes can help teachers to study children's oral language, including participation in singing, chanting, language games, or oral reading. Videotapes can be helpful in documenting and analyzing a wide range of behaviors. Videotapes can also be used to aid discussion about a child with parents and other support personnel who find it difficult to observe the child on a regular basis. A parent's written permission is required to audiotape, videotape, or photograph children. Computers can be useful for storing and quickly retrieving information about children. Figure 2.10 provides guidelines for conducting observations.

Documenting and Recording Child Behavior and Development

All high-quality early childhood programs have some record-keeping procedures to document the development of young children. All approaches, including those developed by the early childhood professional, need to be evaluated for (1) developmental appropriateness, (2) objectivity, and (3) usefulness to early childhood professionals and parents in helping them to understand and facilitate a child's growth, development, and learning.

Early childhood professionals continue their child study and hone their observation skills. At times, early childhood professionals may need to revise or eliminate the use of certain assessment or reporting techniques that are not developmentally appropriate or do not meet standards for professional practice. Additional methods of studying and documenting children's behavior and development may need to be designed and used. In recent years, the use of **portfolio** systems for documenting student performance, processes, and products has proven successful in portraying ongoing growth, development, and learning in individual children (Puckett & Black, 2008; Puckett & Diffily, 2004).

Early childhood professionals are very busy, and not all have an assistant or a teaching team. Consequently, they may need to be creative in devising ways that help them learn more about children in their own environment. As this chapter has briefly

support staff
other people within the educational setting who support the learning and development of young children, such as nurses, social workers, diagnosticians, psychologists, secretaries, and food service and housekeeping personnel

resource persons
people outside the educational setting, usually from health-related fields, who can provide information about young children's development and learning

peers
other children who are the same age as a particular child

portfolio
an assemblage of information derived from various assessment strategies, including representative samples of the child's play creations and academic products

Figure 2.10
Effectively Observing
Young Children

Skilled observation of young children requires certain characteristics of the observer and a naturalistic setting in which children can be observed doing and behaving in a typical manner. Although many observations do indeed occur in contrived or laboratory-type situations, any plan for observation must be clear about what it is that is to be observed and what inferences about child development or individual children can be accurately drawn from the observations in a particular context. To be an effective observer of child behavior and learning, the observer must do the following:

1. Be quite clear about what it is that is to be observed, identifying not only the developmental domain (motor development, language development, social interaction behaviors) but also, more specifically, what aspect(s) of a particular developmental domain (e.g., balance beam skill) will be observed and in what contexts (the classroom, the playground, the gymnasium) the behaviors will be observed.
2. Be clear about how and for what purposes observational information will be used.
3. Have a plan for recording observations (e.g., checklist, time sampling, anecdotal record, running record).
4. Prepare in advance for the observation by reading and learning about the behaviors that will be observed.
5. Determine the most appropriate time of day for a particular observation. (Using the balance beam example, perhaps earlier rather than later in the day or after a rest time would provide more accurate information because fatigue would not have to be considered as an influencing factor.)
6. Establish the best location for the observation to take place, and determine the most unobtrusive location for an observer to be positioned (if it is not an observation that requires the observer to follow about and interact with the child or children being observed).
7. Have all materials assembled and in place (clipboard, pen or pencil, observation forms or other recording instruments, laptop or handheld computer, or equipment such as tape recorder, video camera, or other electronic recording devices).
8. Be as unobtrusive and inconspicuous as possible. In some instances, this means becoming an on-the-run or participant–observer, which entails observing while engaged in a particular activity with a child or group of children. Other times, observations may occur from a particular vantage point. In either case, children who become aware that they are being observed do not behave naturally.
9. Develop the art and skill of empathic objectivity. This sounds like an oxymoron, but it implies the sensitivity to accept individuality in children and sufficient objectivity to draw accurate and meaningful inferences from what is observed.
10. Test your inferences. Would others draw the same conclusions from the same observation situation? Do these behaviors consistently and predictably occur in other situations?
11. Be aware of your own biases, assumptions, knowledge level, and physical or psychological state at the time of the observation.
12. Adhere to a code of ethics that protects the privacy and the integrity of children and their families. Information obtained from child study is never appropriate casual conversation material.

illustrated, there are a variety of ways to study individual children and child development. The following are some guidelines for early childhood professionals to facilitate their child study and observation:

1. Become well acquainted with widely held age-related expectations for growth, development, and learning.

2. Identify times when focused observations might be conducted, and also practice observing on the run.

3. Become familiar with the various techniques for observing and recording child behaviors and characteristics.

4. Practice objectivity. Ask yourself often, "What *actually* happened? Are my descriptions of the event colored by my own feelings or biases? Would all others observing this event agree with my description?"

5. Determine whether additional personnel are needed to carry out observations and assessments. Parent volunteers, student teachers, or child development students can assist in either supervising children or completing checklists, time sampling, or event sampling forms. Where professional judgment (not just counting or determining whether an objective characteristic exists or not) is required, the professional early childhood educator should carry out the task. The educator must ensure that the integrity of the observation or assessment technique is not compromised and that the privacy of the student is maintained.

6. Clothing with pockets is helpful for storing small notepads or index cards and a pencil (for recording observations as they occur).

7. Keep all information about children and their families confidential, never talk to others about the children in their presence, and never share information with anyone who does not have a professional and legitimate reason to have the information.

Do you remember the quote at the beginning of this chapter? Look at it again. More than any other factor, your ability to study young children will be the key to understanding their behavior as well as your own and will make the difference between becoming a skilled early childhood professional or not. Child study is not to be looked upon lightly. Child study coupled with knowledge of child development provides the essential foundation for the developing early childhood professional.

Key Terms

achievement test	event sampling	objectivity
anecdotal record	experimental study	participant–observer
authentic assessment	formal assessment	peers
checklist	hypothesis	perspective-taking
correlational study	informal assessment	portfolio
cross-sectional study	inservice	preprimary
descriptive study	intelligence test	preservice
developmental screening test	interview	random selection
	longitudinal study	rating scale
diagnostic test	narrative observation	readiness test

reflecting-in-action
reliability
replicability
representative sample
resource persons

running record
specimen record
standardized test
support staff
teacher-as-learner

teacher-as-researcher
time sampling
validity

Review Strategies and Activities

1. Review the key terms individually or with a classmate.
2. Select a child to observe during the semester. Keep a journal of your observations. Experiment with several of the observation techniques described in this chapter. (See Figure 2.11 for other resources on how to observe and record child behavior.)
3. Read a child development research study in one of the research journals listed in this chapter.
   a. How would you describe this study: descriptive, longitudinal, correlational, or experimental?
   b. What research techniques or strategies did the researcher use?
   c. What were the limitations of the study?
   d. Describe the population studied.
   e. Did the researcher suggest a need for other related studies? What were the topics?
   f. How can you use the information from the study?

Figure 2.11
Related Resources
That Help in the Study
of Young Children

A number of other resources can be helpful in studying young children. These include the following:

1. Child development research journals such as *Early Childhood Research Quarterly, Journal of Research in Childhood Education, Child Development, Child Study Journal, Early Childhood Education Journal, Journal of Infant Behavior and Development, Merrill-Palmer Quarterly, Developmental Psychology, Journal of Applied Developmental Psychology, Society for Research in Child Development Monographs, Journal of the American Academy of Pediatrics, Journal of Child Language, Cognitive Development, American Educational Research Journal, Research in the Teaching of English, Journal of Experimental Child Psychology,* and *Zero to Three Bulletin*
2. Journals from professional organizations and related groups such as *Young Children, Childhood Education, Dimensions of Early Childhood, Early Childhood Research Quarterly, The Reading Teacher, Language Arts, Science and Children, Mathematics Teacher, Arithmetic Teacher, Teaching Exceptional Children, Journal of Special Education, International Journal of Special Education, Gifted Child Quarterly, Elementary School Journal, Journal of Ethnic Studies, Journal of Children in Contemporary Society, Phi Delta Kappan, Educational Leadership,* and *Journal of Teacher Education*
3. Professional magazines such as *Pediatrics for Parents, Child Health Alert, Child Care Information Exchange, Learning, Instructor, Prekindergarten, Early Years,* and *School-Age Notes*

Further Readings

Bagnato, S. J., Niesworth, J. T., & Pretti-Frontczak, K. (2010). *LINKing authentic assessment and early childhood intervention: best measures for best practices* (2nd ed.). Baltimore, MD: Brookes Publishing Company.

Beaty, J. (2010). *Observing development of young children* (7th ed.). Columbus, OH: Prentice Hall.

Grisham-Brown, J., & Pretti-Frontczak, K. (2011). *Assessing young children in inclusive settings.* Baltimore, MD: Brookes Publishing Company.

Kritikos, E. P., LeDosquet, P. L., & Melton, M. (2011). *Foundations of assessment in early childhood special education.* Columbus, OH: Merrill.

Losardo, A., & Syverson, A. N. (2011). *Alternative approaches to assessing young children* (2nd ed.). Baltimore, MD: Brookes Publishing Company.

Wortham, S. C. (2012). *Assessment in early childhood education* (6th ed.). Columbus, OH: Merrill.

chapter 3
The Family Before Birth

A parent has the potential to gain what is without a doubt the highest satisfaction a human being can enjoy—the gratification of nurturing the development of a child into an emotionally stable and mature young man or woman. There is no greater reward for the adult; there is no greater gift to the child.

—Richard A. Gardner

The decision to have children needs the firm conviction that we are committed to family life and values. We need to be clear that family requires sacrifice, responsibility, and hard work. Fathers need to show their children how a man nurtures.

—Jonathon W. Gould and Robert E. Gunter

After studying this chapter, you will demonstrate comprehension by:

▶ demonstrating an understanding of the roles and perspectives of parents;

▶ discussing issues for families in the United States;

▶ demonstrating knowledge concerning the implications of the presence or absence of choice for parenting;

▶ discussing sociocultural and economic factors associated with decisions to become parents;

▶ discussing emotional and psychological aspects of preparing for parenting;

▶ describing the stages of prenatal development;

▶ describing optimal prenatal development, learning, and care;

▶ describing education for childbirth and parenting; and

▶ explaining the importance of preparing other children for the birth of a sibling.

Understanding the Roles and Perspectives of Parents

Throughout this text, much attention is given to the roles and perspectives of parents in the development of young children. It is important that early childhood professionals be aware of this information for several reasons. First, the behaviors and attitudes of parents directly influence the development of the young child and can do so even before birth, as in cases of poor nutrition, prenatal drug abuse, smoking, and maternal depression. To the extent that parents have knowledge, skills, and resources to guide their choices, decision making, and relationships with their children, growth and development can be supported. Conversely, parental lack of knowledge, skills, and support systems works against healthy parenting, predisposing children to less-than-optimal developmental outcomes.

Second, there are wide variations in family configurations, cultural values and attitudes toward children and parenting, and socioeconomic circumstances that influence decisions to have children and subsequent child-rearing practices. Cognizance of the uniqueness of each family helps educators to relate appropriately and to establish mutually supportive relationships, leading to the third benefit of understanding parental roles and perspectives: that of sharing information. Parents' knowledge of their young child can be helpful to early childhood professionals. In the early childhood profession, collaborating with parents is an important process, which cultivates mutual understanding and respect. For collaborations to be effective, early childhood professionals must have an empathic understanding of the challenges and demands of parenting. For instance, third-grade teacher Marie Gonzalez was upset with Joe's mother for not helping him learn his multiplication tables. Through talking with the school counselor, Ms. Gonzalez learned that Joe's mother was a single parent working at two jobs, including one during the evening hours. There were five children in the family, and they lived in a two-room apartment. An awareness of the demands on Joe's mother helped Ms. Gonzalez to adopt a more empathic attitude toward her. Tutoring by a sixth-grade student during school and help from an older brother provided support for Joe and his learning needs.

Early childhood professionals can learn from parents about their culture, their child's temperament, and their child's development. Remember from Chapter 2 how Mr. Hubbard discussed with Juan's parents how they could work together to help Juan adjust to the child care center. Mr. Hubbard encouraged the parents to bring Juan to the center and stay with him for several short periods before he began to attend full time, and Juan's parents suggested that Juan would feel more comfortable if he could bring his favorite toy or blanket every day. The collaboration between the family and the professional resulted in a great outcome for Juan. Finally, a broad awareness of how modern-day families are faring enhances the early childhood professional's understanding of the many circumstances affecting family life and child development.

Issues for Families in the United States

Through social indicators often reported in popular literature and dramatized in the media, we are all aware of the changing definitions and configurations of this institution we call "family." For some time now, the family has been undergoing changes in composition, gender roles, and parenting responsibilities. Children today are members of families that are described variously by the following characteristics: biological, two-parent families; single-parent families (mother only or father only); blended families and step-parented families; teen parents; coparenting divorced parents; grandparents raising grandchildren; same-sex parents; immigrant families; military families; homeless families; and children living with neither parent in kinship care or foster care homes (Brown, 2010; ZERO TO THREE, 2011).

There are 21,442,864 children under the age of 5 (6.8% of the population in the United States) and 75,582,985 children under the age of 18 (24% of the population in the United States) (National Child Care Information and Technical Assistance Center, 2010). Wide variations occur in both the living arrangements of children and who holds primary responsibility for their care and well-being, as illustrated in Box 3.1. Furthermore, there are wide variations among families in what is known and understood about child growth and development as well as wide ranges in parental (or guardian) dispositions and abilities to relate to and access community resources and opportunities for children that promote and facilitate positive developmental outcomes. These characteristics influence parenting and child-rearing practices and the course of growth and development in individual children.

Data from ChildStats.gov (2010) provide a number of indicators of child and family well-being in the United States. Based on information from the statistical studies

---

Box 3.1   Childhood Living Arrangements

According to *America's Children: Key National Indicators of Well-Being, 2010,* in 2009 for children ages 0–17:

70% of children live with two parents

26% live with one parent. Of the 26% of children ages 0–17 who live with one parent, 79% live with a single mother.

4% live with neither parent but rather with grandparents, foster parents, relatives, or nonrelatives

Source: ChildStats.gov (2010)

of 20 federal agencies, a number of key national indicators are listed and described. Indicators of children's well-being center on such topics as the following:

- *Economic security,* which includes family income and secure parental employment, child poverty, housing, food security and quality of diet, and access to health care
- *Health care,* which includes general health status, having health insurance coverage and a usual source of health care, limitations to activity caused by disabilities or chronic health conditions, childhood immunizations, dental care, low birth weight, infant and child mortality, adolescent mortality, and adolescent births
- *Behavior and social environment,* which includes psychological safety and well-being; family risk behaviors such as cigarette, alcohol, and illicit drug use; and youth victims or perpetrators of violent crimes
- *Education,* which includes family literacy, family reading to young children, early childhood care and education, mathematics and reading achievement, high school completion, youth who are neither enrolled in school nor working, and enrollment in higher education

One factor that often poses challenges for all families and their children is poverty.

Poverty and Child Development

Although we must not view poverty as harmful to all who experience it, children living in poverty are at higher risk for interferences to optimal growth development and sometimes for long-term deleterious effects of certain experiences associated with poverty (Annie E. Casey Foundation, 2010). The income level of the family and the size of the family unit typically define poverty, but families may also be identified as living in poverty based on their adjusted income after subtracting the costs of the family (e.g., child care costs). Based on a January 2011 census report on weighted average poverty thresholds for 2010 (U.S. Census Bureau, 2011), a family of four is living in poverty if its income is less than $22,314. For a family of six people, the poverty threshold is $29,887. The U.S. Census Bureau counted 22.86% of children under 5 years old who live in poverty (National Child Care Information and Technical Assistance Center, 2010). ZERO TO THREE (2009), a national advocacy and training organization concerned with the well-being of infants/toddlers and their families as well as the professionals who work with them, based on research findings, concluded the following:

1. Between 2000 and 2006, the number of children of all ages who were poor increased by 11% while the number of poor infants and toddlers increased by 16%.
2. Child poverty costs the United States an estimated $500 billion a year, due to increased expenditures on health care and the criminal justice system and in lost productivity in the labor force later in life.
3. Families with children under the age of 6 are at a higher risk of experiencing food insecurity (having limited or uncertain availability of nutritionally adequate and safe foods) than those with older children.

Infants born to families experiencing poverty are more likely to be born prematurely and/or to have a low birth weight, often because of poor prenatal nutrition and inadequate prenatal health care (DeFranco, Lian, Muglia, & Schootman, 2008). Mortality rates among

66

gestation
the length of an average pregnancy of 280 days, or 40 weeks, from the first day of the last menstrual period; can range from 37 to 42 weeks

prematurity
a preterm delivery that occurs prior to 37 completed weeks of gestation

low birth weight
a newborn weight of less than 2,500 grams, or 5½ pounds

births to poor mothers are higher. Incomplete **gestation**, or **prematurity**, and **low birth weight**, as we discuss later, carry a number of risks to healthy child development.

Families in poverty struggle with inadequate, unsafe, or unsanitary housing; poor nutrition; limited health care often resulting in children's incomplete immunization history; and higher rates of accidents and illness. These conditions can lead to compromised healthy development among children and their families. Families living in poverty are also faced with challenges associated with low education levels, employability and employment stability, transportation, health insurance, knowledge of and access to community resources, and maintenance of court-imposed child support decisions. ZERO TO THREE highly recommends that to support strong families, including those who live in poverty, families be nurtured through national and state policies and home visiting programs (2011). Another concern of families includes finding quality child care for their children while they are employed.

Nonparental Child Care

Among contemporary child life trends is the increasing need for nonparental child care. ChildStats.gov (2011) reports that results from the United States Census indicate that, in 2005, 50.7 percent of America's children from birth to 2 experienced nonparental care while 73% of children ages 3–6 who were not yet in kindergarten experienced nonparental care. The percentages of employed parents were higher for children living in mother- or father-only families. Table 3.1 illustrates percentages of children birth to age 4 experiencing parental care only and nonparental child care arrangements during mother's work hours. Families needing nonparental child care are often confronted with issues associated with accessibility, affordability, and assurances of the quality of care their children receive.

Table 3.1 Primary Child Care Arrangements for Children Ages 0–4 with Employed Mothers (During Mother's Work Hours)

Type of Child Care	Percent in 2010
Mother care	4.4%
Father care	18.6%
Grandparent care	19.4%
Other relative care	5.8%
Center-based care	23.7%
Other nonrelative care	13.5%
Other	14.1%

Adapted from ChildStats.gov, Forum on Child and Family Statistics (http://www.childstats.gov/americaschildren/tables/fam3a.asp)

chapter 3

Family, Friend, and Neighbor Care

Through employment demands and increased job-related mobility, families experience geographic separations and sometimes isolation from extended families, friends, and community life. Frequent moves associated with employment or other family needs often suppress the development of a sense of membership in a community. Some families have greater skill and adaptability in making new friends, locating support systems, and navigating changes in their lives. Others find it difficult to identify and access the resources of a new community and might be less eager to forge new relationships.

Whether one is raising children in a community in which one has resided for some time or in a new and unfamiliar community, babysitting and child care issues can be a challenge. As the previous discussions reveal, children receive child care in many settings. Many families use formal settings such as licensed child care centers, preschools, and licensed family child care homes. However, quite a number of children receive child care in unlicensed or unregulated informal situations, often referred to as "family, friend, and neighbor" (FFN) care (Susman-Stillman & Banghart, 2008). This includes care provided by grandmothers, aunts, uncles, and other relatives, as well as care provided by friends and neighbors. This type of care is the oldest form of child care, is often the most trusted by children's parents, yet can be the least reliable in situations where routine or daily care is required or employment schedules entail nontraditional or odd hours. The National Center for Children in Poverty (NCCP) (Susman-Stillman & Banghart, 2008) summarized 25 research articles and reports on FFN care. The summary revealed the following:

- FFN care is the most common form of nonparental care in the United States.
- Patterns of use differ by age, with infants and toddlers most likely to be cared for solely by FFN caregivers while preschoolers are more likely to attend multiple care arrangements that include relative care. Children from 6 to 9 years old also spend a considerable amount of time in FFN care.
- Families across all socioeconomic groups rely on FFN care, although families with low incomes are most likely to use FFN care. Family structure (marital status), parents' work status, and parents' work schedules influence parental decisions to use family, friend, and neighbor care (Susman-Stillman & Banghart, 2008).

Stay-at-Home Parents

A concept taken for granted in generations past is the "stay-at-home parent," in which the father or mother chooses to stay home to care for children while the other spouse works.

Although it is more common in two-parent families for mothers than fathers to stay at home, it is reported that, in 2006, there were 159,000 fathers who were not in the labor force primarily so they could provide care for their children (Rochlen, McKelley, & Whittaker, 2010). Data from Rochlen et al. (2010) suggest that stay-at-home-fathers feel well adjusted and content with their marital relationships. This is an example of how views about gender roles within the family are changing in contemporary culture.

Family Leave Time

U.S. Congress and state legislatures are taking a more sympathetic approach to the need for family leave time without penalty of loss of job or employment benefits. The Family and Medical Leave Act of 1993 (FMLA) was the first national policy designed to help

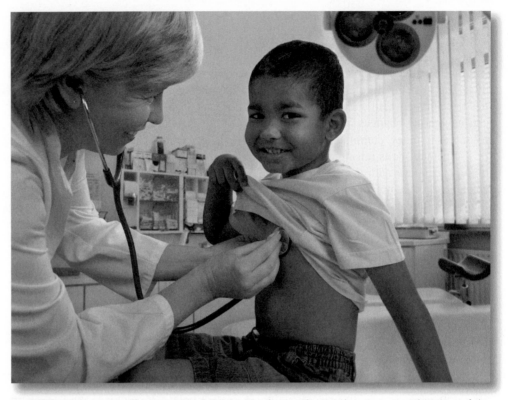

For collaboration to be effective, early childhood professionals must have an empathic view of the challenges contemporary families face. One of those challenges is keeping their children healthy.

working people attend to their work and family responsibilities. Its provisions include unpaid leave to care for a newborn or newly adopted child or a seriously ill family member or to recover from one's own serious health conditions without loss of job security. Because this law provides for *un*paid leave, many employees are unable to benefit from it. However, a number of states are establishing policies that provide for paid family leave time through temporary disability insurance programs and other strategies that cover certain circumstances such as temporary medical disabilities including pregnancy and childbirth. Innovative and family-friendly policy strategies are being conceptualized and implemented in states around the country. This trend reveals a growing awareness of the importance of both mothers *and* fathers to the well-being of their children; however, the United States is far behind other countries in regard to paid maternal and paternal leave. For example, in Sweden, mothers receive paid leave for approximately 15 months and fathers are encouraged to take at least three months of paid leave.

Patterns of Nonmarital Childbearing in the United States

According to the Centers for Disease Control and Prevention (Ventura, 2009), "most births to teenagers (86% in 2007) were nonmarital, 60% of births to women 20–24 were nonmarital, and nearly one-third of births to women 25–29 were nonmarital in 2007." Ventura (2009), summarizing statistics from the National Vital Statistics System, states that childbearing by unmarried women resumed a steep climb since 2002; however, adult women ages 20 and over account for much of these increases. This report attributes the rise in women ages 20 and over to the fact that many couples cohabit, that is, they share the same residence and live as a couple but do not marry. The Census Bureau (Lewin, 2010) reports that 25% of unmarried women who gave birth in recent years were living with a partner of the opposite or same sex.

It is interesting to compare the percentage of nonmarital births in the United States with the percentages in other countries. In 2007, more than 40% of all births were to unmarried women in the United States (Ventura, 2009). Several countries have higher percentages of births to unmarried women: 66% in Iceland, 55% in Sweden, 54% in Norway, and 50% in France. Other countries had lower percentages of births to unmarried mothers: 30% in Germany, 30% in Canada, 28% in Spain, 21% in Italy, and 2% in Japan (Ventura, 2009). In each of these countries, the percentage of births to nonmarried women has increased in recent years.

Is the well-being of the child affected based on whether mothers are married or unmarried? Unfortunately, in the United States, approximately 30% of households headed by a single mother are in poverty, increasing the children's risk for health and education challenges. However, rather than the structure of the family dictating the outcome for children, it seems that living in poverty is the factor that most highly influences the outcomes for children (Moore, Redd, Burkhauser, Mbwana, & Collins, 2009).

The Importance of Early Development and Parenting

During the 1960s, several events stimulated a great deal of research on the early years of life. The translation of Piaget's (1952) work indicated that the early years are critical in the development of intelligence. Benjamin Bloom's (1964) research on human intelligence revealed that the capacity for the development of intellectual potential is greatest during the first four years. The studies of J. McVicker Hunt (1961) documented the importance of environments and early experience in the development of intelligence. Concurrent with the many studies on the intellectual development of infants and young children was an increasing amount of research on the social and emotional development of children. Erikson's (1963) studies of healthy personality, Thomas and Chess's (1977) studies on inborn patterns of behavior or temperament in young children, Ainsworth's (1973) and Bowlby's (1969/2000, 1973) studies on infant attachment, and many others gave rise to interest in early growth and development and the experiences that enhance or impede development.

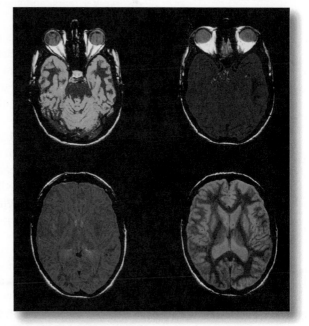

Today, prominent in the professional literature is the research emanating from the biological sciences and neurosciences regarding the earliest developments in the human brain and how environmental influences affect the brain's neurological "wiring." This neurological wiring is said to be most profound during the prenatal to first 10 years of life and results in behavior patterns that remain, for the most part, constant into adolescence and

Advances in technology have made it possible to examine images of the brain's structure and neurological activity.

The Family Before Birth

adulthood. See http://developingchild.harvard.edu for resources on brain development. Professionals in early childhood development, including the pediatric community, are particularly interested in this new emphasis in human growth and development. We refer to the literature on this topic throughout this text.

Meet Jeremy*—Keisha and DeVon Johnson live in a large metropolitan area in the South. Keisha is an accountant, and DeVon is a minister. DeVon grew up in the inner city, where his father was an accountant and his mother was a preschool teacher. Both parents were active in community affairs. DeVon feels fortunate to have grown up with loving parents.

Keisha's parents divorced when she was 7. Although her relationship with her father was close, he was transferred to another company on the West Coast. As a result, she saw him only a few times each year. Keisha's mother was a somewhat distant person, and Keisha never felt emotionally close to her.

After college graduation, Keisha and DeVon married. They worked hard to establish themselves in their respective careers. They traveled, saved their money, and eventually bought a house. When several of their friends began to start their families, DeVon and Keisha felt privileged to share in the discussions about pregnancy, childbirth, and becoming parents. They began to talk about having children of their own. DeVon wanted several children, but Keisha was not so sure. Her own unhappy childhood made her question her ability to be a good parent. Eventually, Keisha went to a counselor to work through her feelings. During this time, she and DeVon read many books about pregnancy, childbirth, and parenting. This process helped Keisha to resolve her fears, and she decided that she could provide a safe and secure childhood for her children.

DeVon and Keisha analyzed their family finances. Between them, they had a comfortable income. Keisha's company provided paid maternity leave, and DeVon's congregation would grant him parental leave. Keisha and DeVon began to investigate possible types of child care for infants. About this time, Keisha's firm, along with several other businesses, decided to establish a child care center, which included an infant room.

Keisha and DeVon had always been health conscious. They exercised regularly and paid attention to their diets. Neither smoked or abused drugs or alcohol. Both had annual checkups. They consulted with their family physician and told her they would like to begin their family. The physician asked for a brief family history and inquired about possible genetic defects. Keisha and DeVon requested the names of several obstetricians whose practice focused on family-centered maternity care.

---

*The vignettes of the childhoods of Jeremy and Angela that lace through this text are intended to illustrate the uniqueness of growth and development in children growing up in different contexts. Angela and Jeremy represent dichotomous family circumstances and are composites of many children the authors have known. Their stories are not representative of any socioeconomic, racial, or ethnic group. The reader is cautioned against applying stereotypical or prejudicial perspectives to their life stories.

Three months later, Keisha missed her menstrual period. She made an appointment with one of the recommended obstetricians, Dr. Susan Windle. DeVon went with Keisha to see Dr. Windle. They were ecstatic when Dr. Windle confirmed that Keisha was pregnant. Dr. Windle took a detailed medical history of both DeVon and Keisha and shared information with them about the early stages of pregnancy. She described the care she would be providing for Keisha and asked for questions. Dr. Windle also discussed various fees and hospital procedures and encouraged Keisha and DeVon to visit the birthing center. She told them about two childbirth classes, the first on general information regarding pregnancy and the development of the baby and the second on Lamaze-prepared childbirth, to be taken near the end of Keisha's pregnancy. As they left Dr. Windle's office, the nurse gave Keisha and DeVon a number of brochures and booklets to read. They celebrated at one of their favorite restaurants. Over a candlelit dinner, they decided to name the baby Jeremy if it was a boy. They were not quite sure about a girl's name. DeVon liked Elizabeth, while Keisha liked Julia, the name of a favorite aunt.

During the beginning of her pregnancy, Keisha's moods varied from elation to mild depression. At times, these mood swings were difficult for DeVon to understand. At their first future parents' class, they found that other couples were experiencing similar problems. Jane, the instructor, explained that these mood swings were caused by the hormonal changes of pregnancy. Keisha, like some of the other women, also reported increased fatigue and nausea. Jane told the class that usually by the end of the first three months, many of these discomforting but normal effects of pregnancy would subside.

DeVon and Keisha made regular trips to Dr. Windle throughout the pregnancy. Keisha ate nutritious and well-balanced meals; increased her intake of fruits, vegetables, and dairy products; and took no medication without the approval of Dr. Windle. DeVon and Keisha attended childbirth classes, visited the hospital, bought furniture and clothes for the baby, and compromised on a girl's name, Julia Elizabeth. They enjoyed talking with other new parents and reading books about parenting, finding that this helped relieve some of their normal feelings of anxiety. They followed the development of their baby with **ultrasound** tests, which indicated that the **fetus** was developing normally and would probably be a boy—Jeremy.

DeVon and Keisha finalized their plans for the baby's care after Keisha returned to work. They discussed their parental leaves with their employers. DeVon wanted to take at least a week off after the baby was born. Keisha decided to return to work when the baby was 6 weeks old. But as the baby's birth drew near, Keisha decided that she did not want to leave her young baby in a group care situation, even though her firm had implemented an excellent program for infants and toddlers. Keisha and DeVon felt more comfortable having someone care for their baby in their home. Keisha looked among members of their congregation for a nanny. After several interviews, Keisha and DeVon chose Breeann. She was 23, had worked for several other families who provided excellent references, had knowledge of young children's development, and demonstrated a love of young children.

Keisha's mother wanted to come to help. DeVon and Keisha had learned from their parenting classes that each couple has to decide whether they want family help with their new baby. Some people can be a great help to new parents, giving them

ultrasound
a technique using sound frequencies that can detect structural characteristics of the fetus and the approximate week of pregnancy

fetus
the developing human from nine weeks after conception to birth

(*continued*)

The Family Before Birth

information about babies' habits as well as helping with household chores. However, some extended families are not very supportive and take control at a time when the new parents should be in charge. Keisha finally decided that, given the somewhat tense relationship she had with her mother, it would be best to invite her mother for a visit after the new Johnson family had a week or two together.

DeVon and Keisha had taken the time to prepare for the optimal development of their baby and to inform themselves about pregnancy and parenting. Now all they had to do was practice the exercises they had learned in the childbirth classes and wait.

Meet Angela—Cheryl Monroe is 15 years old. She lives in an urban area with her mother and four brothers and sisters. Her father died two years earlier leaving the family with significant medical bills. Her grades are barely passing; she has considered dropping out of school, but her mother tells her that it is important to get an education. Every afternoon, Cheryl's mother takes the bus downtown, where she works until midnight cleaning business offices.

Cheryl's dream is to be a movie star or a singer with a rock group. Like most adolescent girls, she is very interested in boys and has been seeing James for about seven months. They have been sexually active and spend most evenings watching TV and listening to music—activities they enjoy together.

It has been four months since Cheryl has had a menstrual period, and her changing body is now reinforcing the idea that she is indeed pregnant. Finally, she shares her suspicions with several of her teenage friends. They generally respond that she is lucky because she will have a cute baby to love her. Eventually, Cheryl tells her mother she is going to have a baby. Her mother reacts with concern, anger, and disappointment. She fears that this will probably mean an end to Cheryl's high school education. She doubts that James will be able to support Cheryl and believes that Cheryl's baby will be another mouth to feed in their already economically stressed household. James is conflicted about his impending fatherhood. He does care for Cheryl and intends to help support the baby from his occasional part-time work. His family intends to share in the responsibility, but they are adamant that he will continue with his plans for college in another state.

Cheryl's mother researches information on community services for teen parents. She goes with Cheryl to a clinic that provides care and services for teen mothers. During her first visit to the prenatal clinic, an examination reveals that Cheryl is six to seven months pregnant. She is counseled on nutrition; told how to sign up for WIC (Women, Infants, and Children), a federally funded program that provides dairy and other food products for pregnant and nursing women and their young children; and scheduled for follow-up visits. They refer her to a group for teen parents and to Early Head Start.

Cheryl spends the last two to three months of her pregnancy working on her studies at home, watching TV, helping out around the apartment, seeing James and her other friends, and visiting the clinic for prenatal checkups. She receives home visits from Early Head Start and participates in the teen parenting group, but her increased knowledge only makes her more worried about her ability to raise a child when she is still a child herself.

Medical personnel feel encouraged from their exams that the baby seems to be developing normally. Ultrasound tests indicate the baby will probably be a girl. Cheryl convinces James to name their daughter Angela. Cheryl and James await Angela's birth.

These two vignettes describe two very different situations into which infants are born. One is planned and potentially optimal. The other is unplanned and potentially at risk. Planning for a family, good health in both parents, and good-quality prenatal care throughout the pregnancy promote optimal development.

Widely disseminated information about the importance of early development and its consequences for later life relationships and achievements has resulted in increased interest among the childbearing/child-rearing population. Ideally, the prospective mother and father decide that they want to become parents because they (1) enjoy children, (2) want to share their love and lives with children as they continue to grow and mature, and (3) are committed to providing opportunities for their children to become well-adjusted and productive members of society. However, nearly 3 million married women in the United States experience an unintended pregnancy each year. "An unintended pregnancy is a pregnancy that is either mistimed or unwanted at the time of conception" (CDC, 2010c). Although most families enthusiastically welcome their unplanned babies, risk factors rise when children are both unplanned and undesired.

Sociocultural and Economic Factors

A number of sociocultural and economic factors affect the quality of life for children and their families. Some of these include the parents' age, the number and spacing of children in the family, cultural differences in prenatal care, and family income. These factors are common to all cultural and economic groups.

Age of Parents

Decisions before pregnancy about whether to complete education, prepare for a specific craft or career, become established in a relationship with one's partner, become economically self-sufficient, and prepare physiologically and psychologically for childbearing and child rearing influence the age at which a family begins or additional children are planned. Two concurrent trends regarding age of first pregnancy are evident in contemporary family life: an increasing tendency for women to postpone first pregnancies until their 30s and a high incidence of teen pregnancies.

The highest rates for first births have generally been, and continue to be, among women ages 20 to 24 years. Data from the National Center for Health Statistics and the Census Bureau (Livingston & Cohn, 2010) reveals that approximately 75% of all births are to women ages 20 to 34, and the average age in 2006 for U.S. women to become mothers was 25. There was an increase from 1990–2008 in the women who gave birth over the age of 35 (9% in 1990 to 14% in 2008). (See http://pewresearch.org/pubs/1586/changing-demographic-characteristics-american-mothers for additional information.)

Most women ages 35 and older have successful pregnancies and healthy infants. As a rule, older parents have more education and greater economic security. One research study found that the increased age of the mother relates to children's higher scores in cognitive tests (Cannon, 2009). Older mothers' desire for children and their maturity motivate them to seek professional prepregnancy and **prenatal** guidance and health care. Such motivations set the stage for conscientious care and nurturing of their offspring. Concerns associated with postponed childbearing center on **fertility**, or the capability of conceiving a child. Generally, fertility peaks for women in their early to mid-20s, then gradually declines until age 30, after which it begins to drop more rapidly. Fertility in men gradually decreases from their teenage years and begins to decline significantly after age 40 as the volume and concentration of sperm changes. Certain types of chromosomal abnormalities have been associated with age of the mother and father (Fisch, Hyun, Golden, Hensle, Olsson, & Liberson, 2003). For instance, Down syndrome, a condition caused by a chromosomal abnormality resulting in mild to severe retardation, has been associated with parents (both mother's and father's ages) who were either quite young or older than age 35; but approximately 80 percent of babies with Down syndrome are born to younger women (March of Dimes, 2009).

The standard age/risk figures for Down syndrome births and other serious conditions resulting from chromosome anomalies are estimated to be as follows (March of Dimes, 2009):

> 1 in 1,250 chance when the mother is age 25
>
> 1 in 1,000 chance when the mother is 30
>
> 1 in 400 chance when the mother is 35
>
> 1 in 100 chance when the mother is 40
>
> 1 in 30 chance when the mother is 45
>
> 1 in 10 chance when the mother is 49

In recent years, news reports of women bearing children in their late 40s and 50s and even beyond have been sensationalized in the media. Studies reveal that women in their 40s and beyond are more likely to suffer from physical conditions that are less conducive to healthy childbearing than younger women. These include **hypertension, gestational diabetes,** anemia, and poor nutrition, which can lead to premature births and low-birth-weight babies, as well as depletion of physical and psychological resources associated with prior childbearing and child rearing (Usta & Nassar, 2008). Based on data from 2005, fetal mortality rate for women over 35 was 15.51. This rate is almost three times the rate for women ages 25 to 29, and closer to the fetal death rate for teenagers under the age of 15 (12.20) (MacDorman & Kirmeyer, 2009). See Box 3.2 for information from the March of Dimes (2011b) concerning how women in their late 30s and 40s (and all women) can have healthy pregnancies.

An interesting phenomenon associated with **fertility rate** is the fact that although births among women in their 30s have increased, there has been a steady decline in the rates of births to teenagers. Birth rates among teenagers declined steadily from the 1991 rate of 61.8 per 1,000 until 2006, when there was a small jump in the birth rate. However, in 2010 the birth rate was 34.3 per 1,000 females aged 15–19, a drop of 3% from the 2009 rate and the lowest rate on record for the United States (Hamilton, Martin, & Ventura, 2011). The general decline in teenage births is attributed to increased contraceptive use (Guttmacher Institute, 2012). However, in spite of a general promising decline from 1991

---

prenatal
the time from conception until birth, an average of 266 days, or 38 weeks

fertility
the capability of conceiving a child

hypertension
high blood pressure

gestational diabetes
diabetes that develops after a woman becomes pregnant

fertility rate
the number of births per 1,000 women ages 15 to 44

Box 3.2   How Women in Their Later 30s and 40s Can Have Healthy Pregnancies

Get checkups and regular medical care.

- Visit your health care provider for a preconception checkup.

- Get tested for immunity to rubella (German measles) and chickenpox before becoming pregnant and consider being vaccinated if not immune. After being vaccinated, wait one month (or until the physician states it would be OK) before trying to conceive.

- Once you are pregnant, get early and regular prenatal care.

- Before and during pregnancy, take a daily vitamin as advised by a doctor.

- Unless recommended by a health care provider who is aware of the pregnancy, avoid drugs of any kind, even over-the-counter medicines or herbs.

Take care of your physical health.

- Begin pregnancy at a healthy size (not underweight or overweight).

- Incorporate foods containing folic acid and folate (the form of folic acid that occurs naturally in foods) into your diet. Good sources include fortified breakfast cereals, enriched grain products, beans, leafy green vegetables, and orange juice.

- Eat no more than 12 ounces per week of fish that have small amounts of mercury, including shrimp, salmon, pollock, catfish, and canned light tuna. (However, limit albacore (white) tuna consumption to 6 ounces or less a week.) Avoid fish that can be high in mercury—like shark, swordfish, king mackerel, or tilefish— altogether. Check with the local health department before eating any fish caught in local waters.

- To avoid toxoplasmosis, an infection that can cause birth defects, don't eat under- cooked meat or change a cat's litter box.

- Do not drink alcohol.

- Do not smoke or expose yourself to secondhand smoke.

Source: Adapted from March of Dimes, 2011b.

to 2010, the United States continues to have the highest rates of unintended and teenage pregnancies among Western nations (Henshaw, 2003).

Many of the concerns associated with later pregnancies hold for teen pregnancies as well. Some pregnancies occur to children as young as 12 years old, compounding the risk factors for both child and mother. Many teenagers fail to recognize the early symptoms of pregnancy and/or acknowledge the pregnancy until they are beyond the earliest stages, and hence they do not obtain timely diagnosis and ongoing professional prenatal health care. They may be ill informed and fearful of pregnancy, have little or no knowledge of available resources, and have limited family support systems and financial resources. Issues with body image and poor prenatal nutrition pose additional

anorexia
a severe disorder, usually seen in adolescent girls, characterized by self-starvation

bulimia
a severe disorder, usually seen in adolescent girls, characterized by binging and then self-induced vomiting

risks to both child and mother. (Nutritional and diet disorders such as **anorexia** and **bulimia** are not uncommon among adolescent girls and young women.) Immature physiology combined with ongoing poor nutrition increases their risk of obstetric complications.

Although not true of all teenagers, some are inclined to engage in risk behaviors such as the abuse of tobacco, alcohol, and other substances; and these individuals are at high risk for sexually transmitted diseases (STDs), particularly when sexual activity involves multiple partners. Sexually transmitted diseases can be carried into pregnancy and result in insult and injury to the developing child (March of Dimes, 2008b).

Some teenage girls want a baby to provide them with the love they feel they have not received from their parents or others who are important to them. They may not realize, however, how challenging single parenting can be or how profoundly dependent their infant will be on them for love and nurturing.

The unmarried father may want to be involved with his child, but a number of barriers can hinder his involvement, including his employment hours and responsibilities, his desire and need to continue schooling, the distance between his and the child's mother's places of residence, and perhaps relationship issues with the child's mother and her family.

Typically, unmarried teenage mothers must rely on their parents or other members of the family for social and economic support. Sometimes the parents of teenage girls feel imposed upon and resent having to sacrifice their time, financial resources, and jobs to help care for their grandchildren. These grandparents may also be caring for the teen mother's siblings and/or their own aging parents. Because of these problems, many teenage mothers and their children come to rely on public assistance.

Reducing the rate of teen pregnancies remains a high social priority. The recent downward trend in rates of teen pregnancies has been attributed to the following reasons:

1. There is greater emphasis on delaying sexual activity because of education, peer groups, and adult mentors.
2. Teenagers have more conservative attitudes about casual sex and out-of-wedlock childbearing.
3. There is a fear of sexually transmitted diseases, which now include AIDS.
4. The availability of long-lasting contraceptive methods has been accompanied by teens more consistent and/or correct use of contraceptive methods.

It is to everyone's advantage to help teen parents complete their educations. Research suggests that teenage mothers who stay in school, limit the number of additional children, and have a successful marriage are similar to mothers who had their first child in their 20s or later (Alan Guttmacher Institute, 2002). Professionals in many fields (e.g., education, social services, pediatrics, public health) are involved in helping teenagers to delay parenting, which so often reduces choices and opportunities for them. Teenagers can be helped to understand the quality-of-life issues related to adolescent pregnancy and that delaying parenthood by completing schooling and seeking job training provides long-term benefits. In the event of pregnancy, teenagers need accurate information about the importance of good prenatal care and competent parenting.

In an effort to help teen parents stay in school, some school districts provide on-campus or near-campus child care. Where this is not feasible, counselors may assist needy teen parents in accessing community resources such as federal or state financial assistance and child care and food subsidies. Many secondary schools offer child development courses.

Some communities provide **home visitor** and **doula** programs to support prospective teenage parents (Abramson, Altfeld, & Tiebloom-Mishkin, 2000). Depending on the sponsoring agency, these programs have varying goals, including the promotion of healthy child development, school readiness, prevention of child abuse and neglect, moral support and guidance for the first-time mother, assisting families with education and employment issues, and assessing and assisting with other family needs. Examples of home visiting programs include the Parents as Teachers Program (PAT), the Home Instruction Program for Preschool Youngsters (HIPPY), and the Comprehensive Child Development Program (CCDP).

The doula is a paraprofessional who provides emotional and physical support to mothers beginning sometime during pregnancy and continuing through labor, delivery, and the first weeks after the infant is born. Depending on the philosophy and resources of the sponsoring community-based agency, doulas are trained to provide education, guidance, and physical and psychological support to expectant families. To encourage mutual trust and close relationships, home visitors and doulas should be selected for their cultural and background similarity with the families whom they help. Studies have shown benefits of doula support that include shorter duration of labor, fewer labor and delivery complications, and lower cesarean rates (Abramson, Breedlove, & Isaacs, 2006; Klaus, Kennell, & Klaus, 2002).

home visitor
a trained nurse or paraprofessional who provides in-home education and support services to pregnant women and families with young children

doula
a Greek word for a female who provides assistance and support during childbirth

Prospective Fathers

Infrequently addressed in scholarly and popular literature are the health and reproductive behaviors of prospective fathers as well as the fathers' roles and desires to be a part of their children's lives. Few health professionals are specifically trained to provide men with reproductive health education and services, and there appears to be a tendency of many men not to seek routine checkups or to pursue professional support systems and guidance regarding reproductive issues and health (Alan Guttmacher Institute, 2003). The concept of fatherhood as limited to breadwinner and weekend family participant is changing to one that views fathers and mothers as equal partners in child rearing. Fathers are more engaged in learning about and participating in the health care and psychological support of their expectant partners. In contrast to generations past, today's fathers may attend prenatal classes and participate in the delivery process, take paternal leave to care for and bond with their newborns, actively participate in the routine care of their infants and children, take an active role in their learning experiences, and provide them emotional support and social interaction.

In unmarried situations and divided families caused by divorce or separation, this dynamic is more difficult to achieve. Sobolewski and King (2005), using a national database, found that 66% of mothers who live apart from their children's fathers say that the fathers have no influence over

Prospective fathers anticipate both the joys and the challenges and demands of raising healthy, well-adjusted children.

The Family Before Birth

childrearing. When parents are unable to negotiate constructive coparenting strategies, the emotional bonding between the infant or child and the absent parent is compromised and the detrimental effects are exacerbated. This, psychologists believe, has enormous implications for the mental health of young children. Scholars refer to a "caregiving system" that surrounds infants and children through their mothers and fathers (Solomon & George, 1996). This system becomes disorganized when coparenting is unsuccessful. Mothers and fathers in such situations may begin to question their own ability to provide for and protect the child and may engage in gatekeeping behaviors that exclude the other parent. Achieving harmonious coparenting partnerships entails "painful, difficult psychological work" (Solomon, 2003, p. 34), and it may require professional counseling to ensure healthy outcomes for both the parents and their children. Fathers are more likely to remain involved with their children if they can work out the coparenting relationships with the mothers of their children, which is often very difficult for both mother and father to do (Soboleswski & King, 2005).

Size of Family and Spacing of Children

Another consideration is the number of children already in the family and their ages relative to the anticipated baby. Some child development experts suggest a spacing of three years between children as optimal for effective parenting and child rearing. Studies of birth and mortality rates around the world have found that when births are separated by less than two years, the infant mortality rate (the risk of dying during infancy) is significantly higher than when births are separated by between 24 and 59 months; however, infant mortality increases again after an interval of 60 months or more. The lowest mortality rate for infants occurs if spacing is between 36 and 47 months (Rutstein, 2008). Closely spaced pregnancies may also result in low birth weight and prematurity.

There are other benefits to spacing, including time and opportunity for the mother's hormonal and physical condition to return to its prepregnancy state and to obtain optimal weight and the physical and psychological stamina to meet the needs of a growing family. It is beneficial to all family members when spacing provides time to adapt family routines and work schedules to a new family configuration and to learn to manage or realign additional home life responsibilities with existing family needs and ongoing commitments.

Children may also benefit from well-spaced pregnancies. The nurturing interactions of parents (mother and father) with infants and siblings can be more focused and extended, providing time for parents and their very young children to successfully form intimate and mutually loving and supportive relationships. Older siblings, as we shall see in later chapters, may benefit from having experienced a longer period of parent–child focus before having to learn to share their parents' time and affections with another child. The infant can benefit from the types of age-appropriate playful and loving interactions and care that siblings can provide.

Couples need time to refocus their psychological energies in ways that meet their own needs, as well as their children's needs. Although achieving a stable and harmonious marital relationship is not a prerequisite to childbearing, studies indicate that the more harmonious a marriage is, the higher is the quality of parent–child relationships. Crockenberg, Leerkes, and Lekka (2007, p. 99) summarized research on the associations between marital conflict and infant emotion regulation. They concluded that "... parents who engage in frequent and intense marital conflicts are more likely than other parents to behave more negatively and less sensitively with their children." This is often referred to as the "spillover effect," in which the effects from one relationship affect another relationship (Susman-Stillman, Appleyard, & Siebenbruner, 2003).

Lower-quality marital relationships that include marital aggression are linked to lower-quality parent–child relationships and children's emotional withdrawal, negative affect, and later behavioral problems. Withdrawal may be an effective strategy for infants to use to avoid their parents' strong, angry outbursts but may lead to the infants' later feelings of anxiety and anger, which then affect their ability to interact effectively with others. The child's temperament may dampen or enhance the negative effects of marital aggression (Crockenberg et al., 2007).

Further, studies suggest that where the mother and a nonresident father maintain a positive relationship, father involvement is greater and child development outcomes more positive than where relationships between unmarried or divorced parents are discordant. It appears that in all types of marital arrangements, whether parents are married, single, or coparenting, the mother–father relationship can be more or less supportive for father's involvement (Susman-Stillman et al., 2003).

Attitudes and Support from Important Others

The attitudes of members of the extended family and of friends and associates often affect prospective parents through words and interactions that are supportive and helpful or nonsupportive and unsettling. The reactions of family members to the pregnancy can influence the perceptions and feelings about childbearing and child rearing that the prospective parents form. Recall the ecological systems theory described in Chapter 1. The concept of circles of influence is typified here, where influences flow reciprocally between the person(s) at the center (prospective parents, in this case) and members of various familial and social systems surrounding them. Parents who will become grandparents, siblings who will become aunts and uncles, friends who may become part of an emotional and social support system that exists beyond the biological family, and colleagues at the workplace who may assist in ensuring family-friendly work expectations all will have their own feelings, needs, concerns, and joys regarding the prospects. Moving outward into the wider circles of influence, the availability and role of the health care professions become important contributors to family and child well-being, as do other social services and education institutions. All of these ecological influences affect the parents' ability to develop positive, secure feelings about the decision to parent, and, hence, help them to prepare for and build positive and secure relationships with their infants (Susman-Stillman et al., 2003).

Economic Considerations in Having a Child

Seldom do we consider the long-term costs of raising a child. When we do, it can be daunting when viewed in the aggregate.

However, perhaps Figure 3.1 can help to clarify the types of expenditures involved in child rearing. Many parents probably believe that they are less financially secure than they would like to be, but the cost of adequately clothing and feeding a child should be considered in making a decision about having a baby. The estimated annual expenditures on a child born in 2010 in the United States vary from almost $9,000 in

Figure 3.1
Amount and Types
of Expenditures for
Children

Source: Lino, M. (2011).
Expenditures on Children
by Families, 2010. U.S.
Department of Agriculture,
Center for Nutrition Policy
and Promotion. Miscellaneous
Publication No. 1528-2010.
U.S. average for the younger
child in middle-income,
husband-wife families with
two children. Child care and
education expenses only
for families with expense.
Retrieved from
http://www.cnpp.usda.
gov/ExpituresonChildrenby
Families.htm

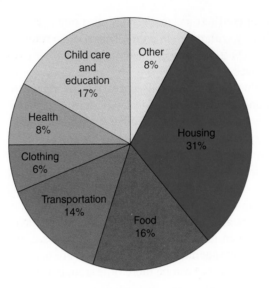

low-income families to $20,000 in high-income families (Lino, 2011). Can the family's financial resources realistically support the child, or will the addition of a child create an undue economic hardship? Ideally, these questions should be considered in family planning.

In addition, lack of adequate economic resources can adversely affect the prenatal health care of the mother and the developing child. Unfortunately, within U.S. society, many families lack access to adequate nutrition and prenatal care. Although some programs, such as the federally funded Supplemental Nutrition Program for Women, Infants, and Children (WIC), provide milk and other essential foods to low-income pregnant women and new mothers, their infants, and their young children, they do not serve all eligible people (USDA, Food and Nutrition Service, 2010). People are often unaware of medical services, and the services that are available may be underfunded and understaffed.

The consequences of poor nutrition and poor prenatal care are reflected in infants who have low birth weight. If these at-risk infants survive, the financial cost of extended hospital care and the social cost of long-term developmental problems constitute major challenges. Solutions to these problems include establishing a network of services that provide appropriate education and health care to families during and after pregnancy.

Emotional and Psychological Aspects of Preparing for Parenthood

Parenting is a stage in life, a personal choice, a psychological transition, a psychobiological condition, a cultural creation, a necessity for the species, a political icon, a state of mind. For some, the word conjures up memories of the past; for others, the anticipated and desired; and for many, an idealization. (Mayes, 2002, p. 4)

This summary description of prospective parenting by pediatrics and psychobiology professor Linda C. Mayes expresses well the physical, psychological, and intellectual milieu associated with decisions to bring children into the world. The transition to

chapter 3

parenting (or to the addition of children to the family) is receiving scholarly attention (ZERO TO THREE, 2011). This transition is a time of anticipation, marked by concerns for the health and well-being of the mother and child and the parents' abilities to meet the physical and psychological needs of another person. It is a time when prospective parents begin to change their mental focus to one that encompasses all that they can imagine parenting might be or require of them. For some, this transition can be unsettling, conjuring anxious, perhaps negative feelings or even resentment. For others, there may be curiosity, joy, and preoccupation in anticipating events to come as the pregnancy progresses. Mixed emotions are not uncommon. It stands to reason that the couple's sense of well-being, both emotional and economic, and their attitudes toward the pregnancy affect their own well-being and both the prenatal and postnatal well-being of their child.

Ideally, the newborn child has a mother and a father whose relationship is stable, mature, and based on mutual love and support. In reality, not all couples are so fortunate, and the idea that a baby can help a troubled relationship is a myth. The demands of adjusting to another family member may only add to an already stressful situation. Couples who have an unstable relationship are wise to seek professional counseling before they decide to become parents.

Reaction of the Prospective Mother

From the discovery that a pregnancy is in progress to the birth of a baby is a time of enormous change in the life of a woman. Over the ensuing weeks, her physique and physiology undergo changes, as will her emotional state. Hormonal changes can precipitate mood swings and feelings of sleepiness, irritability, or mild depression. Family and social support systems become important to her feelings of confidence and well-being.

Because becoming a parent (whether biological or through adoption, foster care, or stepparenting) involves understanding the needs of those who are dependent on others for their care and protection, psychologists today are interested in the extent to which parental **perinatal** mental health is conducive to positive parenting and healthy child outcomes. Mental health problems such as anxiety and depression "have been associated with poor pregnancy outcomes, such as preterm delivery, low infant birth weight, and small-for-gestational-age infants" as well as postnatal depression (Gun-Mette, Slinning, Eberhard-Gran, Røysamb, & Tambs, 2011, p. 1)

perinatal
the period encompassing the weeks before a birth, the birth, and the few weeks thereafter

There is considerable evidence demonstrating that strong spousal or partner support plays a critical role in reducing the intensity and affect of maternal anxiety and depression (Cardone, 2002). Gun-Mette et al. (2011) in a Norwegian study of 50,000 mothers-to-be found that these pregnant women's positive mental health was strongly linked to a good relationships with their husbands or partners during pregnancy. Physicians and public health agencies need to pay particular attention to mothers who do not have adequate emotional support. The authors of the Norwegian study conclude that:

> "All signs of trouble in a woman's adaptation to pregnancy should be taken seriously by obstetricians, nurse midwives, and mental health professionals. Special attention needs to be paid to the woman's relationship with her partner. Early intervention that involves both the woman and her partner may be successfully initiated in some cases to strengthen the foundation for the family's future development" (p. 10)

Interest in perinatal mental health and its accompanying research is encouraging the development of strategies for prevention and intervention with couples who may be at risk for poor outcomes. During the course of pregnancy, the mother begins to form a psychological relationship with her unborn child; she is just beginning to develop a sense of herself as parent to *this* baby (Slade, 2002). Both mothers and fathers must make "room in their minds" for a new person in their lives (Mayes, 2002). Studies seeking to understand how parents make the transition into parenthood have found that toward the end of pregnancy and in the early postpartum period, the fetus and then the infant becomes an increasingly exclusive focus of thought and action, particularly in the mother (Leckman & Mayes, 1999). Preoccupation with the infant's cues and characteristics before and after its birth is common and, indeed, biologically driven through numerous **neurobiological agents** such as estrogen, prolactin, oxytocin, dopamine, and others along with specific genes acting in the brain to promote maternal behavior (Mayes, 2002).

neurobiological agents
hormones and chemicals that facilitate the transmission of information throughout the nervous system

Reaction of the Prospective Father

Concerns for perinatal mental health (or how well prospective parents make room for their new infant) extend to fathers as well as mothers. As with the mother-to-be, and with similar intensity, the father-to-be spends a great deal of time thinking about the pregnancy and about the child who will soon enter his life. The research of Leckman and Mayes (1999) included interviews with couples at selected points in time during the perinatal period and found that men think about becoming fathers, sexual intimacy, and their potency and virility, as well as how they will care for their pregnant partner. The findings of these studies also reveal that father-to-be may wonder about the following:

- how others will view him as a person who has fathered a baby;
- how he will manage the delivery process, including whether to be present or not;
- what types of support are required of him;
- how he will handle the waiting;
- whether the baby will be healthy; and
- how well he will be able to provide for and meet the needs of his partner and their infant (Mayes, 2002).

Because fathers' involvement during pregnancy is associated with fewer fetal deaths and better infant health outcomes, the importance of father involvement during pregnancy was the topic of a recent meeting of the Joint Center for Political and Economic Studies Health Policy Institute (Bonds, 2010) titled Recommendations for Improving Research, Practice, and Policy on Paternal Involvement in Pregnancy Outcomes. The report cited the following:

1. Men are important to maternal and child health.
2. During pregnancy, expectant fathers are open to information, advice, and support.
3. It is essential to provide expectant fathers with the necessary tools to improve their involvement, not only during pregnancy but before, between, and beyond pregnancies.

Several of the recommendations included the following:

1. Health care organizations should promote more father-friendly hospital settings, practices, and policies.

2. There should be mandates that Healthy Start, Early Head Start, Head Start, and other public programs serving children and families develop more "father-friendly" practices and programs. Just as mothers do, fathers benefit from supportive and helpful health care professionals, relatives, friends, and family-friendly employers.

Prenatal Development

It is time to reconceptualize nature and nurture in a way that emphasizes their insepa-rability and complementarity, not their distinctiveness: it is not nature versus nurture, it is rather nature through nurture. If gene expression is inconceivable apart from the environment, then it is useless and potentially misleading to try to finely distinguish the relative importance of nature and nurture in the course of human development. (Shonkoff & Phillips, 2000, p. 41)

Human uniqueness and individuality are caused by the fact that everyone has a different set of inherited characteristics. In addition to **heredity**, everyone has a different **environment**, that is, different relationships, physical settings, interactional, and educational experiences. Even within the same family, each member has a different set of inherited characteristics as well as different experiences. Children are born in different order; and as new family members are added, relationships change and developmental outcomes are unique for each individual child.

For many decades, people have debated the relative influences of heredity and environment on the development of an individual. In certain situations, the influence of heredity or environment may be obvious, but more often behavior is best explained by the interaction of both heredity and environment. In any case, optimal development of an individual depends on both healthy genetic traits and a healthy environment.

Chromosomes and Genes

At conception, the sperm from the father penetrates the mother's egg, or ovum. There is a period of about 24 hours approximately every 28 days during which an ovum is in the position to be fertilized by a sperm. At the point of fertilization, the **chromosomes** of the mother and father unite. Chromosomes are located in the nucleus of a cell and contain thousands of **genes**. This combination of genes from the mother and the father determines a person's genetic potential, or **genotype**. Genes tell cells which proteins to make and influence many characteristics of a person, from the color of the hair and eyes to possible aspects of a person's personality.

Genotype also includes **recessive genes**. These genes are not evident if they are paired with dominant genes. Genes are composed of deoxyribonucleic acid (**DNA**), a molecule that contains the chemically coded information that causes the development of tissues, organs, and physiological functions; it is the blueprint for genetic inheritance.

heredity
the inherited characteristics of humans encoded by genes

environment
the experiences, conditions, objects, and people that directly or indirectly influence the development and behavior of a child

chromosomes
ordered groups of genes within the nucleus of a cell

genes
molecules of DNA that encode and transmit the characteristics of past generations

genotype
the combination of genes inherited from both parents and their ancestors

recessive gene
a gene that carries a trait that may not appear unless a gene for the same trait is inherited from both parents

DNA
deoxyribonucleic acid, the molecule containing the information that causes the formation of proteins that stimulate the development of tissues and organs and affect other genes and physiological functions

The Family Before Birth

Congenital Anomalies

At times, numerical or structural abnormalities of chromosomes can result in incomplete or imperfect cell formation. Many of these abnormalities result in spontaneous **abortion** early in the pregnancy. If the baby is born, these defective chromosomes can result in **congenital anomalies** including malformations and/or mental challenges. Some anomalies may be obvious at birth; others may be internal and not immediately observable, but become expressed at a later age. Examples of diseases or conditions with genetic origins include cystic fibrosis and hemophilia. These disorders occur when both parents' chromosomes carry the gene for them and the infant receives a gene for the anomaly from both parents.

Although the exact causes are unknown, some congenital anomalies are thought to result when two or more combinations of abnormal genes and environmental agents cause a defect. Spina bifida (an opening in the spinal column), anencephaly (a defect in the development of the neural tube during embryonic development that leads to an absent forebrain and an incompletely developed skull), cleft lip and palate, congenital heart disease, and dislocation of the hips may be some of the disorders caused by a combination of genetic and environmental factors.

Another condition that can cause congenital malformation and sometimes stillbirth is the Rh factor, or Rh incompatibility. The **Rh factor** (detected in the rhesus monkey, after which this condition is named) is caused when the mother has Rh-negative blood and the baby has Rh-positive blood. The mother forms antibodies against the fetus as if it were a foreign body. Usually, this condition does not harm the first baby because the formation of antibodies takes time. However, with subsequent pregnancies, the antibodies present in the mother's bloodstream can cross the placenta and attack the blood cells of the fetus. A simple blood test can determine a woman's blood type and Rh factor; further blood testing and antibody screening can determine whether an Rh-negative woman has developed antibodies to Rh-positive blood. Treatments are available to prevent an Rh-negative person's antibody response to Rh-positive blood cells (Mayo Clinic Staff, 2010).

Genetic Counseling and Testing

Genetic counseling can be helpful to a couple whose family histories indicate possible genetic defects or whose fetus has been diagnosed as at risk. As indicated, problems can occur if a child is born to parents who each carry the same harmful trait. Genetic counselors cannot accurately predict whether a child will be born with a disorder, but they can provide information to couples, who can then decide whether to have a child. When conception has already occurred, various tests can provide information about the condition of the fetus. Although this information cannot always predict the extent of the disorder, it may be helpful to parents both medically and for life planning (Rantanen, Pöntinen, Nippert, Sequeiros, & Kääriäinen, 2009).

There are several techniques for determining genetic defects. Testing the blood of the prospective parents can help to determine several possible problems. Sickle cell anemia is a disorder in which the body makes sickle-shaped red blood cells that are stiff and sticky; they tend to block blood flow in the blood vessels of the limbs and organs, which contributes to pain, infection, and organ damage. The U.S. Department of Health and Human Services National Institutes of Health (2011) reports that sickle cell anemia is most common in people whose families come from Africa, South or Central America (especially Panama), Caribbean islands, Mediterranean countries (such as Turkey,

Greece, and Italy), India, and Saudi Arabia. The gene for sickle-cell anemia is present in one in 12 African Americans and the disease occurs in more than one out of every 36,000 Hispanic American births. Tay-Sachs disease, an enzyme deficiency that is seen more commonly in descendants of Ashkenazi Jews, causes neurological degeneration and early death. Maternal serum screening can determine the presence of both sickle-cell anemia and Tay-Sachs disease.

Chromosomal disorders may be detected in the fetus through several prenatal tests. A screening test that used to be called the **alphafetoprotein test (AFP)**—but now is referred to as the maternal serum screening test, the multiple marker screening, the triple screen, or the quad screen—is used to detect disorders in the brain or spinal column. Another procedure, **amniocentesis**, can aid in identifying all chromosomal disorders and more than 100 biochemical disorders including Tay-Sachs disease, cystic fibrosis, and sickle cell anemia. This procedure involves analysis of the fetal cells in the amniotic fluid. These fetal cells are sampled using a large hollow needle inserted into the mother's abdomen. Amniocentesis is recommended when the mother is of advanced age, when the family history indicates that the fetus may be at risk, or if previous tests warrant further examination. The procedure is usually done approximately 15 to 18 weeks into the pregnancy, when sufficient amniotic fluid surrounds the fetus. The results of an amniocentesis can indicate whether a baby has Down syndrome or neural tube defects. The March of Dimes (2011a) reports that amniocentesis carries a small risk of miscarriage (approximately one case in 300 to one in 500.

A third method of determining chromosomal disorders is the **chorionic villus test (CVT)**. A sample of cells is taken from the hairlike projections (villi) on tissue (chorion) in the placenta. The CVT has some advantages over amniocentesis because it can be done as early as the ninth week of pregnancy and the results are usually available in several days.

A fourth technique that is helpful in determining possible problems with the fetus is ultrasound. Ultrasound exams are often used to confirm results of the tests just described. The uterus is scanned with high-frequency sound waves to create an image of the fetus. Parents often share the resulting photos proudly with family and friends, even though early in the pregnancy it is sometimes difficult for nonmedical people to determine exactly where the fetus is in the photo.

The Human Genome

The Human Genome Project is an international research effort begun in 1991 by the U.S. Department of Energy and the National Institutes of Health and coordinated with research institutes in other countries. The initial completion goal was for the year 2003, to mark the 50th anniversary of the discovery of the double helix structure of DNA by James Watson, Francis Crick, and their colleagues. It was completed, at least in rough draft form, ahead of schedule in 2000. It has constructed detailed genetic maps of the human **genome** (the single set of chromosomes characteristic of sex cells, or gametes) and other organisms to localize an estimated 20,000 to 25,000 genes. The outcome of this research is providing detailed information about the structure, organization, and function of human DNA. The information gleaned from this research allows scrutiny of embryonic development for a wider range of physical conditions from rare, inherited ailments to more familiar diseases such as cancer. This process involves the identification of a gene in the cell of a preembryo through a technique called **polymerase chain reaction (PCR)**.

alphafetoprotein test (AFP)
a blood test that can identify disorders in the brain or spinal column in the fetus

amniocentesis
a technique that involves extracting amniotic fluid for the purpose of detecting all chromosomal and more than 100 biomedical disorders

chorionic villus test (CVT)
a test that analyzes samples of the hairlike projections (chorionic villi) of tissue in the placenta to determine chromosomal disorders (can be done earlier than amniocentesis)

genome
the sum total of gene types possessed by a particular species

polymerase chain reaction (PCR)
a procedure used to identify disease-causing genes in an eight-cell embryo

The Family Before Birth

zygote
the first cell resulting from the fertilization of the ovum by the sperm

gender
the maleness or femaleness of the zygote as determined by the kind of sperm fertilizing the ovum (Y sperm: genetically male; X sperm: genetically female)

placenta
an organ attached to the wall of the uterus, which transmits nutrients from the mother to the embryo/fetus and filters wastes from the embryo/fetus to the mother

identical twins
twins whose development began when the zygote split into two identical halves, thus ensuring that both twins have the identical genetic code

fraternal twins
twins whose development began by the fertilization of two ova (eggs) by two sperm, causing each twin to have a different genetic code

embryonic stage
weeks three through eight of pregnancy, during which the major organ systems are formed

teratogens
environmental factors, such as viruses and chemical substances, that can cause abnormalities in the developing embryo or fetus

fetal stage
the stage that begins after the first eight weeks of pregnancy and continues until birth

If the PCR of a single cell from the eight-cell preembryo results in many copies of a target DNA sequence, the preembryo has the disease-causing gene. This process is very expensive and sometimes has to be repeated before a definitive diagnosis can be made.

The Human Genome Project has become one of the most important projects in biology and biomedical science in history, providing information about genetic variation in humans and the identification and measures of risk in individuals for any of a number of diseases, which has the potential for dramatically altering the manner in which diseases are prevented and treated. Also, as a result of the Human Genome Project, a variety of techniques for gene treatments for some genetic disorders are being developed so rapidly that PCR may become obsolete. Nevertheless, PCR can provide information to prospective parents to help them make the decision to avoid passing on a genetically based disease.

Although these techniques can help to detect problems, a number of disorders cannot be determined before birth. Nevertheless, recent medical advances provide new intervention procedures for some conditions. Blood transfusions, special diets, fetal surgery, and other treatments before and after birth can greatly reduce the severity of some conditions. Advances in genetics and genetic programming will continue to provide more information and improved treatments for these and other disorders.

Stages of Prenatal Development

Implantation Stage: Conception to Week Three of Pregnancy. The fertilized cell of a developing human is called a **zygote**. The **gender** of the zygote is determined at conception by the sperm type. If the sperm cell carries an X chromosome, the zygote will develop into a female; if the sperm cell carries a Y chromosome, the zygote will develop into a male.

During the week after fertilization, the zygote travels to one of the Fallopian tubes, where cell division begins. By about the fifth or sixth day, cell division creates two different parts. Inside is the cell mass that gradually develops into a human being. The complex outside cell mass becomes the **placenta**. The placenta transmits nutrients from the mother's bloodstream to the developing embryo and fetus. The placenta also filters out waste from the fetus through the mother's bloodstream. By the end of the second week, the zygote has moved through the Fallopian tube and has become implanted in the uterus.

Sometimes a zygote divides into two identical halves that develop separately, creating **identical twins**. These monozygotic, or one-zygote, twins will look alike, because they have the same genetic code. If two ova (eggs) are fertilized by two sperm, the result is **fraternal twins** (dizygotic, or two zygotes). These twins do not share the same genetic code.

Embryonic Stage: Weeks Three to Eight. The **embryonic stage** is critical to the healthy development of the fetus. It is during the first eight weeks that the major organ systems develop. Exposure to **teratogens**, such as chemical substances, viruses, alcohol, drugs, or other environmental factors, can cause congenital malformations.

Fetal Stage: Week Nine to Conclusion of Pregnancy. By week nine, the embryo has a human-like appearance and is now a fetus. The **fetal stage** continues until birth. During the fetal stage, growth and differentiation in organs and tissues take place. In addition, the weight and size of the fetus increase considerably. Figure 3.2 illustrates critical periods during fetal growth.

chapter 3

Prenatal Age	Significant Developments	Trimester	Significant Developments	Brain and Neurological Growth
Conception to 3–4 weeks	Fertilized egg travels through Fallopian tube; cell division begins; implantation occurs; placenta forms. Central nervous system (CNS) begins to evolve.	F i r s t	Cell division and differentiation create neural plate, which folds inward to form neural tube out of which the embryonic brain forms three major sections: forebrain, midbrain, and hindbrain, which evolve into separate lobes or regions.	First 40 days
4–8 weeks	Embryo is approximately ¼ inch long. All major organs are forming; heart begins to beat; bones form. Buds for arms, legs, fingers, and toes appear. Eyes, ears, nose form.	t r i m e s t e r	Neurons develop within the neural plate and multiply rapidly.	
2–3 months	Brain formation results in disproportionately large head; 20 buds for teeth appear. Liver, spleen, bone marrow produce blood cells; circulatory system is completed. Major organs are maturing in size and function. Fine hair covers the skin. Primitive reflexes move arms and legs.	S e c o n d	Neurons migrate to predetermined destinations, growing axons and dendrites and making first synaptic contact. At 7–9 weeks the brain is about the size of the eraser end of a pencil.	7–9 weeks
3–4 months	Fetus is about 4 inches long and weighs 1 ounce. Sex differentiation has occurred. Fingers and toes are evident. Facial features are distinct; eyelids closed.	t r i m e s t e r	At four months the brain has doubled in size. All neurons of the cerebral cortex have been generated, though their axons are yet to be insulated with myelin, which helps signals to travel.	4–5 months

Figure 3.2   Prenatal Growth and Development

continued

5–6 months

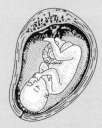

Fetal movement is felt. Heart beat is audible. Eyebrows and finger-nails appear. Vernix caeosa covers the delicate, wrinkled skin.

Sucking reflex emerges; fetus can hear mother's inter-nal sounds and voice. Movements become more deliberate and coordinated.

7 months

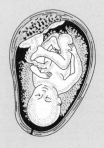

Kidneys have formed and begin to secrete urine; fetus moves, stretches, swallows, sleeps, wakes, and can hear and is growing to 11–14 inches and 2½ pounds. Thumb sucking may occur. Is approach-ing age of viability and has a likelihood of survival if born.

8 months

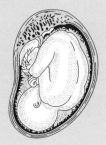

Eyelids open; finger-prints are established; active movement; hiccup and other reflexes are emerging. Fetus is increasing in length and weight; living quarters are becoming cramped and restricting movement. Fetus is gaining weight at a rate of ½ lb/week.

9 months

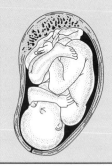

Fine hair disappearing from skin; bones are ossifying; bones in head remain soft and flexible for delivery. Fetus is getting in position for delivery and is 17–21 inches long and weighs 6 to 9 pounds.

S e c o n d   t r i m e s t e r

T h i r d   t r i m e s t e r

Neurons developing at a rate of 250,000 per minute from concep-tion to birth; each will ultimately become con-nected to 5,000–15,000 other neurons.

More neurons have been generated than will ultimately be needed.

Pruning (elimination) of overproduced neurons begins and continues into childhood

Major accumulation of synapse in the prefron-tal cortex continues for several months postnatally.

Infant brain is one-third of its adult size, but its gross anatomy is very similar to the adult brain.

8 months

Synaptic activity is very active at birth. Environmental stimuli increase synaptic and pruning activity as the infant experiences, responds, and adapts.

9 months and first weeks after birth

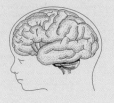

Figure 3.2 *continued*

Prenatal Care

It is important that the expectant mother seek professional prenatal health care as soon as she suspects that she is pregnant. Signs of pregnancy include one or several of the following symptoms: a missed menstrual period, drowsiness and a need for more rest, nausea, and swollen, sensitive breasts. The first eight weeks of pregnancy are critical to the developing fetus because this is the time that all major organ systems develop. Early prevention or detection of problems is important in ensuring the development of a healthy infant.

At the first prenatal visit, medical personnel will run one of several available tests to determine pregnancy. An examination provides basic information about the overall health of the mother-to-be. Blood tests are done to determine whether the prospective mother is anemic or has had **rubella** or whether there could be Rh blood factor. The initial examination may also include blood tests for the hepatitis B virus, urine tests to provide information on blood sugar and protein levels or any current infections, and a Pap test to check for changes of the cervix indicative of cancer. Tests are offered for sexually transmitted diseases including **acquired immunodeficiency syndrome (AIDS)** (caused by **human immunodeficiency virus (HIV)**). Physicians may alert prospective mothers to the dangers of **toxoplasmosis**, a potentially teratogenic parasitic infection caused by contact with cat droppings and raw or undercooked meat. Questions about the prospective mother's and father's medical history, family history, and personal health habits attempt to identify nutritional state, possible substance abuse, and the need for genetic screening. Prospective mothers are counseled about the importance of proper diet and avoiding drugs and radiation and are advised to check with their physicians before taking any medication. It is important that prospective mothers have medical checkups at regular intervals throughout pregnancy as prescribed by a health care professional to monitor for **toxemia** and other potential problems.

Nutrition

The importance to the health and development of the fetus and to the health and well-being of the mother of a balanced and nutritious diet during pregnancy is well documented and widely discussed. Because nutrients are passed from the mother to the fetus through the placenta, it is important for her to maintain a nutrient-rich diet. It is recommended that a woman of normal weight before pregnancy gain 25 to 35 pounds, but this can vary for individuals based on health factors (American College of Obstetricians and Gynecologists, 2011). Women who are underweight or overweight (or carrying twins) may be advised to gain more or less than these amounts, respectively. The physician or other prenatal health care professional plans with the prospective mother an appropriate diet and weight gain regime. The mother may be cautioned against consuming caffeine, alcohol, or calorie-rich/nutrient-poor snacks and junk foods. The appropriate calorie intake per day is determined, and adhering to these instructions helps to ensure a healthy pregnancy.

Both under- and overnutrition can interfere with the healthy development of the fetus. Throughout prenatal development there are **critical periods** during which organs are forming and are particularly vulnerable to insult. Dietary deficiencies can compromise the development and normal functions of developing bodily systems. Further, dietary deficiencies can result in poor health outcomes for the expectant mother.

rubella
a viral disease that can cause birth disorders if the mother contracts it during the first three months of pregnancy (also known as German measles)

acquired immunodeficiency syndrome (AIDS)
a disease that attacks the immune system, causing death from illnesses that the immune system cannot ward off

human immunodeficiency virus (HIV)
the virus that causes AIDS; it can be transmitted from an infected mother to the fetus or embryo via the placenta or delivery fluids

toxoplasmosis
a viral infection that can be transmitted from cat droppings or raw meat to the mother and from her to the fetus or embryo via the placenta, causing birth disorders

toxemia
a disease of unknown cause that occurs in the last trimester and can cause death to both mother and child

critical period
a time of physiological and/or psychological sensitivity during which the normal development of a major organ or structural system is vulnerable to insult or injury

The Family Before Birth

There appear to be generational effects of poor nutrition during pregnancy. An interesting study of grandchildren of Dutch women who were starved during World War II indicates that the effects of malnutrition during the third trimester of pregnancy led to small babies. When these babies became adults, their offspring were of normal expected size. However, when the offspring babies matured into women, they produced underweight infants. Surprisingly, the grandmothers' malnutrition was programmed in utero, affecting the grandchildren. This research suggests that long-term effects of malnutrition may appear over several generations or more (Diamond, 1990).

Teratogens

A teratogen is any agent capable of disrupting fetal growth and producing malformations. Just as nutrients and most medications pass from the mother through the placenta to the developing fetus, so do many other substances, with varying types and severity of consequences. The affect of a particular teratogen depends on its strength or amount and the time it is introduced into the pregnancy. Pregnancy is divided into the first **trimester** (0 to 14 weeks), the second trimester (14 to 28 weeks), and the third trimester (28 to 40 weeks), with dynamic and characteristic growth and development accomplishments in each. This is illustrated in Figure 3.2. Some effects are more profound during one or the other of these trimesters, and some effects are equally damaging throughout the pregnancy. Effects also are related to the affinity of a particular teratogen for a specific type of tissue; for example, lead appears to have its greatest harmful effects on brain and nerve tissue.

Although not exhaustive, Table 3.2 lists types of conditions and teratogens that affect the developing fetus. Consultation with health care professionals helps pregnant women and fathers-to-be to assess their lifestyles and take necessary precautions to avoid toxic or developmentally disruptive fetal development resulting from known insults. Although it may appear that almost anything can have an effect on the fetus or expectant mother, it is not always clear that effects are inevitable for all pregnancies. Little is known about what protects one fetus from a particular teratogen, whereas another might be severely damaged by it. The best precautions include early and continuing professional prenatal care and sensible health habits. Avoiding potentially harmful substances and activities becomes the highest priority. This may mean changing existing habits or lifestyles.

Oral Health

There used to be a belief that women should not receive dental treatment during pregnancy. There was also a belief that a woman loses one tooth with each pregnancy. Now we know that good oral health is important, not just for the woman, but for the fetus she carries. Dental caries, or cavities, are caused by the bacteria streptococcus mutans. This bacteria can be transmitted from mother to child and has been identified as the cause of premature birth, premature rupture of the placenta, and induced premature birth due to **eclampsia** (Dasanayake, Gennaro, Hendricks-Munoz, & Chhun, 2008). Consequently, it is important that women maintain good oral health, not just for themselves but also for their unborn child. None of the procedures at the dentist's office is harmful to the fetus. The second trimester is considered the best time to visit the dentist (Russell & Mayberry, 2008). Of course, not all women can afford to see a dentist. Obtaining dental care for

trimester
the first, second, or third three months of pregnancy

eclampsia
convulsions due to high blood pressure in the mother—a serious condition for the health of the baby and the mother

Table 3.2 Conditions That Affect the Developing Fetus

	Contribution	Detrimental	Potential Effects	Prevention
Prepregnancy checkup.	Establishes relationship with physician of choice. Assesses health history. Recommends and assists with genetic counseling as needed. Assists in planning and spacing of childbearing.	Delayed professional health care.	Ill-timed and/or unintended pregnancy. Failure to diagnose and respond to existing health needs. Lost opportunity to receive recommended pre-pregnancy immunizations and timely genetic counseling.	Talk with family physician. Seek recommendations. Interview two or more recommended American College of Obstetrics and Gynecology Board–certified physicians, licensed general practitioners, or certified nurse–midwives. Visit hospital/birthing center to learn about each one's pro-cedures and expectations. Attend prenatal classes. Select best care.
Prenatal professional health care supervision including early and regularly scheduled examinations.	Early diagnosis and consultation provides an essential health care regime. Anticipates needs, and answers questions. Estimates due date; plans for delivery and perinatal and postnatal care.		Delayed diagnosis and treatment deprives fetus of essential health care during the critical first-trimester development of major body organs and systems and ongoing growth and health oversight.	
Optimal weight gain and maintenance.	Minimizes complications associated with an over- or underweight pregnancy.	Under- or overnutrition.	Deprives fetus of essential nutrients for growth. Compromises all types of fetal growth and development, notably fetal brain growth and neurological development and bone and teeth formation, and risks anemia and low birth weight. Compromises maternal health, and risks pregnancy, labor, and delivery complications.	Learn about and follow recommended nutritional guidelines for pregnancy and lactation, weight con-trol, and exercise routines. Consume fresh natural foods and whole-grain products. Consult with physician about food additives, diet foods, and food and beverages to avoid.
Nutrient-rich diet: protein, carbohydrates, appropriate fats, folic acid, vitamins, and minerals including iron and zinc.	Provides the essential body-building and health-maintaining nutrients to sustain growth and health of oth mother and fetus.			

continued

Table 3.2 continued

	Contribution	Detrimental	Potential Effects	Prevention
Rest, relaxation, sleep.	Optimal state for the secretion of growth hormones necessary to build new body cells.		Obesity increases risk of gestational diabetes with risk of overweight baby with associated heart and kidney diseases and other abnormalities.	
Moderate daily exercise.	Improves circulation, oxygenates the blood, and increases blood supply to the fetus.			Avoid strenuous lifting, pulling, and climbing; not a good time to take up a new sport.
Adequate water and fluid intake.	Maintains body hydration and temperature, assists in elimination of body wastes.			
Dental hygiene.	Contributes to overall health of mother and fetus.	Gum disease.	Associated with preterm and low birth weight.	Regular dental examinations. Dental hygiene.
		Prolonged or excessive maternal stress.	Engages the psycho-physiological fight/flight response, increasing maternal heart rate, constricting blood vessels, and sometimes gastrointestinal disturbances and other symptoms, which in turn may interfere with blood supply to fetus, and less-than-optimal uterine existence.	Follow sensible, healthy daily practices. Enlist spouse or other family members in sharing responsibilities and removing stressors. Assess need for consultation with employer; perhaps a change in hours, workload, or types of responsibilities. Share concerns with physician or health care professional. Seek counseling.
		Certain communicable diseases, e.g., influenza, rubella, rubeola, chicken pox, mumps, viral hepatitis, poliomyelitis, and other viral and bacterial infections.	Variously associated with many anomalies including mental retardation, deafness, blindness, and heart defects.	Seek prepregnancy immunizations as recommended. Consult with physician about preventive measures. Wash hands often; practice good hygiene. Seek immediate medical attention if exposed.

Item	Effects	Recommendation
Caffeine.	A maternal central nervous system stimulant that increases heart rate, urine production, and stomach acid. Associated with low birth weight.	Avoid foods containing caffeine, e.g., coffee, tea, soft drinks, chocolate. Read food and beverage labels.
Artificial sweeteners.	Fetus has difficulty eliminating by-products of saccharine.	Use only on advice of physician.
Over-the-counter medications, vitamin supplements, and herbal remedies.	Variously associated with spontaneous abortion, kidney problems, severe birth defects.	Read food and beverage labels.
		During first visit, tell physician what medications and supplements have been taken. Take only physician-prescribed medications and vitamins, which are essential for, and particular to, each individual pregnancy.
Smoking tobacco or marijuana (first- or second-hand; either occasional or frequent; either partner).	Lowers fertility in men and women, potential damage to sperm, preterm delivery, prematurity, perinatal and neonatal deaths, low birth weight, sudden infant death syndrome. Newborn neuro-behavioral symptoms, e.g., excitability, difficulty calming, nicotine withdrawal symptoms. Later behavioral disturbances, attentional and cognitive difficulties in childhood.	Both parents should stop smoking. Seek professional help to do so if necessary. Avoid second-hand smoke.

continued

Table 3.2 continued

Contribution	Detrimental	Potential Effects	Prevention
	Alcohol.	Fetal alcohol syndrome and other alcohol-related neurodevelopmental disorders, including low birth weight, neurological damage, craniofacial deformity, developmental delay, impaired cognitive abilities (attention, memory, problem solving, abstract thinking), mental retardation, hyperactivity, later behavioral difficulties in childhood.	No alcohol during pregnancy or during fertility efforts.
	Cocaine, opiates, other illicit drugs, or polydrug (multiple drug) use.	Neurological damage, low birth weight, prematurity, neonatal low-arousal states, deficient motor and reflexive activity, higher excitability, abnormal crying behaviors, neonatal addiction and withdrawal symptoms.	No illicit drugs during pregnancy or during fertility efforts.
	Other toxins, e.g., lead, mercury, pesticides, household cleaners, fertilizers and other agricultural products, industrial wastes and emissions, animal droppings, certain insect bites.	Neurological damage, low birth weight, visual impairments, other birth defects, developmental delays in cognitive and language abilities.	Consult with physician about particular exposures and how to avoid known toxins.

Radiation.	Damage to growing cells, miscarriage, malformations, childhood cancers, gene mutations.	X-rays on advice of physician and administered under strict protective guidelines including lead apron shield. Consult with physician about sources of radiation and appropriate precautions.
Sexually transmitted diseases (STDs).	Spontaneous abortion, prematurity, growth retardation, low birth weight, hearing and vision impairments, and other possible birth defects. Some STDs can be transmitted to the infant during pregnancy, labor, and delivery.	Practice safe sex, using condoms and spermicide. Advise physician if exposure is suspected. Both partners may need to be treated.

Sources: ACOG (The American Congress of Obstetricians and Gynecologists). Retrieved from http://www.acog.org

CDC (Department of Health and Human Services Centers for Disease Control and Prevention). (2009b). Sexually transmitted diseases. Treatment guidelines 2006. Retrieved from http://www.cdc.gov/STD/treatment

Eiden, D. (2009). Infants exposed to cocaine in utero react more emotionally to stress. (2009). *The Brown University Digest of Addiction Theory and Application, 28(S3)*, I-II.

Nichter, M., Adrian, S., Goldade, K., Tesler, L., & Muramato, M. (2008). Smoking and harm-reduction efforts among postpartum women. *Qualitative Health Research, 18(9)*, 1184–1194.

Shaw, G. M., Carmichael, S. L., Vollset, S. E., Yang, W., Finnell, R. H., Blom, H., Midttun, O., & Ueland, P. M. (2009). Mid-pregnancy cotinine and risks of orofacial clefts and neural tube defects. *Journal of Pediatrics, 154(1)*, 17–19.

pregnant women in poverty has become a public health issue. Early childhood professionals, in programs like Head Start, may be involved in finding "a dental home" or at least educating pregnant women about the importance of oral health.

Prenatal Learning

What the fetus experiences in utero intrigues us all. Research in recent years suggests that some learning does take place at the sensory level as the central nervous system evolves out of the neural tube and axons and dendrites begin their initial migrations and synaptic activities. Although the information gleaned from in utero experience is sketchy and unrefined, when born, the **neonate** exhibits some remarkable behaviors—following the voice of the mother and sometimes the father, relaxing and sleeping readily to the familiar sound of the mother's heart rhythm, and calming to the scent of her presence. By studying variations in infants' sucking patterns in response to recordings of their mothers' voices, DeCasper and Fifer (1980) found that neonates prefer their mother's voice over that of others. In another study, mothers read *The Cat in the Hat* to their fetuses twice a day for the 6 weeks preceding the due date. After birth, the infants were read both *The Cat in the Hat* and *The King, the Mice, and the Cheese.* The infants demonstrated through their sucking that they preferred *The Cat in the Hat* (DeCasper & Spence, 1986). This study and others suggest that prenatal auditory experiences influence postnatal auditory preferences. Although psychologists have not begun to encourage specific types of extrauterine activities to encourage in utero learning, as we explore the quickly emerging capabilities of the newborn in the next chapter, it will become apparent that the capacity for adapting to various postnatal sensory experiences may well be related to certain sensed prenatal experiences.

Education for Childbirth and Parenting

In the past, women often had control over where they gave birth and who assisted them. With the increased use of anesthetics to relieve pain, physicians began to play the dominant role in directing the birth process, and fathers were usually relegated to the waiting room. Over a period of time, many parents became frustrated over their lack of involvement in one of the most important events in their lives. In addition, in the 1970s and 1980s the increasing number of research studies documenting the negative effects of medication during labor and delivery caused increasing concern among many health care professionals (Sepkowski, 1985; Wilson, 1977). Over time, parents and health care professionals became advocates for educated childbirth and for more active involvement of the parents in the pregnancy, delivery, and care of the newborn in the hospital setting.

Hospitals that specialize in labor and delivery now offer a huge variety of classes. For decades they have offered childbirth classes that explain the stages of delivery and provide some practice in pain management through breathing. Now, a hospital is likely to offer additional classes in breastfeeding, safety-proofing your home, infant care and early parenting, special classes for fathers, prenatal yoga, and infant massage. One hospital Web site also listed these specialty classes: unmedicated childbirth preparation, hypnobirthing preparation, preparing for a c-section, pain management, multiple matters, and private classes for childbirth preparation.

One of the better-known childbirth education approaches is the **Lamaze method** (Karmel, 1959). The Lamaze technique instructs the mother-to-be and her coach, usually

neonate
the newborn from birth to 4 weeks

Lamaze method
a method developed by Fernand Lamaze, which involves training the prospective mother and a partner/coach in breathing and relaxation techniques to be used during labor

the father-to-be, in breathing patterns that help to control pain and discomfort during the different stages of labor. The prospective mother and her coach practice these techniques during the last months of pregnancy.

Prospective parents are given information about the various types of medication and their effects on the fetus and the mother. They are encouraged to discuss their preferred medications with their physicians in advance of delivery. Many Lamaze classes are preceded by a course dealing with general pregnancy and childbirth information. These classes usually occur earlier in the pregnancy and inform the prospective parents about physiological and psychological aspects of pregnancy, childbirth, and parenting.

Some parents-to-be choose to deliver their babies at home with the assistance of a physician or certified nurse–midwife. Although home births provide the prospective parents with more control over the birthing process and can involve family or friends, some risks are involved. If complications arise, hospital equipment and trained specialists are not immediately available.

Many hospitals now provide birthing rooms that allow the mother to remain in one room throughout labor and delivery, with husband and family members often present. Birthing rooms are usually furnished with a homelike decor yet provide all of the necessary medical support services.

Ideally, prospective parents select their obstetrician and hospital with care. An obstetrician who is comfortable with the father's active involvement throughout the pregnancy and who recognizes the value of educated childbirth provides valuable support to the prospective parents. Likewise, a hospital that offers family-involved birthing experiences; allows the father, other children, and close relatives extended visitation privileges; permits the baby to "room in" with the mother; and has classes for new parents on the care and feeding of the newborn provides helpful services to new parents. Such experiences help parents to learn about and get to know their baby and begin to develop confidence in their parenting abilities.

The perinatal period is also seen as a window during which parents may be particularly open to information that will improve their parenting skills. A recent study evaluated a prebirth educational program that emphasized communication and conflict resolution skills along with information about birth and early parenting (Feinberg, Jones, Kan, & Goslin, 2010). At a 3.5-year follow-up, parents involved in the program, Family Foundations, had less stress, more efficacy, less depression, and better coparenting quality than parents in the control group who did not participate in a prebirth educational program. The intervention parents were neither too authoritarian nor too permissive. The children had better self-regulation, better social competency, and fewer behavioral problems.

Some of the health services described in this chapter are not available to all socioeconomic groups. The provision of more extensive coverage to all segments of the population is a concern to child development professionals. As services expand to meet the needs of an increasingly diverse population, programs must be sensitive to the cultural backgrounds of various groups that will use them.

The Importance of Preparing Siblings for the Birth

Preparing brothers and sisters for the arrival of a new baby helps create positive sibling relationships from the beginning. Less jealousy and decreased sibling rivalry later on are the benefits of thoughtful attention to the needs of other children within the family.

For children younger than 3 years of age, parents need to plan some special activities or time spent alone with them after the birth of a new brother or sister. Planning for how and when this will occur can prevent the children from feeling neglected. A doll and various accessories used in the care of young babies can help during times when parents are busy with the newborn. An older brother or sister can feed, bathe, and change the baby just as mother or father does. Siblings can help in preparing the baby's room or bed, gathering clothes, and choosing the baby's name.

Some hospitals have special programs for siblings. Prospective brothers and sisters can visit the hospital to see where their mother and the new baby will stay. Hospital staff members talk to the children about what babies are like and what their care entails. Discussion of the range of feelings about being a brother or sister can also help children deal with their emotions.

Careful thought must be given to who will care for the siblings during the mother's hospital stay. Those who care for them need to be nurturing and understanding of their expressions of distress at separation from their mother and other anxieties. Careful planning for siblings can reduce stress for the entire family and promote positive sibling relationships. Nonetheless, it is normal for siblings to have a hard time during the first weeks and months of a new baby's life, as you will see in Chapter 4.

Siblings often have a special bond.

Anticipating Optimal Outcomes

This chapter has addressed a number of issues regarding optimal conditions preceding the birth of a child. Nevertheless, not all children born to advantaged families have advantaged circumstances during childhood and as adults. Likewise, not all children born into less-than-desirable settings remain disadvantaged. Studies indicate that the forces that create inequality in families are complex and interact in a synergistic process (Garrett, Ferron, Ng'Andu, Bryant, & Harbin, 1994). Werner and Smith (1982, 1992, 2001) studied adolescents who were classified as resilient. These children seemed to have been protected by the following factors: good temperament, small family size, positive parenting patterns, a relationship with a caring adult other than a parent, low levels of family conflict, fewer stressful experiences, and access to counseling and remediation services. Werner (1989) and Werner & Smith (2001) found that early responsibility in caring for a sibling, a grandparent, or an ill or incompetent parent was another factor in the lives of resilient adolescents. In his transcultural study of individual competence, Heath (1977) identified a core set of behaviors including (1) an ability to anticipate consequences; (2) calm and clear thinking; (3) potential fulfillment; (4) orderly, organized approaches to life's problems; (5) predictability; (6) purposefulness;

(7) realism; (8) reflectiveness; (9) strong convictions; and (10) implacability. Finally, self-esteem, coupled with the perception of the individual as one who can cope successfully by the family and others in the culture, was important. Do you think these core behaviors are still important today?

Keisha and DeVon Johnson as well as Cheryl Monroe and James are awaiting the births of their babies. These babies will experience very different sets of circumstances before their births. Chapter 4 shows how these circumstances influence the development of the babies and their family contexts at birth and soon afterward.

Role of the Early Childhood Professional

1. Understand how cultural background and parental behaviors and attitudes directly influence the development of children even before birth.

2. Understand that behaviors and attitudes of parents influence development and learning during prenatal development, after birth, and throughout the early childhood years.

3. Appreciate the challenges associated with family planning and child rearing.

4. Provide information and opportunities for parents to acquire child development knowledge.

5. Understand that parents are valuable sources of information about their children and that early childhood professionals must work in partnership with parents if optimal development and learning are to occur in young children.

Key Terms

abortion
acquired immunodeficiency
   syndrome (AIDS)
alphafetoprotein test (AFP)
amniocentesis
anorexia
bulimia
chorionic villus test (CVT)
chromosomes
congenital anomalies
critical period
DNA
doula
eclampsia
embryonic stage
environment
fertility
fertility rate

fetal stage
fetus
fraternal twins
gender
genes
genetic counseling
genome
genotype
gestation
gestational diabetes
heredity
home visitor
human immunodeficiency
   virus (HIV)
hypertension
identical twins
Lamaze method
low birth weight

neonate
neurobiological
   agents
perinatal
placenta
polymerase chain
   reaction (PCR)
prematurity
prenatal
recessive gene
Rh factor
rubella
teratogens
toxemia
toxoplasmosis
trimester
ultrasound
zygote

Review Strategies and Activities

1. Review the key terms individually or with a classmate.
2. Interview your classmates who are parents. Ask them to share with you some of the following:
   a. Their reactions on finding out they were going to be a parent
   b. Their feelings and reactions as the pregnancy progressed
   c. Reactions of the baby's other parent and of family and friends
   d. The nature of their prenatal care
   e. The types of care and interactions their children required at various times: birth, toddlerhood, 2 to 8 years of age
   f. A typical day as a parent
   g. The joys and challenges of becoming a parent
   h. How becoming a parent has changed their lives
3. Develop a resource file of support services your community provides to prospective parents (e.g., local hospitals, public health centers, prenatal clinics, prenatal and parenting classes, related support groups).
4. Write a research paper on cultural perspectives and practices associated with pregnancy, birth, and parenting.
5. Describe how you think heredity and environment influenced your development. Share with your classmates in small discussion groups.
6. Invite the following speakers to your class:
   a. A genetic counselor to describe and discuss genetic counseling
   b. A Lamaze instructor to describe and discuss the Lamaze method
   c. A La Leche League representative to discuss their perspectives on breastfeeding
   d. A pharmacist to discuss the effects of drugs during pregnancy.

Further Readings

American College of Obstetricians & Gynecologists. (2010). *Your pregnancy and childbirth: Month to month* (5th ed.). Atlanta, GA: Author.

Gonzalez-Mena, J. (2009). *Child, family, and community: Family-centered early care and education* (5th ed.). Columbus, OH: Merrill.

Lerner, C., & Ciervo, L. (2010). Parenting young children today: What the research tells us. *ZERO TO THREE, 30*(4), 4–9.

Michale, J. P. (2008). *Charting the bumpy road of coparenthood: Understanding the challenges of family life*. Washington, DC: ZERO TO THREE Press.

Other Resources

American College of Obstetricians and Gynecologists, www.acog.org. There are many education pamphlets on pregnancy, birth, and postnatal factors available from this site. Following are several examples:

A Father's Guide to Pregnancy (2009)

Family Health History is Important Screening Tool (2011)

Nutrition During Pregnancy (2010)

Routine Tests in Pregnancy (2009)

March of Dimes, www.marchofdimes.com. Local chapters of the March of Dimes provide pamphlets on genetic counseling, prenatal development, and ways to prevent birth defects. These are also available online.

National Scientific Council on the Developing Child. (2010). *Early Experiences Can Alter Gene Expression and Affect Long-Term Development: Working Paper No. 10.* www.developingchild.harvard .edu. This site provides information on how environmental influences can actually change whether and how genes are expressed. The reader can use interactive features that demonstrate how early experiences shape development.

The National Center for Children and Families (NCCF), http://ccf.tc.columbia.edu. This site advances the policy, education, and development of children and families.

USDA. United States Department of Agriculture, Center for Nutrition Policy and Promotion, Cost of Raising a Child Calculator, www.cnpp.usda.gov/calculatorintro.htm. With USDA's Cost of Raising a Child Calculator, you can estimate how much it will annually cost to raise a child. This may help you plan better for overall expenses including food or to purchase adequate life insurance.

chapter 4
The Child and Family at Birth

To be a child is to know the fun of living. To have a child is to know the beauty of life.

—Author Unknown

After studying this chapter, you will demonstrate comprehension by:

▶ describing the stages of labor;

▶ identifying the various types of deliveries;

▶ describing the assessment and care of newborns;

▶ outlining the change in family dynamics at birth, including bonding and reactions of the newborn, parents, siblings, and extended family; and

▶ describing the care of infants with special needs and their families.

The birth of a child is one of nature's profound miracles. Even though there are hundreds of thousands of babies born each day, each new life heightens our sense of wonder. For families, few words or phrases adequately describe the emotions that surround the anticipation, delivery, and first glimpse at their newborn. To the extent that the parents have experienced optimal prepregnancy and prenatal planning and health care, this event is enhanced for them. The nature and health of the pregnancy have been critical to the nature and health of the delivery process and the overall well-being of the newborn. Let us begin this chapter with a description of the delivery process.

Stages of Labor

The average gestation period is 280 days, but it can be shorter or longer by as many as 14 days. Most infants are born between 266 and 294 days. At the end of the gestation period, the fetus has reached full term and is positioned for the birth process. The process, generally referred to as **labor**, is divided into three stages.

The first stage of labor, **dilation**, progresses in three phases:

1. The earliest phase, in which a blood-tinged mucus is discharged from the vagina and the **cervix** begins the dramatic process of enlarging or dilating to make way for easy passage of the baby. Mild **contractions** begin, occurring every 15 to 20 minutes, gradually becoming more regular until they are less than five minutes apart.

2. The active phase, in which the cervix continues dilating to up to 5 to 8 centimeters; the mucous membranes rupture, releasing amniotic fluids; and contractions become stronger and begin to occur about three minutes apart, lasting about 30 to 45 seconds.

3. The transition phase, in which the cervix dilates to 8 to 10 centimeters and contractions occur two to three minutes apart and last about one minute.

The second stage of labor commences when the cervix is fully dilated and contractions become regular and stronger with noticeable rest periods between them. This phase ends with the birth of the baby. The third stage involves light, rhythmic contractions that assist in the expulsion of the placenta. The following vignettes about Keisha and DeVon and Cheryl and James illustrate these processes.

labor
the three stages of the birth process: dilation, birth of the baby, and discharge of the placenta

dilation
the gradual opening of the cervix, which occurs in the first stage of labor

cervix
the opening of the uterus

contraction
the movement of the muscles of the uterus that pushes the baby through the cervical opening and into the birth canal

Stage 1: Dilation to Delivery

It is 6:25 in the morning. Keisha Johnson feels a slight snap in her abdominal area. Amniotic fluid empties from her uterine cavity and soaks the bed linen. Keisha realizes that she is in labor and Jeremy's birth will soon be a reality. Dilation actually began two days earlier, when Keisha's checkup with Dr. Windle indicated that her cervix was dilated 3 centimeters. By the time her baby is born, Keisha's cervix will have dilated to about 10 centimeters (4 inches). This opening is wide enough to allow most babies to be born.

DeVon and Keisha have learned from their childbirth education classes that each labor and delivery is unique. Nevertheless, one or more of the following signs usually indicates that labor is in process: lower backache, indigestion, diarrhea, abdominal cramps, expulsion of the mucous plug, and discharge of amniotic fluid.

Keisha awakens DeVon and tells him what has happened. He excitedly phones Dr. Windle. She tells DeVon that because Keisha's water has broken, it is best that they go to the hospital immediately. Dr. Windle says that she will meet them there in about 45 minutes. Keisha and DeVon dress, gather their bags (which have been packed for several weeks), and drive to the hospital.

Keisha's contractions have been relatively short, lasting about 30 to 45 seconds, and have occurred about every 15 to 20 minutes. During the drive, she uses some of the Lamaze breathing exercises and records the time and duration of each contraction. Keisha and DeVon are greeted at the hospital by obstetrical nurse Maria Lopez. She helps Keisha into a wheelchair and takes her to the birthing room, while DeVon checks Keisha into the hospital. Maria is familiar with Lamaze techniques, so she temporarily takes over as Keisha's coach as the contractions occur.

The birthing room looks very much like a bedroom, attractively furnished in soothing colors. In addition to the birthing bed are a sofa, several comfortable chairs, and a table with four chairs. Unlike the traditional hospital setting, in which mothers are moved to the delivery room before the birth, Keisha will remain in the birthing room for both labor and delivery and for a brief period thereafter. She is free to move around and to take refreshments as needed and permissible. Friends and family can visit, according to Keisha and DeVon's wishes. Dr. Windle and Maria will be on hand to help DeVon and Keisha and provide specialized medical assistance.

The birthing bed is very different from the traditional delivery table on which women lie down with their feet in stirrups. It allows Keisha to recline slightly, and there is a place to rest her legs to help in pushing during the final stage of labor. The position of the birthing bed will relieve pressure on Keisha's back and allow the force of gravity to assist in the birth process.

Dr. Windle soon arrives. She checks Keisha and confirms that she is comfortable, looks over the birthing room and determines that everything is in a state of readiness, and briefs Keisha on the initial procedures that will be taking place. She instructs Maria to set up an intravenous catheter (IV), a very thin, flexible tube placed in an arm vein, through which fluids to prevent dehydration can be administered as needed. The IV is also used to provide medications when necessary to control blood pressure, curtail contractions when labor is premature, augment or induce labor, or provide pain relief medication. This is a common procedure, but it is not routine practice in all hospitals. DeVon enters the birthing room and resumes coaching Keisha and timing her contractions. During this first stage of labor, Keisha's contractions become more frequent and intense. Keisha adapts her Lamaze breathing patterns to the intensity of contractions. She walks around the room or sits in the birthing bed, depending on what feels more comfortable. Because she seems to be experiencing intense pain in her lower back, DeVon rubs her back to relieve the pressure. Throughout labor, Dr. Windle and Maria check in on DeVon and Keisha. At each visit and just after Keisha has experienced a contraction, Dr. Windle places a stethoscope on Keisha's abdomen and listens and records the fetal heart rate. On one or more of these visits, she asks whether DeVon and Keisha would like to listen. Then she places a handheld ultrasound instrument on Keisha's abdomen, and they all listen with awe to the healthy, rhythmic beat of the fetal heart. Dr. Windle assures Keisha and DeVon that labor is progressing normally and that she will return shortly to check on them again.

It is now 10:00 a.m., and Keisha has been in labor at least four hours—possibly longer, because she was asleep when her water broke. Jeremy is on his way into this world.

Now, let's see what is happening to Cheryl Monroe and James. It is four weeks before Cheryl's due date. She and James are watching television at approximately 11:00 P.M. Cheryl does not feel well; she has indigestion and diarrhea. While she is in the bathroom, she notices a mucus-like, blood-tinged discharge on her undergarments. The home visitor who has been helping Cheryl had told her about the signs of labor. Cheryl walks to the living room and tells James and her sister that she thinks the baby is coming.

Cheryl's sister calls the emergency room to tell them of Cheryl's condition. Because it is one month before Cheryl's estimated due date, the emergency room nurse says that Cheryl needs to come to the hospital as soon as possible. James goes to a neighbor who has a car to ask him to drive them to the hospital.

Shortly after midnight, Cheryl's mother arrives home on the bus from her evening job to find the household in an uproar. She quickly gathers clothes and cosmetics into a bag for Cheryl. Cheryl is anxious, and her mother does her best to calm her while they walk to the neighbor's car for the short drive to the hospital. "After all," she says, "millions of women for all time have been having babies; Cheryl can do it, too, and she will be all right." Cheryl's mother and James help her into the large hospital complex, which also has a medical school. Preliminary paperwork about Cheryl has been forwarded by her doctor. It is pulled from the file, and various forms are completed while Cheryl is placed in a wheelchair and taken to an examining room. The examination indicates that labor is well under way. Cheryl is then wheeled to a large room, where she is prepared for labor and delivery. The nurses are kind and efficient, and they talk reassuringly to her.

Because of Cheryl's limited financial resources and the available facilities of her hospital of choice, she does not have access to a private birthing room. Cheryl will share a room and medical personnel with a number of other pregnant women. Because of staff limitations and concern and respect for the other expectant mothers, Cheryl's family and friends are allowed very brief visits in the labor room and no admittance

(continued)

The Child and Family at Birth

to the delivery room. Cheryl's mother, James, and the neighbor are asked to make themselves comfortable in the waiting room. A nurse tells them that he will keep them informed of Cheryl's progress.

A specialist comes in to assess the condition of the fetus. She uses an internal **electronic fetal monitor**, a device that entails inserting through the cervix an electrode, which is carefully attached to the scalp of the fetus to monitor fetal heart rate, and a catheter, which measures the strength of Cheryl's contractions as labor progresses. The monitor indicates that the fetus is in distress. The specialist calls to the delivery room and tells them to prepare immediately for a **cesarean delivery**. Because Cheryl's baby will be **preterm** (a birth that occurs three weeks or more before the due date), the doctor orders an **isolette** to be brought to the delivery room. An isolette is a small crib, which provides a warm, controlled environment for the newborn. It includes attachments that monitor body temperature, heart rate, respiratory rate, arterial blood pressure, and inspired oxygen levels, providing an ongoing assessment of the physiological condition of the infant. Fluids and nutrition as needed can also be given through alternative means when the infant is unable to ingest food through the mouth and intestinal tract.

Stage 2: Birth

Stage 2 of labor begins when the cervix has dilated to 10 centimeters and the head of the fetus pushes through the cervical opening into the vagina. After some time, Keisha Johnson has the urge to push. However, Lamaze training has prepared Keisha to know what to do during this part of labor. She begins a Lamaze breathing technique to help her control the urge to expel the baby. The pains from the contractions become intense, and Keisha tells DeVon that she would like some medication. In their Lamaze class, DeVon and Keisha learned that at times, medication can be necessary and helpful in the birth process. However, it can also have some negative effects, the extent of which is determined by the type of medication, the amount given, and the stage of labor during which it is administered. Discussion with Dr. Windle and Maria reminds Keisha that the most difficult part of labor is almost over and the baby will soon be born. Along with DeVon, they encourage her to continue without any medication because the fetal head has already numbed the vaginal opening. Medication at this point might reduce Keisha's contractions and make her less effective in pushing during the final part of delivery. DeVon also reminds her that continuing without medication will help the baby to be more alert not only at birth, but also for some time afterward (Emory, Schlackman, & Fiano, 1996). Buoyed by their encouragement, Keisha decides to proceed without medication.

Keisha's last ultrasound had indicated that the baby might be large, 8 to 9 pounds. For this reason, Dr. Windle decides to do an **episiotomy**. An episiotomy is a small incision that helps to prevent the opening of the vulva from tearing during the final stages of birth.

It is now close to 3:00 P.M., and it is time for Maria's nursing shift to end. She decides to stay longer because it is almost time for Keisha to give birth. The intense contractions are about one minute apart and last for almost 60 seconds. Dr. Windle and Maria now tell Keisha to push. As she squeezes DeVon's hand, Keisha pushes, and the

electronic fetal monitor
a device used during labor, which is attached to the abdomen of the pregnant woman or the scalp of the fetus to determine the fetal heart rate

cesarean delivery
a surgical procedure during which an incision is made through the abdominal and uterine walls of the mother to deliver the baby

preterm
infants born several weeks before the full term (38 weeks) of pregnancy

isolette
a small crib, which provides a controlled environment for newborns

episiotomy
an incision made in the opening of the vulva to prevent it from tearing during delivery

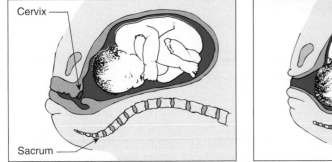

Cervix

Sacrum

(a)

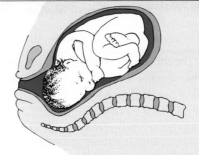

(b)

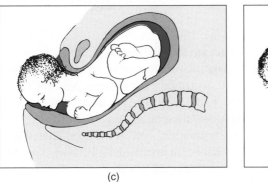

(c)

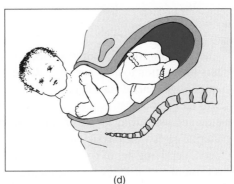

(d)

Figure 4.1
The Stages of Labor

During the first stage of labor (a, b), the uterus contracts, causing the cervix to dilate. In stage 2 (c, d), the baby moves down the birth canal and is pushed out.

baby's head begins to appear. Shortly, with another push, the head emerges. Dr. Windle gently suctions the mucus from the baby's nose and mouth. From the mirror above the birthing bed, DeVon and Keisha have their first look at Jeremy. With the next contraction, Keisha gives another big push, and Jeremy's full body appears. He begins to cry softly. (The stages of labor are illustrated in Figure 4.1.)

The birthing room has been kept a comfortable 78°F, with soothing music playing in the background. This atmosphere provides a calm setting for Jeremy's transition from the comfort and safety of his **in utero** environment to a more demanding **extrauterine** one. Dr. Windle and Maria quickly evaluate Jeremy for any signs of complications. He appears fine and is gently dried off and placed on Keisha's abdomen. Keisha and DeVon speak softly and tenderly to their newborn and begin cuddling him. Jeremy stops crying and looks directly into his mother's eyes. Keisha and DeVon are truly in awe of this little miracle. They look him over from head to toe, touching each little finger as Keisha gently cups her hand around a tiny foot, caressing it as she visually explores Jeremy's delicate facial features. DeVon decides that he looks like one of his brothers. After a while, the blood in the blood vessels in the umbilical cord stops throbbing, and Dr. Windle cuts the umbilical cord.

Guided by Maria, DeVon takes Jeremy and places him on a warmer, a special infant bed equipped with a heat lamp, oxygen, instruments for removing fluid and mucus from the infant's airways, and other equipment and medications needed to attend to the needs of the newborn. Jeremy will be given a warm bath when his vital signs have stabilized, and he will then be swaddled snugly to maintain body temperature and provide a sense of security.

in utero
the environment in which the fetus grows within the uterus

extrauterine
the environment outside of the uterus

The Child and Family at Birth

Stage 3: Expulsion of the Placenta

The third stage of labor involves the expulsion of the placenta and umbilical cord (sometimes referred to as the *afterbirth*) through the cervix. When Keisha's placenta and remaining umbilical cord appear, Dr. Windle and Maria examine them to be sure everything has been completely discharged from the uterus. A very calm and relaxed Jeremy has been enjoying his first bath. Jeremy is dried, then weighed and measured. He weighs 8 pounds, 2 ounces, and is 21 inches long. An identification bracelet matching Keisha's bracelet is placed around his wrist. Jeremy has arrived! What about Angela?

Cheryl is prepared for surgery. Because of her anxiety, the anesthesiologist administers medication to help her relax while preparations are hurriedly completed to begin surgery. A general anesthetic is administered, which puts her to sleep; hence, Cheryl will feel no pain but will be unaware of her child's birth. The physician makes an incision and pulls away layers of skin and abdominal muscle. As Angela is lifted from the uterine cavity, the physician discovers that the umbilical cord is wrapped around her neck, depriving her of oxygen. Angela does not begin breathing on her own. Quickly, a team of pediatric specialists, including a **neonatologist**, is called. Angela is placed in the isolette and taken immediately to the nursery. Cheryl and her family must wait to see their newborn while physicians and health care personnel work to ensure Angela's successful adaptation to extrauterine life.

neonatologist
a physician who specializes in the care and treatment of the neonate, or newborn infant, during the first 4 to 6 weeks

anemia
a condition caused by a lack of red blood cells

Oxygen deprivation can occur in other circumstances, for example, when the placenta detaches too soon during prenatal development, if the mother smokes or has **anemia**, or in cases where mother and infant are Rh incompatible. Mild oxygen deprivation can destroy or damage cell tissue, and in the neonate, brain cell damage is a serious concern. The severity of the effects on the infant depend on the timing and duration of the oxygen deprivation, with outcomes that range from mild to severe seizures, mild to severe motor control abnormalities, and feeding, sleeping, and waking difficulties; to weak and uncoordinated motor controls; to stupor, coma, respiratory arrest, and sometimes death.

The long-term outcomes from oxygen deprivation in infants who survive depend on the extent of neurological damage. Physical/motor and learning disabilities, social and emotional difficulties, and mental retardation are common outcomes of early neurological damage (but not all such problems originate with oxygen deprivation during fetal development and delivery). Electronic fetal monitoring devices, along with other procedures for sampling fetal blood and assessing neonatal neurological signs, are used to assess and prevent or minimize the effects of oxygen deprivation.

breech position delivery
a birth in which a body part other than the head presents itself for delivery first, usually the buttocks, feet, or in some cases the umbilical cord

There are a number of reasons for the performance of cesarean deliveries in addition to complications resulting in oxygen deprivation. Sometimes, the fetus' head is too large to pass safely through the mother's pelvis; or perhaps the fetus is not positioned to make a safe and expeditious journey: the buttocks, feet, shoulder, or other body part may be resting over the cervix, complicating or deterring the delivery process. This is referred to as abnormal presentation or **breech position delivery**. Additional reasons for cesarean deliveries include placenta or cord disturbances, such as premature delivery of the placenta or a prolapsed cord (the umbilical cord descends into the cervix or vagina, competing with the fetus for travel space and impairing blood flow to the fetus), concerns associated with maternal blood pressure or hemorrhaging, prolonged nonprogressive labor, the need to avoid the spread of sexually transmitted disease, and others.

More than 30% of births in the United States today are cesarean section deliveries (Bettegowda, Dias, Davidoff, Damus, Callaghan, & Petrini, 2008). Many people in the medical and allied health professions have begun to question the feasibility and need for the increasing number of cesarean deliveries. "Nonmedical factors suggested for the widespread and continuing rise of the cesarean rate may include maternal demographic characteristics (e.g., older maternal age), physician practice patterns, maternal choice, more conservative practice guidelines, and legal pressures" (National Center on Health Statistics, 2010). Cesarean sections have become more frequent in recent years for preterm births (at gestational age 34 to 36 weeks) and are problematic because, unless they are medically advised, infants born preterm have more breathing problems, feeding challenges, and jaundice (Bettegowda et al., 2008).

Because this procedure is considered major surgery and entails a longer recovery period, it is important to select wisely and conscientiously one's health care professionals and engage in serious conversation about their practices and preferences. Certainly, cesarian section deliveries can be lifesaving for mother or child or both should an emergency arise. The advantages of being in a hospital where immediate response is possible are obvious in such cases. Because prediction of emergencies is impossible, expectant parents are wise to be informed about all procedures that their health care professionals recommend. It can be emphasized, however, that the greatest majority of deliveries proceed normally and without incident.

Fathers may take a more active role in caring for their cesarean-delivered babies than fathers of traditionally delivered infants because of the longer recovery period for the mother.

Forceps may be used to facilitate delivery when there is risk to the fetus. In a forceps delivery, the physician fits forceps around the fetus's head and carefully and gently pulls the fetus through the vagina. This procedure is used only during the second stage of labor and with great skill and caution to prevent injury to the head.

forceps
a surgical instrument, similar to tongs, that is applied to the head of the fetus to facilitate delivery

Assessment and Care of Newborns

Dr. Virginia Apgar (1953) developed a process to evaluate the ability of newborns to cope with the stress of delivery and adjust to breathing independently. The **Apgar score** is usually obtained by observing the newborn at one, five, and sometimes 15 minutes after birth. Five areas of appearance or performance are evaluated: the *a*ppearance (skin color), *p*ulse (heart rate), *g*rimace (reaction to slight pain), *a*ctivity (motor responsiveness and tone), and *r*espiration (breathing adequacy). The initials of these five categories spell APGAR, which helps to make them easy to remember. Each category receives 0, 1, or 2 points. For example, here are the options for the first category:

Apgar score
a score that rates the physical condition of newborns in the areas of *a*ppearance, *p*ulse, *g*rimace, *a*ctivity, and *r*espiration

A = Activity (motor responses and muscle tone)

    0: Limp
    1: Some flexing of limbs
    2: Active motion

As you can see, a baby who is limp would receive a score of 0, a baby who is flexing his or her limbs would receive a score of 1, and a baby who demonstrates active motion would receive a score of 2. Generally, a total score of 7 or more indicates that the newborn is doing well. If the newborn's score is between 5 and 7, there is usually a need for some type of additional care. Infants with a score of 4 or less require immediate medical attention, as such a score indicates a life-threatening situation.

The American Academy of Pediatrics (2005) in its policy statement on breastfeeding recommends that health professionals complete the Apgar testing while the baby is with the mother. AAP emphasizes that "Healthy infants should be placed and remain in direct skin-to-skin contact with their mothers immediately after delivery until the first feeding is accomplished. Dry the infant, assign Apgar scores, and perform the initial physical assessment while the infant is with the mother. The mother is an optimal heat source for the infant. Delay weighing, measuring, bathing, needle-sticks, and eye prophylaxis until after the first feeding is completed" (498).

Brazelton Neonatal Behavioral Assessment Scale
an assessment of 16 reflexes, responsiveness, state changes, and ability to self-calm in the newborn

Another evaluation procedure used to examine a variety of behaviors in newborns was developed by pediatrician T. Berry Brazelton in 1973. The **Brazelton Neonatal Behavioral Assessment Scale** (NBAS) assesses 26 behavioral items and 16 reflexes that newborns possess. This assessment technique requires training because it tries to elicit the infant's highest level of performance and is most commonly used in research settings and on preterm or at-risk infants. The Brazelton Scale helps parents to become aware of the infant's competencies, for example, turning his head toward the sound of his parent's voice or visually tracking a red ball. Parents who have experienced the Brazelton were, after four weeks, more knowledgeable about their infants, had more confidence in handling the infants, and had more satisfactory interactions with their infants than parents who had not experienced the Brazelton assessment techniques (Myers, 1982). Further, fathers who were exposed to the Brazelton Scale were more actively involved with their infants than fathers who had not had the NBAS experience.

The NBAS also helps to identify infants who are unable to control or regulate the various states, ranging from deep sleep to crying. Ill or premature infants and those with immature central nervous systems may cry often, lack the ability to settle themselves, and resist cuddling. Such behaviors can be upsetting and frustrating to new parents. These parents can be provided with continued professional assistance in coping with their infants.

Professionals and researchers use the NBAS to study the influence of ethnicity and culture (Shin, Bozzette, Kenner, & Kim, 2004) and the effects of prenatal exposure to toxins (Higley & Morin, 2004; Stewart, Reihman, Lonky, Darvill, & Pagano, 2000) and as a predictor of later developmental disabilities of low birth-weight and/or premature infants (Ohgi, Arisawa, Takahashi, Kusumoto, Goto, Akiyama, & Saito, 2003). The infant's extreme unresponsiveness may indicate brain damage and/or other

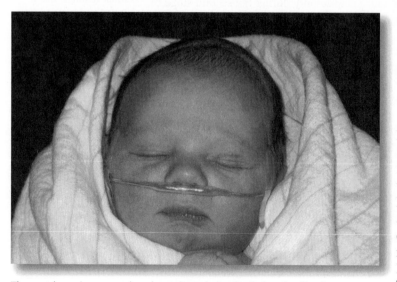

The newborn is assessed and monitored closely during the first hours following delivery.

neurological problems. A low score on the NBAS can also be an indication that health or learning problems could arise.

The NBAS has continued to evolve over the years. The newest tool offered by the Brazelton Institute is the Newborn Behavioral Observations system (NBO). The NBO is a structured set of observations for the clinician and parent to use together

> to reveal the full richness of the newborn's behavioral repertoire, the clinical focus is on the infant's individuality, on the aspects of behavior that make the baby unique and different. In other words, the NBO provides the baby with a voice, with a signature. It gives the baby an opportunity to tell the caregiver who he or she is, if you will, what her preferences are and what her vulnerabilities might be and in what areas she may need support. (Brazelton Institute, 2007)

Newborns are routinely tested for phenylketonuria (PKU), an inborn error of metabolism in which abnormal levels of the enzyme phenylalanine form in the blood. The test involves a simple heel prick to obtain a blood sample and is administered after the infant has consumed a sufficient number of formula or breast feedings for the test to accurately detect PKU presence. If untreated, PKU leads to mental retardation and other abnormalities. When detected and treated within the first three weeks after birth with a specialized diet, developmental outcomes are better than when the diet is started later. Other screening may also take place for suspected inheritable illnesses and abnormalities, such as sickle-cell anemia or thyroid disease. The American Academy of Pediatrics recommends testing for human immunodeficiency virus (HIV, the AIDS virus) in newborns whose mothers' HIV status is undetermined. This is an important precaution because AIDS (acquired immunodeficiency syndrome) can be transmitted to the fetus during pregnancy, labor, or delivery and it is carried in breast milk.

To view the March of Dimes video "A Parent's Guide to Newborn Screening," see www.youtube.com/watch?v=yqQRio1-P6c.

Jeremy's Apgar scores were 9 and 9 on his first and second assessments. A third evaluation was not needed because he was doing well. Angela scored 3, 4, and 5 and required immediate attention, owing to her lack of ability to breathe independently and to her need for ventilation. Dr. Jones, Angela's neonatologist, will return to the nursery later in the day to determine if Angela's condition has stabilized. That afternoon, he reads her charts and examines her. After several days, Dr. Jones and the neonatal staff decide to conduct the NBAS because he notes that Angela seems to have difficulty calming herself when she is in a fussy state. Dr. Jones thinks that he may have to provide Cheryl with some techniques for helping Angela settle into more predictable sleep/wake cycles and eventually to self-comfort with a blanket or soft toy. He will discuss with Cheryl her need to learn to cope effectively with what will most likely be a fussy baby for the first few weeks and an infant who will need frequent small feedings. Cheryl may need additional support from James, members of her family, or an educational or medical home-visiting program.

The length of postpartum hospital stay in uncomplicated deliveries has decreased appreciably over the years, from eight to 10 days in the 1950s to 48 hours or less today. In the 1990s, insurance companies refused to pay for hospital stays over 24 hours if the delivery was vaginal without complications. Horror stories are told of women in labor "toughing it out" in their automobiles on the hospital parking lot until the last minute and then checking themselves into the hospital to deliver, only to be released within hours of the delivery. Concern over the welfare of mothers and their newborns when hospital stays were inadequate prompted considerable debate among physicians, insurance companies, managed care facilities, and families. In 1996, Congress signed the Newborns' and Mothers' Health Protection Act to ensure that payers could not restrict hospital stays for mothers and infants to less than 48 hours after delivery for vaginal births or less than 96 hours for cesearean births, unless the health care provider and the mother agreed that earlier discharge was appropriate (American Academy of Pediatrics, 2010).

In 2010, the AAP released a policy statement titled Hospital Stay for Healthy Term Newborns that included the following: "The hospital stay of the mother-infant dyad should be long enough to allow identification of early problems and to ensure that the family is able and prepared to care for the infant at home" (AAP, 2010). The statement noted that many problems (for example, many cardiopulmonary problems) become apparent during the first 12 hours after birth: "Many problems, however, are not apparent immediately and require a longer period of observation by skilled and experienced health care professionals. All efforts should be made to keep mothers and infants together to promote simultaneous discharge" (2010). The APA policy statement concluded that

> "the fact that a short hospital stay (<48 hours after birth) for term healthy infants can be accomplished does not mean that it is appropriate for every mother and infant. Each mother-infant dyad should be evaluated individually to determine the optimal time of discharge...The timing of discharge should be the decision of the physician caring for the infant and should not be based on arbitrary policy established by third-party payers (2010).

Some managed care programs and/or hospitals provide professional or paraprofessional postpartum home visitors or doulas, particularly to assist first-time breastfeeding mothers, mothers with high-risk infants, and other mothers whose circumstances warrant additional support and follow-up.

Infants with Special Needs

In addition to genetic and chromosomal anomalies (Boxes 4.1 and 4.2), gestational age, birth weight, general health condition, and presence of disease or injury are all markers for determining potential neonatal complications and projecting growth and development challenges facing the newborn. Most infants are born at a gestational age of 40 weeks (give or take two weeks on either side of this age). However, **viability** and integrity of the human organism is compromised at both younger (preterm) and older (postterm) gestational ages.

viability
the capability of sustaining extrauterine survival

Prematurity, Preterm, Late Preterm, Postterm, Low Birth Weight, and Very Low Birth Weight Babies

Most full-term infants are born about 40 weeks after the mother's last menstrual period and are expected to weigh in the range from 5.5 to 7.5 pounds. If an infant is born before 37 weeks gestational age, the baby is considered to be premature or preterm. The March of Dimes (2010) reports that approximately 12% of infants are born

Box 4.1 Examples of Genetic Disorders

Albinism

Color blindness

Cystic fibrosis

Muscular dystrophy

Hemophilia

Huntington disease

Phenylketonuria (PKU)

Sickle-cell disease

Tay-Sachs disease

Box 4.2 Examples of Chromosomal Abnormalities

Down syndrome

Fragile X syndrome

Trisomies (e.g., trisomy 13 refers to an extra chromosome 13)

Turner syndrome

Klinefelter syndrome

prematurely. Premature infants bring low weight and underdeveloped body systems to the challenges in helping them meet the demands of extrauterine living. The March of Dimes cautions:

> You might have read in the newspapers about babies who are born really early and do very well. But, it's important for you to know that those babies are the exceptions. Babies who are born very preterm are at a very high risk for brain problems, breathing problems, digestive problems, and death in the first few days of life. Unfortunately, they also are at risk for problems later in their lives in the form of delayed development and learning problems in school. The effects of premature birth can be devastating throughout the child's life. The earlier in pregnancy a baby is born, the more health problems it is likely to have (2010).

Causes of prematurity include the following:

- "Late or no prenatal care
- Smoking
- Drinking alcohol
- Using illegal drugs
- Exposure to the medication DES
- Domestic violence, including physical, sexual, or emotional abuse
- Lack of social support

- Stress
- Long working hours with long periods of standing
- Exposure to certain environmental pollutants" (March of Dimes, 2010).

This list can be used to prevent prematurity. Women are urged to seek medical care before, during, and after pregnancy and see a physician immediately when experiencing the symptoms of premature birth.

Infants born late preterm (delivery between 34 and 36 weeks) are garnering the attention of the medical community; these preterm infants are more likely than full-term babies to experience emotional and cognitive challenges (Engle, Tomashek, Wallman, & the Committee on Fetus and Newborn, 2007). As stated above, the medical community does not recommend elective cesearean sections prior to 38 weeks, unless there is a valid medical reason for the fetus or the mother, because of research on the effects for infants of being born preterm.

Babies born after 40 weeks are considered **postterm**. "Health risks for the baby and mother increase if the pregnancy is prolonged…and labor is often induced but problems occur in only a small portion of postterm pregnancies" (Cleary-Goldman, Bettes, Robinson, Norwitz, D'Alton, & Schulkin, 2006). Small-for-gestational-age (SGA) babies are delivered close to their due date but are born under 5.5 pounds due to slow growth as fetuses or because their parents are small. If babies are born underweight because of slowed or halted growth as fetus, then they are at risk of health problems (March of Dimes, 2008a). Babies are considered low birth weight (LBW) when they are born less than 5 pounds, 8 ounces. Very low birth weight babies (VLBS) weight are below 1500 grams (approximately 3.3 pounds) and are most at risk for health problems (March of Dimes, 2008a). Causes of LBW and VLBW include multiple births (where the fetuses rarely develop to term in utero), child birth defects, infections in the fetus or mother, smoking, heavy drinking, drug use, inadequate diet, and inadequate prenatal care (March of Dimes, 2008a).

With the expertise, technology, and other resources available to today's medical profession, infants weighing less than 2 pounds have been helped to survive. Although medical science has established means by which very low weight infants can be given a chance for healthy survival, many of these fragile infants face serious health and development challenges. Consider all the systems that need to be in place and functioning in a coordinated manner in the newborn: respiratory, cardiovascular, neurological, endocrine, digestive/gastrointestinal, urinary, and immune. Concurrently, the bones and skeletal system should have taken form and shape with initial **ossification**, and the skin should be sufficiently mature to carry out its functions of temperature regulation by preventing heat and water loss as well as protection from infections. The skin is more efficient when fatty **subcutaneous tissue** has formed. In preterm and low birth weight infants, most, if not all, of these systems are underdeveloped and may fail to function properly.

Responsive care is particularly necessary in the case of preterm and low birth weight infants, who may have a different set of experiences from those of full-term, healthy infants. Many of these infants are born seriously ill and needing immediate treatment or intervention. Immature lungs and associated breathing difficulties are common, as are lack of competence in sucking, swallowing, and taking in and digesting nourishment. The infants' abrupt entry into the extrauterine environment can result in sensory overload from the cacophony of sounds, sights, touch, and activity surrounding

postterm
infants born after 40 weeks of gestation

ossification
the conversion of the softer cartilage of the skeletal system into bone

subcutaneous tissue
tissue that forms beneath the skin

them. They may need immediate and sometimes invasive medical procedures. Because of their need for intensive care, their first experiences may not be in the arms of their mothers or fathers, but in the warmth of an isolette or other infant conveyance to quickly be placed in a life-saving mode of care and attention by neonatal intensive care professionals.

In efforts to make this experience positive and supportive for both infants and family members, most modern-day hospital neonatal intensive care units are structured to

- provide consistency of care by a team of highly trained medical personnel who work closely with one another and with the family to determine an individualized care plan;
- provide a unique and individualized schedule of treatment and interactions that are sensitive to the infant's sleep–wake cycles, levels of alertness, medical needs, and feeding capabilities;
- provide supportive, comforting introductions to and interactions with a primary caregiver who assists parents in becoming engaged and interactive with their newborn (this medical professional coaches parents on how and when to caress, talk soothingly or sing softly, hold a finger, offer a pacifier, feed, rock, diaper, monitor baby cues, and provide other caregiving interactions, thus providing the infant with the comfort and security of his or her family);
- include parents during special examinations or assessments so they may be a comfort to their infant during necessary diagnostic procedures;
- provide a calm and soothing physical environment that controls light, sound, and movements in and about the neonatal intensive care unit;
- provide comfortable family-friendly space and amenities (chair, blanket, drinking water, space for personal items) near the infant, making it possible for family to interact with their infant and converse when appropriate with medical care personnel; and
- provide professional counseling and coaching for siblings as needed and, later, guidance and support to the family in making the transition with their infant from hospital to home upon dismissal (Als & Gilkerson, 1995).

This type of neonatal intensive care is referred to as *developmental care* because of its concern for not only the infant's medical needs but also, importantly, the emotional well-being of both infant and family. Such care acknowledges the strong bond between infants and their parents, which began to form long before the baby was born, and acknowledges parents and other family members as critical to the well-being of the infant. It is believed that this family-friendly developmentally supportive care during the earliest hours and days of extrauterine life and adjustment significantly improves both short- and long-term outcomes for fragile babies.

Kangaroo care is a way of holding a pre- or full-term infant, wearing only a diaper, in skin-to-skin contact with one of the parents. For preterm infants, kangaroo care is practiced for two to three hours a day in early infancy. Researchers have found that kangaroo care helps premature infants regulate their temperature, heart rate, and breathing (Ludington-Hoe, Hosseini, & Torowicz, 2005). Kangaroo care appears to increase the success of breastfeeding, normalize the growth and weight gain of premature infants, and enhance mother–infant bonding (Charpak, Ruiz-Pelaz, & Figueroa, 2005; Dodd, 2005; Mohrbacher & Stock, 2003).

Family Dynamics: A New Social System

The birth of a baby into a family unit establishes a new social system as different relationships and roles are created. Applying Bronfenbrenner's ecological systems theory (1979, 1986, 2004), we note that reactions on the parts of all members of this new social system vary depending on the nature of the pregnancy and birth experience; the size and nature of the family unit; the baby's position in the family unit; family values, attitudes, expectations, and traditions; the health status of family members; and the nature of support from the health care profession and other community services.

For the developing infant, there are expanding circles of influence that gradually enlarge his or her experience and influence developmental outcomes in positive or negative ways. These ecological influences on the infant's growth and development are addressed throughout this text. As we study the numerous influences on human growth, development, and learning, it becomes increasingly difficult to deny the importance of many in the lives of infants and children in modern-day society. Indeed, as the African proverb states, it does take a village to raise a child.

Bonding

bonding
a complex psychobiological connection between parent and infant

Marshall H. Klaus and John H. Kennell are two pediatricians who have conducted research on bonding. They define **bonding** as the establishment of a complex psychobiological connection between parent and infant (Klaus & Kennel, 1982). The bonding process begins to occur perhaps during pregnancy, but most profoundly during those first few moments when the newborn is placed into the arms of eager and emotionally ready parents and the early days and weeks of the infant's introduction into their lives. The bond between child and parent grows and deepens over time, and additional bonds established between children and other family members, close friends, and nonparental caregivers provide emotional nourishment to developing infants and children. (The connection from infant to parent is called *attachment* and grows over time to be expressed most clearly during the latter months of the first year.) In more recent years, the importance of early bonding and attachment has been reemphasized as revelations about early brain growth and neurological development have been published (Gunnar, 1996, 1998; Kemp, 1999; Lieberman & Van Horn, 2008; Schore, 2001; Schuder & Lyons-Ruth, 2004). Its influences on healthy social and emotional, developmental, and cognitive outcomes are now being documented. As we see in the chapters on infancy and on social/emotional development, bonding and attachment are critical to early brain growth and neurological development, which sets the stage for long-term healthy emotional, social, and cognitive outcomes.

Reactions of the Newborn

Reactions of newborns vary according to the quality of their prenatal existence and the extent to which optimal development was achieved, the labor and delivery experience, the nature of their parents' responses to them, and the infant's personality and temperament. Heretofore, the uterus has provided a comfortable and consistent temperature and constant nourishment. The infant has grown accustomed to the rhythm of the mother's heartbeat, which is considered one of the most important sensory cues during prenatal development (Perry, 1998); the sounds of the mother's voice (DeCasper & Spence, 1986;

Fifer & Moon, 1995); and the ebb and flow of her daily activities of rest, sleep, work, and play. After the arduous birth process, the infant must adjust to breathing independently; take an active role in the feeding process; adapt to variable room temperatures; become efficient in the use of all of the senses to see, feel, smell, taste, and hear; and begin the long, exciting journey of self-discovery and learning. Fortunately, most infants are resilient and possess many capabilities that help them to adjust and embark on the growth journey. Good-quality prenatal care, a normal labor and delivery process, warm and positive interaction with parents, and good-quality care from the medical profession are critical ingredients for the newborn's optimal adjustment.

Reactions of the Mother

Good-quality prenatal care, educational preparation for childbirth and parenting, a successful labor and delivery, and a supportive family all help the mother to adjust to her new role. However, even new mothers who enjoy optimal pregnancy and delivery conditions can feel overwhelmed, tired, and depressed.

In most instances, giving birth is a very rigorous event demanding a great deal of physical and emotional energy. After delivery, the mother's body begins to undergo dramatic hormonal adjustments as it returns to its nonpregnant state. Fluctuations in hormone levels can create mood swings and depression. In addition, caring for a newborn who needs to be fed every few hours around the clock can be tiring for most mothers and fathers.

The need to deal with the realities and responsibilities of parenting following the emotional high of anticipation of the baby's birth can be overwhelming. In addition, many mothers think that they should feel instant maternal love for their babies. If they do not, they feel confused or guilty. Some find that they do not bond immediately with their infants, sometimes taking several days or weeks to recover from pregnancy and birth and turn their thoughts and emotions from inward concerns (characteristic of pregnancy) to an outward focus on their infant's needs.

New mothers often have many questions about their babies' behavior, particularly eating and crying behaviors. A classic study of parents' views of early childhood development found that of three developmental domains—emotional, social, and intellectual—parents thought that they would have the greatest influence over their children's emotional development in spite of the fact that one in four reported having the least information about how children develop emotionally (Melmed, 1997). Books and advice from family, friends, and the medical profession can be helpful. At times, however, the mother's reading of her baby and her "maternal instinct" may be the best guides to responding to her infant.

The nurses at the hospital advised Keisha to bathe Jeremy when he awakened from his afternoon nap and then feed him after his bath. Hungry, Jeremy cried more and more intensely during his bath. Keisha became fearful that Jeremy would come to dislike bathtime. On her own, Keisha decided to feed Jeremy first. She could see Jeremy relax as his tummy became full. After a time for burping and cuddling, Keisha gave a relaxed and happy Jeremy his bath.

The Child and Family at Birth

After several days in the nursery, Angela seems to be breathing more easily. Her skin tone has improved, and the usual weight loss after birth has not been as great as the doctors feared. Angela weighed less than 5 pounds at birth and was 14 inches long. The doctors tell Cheryl that they want to keep Angela in the nursery for a few more days just to be sure she is breathing independently and gaining weight.

At Dr. Jones's direction, Cheryl and James have been visiting Angela in the nursery several times a day. Angela cries frequently, which can be expected in preterm babies with her complications. The nurses tell Cheryl that it is important to respond to Angela's cries because she is trying to communicate hunger, discomfort, or boredom. Cheryl replies that one of her hospital roommates told her that picking up crying babies can spoil them. The nurses reassure Cheryl that this is not the case. Cheryl feels confused. She has noticed that when she visits Angela and Angela has been crying, touching her and talking to her in a soothing voice do seem to calm her. The nurses teach her how to use kangaroo care to hold and help regulate her premature baby. Maybe the nurses are right.

Cheryl and James have felt extremely stressed by Angela's special needs. Visiting the nursery has been a bewildering experience for them. Cheryl wonders whether Angela will cry as much when she comes home. She is glad she will be at home without Angela for a while, but these thoughts make her feel guilty. The nurses tell her that she should visit Angela during the days that the baby needs to remain in the nursery. Cheryl wonders how she will get there, as her family has no car and little money for public transportation. Cheryl's Early Head Start home visitor organizes times when neighbors and friends can take Cheryl and James to visit Angela. Cheryl notices that she, too, feels like crying much of the time and often feels the need to withdraw from the company of others. Her mother is concerned about her and wonders how they will manage when Angela leaves the nursery.

Depending on the study, it is estimated that between 26 and 85 percent of childbearing mothers experience the "baby blues," after giving birth, which includes feeling overwhelmed, exhausted, and irritable for approximately two weeks. Approximately 10% to 20% experience **postpartum depression**, which includes frequent episodes of crying or weepiness, feelings of inadequacy or guilt, and lack of interest in the baby, family, or activities for more than 14 days. This level of depression may require medical attention, home visits from professionals, and/or psychotherapy (Halbreich & Karkun, 2005). In rare cases, **postpartum psychosis** occurs, in which the mother's moods, delusions, and bizarre behaviors make her a danger to herself and others, including her children. This is considered a psychiatric emergency, and hospitalization and medical attention are required.

Chemical changes in the brain can cause postpartum depression symptoms of emotionality, sleep, and eating disturbances and altered energy levels (Epperson, 2002). In the great majority of cases, as hormonal levels and body shape return to their prepregnancy states, energy level increases as does confidence in mothering. Hormonal changes, medications, fatigue and loss of stamina, preexisting anxieties exasperated by infant care responsibilities, unresolved emotional conflicts, lack of support from the father or other family members, and economic or work-related issues are some of the possible contributors to postpartum depression.

postpartum depression
a period of depression that affects most mothers for a few days and in some cases for weeks and months after childbirth

postpartum psychosis
a psychological condition associated with severe depression following childbirth in which there is a loss of insight, good judgment, and coping strength; sometimes there is a loss of touch with reality

Sometimes, postpartum depression may be a continuation of depression occurring during pregnancy, which may or may not be related to the pregnancy itself.

Depending on the extent and duration of the depression during pregnancy, there is evidence that perinatal maternal depression predicts less optimal mother–child interactions and infant insecure attachment (Teti & Towe-Goodman, 2008) as well as negative effects on the development of the infant's stress systems and ability to regulate emotions (Waxler, Thelen, & Muzik, 2011). Knitzer, Theberge, and Johnson (2008) wrote a policy brief on maternal depression that emphasizes the importance of a responsive early childhood policy framework for reducing maternal depression because of its negative impact on families and children. Friends, relatives, and the medical profession need to be sensitive to depression prepregnancy, during pregnancy, and postpartum and provide guidance, support, or treatment as needed.

Reactions of the Father

Recently, more attention has been given to the reactions of prospective fathers. They worry about whether they will be good fathers, whether they will please their wives, the added financial responsibility, possible changes in their relationship with their wives, and lack of freedom. If there are siblings, fathers wonder how they will respond to and meet the needs of the new brother or sister. The increasing need for two incomes to support a family and family-centered maternity care have encouraged many fathers to become more involved in the birth and care of their children. The mother's perception of the father's role influences the types of interactions and responsibilities that she encourages.

Further, it is evident that positive mother–father relationships influence the extent to which fathers become engaged in the care and nurturing of their infants. Several studies indicate that distressed parental relationships impede both parents' abilities to meet the needs of their children (Cabrera, Hofferth, & Chae, 2011; Susman-Stillman, Appleyard, & Siebenbruner, 2003).

In the case of the nonresident father, the stereotype of avoidance of parental responsibilities appears to be inaccurate. Studies reveal that most fathers choose to be involved with their infants at birth and intend to stay connected and involved (Teitler, 2001), and where there is intent to marry the child's mother, the father is particularly engaged in the care of their infant (Carlson & McLanahan, 2002). Studies completed in the 1980s indicated that a father's participation in the preparation for the birth, delivery, and early care of the baby leads to later positive interaction patterns with his child (Klaus & Kennell, 1982; Parke & Sawin, 1981). This research must be further validated with multiple racial/ethnic groups and with a variety of birthing methods.

Do fathers from different race/ethnic groups differ in their play, verbal interactions, and caregiving styles? Cabrera, Hofferth, and Chae (2011) studied these aspects of father engagement across different groups including Caucasian, African American, and Latino fathers in a sample of 5,089 infants and their families drawn from the Early Childhood Longitudinal Study-Birth Cohort (ECLSB). These authors found that African American and Latino fathers had higher levels of engagement in caregiving and physical play activities with their infants than Caucasian fathers but found no differences in race/ethnicity for verbal stimulation. However, fathers' education level predicted fathers' higher levels of verbally stimulating activities with their infants. This research informs the early childhood professional to observe the dynamics within families in order to work more respectfully and responsively with families from a variety of racial/ethnic groups.

As DeVon watches Keisha breastfeed Jeremy in the hospital, he sometimes feels left out. In some ways, he wishes that Keisha had not decided to nurse Jeremy. He knows that breast-fed babies have more immunity to illness and that a mother's milk is more suited to infants' immature digestive systems than formula, but if Jeremy were bottle fed, DeVon could take part in feeding him.

DeVon mentions these feelings to Keisha. They discuss the fact that after a few weeks of initial breastfeeding, she will be able to express milk (manually or with a breast pump) from time to time for bottle feedings. She will discuss this option with her physician.

Reactions of Siblings

Even though parents prepare children for the birth of a new brother or sister, many adjustments must be made. Stewart, Mobley Van Tuyl, and Salvador (1987) studied middle-class families with a firstborn child of 2, 3, or 4 years of age over a 15-month period. Findings indicated that these firstborns spent much time trying to get their mothers' full attention and that their strategies followed similar patterns regardless of age (Stewart et al., 1987).

During the first four months after the birth of a brother or sister, the firstborns engaged in such behaviors as baby talk, using baby table manners, demanding a bottle or pacifier, and regressing in toileting behaviors. Other acting-out behaviors included verbal and physical confrontations with the parents, infant, and even inanimate objects. At times, the firstborn children were whiny, withdrawn, and clingy and had a need for a security blanket or toy. By the fourth month after the birth of the baby, displays of imitation or confrontation usually disappeared. Anxiety behaviors continued, however. Four months later, when the new brother or sister was around 8 months old, the older siblings again used confrontational strategies. According to the researchers, these behaviors were explained by the baby's increasing mobility and responsiveness.

Parents can help their older children adjust to a new brother or sister by talking with them about the needs of the baby.

The brothers and sisters said that they helped to care for the new baby. Ninety-five percent of the mothers confirmed this behavior. More than half the siblings said they liked to cuddle the new baby. During the last visit, when the new baby was just more than 1 year old, 63% of the firstborns said that they were ready for a new baby.

Siblings of the same gender were reported to show a higher incidence of all types of behaviors. Fathers seemed to help out and give the firstborns needed attention. By the end of the study, the fathers were talking and playing with their firstborns as much as the mothers were. This study indicates that at least in some middle-class families, the attention-getting behaviors of firstborns are normal; fathers can help to meet their need for attention; and in spite of the obvious negative feelings of firstborns, they also have positive attitudes toward the new baby.

Parents can help their older children to adjust to a new brother or sister if they talk about the baby's needs and involve the older sibling in making decisions regarding the infant. Explaining the infant's behaviors and pointing out his or her interest in the older sibling can also facilitate positive interactions.

Reactions of Extended Family

Reactions of extended family can vary and also affect the immediate family of the new-born. Grandparents are usually thrilled. However, comments sometimes suggest mixed or negative feelings about the birth of a grandchild. Grandparents often view the birth of a grandchild as a sign that they are getting older. Adjusting to the aging process can be difficult for some. At times, feelings of failure or inadequacy that the grandparents experienced as parents can surface and create tension.

Keisha's mother had not been successful at breastfeeding, and she kept telling Keisha that Keisha's breasts were too small to feed Jeremy. Fortunately, Keisha's childbirth classes had given her background information about the physiological process of nursing. She calmly responded to her mother's concerns, explaining that the glands and not the size of the breasts stimulated milk production. Keisha also pointed out that the baby's sucking increased the supply of milk. This information seemed to relieve Keisha's mother.

Because many prospective parents today attend childbirth classes, they have up-to-date information. At times, this may contradict some of the ideas about parenting held by grandparents. Grandparents may feel unsure about what they should do. This insecurity may be viewed as a lack of interest in the grandchild or the new parents. In addition, some grandparents find it difficult to allow their children to become parents. The grand-parents have been in control in their role as parents, and they feel a need to stay in control rather than allowing their child to take charge of his or her new family.

At times, the new parents' siblings may feel jealous at all the attention the new parents are receiving. Becoming an aunt or uncle also involves adjusting to a new role. If there has been a great deal of competition between the new parent and his or her siblings, old feelings of rivalry can surface and persist even when the sibling becomes a parent, and cousins can be pitted against one another.

Nevertheless, many extended family members can provide information, needed support, and encouragement to the new parents. The reactions of the extended family add to the complexity of relationships surrounding the birth of a baby. An awareness of some of these feelings and their possible causes can help new parents to better understand and cope with these behaviors and feelings.

We hope that this chapter has made you more aware of the complex set of circumstances that affect newborns and their families. An awareness of these factors and dynamics can facilitate a more complete understanding of young children and their families. A positive birth experience and adjustment of all family members to the newborn can pave the way for a child to "know the joy of living" and for the parents to enjoy and celebrate "the beauty of life" (see the quote at the beginning of this chapter).

DeVon, Keisha, and Jeremy Johnson have had optimal circumstances for beginning their lives as a family. Cheryl Monroe, James, and Angela have not been as fortunate. The following chapters continue the story of the growth and development of Jeremy and Angela.

Role of the Early Childhood Professional

● Working with Families with Newborns

1. Become knowledgeable about factors that influence optimal prenatal development and successful deliveries.

2. Respond to parents' interests and desires for information about early growth and development; help parents to become aware of the critical development that occurs during the first three years.

3. Help parents to understand and respond appropriately to the reactions of siblings to a new baby. Provide suggestions for preparing siblings for a new baby and helping them to adjust to a new member of the family.

4. Respond in empathic and helpful ways to changes in classroom behavior in young children during the weeks after the birth of a sibling.

5. Become knowledgeable about community resources that are available to families with infants, and be prepared to share information with families when appropriate.

6. Become knowledgeable about community resources that are available to families with infants with special needs, and be prepared to share information with families when appropriate.

Key Terms

anemia
Apgar score
bonding
Brazelton Neonatal Behavioral Assessment Scale
breech position delivery
cervix
cesarean delivery

contraction
dilation
electronic fetal monitor
episiotomy
extrauterine
forceps
in utero
isolette
labor

neonatologist
ossification
postpartum depression
postpartum psychosis
postterm
preterm
subcutaneous tissue
viability

Review Strategies and Activities

1. Review the key terms individually or with a classmate.

2. Interview several parents of newborns from varied cultures. Ask them to share the following with you and compare and contrast their answers.

   a. The delivery and hospital experience

   b. Opportunities for and experiences with bonding after delivery

   c. The challenges they experienced and the adjustments they needed to make during the first two months after the baby's birth

   d. Reactions of immediate and extended family to the baby's birth

3. Invite an obstetrical or pediatric nurse to your class to discuss the following:
   a. The care of a newborn infant
   b. The care of an at-risk infant
   c. The care of the mother
   d. Support for the family
   e. Evaluation of the newborn, including the Apgar and Brazelton scales and other assessment tools
   f. Follow-up support
4. Discuss the short- and long-term implications of good-quality prenatal and neonatal care.

Further Readings

Bowman, B., & Weissbourd, B. (2010). The gift of grandparents: Supporting the next generation of infants, toddlers, and families. *ZERO TO THREE, 30*(4), 22–27.

ZERO TO THREE. *Daddy, Papi, Papa, or Baba: The influence of fathers on young children's development.* www.zerotothree.org/about-us/funded-projects/parenting-resources/podcast/daddy-papi-papa-or-baba.html.

Other Resources

American Academy of Pediatrics, www.aap.org. This is the official Web site of the American Academy of Pediatrics—an organization of 60,000 pediatricians committed to the attainment of optimal physical, mental, and social health and well-being for all infants, children, adolescents, and young adults. This site provides extensive information on health topics and resources, advocacy, policy statements, and pediatric clinical practice guidelines, as well as articles published in the American Academy of Pediatrics journals and periodicals.

American Society for Reproductive Medicine, www.asrm.org. The Vision of the American Society for Reproductive Medicine (ASRM) is to be the nationally and internationally recognized leader for multidisciplinary information, education, advocacy, and standards in the field of reproductive medicine. The ASRM is a nonprofit organization whose members must demonstrate the high ethical principles of the medical profession; evince an interest in infertility, reproductive medicine and biology; and adhere to the objectives of the society.

Child Trends, www.childtrends.org. This is a nonprofit, nonpartisan research center that studies children at all stages of development. The site provides child trends research including excellent graphs for child poverty, child welfare, early childhood development, K–12 education, fatherhood and parenting, health, use of data for evaluation, indicators of child well-being, marriage and family, positive development, teen sex and pregnancy, and youth development. This is an important Web site to visit regularly.

Guttmacher Institute, www.guttmacher.org. This Web site provides policy information, slide shows, audio clips, archived reports, fact sheets, and publications on abortion, adolescents, contraception, HIV/AIDS and STIs (sexually transmitted infections), men, pregnancy, services and financing, sex and relationships, and technology and bioethics.

chapter 5

Brain, Perceptual, Motor, and Physical Development of the Infant

Infancy conforms to nobody—all conform to it.

—Ralph Waldo Emerson

After studying this chapter, you will demonstrate comprehension by:

▶ outlining principles of development related to the physical and motor development of infants from birth to the end of the first year;

- discussing cultural influences on prenatal and infant growth and development;
- describing earliest brain growth and neurological development;
- describing major physiological competencies of the infant;
- identifying expected patterns of physical and motor development during the first year;
- discussing major factors influencing physical and motor development;
- discussing contemporary infant health and well-being issues; and
- suggesting strategies for promoting and enhancing physical and motor development during the first year.

To make room for incoming expectant mothers in the prenatal care unit, Cheryl has been moved to a semiprivate room down the hall. Between school and work schedules, James has tried to be with Cheryl as much as possible. Today, members of her large extended family and one or two of her close friends have gathered eagerly around Cheryl in the hospital room to share in the joy of Angela's birth. Because Angela is receiving special attention in the neonatal intensive care unit, they are also concerned for her well-being. Family and friends stroll quietly into and out of Cheryl's room, returning from viewing the newborn through a window to the neonatal intensive care unit. They share their observations and excitement: "She's so beautiful, so tiny." "She was awake and squirming. I believe she has James's eyes; I always thought James and his brother had those same beautiful eyes." "She seems a little upset with all those nurses fussing over her." "Cheryl was a calm and easy baby," muses her mother. "I remember Cheryl being a crybaby when she was little," chirps one of her siblings. "No, you were the crybaby, not me," quips Cheryl in a characteristic sibling retort. Happy banter continues among Cheryl and her friends and family: "Can she see yet?" "Do you think she knows your voice?" "She is so tiny, will she be normal and healthy?"

Principles of Brain, Perceptual, Motor, and Physical Development

Cheryl and her friends have many questions about this tiny baby. They aren't sure what she can see or do. Cheryl's Early Head Start home visitor has been able to tell her many things about how Angela's brain and body will grow, thanks to knowledge gained by many decades of research. Cheryl has been learning about caring for her new baby to keep her healthy and safe. She has been learning about how Angela's abilities to see, hear, taste, and smell will become more sophisticated. She has some ideas about how Angela will begin to use her body for movement. To her concern, she is also thinking that the family's apartment is not going to be safe when Angela begins crawling and that her own diet of fast foods, noodles, snacks, and sweets will not be healthy for her baby.

This chapter will describe the development of four highly interrelated systems of great interest to professionals and new parents: the brain, perception, motor, and physical health and growth. Innovations in technology have made each of these systems visible, with research illuminating how they work. Many of the basic principles of development in these systems apply to the other domains. They all have to do with immature systems that grow, learn, and change because of interaction between inborn capacities and the environment. Alison Gopnik phrases it well:

> Far from being mere unfinished adults, babies and young children are exquisitely designed by evolution to change and create, to learn and explore. Those capacities, so intrinsic to what it means to be human, appear in their purest forms in the earliest years of our lives. (2010, p. 81)

The Infant Brain

A growing body of scientific evidence shows that early influences—whether positive or negative—are critical to the development of children's brains and their lifelong health. (National Scientific Council on the Developing Child, Center on the Developing Child, 2011a)

The infant brain begins developing at three weeks—gestation—and continues to develop throughout one's lifetime. At no time, however, does the brain grow as quickly as it does prenatally and in the first three years of life. During these years, the brain is at its most resilient and its most vulnerable state. As the young brain is creating over 3 million connections each second, it is most open to learning. If some part of the brain is not working, another part may be able to take on its function. Unfortunately, this high generation of connections within the **neural network** also means that the young brain is particularly vulnerable to damage through physical insult, stress, and toxins. This section describes how we are now able to study the brain, how the brain develops prenatally and in the first year of life, and factors that threaten healthy brain development.

neural network
circuits created by connections of neurons

Windows to the Brain

Recent advances in technology, neuroscience, and medicine have made it possible to study with amazing precision the neurological development of young children. We are able to see which sections of the brain are activated by different stimuli and compare the brains of, for example, typically developing children with those of children with autism (Courchesne, Pierce, Schumann, Redcay, Buckwalter, Kennedy, & Morgan, 2007; Shaw et al., 2008). Imaging technology such as the following are used:

- *High-resolution ultrasound recordings*, a noninvasive technique that creates a sonogram picture of the fetus or other soft tissues using sound waves.
- *Computerized axial tomography* (CAT scan) is a noninvasive procedure that uses computers to provide multiple-angle pictures of the brain, giving information about its structure.
- *Positron emission tomography* (PET scan) uses radioactive dye, either injected or ingested, to view not only the structures of the brain, as with the CAT scan, but also complex neurological activity as it takes place in various parts of the brain.
- *Magnetic resonance imaging* (MRI), also a noninvasive technique, employs magnetic fields, radio frequencies, and computer technology to produce high-contrast images that allow scientists to examine various anatomical features of the brain.
- *Functional MRI* (fMRI) combines imaging of activity in the brain with MRI images of the brain's structure.

Box 5.1 Culture and the Brain

The relatively new ability to watch the brain in action has demonstrated that cultural differences may cause the brain architecture to develop differently (Zhu, Zhang, Fan, & Han, 2007). American and Chinese men were asked to evaluate traits of themselves and traits of others. For American men from an individualistic culture, when asked to evaluate their own honesty and then their mother's honesty, the brain activity is very different. When Chinese men were asked the same questions, their brain activity was the same whether considering themselves or someone close to them. The researchers suggest that the collectivist culture, with its deep value for close relationships, causes the brain to develop differently from the individualist culture. Another study involved showing American and Japanese men a silhouette of a person in a dominant pose or in a submissive pose. From historical data demonstrating an American value for dominance and an Asian value on submission, the researchers hypothesized that the brain's limbic system would activate only when viewing the posture preferred in their culture. In fact, the brain's reward circuitry did activate only in response to their culture's favored posture (Freeman, Rule, Adams & Ambady, 2009). These and similar studies suggest that culture directly affects the neural network of the brain.

- *Magnetoencephalogy* is a very new technology that allows us to see changes in the magnetic fields of an infant's brain as he is thinking.
- *Video-enhanced microscopy* combines microscopic images with video technology to examine the characteristics and activity of minute particles in living tissue.

New technology is constantly being developed and will continue to vastly increase our knowledge of the human brain. Box 5.1 shows one example of this additional insight.

Earliest Brain Growth and Neurological Development

During the first weeks of prenatal development, the **neural tube** (which develops into the spinal column and brain) emerges out of the **embryonic cell mass.** Specific cells along the length of the tube develop into **neurons,** or nerve cells. During prenatal development, neurons are forming at a startling rate of 250,000 per minute. Neurons are tiny; it is estimated that 30,000 of them can fit into a space the size of a pinhead. The spinal column, brain, and a spectacular network of nerve cells make up the nervous system. The nervous system has three interrelated functions: to receive and interpret information about the internal and external environment of the body, to make decisions about this information, and to organize and carry out action based on this information.

During the embryonic period, neural cells that will form the parts of the nervous system grow from germ cells, which divide repeatedly, generating new cells. This process of generating new cells ceases before an infant's birth. Hence, infants are born with a lifetime supply of nerve cells, or neurons—more than 100 billion, which before birth have already formed more than 50 trillion connections. No new cells develop, but these cell bodies continue to grow **axons** (usually a single long fiber), which convey information *away* from the cell body, and **dendrites,** branches that convey information *toward* the

neural tube
the rudimentary beginning of the brain and spinal cord

embryonic cell mass
the developing fertilized ovum during the first three months of pregnancy when cells are dividing rapidly to form the fetus

neuron
a type of cell that conveys information; a nerve cell

axon
a branchlike projection from the neuron that carries information away from the cell body

dendrites
branches from the neuron that carry information toward the cell body; a neuron can have several dendrites

Figure 5.1
Myelination of Nerve Cells

The growth of myelin, or fatty tissue, around the nerve cells of the brain coincides with development of the auditory system, rapid language development, and increased processing of visual, spatial, and temporal information.

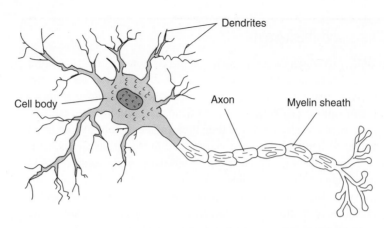

synapses

the point of contact between nerve fibers

neurotransmitter

a chemical that facilitates the transmission of information through the synapse

grey matter

neuronal cell bodies involved in muscle control, sensory perception, memory, emotions, and speech

atrophy

waste away, diminish in size and/or function

myelin

a fatty substance surrounding the axons and dendrites of some neurons, which speeds the conduction of nerve impulses

glial cells

supporting cells, which serve to protect and insulate (as in myelin) cells in the nervous system

cell body, which will travel in designated pathways to connect at **synapses** to form a very dense and complex system of connections. Neurons communicate through these synapses either through certain chemicals known as **neurotransmitters** or by the transmission of electrical currents from one neuron to another. During infancy and the first year of development, these connections are bursting forth at an astounding rate. By the end of the infant's first year, the brain volume grows by 101% and is two-thirds of its adult size; **grey matter** (containing neuronal cells) has increased by 149% (Knickmeyer et al., 2008). By the end of the second year, it is about four-fifths of its adult size. (See Figure 5.1.)

Environmental sensory stimuli, memories, and thoughts cause the brain to develop its own unique circuitry and determine which connections will last (or become "hard wired") and which connections will be so weak that they **atrophy** and die. Connections that are not used frequently enough are pruned away or sometimes rerouted to another compensating or perhaps less appropriate or debilitating connection. Studies of infants and young children who have *not* received healthy, consistent, predictable, repetitive sensory and emotional experiences during this critical period of growth and development have been shown to have significantly smaller brains and abnormal brain development (Perry, 1998).

During the early growth of nerve cells, **myelin,** which is a fatty tissue made up of **glial** membrane, begins to wrap around the axons and dendrites. Myelin promotes the efficient transmission of messages along the neurons and strengthens synapses. (See Figure 5.1.)

Its growth coincides with the refinement of vision and hearing systems, motor development, language, certain cognitive processes, and the expression and control of emotions. All experiences affect neurological development by strengthening the synapses. Over the life span of an individual, many nerve cells die as a consequence of the prenatal production of more cells than are actually needed or than can survive to adulthood and through lack of use. Consequently, reduction of the number of neurons present at birth occurs throughout development, resulting at adulthood in half the original number of cells. Figure 5.2 outlines the sequence of neuron development.

Stress Hormones and the Developing Brain

In utero, the fetus is awash in the mother's hormones. After birth, the infant produces his or her own hormones in response to the environment. Two hormones that are produced when a person is under stress are cortisol and adrenylin. The Center

1. Fertilization (ovum/sperm)
2. Cell division
3. Formation of neural plate
4. Evolution of neural tube
5. Cell proliferation (rapid formation of nerve cells called neurons)
6. Migration of primitive neurons
7. Cell differentiation into
   a. ectoderm, which evolves into outer surface of the skin, nails, teeth, lens of the eye, inner ear, brain, spinal cord, and nerves
   b. endoderm, which evolves into digestive system and lungs
   c. mesoderm, which evolves into bones, muscles, circulatory system, skeleton, gastrointestinal track, and inner layers of the skin
8. Growth of axons and dendrites
9. Myelination of axons
10. Synaptogenesis (formation of chemical and electrical contacts between nerve cells)
11. Neuronal and synaptic death (or pruning of redundant nerve connections)

Figure 5.2
Sequence of Neuron Development

for the Developing Child at Harvard frames pre- and postnatal stress as occuring in three different levels: positive, tolerable, and toxic. Positive stress might occur as an infant tries over and over to pull up to a stand. She may feel frustrated, but with loving support from a responsive adult, she will manage her frustration and keep trying. Tolerable stress is a response to a very significant event, such as the birth of a sibling, wherein the infant is supported in managing her feelings by a loved one. Toxic stress is "chronic, uncontrollable, and experienced without support from an adult" (National Council on the Developing Child, 2005, p. 3). If a young child chronically experiences more stress than she can handle, the hormonal response system may be set off in even mild situations or it may shut down and not react at all. Sustained activation of the stress response systems can decrease the size of the brain and cause memory, learning, and behavior problems later in life.

Sensitive Periods

Of special interest to child developmentalists is the concept of *sensitive periods,* which are identified periods during growth and development when certain synaptic activity can be strengthened if infants and young children are provided appropriate experiences. From recent studies of prenatal and infant neurological development and brain growth, it is evident that the first three years are critical, particularly for the neurological development that is associated with attachment, control of emotions, ability to cope with stress, vision, and motor development. Table 5.1 illustrates these sensitive periods.

During the prenatal period, neurological development emerges intrinsically as a result of the properly timed activation of genes, which is not dependent on external input or neural activity (Delcomyn, 1998). However, during later prenatal development and the early months and years of infancy and early childhood, external input is critical to neurological development. Environmental input stimulates electrical activity in neurons, resulting in the process of circuitry building, or "wiring," of the neurological system as nerve cells grow axons and dendrites, which navigate toward their targets, forming important connections for the relay of messages throughout the body.

Table 5.1 Sensitive Periods in Early Brain Growth and Neurological Development

Age	Developmental Domain
Birth to 2 years	Social attachment, ability to cope with stress
Birth to 3 years	Regulation of emotions
Birth to 2 years	Visual and auditory acuity
Birth to 3 years	Vocabulary
Birth to 5 years	Motor development and coordination
Birth to 10 years	First- and second-language development
Birth to 5 years	Mathematical and logical thinking
Birth to 10 years	Music appreciation and learning

plasticity
the ability of some parts of the nervous system to alter their functional characteristics

The fact that the nervous system can be shaped by neural activity aroused by environmental stimuli is evidence of the brain's **plasticity,** which is most apparent when neuron connections are forming. This means that an individual's brain has the remarkable ability to change and compensate for problems if intervention is timely and intensive. However, inappropriate or negative experiences, as with child abuse and neglect, have been found to interfere with normal wiring of the brain, resulting in adverse developmental outcomes (Chugani, 1997; Glaser, 2000; Perry, 1993a, 1993b). These early environmental stimuli have important implications for the development and integrity of the sensory and motor systems and for various types of growth and development throughout the life span. Missed prime times or opportunities, for the most part, are ameliorated by timely interventions that include consistent and appropriately challenging, nurturing, and enriching experiences.

After this brief synopsis of early neurological development and brain growth, we are now prepared to look more specifically at the present and emerging capabilities of the newborn.

subcortical
refers to the portion of the brain just below the cerebral cortex, which is responsible for controlling unlearned and reflexive behavior

cerebral cortex
the outer layer of the cerebral hemisphere, which is mostly responsible for higher mental functions, sensory processing, and motor control

survival reflexes
reflexes essential to sustaining life

Reflexes

The *neonatal period* is usually defined as the first four weeks of life and is a critical period in infant development. Many physiological adjustments required for extrauterine existence are taking place. In this period, the nervous system is expressed, in part, through reflexes, inborn movement patterns that help the infant adapt to new surroundings and new demands. Many reflexes are present before birth. Reflexes are unlearned, automatic responses to stimuli resulting from earliest neuromuscular development. For the most part, these early reflexes are a function of **subcortical** (brain stem and spinal cord) mechanisms, but some cortical control is evident. The **cerebral cortex** is the part of the brain that is responsible for perception, memory, and thinking. Figure 5.3 illustrates the regions of the brain and their respective responsibilities.

Some reflexes are called **survival reflexes** because they are necessary for the infant to sustain life. An obvious example is breathing. The birth cry, which sometimes occurs

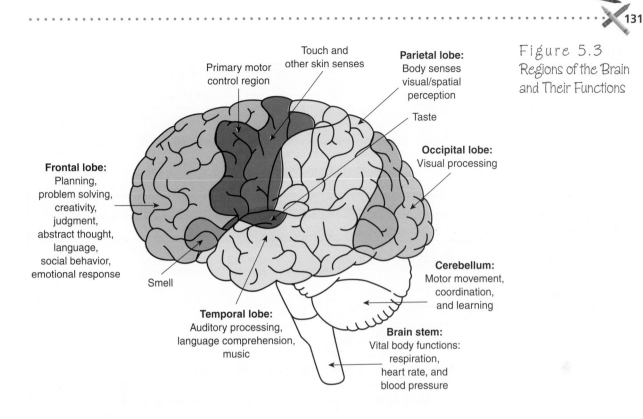

Figure 5.3
Regions of the Brain
and Their Functions

before the infant is fully delivered, sets the respiratory mechanisms in motion, oxygenating the red blood cells and expelling carbon dioxide from the lungs. Gagging, sneezing, and hiccupping reflexes are present before and after birth.

Most subcortical or **primitive reflexes** gradually disappear as the cerebral cortex matures and begins to direct and control bodily movements and behaviors. Some reflexes such as breathing and other involuntary functions, including bladder and bowel control, may continue to have elements of both subcortical and cortical control. The developmental course of the individual reflexes varies. Some disappear in the first few days; others vanish within the first 12 to 18 months; and still others persist throughout life, becoming more precise and organized.

In preterm infants, subcortical reflexes are frequently not evident at birth but appear soon thereafter. Premature infants often exhibit weak rooting and sucking responses. Continued absence or weakness of these early reflexes suggests delayed development or dysfunction in the central nervous system. In premature infants, these early reflexes disappear somewhat more slowly than they do in full-term infants. Table 5.2 lists some major reflexes observed in early infancy.

In addition to an impressive array of reflexes, there are other early behaviors of special interest. They are infant psychological states and activity levels, sensory capabilities, and expected growth and development patterns.

primitive reflexes
reflexes controlled by subcortical structures in the brain, which gradually disappear during the first year

Sleep Behavior

An eagerly awaited milestone in infant development is the ability to sleep through the night. Sleeping patterns of infants are often the subject of conversation with proud (or tired) parents. Researchers also are interested in infant sleep patterns. Patterns,

Table 5.2 Major Reflexes Present in Infancy

Reflex	Description
Survival Reflexes	
Breathing reflex	Inhales/exhales, oxygenating the red blood cells and expelling carbon dioxide.
Rooting reflex	Turns in the direction of a touch on the cheek as though searching for a nipple. Serves to orient the infant to the breast or the bottle.
Sucking and swallowing reflex	Stimulated by a nipple placed in the mouth; allows the infant to take in nourishment.
Eyeblink and pupillary reflex	Eyes close or blink; pupils dilate or constrict to protect the eyes.
Primitive Reflexes	
Grasping reflex	Holds firmly to an object touching the palm of the hand. Disappearance around the fourth month signals advancing neurological development.
Moro reflex	Often referred to as the *startle reflex*; a loud noise or sudden jolt causes the arms to thrust outward, then return to an embrace-like position. Disappearance around the fourth or sixth month signals advancing neurological development.
Babinski reflex	Toes fan outward, then curl when the bottom of the foot is stroked. Disappearance by the end of the first year signals advancing neurological development.
Tonic neck reflex	A "fencing pose," often assumed when sleeping—head turned to one side, arm extended on the same side, and opposite arm and leg flexed at the elbow and knee. Disappearance around 7 months signals advancing neurological development.

characteristics, and problems of sleep in young children make up a large body of literature. In the past two decades, the connection between sleep and brain development has been a major field of study.

Sleep patterns change as infants mature. Newborn infants usually sleep a total of approximately 16 to 20 of 24 hours. The longest period of sleep may be around two hours during the first days. By 4 to 6 weeks of age, the infant may be sleeping a total of 12 to 14 hours a day, taking as many as seven "naps" during a 24-hour period. By 6 months, sleep duration among infants averages 14.2 hours, with decreasing daytime sleep and increasing nighttime sleep, and by three years of age, children average 12.5 hours of sleep a day (Iglowstein, Jenni, Molinari, & Largo, 2003).

Some infants sleep a six-hour night by the fourth week after birth, but some do not sleep through the night until they are 7 or 8 months old. Some infants sleep more during the day and others sleep more at night, but most infants seem to sleep for longer periods at night. There is great variation in both the amount and type of sleep exhibited in infancy. There are also differences in infants concerning how long they stay awake, are fussy, or are crying.

In his book *Touchpoints,* Brazelton (1992, p. 59) describes six states of infant consciousness:

1. Deep sleep: The infant breathes deeply, eyes are shut, any movements are jerky
2. Light, or REM (rapid eye movement) sleep: Breathing is shallower and irregular, infant may suck, may startle
3. Indeterminate state: Occurs as the infant wakes up or goes to sleep, may squirm, eyes open and close again, may have frowning face
4. Wide-awake, alert state: Movements are organized, eyes open, open to interaction and communication
5. Fussy, alert state: Often follows the alert state, movements are jerky, breathing irregular, may have difficulty controlling his/her movements
6. Crying: A cry could be painful-sounding; demanding and urgent; bored; or rhythmic but not urgent

By observing eye movements beneath the eyelid during sleep, the infant's sleep phase can be determined. There are two sleep phases: *rapid eye movement (REM)* and *nonrapid eye movement (NREM)* sleep. REM sleep is characterized by closed eyes; uneven respiration; limp muscle tone; intermittent smiles, grimaces, sighs, and sucking movements; and rapid eye movement beneath the eyelids as though the infant is dreaming. NREM sleep ranges from eyes partially open or still closed and a very light activity level with mild startles, to alertness but minimal motor activity, to eyes open with increased motor activity and reactions to external stimuli, to crying, sometimes quite intense.

Sleep researchers believe that REM sleep is vital to growth of the central nervous system. There is some evidence that during an infant's non-REM sleep the activities of the day may be replayed and consolidated in the brain, increasing the strength of synaptic connections and building neuronal networks (National Center on Sleep Disorders Research, 2003) Certain gene expressions that enhance the plasticity of the brain may also occur during REM sleep. This plasticity helps the brain share functions if one part of the brain is damaged or if certain brain activities are more salient for a particular culture. Establishing this early plasticity is linked to learning and memory in adults (Frank, Issa, & Stryker, 2001).

Observations of infant sleep states and patterns help physicians to identify central nervous system abnormalities. For instance, preterm infants generally display a greater amount of REM sleep. There is some evidence that infants suffering from brain injury or birth trauma may exhibit disturbed REM/NREM sleep patterns.

Sleep and Maternal Depression. A connection between infant sleep problems and maternal postpartum depression is discussed by researchers. A seminal work from 2001 proposes that maternal depression can interfere with infant sleep and difficult infant sleep habits can contribute to depression (Hiscock & Wake, 2001). This suggests a transactional theory of development, as described in Chapter 1. An Israeli study had similar findings, that adult behavior strongly influenced sleeping patterns *and* fragmented infant sleep had serious effects on the mother's well-being (Sadah, Tikotzky, & Scher, 2010). Infants with sleeping difficulties are likely to still have them when they are 3. They are also at greater risk for depression. Parents can usually resolve these problems by following the health care provider's advice to build in routines and help the infant learn to soothe himself or herself (Armitage, Flynn, Hoffman, Vazquez, Lopez, & Marcus, 2009).

Sleep and Obesity. In the past several years, a link has been established between sleep disturbances in infancy and later child obesity. A prospective study at a consortium of universities found that "Daily sleep duration of less than 12 hours during infancy appears to be a risk factor for overweight and adiposity in preschool-aged children" (Taveras, Rifas-Shiman, Oken, Gunderson & Gillman, 2008). A multi-national study identified eight factors that contribute to childhood obesity, but deficient sleep acted as an independent, direct factor (Reilly et al., 2005). Experts suggest routines at bedtime; putting babies on their backs in the crib while they are drowsy; and briefly assuring infants that you are there if they waken during the night.

Jeremy, now 4 months old, is usually quite content at bedtime. His mother usually holds him in her lap for a while after the evening feeding while he drifts into drowsiness and then into irregular sleep. Her soft voice hums to him while he drowses in her arms. Sensing his readiness for the crib, she carries him to his room. Placing him quietly on his back in his crib, she continues to hum. She rubs his tummy softly and then leaves the room after observing that he will soon fall soundly to sleep.

However, on this particular evening, Jeremy resists sleep. His eyes are open and scanning his surroundings, but he appears tired and cries sporadically. Tonight, he is what most parents would call "fussy." His mother, also tired, wishes that some magic formula would soothe him and help him to rest. Nevertheless, after determining that Jeremy is not hungry, his diaper does not need changing, and his clothing is comfortable, she follows her established routine with him, sustaining each phase slightly longer. After being placed in his crib, he rouses somewhat and cries resistively while Keisha gently strokes his tummy. Although he has not fallen into sound sleep, he is calm. She then leaves the room and soon he is sound asleep.

The Importance of Routines. Predictable, unhurried bedtimes with regular routines help the reluctant infant to separate from the family and fall asleep more readily. Routines may include a relaxed bath time during which the interaction between parent and child is enjoyable, followed by being held in the parent's lap, rocked, and sung to softly. Cuddling a soft stuffed toy while being held focuses attention away from more stimulating activities occurring around the infant. This routine is followed by being placed in bed with a moment of slow caresses and a kiss on the cheek, a whispered "good night," and then departure from the room. The American Academy of Pediatrics recommends that infants be placed on their backs (supine position) to sleep (Figure 5.4). This position for sleep has been widely publicized through the National Institute of Child Health and Human Development and the American Academy of Pediatrics Back to Sleep campaign, which was launched in 1994 to reduce the risk of sudden infant death syndrome (SIDS) (American Academy of Pediatrics, 2011). SIDS is discussed later in this chapter.

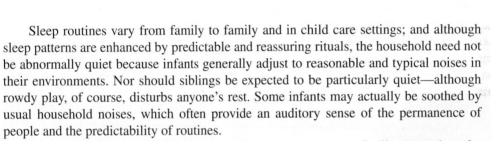

Figure 5.4
Recommended Best
Sleep Position for
Infants

Sleep routines vary from family to family and in child care settings; and although sleep patterns are enhanced by predictable and reassuring rituals, the household need not be abnormally quiet because infants generally adjust to reasonable and typical noises in their environments. Nor should siblings be expected to be particularly quiet—although rowdy play, of course, disturbs anyone's rest. Some infants may actually be soothed by usual household noises, which often provide an auditory sense of the permanence of people and the predictability of routines.

Similar routines in out-of-home child care arrangements facilitate naptime for infants and reassure them of the support of their caregivers. As with noise levels at home, rest times away from home can be scheduled during periods of the day when noise levels are at a minimum; however, there is no need to expect that all noise can be curtailed during group care naptimes.

perception
the physiological process by which sensory input is interpreted

proprioceptive system
stimuli that are connected with the position and movement of the body

Perception

The infant's sensory equipment is remarkably operative at birth. Neonates are capable of seeing, hearing, tasting, smelling, and responding to touch. The neonate takes in and processes information to a much greater extent than we might expect. Development of **perception** begins as the infant seeks and receives information through the senses. We normally talk about five senses: touch, taste, seeing, hearing, and smell. In recent years, scientists often add the **proprioceptive system** that gives us information about our own body's posture and the vestibular system that helps us balance.

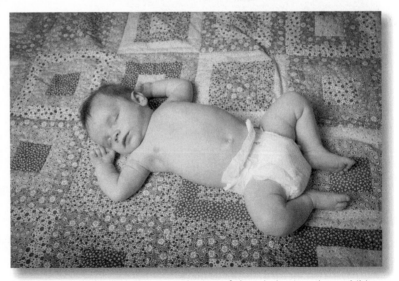

Infants vary in both the amount and types of sleep behaviors they exhibit.

Brain, Perceptual, Motor, and Physical Development of the Infant

Touch

Scientists believe the sense of touch emerges between 7½ and 14 weeks of embryonic development. Skin, muscular, and inner ear (vestibular) senses are more mature at birth than are the other senses (Gottfried, 1984). The sense of touch, particularly around the mouth area, is especially acute and facilitates infant rooting and nursing. Certain other parts of the body are sensitive to touch. These include the nose, skin of the forehead, soles of the feet, and genitals. Most of the reflexes listed in Table 5.2 are stimulated by touch. In addition to touch, the skin is sensitive to temperature, pressure, vibration, tickle, and pain.

For obvious ethical reasons, little research exists on sensitivity to pain. Contrary to the previous notion that neonates do not experience great pain, we now know they do. A seminal study of pain associated with infant circumcision procedures has helped to advance knowledge about infant pain. By analyzing the recorded vocalizations of newborn males during circumcision, researchers identified significant differences in vocalizations as each step of the procedure became more invasive (Porter, Miller, & Marshall, 1986). Some surgical procedures that were previously thought to be painless for newborns are now accompanied by analgesia or anesthesia whenever possible (American Academy of Family Physicians, 1996; American Academy of Pediatrics & American College of Obstetricians and Gynecologists, 1992; Ryan & Finer, 1994). There is also evidence that prolonged pain may have adverse consequences (Fitzgerald & Walker, 2009). Recognizing that infants do indeed experience pain with various medical procedures, research continues to identify safe methods for reducing pain. For instance, it has been found that giving newborns a drink of a sucrose solution moments before the routine heel prick to test a blood sample for the presence of PKU appears to reduce the pain of the procedure (Blass & Shah, 1995).

As discussed in Chapter 4 of this book, studies of preterm infants have found that touch plays a very significant role in their development. Many nurseries encourage parents of preterm infants in particular to gently hold and caress them (when the infant's physical condition permits). When the infant cannot be held, gently caressing the infant in the isolette is encouraged. In some hospitals, volunteers hold, rock, and softly stroke these small and vulnerable babies. A study by T. M. Field and her colleagues (1986) found that preterm infants who were gently touched and caressed several times each day gained weight faster than preterm infants who did not receive this

Touch is important for an infant to thrive.

regular stimulation. These infants also exhibited advanced mental and motor development at the end of the first year compared with the control group infants.

Skin-to-skin holding (or kangaroo care) also has been shown to increase respiratory stability and more restful sleep in newborns (Ludington-Hoe et al., 2005). Further, during skin-to-skin contact, mothers were shown to exhibit more positive adaptation to infant cues, and their infants were more inclined to hold their gaze on their mothers.

> "Health professionals are increasingly recognizing that skin-to-skin contact between mother and baby immediately after birth has important and significant health benefits for all babies" (Vincent, 2011).

In one study, it was found that when their infants were 3 months of age, both mothers and fathers who engaged in kangaroo care exhibited more sensitivity and a more nurturing home environment, and their infants scored higher on the Bayley Mental Developmental Index than did the control group who did not engage in such care during the infants' first days and weeks (Feldman, Eidelman, Sirota, & Weller, 2002). Feldman et al. speculated that along with its effect on improving parental mood and interactions with the infant, there is a direct influence on infant development by contributing to neurophysiological organization.

The importance of touch and the infant's need for it have been of interest to researchers for years. One study (Diego, Field, Hernandez-Reif, Deeds, Ascencio, & Begert, 2007) found that infant massage was related to higher weight gain among infants. Lack of soothing tactile sensations during infancy has been associated with delays in cognitive and affective development (Feldman et al., 2002). Thus, in addition to the sheer pleasure experienced

Hugging that is responsive to the infant's needs provides important tactile stimulation.

by both infant and caregiver that hugging, rocking, caressing, and patting bring, these experiences provide the infant with the tactile stimulation that is essential to perceptual and sensory development.

Vision

The neonate's vision functions well at birth, but visual acuity is imperfect, with a tendency toward nearsightedness (Spierer, Royzman, & Kuint, 2004). Visual skills that need to be learned include coordinating the use of their eyes together and learning to keep what they are looking at in focus. At the same time they are learning to visually separate relevant from irrelevant features within their sight. Perceptual learning is a term used to describe how humans use perceptions such as sight to learn and then what is learned affects what is seen. For example, the infant "sees" her father over and over. Her father's shape and features become familiar and important to the child. So when her father is within her sight she "sees" her father with intent and focus, and the background sights are not as visually compelling.

Perhaps the most important point is that the infant actively uses perception for learning. The '60s, '70s, and '80s researchers pioneered very interesting research concerning infants' visual abilities. In his pioneering studies of infant visual preferences, Fantz (1961) found that infants prefer human faces, enjoy bold patterns such as checkerboards or bull's-eye patterns, and tend to look at the edges of the designs or at the point where two contrasts come together. Haith (1966) and Samuels (1985) found that infants watch more intently a face that is active, smiling, talking, blinking, or laughing. Although bold patterns appeared to hold the infant's attention, research demonstrated that infants exhibit interest through fixed gazes in color, showing a preference for blue and green objects over red ones (Adams, Mauer, & Davis, 1986). Bornstein (1984, 1985) also found that infants respond to differences in colors and suggested that later ability to categorize by color, thought to be a result of cognitive development, has its origins in the earliest visual perceptual processes. Researchers found that 18- to 20-week-old infants looked longer at a face (preferred) making a sound that they heard simultaneously, rather than a face making a different sound than one they were hearing (Kuhl & Meltzoff, 1984, 1988). Others have found that infants attend longer to a face that imitates their own facial movements and expressions (Winnicott, 1971).

More research has continued the innovative research on visual skills. Turati, Cassio, Simian, and Leo (2006) designed research to determine if newborns' ability to recognize individual faces is based more on the specific features of a face or the general configuration of the face. Their conclusion (at this time) is that newborns use the general configuration to recognize faces, but as the cortical system in the brain develops as a function of experience (the neoconstructivist view), infants use more specific clues to identify faces. The importance of this research for early childhood professionals is twofold: (1) infants are prepared at birth to learn about objects including faces because they can recognize these based on how they are shaped, and (2) experience (exposure to faces) influences how the brain develops to enable the child to recognize people based on their specific features.

By 10 to 11 months, infants use their visual skills to learn about objects in their world. They follow the gaze of an adult who is looking at an object with eyes opened more than the direction of an adult who has her eyes closed. The researchers who completed this

work, Brooks and Meltzoff (2005), concluded that older infants begin to use their own visual skills to understand adult looking in a new way. They begin to understand that adults are "visually connected to the external world" (p. 535). As infants begin to understand that an adult's gaze has meaning, they also begin to say their first words.

Hearing

There is remarkable evidence that fetuses hear at least by 30 weeks, as their heart rate increases when hearing their mothers' voices but decreases when hearing strangers' voices. At birth, although the passages of the ear (eustachian tubes and external canal) may still contain amniotic fluids for the first few days after birth, the newborn hears fairly well. After the fluids are absorbed, the neonate responds vigorously to various sounds in the environment. The infant is startled by loud noises and soothed by soft sounds.

Neonates are particularly responsive to the human voice. The neonate often stops crying when spoken to, visually scans for the source of the voice, and attempts to vocalize. Newborns can differentiate between sounds and prefer the sounds of their own language and their mother's voice (McGaha, 2003).

It has been estimated that approximately two to three in 1,000 otherwise healthy infants has inherited hearing loss present at birth (congenital) (Centers for Disease Control and Prevention [CDC], 2010b), one to three infants per 100 well neonates have significant bilateral hearing loss (both ears), and among infants in neonatal intensive care, the incidence reported to be two to four per 100 neonates (Hay, Levin, Sondheimer, & Deterding, 2011). Because hearing loss in infants, if left undetected and untreated, can lead to speech and language delays, learning difficulties, and social and emotional problems, the medical profession makes every effort to screen infants before they are 6 months old. The American Academy of Pediatrics and other health care organizations have launched a campaign to ensure that newborns are screened for hearing loss before they leave the hospital so that timely comprehensive evaluation and intervention services can be provided. As of 2005, the American Academy of Pediatrics (2007) reports that 95% of newborn infants in the United States were screened for hearing loss before they left the hospital.

Taste

Newborns are very responsive to variations in taste. The taste of milk seems to elicit a reaction of satisfaction in infants. Infants prefer sweet tastes and usually react negatively to sour, bitter, or salty tastes (Steiner, 1979). Because flavors from the mother's diet are carried in the amniotic fluids and swallowed by the fetus, and breast milk also carries flavors from the mother's diet, the question could be asked whether the fetus develops an affinity for certain tastes. In an experiment in which expectant mothers were asked to include carrot juice in their diets four days per week for the last trimester of their pregnancies and during the early weeks of breastfeeding, it was noted that compared with infants whose mothers did not drink carrot juice during this same period, when infants were old enough to be introduced to solid foods, they favored carrots. This study leads us to suspect that flavors from the mother's typical diet during pregnancy and lactation influence the infant's acceptance and enjoyment of similar foods when the infant is weaned to solid foods. Foods consumed by different cultures in their typical diets, then, are more likely to be favored by children as they are introduced to solid foods (Mennella, Jagnow, & Beauchamp, 2001). Early experiences with tastes from the mother's amniotic fluids affect the infant's taste acceptance.

Smell

Infants sense a variety of scents and turn away from noxious odors such as vinegar or alcohol. Odors motivate babies to move. Infants who are breast-fed, but not those who are bottle-fed, choose to turn their heads to smell their mother's breast pad at 5 days of age rather than another woman's (MacFarlane, 1977), and more newborn infants move toward a pad carrying their mother's breast odor than a clean pad (Varendi & Porter, 2001). Newborns' sense of smell may be why newborns who are placed on their mother's stomach immediately after birth move toward the mother's breasts and begin feeding.

Motor Development

Growth and development during this first year are both dramatic and significant. According to Sandra Anselmo, "In no other one-year period until puberty are there so many physical changes. The changes in infancy are measured in terms of days and weeks rather than in terms of months and years" (1987, p. 148).

For decades our understanding of motor development in children was influenced by the maturation theory of Arnold Gesell. Gesell (1928) tracked the ages and sequences of motor development. His subjects were from "Western, Educated, Industrialized, Rich, and Democratic" societies (referred to as WEIRD in psychology) (Johnson, 2010), and his results can only be applied to this population. All of the developmental norms he established, which we still use in assessing development, were intentionally based on only one population because it was seen as the most accomplished population. As Karasik and colleagues (2010) put it

> Such normative templates are the current, accepted gold standard of motor development and are regarded as prescriptions of what is desired, rather than relatively narrow descriptions of what may be acquired. (p. 35)

Culture

Karasik et al. (2010) assert that our Western history of understanding motor development has been "a search for universals" (p. 35), the assumption being that something as basic as motor development must be inborn and the same across cultures. However, cross-cultural studies demonstrate that experiences tied to both culture and environment directly affect motor development. In many areas of the world, especially where walking great distances or running with speed are important skills, caregivers actively massage and exercise a baby's limbs and create early walkers. On the other hand, some cultures restrict movement by carrying babies all day or, as in Northern China, keeping the baby prone on a bed of sandbags for toileting training. These babies tend to walk later than WEIRD babies.

Dynamic Systems Theory

Eleanor Gibson's dynamic systems theory is the prevailing theory in motor development. Esther Thelen, another important figure in developmental psychology, suggested that dynamic systems theory could be demonstrated with motor development but might be used to describe all development. Thelen found that the traditional maturationist theory did not explain her observations of infant movement. Maturation theory depended only on the aging of the brain and the nervous system and assumed that developmental

changes were continuous, connected to each other; that rolling led to crawling to walking because the brain was maturing. Thelen believed that more than the nervous system was involved:

> Infants' body weights and proportions, postures, elastic and inertial properties of muscle and the nature of the task and environment contribute equally to the motor outcome. Moreover, infants seemed to be exquisitely sensitive to changes in the tasks, and able to "self-assemble" new motor patterns in novel situations. (Thelen & Bates, 2003, p. 380)

Thelen believed that young children are constantly being invited by the environment to change their posture or their form of locomotion. That environment includes their own bodies. Thelen noticed that infants often went through periods of rhythmical repetitions with parts of their body just before they would do something new. For example, they would rock on hands and knees before crawling or wave their arms before reaching. At first, these actions don't seem to have a purpose, but then a more goal-directed ability emerges. For example, reaching is not a precursor to pointing; reaching has a goal of getting something while pointing is a social interaction.

Adolph, Berger, and Leo (2011) developed some very elegant experiments to see if cruising and walking are an example of continuous development (one action builds basic skills that lead to the other, more complex action) or are an example of a dynamic system of development wherein the environment and physical changes in the baby bring about a qualitative change—a new skill altogether. Infants usually crawl and cruise at the same time, storing up many hours of skills and experience before walking. The researchers built a raised platform with railings on the sides and a very steep decline a few feet in. They wanted to know if infants having gained spatial knowledge in one action could use that knowledge within another action. New crawlers would come to the edge and keep going, falling off the platform (although every infant was caught by a research assistant). When the experienced crawling infants came to the decline, they stopped and refused to crawl any further. When these same infants were new cruisers and they cruised on the platform, holding on to the handrail, and got to the sudden decline, they would step right off the edge. They could not use their spatial knowledge from another posture. However, if there was a gap in the handrail, the cruisers would make a judgment as to whether they could manage a gap of that length. New walkers on the platform, without handrails, would also walk right off the edge. These studies, and others, demonstrated that motor development is not continuous but occurs in a dynamic system with the infant demonstrating his or her flexibility to adjust to and learn from new situations.

Expected Patterns and Developmental Possibilities

Recall the examples of cross-cultural variations in child growth and development. Timing, sequence, and form of development can vary among and within cultures. As we described earlier in this chapter, current thinking about expected patterns of growth and development calls for a consideration of geographic, cultural, and socioeconomic factors that facilitate (or in some cases impede) growth and development. Parental goals and expectations influence growth and development through the types and timing of educational or enrichment opportunities they provide, the quality and quantity of play they encourage, and the behaviors they elicit through their interactions with their children (Bronfenbrenner, 1986;

Garrett et al., 1994; Ogbu, 1981). Therefore, in studying Table 5.3, remember that these milestones are based on a WEIRD population. So, consider the ages as approximations and recognize that the sequence may indeed vary.

Table 5.3 Developmental Possibilities in Motor Control During the First Year

Age	Motor Development
Birth–3 months	Supports head when in prone position
	Lifts head
	Supports weight on elbows
	Hands relax from the grasping reflex
	Visually follows a moving object
	Pushes with feet against lap when held upright
	Makes reflexive stepping movements when held in a standing position
	Sits with support
	Turns from side to back
3–6 months	Slaps at bath water
	Kicks feet when prone
	Plays with toes
	Reaches but misses dangling object
	Shakes and stares at toy placed in hand
	Head self-supported when held at shoulder
	Turns from back to side
	Sits with props
	Makes effort to sit alone
	Exhibits crawling behaviors
	Rocks on all fours
	Draws knees up and falls forward

continued

Table 5.3 continued

Age	Motor Development
6–9 months	Rolls from back to stomach
	Crawls using both hands and feet
	Sits alone steadily
	Pulls to standing position in crib
	Raises self to sitting posture
	Successfully reaches and grasps toy
	Transfers object from one hand to the other
	Stands up by furniture
	Cruises along crib rail
	Makes stepping movements around furniture
9–12 months	Exhibits "mature" crawling
	Cruises holding on to furniture
	Walks with two hands held
	Sits without falling
	Stands alone
	May walk alone
	Attempts to crawl up stairs
	Grasps object with thumb and forefinger

Physical Characteristics

Birth weight and birth length are always of interest to parents, grandparents, and health care professionals. Although birth weight and birth length often make for proud conversation, physical measurements are quite significant in the context of infant health and developmental outcomes. Low birth weight, for instance, has serious implications for survival and for subsequent normal development.

The average birth weight for full-term infants is 7½ pounds, with a range from 5½ to 10 pounds. Boys usually are slightly heavier than girls at birth. Birth length ranges from 18 to 22 inches, with an average of 20 inches. The neonate frequently loses weight in the

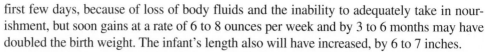

first few days, because of loss of body fluids and the inability to adequately take in nourishment, but soon gains at a rate of 6 to 8 ounces per week and by 3 to 6 months may have doubled the birth weight. The infant's length also will have increased, by 6 to 7 inches.

During the second half of the first year, gains in weight and length decelerate somewhat, but growth continues at a rapid pace. Weight may increase by 4 to 6 ounces weekly. By the first birthday, infants may have tripled in weight and grown 10 to 12 inches since birth. If growth were to proceed at such pace, an 18-year-old would measure more than 15 feet tall and weigh several tons! Fortunately, growth slows appreciably after the first two years.

Weight and height are observable characteristics. Although this outward growth is readily observable, significant internal growth is taking place as the central nervous system matures and bones and muscles increase in weight, length, and coordination.

The soft bones of early infancy gradually *ossify* as calcium and other minerals harden them. At first, the bones are soft and pliable and are difficult to break. They do not support the infant's weight in sitting or standing positions. The skull bones are separated by **fontanelles** (often called "soft spots"), which may compress to facilitate passage through the birth canal. These fontanelles tend to shrink after 6 months and may close between 9 and 18 months.

fontanelles
membranous spaces between the cranial bones of the fetus and infant

Interestingly, the bones of the skull and wrists ossify earliest, and the wrists and ankles develop more bones as the child matures. Girls may be several weeks ahead of boys in bone development at birth. Physicians may use X-rays of the wrists to determine the **skeletal age** of a child. Such X-rays reveal the number of bones in the wrist along with the extent of ossification. This information assists in assessing expected growth progress and diagnosing growth disorders and disease.

skeletal age
a measure of physical development based on examination of skeletal X-rays

Although infants are born with all the muscle cells they will ever have (Tanner, 1989), there is a large amount of water in muscle tissue. Gradually, as protein and other nutrients replace this cellular fluid, the strength of the muscles increases.

Because neurological development and brain growth are rapid during prenatal development and the first year, head circumference measures provide a useful means for evaluating the status of the central nervous system in infants and young children. Small-for-age head circumference measurements at 8 months to 2 years of age may indicate central nervous system anomalies that are associated with developmental delay. As is true of other organs, not all parts of the brain develop at the same rate. At birth, the brain stem and the midbrain are the most highly developed. These areas of the brain control consciousness, inborn reflexes, digestion, respiration, and elimination.

The cerebrum and the cerebral cortex surround the midbrain and are significant in the development of primary motor and sensory responses. The nerve cells that control the upper trunk and arms mature before those that control the lower

As a rule motor development proceeds from the upper region of the body to the lower.

trunk and legs. Observation of infant motor activity reveals a growing number of skills that use the muscles of the neck, arms, and hands, skills that precede the abilities to turn over, sit up, or crawl. By 6 months of age, the cerebral cortex has matured sufficiently to control most of the infant's physical activity. At this point in growth and development, many reflexes of early infancy should be fading, signaling maturation of the neurological system.

Infants with Special Needs

Infants whose prenatal development was less than optimal owing to the challenges of poverty, maternal health complications, inadequate nutrition, toxic stress, or teratogenic disturbances to fetal development or those who experienced prematurity or other birth trauma are most often infants identified as being *at risk*. Their growth and development is expected to have challenges that may require specialized care, treatment, and educational practices. Infants who are at risk for poor or delayed development or who have disabling conditions require assessment and identification that lead to timely diagnosis and intervention. The Apgar Scale, the Brazelton Neonatal Behavioral Assessment Scale, the Bayley Scales of Infant Development, and the Bayley Infant Neurodevelopmental Screener are examples of tests that are frequently used to provide initial and diagnostic information.

In addition to earliest possible intervention, infants with special needs require knowledge and special sensitivity on the part of their caregivers. Sometimes, the challenges of caring for an infant with special needs can be daunting for parents, family members, and nonparental caregivers. Today, Part C (formerly Part H): Early Intervention Program for Infants and Toddlers with Disabilities (Birth Through Age 2) of the Individuals with Disabilities Education Act (Individuals with Disabilities Education Act, 2009) provides federal funds to states for services specifically for children birth through age 2 and provides funds to develop, establish, and maintain a statewide system that offers early intervention services. The law provides for the following three groups of children:

1. Infants and children who have a measurable developmental delay in one or more of the following developmental domains: cognitive, physical, language/communication, social, emotional, adaptive/self-help, and behavior.
2. Children who have a diagnosed physical or mental condition that could result in a developmental delay (e.g., Down syndrome, sensory impairments, cerebral palsy, autism).
3. Children who are at risk of experiencing developmental delay, as determined by the state, if intervention is not provided.

Recognizing the importance of the family in the child's development, the law (IDEA, 2004) provides supports and services to help families by mandating that intervention services be provided in "the most natural environment," the types of settings in which infants and toddlers without disabilities would participate. This means that child care programs, nursery schools, public schools, and family care settings must make provisions to successfully integrate infants and toddlers with special needs into their programs. This includes providing additional and sometimes specialized training for adults who are responsible for the children, developing appropriate communicative and interactive skills, adapting physical environments, integrating remediation and intervention strategies into a developmentally appropriate curriculum, and effectively working with parents.

Relationship of Physical and Motor Development to Social and Emotional Development

Increasing physical and motor abilities during the first year expand the infant's social and emotional horizons. By communicating hunger, pain, and happiness cues through crying, cooing, and other vocalizations, infants learn that they can draw others into interactions with them. When these interactions are positive and supportive, infants learn to trust parents, caregivers and themselves to meet their needs. Each new developmental milestone brings with it new sets of behaviors and new types of interactions between infant and caregivers. For most infants, each new ability elicits encouragement, praise, and joy supporting an emerging sense of self.

As the infant becomes more mobile, safety becomes a real and immediate concern. As motor abilities increase, parents, siblings, and caregivers often begin to perceive the infant as more "grown up" and may unwittingly attribute greater self-sufficiency to the infant than is really the case. Misattributions—for example, expecting the infant to hold her own bottle for feeding, judge the depth of a stair step, or manage playthings designed for older children—compromise the infant's safety and deflate an emerging sense of confidence. Concerns about safety bring about new forms of communicating, which include facial expressions, voice tone and pitch, and verbal cautions and commands. Keeping children safe while encouraging the types of activities that enhance motor development requires both vigilance and understanding. Undue restraint and excessive restrictions, particularly if delivered in impatience and anger, frighten and confuse the infant. Such interactions can reduce children's emerging self-confidence and willingness to explore, learn, and express themselves. Overuse of restrictions, such as saying "no" and "don't touch," can cause infants to associate negative and disapproving responses with the people who mean the most to them. Attempts to explore and investigate and to try out emerging skills are hindered, as is the confidence and independence that new skills bring. It is better to establish safe, "child-friendly" environments with supervision that offers substitutes and distractions than to impose constant verbal restrictions (Meyerhoff, 1994).

Relationship of Physical and Motor Development to Cognition

Motor experiences in infancy form the basis of meaning in earliest cognitive development. An environment that is rich in sensory input—sights, sounds, tastes, aromas, textures, and movement—has been shown to enhance brain growth and neurological development in infants (Shore, 1997/2003). Talking, singing, sharing books, and interacting socially with the infant provide needed input for a rapidly developing mind. An environment that encourages social interactions and freedom to explore is essential to a well-integrated neurological and cognitive system.

Factors Influencing Physical and Motor Development

Genetic Makeup

Each infant is a unique individual with a special genetic endowment. This genetic endowment is observable in physical features such as eye, hair, and skin color; shape and size of facial features; body build; activity levels; and so on. It may also be related to mental and social-emotional characteristics such as temperament, some forms of mental retardation, and certain health and psychological disorders. Research in genetics is beginning to pinpoint the influence of heredity on less observable characteristics such as size and functioning of the internal organs, susceptibility to disease, psychological strengths and disorders, and numerous other facets of human individuality. Gene mapping research holds promise for identifying genetic anomalies and perhaps gene therapy to alleviate or minimize the influence of certain genes on developmental outcomes. Screening tests during pregnancy to detect genetic abnormalities allow for early identification and consideration of appropriate intervention strategies.

Integrity of Prenatal Development

Chapter 3 described very rapid development during the prenatal period. To the extent that this critical period in growth and development is protected from hazard, the integrity of the fetus is ensured. As reviewed in Chapter 3, studies of the vulnerability of the fetus during various prenatal stages indicate that there are both immediate and long-term effects of unhealthy intrauterine environments. Infants who benefit from a healthy prenatal journey—one that is free of drugs, toxins, poor nutrition, maternal stress, and other environmental hazards—are less likely to experience the myriad and sometimes devastating health, growth, and developmental outcomes associated with poor or inadequate intrauterine environments.

Socioeconomic Circumstances

Infant and family well-being depend on adequate food, shelter, clothing, transportation, and preventive and medical health care. The extent to which these family needs are met is dependent on income and available resources both within the family and in the community. Knowledge about, eligibility for, and willingness to access local, state, and federal assistance programs such as the U.S. Special Supplemental Nutrition Program for Women, Infants, and Children (WIC) and the State Children's Health Insurance Program (SCHIP) also contribute to infant and family well-being. Population studies for the year 2010 reveal that 19% of U.S. children lived in families with incomes below the poverty line, and 7% of U.S. children lived in extreme poverty (ChildStats.gov, 2010).

Poverty has both immediate and long-term effects on child growth, development, and learning. Children living in poverty are more likely to experience food insecurity, leading to poor or inappropriate diets and malnutrition, and limited or neglected health care, including failure to immunize. They are less likely to have dental assessments and have timely treatment for diseases, infections, and injuries. They may have limited or no attention to psychological needs. Families whose energies are taxed by overwhelming economic issues may have little to share with children for nurturing, playful interactions, and enriching learning opportunities. Families receiving welfare assistance or making transitions to the workforce or work training may find the cost of child care for infants prohibitive and often use friend and family care.

General Health and Freedom from Disease
Regular Health Checkups and Immunizations

Regular visits to the pediatrician or family health care specialist are necessary to monitor the infant's progress in growth and development; assess nutritional needs; treat infections, allergies, and illness; and administer disease-preventing immunizations. The American Academy of Pediatrics recommends preventive health care visits for healthy infants and children at 1, 2, 4, 6, 9, 12, 15, and 18 months, then annually from ages 2 through 6, and then every two years through adolescence. More frequent visits may be necessary for children with special needs and between regular checkups as the need arises. Newborns are routinely tested for phenylketonuria (PKU), an inborn error of metabolism in which abnormal levels of the enzyme phenylalanine form in the blood; if untreated, PKU leads to mental retardation and other abnormalities. When detected and treated within the first three weeks after birth with a specialized diet, developmental outcomes are better than when the diet is started later. In addition to checking growth progress through weight, height, and head circumference measurements, the physician and parent have an opportunity to discuss the child's growth and development, preventive health care measures, individual nutritional requirements, treatment of allergies, and other health and developmental concerns.

Fortunately, immunizations now prevent many life-threatening diseases in infants and children, and promising new vaccines are on the horizon. Infants and young children receive a standard series of immunizations against hepatitis B, diphtheria, tetanus, pertussis (whooping cough), *Haemophilus influenzae* type B, polio, measles, mumps, and rubella. All of these immunizations need to be given to children before they are 2 years old to protect them during their most vulnerable early months and years. Recommended vaccination schedules are updated annually and published every January. The American Academy of Pediatrics, in collaboration with the U.S. Centers for Disease Control and Prevention and the American Association of Family Physicians, develops the schedule; and through their practices, doctors (and local health departments) advise parents of any revisions or additions to the immunization schedule. They also provide information about new or improved immunizations and alternative methods for administering

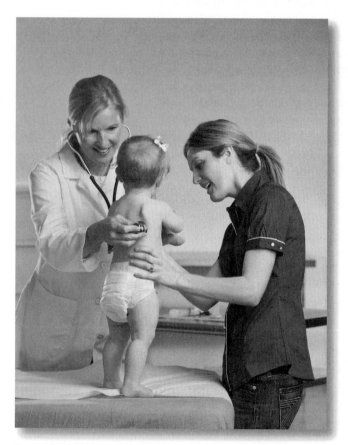

Preventive health care is provided through regular checkups and immunization.

them (e.g., nasal sprays, skin patches, time-release pills, genetically engineered food products). Additional vaccines are also available and administered when advisable, including chicken pox and rotavirus vaccines. (Rotavirus is responsible for the most common cause of diarrhea in infants and young children. Untreated diarrhea is a serious childhood infection and can be life threatening.) On the horizon are many new and improved vaccines including vaccines for ear infections, asthma, strep throat, juvenile diabetes, multiple sclerosis, AIDS, and some forms of cancer. Advances in genetics and immunology research are truly ushering in a new generation of vaccines and disease prevention and treatment practices.

The National Childhood Vaccine Injury Act (42 U.S.C. §300 aa-26) requires that physicians provide information about the vaccine that has been published by the Centers for Disease Control and Prevention to a child's parent or legal representative before vaccination. The physician or health care professional administering the vaccine must ensure that the person authorizing the vaccine reads and understands the vaccine information materials. The risks and benefits of immunization are discussed further in Chapter 8.

Dental Health

The first teeth begin to erupt between 5 and 9 months of age. The first teeth to erupt are usually the two lower middle incisors, followed in a few months by the four upper middle incisors. By the end of the first year, most infants have these six teeth. The complete set of 20 teeth does not erupt until around 2½ years. Pain associated with the eruption of teeth varies among infants. Some infants cry, are sleepy and fretful, seem to want to chew something, and drool considerably. Others appear to feel no pain or discomfort and may, to the surprise of their parents, present a "toothed" smile.

Care of teeth during the first year includes cleaning the infant's gums, tooth pads, and first teeth with gauze and beginning the use of a very soft infant toothbrush after several teeth have erupted. This is not too early to get established with a dentist for assessment of dental needs and guidance on how to care for infant teeth and prevent cavities.

Nutrition

The role of nutrition in ensuring optimal growth and developmental outcomes is paramount during prenatal development and infancy. During this period of very rapid growth, brain growth is particularly dramatic. Studies have linked impaired functioning of the central nervous system to iron deficiency in the early months of life (Algarin, Peirano, Garrido, Pizarro, & Lozoff, 2003; Roncagliolo, Garrido, Walter, Peirano, & Lozoff, 1998) and to later cognitive and behavioral outcomes in childhood and adolescence (Lucas, Morley, & Coles, 1998). Adequate nutrition helps to prevent illnesses and ensures the developmental integrity of the individual.

A major task of the newborn is that of learning to take in nourishment. This task is a complex one in which sensory–motor physiological capabilities, sleep/wake state, and focus of attention must all be coordinated. The reflex sucking system comes into play as the infant learns to coordinate sucking, swallowing, and breathing efficiently during the nursing process.

Although most infants have little difficulty orally grasping the nipple of the breast or the bottle, sucking, swallowing, gagging, burping, and digesting, premature and SGA

gavage feeding
introducing fluids or foods
through a tube passed
orally or through a nasal
passage into the stomach

colostrum
the first fluid secreted by
the mammary glands soon
after childbirth, before
true milk is formed

infants may have greater difficulty. Some of these fragile or ill infants may require **gavage feeding.** Newborns are always observed and assessed for feeding readiness and competence.

Breastfeeding. Because of its biochemical composition, breast milk is uniquely suited to the infant's immature digestive system. It provides initial advantages through **colostrum,** the milk that precedes mature breast milk in the first several days after delivery. Colostrom provides immunity to a number of infections when the mother carries the immunities and is rich in the nutrients a newborn needs. Mature breast milk is secreted between the third and sixth day after childbirth and changes over time (as long as breastfeeding takes place) to match the changing needs of the growing infant. For the first 6 months, except for vitamin K, vitamin D, and, if the mother is a vegetarian, vitamin B12, breast milk provides all the fluids and nutrients an infant needs to be healthy and provides anti-inflammatory factors that decrease the incidence of respiratory and gastrointestinal infections (Hay et al., 2011, p. 7–8).

The American Academy of Pediatrics Section on Breastfeeding, American College of Obstetricians and Gynecologists, American Academy of Family Physicians, Academy of Breastfeeding Medicine, World Health Organization, United Nations Children's Fund, and many other health organizations recommend exclusive breastfeeding for the first 6 months of life. Exclusive breastfeeding is defined as an infant's consumption of human milk with no supplementation of any type (no water, no juice, no nonhuman milk, and no foods) except for vitamins, minerals, and medications. Exclusive breastfeeding has been shown to provide improved protection against many diseases and to increase the likelihood of continued breastfeeding for at least the first year of life (American Academy of Pediatrics, 2005). Parents can discuss exclusive breastfeeding with their pediatrician or family doctor to determine whether exclusive breastfeeding is best for their particular baby.The American Academy of Pediatrics has developed a Breastfeeding Initiatives Web site (www2.aap.org/breastfeeding) with recommendations, advocacy materials, and resources for parents, professionals, and community agencies.

In 2011, the Surgeon General of the United States released a "Call to Action to Support Breastfeeding," citing beneficial health, psychosocial, economic, and environmental effects and endorsement of breastfeeding as the best nurtrion for infants. This "Call to Action" cited research documenting the benefits of breastfeeding to both infant and mother.

For infants, the possible benefits include:

- Decreased risk for a number of acute and chronic diseases, including diarrhea, lower respiratory infection, otitis media (infection of the middle ear canal), and allergies such as eczema and asthma.
- Possible protection against sudden infant death syndrome (SIDS), insulin-dependent diabetes mellitus, and gastrointestinal infection
- Lower rates of childhood obesity
- Receiving the most nutritionally beneficial food

For mothers, the benefits of breastfeeding are equally impressive:

- Bonding more closely with their babies
- Reduced risk of postpartum depression
- Economic benefits because the family doesn't have to buy formula (savings of approximately $1,200 to $1,500)

- Burning of more calories, resulting in earlier return to prepregnancy weight
- Convenience because the breast milk has been "properly stored," comes already prepared, and is ready to serve at the appropriate temperature. It can be pumped and stored for feedings when mother must be away or when other members of the family wish to participate in feeding the infant.

Certain health conditions, for example, untreated, active tuberculosis, may preclude breastfeeding (Centers for Disease Control and Prevention (CDC), 2007). Breastfeeding employed mothers may find it difficult to continue breastfeeding. Any mother can tell you that breast pumps (manual or electric pumps used to express milk for later use) make them feel less than human, can be painful, and take time; however, they will also tell you that the time is worth it if they can give their baby breast milk. In many states, workplaces are required to provide a room for breastfeeding mothers to pump milk; however, there still may be a stigma attached that discourages mothers to do so. Please see Box 5.2 for what employers can do to support breastfeeding.

Although many babies are quite capable of "latching on" to the mother's nipple during the first hour after birth, many mothers will need help from lactation specialists

Box 5.2   Mother-Friendly Employers

Many mothers juggle parenting responsibilities and working outside the home. Women who return to work and choose to continue breastfeeding their infants benefit from business practices that are mother friendly. Businesses, as well, benefit through reduced absenteeism, reduced employee turnover, shorter maternity leaves, increased productivity, recruitment incentive, fewer health insurance claims, and a positive image in the community. A number of states have enacted laws or policies that recognize businesses that are mother friendly. Such policies include the following:

- A workplace atmosphere that supports a woman's choice to breastfeed her infant
- Work schedule flexibility that provides timely breaks for lactating mothers to breastfeed their infants or to express breast milk
- A private lactation room that is equipped with a sink and a clean, safe water source for hand washing and for rinsing breast pump equipment, comfortable furnishings, an electrical outlet, a phone, and a locking door or an appropriate "reserved" sign
- Access to hygienic storage (e.g., refrigerator, ice chest) where breast milk can be kept cool, safe, and free from contamination
- A procedure for informing employees of the employer's mother-friendly policy

Mother-friendly businesses may also provide:

- Prenatal or postpartum classes on breastfeeding and infant nutrition through their wellness programs
- The services of a lactation consultant
- Literature and other resources on infant feeding and nutrition

Brain, Perceptual, Motor, and Physical Development of the Infant

or nurses to learn how to help the baby latch on correctly. They will need ongoing support to continue breastfeeding, especially if breasts become sore during the first few days or weeks of breastfeeding. Adolescent mothers may lack confidence to breastfeed (Mossman, Heaman, Dennis, & Morris, 2008). For mothers who cannot breastfeed their babies, milk banks are available in the United States, but parents will want to be sure that milk storage standards meet federal and state guidelines for safe and healthy breast milk.

There are certain foods and substances to be avoided if the mother chooses to breastfeed. Some foods ingested by the mother may alter the content and character of the milk and may also disagree with the infant's delicate digestion and absorption system. Some medications can be dangerous for the infant, but some are not. Both prescription and nonprescription drugs should be used only on the advice of a physician. Illicit drugs, alcohol, and caffeine have all been shown to have dangerous adverse effects on the nursing infant. Certainly, smoking while breastfeeding should be avoided because the effects of secondhand smoke are now well documented. Indeed, secondhand smoke has been shown to increase the incidence of asthma, wheezing, and chronic bronchitis and the risk of SIDS (American Academy of Pediatrics, n.d.).

Human Milk Banks. Few health care professionals today would not encourage breastfeeding. However, some mothers may be unable to breastfeed for various reasons (infant's health status and hospitalization needs, mother's health, medications, disabilities, employment, adoption) or may simply choose not to do so. For some of these mothers and infants, there is the option to provide human milk provided by human milk donor banks, wherein human milk is obtained from well-screened donors, pasteurized, and made available to eligible applicants. There are six regional human milk banks in North America, five of which are members of the Human Milk Banking Association of North America (HMBANA). HMBANA member banks must follow stringent guidelines based on recommendations from the U.S. Centers for Disease Control and Prevention and updated yearly and take additional precautions to protect against the transmission of infectious diseases (HMBANA, 2011).

Formula Feeding. For personal or health reasons, a mother may decide not to breastfeed her baby. The decision to provide formula is best discussed with a pediatrician or pediatric health care specialist to ensure the most suitable product for the infant. Research to improve the nutritional content, quality, and digestibility of commercial formulas has evolved over many decades and is ongoing. The U.S. Food and Drug Administration bases its regulations of infant formula on standards developed by the American Academy of Pediatrics Committee on Nutrition. Today's formulas are designed to simulate human milk and provide essential proteins, fats, carbohydrates, vitamins, and minerals. Thus, the choice to provide formula instead of human milk during the first months is certainly a viable option. Formula can also be used as a supplement for breast milk when the mother must be away or chooses to omit a feeding or the mother's breast milk is inadequate. In addition, there are special-purpose formulas for specific nutritional or medical needs. A 2005 report from the American Academy of Pediatrics warns against using well water to prepare formula or food as there are potentially dangerous nitrates that can cause a dangerous blood condition that limits oxygen in the baby's circulation system. If it is necessary to use well water, then it should be tested for nitrates (American Academy of Pediatrics, 2005).

To ensure optimal benefit from formula feeding, formula must be mixed according to the directions supplied by the manufacturer and prescribed by the infant's pediatrician. Overdiluted formula has less nutritional value and may fill the infant's stomach but not provide enough nutrients and calories to sustain growth. Overdilution is often a problem in economically disadvantaged families, who dilute the formula to make it last longer and thus reduce its cost. In addition to failing to meet the infant's nutritional needs, overdiluting can lead to **water intoxication,** a very serious condition that can cause brain swelling and convulsions in infants. Underdiluted formula may also cause problems. Because of water loss through urine, feces, regurgitation, fever, or vomiting, underdiluted formula can fail to meet the infant's need for fluid intake, leading to dehydration and other complications.

water intoxication
a dangerous, potentially life-threatening physiological condition caused by overconsumption of water apart from or in overdiluted formula or juices

Other precautions need to be taken in feeding an infant. Bottle-fed infants must be held in a comfortable position during feeding. The bottle should never be propped. Because the infant lacks the motor skills necessary to move the propped bottle, there is a high risk for choking and asphyxiation. Propping the bottle has other risks as well. When the infant is lying down while bottle feeding, bacteria grow in the pooled liquid in the mouth and cheeks, then make their way to the eustachian tubes, resulting in painful and potentially damaging inner ear infections. Tooth decay in older infants can also occur when formula stays in the mouth too long, coating the teeth with sugars.

Infants' psychological need to be held when being fed is also important. Whether breast- or bottle-fed, infants experience both physical and emotional closeness to their parent or caregiver while being held and cuddled during feeding. Calm, unhurried feeding times contribute to the infant's sense of well-being and trust and enhance the bond between infant and caregiver.

Satiety. Sensitivity to the infant's hunger and **satiety** cues also enhances infants' trust in both themselves and their caregivers. Overfeeding or underfeeding results when adults fail to recognize these cues. Turning the head away from a nipple, facial expressions of distaste, and other bodily attempts to refuse food are the infant's way of communicating satiety. Allowing infants to eat what they need without insisting on further intake helps infants to recognize their own feelings of hunger or fullness. Adults must also avoid giving food indiscriminately in an attempt to curtail crying. Not all crying is hunger related.

satiety
the feeling of having consumed sufficient food to satisfy hunger

All infants need to be fed on demand. However, for most healthy infants after the neonatal period, feeding schedules break into four-hour intervals. Some infants may need to be fed every three hours; smaller infants will need food every two hours. Caregivers soon learn to adjust to these rhythms, knowing that as the infant grows and matures, the schedule will become more predictable.

Solid Foods. To breastfeed or drink from a bottle successfully, infants before approximately 4 months have a tongue pushing reflex. This reflex begins to disappear around 4 months. Eating solid foods is a different developmental task than sucking and swallowing liquids. Now the infant must mouth or chew the food to soften it, experience its texture as well as its taste, move it to the back of the mouth, and successfully swallow it. This task is not always well coordinated, as is demonstrated by the infant's need for a bib. Before being fed solid foods, the infant should be able to sit with support and have good head and neck control.

Contrary to a somewhat common belief, early introduction of solid foods does not assist the infant in sleeping through the night. Hunger does awaken infants in the night, but nutritionists advise that the decision to introduce solid foods must be based on the infant's need for the nutrients provided by solid foods and on the infant's physiological readiness to handle solid foods, which usually emerges between 5 and 6 months of age.

The introduction of solid foods often begins with iron-fortified cereals, although some physicians may recommend pureed fruits and vegetables. New foods are introduced one at a time, and usually once a week, to accustom the infant to this new experience and to detect any allergic reaction to specific foods. As the infant's intake of solid foods increases, the infant still needs breast milk or formula. Cows' milk does not have the nutrition that an infant needs. Neither sugar nor salt should be added to foods given to infants; their immature digestive systems do not handle added seasonings well.

As the infant grows and learns to eat a variety of foods, care must be given to provide a balanced diet consisting of foods selected from the vegetable, fruit, meat, grain, and cereal groups. Foods selected for the youngest eaters should be appealing in color, flavor, texture, and shape. Self-feeding foods, foods that can be held in the hand or grasped from a tray, must be easy to chew and swallow. Mealtimes should be unhurried and pleasant.

Food Safety. In providing solid foods to an infant, several precautions must be taken. Foremost is avoiding food contamination. Foods should be fresh and properly stored. Adults must observe scrupulously hygienic procedures for preparing and serving baby meals: washed hands; clean utensils; foods kept at appropriate hot or cold temperatures; and covered, sanitary, and refrigerated storage of unused portions. It is best not to reheat leftover baby food because illness is caused by microorganisms that grow in foods at room temperature.

Some foods cause particular problems for infants and young children. For instance, honey and corn syrup have been found to contain ***Clostridium botulinum,*** the organism responsible for **botulism.** In infants younger than 1 year old, the immature gastrointestinal tract allows this organism to become active and potentially lethal (Hay et al., 2011). Foods that have caused choking in infants and young children include hot dogs and other chunks of meat, peanuts, grapes, raisins, hard or chewy candy, carrots, popcorn, fruit gel snacks, and chewing gum. Selection of nutritional substitutes for these foods and close supervision as the infant learns to handle new foods are imperative. Infants and small children should not be given foods to eat in a moving vehicle or as they are toddling about because movement increases the risk of choking.

Calorie Needs. Concerns about obesity, cholesterol, and other diet-related health problems have led some parents to mistakenly believe that reducing fat and calories in the infant's diet is necessary. Quite the contrary is true. Body size, proportions, and composition are in a period of very rapid change. The infant's calorie needs per unit of body weight far exceed those of older children and adults to maintain their rapid growth. In the absence of teeth, infants depend on consuming sufficient amounts of breast milk or formula to meet their increased caloric needs. In addition, during the last trimester of prenatal development and during the first few years of postnatal development, myelination of nerve fibers takes place. Fat is a major component of myelin (the tissue that surrounds the nerves as they mature) and, as such, is an essential part of the infant's diet if optimal neurological integrity is to be obtained.

Clostridium botulinum
the bacterium that causes botulism

botulism
a potentially fatal form of food poisoning

Colic. *Colic* is abdominal discomfort that occurs in infants 2 weeks to 3 months of age. It is characterized by irritability, fussing, or crying, sometimes for more than three hours per day and occurring as often as three days per week. It can be quite painful for the infant and distressing to parents. Why colic begins to appear at this age is unclear. Some suggested causes are foods passed through breast milk, such as caffeine and chocolate; sensitivity to formula; medicines passed through breast milk; and/or a specific bacteria in the intestine. Some infants seem more prone to colic than others, and no universal treatment exists because the causes vary. Physical examination by a pediatrician may be needed to determine whether more serious problems exist.

Some preventive measures can be taken to reduce the incidence of colic. These include feeding in an unhurried and calm manner; burping at regular intervals during feeding; avoiding either over- or underfeeding; and, with a physician's help, identifying possible food allergies. Kaley, Reid, and Flynn (2011), in a summary of the research on colic, emphasize that colic can have a harmful effect on a family and the infant, so it is important that solutions are found with each child. When colic occurs, holding the infant upright or laying the infant prone across the lap, swaddling, or moving gently with the baby may be helpful. Sometimes, changing caregivers helps. A tired and frustrated parent or caregiver whose attempts to soothe the infant have met with failure may, if these efforts continue, exacerbate the tensions in both the infant and the caregiver.

Safety

The infant's growing mobility and inclination to put things in the mouth lead to a number of health and safety issues. The most common safety concerns during the first year are automobile accidents, falls, burns, choking or suffocation, poisonings, and drowning. Adult failure to recognize the infant's changing abilities and curiosities is often the reason infants get injured.

Infant Spaces and Furnishings. The infant's surroundings must be sanitary and frequently examined for potential dangers: objects on the floor that could scratch, cut, or go into the mouth (e.g., balloons, coins, marbles, small toy parts, buttons, safety pins); exposed electrical outlets and electrical wires that could be pulled or mouthed; furnishings that topple easily; toxic substances within easy reach (e.g., medicines, cosmetics, household cleaning and gardening supplies, arts and crafts products); poisonous plants; swimming pools, bathtubs, and other bodies of water; hot water faucets and unsanitary toilet bowls; and many others.

All baby equipment and clothing should be selected according to current safety standards. These standards apply to bassinets, cribs, car seats, carriages, swings, playpens, jogging strollers, pacifiers, toys, and all other baby supplies and equipment. The Consumer Products Safety Commission regularly publishes information about safe products for children and items that have been recalled because of the hazards they pose. Parents and caregivers can avail themselves of this information at no cost, a responsible thing to do to prevent unnecessary (and sometimes lethal) injuries to infants and children. (See the Further Readings and Other Resources sections at the end of this chapter.)

Transportation. Beginning in infancy, automobile child safety seats must be consistently used in transporting an infant or a young child in a motor vehicle. Responding to the fact that more children are killed and injured in automobile accidents than from any other type of injury, every state now requires that infants and children be properly restrained when riding in a vehicle. Proper use of infant safety seats helps to prevent death and injury. The Federal Motor Vehicle Safety Standard Act 213 mandates that passenger safety seats manufactured after January 1981 must meet certain standards for design and use. However, this law did not prohibit the sale of infant passenger seats manufactured before this date. Consequently, some unsafe infant passenger seats may still be on the market through hand-me-downs, garage sales, and thrift shops. Since September 1, 1995, the National Highway Traffic Safety Administration has required that all manual safety belts have a lockable feature to lock them securely around child safety seats and that they be properly tethered to the adult seat back. Many automobile manufacturers now have integrated safety seats for children and other automobile child safety features.

In March 2011, the National Highway Traffic Safety Administration released new child car seat guidelines:

> The new guidelines advise parents to keep children in rear-facing, forward-facing, and booster seats for "as long as possible" before moving them up to the next type of seat. For example, NHTSA recommends parents keep young children in rear-facing seats as long as they fit within the height and weight limits set by the car seat manufacturer. The new guidance is in line with a new policy statement issued by the American Academy of Pediatrics, which recommends young children be placed in rear-facing car seats until age 2. (National Safety Council, 2011).

Car seat manufacturer's instructions should be conscientiously followed because incorrectly installed and secured car seats place children at risk in the event of a sudden stop or accident. Begin consistent (never wavering) use of car seats and restraints in infancy, and as children get older, the use of appropriate vehicle safety restraints will become an established habit.

State law requires car seats for all infants, and hospitals cannot allow a newborn to travel home without a properly installed car seat. Sleeping in a typical car seat, however, may be detrimental to premature infants born before 37 weeks' gestation or infants with respiratory challenges. Bull and Engle (2009) recommend that hospital personnel observe premature infants in the family-purchased car seat for a minimum of 90 to 120 minutes to detect apnea, bradycardia, and oxygen desaturation before allowing the premature infant to ride home. To ease respiratory challenges, certain infants may require a car bed rather than a car seat, but parents should use these only when recommended by a physician (Bull & Engle, 2009). Physicians recommend that children only sleep in car seats during travel and not at other times during the day (Bull & Engle, 2009).

Proper use of approved safety seats helps to prevent serious injuries or death.

Toys. Wise selection of toys for infants involves choosing toys that are constructed of pieces too large to swallow;

are lightweight and easily grasped; and are free of sharp edges, projectiles, batteries, or small removable parts. They should be made of washable, nontoxic materials and should be sturdy enough to withstand vigorous play. Toys should be selected for their sensory appeal and should be age appropriate for the infant who will play with them.

Issues in Infant Development
Infant Mortality Rates and Risks

Infant mortality rates (deaths during the first year of life) in the United States appear to be decreasing but remain alarmingly high for a modern industrialized and technologically advanced nation. Despite great strides in medical and child health protection over the years, in 2004 the infant mortality rate for all races was approximately 7.0 deaths per 1,000 live births (Federal Interagency Forum on Child and Family Statistics, 2007). In the United States, an African American infant is more than twice as likely to die during the first year as an Anglo infant (Children's Defense Fund, 2002). The causes of neonatal and infant deaths among all races relate to poor prenatal and newborn care, prematurity and low birth weight, congenital malformations and diseases, and complications associated with certain **syndromes,** including fetal alcohol syndrome, fetal tobacco syndrome, fetal marijuana syndrome, chemical withdrawal syndrome, and sudden infant death syndrome (SIDS). A brief discussion of SIDS at this point might be helpful.

syndrome
a group of combined symptoms that characterizes a physiological or psychological disorder

Sudden infant death syndrome is the sudden and unexpected death of an apparently healthy infant during the first year. It is the most common cause of death between 1 and 6 months of age, peaking between 2 and 4 months of age. It is estimated that 90% of SIDS deaths occur before the age of 6 months (American Academy of Pediatrics, 2011). It is sometimes called sudden unexpected infant death syndrome or sudden unexplained infant death syndrome (SUIDS).

In the past, it was thought that infants who died in their cribs had smothered in their covers (thus the term *crib death*). However, since its identification as a syndrome in the 1960s, this perplexing phenomenon has commanded considerable research, and its actual cause or causes are still difficult to pinpoint. In a new policy statement, the American Academy of Pediatrics provides these guidelines for a safe sleeping environment to prevent SIDS: supine positioning, use of a firm sleep surface, breastfeeding, room-sharing without bed-sharing, routine immunization, consideration of a pacifier, and avoidance of soft bedding, overheating, and exposure to tobacco smoke, alcohol, and illicit drugs (2011).

In a rigorous yet elusive search for causes over the past three decades, scientists have identified a number of factors associated with SIDS. Although these factors are not causes in themselves, they have helped researchers to identify high-risk populations. The following factors have been associated with SIDS:

- late or no prenatal care
- prematurity
- LBW and low Apgar scores
- male gender
- **apnea**
- sleeping in prone position (on the tummy)
- sleeping on soft surfaces

apnea
absence of breathing for a period of up to 20 seconds

Brain, Perceptual, Motor, and Physical Development of the Infant

- maternal age younger than 20 at first pregnancy or younger than 25 during subsequent pregnancies and an interval of less than 12 months since the preceding pregnancy
- multiple births
- maternal history of smoking, drug abuse, or anemia
- sibling(s) who died of SIDS (American Academy of Pediatrics, Task Force on Sudden Infant Death Syndrome, 2005).

In a small proportion of SIDS cases, child abuse is suspected (American Academy of Pediatrics, Task Force on Sudden Infant Death Syndrome, 2005).

A number of theories have attempted to explain SIDS. Some have implicated heredity; others have suggested upper respiratory viruses or a bacterium such as *C. botulinum;* still others have proposed **metabolic** disorders, allergies, **hyperthermia** and **hypothermia,** and central nervous system abnormalities. One popular explanation relates to the infant's cardiovascular system. Studies have found, in a number of cases, an abnormality in the brain area controlling breathing and heart rate (National Institute of Child Health and Human Development, 2006). Subsequent studies suggest that SIDS may be caused by abnormalities in the brainstem, which can be associated with delayed development of arousal along with immature cardiovascular and cardiorespiratory control. During sleep, the infant may not arouse sufficiently to breathe efficiently (American Academy of Pediatrics, Task Force on Sudden Infant Death Syndrome, 2005). However, not all infants studied exhibited this abnormality, so this theory awaits additional research. In spite of years of research, scientists are still unable to identify a specific cause or causes.

The incidence of SIDS appears to have decreased in recent years, owing in part to a *Back to Sleep* campaign. The Back to Sleep campaign has attempted to educate parents and child care personnel about SIDS and the importance of placing infants on their backs to sleep, as a preventive strategy, rather than on their stomachs. The American Academy of Pediatrics no longer recommends placing infants on their sides, because recent studies have revealed this position to be less safe than the on-the-back (supine) position (American Academy of Pediatrics, Task Force on Sudden Infant Death Syndrome, 2005). This practice of supine positioning is now widespread, and the overall SIDS rate has been reduced by 50% since 1992. You can view tables exploring the decrease in SIDS and order free publications and brochures from the Back to Sleep Education Campaign at www.nichd.nih.gov/sids/sids.cfm.

Box 5.3 highlights additional recommendations from the American Academy of Pediatrics to prevent SIDS.

Researchers also recommend the mother provide exclusive breastfeeding (without bottle feeding) to reduce the incidence of SIDS (Hauch, Thompson, Tanabe, Moon, & Vennemann, 2011).

Child Maltreatment (Abuse and Neglect)

Child maltreatment (abuse and neglect) is discussed in Chapter 8; however, we want to emphasize the importance here of *never shaking a baby* or leaving an infant with someone who has difficulty controlling his/her anger. Frustrations over infant crying, colic, diaper soiling, eating, sleeping, and other stresses, as well as maternal depression, family stress, and lack of knowledge about child development, may provoke an adult to become abusive. A common form of infant abuse is known as **shaken baby syndrome** and appears mostly in infants younger than 6 months of age. Shaking an infant or small child can

metabolic
pertains to the body's complex chemical conversion of food into substances and energy necessary for maintenance of life

hyperthermia
a very high body temperature

hypothermia
a below-normal body temperature

shaken baby syndrome
head (intracranial) or long bone injury caused by forceful shaking or jerking of an infant; may result in serious injuries (including blindness) and often death

Box 5.3 Sleeping Practices of Infants that the American Academy of Pediatrics (2005) Recommends to Prevent Sudden Infant Death Syndrome (SIDS)

(1) Place infants on their backs for sleep
(2) Avoid loose bedding
(3) Avoid soft sleeping surfaces
(4) Avoid overheating
(5) Consider a pacifier for sleep
(6) Use room-sharing without bed-sharing
(7) Avoid prenatal and postnatal tobacco exposure

cause serious physical and mental damage and even death. "The brain rotates within the skull cavity, injuring or destroying brain tissue…blood vessels feeding the brain can be torn, leading to bleeding around the brain." You will find these quotes and more information on a special Web site that has been created to provide information and resources for parents and professionals: www.dontshake.org.

Role of the Early Childhood Professional

Facilitating Physical and Motor Development in Infants

1. Advocate for adequate and appropriate food, clothing, and shelter for families.
2. Encourage (and assist where possible) families to access professional medical and health care supervision.
3. Be ever vigilant for infants who may need early identification and assessment of special needs and timely intervention.
4. Provide sanitary and safe surroundings for infants.
5. Provide sensorimotor stimulation through engaging responsive interactions, sensory-rich environments, and opportunities to explore.
6. Provide an encouraging, supportive, and predictable atmosphere of love, acceptance, and socially and emotionally satisfying interactions.
7. Provide guidance that is positive and instructive in helping the increasingly mobile infant to discover his or her capabilities in an atmosphere of both physical and psychological protection and safety.
8. Establish collaborative and supportive relationships with parents of infants.
9. Stay abreast of health and safety alerts, regulations, and laws to protect infants and young children.
10. Become aware of community resources that address the needs of infants and their families.

Brain, Perceptual, Motor, and Physical Development of the Infant

Key Terms

apnea
atrophy
axon
botulism
cerebral cortex
Clostridium botulinum
colostrum
dendrites
embryonic cell mass
fontanelles
gavage feeding

glial cells
grey matter
hyperthermia
hypothermia
metabolic
myelin
neural network
neural tube
neuron
neurotransmitter
perception

plasticity
primitive reflexes
proprioceptive system
satiety
shaken baby syndrome
skeletal age
subcortical
survival reflexes
synapses
syndrome
water intoxication

Review Strategies and Activities

1. Review the key terms individually or with a classmate.

2. Compare infant formulas and baby foods that are available at your local supermarket. What nutrients are listed on the labels and in what proportions? How do these foods differ? How are they alike? What considerations are essential in the selection of a formula or a solid food for individual infants?

3. Invite a Child Protective Services professional from your state or regional health and human resources department to talk to the class about child abuse and neglect. What is the responsibility of the early childhood professional in dealing with abuse and neglect of young children?

4. Visit an accredited child care center or a family day care home that cares primarily for infants. Make a list of health and safety precautions practiced by the child care-givers and staff in these settings.

5. Identify and investigate support services and infant care programs for infants with special needs and their families.

6. Discuss with your classmates the issues surrounding infant health and safety and identify ways the early childhood professional can address these issues.

Further Readings

Centers for Disease Control and Prevention, www.cdc.gov/nchs/data/databriefs/db18.htm.
- ADHD
- autism
- birth defects
- fetal alcohol syndrome
- HIV/AIDS
- newborns born addicted to pain killers
- safety—injuries, brain injury, violence, safety
- health
- traumatic brain injury

National Center on Shaken Baby Syndrome, www.dontshake.org. Describes the physical consequences of shaking.

National Sudden and Unexpected Infant/Child Death and Pregnancy Loss Resource Center, www.sidscenter.org. Displays information collected from national, state, and local SIDS/infant death programs, as well as perinatal, stillbirth, maternal and child health, and bereavement organizations. New resources include:

- Addressing Racial Disparities in Infant Sleep Practice: New Perspectives and Recommendations: ASIP/AMCHP Webinar #4 (9 December 2010), including resources and Webinar archive
- Acueste a Su Bebé Boca Arriba Para Dormir: Spanish translation of Helping Baby Back to Sleep
- Hot Topics in Infant Safe Sleep: An Interactive Workshop with Rachel Moon, M.D., from the ASIP-Pregnancy Loss and Infant Death Alliance 2010 International Conference on Perinatal and Infant Death (November 2010)
- Helping Babies, Healing Families: Program Manual and Trainer's Guide (winner of a 2010 APEX Award for Publication Excellence in the Education and Training/Electronic & Video Publication category)
- New Bibliographies: Apparent Life-Threatening Events (ALTE); Sudden Unexpected Infant Death; Aspiration or Choking and SIDS; Breastfeeding and SIDS
- New Research Bibliography: SIDS and Related Research Published in 2010: Web Portal PDF

Other Resources

American Academy of Pediatrics, www.aap.org.
Consumer Product Safety Commission, www.cpsc.gov. Hotline: 1-800-638-2772.
National Association for Child Care Resource and Referral Agencies, www.naccrra.org.
National Association for Sport and Physical Education, www.aahperd.org/naspe.
National Child Care Information Center (NCCIC), http://nccic.org.
Pediatrics for Parents, www.pedsforparents.com.
United States Breastfeeding Committee, www.usbreastfeeding.org.
ZERO TO THREE, Brain Development, http://main.zerotothree.org/site/PageServer?pagename=key_brain.
ZERO TO THREE: The Power of Movement in the Child's First Three Years: On the Move, www.zerotothree.org/site/DocServer/OntheMoveEnglish.pdf?docID=802&AddInterest=1153.

chapter 6
Emotional and Social Development of the Infant

In order to develop normally, a child requires progressively more complex joint activity with one or more adults who have an irrational emotional relationship with the child. Somebody's got to be crazy about that kid. That's number one. First, last, and always.

—Urie Bronfenbrenner

After studying this chapter, you will demonstrate comprehension by:

► identifying important theories associated with emotional and social development;

► describing the potential effects of earliest emotional and social experiences on brain growth and early neurological development;

► relating the concept of essential experiences to emotional and social development during the first year;

► identifying major emotional and social milestones in infancy;

► describing factors that influence emotional and social development; and

► describing the role of adults in facilitating healthy emotional and social development in the infant.

Emotional development in infancy provides the basis for the child's ability to manage his or her reactions to experiences, to effectively express and read emotions, to develop a sense of identity, and to develop an attachment relationship. These basic skills, if successfully established, provide a healthy foundation for mental health, relationships, and learning. Social development in infancy provides the basis for effective social interactions, positive social relationships, and participation in social relationships, with adults and peers, that are mutually satisfying for both partners. Early social competence provides a foundation for meaningful relationships and abilities to negotiate and resolve differences. These two areas of development are closely related, but for fuller understanding, we will present the neurobiology of and theories of both social and emotional development and then discuss emotional development and competence separately from social development and competence.

The Neurobiology of Emotional and Social Development

Emotional development is actually built into the architecture of young children's brains in response to their individual personal experiences and the influences of the environments in which they live. In fact, emotion is a biologically based aspect of human functioning that's "wired" into multiple regions of the central nervous system that have a long history in the evolution of our species. (National Scientific Council on the Developing Child, Center on the Developing Child, 2004a, p. 2)

Neurological Wiring

Although a great deal of genetically driven neurological development has taken place prenatally, external stimuli come importantly into play at birth and exert further influence on the formation of the brain's neurological circuitry. This neurological wiring is forming during the first three years for some developmental achievements and continues up to seven to 10 years for others. Indeed, the brain continues to change its "wiring diagram" throughout life, overproducing and pruning synapses during childhood and adding synapses as new learning is achieved during adult life (Greenough, Gunnar, Emde, Massinga, & Shonkoff, 2001).

The neurons, or brain cells, in the young infant's brain are making 300 million connections each second. The connections, or synapses, each record a bit of information the child takes in through his senses and through his own bodily experiences. For young infants, the repeated experiences of being tired, hungry, wet, or otherwise uncomfortable are being recorded through their ongoing synaptic connections. These experiences include both a physical component and an emotional component. Both components are building the architecture of the brain through synaptic formation. The relief and comfort provided by a responsive adult are also experienced physically and emotionally— and are also continuously changing and building the architecture of the brain. If the infant is neglected and left to cry, that experience is also captured by the ever-changing brain. The infant feels stressed, and that can have deleterious effects on the child's brain and ways that he or she interacts with others.

Brain Responses to Stress

In the first year of life, almost every moment is experienced both emotionally and socially (National Scientific Council on the Developing Child, Center on the Developing Child, 2004b). The depth of the child's emotional experience and the support given by adults to help the child manage those feelings produce the foundation for both attention and social capacities. It appears that strong, secure attachment to a nurturing caregiver can provide a protective biological structure that functions to buffer an infant against the later effects of stress or trauma (Gunnar, 1996; Gunnar & Cheatham, 2003).

cortisol
a steroid hormone produced by the adrenal gland and released in response to stress

Meghan Gunnar and her associates at the University of Minnesota studied levels of a steroid hormone known as **cortisol** in children's reactions to stress (Gunnar & Quevedo, 2007). "Healthy human beings have low levels of cortisol" (Gunnar & Cheatham, 2003, p. 203). However, cortisol's level increases when a person experiences physiological or psychological stress or trauma. The negative effects for young children with elevated cortisol levels because of stress are many!

Elevated cortisol affects metabolism, has been associated with depression, circulatory and heart disease, growth failure, and suppression of the immune system, and, when chronic, can lead the brain to respond to everyday events as threatening and stressful (Gunnar & Cheatham, 2003). This interpretation of events as threatening affects children's self-regulation of emotions, quality of relationships, and emotional health.

The National Scientific Council on the Developing Child's report on Stress and the Architecture of the Brain (2006) summarized research on the harmful effects of stress in the following way: "We now know empirically that exposure to frequent stress causes the release of harmful chemicals in a child's developing brain that can impair its physical growth and make it harder for neurons to form connections with each other." Neuroscientists now caution that stressful or traumatic experiences in infancy and early childhood, when prolonged and uninterrupted by successful intervention strategies, can undermine neurological development and impair brain function (Chugani, Behen, Muzik, Juhasz, Nagy, & Chugani, 2001; National Scientific Council on the Developing Child, Center on the Developing Child, 2005). Shore (1997/2003), who wrote *Rethinking the Brain: New Insights into Early Development,* emphasized that continuous or traumatic feelings of fear and hopelessness result in a brain structured to survive in a chaotic and dangerous world, which then negatively affects the child's social behavior, making the child more suspicious and less trusting, for example.

This recent research emphasizes that adults must try to reduce excessive stress for infants and toddlers. All infants and toddlers, however, experience stress. As a very tired 27-month-old grandson related to his grandmother after a ride home from the zoo with his mom and dad, "I cried and cried and cried—sad." While this was a rare case of being "sad" for this child, many infants and toddlers experience *frequent* stress that is harmful to their physical growth and optimal development.

It is believed that the infants' ability to express and control emotions (self-regulation) has biological origins derived from the types of care, nurturing, and supportive interactions that stimulate specific neurological connections (Gunnar & Cheatham, 2003; Gunnar & Quevedo, 2007; Perry, 1996). Early experiences quite literally shape the biological systems (neurological "wiring" and chemical characteristics) that underlie expressions of emotions. Children who have been abused, abandoned, neglected, and otherwise emotionally maltreated suffer impaired ability to regulate their emotional responses because of abnormal migrations of neurons and synaptic activity (Perry, 2006; Teicher, 2000, 2002; U.S. Department of Health and Human Services, 2009). Children who suffer chronically high levels of cortisol have been shown to exhibit more developmental delays in cognitive, motor, and social development than other children (Gunnar, 1996).

Secure attachment and affectionate warm relationships buffer the effects of stress for infants and toddlers. An infant's warm **attachment** (a connection between an adult and child that contributes to the child's feelings of safety) to his or her primary caregiver can block stressful hormones in frightening situations. In her interesting research on the effects of stress and the relationships that provide a protective stress blocker, Gunnar observed how infants react to the frightening experience of immunizations in the doctor's office. The surprised (shocked) face of an infant when the needle is stuck into his or her leg after the smiling doctor tried to make him or her feel at ease is only surpassed by the heart-rending cries that accompany the look. Gunnar found that a secure attachment of the infant with his parent blocked the baby's hormonal response to the stressful situation. In warm, affectionate relationships, infants seem to be more resilient in the face of stress. On the other hand, an insecure infant overreacts, producing elevated levels of stress hormones. Interestingly, children of mothers who experienced excessive stress while the children were infants may be more sensitive to stress as they grow older (Essex, Klein, Cho, & Kalin, 2002). When parents are stressed, infants may feel this stress on an emotional and physical level.

attachment
a strong emotional relationship between two people, characterized by mutual affection and a desire to maintain proximity

Earliest nurturing experiences and strong parent–child bonds during the first year appear to build inner strength (both biological and psychological) against the harmful effects of stress and trauma, a strength that remains evident as children get older. School-age children who have enjoyed secure attachment dynamics during infancy and early childhood exhibit fewer behavior problems when stress or trauma confronts them.

Researchers are studying state-of-the-art treatments that can prevent, remediate, or undo these neurobiological effects (NCTSN, 2011). Gilgun (2001) also identified protective factors that include the following:

- "Close, long-term relationships with other persons who (1) model pro-social behaviors, (2) are emotionally expressive and facilitate emotional expressiveness, (3) praise and encourage pro-social behaviors…"
- "[A] favorable sense of self that challenges images of the self as bad and powerlessness…"
- "An affirming ethnic and cultural identification…" (p. 5)

The Importance of Neurobiological Studies

Revelations about early brain growth and neurological development support many theoretical perspectives on child development. Among them, the notion that there are periods during growth and development in which experiences seem to have greater or lesser effect on the changing organism holds sway across the spectrum from theory to hard data from the biological and neuroscientific fields. Whether we are talking about "stages" or "sensitive periods," the concept of periods of vulnerability in which certain experiences enhance or thwart emerging development is an important one. The long-term effects of early experiences are also supported through neurobiological studies. Even though one can always learn new ways of thinking and behaving, the fact that neurological development is in a period of profound growth during the first three to 10 years suggests the critical need for appropriate experiences. Thus, for example, the long-held theoretical perspective on the importance of early bonding and attachments is affirmed through contemporary neurobiological discoveries. Further, although genetics remains the determinant of many traits and characteristics, the human organism remains dependent on its environment for the opportunity to develop optimally—a perspective that is reinforced through scientific data on how the human brain becomes neurologically wired.

An Overview of Theories on Emotional and Social Development

Before we began seeing emotions as electrical firings and hormone releases in the brain, many scientists theorized about the development of emotions and social relationships.

A brief look at the ideas of Freud, Erikson, and Piaget can be seen in Table 6.1.

Psychosocial Theory

Erikson's psychosocial theory frames some issues of emotional development in ways that continue to be so helpful that it deserves more explanation. By expanding on Freudian theory, Erikson identified eight stages of psychosocial development, each representing

Table 6.1 Freud, Erikson, and Piaget's Theories of Social and Emotional Development

Name	Important Concepts
Sigmund Freud Psychoanalytic Theory (1933)	• Early experiences shape personality • People are born with hidden psychosexual desires that manifest in different areas of the body at different ages • Behaviors are governed by unconscious desires and hidden motives • Introduced idea of stages of development • Successful resolution of stage-related conflicts over time should lead to healthy development • Introduced concept of **fixation**
Erik Erikson Psychosocial Theory (1994)	• Early experiences shape personality • Eight stages, each a conflict to be resolved • Biology and society together create conflicts
Jean Piaget Constructivist Theory (1952, 1954)	• Proposed that persons were the first interesting objects. • In first year, child realizes people and objects exist even when they are not present—*object permanence*

fixation
in psychoanalytic theory, a point in development that becomes fixed, failing to move forward to more mature forms

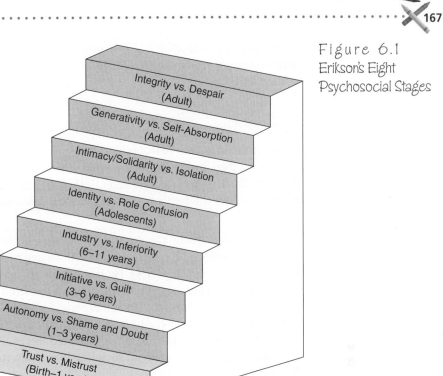

Figure 6.1
Erikson's Eight
Psychosocial Stages

stage-related psychological conflicts to be resolved in order for the individual to proceed successfully to the next and subsequent stages leading to healthy personality development (see Chapter 1 and Figure 6.1). These conflicts result from an individual's biological maturation and expectations imposed on the individual by society.

According to Erikson's theory (1994), the first year of life is a critical period for the development of a sense of trust. The conflict for the infant involves striking a balance between trust and mistrust. This primary psychosocial task of infancy provides a developmental foundation from which later stages of personality development can emerge. Resolution of the trust/mistrust conflict is manifest in a mature personality by behaviors that basically exhibit trust (of oneself and others) but maintain a healthy amount of skepticism. Infants learn to trust when their caregiving is characterized by nurturing and warm interactions and predictable routines. Needs for food, comfort, and satisfying interactions are met through a responsive and protective environment. Infants depend on their caregivers to come when beckoned; to interact with them in warm, supportive, and affectionate ways; and to respond appropriately to their many physiological, social, and emotional needs. When caregiving is responsive to infant cues, infants learn to trust their own ability to signal needs and to elicit caregiver attention. This helps to establish not only trust in others, but also trust in oneself.

Mistrust arises when the infant's caregivers fail to adequately respond to cues of hunger, discomfort, boredom, and other needs or do so in inconsistent and unpredictable ways. Infants who are subjected to neglect, rejection, or inappropriate expectations or infants who are repeatedly left to "cry it out" learn that other people cannot be trusted. Equally detrimental is the failure to learn to trust oneself and to gain a sense of self from positive and responsive interactions with others achieved by one's own efforts. Failure to develop a sturdy sense of trust undermines the ability to succeed in resolving the psychosocial challenge of autonomy versus shame and doubt during the toddler period.

Cognitive Theory

Cognitive theorists believe that infants have capabilities when they are born that drive them to construct their knowledge of emotions and social relationships from their experiences. Cognitive theorists such as Bandura (1997, 2001) describe the importance of observation and imitation for children's emotional and social learning.

reciprocal determinism
a socialization process through which the individual both influences and is influenced by the environment

socialization
the process by which individuals acquire the accepted behaviors and values of their families and society

social cognition
the ability to understand the thoughts, intentions, and behaviors of oneself and others

Social Cognitive/Learning Theory. Bandura advanced the importance of observation and imitation in childhood behavior and first illustrated his theory through his famous Bobo doll experiment (see Chapter 1). He brought into focus the importance of role models in shaping the behaviors of children. Bandura proposed that human beings are not simply passive recipients of information and experience, but use sophisticated cognitive abilities to draw on past experiences to think about the consequences of their behavior and anticipate future possibilities. Bandura furthered the concept of **reciprocal determinism.** As infants and children undergo **socialization** within their families and cultural groups, their own unique characteristics, behaviors, and levels of understanding affect the manner in which they respond to people and events. But, equally influential is the fact that the unique characteristics of the infant's social environment also affect the infant. Unlike age/stage theories, social learning theory suggests that the course of development for any individual depends on the kinds of reciprocal social learning experiences encountered. The individual's responses and interactions change over time as the individual matures and his or her social experiences expand.

From the foregoing, we are directed toward a discussion of how children develop understanding of behavior and behavioral expectations. **Social cognition** is the ability to understand the needs, feelings, motives, thoughts, intentions, and behaviors of oneself and others (Bandura, 1997, 2001). As infants develop a basic sense of trust, they learn to associate certain behaviors with the solicitation of certain responses from their caregivers. This awareness marks the beginning of the development of social cognition.

Imitative behaviors become a means of both social cognition and interpersonal communication. Imitations seen in games of pat-a-cake and peek-a-boo and in learning to kiss or wave are behaviors indicative of emerging social cognition. As the infant experiences these social interactions and finds them pleasurable, the motivation to repeat them emerges. These and other forms of infant interpersonal communications contribute to social cognition and competence and have implications for later language and cognitive development (Strid, Tjus, Smith, Meltzoff, & Heimann, 2006).

Spelke's Core Systems Theory. This theory proposes that infants may be born with a core knowledge for recognizing potential social partners by seeing themselves as members of a group, an "us versus them" sensibility. In studies, infants preferred looking at faces of people of their same race (Baron & Banaji, 2006) or of the same gender as their primary caregiver (Quinn, Yahr, Kuhn, Slater, & Pascalis, 2002). They looked longer at people speaking their home language (Kinzler & Spelke, 2005) and were more likely to take a treat from someone who spoke their home language (McKee, 2006). Spelke believes that this core knowledge served an evolutionary purpose of helping infants identify their primary caregivers, but it is sometimes misinterpreted as inherent racism. Infants aren't racist; they are just using their innate perceptual capabilities.

Contextual Theories

These theories emphasize the social context of learning. Contextual theories such as Vygotsky's sociocultural, Bronfenbrenner's bioecological, and Dynamic systems focus on the importance of the type of moment-to-moment interactions, culture, and community for the developing child's emotional and social development.

Sociocultural theory is sometimes referred to as a social constructivist theory. Sociocultural theorists believe that infants are born with cognitive functions such as attention and memory; however, their immediate and historical culture influences them and they, in turn, influence their culture. Adults in different cultures, for example, may scaffold infants' emotional and social development in different ways. In some cultures, infant/toddler peer relationships are valued while in other cultures peers may not become important until age 3 or even age 5.

Contextualistic theories such as the bioecological theory of Bronfenbrenner give us insight into infant development during the first year. Again the reader is referred to Chapter 1 for a description of this theory. In terms of social and emotional development of the infant, it is important to note that during the first year, a microsystem (Bronfenbrenner, 1986, 2005) surrounds the infant, exerting primary influence through the home and family and through nonparental caregivers and the settings in which this occurs. As infants grow and change, their needs and capabilities change, resulting in changes in both their physical and interactive environments. For instance, when infants begin to roll over and sit alone, they can be provided greater space for movement and a different array of toys than they previously experienced to support their emerging motor activity, and they are more comfortable in a high chair for feeding. These abilities change appreciably the types of safety protections imposed on the infant and the types of interactions between the infant and objects and people in their environment. These supports and interactions then produce more changes in the growing infant, and as circles of influence enlarge, this type of reciprocal influence becomes a continuous process. The growing child affects his or her environment and the environment affects the growing child (Sameroff, 1999).

Emotional Competence and Development

During the first three years, infants and toddlers have four major challenges in emotional development: managing or regulating their reactions to internal and external events, learning to express and understand the expression of emotions, developing an attachment relationship, and beginning to develop a sense of identity or self-awareness. Each child is born biologically prepared to master these challenges given a responsive and supportive environment.

Regulation

Newborns and very young infants are easily overwhelmed by feelings of discomfort that they cannot rectify. Feeling cold, wet, tired, hungry, or alone might set off a strong, uncontrollable emotional reaction of crying, shaking, and moving arms and legs. During this period, a calm adult can be very helpful in soothing the infant and providing the warmth, food, rest, or comfort needed. As the baby calms, he begins to orient his eyes and attention to the responsive adult. As difficult sensations are managed or regulated, the ability to quietly pay attention to the world returns.

Very young infants usually need help in regulating their reactions to internal or external events (Thompson, 2009). In time they begin to learn ways to help manage the intensity of their own reactions; curling up, sucking a hand or fingers, wedging against the side of a crib, or effectively summoning help with their own cry. When adults are with young infants, it is important that they recognize these self-comforting strategies as the infants' attempts to self-regulate. Without these strategies or adult support to regulate their emotions and reactions, infants can "fall apart."

Maternal (or other important caregivers') sensitivity in responsiveness is generally recognized as being the most effective support for developing regulation. When an infant cries and an adult comforts the child, the infant begins to understand that he is not alone, emotions can be expressed, and positive strategies can be learned to regulate his emotions. "Associations between positive emotions and the availability of sensitive and responsive caregiving are strengthened during infancy in both behavior and brain architecture" (National Scientific Council on the Developing Child, Center on the Developing Child, 2004a, p. 2.)

Increasingly, emotional regulation is being seen as an aspect of emotional reactivity. It is a major contributor to the child's ability to attend and learn. Children may have a difficult time learning if they react strongly to external events as this takes their attention away from the learning task. On the other hand, self-regulation strategies may become maladaptive, especially in the face of environmental adversity (Thompson, Lewis, & Calkins, 2008). For example, if a young child is continually under stress, he may not trust a primary caregiver enough to signal his needs and rather constantly withdraw with thumb in mouth in an attempt to self-regulate.

Maine's Early Learning Guidelines for "Supporting Maine's Infants and Toddlers" (www.maine.gov/education/fouryearold/documents/infantsandtoddlersguidelines.pdf) has a section on how caregivers can support infants' self-regulation in a variety of ways.

Emotional Expression

In addition to the readily observable emotional states of contentment and distress, the infant displays an array of emotions, including affection, joy, surprise, anger, fear, disgust, interest, and even sadness. The newborn shows interest and surprise when something catches his attention and smiles at a pleasing sound or when hunger has been satisfied. A sudden jolt or loud noise may evoke surprise and distress. The infant may show anger or even rage at being restrained or uncomfortable.

A number of scholars who studied emotions in the 1990s have suggested sequences for the emergence of discrete emotions (e.g., Brazelton, 1992; Denham, 1998; Izard, 1991; Lewis & Haviland-Jones, 2000; Sroufe, 1996). For instance, it is believed that distress, disgust, and surprise are expressed by newborns, whereas anger and joy emerge during the first 4 months and fear and shyness emerge between ages 6 months and 1 year.

Although most emotions seem to be present from birth, differences in emotional responses occur as the infant gets older. The most significant changes in emotional and social responses in infants occur during the period from 6 to 12 months, owing primarily to significant emerging cognitive development (Ball & Wolfe, 2004). The abilities to recall the past, sense discrepancies, and attend to expressions of emotion in caregivers contribute to these differences (Lamb, Morrison, & Malkin, 1987).

Attachment

The subject of infant bonding and attachment has received considerable attention in both the professional and the popular press for many decades. Recall from Chapter 4 that *bonding* (Klaus, Klaus, & Kennell, 2002) refers to the strong emotional tie between the mother or father (or caregiver) and the infant, usually thought to occur in the early days or weeks after delivery. Attachment emerges gradually during the first year. It is based on the quality of the interactions between the child and the parent or primary caregiver and it describes the sense of safety a child feels in proximity to the adult. It is currently one of the foremost concerns in the mental well-being of infants.

Infants can express a variety of emotions.

During the 1950s and early 1960s, John Bowlby, a psychiatrist and pioneer in the study of attachment, published a series of papers based on extensive research on mother–child attachments and separations. These papers, later enlarged and refined, were published in three volumes (Bowlby, 1969/2000, 1973, 1980) and have provided the impetus for continuing scholarly research.

Studying delinquent boys in institutions, Bowlby focused on their inability to form lasting relationships with others. Bowlby attributed this inability to the lack of opportunity to form an attachment to a mother or mother figure during infancy. Other delinquent boys in the same institutions, who had early relationships with a meaningful adult, were better able to show some compassion to others. He also studied children who, after experiencing strong infant–mother attachments, were separated from their mothers for extended periods of time while the mother was hospitalized having a second child. He observed that these children resisted comforting or close human ties. Bowlby was convinced that to understand these behaviors, one should examine infant–mother attachments. However, studies of attachment highlight the critical need to form attachments to several significant adults, not just the mother, during the early months and years and suggest that failure to do so may have a lifelong effect on healthy social and emotional development (Ainsworth, 1973; Bowlby, 1973; Bretherton & Walters, 1985; Robinson, 2002; Zeanah, Mammen, & Lieberman, 1993; Zeanah, Scheeringa, Boris, Heller, Smyke, & Trapani, 2004; Zeanah & Smyke, 2008).

Bowlby (1999) proposed a sequence for the development of attachment between the infant and others.

The sequence is divided into four phases:

Phase 1 (birth to 8 to 12 weeks): Orientation and Signals with Limited Discrimination of Figures. During this phase, infants orient to people in their environment, visually tracking them, grasping and reaching for them, and smiling and babbling.

The infant often stops crying on seeing a face or hearing a voice. These behaviors sustain the attentions of others and thus their proximity to the infant, which is the infant's goal.

Phase 2 (2 to 7 months): Orientation and Signals Directed Toward One (or More) Discriminated Figure(s). The infant's behaviors toward others remain virtually the same except that they are more marked in relation to the mother or perhaps the father. Social responses begin to become more selective; however, the social smile is reserved for familiar people, whereas strangers receive a long, intent stare. Cooing, babbling, and gurgling are more readily elicited by familiar people. A principal attachment figure begins to emerge; and the infant develops expectations for how the favorite adult(s) will respond.

Phase 3 (7 months to 24 months): Maintenance of Proximity to a Discriminated Figure by Means of Locomotion as Well as Signals. Infants show greater discrimination in their interactions with people. They become deeply concerned for the attachment person's presence and cry when that person starts to leave. Infants will monitor the attachment person's movements, calling out to the person or using whatever means of locomotion they have to maintain proximity to the person. The attachment person serves as a base from which to explore and is followed when departing and greeted warmly upon return. Certain other people may become subsidiary attachment figures; however, strangers are now treated with caution and will soon evoke emotions of alarm and withdrawal.

separation anxiety
fear of being separated from the attachment person

During phase 3, two very predictable fears emerge. **Separation anxiety** occurs as the relationship between the infant and the attachment person becomes more intense and exclusive. The infant cries, sometimes quite vociferously, on the departure of the attachment person and exhibits intense joy on reunion. Although this phase can be disconcerting for parents and primary caregivers, it is nevertheless a healthy aspect of social and emotional development. To the extent that adults respond to separation anxiety in supportive and empathic ways, the child can gain trust and confidence in their caregivers and in their own self-comforting strategies. Figure 6.2 offers suggestions for caregivers during this difficult phase.

stranger anxiety
fear of strangers, characterized by avoidance, crying, or other distress signals

Stranger anxiety is another characteristic fear of phase 3. Occurring around 7 to 8 months of age, the infant's stranger anxiety is characterized by intense or lengthy stares and crying at the sight of an unfamiliar person. Alarmed, the infant will cling tightly to the attachment person and resist letting go. Stranger anxiety, like separation anxiety, signals maturing cognitive, social, and emotional development and can lead to healthy trust and mistrust when responded to in supportive and helpful ways. Figure 6.3 includes suggestions for dealing with stranger anxiety.

Phase 4 (after 2 years): Formation of a Goal-Corrected Partnership Behavior. Before this phase, the child is unable to consider the attachment person's intentions. For instance, the suggestion that "I will be right back" is meaningless to the child, who will insist on going along anyway. By age 3, the child has developed a greater understanding of parental intent and can envision the parent's behavior while separated. The child is now more willing and able to let go and can be more flexible. According to Bowlby, "…the groundwork is laid for the pair [attachment figure and child] to develop a much more complex relationship with each other, one that I term a partnership" (1969/2000, p. 268).

Figure 6.2
A Sensitive Response
to Separation Anxiety

- Recognize that new experiences present new challenges for the infant; some of these challenges can be quite unsettling, maybe even alarming.
- Provide predictable, unhurried schedules, particularly when introducing the infant to new experiences.
- Begin to accustom the infant to short separations at home by
  - maintaining visual and auditory contact by leaving the infant's door open at nap and bedtimes; and
  - maintaining voice contact across rooms and, when departing the room of a protesting infant, providing softly spoken verbal assurances.
- Ritualize bedtimes and naptimes (e.g., provide a slower pace, soften volume on TV, give a bath and a change of clothing, brush teeth, read a story, rock and sing, kiss goodnight, and tuck in bed).
- Provide prior opportunities for the infant to become familiar with a new babysitter or child care arrangement.
- Select caregivers on the basis of their ability to respond to the infant's unique rhythms and temperament.
- Familiarize the caregiver with the infant's routines and preferences.
- Have available for the infant any special blanket, stuffed toy, or other object from which the infant gains comfort.
- Ritualize departure time: hug, kiss, spoken good-byes, wave, and so on. Never slip away when the child is not looking; rather, let the infant develop confidence in the arrangement.
- Anticipate the new experience with pleasure.
- Be dependable. First separations should be brief, and reunions should be unwaveringly predictable.

Bowlby's student and colleague, Mary Ainsworth, studied different patterns in attachment behaviors (Ainsworth, 1967, 1973; Ainsworth, Bell, & Stayton, 1974; Ainsworth & Wittig, 1969). Using her *Strange Situation* test, Ainsworth and her colleagues attempted to delineate individual differences in the quality of attachments that infants form. She devised a series of eight episodes designed to induce increasing

Figure 6.3
A Sensitive Response
to Stranger Anxiety

Learning to distinguish mother and father from others is an important task in infancy, and for many of today's infants, adapting to a nonparental caregiver may be an added task. The parent or caregiver must recognize that fears in the first year relate to new learnings and limited experiences.

- Discourage an unfamiliar person from immediately attempting to hold the infant.
- Provide ample time for the infant to assess the stranger and sense your reaction to him or her.
- When introducing the infant to a new caregiver, invite the person to visit. Spend time together, allowing the infant time to accept this new person into his or her world.
- During this session, let yourself serve as the secure base from which the infant can venture forth to make friendly overtures with the new acquaintance.
- Allow the infant to "control" the encounter, deciding when to approach and when to retreat.
- Provide the infant with familiar and comforting objects to hold.
- The confidence of older siblings who are already familiar with the "stranger" may encourage the infant's comfort and acceptance.

anxiety in the infant. The episodes, lasting 30 seconds to three minutes or so, created eight pairing situations that included the following:

1. the mother with the infant,
2. the mother and infant with a stranger,
3. the infant alone with a stranger, and
4. the infant being united with the mother.

She recorded and analyzed exploratory behaviors, reactions to strangers, reactions to separation, and infant behaviors on reuniting with the mother after separation.

From her studies, Ainsworth identified three categories of attachment:

1. Insecure attachment: anxious and avoidant
2. Secure attachment
3. Insecure attachment: anxious and resistant

Securely attached infants were found to be visibly upset upon separation from the mother and greeted her heartily and sought close physical contact with her on reunion. In their mother's presence, these infants more willingly explored their environments and were friendly with the stranger.

Insecurely attached, anxious/avoidant infants showed little distress when the mother departed and no great joy upon her return, generally avoiding contact with her, concentrating their attention on the toys while maintaining a sense of where their mother was. With strangers, they behaved similarly, tending to avoid or ignore them.

Insecurely attached, anxious/resistant infants were less likely to explore when the mother was present and were distressed when she departed. The reunion was strained, as the infant maintained proximity but resisted the mother's efforts at physical contact, displaying apparent anger at her absence. These infants were quite wary of strangers, even with the mother present.

Another classification of attachment, described by Main and Solomon (1990) as "disorganized," suggests that disorganization or conflicted feelings and behaviors expressing stress or anxiety can occur. Risk factors associated with disorganized attachment include maladaptive parental behavior, abuse, neglect, maternal mental health, poverty, and absence of or failure to access intervention services (Sameroff, 1999). Expressions of these disorganized attachment behaviors increase in frequency as the severity of the risk factors increases. Some researchers believe that disorganization of attachment patterns may foretell later hostile behaviors in children (Fagot, 1997; Gauthier, 2003; Schneider, Atkinson, & Tardif, 2001). Avoidant attachments are also thought to predict later antisocial behaviors (McElwain, Cox, Burchinal, & Macfie, 2003; Rubin, 2002).

On the positive side, a large body of research found that securely attached infants:

- formed early attachments between 1 and 4 months of age as a result of their primary caregivers' sensitive responses to their cues;
- exhibited trust in their primary caregivers' availability;
- developed self-regulation;
- progressed toward autonomous behaviors more easily;

- exhibited more confidence in exploratory behaviors;
- played with toys and other objects more than insecurely attached infants;
- enjoyed greater involvement and success in peer interactions as they got older (Cassidy & Shaver, 2008).

Bowlby and many other researchers propose that the attachment relationship is not only vital to the child's mental well-being, but is used by the child as the template for all later relationships (1969/2000, 1988).

What did securely attached infants experience that their less successfully attached age-mates did not? Do certain parental characteristics facilitate the attachment process? A number of researchers suggest that the mothers (or primary caregivers) of these infants exhibited more sensitive and responsive behaviors toward them. These primary caregivers:

- were more involved with their infants;
- were sensitive to their infants' behavioral cues;
- were readily accessible and emotionally available;
- were predictable;
- responded to their infants in developmentally appropriate ways;
- generally exhibited more positive behaviors and interactions and expressions of affection;
- enjoyed close physical contact with their infants;
- encouraged exploratory play and timed their interactions strategically so as not to intrude in their infants' play;
- had a sense of when to interact (Ainsworth, Bell, & Stayton, 1974; Cassidy, Belsky, & Fearon, 2006; Fagot, 1997; Honig, 2002; Shaver & Fraley, 2008).

Many scholars view the security or insecurity of the infant–mother attachment as influencing the quality of all other relationships. However, Main and Weston (1981) determined that infants can form independent attachments to both mothers *and* fathers resulting from the types of interactions they have with each. Moreover, these scholars found that infants who have established secure attachments with both parents are more empathic during the toddler years to an adult in distress. Recent researchers have determined that while infants are capable of becoming closely attached to more than one caregiver, they tend to place these attachment people in an internal hierarchy or preference order (Lieberman & Zeanah, 1995). Studies have found that when infant–mother attachments were insecure, secure infant–father attachments buffered the effects. Although Belsky and Rovine (1988) found that infants in nonmaternal care of less than high quality for more than 20 hours per week were at risk of developing insecure attachments with their mothers, this did not occur among infants who were cared for by their fathers in their mothers' absence. Hence, it appears that fathers can play a critical role in healthy attachment behaviors (Goodsell & Meldrum, 2010), and attachment researchers are taking a more family approach that includes the role of the father (Bretherton, 2010). Fathers' play, sensitivity, and responsiveness with their infants have been found to predict attachment classifications at 16 years of age (Grossmann, Grossmann, Fremmer-Bombik, Kindler, Scheuerer-Englisch, & Zimmermann, 2002; Trautmann-Villalba, Gschwendt, Schmidt, & Laucht, 2005). Fike (1993) provided suggestions for both meeting fathers' needs for interaction

As with parents and their infants, siblings also form loving attachments.

with their children and fostering the very important relationships that develop between infants and fathers that still hold true today. Fathers should:

1. understand the importance of setting positive expectations for their infants and practice a mental attitude of expecting positive relationships to develop;
2. appreciate the importance of holding, cuddling, and playing with their infants;
3. become involved in the daily lives of their infants through routines such as feeding, changing, bedtime and playtime routines, and so on;
4. become aware of the day-to-day events unfolding in their infants' lives;
5. communicate verbally with their infants in tones of approval and acceptance; and
6. nurture their infants through attitudes, deeds, and actions that communicate the infants' unique worth.

Both Lamb (2005) and Lewis (2005) emphasize the importance of social networks, including parents and family members (including siblings, peers, and child care providers) as important for children's development. Lamb (2005) "discusses research findings which document the ways in which an array of individuals shape children's behavior and characteristics from infancy" (p. 108). Lewis (2005) states that "The classical attachment theory holds to the notion of a monotropic model. Such a model leads to a view of the mother as first and most important figure in an infant's life. A polytropic view of attachment moves us toward a model of simultaneous and multiple attachment figures" (p. 8). Lewis (2005) also emphasizes that "A review of children's peer relationships, including siblings, leads to the consideration of a social network model in which a variety of different people satisfy a variety of different needs of the child" (p. 8). (See Box 6.1 for Diversity Perspectives concerning parental value for children's independence or interdependence.)

This expanding research on attachment has been enormously helpful to the early childhood professional by:

- emphasizing the importance of the first year for the development of parent–child bonds;
- affirming the ameliorative potential for other attachments (family members, child care providers) when parental (or primary caregiver) attachments are insecure;
- affirming the importance of nonparental caregivers in complementing and supporting parent–child attachments; and
- supporting the need for professional intervention when parent–child relationships are dysfunctional.

Box 6.1 Diversity Perspectives: Independence and Interdependence

These two words describe a very basic difference between most of the cultures of the world. Some, mostly Western countries, emphasize growing autonomy and self-reliance as signs of maturation. These cultures value independence. Other cultures see maturation as increasing connection and responsibility to others. These cultures value interdependence. In infancy, these values are often visible in the sleeping arrangements for the family. Independent cultures value infants sleeping alone in a crib and learning to sleep through the night by self-comforting. Interdependent cultures have the infant sleep with the mother, both parents, or possibly the siblings (Oskar & O'Connor, 2005; Small, 1998).

The U.S. Consumer Product Safety Commission (CPSC) and the American Academy of Pediatrics recommend that infants *not* sleep with their parents (American Academy of Pediatrics, Task Force on Infant Sleep Position and Infant Death Syndrome, 2002; American Academy of Pediatrics, Task Force on Sudden Infant Death Syndrome, 2005), stating that the practice puts babies at risk of suffocation, strangulation, and SIDS and that while co-sleeping is prevalent in many countries, parents in these countries generally sleep on firmer surfaces than do parents in the United States. Also, McKenna and Dade (2005) emphasized that there are many kinds of co-sleeping, including babies sleeping in the same room but not in the same bed as parents.

As you consider cultural differences, there is research that supports the following: sudden infant death syndrome occurs in higher rates among co-sleepers when a mother smokes, in poverty environments, among African Americans who live in urban environments, when bedding is soft, and when the baby is in a prone (face-down) position (McKenna & Dade, 2005).

Self-Awareness or a Sense of Identity

It is believed that to become a participant in the give-and-take of a relationship, the infant must first develop a sense of self as distinct and apart from others (Lewis, 1987; Lewis & Brooks-Gunn, 1979). Emotions such as love, hate, jealousy, and guilt—the types of complex emotions that are evoked through relationships with others—are related to an individual's sense of self. Infant psychiatrist Daniel Stern believes that the infant must always be aware of herself as a separate entity. From the moment of birth, touching oneself feels different from having someone else touch you, closing your eyes is different from having someone else turn off lights. He says that the development goal is not differentiating one's self from others but achieving closeness to others (Stern, 2008).

Self-recognition is an aspect of self-awareness. When a 2-year-old looks at a picture of herself and someone says, "Who's that?" the child might exclaim loudly, "That's De-De," a name that her parents call her. She is recognizing her own image as representing herself. Self-recognition has been assessed in a variety of ways, but the mirror assessment may be the best-known strategy. Researchers add a red mark on the nose of a toddler and then place the child in front of a mirror. If the child touches his own nose, this indicates that the child realizes that the image is of himself, thus the child shows self-recognition.

Emotional and Social Development of the Infant

Many theorists believe that the task of understanding that one is separate from others is the major emotional task of infancy. Five periods in the development of self–other differentiation were identified by Lewis in 1987, and these periods are supported by research more than 20 years later.

Period 1 (0 to 3 months) is characterized by reflexive interactions between the infant and caregivers and objects.

Period 2 (3 to 8 months) is a period in which the infant, through increasing numbers of experiences with others, progresses toward greater distinction between self and others, but the child may not make these distinctions in all situations.

Period 3 (8 to 12 months) is a period in which self–other differentiation appears to be accomplished; the infant evidences awareness of self as different and permanent in time and space.

Period 4 (12 to 18 months) is a period in which self-conscious emotions such as embarrassment and separation anxiety begin to emerge, as does the ability to recognize oneself in a mirror or photo image.

Period 5 (18 to 30 months) is a period in which self-definition begins to emerge, in which the infant can refer through language to his or her age, gender, and other defining characteristics.

The emergence of self-awareness depends on cognitive development—the ability to make mental "like me"/"not like me" distinctions. Self-awareness is also dependent on social experiences. Infants develop their understanding of self and subsequently a self-concept through their social interactive experiences with others: how others respond to them. As we will see in later chapters, self-concepts are continually being modified as new abilities emerge and social interactions expand beyond primary caregivers.

Temperament

Whether or not infants know they are separate people, parents certainly learn very quickly that infants can be very different from one another. From birth, infants display distinctive personality characteristics, the study of which has intrigued parents and researchers alike. Quite often, discussions of personality center on temperament, a characteristic that is believed to be at least in part influenced by genetic endowment (Plomin, 1987; Rothbart, Ahadi, & Evans, 2000).

During the 1980s and 1990s, researchers focused on various dimensions of temperament, such as emotionality (the extent to which events can be upsetting), activity (types and pace of behaviors), and sociability (the desire for social proximity and interaction versus shyness or withdrawal) (Buss & Plomin, 1984; Kagan, 1997; Kagan, Snidman, & Arcus, 1992). In studying individuality in children, Stella Chess and Alexander Thomas (1987, 1996) identified a number of dimensions of behavior that are associated with temperament. (See Figure 6.4 for a description of the nine dimensions of temperament).

By gathering information about these behaviors described in Figure 6.4 in large numbers of children, Chess and Thomas were able to delineate three main types of temperament:

1. *The easy temperament.* The child is usually easygoing, even tempered, tolerant of change, playful, responsive, and adaptable. The child eats and sleeps with some regularity, is easily comforted when upset, and generally displays a positive mood.

Dimension	Definition	Example of Infant Behavior
Activity level	Amount of physical movement	Phin moves most of the time—even in his sleep. Lana often seems content to sit and watch the other babies move.
Biological rhythms	Regularity of eating, sleeping, elimination	Phin often is hungry one day but not the next day. Lana quickly seems to get into a routine of eating every three hours.
Approach/ withdrawal	Comfort in new situations	Phin seems very comfortable in new situations—he will crawl over to a stranger (as long as he can see his dad). Lana often cries and whimpers in new situations.
Mood	Amount of time in pleasant, cheerful mood as opposed to fussing, crying, or resisting others	Phin seems in a cheerful mood almost every day. Lana fusses quite a bit of the time.
Intensity of reaction	Energy level of emotional expressions	Phin reacts loudly with squeals and shouts when he bangs a toy on the ground. Lana fusses quietly or reacts quietly when playing.
Sensitivity	Response to sensory information, including light, sounds, textures, smells, tastes	Phin tries new foods and does not fuss when he touches foods of different textures. Lana seems hesitant to touch or eat new foods.
Adaptability	Ability to manage changes in routine or recover from being upset	Phin has a hard time moving back into a routine of sleeping during the night after visits to Grandma's. Lana seems to welcome her bed and moving back into her usual routines after visits to Grandma's.
Distractibility	How easily the child's attention is distracted	While playing with a new toy, Phin turns his head to listen to a truck go by, then runs to the door when he hears an airplane. When Lana starts playing with her toys, it is often difficult to distract her to go to bed.
Persistence	How long a child will stay with a difficult activity before giving up	Phin tries to make new toys work, but will move quickly on to another toy if he can't. Lana will sit for long periods of time, turning a toy over and over and trying to make it work.

Figure 6.4
The Nine Dimensions of Temperament and Examples

Source: Adapted from Thomas, Chess, Birch, Hertzig, & Korn (1963) (examples added)

2. *The difficult temperament.* The child is slower to develop regular eating and sleeping routines, is more irritable, derives less pleasure from playtime activities, has difficulty adjusting to changes in routines, and tends to cry louder and longer than more easily soothed children.

3. *The slow-to-warm-up temperament.* The child displays only mild positive or negative reactions, resists new situations and people, and is moody and slow to adapt. The slow-to-warm-up child may resist close interactions such as cuddling.

The easy child's behaviors provide positive feedback and reinforcement to caregivers and, in so doing, influence the kinds and amounts of attention the child will receive throughout early development. More often than not, these children experience what Chess and Thomas (1987, 1996) called a "goodness of fit" between themselves and the personalities and expectations of their caregivers. *Goodness of fit* is defined as a principle of interaction in which

> the organism's capacities, motivations and styles of behaving and the demands and expectations of the environment are in accord. Such consonance between organism and environment potentiates optimal positive development. Should there be dissonance between the capacities and characteristics of the organism on the one hand and the environment opportunities and demands on the other hand, there is poorness of fit, which leads to maladaptive functioning and distorted development. (Chess & Thomas, 1987, pp. 20–21)

Infants who are described as temperamentally difficult may fail to elicit appropriate nurturing and support from their caregivers. Adults who find this temperament hard to respond to may become punitive, overly demanding, or perhaps inconsistent and appeasing in their interactions. They may be vague or unclear with their child about their expectations or perhaps their acceptance of the child. The adults may feel inadequate to their task, helpless, and confused. Poorly prepared to deal with a difficult temperament, these adults may engage in power struggles for control. Obviously, a challenging fit between the adult and child emerges in these situations and holds potential for ineffective and negative relationships and childhood behavior disorders that can persist into adulthood.

The slow-to-warm-up child generally does not present substantial difficulties in the adult–child relationship. However, this child, being slower to adapt and reticent with new acquaintances and situations, may not receive persistent efforts on the part of caregivers to maintain positive interactions.

Not all children fall neatly into these categories; easy children are not always easy, difficult children are not always difficult, and slow-to-warm-up children are not

Nurturing caregivers and siblings facilitate positive outcomes for infants.

always reticent. However, these descriptions help us to appreciate wide variations in infant and child personalities. Recognizing and appreciating individual differences help adults to respond appropriately to these behaviors. Adults must be cautious in applying these categories, however. Self-fulfilling prophecies may occur in which the child behaves according to adult expectations. If adults ascribe labels and misunderstand the infant's cues, they may fail to support the infant's needs for positive and nurturing interactions, regardless of temperament or personality type. Recent research gives additional insight into how child-rearing practices can modify temperament significantly.

Infants with irritable temperaments are less anxious or depressed at ages 2 and 3 and exhibit fewer behavior problems with mothers who are more sensitive (Shaw & Vondra, 1995; Warren & Simmens, 2005), have positive affect and are less intrusive (NICHD Early Child Care Research Network, 2004), and use positive, more sensitive guidance strategies (Belsky, Hsieh, & Crnic, 1998). "Not all difficult infants evidence behavior problems in the preschool years, and there are often complex interactions between child characteristics and aspects of parental behavior that together predict which difficult children will and will not show problem behavior at later ages" (NICHD Early Child Care Research Network, 2004, p. 45). If there is goodness of fit between infants and their environments, there are positive outcomes that carry over into later development.

Cheryl's mother finds it difficult to work as an office cleaner and help to care for Angela. Cheryl goes to school and feels fortunate that Angela can be in an Early Head Start that provides child care and home visits to the family. On the weekends, however, the older siblings in the family have been called on to help with babysitting; but that has not always worked out, owing to their own childhood needs for play and socialization and desires to succeed in school.

James has tried to be helpful, but his visits to his infant daughter are becoming less and less frequent. His need to work and his desire to stay in school consume his time and energies. His feelings for both Cheryl and their baby are becoming ambivalent and confused, and he sometimes feels depressed. He isn't sure what his role should be.

Cheryl has experienced mixed feelings as the realities of constantly having to meet an infant's needs become more apparent. She isn't sure of James anymore and anticipates that they will probably split up soon. She feels sad, but she does not blame him. She is tired most of the time, since she has returned to school and her classes have become quite demanding. Sometimes she feels like a failure at school and at mothering, and her baby seems cranky much of the time.

Cheryl's mother frequently shares her frustrations with a friend at her church, including the difficulties of making a living and raising a two-generation family. When it becomes difficult to pay the rent for the apartment, Cheryl and her mother decide that they have to move. Cheryl wants to move to a house in the same neighborhood so Angela can continue in the Early Head Start Program. After searching for several months and finances becoming even more challenging, they find a small house in a neighborhood on the other side of the city. Cheryl's mother finds a high school in the area that provides on-site child care for teenage mothers. Cheryl chooses to take advantage of the child care program.

Cheryl doesn't want to move, yet she feels that she has no choice. She will miss James and her other friends. James offers to help; he will borrow his brother's pickup truck and will help them to prepare the new house for occupancy. Cheryl is pleased at this show of caring and thinks that maybe her relationship with James can continue.

Meanwhile, Angela has experienced a constant turnover in caregivers. At age 8 months, her sleeping patterns are still irregular and unpredictable. She is hungry at

(continued)

Emotional and Social Development of the Infant

odd hours and is a finicky eater. She cries easily and often, continuously demands the company of others, and vigorously resists being put to bed. She can be quite playful, however, and enjoys the attention of her school-age aunts and uncles. She responds readily to Cheryl, but her relationship with her grandmother seems more comforting. She watches the comings and goings of all the family members and frets or cries when left in her playpen as others leave the room. Both Cheryl and her mother care deeply for Angela and want her to be a happy, cheerful baby.

Jeremy's experiences have been quite different. His social and emotional world has included his mother, his father, Phyllis (his child care provider), and an occasional visit from grandparents and trips to the church nursery. Except for his bouts with colic, Jeremy's routines of sleeping and eating are generally without incident. Bathing, dressing, playing, and interacting with Phyllis and his parents are, for the most part, relaxed, predictable, and enjoyable.

Keisha, now back at work, is making every effort to maintain a sense of order in their lives, but meeting Jeremy's needs has at times overwhelmed her. Keisha and DeVon talk frequently and frankly about the dramatic change in their lifestyle, daily schedules, social life, and physical stamina.

DeVon feels a need and a desire to nurture Jeremy and misses the child when he is at work. Jeremy has become his "buddy," and DeVon cherishes the smiles, the reaching toward Daddy's face when being held, and the pounding at his legs with uncoordinated hands to get attention or to be held. Dinnertimes are not always serene, nor are bedtimes, yet Keisha and DeVon both savor the changes they are observing in their growing baby. Indeed, Jeremy has a distinct personality. Does he take after DeVon's side of the family or Keisha's? Together, they anticipate Jeremy's changing looks, behaviors, and interactions with each of them.

Because Jeremy's routines have been mostly predictable and pleasurable, with the adults in his world responding to his cues in focused ways, his sense of trust is emerging, and he has learned which cues result in which responses from others. At 8 months, however, he is beginning to fret on separation from his parents and sometimes from Phyllis. He is especially wary of strangers and seems to need more close physical contact than usual. He also cries more frequently than he used to and is especially difficult in the mornings when Keisha and DeVon are scurrying to dress and leave for work.

Social Competence and Development

Infants are developing social competence as well as emotional competence during the first year of life. They seem to be programmed to interact with and obtain the attention of others who take care of them. In other words, infants are social beings primed for human relationships. They interact with those who consistently and sensitively take care of them with back and forth, turn-taking interactions. They show interest in peers, and they gaze at, touch, and take toys away from other infants in social settings. In the following section, two aspects of social behavior in infants are explored—social smiles and interactions with others.

Social Smiling and Facial Expressions

Authors Strathearn, Fonagy, and Read (2008) ask, "What's in a smile?" (p. 40). These authors wanted to know how a mother's brain responds to infant facial cues, so they showed 28 first-time mothers novel face images of their own 5- to 10-month-old infant and a matched infant that the mothers did not know. In response to their own babies' smiles (not sad faces), but not to a strange baby's smile, "an extensive brain network seems to be activated" (p. 40) that is likely to result in responses to their own infant. This interesting research paves the way for researchers to explore further the neural basis for mothering and fathering behaviors. Smiles and other facial expressions are one of the primary ways that infants communicate.

Smiles observed in the neonate are thought to be triggered by internal stimuli associated with the immature central nervous system. Researchers in the 1970s and 1980s discovered a developmental pattern for smiling (Campos & Stenberg, 1981; Emde & Harmon, 1972) that proceeds from internal stimuli to external elicitations as infants interact with their social environment. At first, infants smile at faces regardless of facial expression. Then, from 3 to 7 months, they begin to notice and respond to differences in facial expressions. This ability is a crucial developmental step toward reading others' emotions during social interactions.

Social smiles appear in the third month (Huang, Chen, Haiso, & Tsai, 2006). It is believed that when the infant can remember and recognize the face and perhaps the voice of the primary caregiver, smiling

Social smiling emerges as infants recognize the faces and voices of responsive caregivers.

becomes more social and is more likely to occur in the presence of a responsive, sensitive, affectionate person. As infants get older, they become more discerning in their smiling behavior, choosing to smile at familiar faces, voices, and interactions over unfamiliar ones. Yet the frequency of smiling increases with age. Cognition seems to play a major role in the emergence of smiling that is triggered by external stimuli.

Infant Interaction Patterns and Play Behaviors

In the first few weeks of life, the neonate's interaction patterns relate primarily to survival needs, signaling those needs to parents and caregivers through crying, squirming, and fretting. As the infant becomes more alert and begins to study the faces and responses of parents and to distinguish his or her primary caregivers from others, the infant's responsiveness increases. As experiences with others expand during the first year to include siblings, grandparents, nonparental caregivers, and in many cases other infants and young children, interactive strategies emerge and become more complex.

Emotional and Social Development of the Infant

Siblings may need to be coached on how to safely interact with an infant.

Infants' efforts to interact are characterized by gazing for some time at a face, reaching toward it, imitating facial expressions, and visually and auditorially tracking a person. Socially, the infant enjoys being gently tickled and jostled; responses include cooing, gurgling, babbling, kicking, and wiggling. Such behaviors elicit playfulness, attention, and encouragement from others.

Around age 5 months, interest in other children and siblings increases. The infant engages in prolonged onlooker behavior when placed in the same room with other children. Some consider this to be an early stage of social play development. Observing others is entertaining in and of itself, and infants derive considerable pleasure from simply being near the action.

Interest in siblings is particularly profound during the latter half of the first year. It is generally thought that playful and responsive siblings increase infant sociability. Some scholars believe that the infant's sociability itself influences the amount of attention received from siblings (Lamb, 1978). In any event, infants can be extremely interested in their siblings, following them around, imitating them, actively seeking their attention, and exploring their toys and other belongings. Siblings can be taught to respond to the infant in gentle and playful ways. Around 6 to 8 months, the infant will participate in games, such as peek-a-boo and pat-a-cake, and infant-initiated reciprocal activities, such as repeatedly dropping a toy to be retrieved, handed back to the infant, and dropped again.

How infants respond to other infants has been the focus of a number of studies (Sanefuji, Ohgami, & Hashiya, 2006). Infants will react to the sound of another infant's cry and show an awareness of the presence of another infant. At 6 months of age, the infant will reach toward another infant, watch intently, and perhaps smile and make friendly sounds. At this age, infants have been shown to respond positively to one another in groups of two and generally to find other infants intriguing. Sanefuji et al. (2006) discovered that 6-month-olds and 9-month-olds preferred to look at babies their own age. An infant may crawl into or fall on another infant in clumsy efforts to interact, yet infant–infant interaction is seen to be positive despite its awkwardness. See Maine's Infant-Toddler Early Learning Guidelines (http://www.maine.gov/education/fouryearold/documents/infantsandtoddlersguidelines.pdf) for an example of how teachers/caregivers can support peer interactions.

Infants with Special Needs

In the first year of life, infants are surprisingly vulnerable to emotional and social disabling conditions. Some disabilities can be successfully treated, some at least respond well to early intervention. In this section, we will describe failure to thrive, attachment disorders, and early warning signs of autism.

Attachment Disorders

Reactive attachment disorder (RAD) can occur when an infant or child is maltreated or raised by an ever-changing group of caregivers, as in an institutional setting. RAD may appear as a child who is *emotionally withdrawn and inhibited* or as a child who is *disinhibited and indiscriminately social*. The emotionally withdrawn child does not respond to attempts at engagement. The indiscriminate child will show inappropriate affection to strangers (Zeanah & Smyke, 2008). Another form of attachment disorder that focuses on the relationship is called a *secure base disorder* (Lieberman & Pawl, 1988). This occurs when the child has a discriminated relationship with an adult but the relationship is severely disturbed. These disorders may result in serious psychiatric disorders later in life, although interesting prevention and intervention programs reduce the rate of disorganized attachment through video feedback concerning interactions with the infants (Juffer, Bakermans-Kranenburg, & van Ijzendoorn, 2005).

Autism

In recent years, considerable gains have been made in early detection of autism. The Centers for Disease Control and Prevention states that an average of one in 110 children in the United States has an autism spectrum disorder (ASD). Children with ASD have significant social, communication, and behavioral challenges (Centers for Disease Control and Prevention (CDC), 2011a). The Autism Society (2012) identifies symptoms of ASD as the following:

- Does not babble or coo by 12 months
- Does not gesture (point, wave, grasp) by 12 months
- Does not say single words by 16 months
- Does not say two-word phrases on his or her own by 24 months
- Has any loss of any language or social skill at any age
- Little or no eye contact
- Lack of interest in peer relationships
- Lack of spontaneous or make-believe play
- Persistent fixation on parts of objects

Early identification is essential to improve the outcomes for children, and researchers are hard at work trying to identify ASD in the first and second years of life (Busco & Barclay, 2007; Landa, 2008). One test that seems to have predictive value is a failure of the infant to respond to his or her name by 12 months of age. Most infants will turn around when a speaker says the child's name behind the child's back (Nadig, Ozonoff, Young, Rozga, Sigman, & Rogers, 2007). Other researchers (Shumway & Wetherby, 2009) found that children at 18 to 24 months of age who were later diagnosed with ASD communicated at a significantly lower rate than children who were typically developing and children with developmental delays. This research on early identification is critically important because early intervention reduces the effects of ASD and leads to increased social interaction and communicative competence (Landa, 2008).

The cause of ASD is unknown; however, research is being conducted on genetic factors and environmental factors, including metabolic imbalances, viral infections, and exposure to environmental chemicals (Autism Society, 2012).

Factors Influencing Social and Emotional Development in Infants

From the foregoing, we are now able to list a number of factors that influence social and emotional development during infancy. They include the following.

Success and Quality of Attachments

Success and quality of attachment behaviors have been shown to affect the manner in which the brain processes social and emotional information and becomes wired for positive affect. This has long-term implications for social and emotional development and the development of social and moral competence during later childhood.

Essential Experiences

Essential experiences occurring during opportune periods of brain growth and neurological development are simple, inexpensive, and usually come naturally but can be enhanced through conscientious effort on the part of infant caregivers (see Box 6.2). Early experiences that promote optimal early brain growth and neurological development establish a biological buffer against later stresses and enhance the ability to learn.

Box 6.2 Essential Experiences in Infancy

Developmental Domain	Essential Experiences
Social attachment and the ability to cope with stress	Consistent care that is predictable, warm, and nurturing. Gentle, loving, and dependable relationships with primary caregivers. Immediate attention to physiological needs for nourishment, elimination, cleanliness, warmth, exercise, and symptoms of illness. Satisfying and enjoyable social interactions, playful experiences, and engaging infant toys.
Regulation and control of emotions	Empathic adult responses and unconditional acceptance of the child's unique characteristics and personality traits. Adult expectations that are appropriate for the age and the individual. Guidance that is instructive and helps the child to learn about emotions and that suggests appropriate ways and contexts for the expressions of emotions. Relationships that are psychologically safe, that is, free of threat, coercion, teasing, or physical or psychological neglect or abuse. Opportunities to engage in socially and emotionally satisfying play.

---

continued

Box 6.2 *continued*

Developmental Domain	Essential Experiences
Vision and auditory acuity	Regular vision and hearing examinations by health care professionals. Interesting and varied visual and auditory fields accompanied by verbal interactions that label and describe. Personal belongings, toys, and baby books that enlist interest in color, shape, texture, size, pattern, sound, pitch, rhythm, and movement. Experience with many forms of music, song, and dance.
Motor development and coordination	Opportunities and encouragement to use emerging muscle coordinations in safe and interesting surroundings. Supportive and positive interactions for effort. Play space, equipment, and toys that facilitate both large and small motor coordinations.
Vocabulary and language development	Rich verbal interactions that respond to the infant's efforts to communicate. Engaging the infant in talking, chanting, singing, sharing, picture books, telling stories, and sharing poems and rhymes. Toys and props that encourage pretend play. Conversations characterized by varied topics, interesting vocabulary, and engaging facial expressions and voice inflections. Interesting and enlightening firsthand experiences. Focused and responsive interactions in both native and second languages. Opportunities to converse and sing in either language.
Cognitive development	Toys and learning materials that encourage manipulations and constructions, dumping and pouring, pushing and pulling, dropping and retrieving, and hiding and finding. Toys and props that encourage and support pretend play. Social interactions that facilitate explorations and play. Baby books that introduce familiar objects, labels, and simple stories. Selected recorded music, or pleasing instrumental music and singing.

Sociocultural Experiences and Relationships Within the Microsystem

Because the first sphere of influence on child growth and development occurs within the microsystem that includes the infant, the family, and other caregivers, the child's cultural heritage comes strongly into play.

Cultural contexts influence social and emotional development through the perceptions, values, goals, and expectations associated with child rearing held by the child's particular cultural group. Expressions of emotions, expectations, and encouragement of infant responses; tolerance for infant behaviors; and perceived parental roles vary among and within cultures. Attitudes toward feeding, crying, holding, and clothing; the nature and amount of language to which the infant is exposed; and attitudes toward sickness and health, medicine and social services, religious belief systems, and many other issues provide the cultural contexts through which infant social and emotional development emerges (Bornstein & Cheah, 2004; Casper, Cooper, Finn, & Stott, 2003).

Socioeconomic status also plays a role in the family dynamics surrounding children and child rearing. Of particular concern are families of very low socioeconomic means. For some (but certainly not all) families of low socioeconomic status, survival needs can supersede the social and emotional needs of children and the physiological needs for adequate food, health care, and medication. The difficulties of surviving may be so overwhelming that they interfere with healthy parent–parent and parent–child interactions. Children in such families may be hungry and/or cold, suffer more illnesses, and even be neglected or abused. Parental efforts to provide food, clothing, shelter, and transportation for the family may be thwarted. Attending to the social and emotional needs of children is precluded by fatigue, frustration, anxiety, and sometimes resentment or a sense of futility. Personality development of infants in these situations can be at risk.

For such families, high-quality child care can provide a much-needed support system. The professionals involved may provide access to needed social and health care services, job counseling, and parenting education. Along with a full day of good-quality nurturing and socially and emotionally sound interactions, the infant is given an improved chance at healthy development. The relief from the stress associated with child rearing and the assurance that the infant is well cared for during a number of hours of the day (or night) should provide some relief for the parents in these potentially unhealthy situations.

Within the child's microsystem, the integrity of all of the entities within that system is important. Family health and freedom from discord or dysfunction, economic security, and overall psychological and social well-being are important contributors to infants' social and emotional development and its manifestation in later years.

Interactions That Promote Social Cognition

Social interactions that provide opportunities to observe, imitate, and reference positive and supportive behaviors of others in their family and cultural groups help infants to develop social cognition. Learning to read facial expressions, body language, and other cues in their social interactions helps infants to begin to notice and regulate their own feelings and behaviors. Positive and supportive social interactions with others promote self-awareness and positive feelings.

Goodness of Fit with Caregivers

The child's personality, which includes characteristic temperament, influences the frequency and types of interactions with others that the child receives. The extent to which adults who care for infants can respond appropriately to different temperament profiles determines the extent to which there can be goodness of fit between infant and caregiver, leading to positive personality outcomes. Because temperament is genetically influenced to some extent, it falls on the adult to make appropriate adaptations to the infant's expressions of need while encouraging and modeling socially acceptable behaviors and providing unconditional acceptance of the child's uniqueness.

Nonparental Child Care

Nonparental child care is a necessity for millions of U.S. families. It is estimated that each day, 12 million children spend a part or all of their day in nonparental care, and many of these children have been enrolled by 11 weeks of age (Children's Defense Fund, 2005). Because the early years of life are critical ones and because parents are increasingly depending on child care, it is essential that nonparental care be of the highest quality. High-quality child care is more expensive for infants and toddlers than for older children. Wise selection of child care for infants and toddlers involves seeking well-trained, knowledgeable, and sensitive adults who have the personal qualities a parent determines will be good for their child. Adult-to-child ratios in group programs serving infants and toddlers ideally should be no more than one adult to three children (ZERO TO THREE, 2012). The home or center should meet health and safety standards, and the daily routines should be warm, supportive, infant friendly, engaging, responsive, and satisfying. High-quality nonparental child care can be an enormous source of comfort to parents who need it. However, many families lack knowledge about how to choose high-quality child care, and the cost of such care often exceeds the family's ability to pay for it.

An increasing number of infants are receiving nonparental child care. Many enter nonparental child care arrangements as early as 6 weeks of age. These arrangements include care by a member of the child's extended family (grandparent, aunt, uncle, cousin, older sibling), neighbor, in-home babysitter, family day home, and child care centers. The quality of infant care programs is always a major concern, and parents need to be discerning in their choices of individuals who will care for their infants. Those who provide infant care have a moral and ethical responsibility to be knowledgeable about infants' needs and the critical nature of early neurological and physiological development and the essential experiences needed to foster optimal growth and development. Through state licensing laws and standards, accreditation standards of the National Association for the Education of Young Children, and standards such as those set by the joint efforts of the American Public Health Association and American Academy of Pediatrics, providers can assess their facilities, programs, and interactive environments and make continuous efforts to improve and enrich their programs so that parents who enlist their services can be confident in the choices they have made and the children they serve can benefit.

At the end of the 1980s, several researchers proposed that long hours (20 or more) in nonparental child care can impede the development of secure attachments between infants and their mothers (Belsky, 1988; Belsky & Rovine, 1988). Other studies did not support this perspective. More recently the longitudinal NICHD national study of more than 1,000 children has attempted to explore the complex variables that influence the outcomes for children who have or have not attended child care, as well as the influence of various types of child care (family, center, etc.), hours of use, and the quality of care (Belsky, 2006a, 2006b; NICHD Early Child Care Research Network, 1994, 1997, 1999, 2000, 2001, 2002a; Vandell, Belsky, Burchinal, Steinberg, Vandergrift, & the NICHD Early Child Care Research Network, 2010). When the children were 1 year of age, the researchers found the following: "Significant interaction effects revealed that infants were less likely to be secure when low maternal sensitivity/responsiveness was combined with poor quality child care, more than minimal amounts of child care, or more than one care arrangement" (NICHD Early Child Care Research Network, 1997, p. 68). At age 3, more hours of care predicted less maternal sensitivity and less child engagement; however, for children in care, higher-quality care predicted higher maternal sensitivity (NICHD Early Child Care Research Network, 1999). In other analyses, positive, responsive caregiving was found to be significantly related to outcomes for children (NICHD Early Child Care Research Network, 2001). The important points are that maternal sensitivity, the quality of child care, and the responsiveness of the caregiver are of utmost importance for positive outcomes for children. Quality of infant care programs is usually defined in terms of involved, sensitive, and developmentally appropriate caregiving; low infant-to-caregiver/teacher ratios; and small groups (the younger the child, the smaller the group should be).

Earlier in this chapter, we discussed the importance of the mother's and father's sensitivity and responsiveness to their infant's signals. It follows that the infant's nonparental caregivers must also be sensitive and responsive. Stressing the importance of high-quality child care programs, Raikes (1993) focused on how the amount of time an infant spends in the care of a "high-ability" teacher affects infant–teacher attachment. Because a secure attachment with a caring and nurturing caregiver can buffer the stress of parental separation, such an attachment can prove to be quite important. It is also thought that such child–caregiver attachments may even compensate for insecure parental attachments. Raikes's study was based on the following premises:

- High-ability caregivers/teachers support and facilitate the infant's developing sense of trust, predictability, and control.
- Experience with infants allows teachers to become fully acquainted with infants' personalities, that is, what upsets, excites, amuses, and bores infants.
- History in a relationship is required for secure attachments to develop.
- Infants' cognitive, social, emotional, and language development depend on quality relationships.

Raikes found that at least 9 months with the same caregiver/teacher provides the best opportunity for the infant to form a secure attachment. She proposed that rather than "promoting" infants at age 6 or 7 months, as is quite common in child care programs, a "new standard for excellence" in the field would keep infants and high-ability teachers together beyond 1 year of age.

Among the most important qualities of infant care in terms of healthy social and emotional development are *consistency, predictability, responsiveness,* and *continuity* of care. Although personalities and adult responses to infants vary greatly, infants need their different caregivers (mother, father, siblings, nonparent caregivers) to respond to their cues in relatively similar and nurturing ways (consistency). Also, the infant needs to trust that certain events will occur in reasonable order and with some predictability. Earliest experiences that are marked by predictability of routines, hunger satisfaction, comforting closeness, and reliable and prompt response to bids for attention and expression of need build a sense of trust that is critical to healthy social and emotional development.

Responsiveness refers to caregivers' knowledge of, sensitivity to, and acceptance of the infant's communication cues; individual temperament, rhythms, and interaction patterns; and other characteristics that make the infant unique. While many infants are cared for by nonparental caregivers during their parents' working hours, continuity of care is maintained when the infant experiences a minimum number of caregivers during the course of a day, week, and the first 3 years. Many child care centers today provide a **primary caregiver** to infants in an effort to reduce the number of adults to whom the infant must adapt. This practice enhances the infant's sense of order and facilitates opportunities to form positive relationships and, perhaps, healthy attachments between infant and nonparental caregivers.

primary caregiver
the person primarily responsible for the care and nurturing of a child

The vignettes about Angela and Jeremy earlier in this chapter reveal two very different situations in the quality and consistency of care each infant is receiving. Angela's routines are less predictable; so are her caregivers. After their move, the quality of care Angela is receiving is not optimal, and the opportunity for her to develop stable, trusting relationships is tenuous.

Jeremy, however, is experiencing daily schedules and routines that are neither rigid nor inflexible yet are predictable to him. His caregivers are limited in number, and each responds effectively to his cues for attention and other needs. In both cases, the infants are being provided with nonparental care while their parents are away at school or work.

Earlier in this chapter, the effects of cortisol on the child's reactions to the environment were discussed. The quality of child care affects whether the levels of cortisol increase or decrease during the day. If an environment is nonstressful, young children's cortisol levels typically decrease during the day. However, in child care centers where young children are not receiving individualized, focused attention from the caregivers, children are likely to experience increases in their cortisol levels during the day. This increase in cortisol levels indicates that the children are experiencing stress (Dettling, Gunnar, & Donzella, 1999). Young children need responsive environments to ensure that cortisol levels decrease during the day.

Young children who have irritable temperaments and poor self-regulation skills have the highest increase in cortisol in low-quality child care during the child care day (Dettling, Parker, Lane, Sebanc, & Gunnar, 2000). Children who withdraw from peers, are rejected by peers, or have challenging temperaments need focused, caring attention to develop positive relationships with others (Gunnar & Cheatham, 2003).

Communication between parents and caregivers is also important in nonparental child care. The accreditation standards of the National Association for the Education of Young Children and other standards set by funding entities encourage frequent interactions and mutual support. The amount of parent–caregiver interaction varies appreciably among child care settings, yet frequent and meaningful communication is predictive of the quality of the child care program.

Emotional and Social Development of the Infant

Figure 6.5
Characteristics
of High-Quality
Child Care

1. Trained, knowledgeable, nurturing, and committed caregivers
2. Safe, sanitary, healthy environment for infants and children
3. Low child–adult ratios, with emphasis on providing primary caregivers to individual infants over extended periods of time
4. Cognitively and linguistically enriching, socially stimulating, emotionally supportive environment and caregivers
5. Sensitive, appropriate, antibias interactions and activities for all children
6. Sensitivity to parental needs, goals, and concerns
7. Exceeds local and/or state licensing standards
8. Accredited through the National Association for the Education of Young Children or other nationally recognized accrediting agency

Parents need to assess their infant's responses and well-being on an ongoing basis. Are positive and nurturing relationships developing among all who share in the care and nurturing of the infant? Does the infant need the routine at home to be more like that of the infant care program, or vice versa? Is the infant overtired or overstimulated from the day's experiences? What is the parent doing to ensure consistency, predictability, responsiveness, and continuity in the infant's life at home? Are the infant's health and safety paramount to all caregivers? Is the infant exhibiting a basic sense of trust, secure attachments, healthy emotional development, and enjoyment of parents and other caregivers? Qualities to assess in seeking appropriate infant care are listed in Figure 6.5. Parents should make informed choices for themselves and their infants, choosing according to the infant's unique developmental needs and the caregiver's ability to meet those needs adequately and appropriately.

Overall Health, Safety, and Freedom from Stress

Certainly, we can assume that healthy infants are better equipped to deal emotionally and socially with their environments than less healthy infants. Obstetric and pediatric supervision during prenatal development and infancy provides preventive and corrective measures to facilitate healthy development. Proper nutrition and socially and emotionally satisfying interactions are essential to this health.

Role of the Early Childhood Professional

Promoting Social and Emotional Development in Infants

1. Provide warm, loving, supportive, predictable, consistent, and continuous care.
2. Respond readily to the infant's cues for food, comfort, rest, play, and social interaction.
3. Recognize that crying is the infant's way of communicating needs.
4. Be aware of sensitive periods relating to attachment behaviors, separation, and stranger anxiety, and respond in supportive/empathic ways.
5. Be aware of windows of opportunity and the need for certain essential experiences to promote optimal brain growth and neurological development.
6. Provide responsive and satisfying social and emotional interactions.

7. Respond readily to the infant's playful overtures.

8. Recognize and accept the infant's unique temperament and ways of interacting with others.

9. Recognize and respond in accepting and supporting ways to the infant's various emotional displays.

10. Recognize children's and families' behavior as adaptive to their environment. Although, their behavior may not be adaptive in the long run, the personal and physical environment for the child and family may need to change in order for them to change their behavior (ecological view).

Key Terms

attachment
cortisol
fixation

primary caregiver
reciprocal determinism
separation anxiety

social cognition
socialization
stranger anxiety

Review Strategies and Activities

1. Review the key terms independently or with a classmate.

2. Discuss with classmates the differences in the early lives of Angela and Jeremy. In terms of social and emotional development, what kinds of experiences are these infants having? What are the characteristics of the environmental contexts in which each child is developing? What suggestions can you make to enhance the social and emotional development of each child?

3. Review the qualities of a good infant care center. Visit a NAEYC-accredited or other high-quality child care center in which infants are enrolled.

   a. Describe the frequency and nature of the interactions between adults and infants:

      i. What strategies do infants use to summon attention to their needs?
      ii. What self-comforting strategies do infants employ?
      iii. What adult behaviors elicit and help infants develop a sense of trust?
      iv. How do adults respond to infants who are difficult to console?
      v. How is infant attachment behavior displayed?
      vi. How is playfulness displayed? Encouraged?

   b. Observe the infants' reactions to other infants. What behaviors do they exhibit?

   c. How did the infants respond to you as a stranger? Did younger infants respond differently than older infants?

   d. How are parents' needs and concerns addressed?

   e. How do the early childhood professionals nurture the social and emotional development of developmentally challenged infants?

4. Interview a parent to discuss how she or he juggles work and parenting. Does this person feel generally positive about his or her lifestyle? What has this parent found to be challenging? Most satisfying?

5. How might parents and/or primary caregivers ensure that infants develop a healthy sense of trust? Develop a list of dos and don'ts.

Further Readings

Honig, A. S. (2010). Keys to quality infant care: Nurturing every baby's life journey. *Young Children, 65*(5), 40–47.

Newton, E. K., & Thompson, R. A. (2010). Parents' views of early social and emotional development. More and less than meets the eye. *ZERO TO THREE, 30*(4), 10–16.

Pizzolongo, P. J., & Hunter, A. (2011). I am safe and secure. Promoting resilience in young children. *Young Children,* 67–69.

Wittmer, D. S. (2008). *Focusing on peers: The importance of relationships in the early years.* Washington, DC: ZERO TO THREE Press.

Other Resources

National Scientific Council on the Developing Child, http://developingchild.harvard.edu/index.php/activities/council.

Working paper #1: *Young children develop in an environment of relationships*

New research shows the critical impact of a child's "environment of relationships" on developing brain architecture during the first months and years of life. This report summarizes the most current and reliable scientific research on the impact of relationships on all aspects of a child's development and identifies ways to strengthen policies that affect those relationships in the early childhood years.

Working paper #2: *Children's Emotional Development Is Built into the Architecture of Their Brains*

This report presents an overview of the scientific research on how a child's capacity to regulate emotions develops in a complex interaction with his or her environment and ongoing cognitive, motor, and social development. It then discusses the implications of this research for policies affecting young children, their caregivers, and service providers.

Working paper #4: *Early Exposure to Toxic Substances Damages Brain Architecture*

This report summarizes the complex scientific research on which toxins present the greatest risk at various stages of brain development, addresses popular misconceptions about the relative risk and safety of some common substances, and suggests policies that can help reduce the enormous human and economic costs of exposure to toxins during development

Center on the Developing Child, http://developingchild.harvard.edu/index.php/activities/council.

Brain Hero: This three-minute video adapts the visual sensibility of interactive game models to a video format.

ResilienceNet, http://resilnet.uiuc.edu.

chapter 7

Cognitive, Language, and Literacy Development of the Infant

Nature has plainly not entrusted the determination of our intellectual capacities to the blind fate of a gene or genes: she gave us parents, learning, language, culture and education to program ourselves with.

—Matt Ridley

After studying this chapter, you will demonstrate comprehension by:

▶ describing aspects of the neurobiology of cognitive, language, and literacy development

▶ recognizing theoretical perspectives on cognitive, language, and literacy development;

▶ describing cognitive development during the infant's first year;

▶ describing language development during the infant's first year;

▶ describing earliest literacy behaviors;

▶ relating cognitive, language, and literacy development to other developmental domains;

▶ identifying major factors influencing cognitive, language, and literacy development during infancy; and

▶ suggesting strategies for promoting and enhancing cognitive, language, and literacy development in infancy.

Cognitive development in the first year of life has several components. First, the processes of learning, often referred to as approaches to learning, are established in the brain in the first three years of life. These include curiosity, memory, exploration, constructing knowledge, solving problems, persistence, imitation, and the ability to focus attention. They learn concepts such as cause and effect, **object permanence,** use of tools, use of space, language, and early literacy. Infants learn how to be partners in relationships, how to be members of their families, and the values and rules of their culture. The development of language and other communication strategies and the early beginnings of literacy are among the most important accomplishments of the first year.

cognitive development
the aspect of development that involves thinking, problem solving, intelligence, and language

object permanence
the realization that objects and people continue to exist even though they may not be visible or detected through other senses

Neurobiology of Cognitive, Language, and Literacy Development

In the first year of life, infants are creating the processes that will build the foundation for later **executive function.** These processes include **working memory, inhibitory control,** and **cognitive flexibility** (National Scientific Council on the Developing Child, Center on the Developing Child, 2011a). (See Box 7.1.)

executive function
the brain's ability to plan, stay focused, process information, and filter out distractions

working memory
aspect of memory that refers to the capacity to remember and manipulate information

---

Box 7.1 Executive Functions of the Brain

These early foundations of executive function carry three important messages about development:

"First, executive function skills are crucial building blocks for the early development of both cognitive and social capacities. Second, both normative differences in the nature and pace of individual developmental trajectories and the impacts of significant adversity will affect how the development of executive functioning will unfold for any given child. third, several interventions focused on supporting the development of specific executive function skills have demonstrated at least short-term effectiveness, with evidence also emerging that they may have impacts on other aspects of learning as well" (National Scientific Council on the Developing Child, Center on the Developing Child, 2011a, p. 5).

---

inhibitory control
the skills of paying attention, filtering out distractions, and regulating thoughts and actions

cognitive flexibility
the ability to be mentally flexible and adjust to new situations

Figure 7.1 Parts of the Brain Related to Executive Functioning

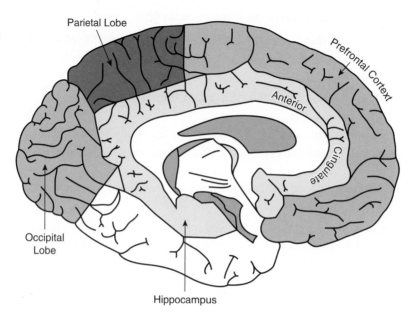

Executive function skills (staying focused and being able to control impulsive behaviors) are foundational to both learning and social relationships. The gradual acquisition of these skills corresponds to the growth of the prefrontal cortex, the anterior cingulate, the parietal cortex, and the hippocampus (see Figure 7.1). As these regions mature, they interconnect the areas of executive function with the areas that respond to threat and stress. This underscores the likelihood that strong emotions can harm higher functioning but, also, that higher brain functioning may mitigate events that stress the brain.

The rapid brain growth and neurological development in very young children include a process known as myelination in which fatty tissue forms around the nerve cells, facilitating the transportation of impulses along the neurons. Rapid growth and myelination in the brain coincide with the development of the auditory system, rapid language development, and increased processing of visual, spatial, and temporal (or time) information. Simultaneously, these increased connections promote better processing of information, and their presence in the speech center of the brain facilitates the development of symbolization and communication. Gains in short-term memory and small motor skills are also attributed to the rapid myelination occurring at the ages of 4 and 5.

Also, as we discussed in earlier chapters, the structure and functions of the neurological system are determined by the interplay of experience and an individual's genetically programmed growth and development. In terms of cognitive, language, and literacy development, of particular importance in earliest brain growth and neurological development is the nature or quality of the child's first interpersonal relationships. As Siegel (1999) stated, "human connections shape the neural connections from which the mind emerges" (p. 2).

How do these and similar studies influence our thinking about the human brain? Obviously, ethics and common sense prevent the types of environmental controls and anatomical examinations of humans that are possible with laboratory rats. Nevertheless, scientific examination of donated human brain specimens during the early decades of brain research corroborated findings such as those described earlier; contemporary technological techniques for examining neurological activity support these early findings (de Zubicaray, 2006) In short, scholars can now assert that enriched and mentally stimulating environments increase the growth and branching of dendrites and thicken the human cortex. (See Figure 7.1.) Further, scientists can trace the emergence of various types of development, vision, hearing, motor controls, language, and so on through periods of sensitive and rapid growth, delineating certain periods in growth and development when selected experiences have their greater impact. Although brain enrichment is possible throughout the life span, childhood and adolescence appear to be the optimal period for neural development—a time when **neural connectivity** and **pruning** and refining are most prolific.

An Overview of Theories on Cognitive, Language, and Literacy Development

Understanding how we learn and communicate has always fascinated philosophers and scientists. At the extremes were beliefs that the mechanisms for learning are entirely within the person (the nature or nativist argument) or that a person's knowledge comes directly from the environment (the nurture or empiricist position). Today we know that people are born with some mechanisms for learning *and* that the act of learning is highly dependent upon the environment.

Cognitive Theory

The most familiar theory of cognitive development is Jean Piaget's **constructivism** (1952). Foremost among Piaget's contributions to early childhood education is the idea that children actively construct knowledge from their environment and meaning from their experience. He also recognized that the thinking processes and problem-solving abilities of infants and young children are quite different from those of older children and adults. Piaget identified six substages of sensorimotor development in children birth to 24 months. These stages are described in Table 7.1.

You may remember from Chapter 1 that accommodation is a process by which a previous schema (experience or concept) is modified to include or adapt to a new experience. For example, the breast-fed infant who is changed from breastfeeding (existing schema) to bottle-feeding (new experience) must alter sucking behaviors to succeed with the new experience, the bottle. This altered sucking behavior is an example of accommodation to a new environmental demand. Each assimilation of an experience is complemented by accommodation to that experience, and this leads to **adaptation.** Adaptation to an event or experience brings about equilibrium between the individual and her or his environment.

To some degree, all learning theorists today believe that infants and toddlers actively construct knowledge from their environment and meaning from their experiences. For

neural connectivity
the organized connections that occur between neurons (nerve cells) in the brain

pruning
the reduction of neurons and synapses in the brain which leaves a more efficient system

constructivism
a term used to describe learning as an active process of creating meaning

adaptation
the process by which one adjusts to changes in the environment

The infant's sensory capabilities are remarkably operative at birth.

Table 7.1 Piaget's Sensorimotor Substages

Stages/Ages	Characteristics	Implications for Interactions and Education
1. Reflexive (0–1 month)	Reflexes that have been dominant since birth are modified as the infant experiences an increasing variety of sensory stimuli and interactions with the environment. Piaget believed that the infant constructs schemata from the sensory experiences of these first weeks.	Interact in ways that stimulate the infant's sense of touch, taste, sight, sound, and smell. The human face or voice, the positioning in the mother's arms before breastfeeding, and the sounds and rhythms of the household are sources of early schemata.
2. Primary circular reactions (1–4 months)	Repeats actions that previously happened by chance; reflexes become more coordinated. At this time, infant reactions center on bodily responses. For example, the infant can now purposefully bring the thumb to the mouth to suck. During this stage, the infant engages in other purposeful motor activity. This period is called primary because of its focus on bodily responses; it is called circular because the infant repeats the activities over and over again. This repetition may be the first indication of infant memory.	Provide sensory-stimulating toys and objects such as rattles, mobiles, baby books, recorded familiar voices, or pleasing music. Engage in warm, affectionate turn-taking with the infant, e.g., infant coos, you coo and smile while looking at the infant's eyes. Wait for the infant to take a turn.
3. Secondary circular reactions (4–10 months)	The infant intentionally repeats behaviors or pleasurable actions; the notion of object permanence emerges. It is called secondary circular because it involves the infant's growing awareness of objects and events outside his or her body. Through chance events, the infant learns that he or she can make things happen to external objects. For example, the infant hits the bath water, and a big splash results. This novel experience generates interest and a desire to repeat it; and repeat it the infant does, motivated by both curiosity and pleasure.	Provide clean, safe objects and toys; play hide and seek; continue to talk or sing when moving out of the child's auditory or visual field; play repetitive games like peekaboo.
4. Coordination of secondary schemes (10–12 months)	Applies previously learned behaviors and activities to new situations; imitative behaviors emerge. This is the period in which the infant's intentional behaviors are clearly evident. Imitative behaviors signal the infant's growing ability to learn through observing the behavior of others. Play becomes more clearly differentiated from other means/end activities and is enjoyed for its own sake.	Provide familiar toys, dolls, stuffed animals, blankets, and clothing; encourage imitation, provide encouraging verbal feedback.
5. Tertiary circular reactions (12–18 months)	Cause-and-effect discoveries; seeks proximity and playful interactions with persons to whom attachments have been formed; repeats novel experiences.	Respond positively to interaction overtures; provide toys that stack, nest, roll, open, close, push, pull, and are easily manipulated; talk, label, and pretend with child.
6. Symbolic representation (18 months–2 years)	Applies learned skills to new situations; begins to think before acting; applies learned experiments with new uses for familiar objects; represents objects or events through imagery.	Provide verbal labels for objects and events; encourage and provide props for pretend play; provide social interaction with other children; encourage and provide props and safe equipment for large motor activity.

example, Harlan, a 2-year-old, watched his dad throw a ball across the yard. Harlan picked up a ball, too, and tried to throw it as hard as he could. He ran and picked up the ball and tried again. Each time, through his actively constructing knowledge about the ball, how balls travel through space, and watching the ball fall, he improved his skill of throwing. This is an example of how young children are constantly processing information and adjusting their behavior accordingly. However, theorists differ signficantly concerning what children bring to the learning experience and how they integrate the information. Core knowledge theorists, who were introduced in Chapter 1, think that babies are born with an inclination to learn the things that support survival.

Core Knowledge. The theory of core knowledge asserts that it would be impractical, in terms of evolution, to be born having to discover all of the information one needs in the world. It would be equally impractical to be born with a set of knowledge that was developed in prehistoric times and of no relevance to life in the 21st century. It would be very practical, on the other hand, to have an internal system (or systems) prepared to learn those things that are most important for survival. That system (or systems) would need to be flexible, to be able to learn different things as cultures change over time. Some theorists suggest that there is one cognitive system that allows the human being to learn anything; others believe there are thousands of systems, each one specific to a certain kind of information.

Leading cognitive researcher Elizabeth Spelke (Spelke, 2000, 2003) suggests in her core knowledge theory that evolution has provided human beings with a core set of learning systems that would be most important for survival but are flexible enough to respond to new information. These core systems of knowledge predispose human infants to attend to certain kinds of information and organize them with meaning. As discussed in Chapter 1, four of the systems are Object Representation, Agents, Number, and Geometry.

Human infants are able to create mental representations of objects when the objects display the following spatial-temporal principles: "cohesion (objects move as connected and bounded wholes), continuity (objects move on connected, unobstructed paths), and contact (objects do not interact at a distance)" (Spelke & Kinzler, 2007, p. 90). If these principles are inborn, the infant is able to discern the boundaries of objects such as her blanket, complete shapes of objects that move partially into or out of view such as his mommy's face, and predict where moving objects will stop. Infants are able to represent only three sets at a time.

Agents (e.g., people) are recognized as using intentional actions to achieve goals. Actions are efficient, contingent, and reciprocal. If agents have faces, an infant uses her gaze to interpret, for example, her father's intent. In addition, infants do not recognize inanimate objects as having goals and will only imitate animate objects.

The core number system has its own unique characteristics. Number representations are imprecise and become

As infants gain greater mobility through crawling, pulling themselves up, and walking, they make surprising discoveries.

Cognitive, Language, and Literacy Development of the Infant

more imprecise as the numbers grow larger. Number representations are abstract and apply to sounds, objects, or sequences of actions. Finally, number representations are subject to addition and subtraction. Young infants can discriminate between sets of objects at a ratio of 2:1.

The geometric system is used to orient oneself in space. The child of 4 is able to make use of distance, angles, and direction to create a mental representation of the surface layout of his environment (Spelke, Ah Lee, & Izard, 2010). This will be discussed further in Chapter 13.

Neoconstructivism. Some contemporary scholars of cognitive theory (neo-Piagetians, as they are often called) have challenged a number of Piaget's cognitive development assumptions and "consider Piaget in a new light." For instance, Bower (1982) and Wishart and Bower (1985) challenge the notion of object permanence in the infant at 6 to 8 months. Although Piaget proposed that an infant will not search for an object hidden behind a screen because the infant believes that the object no longer exists, Bower believes immature space perception may explain the infant's failure to search. He suggested that from the infant's point of view, the screen has replaced the hidden object, and two objects cannot occupy the same space. Bower believes that Piaget underestimated what infants come to know about objects and that their failure to search for or locate a hidden object may represent a lack of spatial knowledge rather than a lack of knowledge of object permanence. Bower suggests that infants as young as 5 months old will not only anticipate the reappearance of an object that has been moved to a position behind the screen, but will attempt to look for it when a different object or no object appears when the screen is removed.

Other researchers challenged Piaget's notion that infants must do something to or with objects or people in their environment for cognitive development to occur. These scholars suggested that there may be other pathways through which cognition emerges. Studying infants and young children with impaired vision, hearing, and/or motor abilities, they demonstrated that cognitive development proceeds nonetheless (Bebko, Burke, Craven, & Sarlo, 1992; Furth, 1992a, 1992b, 1992c; Mandler, 1990, 1992). The belief is that infants, through their perceptual abilities and mental imagery, are able to form concepts with and without direct interaction with objects or people and can do so earlier than Piaget proposed.

Neoconstructivism represents a new science of cognitive development (Johnson, 2010). While believing that Piaget's fundamental ideas were sound—"a biologically prepared mind interacts in biologically evolved ways with an expectable environment that nevertheless includes significant variation" (Johnson, 2010, p. vi)—neoconstructivists attempt to incorporate all of the exciting research on the processes of how children learn, including how environmental input is integral to cognitive development.

Social Cognitive/Learning Theory. This theory emphasizes the importance of role models for learning. Social cognitive/learning theory (Bandura, 1977, 1997; Bandura & Walters, 1963), which is an outgrowth of the behaviorist philosophy, places more emphasis on cognitive processing and emphasizes the role of imitation in cognitive development. Many behaviors are learned simply by watching others, and much learning occurs in social situations. It is believed that very young infants can imitate the facial expressions of others (Meltzoff, 1989, 1995) and that infants may have an innate ability to compare information received through different modalities, such as vision, hearing, and their body movements. They then use this information to coordinate imitative behaviors on the basis of actions observed in others.

Contextual Theory

Dynamic Systems Theory. Edward Tronick (2007) combines Bruner's (1983) view of humans as meaning makers with dynamic systems theory. Tronick sees humans as purposeful and

> ... as complex systems, as heirarchical multileveled psychobiological systems that constantly work to gain energy and meaningful information to make sense of their place in the world. (p. 2)

Young children are "meaning makers," as you will see in the cognitive and language sections that follow, who constantly strive to understand such things as cause/effect and how to communicate with others.

Summary of Theories on Cognitive Development

The technology that allows us to watch the brain in action is driving the development of current theories. Although the cognitive theories emphasize brain structures that organize young children's thinking (internal mechanisms) and the contextualists emphasize the importance of the environment, both camps further our understanding of early learning.

Increasingly, our theories are attempts to bring together scientific data in understandable ways that would account for the learning and development we observe. There are four main points on which current theorists would generally agree:

1. Skill and knowledge are actively constructed by the infant and toddler through observations and interactions with the environment.
2. The healthy brain develops within a context of loving, responsive, ongoing relationships.
3. The brain is somehow predisposed to make sense of the world.
4. Development is dynamic rather than continuous.

Language Development Theories

Neoconstructivist. Kuhl (2000) represents the neoconstructivist view of language acquisition. In an article titled "A New View of Language Acquisition," she describes how infants have the cognitive abilities to pick up the statistical properties of speech when they are exposed to language.

> At the forefront of debates on language are new data demonstrating infants' early acquisition of information about their native language. The data show that infants perceptually "map" critical aspects of ambient language in the first year of life before they can speak. Statistical properties of speech are picked up through exposure to ambient language. Moreover, linguistic experience alters infants' perception of speech, warping perception in the service of language. Infants' strategies are unexpected and unpredicted by historical views. A new theoretical position has emerged... (p. 11850)

Another prominent theory proposed an inborn capacity for learning language called the **language acquisition device (LAD)** (Chomsky, 1968, 1980, 1993). The LAD is

language acquisition device (LAD)
an innate mental mechanism some theorists believe makes language development possible

described as a set of innate skills that enable children to infer phoneme patterns, word meanings, and syntax from the language they hear. This skill facilitates the child's attempts to communicate.

These nativist and instinctual perspectives assume a biological basis for human language; one that supposes that language emerges because there are specialized structures in the brain and neurological systems of humans. Studies of language development in children with hearing loss, of children who have suffered brain injury to the left-brain hemisphere, and of people who attempt to acquire a new language after early childhood have demonstrated that there is a critical period or window of opportunity for language development. For example, when infants who are deaf are raised by parents who communicate through signing, the infants learn sign language in the same manner and with the same ease as hearing infants learn spoken language and come to use this form of communication quite competently as they get older. Deprived of opportunities to learn sign language from infancy onward, deaf children struggle as they get older to gain skill in signing and seldom truly master this form of communication (Yoshinaga-Itano, 1999, 2000, 2001). Because of the plasticity of the language-learning circuitry in the brain, children with left-brain hemispheric injury or removal recover language to a greater extent than do adults with comparable injury. For the same reason, younger immigrants acquire a new language, including accents and inflections, more completely and accurately than do their teenage or adult relatives. Between birth and age 6 appears to be a biological prime time for the acquisition of language.

Contextual Theory. Contextual theorists propose that there is not one true reality. As discussed in Chapter 1, these theories pay more attention to the influence of the environment, culture, time, space, and system on child and family development rather than the brain's built-in mechanisms. Contextual theory has application to cognitive and language development.

The social interactionist point of view emphasizes the importance of the infant's interactions with caregivers in which vocal exchanges occur (Bruner, 1983; Golinkoff, 1983). These researchers recognize the communicative aspects of these early vocal exchanges and the emotional satisfaction that accrues from successful exchanges between caregiver and child. Indeed, language in humans is dependent on having other humans with whom to communicate. Bruner (1983), in response to Chomsky's LAD, proposed that children must have a LASS—a Language Acquisition Support System.

A social interactionist view of language development takes into consideration the interplay of many factors, including the biological underpinnings of language, maturational patterns, cognitive development and the role of imitation, teaching and learning, and the necessity of social interaction. Through an interactive process, these factors play off one another in ways that encourage or impede language development.

A sociocultural view of language development (Vygotsky, 1978) emphasizes how social interaction within cultural groups plays a crucial role in language development. Young children are socialized into a community of language learners through language dialogue with adults or peers who are more capable language speakers. Children learn how to speak, when to speak, and how to use different forms of language (e.g., in church and at home) within a cultural context.

Still another contextual theoretical perspective that is important in the discussion of cognitive, language, and literacy development is one in which development and social

Box 7.2 Diversity Perspectives: Babies from Different Cultures

In the 2010 movie *Babies,* four babies from very different cultures are followed from birth to their first birthdays. The children are from Mongolia, Namibia, Japan, and the United States. Without narration, the video demonstrates the parent–infant relationships, the environment, and how parents in these different cultures care for and educate their babies. Play materials vary from glossy, manufactured learning toys to sticks, rocks, and dirt. The most striking similarity, however, is how the babies are always near their parents, receiving the touch or word that keeps them safe and interested in their explorations.

interaction are viewed as reciprocal influences on one another. Stated quite simply, this theory supposes that the growing and developing child influences and is influenced by his or her environmental context. Bioecological systems theory (Bronfenbrenner, 1977, 1986; Bronfenbrenner & Ceci, 1994) describes cognitive (and language and literacy) development as being integral to the social and cultural context in which an individual grows and develops. Development in all domains (physical/motor, psychosocial, and cognitive, language, and literacy) is viewed as an interactive process between the individual and a variety of social and cultural influences. Cognition continually changes as learning contexts change. For an example of cultural variations, see Box 7.2.

Summary of Theories

Cognition, language, and literacy, then, are determined by many factors, including observation and imitation, but also opportunities to explore and discover in a variety of situations, both independently and in the company of others as well as through coaching and direct instruction. From this perspective, development may or may not proceed in all domains simultaneously. The degree of influence and rate of development in specific developmental domains depend on the context and nature of the environmental input and the nature and responses of the learner at a given point in time. The following vignettes also illustrate this interactive process.

Jeremy, lying in his crib, is intently watching a yellow soft-sculpture airplane dangling from the mobile above him. He kicks and squeals with glee, then stops and stares at the object bouncing above his crib. Lying still, he seems to notice that the object stopped swinging; when he kicks some more, the object begins to swing again. The entertainment is quite exhilarating and is repeated several times.

Phyllis, Jeremy's babysitter, noticing his playfulness and his interest in the mobile, recognizes that Jeremy has discovered the link between his own bodily movements and the subsequent jiggling of the colorful airplane. She approaches, detaches the airplane from the mobile, and holds it within Jeremy's reach while saying to him, "Do you want to hold the airplane? I think you like this bright toy, Jeremy."

(continued)

Cognitive, Language, and Literacy Development of the Infant

Distracted from his previous activity, Jeremy's kicking subsides. He stares at the soft toy, looks at Phyllis (a bit puzzled), then back again at the toy. His eyes then travel to the mobile above where the airplane had been, then back to Phyllis and the toy in her hand. He reaches for the airplane, grasps it and brings it to his mouth momentarily, then drops it, only to return to the original activity of kicking and watching the mobile. Somehow it isn't the same, and he immediately tires of the effort and begins to fret.

Jeremy is now 6 months old. His motor activity that caused the mobile to bounce and swing was entertaining in and of itself. Jeremy was discovering that his actions could make the airplane wiggle. However, playful infants attract their caregivers' attention. Phyllis could not resist getting in on the action, but when she did, Jeremy was presented with a choice that was perhaps difficult for him to make: reach for and hold the toy airplane, interact with Phyllis, or continue the pleasurable activity of kicking and watching the mobile move.

Although her timing and assumption about what would please Jeremy at that moment missed the mark, Phyllis was supporting Jeremy's cognitive development by noticing what held his attention, naming the object, and bringing it within his reach. Observant adults soon learn to synchronize their interactions with the infant's, recognizing when to enter an activity and when to leave the infant to her or his own explorations.

Angela, now 8 months old, is in her high chair. She still has some difficulty sitting alone and slides under the tray, only to be restrained by the high-chair safety strap between her legs. Cracker crumbs are in her hair, on her eyebrows, between her fingers, clinging to her clothing, and sprinkled about on the floor on both sides of her chair. James and Cheryl, seated at the table nearby, have just finished their take-out burgers and are arguing over James's dating activities. It seems that James is seeing some other girls now, and Cheryl is very unhappy about it.

Angela slides under the high-chair tray and frets in discomfort. James offhandedly pulls her back into a seated position and continues his emotional discussion with Cheryl. Angela begins to cry intermittently. Cheryl places another cracker on the high-chair tray while continuing her emotional conversation with James. Quieted momentarily, Angela bangs the cracker on the tray, holds what is left of it over the floor, then releases her grasp and watches the cracker fall to the floor. Sliding under her tray again, she begins to cry, this time more forcefully. Cheryl pulls her back to a seated position, but this does not comfort or quiet her. James, tired of arguing and a bit distracted by the baby's crying, decides to leave.

Frustrated and angry, Cheryl picks up Angela, scolds her about the mess, takes her to the sink to wash her face and hands, and then puts her in her playpen, even though Angela is fretful. Unable to respond to Angela's needs—her own are overwhelming at this time—Cheryl turns on the TV, props her feet up on the coffee table, and lapses into sadness.

Unable to elicit her mother's attention, Angela cries awhile longer. Defeated and tired, she picks up her blanket, puts her thumb in her mouth, watches her mother, and listens to the sounds of the television set until she finally falls asleep.

Angela's predicament involves social and emotional, physical/motor, and cognitive aspects. At 8 months old, what are Angela's cognitive needs? How would you characterize the social and emotional dynamics in this setting between Angela and her caregivers? What does her behavior suggest about her physical/motor development and needs?

Are any apparent constraints to her cognitive development illustrated in this vignette? What alternative activities might be provided for Angela that might engage her attention and contribute to her cognitive development while the adults continue their discussion? What theoretical perspectives can you apply to each of these two scenarios? Let's continue to explore these and other facets of cognitive development.

During the first year, infants become aware of their own bodies, noticing and gazing at their hands; clasping them together; sucking on fists and fingers; and playing with feet, toes, and genitalia. Emerging coordination of motor skills leads infants to use their bodies and their abilities to explore, experience, and discover. Now there are infinite avenues for learning. The ability to grasp and let go leads to handling, mouthing, and experimenting with a variety of playthings. As the infant manipulates a variety of objects, information about his or her surroundings is being mentally constructed. The ability to sit, pull to a standing position, cruise around furniture, and return to a seated position provides variety to the infant's sensory experiences and increases the sources of information. The mobility provided by crawling and walking further extends the infant's explorations, experiences, and discoveries.

Cognitive Competence and Development

A 1-year-old fumbling to fit a plastic cylinder into a shape box may not strike you as the next Einstein, but in this first year, his brain has created the foundation with which he will approach the lifetime of learning ahead of him. Approaches to learning is the term used to describe the mental qualities one brings to gathering and storing new information. In the first year of life, infants are developing the capacity for curiosity, memory, exploration, constructing knowledge, solving problems, persistence, imitation, and the ability to focus attention. These skills allow the infant to confidently engage with the people and things in his world and, through that engagement, learn about himself, others, relationships, physical properties of objects such as spatial relationships, and cause and effect. The infant's ability to master these skills is largely dependent on the presence of a responsive, invested adult. It is the adult who helps the infant stay focused, to feel safe exploring, and to manage frustration when a first or second try doesn't bring about the desired results.

In this section, we'll describe desired approaches to learning and some of the concepts infants learn in the first 12 months. These include cause and effect, object permanence, use of tools, use of space, language, early literacy, and basic math and science. Infants also learn how to be partners in relationships, members of their families, and the values and rules of their culture.

Playful interactions contribute to early cognitive development.

Cognitive, Language, and Literacy Development of the Infant

Approaches to Learning

The earliest learning experience is within the parent/caregiver–infant relationship. As the adult helps the infant to be calm and alert for short periods of time, the infant is developing the ability to pay attention to one thing (usually the adult's face) while filtering out the massive amounts of visual and auditory information in the environment. Without the foundational ability to pay focused attention, learning would be impossible. Current researchers describe early learning as computational, meaning that infants pick up on regularities of patterns in their environment and attend to them—before they can even handle objects or use language (Meltzoff, Kuhl, Movellan & Sejnowski, 2009).

Social cues from adults help infants know to what they should attend. The attitudes of adults toward the infant's actions tell the infant if exploration and curiousity are encouraged. Depending on how the adult plays with the child, the adult can support exploration and curiosity, can help the child persist with a task that is frustrating and solve the problems posed, as well as provide predictable routines and interactions that promote memory.

Oregon's Early Learning Foundations that emphasize attitudes and skills considered important for birth to age 3 children's development in the approaches to learning area can be found at www.ode.state.or.us/search/page/?id=1352.

Imitation

Infants learn from adults in many ways, primarily through imitation. When an infant observes an adult's behavior, the area of the infant's brain that is watching (perceiving) the action activates, but so does the responding part of her brain that would activate if she were the one performing the action (Hari & Kujala, 2009). For example, within an hour of birth, a newborn will imitate an adult opening his mouth or sticking out his tongue. This is before the infant has ever seen her own face in a mirror or has any reason to know she is of the same species (Meltzoff & Moore, 1977). It is because the perceptual and action areas of the brain overlap.

Shared Attention

Shared attention is another powerful learning mechanism in the first year. "Joint attention (shared attention) is when an individual is engaged with a social partner around an event or object" (Röska-Hardy & Neumann-Held, 2010, p. 89). It is usually characterized by a shifting of eye gaze between the object and the social partner. Infants are able to follow the adult's eye gaze between 3 and 6 months. Between 6 and 9 months, the infant can initiate the shared attention by pointing and vocalizing to the adult. At that time, the adult can also use pointing or language to draw the child's attention to an event or object. As in imitation, this form of social learning is an efficient way to transmit language, information, and culture.

Cause and Effect

In infancy, we tend to think of mastering cause and effect as the moment when the child learns that flipping the light switch turns the light on and off or the various knobs make the busy box lids fly up. In fact, determining cause and effect requires the infant to sort out and segment a continuous stream of observed actions into meaningful pieces and then to determine which of those actions might have made other actions occur (Buchsbaum, Griffiths, Gopnik, & Baldwin, 2009). Researchers describe this sorting out as computational, attending to patterns that recur and seem to make other actions happen, as opposed to patterns that recur but do not appear to cause other actions to occur (Baldwin, Baird, Saylor, & Clark, 2001). There is so much mental processing, some call it computation, that makes up the learning that we used to understand on a simpler behavioral level.

Object Permanence

Object permanence is the understanding that a particular, unique object continues to exist even when out of perceptual (sight, touch, or hearing) contact (Moore & Meltzoff, 2010). Object permanence includes understanding that an object or person exists even when out of direct contact *and* that when perceptual contact is regained, the identity of the object as the original object is recognized. It is considered one of the first experiences of working memory in the cognitive development of infants.

Use of Tools

Even in infancy, human beings are able to use tools to achieve their goals. The adults are the first tools used by infants. Infants use cries, facial expressions, reaching, and pointing to let adults know what is needed of them. In the first year of life, infants may use spoons and forks to carry food, markers to draw, and sofas to cruise along. Infants may discover how to use an object as a tool or may learn through imitation. Ten-month-old infants are able to discern the goal of an adult's tool use by watching them and will try to use the tool to achieve the same goal given time to practice using the tool (Sommerville, Hildebrand, & Crane, 2008).

Use of Space

During the first year of life, infants understand that two objects cannot occupy the same space, that an object looks bigger or smaller depending on the distance, and what objects might fit inside of other objects. Infants who crawl or walk during the first year develop a sense of depth perception and begin to make judgments about how steep an incline or decline they might be able to manage (Adolph, Eppler, & Joh, 2010). Understanding of spatial relationships derives from both handling of objects and being able to move through space.

Infant Developmental Possibilities in Cognitive Development

Although cultural expectations for development differ, there are age-related possibilities that provide a general guideline for thinking about a sequence of development (see Table 7.2). Keep in mind that infants may skip a step or attain a milestone earlier or later depending on both genetic conditions and environmental restraints or emphasis.

Table 7.2 Developmental Possibilities in Infant Cognitive Development

Between birth and 4 months, the child	as a newborn—follows moving toys with eyes
	explores new objects by mouthing
	exhibits increased attention to the external world
By 4 to 8 months, the child	explores by touching, shaking, and tasting objects
	tries to get his thumb to his mouth
	discovers that objects exist even when they're out of sight; watches and looks for hidden toy
	pulls string to get toy out of reach
	explores cause and effect by banging objects together or on a surface
	may drop objects to see what happens
	exhibits improving memory—stranger anxiety and separation anxiety occur when baby doesn't see a familiar face
By 8 to 12 months, the child	imitates actions
	holds one toy in one hand and explores it with the other hand
	uses and understands a few gestures; can use a few signs if taught sign language
	exhibits improving memory—looks for toy that is out of sight

Language Competence and Development

One of the most remarkable cognitive achievements of early childhood is the acquisition of language and the ability to communicate with others. Communication refers to imparting or exchanging information while language refers to a structured system of talking or writing. Language also refers to nonverbal communication such as sign language, a system of communication that refers to the use of gestures to communicate. "Infants learn language(s) with apparent ease, and the tools of modern neuroscience are providing valuable information about the mechanisms that underlie this capacity" (Kuhl & Rivera-Gaxiola, 2008, p. 511). From crying to a variety of interpretable vocal utterances, the infant begins to cognitively construct a very complex communicative system.

This system includes focusing attention on another person, gazing and gesturing at sources of sounds, associating certain sounds and voices with particular events and people, perceptually processing what a word is, developing reciprocity in verbal interactions (as when adult and infant coo back and forth to each other), and learning to use communicative systems to convey needs, feelings, and new learning. Infants are intensely social, fixing their gaze on the faces of those who talk and sing to them, and are sensitive to the emotional tone of their caregivers. Infants have such a strong desire to communicate that, quite interestingly, in the absence of speech, infants demonstrate remarkable communicative competence.

> ## Box 7.3 An Example of Infant-Directed Speech
>
> Parent with Her 5-Month-Old Infant Addy
>
> Parent: "Good morning" in a lilting voice to Addy who has just woken up in her crib (waits for Addy to respond)
>
> Addy: Smiles and coos, "Ahh"
>
> Parent: "Ahh," repeating Addy's sounds. "Are you ready to get up?"
>
> Addy: Smiles and puts out her arms to be picked up.
>
> Parent: Picks up Addy and carries her to the window. "Look, a bird" pointing to a bird on a branch outside the window.
>
> Addy: "ba" "aah"
>
> Parent: "Yes, bird" emphasizing the word "bird."

In addition, all over the world, many parents, siblings, and children older than the infant adjust their speech styles when talking to infants, using the simplest words, a higher pitch, hyperarticulation, and an exaggeration of certain vocal sounds and expressions, thus coaxing language along (Bryant & Barrett, 2007; Matsuda et al., 2007; Thiessen, Hill, & Saffran, 2005). This altered speech is often referred to as babytalk; **motherese, fatherese,** or **parentese; or infant- or child-directed speech**. Infant-directed speech makes language learning easier for infants because IDS speech facilitates infants' ability to segment speech into words (Thiessen, Hill, & Saffran, 2005). (See Box 7.3 for an example of IDS.)

motherese
modifications in the mother's speech when talking with infants and young children

fatherese
modifications in the father's speech when talking with infants and young children; can differ from motherese

parentese
modifications in the parent's speech when talking with infants and young children

child-directed speech
speech that has qualities of elevated pitch, conspicuous inflections, long pauses, and exaggerated stress on syllables

Receptive Language

Infants are listening to and learning the language or languages spoken with them during the first year. Receptive language involves the ability and willingness to receive information. We know that infants are listening, observing, and making sense of language.

From before birth, infants seem to be preprogrammed to communicate. They respond readily to the sound of the human voice and have been shown to distinguish the voices of their mothers from other female voices and to prefer their mothers' voices over strangers' voices (Kisilevksy et al., 2009). When researchers used a loudspeaker approximately 10 centimeters above the mothers' abdomens to play a recording of the babies' mothers reading a passage, the fetuses' heart rate increased. When a stranger's voice reading a passage was used, the fetuses' heart rate decreased. The authors of the research state that this finding demonstrates both a genetic expression of neural development and the importance of experience—fetuses' listening to their mothers' voices in utero.

During the first year of life, opportunities to hear the language of others and observe its use in daily interactions as well as being gently talked and sung to bring about comprehension long before the physiological structures that produce speech are mature. Hence, we see language comprehension evolve as infants begin to understand what is said to them but, as yet, are unable to speak. Infants' ability to process language is truly amazing. There is a structure to language, and infants are very actively trying to

Infants enjoy and benefit from listening to the words in baby books.

figure out that structure. As adults talk to infants, they may say short sentences, such as "There is a bird." But how do infants figure out what is a word in that sentence?

Infants are working hard to make sense of language by using auditory or prosodic clues (the patterns and rhythms of sounds) to separate strings of sounds into words (Seidl, 2007). Six-month-olds, who we know can't talk yet, even prefer to listen to words rather than non-sense syllables (Shi & Werker, 2001). Romberg and Saffran (2010) study how infants use statistical learning to learn their native language during the first year by figuring out which sounds are more likely to follow other sounds in words (Singh, Morgan, & White, 2004). These research studies provide more evidence that infants are trying to discover patterns of sounds that are typically used by adults when speaking to them.

By 1 year of age, if infants have experienced a rich language environment, they can easily distinguish between words. In one research study, a 1-year-old looks at images or objects on a screen and a researcher tracks the baby's eye movements when a researcher says the name of one of the objects. She looks less at the picture of the dog when the researcher says "Tog" than when the researcher says "Dog" (Swingley, 2008). The baby is recognizing words although she can't speak them yet.

Remember from Chapter 5 that infants during the later part of their first year begin to look at a target more if an adult turns her head toward the target with eyes open rather than closed-eyed. These researchers, Brooks and Meltzoff (2005), found that infants who followed an adult's gaze at 10 to 11 months had higher language scores at 18 months.

What does all of this research on infants' remarkable capabilities to process sounds and words to communicate mean for a parent or teacher? It means that adults must show genuine interest and delight in infants' sounds and toddlers' words, label objects and experiences for the child, communicate through imitating infants' sounds, and talk about what an infant is observing.

Expressive Language

The development of speech in the first year of life varies from child to child. A few children speak in sentences by the end of the first year. Others use only one-word "sentences" that can be understood only by those who participate consistently in the infant's everyday care. Infant crying communicates a variety of messages—hunger, discomfort, distress, anger, or boredom—and does so through different intonations and patterns, which become recognizable to the infant's parents and other caregivers. Primary caregivers soon learn to interpret the sounds and intensities of the infant's cries and respond appropriately. Around age 4 weeks, infants make small, throaty noises that are perhaps precursors to the vowel sounds that will begin to appear around 8 weeks. Infants discover their own voices around 12 weeks and enjoy gurgling and cooing, repeating the same vowel sound over and over, with perhaps some variation in tone. The infant is content to play with his or her voice alone or in concert with a parent or caregiver. Laughing aloud also occurs about this time.

Around 6 months of age, babbling begins to occur in which the vowel sounds are combined with the consonants *m, p, b, k,* and *g.* Babbles such as "bababa" are repeated over and over in succession, producing **echolalia.** Also, young children learning sign language use "manual babbling," making approximations of signs with their hands. Hearing babies learning sign language babble silently on their hands (Petitto, Holowka, Sergio, Levy, & Ostry, 2004). Some scholars believe that regardless of culture or locale, infants from all over the world produce similar babbles during the first 6 months of life (MacNeilage & Davis, 2000). However, as infants get older, linguists are able, through the use of careful listening of infant vocalizations, to distinguish subtle differences in the babbles of children in different environments exposed to different languages (Engstrand, Williams, & Lacerda, 2003; von Hapsburg & Davis, 2006). Also, babbling among infants with hearing loss has been found to be different in quality than babbling among infants without (von Hapsburg & Davis, 2006). But, why does the quality of children's babbling begin to differ around 7 to 9 months?

Researchers conclude that beginning at approximately 7 months babbling becomes more varied in intonation, loudness, and rhythm and additional consonants are produced as infants *imitate the sounds* of the language(s) they are hearing. During the latter half of the first year, infants are learning about and imitating the sounds of their native language (Kuhl, Tsao, & Liu, 2003).

Around 8 to 10 months, the infant may vocalize with toys, as though talking to them. Streams of babbles that sound like a conversation occur, yet no meaningful words emerge in this rich array of sounds. The infant may use sounds that approximate words or are his or her own creation to represent objects or events. These sounds are called **vocables** (Ferguson, 1977). Later in this period, the infant may have learned a few isolated words. Sometimes, the streams of babble include the interjection of an occasional word, creating a kind of pseudolanguage.

By the end of the first year, the infant may use one or two words correctly and comprehend simple commands and phrases, such as "no-no" and "bye-bye," and some nonverbal language in the form of gestures, such as "come to Daddy" and "peekaboo." Infants respond to their own names, and **holophrases,** in which one word or syllable represents a whole sentence, may emerge (e.g., "baba" means "I want my bottle").

Of interest to researchers and parents alike is the emergence of first words. Katherine Nelson refers to the infant's growing awareness of two different worlds: objects and people (Fivush, Hudson, & Lucariello, 2002; Nelson, 1996; Nelson & Lucariello, 1985). During the latter half of the first year, infants begin to realize that these different entities provide different experiences. Nelson argues that coordination of these two worlds is essential for the development of language. First words are often overgeneralized; for instance, "ball" may come to represent all toys, not just the child's ball. Nelson places some emphasis on the interactive experiences infants have with adults who are aware of and in tune with emerging language. Parents and caregivers who engage in focused "conversations" with their infants and continually provide names and descriptions of objects and events around them support and enhance language development during this important period.

echolalia
replication in repetitive fashion of the sounds of another speaker in an infant–other turn-taking "conversation"

vocables
early sound patterns used by infants that approximate words

holophrase
the use of one word to convey a phrase or a sentence

Cognitive, Language, and Literacy Development of the Infant

The back-and-forth, turn-taking conversations that build relationships are key during the first year of an infant's life, and infants use their facial expressions of frowning and smiling, their gestures, and their sounds to communicate. Infants have a desire to communicate and use gestures that include movement of fingers, arms, and hands, facial features, and body motions (Crais, 2009). Most parents and teachers (and the infant) are so happy at the end of the first year when the infant can wave bye-bye, often with a hand turned so that the fingers are pointing toward the infant. Crais (2009) reported that infants communicate the following meaning through gestures:

- Protests 6 to 8 months
- Requests for actions 6 to 8 months
- Requests for objects 6 to 10 months
- Comments 8 to 11 months
- Answering 13 to 16 months

Crais (2009) also reported that 9- to 12-month-old children later identified with autism spectrum disorder used far fewer gestures than typical children did.

Another question that parents and teachers often ask is, "Should children be exposed to two languages during their first year of life?" (See Box 7.4.)

Pragmatics

The term *pragmatics* includes the functions of language and how language is used in different contexts. Turn-taking is one of the key aspects of communication that we all use when talking with others, and infants learn how to turn-take in the first year of life. The infant coos while looking at his grandmother and the grandmother coos back while gazing at the infant and touching him softly. The infant maintains his cooing attention as the adult scaffolds his engagement by listening, responding, and touching to help the infant stay regulated. Through this type of turn-taking, with the adult waiting for the infant to take a turn, infants learn one of the most important rules of communication.

Box 7.4 Diversity Perspectives: Second Language Acquisition

Should infants be exposed to two or more languages during the first year of life? What do you think based on the following research?

Because infants are "tuning" in to the sounds they hear in their language, between 6 and 12 months of age, infants begin to lose their ability to discriminate phonetic sounds in foreign languages, unless they are exposed to those languages. English-learning infants exposed to five hours of infant-directed Mandarin Chinese between 9 and 10 months of age were able to continue to discriminate Mandarin sounds not found in English, whereas a control group of infants' ability to hear Mandarin phonetics declined (Kuhl, Tsao, & Liu, 2003). This research demonstrated that infants are capable of continuing to distinguish the sounds of a foreign language after 9 months of age *if* they hear the language by socially interacting with an adult, rather than hearing the language on a DVD.

Edward Tronick (2007) writes about his Mutual Regulation Model (MRM) of adult–infant interaction. "The MRM sees infants as part of a dyadic communicative system in which the infant and adult mutually regulate and scaffold their engagement with each other and the world by communicating their intentions and responding to them" (p. 1). Infants need conversational partners who affectionately engage them. Definitely talk with infants in responsive ways from the moment they are born.

As with other areas of development, most children follow a predictable pattern, but not all children proceed through the sequences at the same rate. A common sequence for language development during the first year is illustrated in Table 7.3.

bilabial trills
the production of sounds such as *m, b,* and *p* that are formed in the front of the mouth with the lips closed and move from the lips toward the back of the mouth (other structures for the articulation of sounds include the lips, teeth, roof of the mouth, and tongue)

Table 7.3 Developmental Possibilities in Infant Language Development: Receptive, Expressive, and Pragmatic Language and Communication Development

Age	Language Development
Birth to 4 Months	Communicates through crying, fretting, and other reflexive vocalizations: coughing, burping, sneezing
	Gazes into the eyes of the caregiver
	Searches and attends to voices
	Begins to distinguish speech sounds
	Sensitive to the emotional tone of voices
	Produces some vowel sounds when cooing/gooing
	Smiles and chuckles
From 4 to 8 months	"Plays" with voice and sound making
	Appears to experiment with contrasts in loud and soft sounds; low- and high-pitched sounds
	Produces "raspberries" (**bilabial trills**)
	Sustains some vowel sounds
	Combines some vowel and consonant sounds and begins to babble
	Produces strings of the same sounds: "mamamama," "bababababa," "dadadadada"
	Produces strings of two or three different sounds, such as "dabagiba"
	Replicates in repetitive fashion the sounds of another speaker in an infant–other turn-taking "conversation" (echolalia)
	Points and gestures
From 8 to 12 months	Babbling takes on the tone and inflections of "real talk" (referred to as jargon or conversational babble)
	Jargon may be accompanied by body language cues, such as nodding, tilting, or shaking head, making eye contact, gesturing, and exaggerated intonations
	Jargon can take the form of communicating, conveying a need or desire (e.g., request for the bottle, rejection of interaction, request to be picked up)
	Jargon can represent engagement in vocal sound play enjoyed in and of itself
	Early words emerge from jargon
	Understands and imitates communicative gestures (bye-bye, throw a kiss, "applause" clapping)
	Babbles and early words coexist for a time

Cognitive, Language, and Literacy Development of the Infant

Two infants enjoy listening to a story and looking at the pictures.

Early Learning Guidelines, developed in many states, also identify the skills that infants acquire and the suggested supportive learning experiences. For information on Massachusetts' Early Learning Guidelines for language development, see www.eec.state.ma.us/docs1/Workforce_Dev/20110519_infant_toddler_early_learning_guidelines.pdf.

Literacy Competence and Development

Literacy has its origins in a variety of infant experiences and sensations. Listening to and engaging in vocal interactions with others, tuning into the sounds and rhythms of the voices and language surrounding them, observing the facial expressions of their caregivers, and visually fixating on objects of interest begin the journey toward literacy. On the basis of the belief that the origins of literacy occur in infancy, researchers in language and literacy development suggest that infants benefit from and enjoy sharing chants, rhymes, songs, playful games of peekaboo and pat-a-cake, and baby books with their parents and caregivers. Hearing softly spoken language with the rich intonations that accompany stories and songs is an enriching and enjoyable auditory and cognitive experience for infants, which leads to heightened interest in both the spoken word and books (Wittmer & Petersen, 2012).

Further, infants can be provided appropriate baby books to view and handle, beginning with heavy cardboard baby books using very simple pictures of single familiar items. The board book (as this type of book is called) can be stood in the corner of the crib or within the infant's view to provide an engaging visual experience. As the infant gains motor controls and can reach and bring items to his or her mouth, a different type of book is preferable, one that is made of fabric or another soft, washable material. Gradually, as infants become less physical and more visual in their relationships with books, their interest in the pictures and stories of books increases. Using baby books to engage older infants in very simple point-and-name activities ("This is a ball," "See the kitten?") engages the infant, enhances interest and curiosity, and begins a process whereby infants begin to form visual symbolic representations in their minds. Types of books that are recommended for infants during the first year of growth and development are described in Box 7.5.

Infants with Special Needs

Many delays in cognitive, language, and literacy development are not identified during the first year of life. For the earliest intervention in these areas, we look to biological conditions that are likely to cause delays. This section describes the most common, Down syndrome.

Box 7.5 Types of Books Recommended for Infants

Format for very young infants

Board books that can stand in the corner of the crib or on the floor in view range

Colorful or black-and-white illustrations

Lead-free and nontoxic construction materials (including inks, adhesives, and paper or cardboard content)

Rounded edges (no staples, spirals, or other sharp or detachable parts)

Content and illustrations of baby books

Image of one simple object per page (point-and-say books)

Familiar objects such as baby bottle, soft stuffed toy, ball, cup, sweater, cap

Enlarged photographs (bound into a board book) of familiar faces: mother, father, sibling, grandparent

Enlarged photographs (bound into a board book) of familiar objects unique to the child's environment (crib, table lamp, stuffed toy, rocking chair, high chair)

No print message necessary; spoken labels provide important auditory engagement

Format for older infants when books can be grasped, mouthed, and held

Washable cloth books

Washable soft plastic or vinyl books

Lead-free and nontoxic construction

No small removable parts

Rounded or soft edges

Content and illustrations of books for older infants

More point-and-say books with expanding "vocabulary" of familiar objects or "story" content

Touch-and-smell books

Simple illustrations (avoiding too many items per illustration and per page)

Simple one-word print labels accompanying illustrations

Simple one-, two-, or three-line story, increasing the story length and complexity only slightly as the infants get older and engagement is revealed

Simple one-to-one correspondence books (one item, two items, three items per page in successive pages to no more than five items)

Down Syndrome

Down syndrome is the most common birth defect. Down syndrome is a condition in which an infant is born with 47 chromosomes instead of the usual 46. The extra chromosome is usually an extra copy of chromosome 21, and the condition is often referred to as Trisomy 21. Down syndrome results in a predictable set of physical features including short stature, a smaller, somewhat rounded head, and eyes that are rounded rather than pointed at the inside. Other physical signs include low or hypotonic muscle tone, a single crease across the palm, and a flattened nose. Delays in learning and language are usually a part of the syndrome. Early intervention is extremely helpful in motor, learning, language and behavior issues. Infants and toddlers with Down syndrome tend to be very easily included in child care and education programs, with the support of the family and the early intervention team.

Factors That Influence Cognitive, Language, and Literacy Development

Think again about Jeremy and Angela. From the descriptions of their lives so far, several factors influencing development in these areas are becoming evident. Compare the lives of Jeremy and Angela in terms of the factors that influence cognition, language, and literacy.

1. Full-term infants get off to a healthier, less vulnerable start in life. Optimal health from the beginning facilitates all development—physical and motor, psychosocial, cognitive, language, and literacy.
2. The integrity of the sensory mechanisms, particularly hearing and vision, influences the extent to which these modalities can support and enhance learning and the extent to which compensating mechanisms come into play.
3. Proper nutrition is essential to good health and supports optimal brain and neurological development. There is evidence that appropriate and adequate nutrition during the earliest months is critical for brain growth and neurological development; in severe cases of malnutrition during the first 6 months, the deleterious effects can be irreversible.
4. Environments that support the infant's cognitive, language, and literacy development with engaging social interaction, enriching sensory stimuli, opportunities for motor exploration, and appropriate playthings and baby books promote optimal development.
5. Interactions with others who are responsive, supportive, and stimulating enhance not only the psychosocial development of the infant, but cognition, language, and literacy development as well.

Every child is born with the capacity to learn, master his or her home language, and become literate. However, genetic endowment or even a predisposition to learn is not enough to guarantee learning. Information is at least partially culturally based, and infants need responsive adult partners to help them focus their attention and understand what is occuring around them. Adults may facilitate and enhance infant cognition, language development, and emerging literacy in a number of ways. However, development cannot be hurried, and any efforts should first take cues from the behaviors of the infant. Having too many stimuli, inappropriate toys, visually and auditorially overstimulating environments, and expectations that exceed current capabilities bombard the infant is confusing and can impede optimal psychosocial and cognitive development. In confusing and overstimulating circumstances, infants become irritable and stressed, sometimes become depressed, and may exhibit problems with eating, sleeping, attending, and playing. An appreciation of the infant's own developmental timetable guides parents and caregivers.

The adult is most helpful by paying attention to the infant's signals and interests, providing a responsive and supportive relationship, and offering experiences that are enjoyable and interesting to the infant. Toys and materials should react contingently to the child's actions, e.g., a bell rings when the child pushes the red button on a toy. Time should be spent in the natural, outdoor environment for learning and language enrichment.

Role of the Early Childhood Professional

Promoting Cognitive, Language, and Literacy Development in Infants

1. Engage readily in social interaction with the infant, responding to the infant's cues for social and emotional support.

2. Provide an enriched social environment that includes opportunities for the infant to watch, interact with, and feel and be a part of the family or child care group.

3. Provide a safe, supportive, and nurturing environment that encourages exploration.

4. Provide a sensory-rich environment, including vocal and verbal interactions with the infant, soft singing, shared baby books, story reading, bright and cheerful surroundings, visual access to windows, simple, uncluttered pictures on the wall, and other visual attractions.

5. Provide appropriate auditory stimuli, including talk and laughter, singing, chanting, reading, CDs, and other sources of interesting sounds, such as wind chimes.

6. Vary tactile stimuli with appropriate stuffed toys and soft sculptured items made from a variety of textures.

7. Periodically alter the child's scenery: Move the crib to another side of the room, move the high chair to another side of the table, occasionally change the visuals on the wall around the crib or play areas.

8. Provide safe, simple, engaging, age-appropriate toys and crib items, and replace them when the infant's interest in them wanes.

9. Explore the surroundings with the infant, saying the names of objects, carrying him or her about, gazing into the mirror, pointing to a photograph on the wall, looking through the window, finding the lowest kitchen drawer and examining its safe and intriguing contents, and so on.

10. Take infants on brief outings with you. Talk about where you are going, what you are doing, and what you are seeing. Name objects, places, and people as you go.

11. Place an older infant's toys on low, open shelves for easy access and clean-up.

12. Respond with focused interest and enthusiasm to the infant's attempts to initiate playfulness and interaction.

13. If the child is learning a language at home that is different from that in a program, learn key phrases of the child's first language from family members to use with the infant—especially words of endearment or songs,

14. Work closely with infants' families to encourage talking with infants and reading to them during the first year. Share information on the types of books that infants enjoy.

Key Terms

adaptation
bilabial trills
child-directed speech
cognitive
    development
cognitive flexibility
constructivism

echolalia
executive function
fatherese
holophrase
inhibitory control
language acquisition
    device (LAD)

motherese
neural connectivity
object permanence
parentese
pruning
vocables
working memory

Review Strategies and Activities

1. Review the key terms individually or with a classmate.

2. This and other chapters have introduced a variety of theories associated with growth and development in young children. Angela and Jeremy have provided examples of development during the first year. Reread the stories of Angela and Jeremy appearing in previous chapters. On the basis of what you have learned so far about child development, make a list of your observations about Angela's and Jeremy's development and reflect on their potential. Discuss and compare your lists and reflections with those of your classmates.

3. Visit an infant care program that offers age-appropriate opportunities for cognitive, language, and literacy development. What types of interactions take place in these settings? How is cognitive, language, and literacy development supported through the activities and materials provided for infants?

Further Readings

Jalongo, M. R. (2011). *Early childhood language arts* (5th ed.). Upper Saddle River, NJ: Pearson.

Oakes, L., Cashon, C., Casasola, M., & Rakisoon, D. (Eds.). (2010). *Infant perception and cognition: Recent advances, emerging theories, and future directions*. New York: Oxford University Press.

ZERO TO THREE. (2008). *Caring for infants and toddlers in groups: Developmentally appropriate practice* (2nd ed.). Washington, DC: Author.

Other Resources

First Signs (Resources on Children with Autism), www.firstsigns.org.

Links to Child Care, Head Start, and Early Head Start Sites, www.acf.hhs.gov.

Early Head Start National Resource Center, www.ehsnrc.org.

U.S. Department of Health & Human Services. Administration for Children & Families. ECLKC Early Childhood Learning & Knowledge Center. Cultural and Linguistic Responsiveness, http://eclkc.ohs.acf.hhs.gov/hslc/tta-system/cultural-linguistic.

ZERO TO THREE, http://main.zerotothree.org/site/PageServer?pagename=key_language.

    Early Language & Literacy

    Getting Ready to Read

    Dual Language Development: Double the Benefit

    New Video: Promoting Early Language and Literacy Development (Play the video from the Web site)

    Early Experiences Matter

Perceptual, Motor, and Physical Development; Health and Nutrition: Ages One Through Three

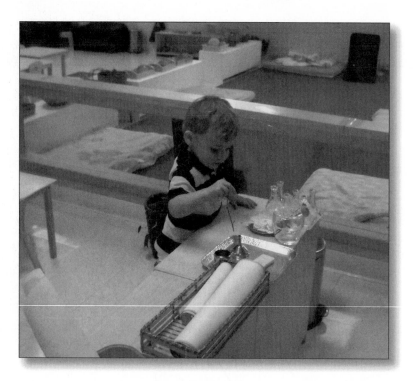

Little children are not logical—they are motor. To give a child joy, give him something to do.

—Lucy Gage

After studying this chapter, you will demonstrate comprehension by:

▶ describing perceptual competence and development;

▶ identifying developmental landmarks in physical and motor competence;

▶ identifying issues concerning children with special needs;

▶ describing the relationship between physical–motor development and social/emotional development;

▶ discussing health and well-being issues that are relevant from ages 1 through 3;

▶ discussing issues in perceptual, motor, and physical development and how health and nutrition influence these types of development; and

▶ suggesting strategies for enhancing physical and motor development from ages 1 through 3.

Following the dramatic changes of the first year of life, the second and third years are marked by an impressive development of competence in all areas. This chapter will describe development in perception, large and fine muscle control, and physical growth. This is followed by a section on healthy practices for this age group.

Perceptual Competence and Development

Growth and development are influenced by the integrity and functioning of the sensory mechanisms. Of particular interest is the normal functioning of vision and hearing.

Vision

Although a normal adult's visual acuity (how well one sees) is 20/20, a newborn's is about 20/600, which means that something 20 feet away is seen by the newborn with the clarity of what an adult would see if the object were 600 feet away. This improves rapidly over the first 6 months to about 20/100, and by age 3, visual acuity has reached about 20/30. It is not until around age 5 that children reach 20/20 visual acuity (Boothe, Dobson, & Teller, 1985).

Because of rapid development during the first years, regular eye examinations are recommended to ensure early detection of any problems with the eyes that could result in visual impairment. Children who received oxygen at birth, were premature or had a low birth weight, or have congenital anomalies are at high risk for eye abnormalities. Their vision should be regularly monitored during infancy and early childhood. Pediatricians include basic eye exams during well-child check-ups, but optometrists suggest more thorough exams annually. Behaviors and physical characteristics suggestive of visual problems observed in infancy and very young children are listed in Box 8.1. These symptoms indicate a need for professional evaluation and intervention.

Hearing

Like vision, hearing influences the course of growth and development of young children, and, as with vision, early diagnosis and intervention are critical. Hearing impairment is classified according to its physiological basis. Conductive hearing impairment is caused by some barrier in the outer or middle ear that prevents sound waves from traveling to the inner ear, such as when there is fluid in the ear, wax buildup, or middle ear infection (i.e., otitis media); sometimes the structures of the ear did not develop properly or were injured. Conductive hearing impairment interferes with the child's ability to understand

Box 8.1   Behaviors Suggestive of Visual Problems in Infants and Toddlers

Persistent misalignment of the eye such as crossing of the eyes (**strabismus**)

Eyeballs that flutter quickly from side to side or up and down (**nystagmus**)

Inability to track a moving object

The presence of a white pupil suggestive of cataract or other condition

Pain or redness in one or both eyes

Persistent watery eyes

Sensitivity to light

Thick, colored discharge from the eye

Frequent squinting or rubbing the eyes

Uncharacteristic tilting or turning the head "to see"

Eyelids that droop

Eyes that appear to bulge

strabismus
a condition referred to as *crossed eyes,* in which one or both eyes turn in, out, up, or down

nystagmus
involuntary and jerky repetitive movement of the eyeballs

cochlear implant
an electronic device placed in the skull, which, with help from an external hearing aid, enhances the detection of sound

speech sounds and, if prolonged, can delay speech and language development. If left undetected and untreated, conductive impairments can lead to permanent hearing loss, but most can be corrected through antibiotics or surgery (Deiner, 1997). Ear tubes are often inserted surgically when fluid in the ear or ear infections are chronic. The tubes relieve the problem and fall out in six to 12 months (Mayo Clinic Staff, 2011).

Hearing impairment may also be a result of sensorineural injury to the inner ear and/or the nerve to the brainstem, as can occur with tumors, brain injury, prenatal infections, anoxia, some genetic anomalies, and some childhood diseases such as bacterial meningitis, chicken pox, measles, and mumps. Contemporary surgical procedures such as the **cochlear implant** help some profoundly impaired children to hear. Other amplification devices may be prescribed for children with hearing impairments, and language development may include learning sign language and lip-reading techniques. The symptoms of hearing loss may be confused with the language delays of the autism spectrum. One recent study showed that toddlers with autism had greater receptive language deficits than children with other developmental delays (Weisnmer, Lord, & Esler, 2010).

It is difficult to detect hearing loss in infants through observation. In the absence of newborn screening, hearing loss may not be detected before the child is 1 or 2 years old, an age at which important opportunities for language development and intervention have been missed. Newborn screening through the American Academy of Pediatrics Early Hearing Detection and Intervention program helps to identify infants in need of intervention. Failure to identify hearing loss before 6 months of age is associated with delayed speech and language development. However, where regular physical examinations provide hearing evaluations, interventions can be prescribed with the goal of helping infants to develop language commensurate with their cognitive development (American Academy of Pediatrics, 2007). The more severe the hearing impairment, the more likely it is to be noticed by untrained observers. Early detection and intervention makes a significant

> **Box 8.2** *Behaviors Suggestive of Hearing Problems in Infants and Toddlers*
>
> Failure to turn in the direction of sounds
>
> Pulling or rubbing ears
>
> Turning or tilting the head toward the source of a sound
>
> Staring at a speaker's mouth
>
> Easily startled by sound
>
> Inattentiveness
>
> Failure to follow directions
>
> Delayed speech and language development
>
> Frequent ear aches, colds, or allergies

difference in children with many different causes of hearing loss (Paul & Roth, 2011). Children with hearing impairments may display any or a combination of the behaviors listed in Box 8.2.

Perceptual–Motor Development

Perception is a neurological process by which sensory input is organized. It involves all of the senses. For instance, visual perception involves the ability to recognize and discriminate faces, patterns, sizes, shapes, depth, distance, and so on. Auditory perception involves the use of auditory clues to identify people, objects, and events and to discern such qualities as distance, speed, and space. Tactile–kinesthetic perception provides information relating to touch, textures, temperature, weight, pressure, and one's own body position, presence, or movements. Olfactory (smell) and taste perceptions provide additional information for the recognition, discrimination, identification, and location of experienced events and objects.

Perceptual–motor development refers to the interrelationships between a child's perceptions and motor responses. Because perceptions derive from the senses and provoke awareness, motor development and perception are interdependent, and each influences learning. Space, depth, and weight perceptions, for example, depend heavily on locomotor experiences for their development. Expecting a large, hollow block to be heavier than it actually is, a child may brace himself or herself to lift it, only to discover that the block did not require such muscular readiness. Such an experience enhances weight perception. Child development observers are interested in the effective integration of perceptual and motor development. When perceptual and motor abilities are integrated, the child uses visual, auditory, tactile, or other sensory data to plan and carry out motor activities more efficiently. By the same token, perceptions are modified as a result of motoric experiences. Imitating another child's scribbles is an example of visual–motor integration. Responding to the rhythms of music is an example of audio–motor integration. Curling into one's own cubby at the child care center is an example of kinesthetic–motor integration.

perceptual–motor
interrelationship between sensory information and motor responses

Jeremy is now 13 months old. He is aware of his parents' delight in watching him attempt his first steps. Feet widespread, arms bent at the elbows, reaching upward for balance, he lifts one foot to step, loses his balance, and tumbles sideways. On the next attempt, he is able to toddle two or three steps before falling. His new skill is thrilling but also somewhat frightening. His parents clap, laugh, coax, and praise him profusely with every attempt. Tiring, he reverts to a more expedient mode of locomotion and crawls easily to his mother's outstretched arms.

Jeremy's parents have attempted to provide space for Jeremy's increasing mobility. Furnishings are arranged to provide obstacle-free movement and to eliminate sharp edges or items over which he might trip. Jeremy especially enjoys climbing the three steps to the front door on returning from an excursion, and now that he is learning to walk, his mother experiments with his stair-climbing skills.

Holding both hands from behind him, mother and Jeremy walk toward the three steps to descend. At first, Jeremy thrusts one foot forward into the air, bringing it back to the level of the first step, as though he were walking on a level plane. Consequently, his mother must rescue him, or he will tumble down the steps. Not too happy with this effort, Jeremy returns to a crawling position and proceeds to back his way down the steps.

Jeremy's motor behaviors illustrate some aspects of perceptual–motor development. Jeremy's parents are aware that his space and speed perceptions are faulty, so they have arranged their living spaces to accommodate his poorly coordinated movements and lack of space perception. Also, Jeremy's mother's experiment reveals Jeremy's lack of depth perception. Jeremy's visual, kinesthetic, and/or depth perceptions have not yet become coordinated. In such cases, one would assert that 13-month-old Jeremy needs more time for visual–motor abilities to become integrated. It will be some time before he masters descending steps in an upright-forward position (typically, children do not descend stairs smoothly and unassisted until around age 4). Visual–motor development is enhanced through opportunities to use developing locomotor abilities and small motor skills. Body awareness, balance, rhythm, space, and temporal awareness increase as toddlers explore their surroundings and experience their body movements and abilities.

Angela is also 13 months old. Her motor development is somewhat, though not dramatically, delayed. (Recall that Angela experienced a premature delivery, complicated by anoxia.) Measured against the usual age ranges for emergence of motor skills, Angela has performed approximately 2 to 3 months behind expectations for full-term infants. Nevertheless, her development appears to be quite normal, but she exhibits more excitability, restlessness, and frustration, which is not unusual for preterm infants. Her excursions about the house are far-reaching when she is allowed to explore beyond the playpen or crib.

Cheryl, now 16 years old, has had a relatively happy and successful year in her new school. With help from the child care center on her high school campus, Cheryl is learning to juggle parenting and education. She is taking a child development course and is thrilled to learn about the different stages and abilities Angela is exhibiting. Angela has ample opportunities to explore throughout the day at school and Cheryl is learning to provide an environment at home in which Angela can explore—but with older children around, the places Angela wants to explore are often hazardous. Consequently, at home Angela is often relegated to the playpen, sometimes for lengthy periods. She cruises around the playpen, watches the other children, listens to the television, and cuddles her soft toys. She enjoys dropping small blocks into a bucket and then dumping them out. The older children bring her other items to play with, and when she gets fussy, they increase their verbal interactions with her, playing games such as peekaboo or "which hand is the toy in?" Angela's environment is verbally rich and interactive.

The limited visual and tactile–kinesthetic environment of the playpen, however, has further delayed Angela's perceptual–motor integration. Limited opportunities to develop perceptual–motor integration could place Angela at risk for learning difficulties later on.

Physical and Motor Competence

By the end of the first year, the infant has made dramatic developmental strides in all areas of development: sensory, physical/motor, social, emotional, cognitive, and language. Of special interest to parents and child development observers is the physical growth that proceeds quite rapidly and its accompanying repertoire of motor skills. Indeed, some of the first large motor skills—pulling up, standing alone, and taking the first steps—evoke excitement, praise, and celebration. These milestones signal the beginning of a new period in child development, typically referred to as the *toddler period*. This period extends from age 1 through age 2 and into the third year.

General Physical Characteristics

The rapid growth rate of infancy decelerates somewhat during the second year. For example, whereas the infant's birth weight typically triples during the first year, the toddler gains around 5 to 6 pounds during the second year. Similarly, the infant's length, which increased by about 10 to 12 inches during the first year, is followed by growth of about 5 inches during the second year.

Body proportions begin to change from the short, rounded characteristics of the 1-year-old to a leaner, more muscular build by age 3. However, the head is still large in proportion to the rest of the body (making up one-fifth of the total body length at age 1) and gives the toddler a top-heavy appearance. The toddler's early attempts to walk result in posture characterized by a protruding abdomen, arms held upward and feet spread wide apart for balance (not always successfully), and a leading forehead. Awkward and unsure locomotion, body proportions, and characteristic posture make the term *toddler* quite appropriate for this period in child growth and development. By age 3, changes in body build and proportions lower the center of gravity from the upper regions of the body to the midsection, facilitating more coordinated locomotion and a leaner, more upright body profile.

Recall that brain growth and neurological development during the first 3 years are quite rapid, as neurological connections proliferate in an extensive and profoundly complex manner. When examining infants and toddlers, pediatricians often measure the circumference of the child's head, but this measure is not taken routinely after age 3. Head circumference during these first 3 years is significant in physical examinations because it helps the physician assess ossification of the cranial bones as the fontanelles close and evaluate brain growth and the status of the central nervous system. Although the head circumference at birth is greater than that of the chest, it is about equal to the chest circumference when the child is about 1 year old.

Facial proportions are also changing. The infant and young child have rather high, rounded, and prominent foreheads, resulting from early and rapid brain and cranial growth. Because of this early growth pattern, facial features make up a smaller portion of the facial area than they will as the child gets older. The face is round with a small jaw and a small, flat nose. The eyes are set close together, and the lips are thin. Over the course of the next few years, facial proportions will change, and the child will lose the "baby face" appearance.

The eruption of teeth contributes to changes in facial proportions. By age 1, six to eight teeth may have appeared; but in some children, teeth appear at a much slower rate, and some have no more than three or four teeth by their first birthday. By age 2½ to 3, most children have all 20 of their **deciduous teeth** ("baby teeth"), as illustrated in Figure 8.1 (American Dental Association, 2011). Deciduous teeth, also called *primary* teeth, tend to appear sooner in boys than in girls. However, girls, who are generally thought to progress toward maturity more rapidly than boys in most areas of development, will be slightly ahead of boys in the eruption of permanent teeth.

Changes in other body proportions are also evident. Look at Figure 8.2, and notice the changes in body proportions from fetal development to adulthood. Notice that the arms of the infant seem long and the legs quite short in proportion to the trunk. Then compare the arm and leg lengths with those of the preschool age child. As the legs grow longer, the arms appear shorter, and the head accounts for a much smaller proportion of the body length.

Skeletal development is characterized not only by an increase in size, but also by changes in the number and the composition of bones. Beginning in the fetal period with soft, pliable cartilage, which begins to ossify around the fifth prenatal month, bones gradually harden as calcium and other minerals are absorbed. Not all bones grow and develop at the same rate. The cranial bones and long bones of the arms and spine are among the first to ossify. The bones of the hands and wrists tend to mature early and serve as valuable indicators of general growth progress in the child (Tanner, 1989).

deciduous teeth
the first set of teeth, which erupts during infancy; also called temporary or baby teeth; later replaced by a set of 36 permanent teeth

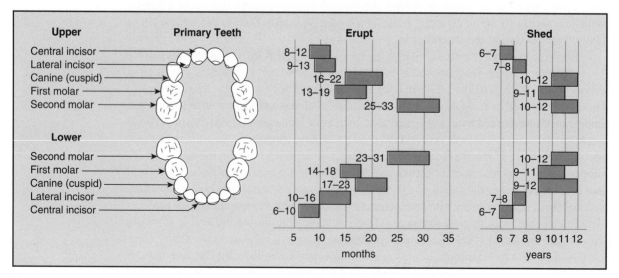

Figure 8.1   Typical Sequence of Eruption of Primary Teeth

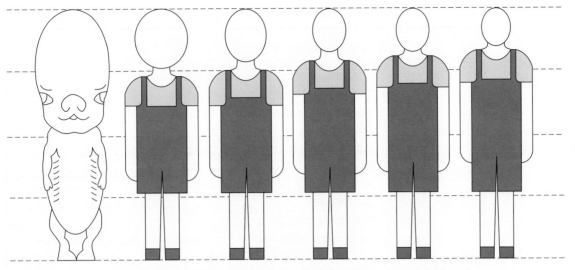

Figure 8.2   Changes in Body Proportion from Fetal Development to Adulthood

The amount of **adipose** (fatty tissue) children have depends on a number of factors, including heredity, body type, nutrition and eating habits, activity levels, and exercise opportunities. During infancy, adipose tissue develops more rapidly than muscle. However, children tend to lose adipose tissue toward the end of the first year and continue to do so during the next few years as they become upright and more mobile. The decrease will continue until about age 5, when increases in weight will result from skeletal and muscle growth.

Development of **locomotion** refers to the growing ability to move independently from place to place. Like other areas of development, motor development follows the law of developmental direction, that is, a head-to-foot direction with control over muscles of the upper regions of the body preceding control over muscles in the lower regions. This development parallels neural development, which also proceeds in a head-downward pattern. Brain development, particularly of the cerebellum, which is involved in posture and balance, is rather rapid between 6 and 18 months of age. Thus, neural and muscular development in tandem with changing body proportions facilitates locomotion and does so in a fairly predictable sequence.

adipose
tissue in which there is an accumulation of connective tissue cells, each containing a relatively large deposit of fat

locomotion
the ability to move independently from place to place

Expected Growth Patterns and Developmental Possibilities

By the end of the first year, children often have mastered such motor skills as rolling over, sitting unassisted, crawling, pulling up, and perhaps standing alone. Between the ages of 10 and 15 months, the child may walk when held by one hand or walk alone. He may pull to a standing position and "cruise" by holding onto furniture. These activities are referred to as *large motor* activities because they enlist the use and coordination of the large muscles of the arms, trunk, and legs. Because these muscles generally mature earliest, children master large muscle skills sooner than small muscle skills such as handling a spoon, a crayon, or buttons.

Large Motor Development. Large motor development usually follows predictable patterns. Table 8.1 identifies **developmental possibilities** of the period from ages 1 to 4. Review Table 5.3 and notice how motor development progresses from birth to age 1 and

developmental possibilities
significant events during the course of growth and development

Table 8.1 Developmental Possibilities in Large Motor from Ages 1 Through 4

Age	Motor Development
12–18 months	Pulls to standing position holding onto furniture
	Throws objects from crib
	Walks with two hands held
	Crawls up steps
	Rolls a large ball, nondirected, using both hands and arms
	Attempts to slide from lap or high chair
	Begins to make shift from crawling to walking
	Stands alone
	Climbs onto a chair
	Takes two or three steps without support with legs widespread and arms held forward for balance
	Gets into a standing position unassisted
	Squats to pick up an object
	Reverts to crawling when in a hurry rather than attempting to walk
	Cannot yet make sudden stops or turns
	"Dances" in place to music
18–24 months	Bends to pick up objects
	Walks without falling
	Pulls, drags toys
	Seats self in a child's chair
	Walks up and down stairs assisted
	Walks backward
	"Dances" to music moving about
	Mimics household activities: bathing baby, sweeping, dusting, talking on telephone
24–36 months	Runs
	Walks on toes
	Jumps in place
	Kicks a large ball
	Imitates rhythms and animal movements; e.g., gallops like a horse, waddles like a duck
	Throws a ball, nondirected
	Catches a rolling ball
	Jumps in place
	Rides a tricycle
	Walks stairs one step at a time
	Jumps from lowest step
	Attempts to balance standing on one foot

Table 8.1 continued

Age	Motor Development
36–48 months	Balances on one foot
	Hops, gallops, runs with ease
	Avoids obstacles
	Stops readily
	Walks on a line
	Jumps over low objects
	Throws a ball, directed
	Enjoys simple dances and rhythms

from ages 1 through 3. Notice the impressive array of large motor coordinations and skills that emerges during this first 36 months. However, there are individual differences in rates and sometimes sequences of development in all aspects of child growth and development. Any such sequence of developmental events, as listed in Table 8.1, can provide only approximations with which to observe and understand emerging abilities. Awareness of expected sequences, though, can help parents and teachers prepare for possible next steps in development.

Small Motor Development. Equally dramatic, but probably not always as obvious, is the emergence of small motor development. Small muscle development and motor skills proceed from the head downward and from the central axis of the body outward. This means that the coordination of the smaller muscles of the wrists, hands, and fingers is preceded by, and for the most part dependent on, the coordination of the large muscles of the upper trunk, shoulders, and upper arms.

prehension
the coordination of fingers and thumb to permit grasping

flexors
muscles that act to bend a joint

extensors
muscles that act to stretch or extend a limb

The abilities to reach, grasp, manipulate, and let go of objects become more precise during the second year. Coordination of eyes and hands improves rapidly during the toddler period, and with ever-increasing locomotor skills, exploratory behaviors expand. Thus, locomotion, in tandem with improving eye–hand coordination, facilitates learning. Successful exploration depends on coordination of large muscles, small muscles, vision, and hearing.

By age 1, **prehension,** the ability to use the thumb and fingers in opposition to each other has become reasonably efficient. Recall that during the first year of development, the grasping muscles (**flexors**) are stronger than the releasing muscles (**extensors**). During the toddler period, grasping and letting go become more efficient. Pouring objects from a container and then putting them back into the container one by one can be an absorbing activity, requiring both grasping and releasing. This development is illustrated in Figure 8.3.

Large motor development is facilitated when infants can safely explore their surroundings.

Perceptual, Motor, and Physical Development; Health and Nutrition: Ages One Through Three

12 weeks: reflexive; ulnar side dominant

16 weeks: mouthing of fingers and mutual fingering; holds object placed in hand

20 weeks: primitive squeeze; raking with fingers only, no palm or thumb involvement

24 weeks: palmar or squeeze grasp; still no thumb involvement; eyes and hands combine for grasp

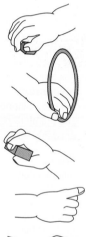

28 weeks: radial-palmar or whole-hand grasp; radial side stronger, thumb begins to adduct, unilateral approach (one hand); transfers from one hand to the other

32 weeks: inferior scissors grasp, thumb is adducted, not opposed

36 weeks: radial-digital grasp; fingers on radial side provide pressure to object, thumb begins to move forward in opposition

40 weeks: inferior-pincer grasp; thumb begins to move toward forefinger; beginning of voluntary release

44 weeks: neat pincer grasp with slight extension of the wrist

52 weeks: opposition or superior-forefinger grasp; wrist extended and deviated to ulnar side for efficient grasp; smooth release for large objects and awkward for small objects

Figure 8.3 Sequential Development of Grasp

Source: Assessing Infants and Preschoolers with Handicaps, by D. B. Bailey and M. Wolery, 1989; Upper Saddle River, NJ: Prentice Hall, Copyright 1989 by Prentice Hall, Inc. Reprinted with permission.

Keep in mind that multiple biological and environmental influences affect both the sequence and timing of motor abilities. These influences have origins in prenatal and infant developmental histories, cultural expectations, nutritional status, general health and well-being, and opportunities and encouragement to use emerging capabilities. Table 8.2 identifies the developmental possibilities in small motor development from ages 1 through 4.

chapter 8

Children with Special Needs

Toddlers with cerebral palsy are among those most likely to struggle with motor difficulties. Cerebral palsy is a group of disorders that is caused by damage to the brain. Sometimes it is because the brain went without oxygen for a period of time. Cerebral palsy (CP) may develop in the womb, during the birth process, or anytime in the first 2 years of life. It can affect motor, learning, hearing, seeing, and thinking functioning. The effect may be on a continuum from mild, with very little effect, to severe, where the person has almost no voluntary control of her body and could have brain damage that leaves her unable to learn or speak. Severe motor issues, however, do not necessarily mean learning difficulties will occur. A good example is Christopher Nolan, an Irish poet and author of the autobiography *Eye of the Clock.* Unable to voluntarily move any part of his body below his neck, Nolan is an eloquent, prize-winning poet who began writing on a typewriter with a stick strapped to his forehead.

Cerebral palsy cannot be cured, but it is not progressive. Whatever damage there is will remain stable. Early intervention can make a considerable difference in the abilities of an infant or toddler with CP. An occupational therapist might work with the child to unclench his fist and use his fingers independently and in efficient grips or help him control his head and neck.

Prehension, the ability to use thumb and fingers to grasp small objects, emerges during the first year.

Table 8.2 Developmental Possibilities in Small Motor Development from Ages 1 Through 4

Age	Motor Development
12–18 months	Picks up small objects with pincer movement
	Drops and picks up toys
	Releases a toy into a container
	Knocks over a tower with a wave of the hand
	Throws objects to the floor
	Finger-feeds efficiently
	Uses a spoon awkwardly
	Stacks two cubes after demonstration
	Pours objects from a container
	Builds a tower of three or four cubes
	Holds two cubes in one hand
	Takes off shoes, socks
	Points to things
	Uses a cup for drinking
	Feeds self efficiently

continued

Table 8.2 continued

Age	Motor Development
18–24 months	Manages a spoon and a cup awkwardly at times
	Turns pages of a book, two and three pages at a time
	Places large pegs in a peg board
	Holds a crayon in a fist
	Scribbles
	Squeezes a soft squeak toy
24–36 months	Builds a tower of five to seven cubes
	Strings three or four large beads
	Turns the pages of a book one page at a time
	Imitates demonstrated vertical and circular scribbles
	Manages a spoon and a cup with increasing efficiency
	Lines up objects in a "train" sequence
36–48 months	Builds a tower of 8 to 10 cubes
	Approximates a variety of shapes in drawings
	Feeds self with few spills
	Unbuttons front clothing
	Zips, handles various simple fasteners
	Works puzzles of three to six pieces
	Handles books efficiently
	Exhibits hand preference
	Spreads butter and jam on toast
	Dresses and undresses with assistance

Early interventionists may supply families or early childhood care and education programs with equipment that will help the child achieve optimal outcomes. These may include switches that are used to turn toys on and off by pressing on a disk, sipping or breathing into a tube, or holding the head upright with a switch on a forehead band. This introduction to technology—and cause and effect—may begin a lifetime of increased independence as the child later learns to use an electric wheelchair or other adapted equipment.

Programs should perform ongoing assessment of physical and motor abilities, with special attention to movement competence and emerging large and small motor abilities, including but not limited to the following:

1. Motor functioning
   - Reflexive reactions
   - Posture
   - Balance

- Flexibility
- Voluntary movements
- Transitional movements as in moving from sitting to standing
- Mobility preference patterns
- Eye–hand, eye–foot, and hand–mouth coordination
- Prehensor and grasping/releasing abilities
- Chewing and swallowing efficiency

2. Early intervention services may include the following:
   - Providing appropriate physical and occupational intervention and therapies
   - Providing ongoing assessment, guidance, instruction, and, where needed, adaptive equipment to assist and facilitate emerging motor and self-help abilities
   - Adapting purposeful activities and daily routines to facilitate and enhance physical and motor development
   - Providing high-quality, inclusive early childhood education programs and skilled professionals to ensure optimal developmental progress (Mahoney, Robinson, & Perales, 2004)

Many disabling conditions, when recognized and identified early in the child's development, can be treated and ameliorated. Regular physical examinations and ongoing observations of growth and developmental trends in individual children help to ensure that any unusual developmental events are not overlooked and are responded to in an appropriate and timely way.

Many types of intervention programs and services are available for children and families with special needs. Research in genetics and the neurosciences provides guarded hope for the amelioration and perhaps the alleviation of some disabling conditions in children. As new strategies are designed to identify and examine the molecular origins of specific heritable and congenital anomalies, the scientific community will be better able to direct efforts toward prevention as well as intervention and correction of many disabling conditions. The potential exists to identify the specific points during growth and development from conception through the early years when specific risk factors influence a particular growth trajectory. The potential for intervening with gene and/or drug therapy, neurological intervention through timely environmental and social interaction adjustments, and other strategies holds enormous promise for the field of child development.

Intervention programs for toddlers with special needs involve meeting the child's immediate physical, health, and psychological requirements, supporting parents' priorities for their children (family-centered practice), providing support systems for parents, adapting environments (home and out-of-home child care arrangements), serving children in natural environments (where you would find any child in a community), providing ongoing assessments and therapies as required, providing assistive technologies as needed to facilitate self-help efforts, and coordinating services and supports needed by the child and the family. All young children have a right to participate "actively and meaningfully within their families and communities" (Sandall, McLean, & Smith, 2000, p. 9). It is the role of professionals in early intervention to support families as they provide learning opportunities for their children during routines at home and in inclusive settings in the community.

Relationship Between Physical/Motor and Emotional and Social Development

self-efficacy
the feeling that one's efforts are effective; the perception that one can succeed

Each new motor skill contributes to the child's emerging self-concept and sense of **self-efficacy.** The toddler's early definitions of self are based on his or her interactive experiences with parents, primary caregivers, and important others. These relationships and the toddler's increasing awareness of his or her own capabilities form the basis for body awareness and an emerging self-concept. Self-concept development is a gradual process, which continues throughout childhood and is subject to positive and negative changes as experiences and relationships expand.

Older infants and toddlers demonstrate an emerging self-concept by focusing on certain aspects of their bodies and emerging abilities. Pointing to and naming their body parts; telling their names; holding the appropriate (or approximate) number of fingers to convey their ages; saying "Look at me!" as they demonstrate a new skill; and insisting on doing things for themselves such as pulling off socks and shoes, holding their spoon or cup, and preferring to walk rather than being carried are all indications of the child's emerging body and self-awareness. Important aspects of self-concept development are the child's increasing efforts to be self-sufficient, his or her growing awareness of gender differences, and the self-governance that comes with bladder and bowel control.

Self-Help Efforts

The desire to do things for themselves emerges early when infants choose to hold their bottles, use their hands and fingers to feed themselves, retrieve and relinquish toys and other belongings, and efficiently (vocally, verbally, or through body language) communicate

This toddler's new motor skills increase his emerging self-confidence.

their needs to others. The toddler's increasing sense of self parallels a growing desire for independence or autonomy (self-governance) in some cultures. In others, this period signals an increasing ability to cooperate.

Mobility, aided by refinement of large motor abilities and increasingly skilled use and coordination of eyes and hands through small motor development, facilitates the child's emerging self-help skills. Awkward yet determined attempts at dressing and undressing (usually starting with the removal of shoes and socks or perhaps a diaper), following simple directions, enjoying fetch-and-carry activities, using a washcloth to wash the face after meals, washing hands, bathing, brushing teeth, and reporting simple events ("I broke it") are examples of early self-help abilities. Spills, accidents, and delays are common. Patience, support, and encouragement are needed during these often tedious, time-consuming, and sometimes frustrating early efforts. As toddlers become more successful in their attempts at self-help, their sense of pride and positive self-regard grows, and they are motivated to continue their efforts, becoming more and more efficient with practice and experience. As we discuss in the next chapter, the child's growing sense of independence needs support if healthy social and emotional development is to emerge. Mishandling of these early self-help efforts by reprimanding, cajoling, punishing, or offering other negative responses discourages young children and can lead to dependent, defiant, and other negative behavioral outcomes. Recognizing this as an important aspect of growth and development, adults can anticipate the time it takes for young children to manage self-help tasks and allow for it as much as possible. When time is an issue, determine what the child can do while other tasks are being performed by the adult—for example, "I'll pack the diaper bag, while you pull on your socks. Good, thank you. Now I'll put on one shoe and you put on the other. OK, your shoes on on. Now you go and get your blanky, while I get your sweater; then we will be ready to go to Grandma's house."

Body and Gender Awareness

Body awareness emerges with the acquisition and repetition of each new motor skill. Motor abilities, once discovered, are repeated over and over. Throwing an object from the crib, pulling to a standing position beside furniture and dropping back to a seated one, dumping toys from a container, climbing a staircase, and opening a drawer are some of a myriad of activities for which repetition is, in and of itself, quite pleasurable for the toddler. The intrinsic thrust toward growth and development and the ever-present desire to do more mature things drive toddlers to repeat and repeat actions until new challenges command their attention. Encouragement and praise from their caregivers forward this development. Mastering skills gives toddlers a sense of control or empowerment and an enhanced awareness of their capabilities. For the toddler, this is an exhilarating time. It is also a time for close adult supervision.

Body awareness is also an outgrowth of a child's increasing ability to name body parts. Toddlers enjoy learning the names of their body parts: eyes, ears, nose, mouth, feet, toes, stomach, ribs, and so on. Naming body parts and demonstrating what they can be willed to do often become a game, with the adult asking for identification and delighting in the toddler's answers. These early body awareness experiences are part of a sense of identity that includes an awareness of gender and gender-related behaviors.

Discriminations between male and female emerge during the first year (Brooks-Gunn & Lewis, 1982). **Gender awareness** (the realization that men and women, girls and boys are different) and **gender identity** (the realization of being either male or

body awareness cognizance of one's body, its parts, its functions, and what it can be willed to do

gender awareness the realization that men and women, girls and boys, are different

gender identity the cognizance of being male or female

female) is usually established by age 2½ to 3. Gender awareness involves labeling one-self and others according to gender, an assessment that is usually derived from external characteristics such as the clothing people wear, the toys they own or choose to play with, the way they wear their hair, and so on. Very young children often assume that simply by changing such external characteristics as these, they can become a different gender. Gender role stereotypes have their origins in these early attributions (Wellhousen, 1996). However, a recent study showed that toddlers of unmarried mothers had much less stereotypical judgment, probably because they witnessed their mothers doing androgynous tasks (Hupp, Smith, Coleman, & Brunell, 2010).

Toddlers may demonstrate emerging gender awareness through curiosity about their and others' anatomies. Curiosity about body parts of others is unabashed and straightforward. The toddler may touch mother's breasts, watch intently as father urinates, become intrigued by the body parts of siblings, and explore their own genitalia. These behaviors reflect normal curiosity, are harmless, and represent the child's growing body awareness and the early stages of **sexuality** (Chrisman & Couchenour, 2002).

Sexuality develops in stages from infancy through adulthood, just as other aspects of human functioning do, and distinct differences exist between childhood sexuality and adult sexuality.

Childhood sexuality is marked by curiosity and play, spontaneity and openness, and sensuality and excitement. Adult sexuality is characterized by knowing and consequential behavior, self-consciousness and privacy, and passion and eroticism (Rothbaum, Grauer, & Rubin, 1997). Hence, the meanings that young children attach to gender differences and sexual behaviors are distinctly different from those of adults. Children's sexuality is characterized by interest in the body and its functions, labels for body parts, and experiments with adult language associated with the body and its functions. Young children are usually quite comfortable in their own skin and are not always as concerned about privacy (which is learned behavior). Hence, they are open and direct with their curiosities, questions, and sexuality behaviors. These behaviors are often unsettling to adults, particularly if the adults attach adult meanings and their own feelings and values to the behaviors and fail to recognize that young children's sexuality behaviors are not accompanied by the hormonal underpinnings and eroticism that characterize adolescent and adult sexuality.

Parents and adults who work with young children should respond in a manner that does not convey shock, embarrassment, or reprimand. Sometimes, simply naming the body parts is all that is required. It is appropriate to use correct anatomical terms such as *urinate, bowel movement, breasts,* and *penis,* as this assists the toddler's understanding and helps to prevent the development of misconceptions. One 2-year-old, sitting in a grocery store shopping cart, used this information and announced, "My bladder is full" to the great amusement of the produce aisle shoppers. Further, it is appropriate to talk about and set clear limits about public and personal behaviors, modesty and privacy, and appropriate language to use and in what contexts. Such discussion should be matter-of-fact, respectful, and free of accusation or shame.

Questions that often accompany the toddler's curiosity about gender should be answered in simple, sensitive, and nonjudgmental ways. Toddlers have many questions about why girls and boys are different, why they use the toilet in different ways, how babies get in a mommy's tummy, why girls don't have a penis, and the like. Matter-of-fact answers that are simple enough for the child to understand are all that is required at this age. What is most important is that children feel psychologically safe in asking

sexuality
the relational, biological, and procreational aspects of gender

questions. Shock, embarrassment, or reprimand stifles healthy communication between adult and child and conveys negative messages about the human body—the child's and those of others. Rather, adults need to be approachable on topics relating to human anatomy, gender, and sexuality and should refrain from elaborate technical or value-laden discussion. Answering questions as they arise is always preferable to postponement to a later time (or age), deferring to the other parent or another adult, or arranging a certain time for a formal discussion. Such strategies convey confusing messages to children who have asked what are reasonable questions to them.

Toilet Learning

In infancy, the elimination of body wastes occurs involuntarily as a reflexive activity when the bladder or bowels need emptying. During the first year or so, the infant must develop a conscious awareness of the feelings of bowel and bladder fullness and develop some control over anal and urethral sphincters. Such control cannot occur until certain nerve pathways have developed and matured. The toddler must have developed some language and locomotor skills to signal a need to caregivers, get to the toilet in due time, manage clothing, and then manage toileting itself. This is not a small order.

Toilet learning is a gradual maturational process that extends over a period of several years. It is not, as the term *toilet training* implies, something that can be taught at some predetermined age. Instead, parents and caregivers learn to respond to the child's readiness cues. Toilet learning depends on complex neurological development. Usually, bowel control precedes bladder control. A number of physiological events must have occurred before bowel and bladder controls develop. Neurological development brings consciousness of bladder and bowel discomfort. Certain large motor skills that are required for getting to and using toilet facilities must be in place, along with the fine motor skills necessary for handling clothing. Verbal skills (or, in the beginning, body language cues) are necessary to express the need for assistance, and the conscious ability to control the sphincters that hold and let go must be present. These developments emerge over an extended time, and toileting remains a relatively unskilled activity well into the preschool years.

toilet learning
a gradual maturational process in which the child gains control over elimination

Between the ages of 18 and 20 months, the toddler begins to indicate an awareness of soiled diapers, may attempt to remove the diaper, and may employ idiosyncratic words to describe the need to urinate or defecate. These are early signals that toilet learning is in progress. Overresponding to these cues with expectations that control is imminent can yield disappointing results. Certainly, attempts to impose rigid toileting schedules are doomed, but being aware of the times of day when toileting seems to occur with regularity—for example, on waking from a nap, soon after breakfast, or first thing in the morning—helps adults to begin a system of inquiries or reminders that help the child to notice the need and willingly proceed to the toilet. Insistence is counterproductive, as is reprimand, shaming, or punishing. Indeed, undue pressure from adults only prolongs the process by creating stress, anxiety, or power control situations that have negative effects on both child and adult and on the adult–child relationship. The child needs to experience adult patience, assistance, encouragement, and praise for efforts as toilet learning proceeds. Toileting accidents should be treated respectfully, for many will occur before mastery is achieved; again, embarrassment or punishment do little to enhance this complex developmental process.

When a child is interested in using the toilet but continues to have great difficulty with bowel movements, the problem may be physical. For some children, the intestines do not move the stool along. The stool becomes impacted and can't be passed without pain. This condition is called encopresis and should be treated by a pediatric gastroenterologist.

Some children may achieve control over their toileting needs by age 2, others may lack such control until age 3 or 4, and still others may not be free of occasional toileting accidents before age 5 or 6. Once control seems to be established, children will have relapses for a variety of reasons: impending illness, diarrhea, bladder infections, sound sleep, being too busy to notice the need, excitement, anxiety, or psychological trauma, to mention some. Toddlers sometimes revert to precontrol stages when family life is altered in some manner: a family move, a new baby, hospitalization of a family member, a death or divorce in the family, or even an unusually exciting and happy event such as a birthday party or holiday celebration. Adults should expect uneven development in toilet learning and should not show disappointment when the toddler is unsuccessful. The positive and supportive manner in which adults handle toilet learning will be instrumental in ensuring continued control and healthy attitudes toward the human body and elimination.

Theorists have related body and gender awareness experiences and toilet learning to social and emotional development. Erikson (1963), for instance, related toilet learning to the child's developing sense of autonomy (self-governance) or feelings of shame and doubt and suggested that its healthy management has far-reaching effects on psychosocial development.

Health and Nutrition

This section elaborates on topics that were introduced in Chapter 5 and includes some additional topics. You may wish to review the relevant section in Chapter 5 before reading the following.

Nutrition

The visible effects of prolonged malnutrition on young children are seen almost daily in television newscasts and philanthropic solicitations for help for children in underdeveloped countries. Hollow eyes, protruding abdomens, and skeletal bodies are disturbing features of seriously malnourished children. Nutrition-related health problems exist not only in third-world countries, but in all cultures around the world. Poor nutrition is associated with impaired neurological and physical development, poor cognitive outcomes, numerous health and disease issues, compromised immune systems, and vulnerability to environmental toxins. Indeed, a recent study by the Centers for Disease Control and Prevention reported the identification of nutritional rickets, a condition that causes weak or deformed bones, among some children in the United States, although the disease is rare in this country. The children who were identified as having rickets were breast-fed as infants and toddlers, but did not receive recommended vitamin D supplements (Centers for Disease Control and Prevention (CDC), 2001). In 2003, the American Academy of Pediatrics (AAP) developed guidelines for vitamin D intake and revised them in 2008 (Wagner, Greer, & the Section on Breastfeeding and Committee on Nutrition). Always check the AAP's Web site for up-to-date information (www.aap.org).

Food provides the nutrients young children need to grow and develop strong minds and bodies and the energy required to play, think, and learn. Helping toddlers to learn to eat and enjoy the types of food that ensure proper nutrition involves (1) wise selection of nutritious foods, (2) appealing preparation and presentation of new foods and including the child in the preparation of snacks and meals, (3) mealtime social and emotional climates that are conducive to food enjoyment and digestion, and (4) respect for the child's satiety and food preferences.

Because the young child's immune system is immature, protection from food-borne illnesses is crucial. The child's eating surfaces and utensils must be scrupulously clean, and toddlers can be taught to wash their hands and faces before and after eating. Food should be properly cleaned, cooked, and prepared and served at the appropriate temperature. It should be served in manageable portions. Finger foods should be peeled (when appropriate) and cut into small, manageable pieces. All food served to toddlers should be a size and consistency that the young child can mouth, chew, and swallow. Foods that can cause choking should be avoided. Foods that are likely to be aspirated include hot dogs, meat (beef, pork, chicken) in chunks that are too large and too tough to chew and swallow easily, peanuts and other nuts, popcorn, grapes, carrots, round hard candies, stiff chewy candies (taffy, caramels), and chewing gum.

Wise Selection of Nutritious Foods. The toddler's daily dietary plan should consist of food selected from the following five food groups: (1) breads, cereals, rice, and pasta; (2) vegetables and fruit; (3) milk, yogurt, and cheese; (4) meat, poultry, fish, beans, and eggs; and (5) fats, oils, and sweets (sparingly). Fatty foods and sweets need not be eliminated from the toddler's diet, but should be included judiciously. Recall from Chapter 5 that young children should not be placed on low-fat diets except on the advice and guidance of a pediatrician or health care professional. However, many foods that are marketed to young children are inappropriately high in sugars and fats and should be selected only on the basis of their contribution to the overall dietary needs of the young child. Furthermore, overreliance on any of the food groups deprives the growing child of other vital nutrients. Because different foods contain different combinations of nutrients and other substances necessary for growth and health, a variety of food choices is necessary. No single food or meal plan can supply all of the essential nutrients. If the child does not eat from each food group each day, don't worry. Consider the overall nutrition over the course of several days.

Appealing Preparation and Presentation of New Foods; Including the Child in Preparation. Toddlers are just beginning to get acquainted with many solid foods and beverages other than milk. They are being introduced to a variety of food tastes, textures, colors, consistencies, and temperatures. Acceptance of new food experiences depends on the *v*isual, *o*lfactory, *t*exture, and *t*aste (VOTT) appeal of the food. As with older children and adults, foods that fail the VOTT test have a high rejection rate. New foods are best introduced in very small portions with another, familiar food

Toddlers enjoy eating together.

Perceptual, Motor, and Physical Development; Health and Nutrition: Ages One Through Three

that the child has an established taste for and likes. To engage interest, the food can be named in a manner that informs and responds to the child's curiosity: "You have never had spinach before; this is spinach." If it is at first rejected, the food can be reintroduced from time to time until a taste is acquired. Encouraging children to taste new foods but not insisting on their eating the whole serving gives them an opportunity to learn about the food in a positive context.

Toddlers enjoy helping with food preparation and are often more willing to try foods they helped to cook. They enjoy stirring, spreading, pouring, and mixing. You are likely to see them repeating these activities later in their play.

Mealtime Social and Emotional Climates Conducive to Food Enjoyment and Digestion. Toddlers are gaining independence in feeding themselves: finger feeding, using a spoon, and drinking from a cup—all of which involve the development of chewing and swallowing and eye–hand and hand–mouth coordinations. It takes focus and concentration to do these things well. Playful distractions and negative interactions interfere with this process. Laughing, talking, or crying with food in the mouth increases the risk of choking. Pleasant conversation and positive role models during mealtime help toddlers to focus on eating and to eat enough to satisfy their hunger. Mealtimes should never be a time to reprimand or discipline, nor should food be used to reward or punish. Using food in this manner attaches the wrong meaning to it and leads to the individual's use of food to satisfy psychological instead of physiological needs (e.g., eating when feeling unhappy, bored, angry, or self-defeated or rejecting food to self-punish or to rebel against frustrating situations).

Respect for the Child's Satiety and Food Preferences. Toddlers' appetites vary from meal to meal and day to day and are not quite as commanding as during infancy, when growth was so rapid. Nevertheless, toddlers should be offered three nutritious meals and two nutritious snacks each day. Serving sizes should be small yet sufficient to satisfy the child's hunger. Large serving sizes can discourage the young child. Tastes and food preferences also vary from day to day, often according to temporary whims. Whims are no cause for concern as long as, over the course of two or three days, children are offered a variety of nutrient-rich foods from which to choose. Because of the toddler's short attention span, mealtimes should not be too prolonged. Taking cues from the child, the adult can end the meal when it is clear that the child is no longer hungry. Minimal intake at one or two meals is no need for concern. Healthy children generally eat sufficient amounts of food to satisfy them. Avoiding nonnutritious sugary or fatty between-meal snacks increases the child's enjoyment of mealtime and enhances his or her intake of essential nutrients provided by well-balanced meals and snacks. However, if the timing or content of a meal is such that the child is hungry at a later time, providing a nutritious snack helps to fill his or her nutritive needs and sustains the child until the next meal. Finally, it is important to note that it is the adult who purchases, prepares, and offers nutritious foods to children. However, it is the child who knows when he or she has had enough to eat and when a particular food holds no appeal.

Rapid growth during the preschool years makes regular health assessment check-ups imperative. In general, children need to be examined two or three times during the second year and one or two times per year thereafter. This schedule helps to ensure that immunizations are kept current and that emerging developmental and health care needs are addressed as they arise. In addition to the general developmental and health examinations, children may be tested for anemia, lead levels in the blood, and any other unusual symptoms.

Because infectious diseases can spread rapidly among children in groups, child care and early education programs adopt attendance and participation policies. These policies address conditions or symptoms that require isolation, exclusion, or temporary dismissal. The American Public Health Association and the American Academy of Pediatrics (2002) published recommended guidelines in *Caring for Our Children: National Health and Safety Performance Standards: Guidelines for Out-of-Home Child Care Programs.* The third edition was published in 2011. For information on this and other health and safety topics relating to children in groups, the reader is referred to this thorough and comprehensive set of standards (http://nrckids.org/). Some obvious signs require immediate attention such as fever, uncharacteristic lethargy, irritability, crying, difficulty breathing, diarrhea, vomiting, mouth sores, rash, infestations such as head lice, scabies, or symptoms of any of the communicable diseases. Individuals who care for children on a daily basis are better prepared to address these health issues when they are armed with knowledge of common symptoms and behaviors and how to respond to children who are ill or injured, as well as how to prevent the spread of illness among children.

A growing concern for scientists is the increasing prevalence of bacteria that are antibiotic resistant, that is, the antibiotics used to combat some infections are no longer effective. Antibiotics can be powerful allies in the treatment of infectious diseases but are designed to cure *bacterial* infections. Antibiotics are ineffective in treating *viral* infections. The more often a child is treated with antibiotics, particularly when the illness is caused by a virus, or when the entire course of antibiotic treatment is not taken, the higher the risk becomes for untreatable bacterial infections. This is explained by the fact that each time an antibiotic is prescribed, sensitive bacteria are killed, but resistant bacteria are left to grow and multiply. These resistant bacteria do not respond to the antibiotic, so the illness is unaffected and persists and may increase in severity. These antibiotic-resistant bacteria may be spread to others as well.

The child's physician, who may advise a parent or caregiver to allow a particular ailment to run its course without medication, best determines the need for antibiotics for infections and illnesses such as ear infections, sinus infections, cough, bronchitis, sore throat, and colds. A related concern under investigation is the use of antibiotics in agriculture, which creates drug-resistant strains in the food supply (Shea, 2003).

Immunization Benefits and Risks

Immunizations are the world's best defense against many debilitating and life-threatening diseases. Before vaccinations became widely used, infectious diseases killed thousands of children and adults each year in the United States and around the world. Indeed, even today in parts of the world where vaccinations are not widely administered, children and adults still suffer the devastating effects of many of the diseases that have been virtually eradicated in the United States. Table 8.3 lists vaccine-preventable diseases and their risk characteristics.

Because infants are particularly vulnerable to infections, it is important to begin immunizations during infancy. A precise immunization schedule is designed to provide immunizations at appropriate age intervals and doses for each preventable disease. Although breastfeeding supplies some protection against some infections, such as colds,

Table 8.3 Vaccine-Preventable Diseases

Disease	Characteristics and Risks
Chicken pox (varicella)	Characterized by fever, blistery, itchy rash; can cause pneumonia or death
Diphtheria	Characterized by a thick coating in nose or throat, which can lead to breathing obstruction, heart failure, paralysis, or death
Haemophilus influenzae type B (Hib) infection	Causes meningitis; swelling of the membranes surrounding the brain and/or spinal cord; also causes pneumonia and other diseases
Hepatitis B	Causes severe liver disease, liver cancer; can lead to death
Measles	Characterized by a rash, conjunctivitis, cough, and fever; can lead to pneumonia, seizures, brain damage, or death
Mumps	Characterized by fever, headaches, and swollen glands under the jaw; can lead to hearing loss and/or meningitis
Polio	Characterized by fever, stiffness in the neck and shoulders, headache, muscle spasms; can result in paralysis and death
Rubella (3-day measles)	Characterized by rash and fever; particularly dangerous for pregnant woman, who could miscarry or give birth to an infant with serious problems including brain damage, heart disease, and other anomalies
Smallpox	Characterized by high fever, headache, backache, pustular blisters that form pockmarks; high risk of death; *note:* this disease has been considered eradicated, and vaccinations for it were halted in the United States in 1972; however, the threat of bioterrorism around the world suggests that there could be a time when this vaccination should be reinstituted for some populations
Tetanus (lockjaw)	Characterized by severe muscle spasms; high risk of death

ear infections, and diarrhea, it does not stimulate the infant's immune system to fight infection against specific diseases. Therefore, breastfeeding, for all of its benefits, is not effective in preventing contagious, vaccine-preventable diseases.

In recent years, concern about the safety of some vaccinations has arisen. Reports of risks associated with various vaccines have resulted in the reluctance of some parents to have their children immunized. Modern-day vaccines are getting safer and more effective with continuing research and ongoing review by physicians, researchers, and public health officials. Vaccines are required to meet very strict safety standards of the U.S. Food and Drug Administration (FDA) before they are approved. Further, the FDA and the U.S. Centers for Disease Control and Prevention (CDC) closely monitor every vaccine as long as it is in use. In 1990, the FDA and the CDC established the Vaccine Adverse Events Reporting System (VAERS) to collect and analyze all reports (from anyone who wishes to submit one, including parents) of possible adverse reactions. Such reporting has led to a database from which analysis and large-scale research studies can be generated to determine whether a reaction is vaccine associated or has origins that are unrelated to the vaccine.

Although it is true that serious adverse effects from vaccines have occurred, the incidence of these events is extremely rare. Hence, scientists and parents must weigh the *benefits* against the *risks* of a particular vaccine. Generally, scientists conclude that the chance of serious complications (including death) from the disease itself is many times higher than is the chance of vaccine-related complications.

During the past decade, the prestigious Institute of Medicine (IOM) has conducted extensive reviews of the scientific studies and medical literature on health problems occurring after vaccination. The IOM provides the health care community its findings from these objective and thorough reviews. A list of these reports is available through the Web site of the Allied Vaccine Group, a linked group of organizations committed to providing valid scientific information about vaccines (see Other Resources at the end of this chapter).

Immunizations are required when children are enrolled in child care settings and schools. All 50 states have immunization laws. Each state determines which vaccines are required by state law. Most states rely on the vaccination schedules recommended by the Committee on Infectious Diseases of the American Academy of Pediatrics, the Advisory Committee on Immunization Practices of the Centers for Disease Control and Prevention, and the American Academy of Family Physicians. Child care and school vaccination laws are designed to prevent outbreaks of contagious diseases. Unvaccinated children are at high risk of contracting and spreading a preventable disease.

As of August 2003, all 50 states have passed laws allowing for certain exemptions. States may exempt children from the immunization requirements on the basis of medical, religious, or philosophical reasons. However, to be enrolled in child care programs and schools, families must present state-required documentation to support their request for exemption. Should an outbreak of a disease occur in a school or child care setting, children who have not been immunized may be prevented by law from attending until the outbreak is over.

Other Communicable Diseases and Health Issues

There are a number of additional health issues associated with very young children. Among the more prominent ones are the rising incidence of childhood asthma, the control of HIV/AIDS disease, and the reappearance of diseases once thought to be eradicated in the United States.

Asthma. Childhood asthma is a chronic disease that makes airways (bronchial tubes) sensitive to irritants. It affects 6.2 million children under the age of 18 (Healthy Children.Org, 2012). Because this disease can slow growth and development and can be potentially life-threatening, it is important to determine the types of triggers to an asthma episode and, where possible, control or eliminate exposure. Some common irritants and risk factors are cigarette smoke; pet dander; household dust, particularly dusty bedding, pillows, or stuffed toys; strong odors; certain foods; cockroaches; hay; dry leaves and pollen; emotional disturbances; overexertion; and seasonal and weather changes. The family's health care professional can provide appropriate therapies, medication, and guidance regarding control of triggers to asthma. Parents have a responsibility to communicate with their children's nonparental caregivers about their child's particular health care needs. Personnel in child care settings and schools may need to assess their environments for potential asthma triggers and be clear about how to respond to a particular child's asthma episode. The Caring for Our Children (http://nrckids.org/) materials include a *Special Care Plan for a Child with Asthma* that early care and education programs are encouraged to complete with the family. This Special Care Plan provides information on the typical signs and symptoms of the child's asthma episodes, known triggers for the child's asthma, and activities for which the child has needed special attention in the past.

HIV/AIDS. The human immunodeficiency virus (HIV), which causes acquired immunodeficiency syndrome (AIDS), is a disease that has risen rapidly in prevalence among heterosexual men and women, including adolescents. HIV attacks the immune system, rendering it ineffective in fighting infectious diseases. It is spread through sexual contact, intravenous drug use, and, in very rare cases, blood transfusions and organ transplants. This disease can be transmitted to the fetus during prenatal development, labor, and delivery and through breastfeeding. However, certain medications during pregnancy can reduce the chance of a mother passing HIV to an infant. For this reason, the American College of Obstetricians and Gynecologists (2011) recommends that all pregnant women be tested for HIV so treatment can be initiated if needed.

If the mother of a newborn is known to have HIV, then testing of HIV in the infant is recommended before 14 days of life, at 1 to 2 months of age, and at 3 to 6 months of age. If any of these tests is positive, repeat testing must be done to confirm the diagnosis. Treatment can begin immediately (American Academy of Pediatrics, Read, & the Committee on Pediatric AIDS, 2010). Guidelines for the care of children with AIDS in child care settings include protection of both the child who has AIDS and other children and adults (American Academy of Pediatrics, American Public Health Association, National Resource Center for Health and Safety in Child Care and Early Education, 2011). Of critical importance is the strictest regime to prevent infants and toddlers from consuming milk or juice from bottles or cups used by another infant. Further, when **standard precautions** are used in responding to incidents that involve exposure to blood or blood-containing body fluids and tissue discharges, the potential spread of disease is reduced.

standard precautions procedures involving the use of protective barriers such as nonporous gloves, aprons, disposable diapers and diaper table paper, disposable towels, and surfaces that can be sanitized to reduce the risk of exposure to pathogens

Resurgence of Communicable Diseases. Resurgence of diseases thought to be under control within a given population is always a concern to health care professionals, who diligently strive to prevent the spread of disease particularly among children. Because of state laws that allow for certain exemptions for religious or philosophical reasons, unimmunized children who contract a disease can spread it to others, both adults and other unimmunized children. The increase in cases of measles, whooping cough, and polio in recent years in the United States has been attributed to:

1. failure to fully immunize;
2. immigrants and vacation travelers who have or carry the disease from locations around the world where the disease exists;

3. diseases such as HIV that compromise a person's immune system; and

4. the fading of immunity provided by vaccination to a disease as a person enters adulthood. Whooping cough, a highly contagious respiratory tract infection, has been increasing among teens and adults because of fading immunity (Mayo Clinic, 2009). See Table 8.3 for a list of vaccine-preventable diseases.

In recent years, tuberculosis (TB), generally thought of as a disease of the past, has reemerged as a serious public health problem (Mayo Clinic, 2011). The CDC (2011) reports that 11,545 TB cases (a rate of 3.8 cases per 100,000 persons) were reported in the United States in 2009. Both the number of TB cases reported and the case rate decreased compared to 2008 (CDC, 2011). In 2009, 646 children under the age of 14 in the United States (6% of all cases) were infected with TB. The CDC (2010) reports that the TB bacteria usually attack the lungs but can attack kidneys, spine, brain, and other parts of the body.

People with latent TB infection cannot spread the disease and may not even know that they have it. However, if the TB bacteria become active in their bodies, people become sick and can spread the disease by spreading bacteria through the air when they cough, sneeze, speak, or sing. Both types of TB can be diagnosed through a tuberculin skin test or special TB blood test. With appropriate medical diagnosis and treatment, TB can be cured in most cases. Treatment involves drug therapy over a six- to 12-month period. Early diagnosis and treatment of tuberculosis are necessary steps in preventing the spread of the disease (CDC, 2011).

Sleep. Adequate amounts of sleep and rest contribute to general health and a sense of well-being. The need for sleep decreases as children get older. The average hours of sleep for 6-month-old children is 14.2 hours a day, including naps (Iglowstein, Jenni, Molinari, & Largo, 2003). By 2 years of age, Iglowstein et al. (2003) found that toddlers sleep an average of 13.2 hours a day. They may take one or two short naps or one long nap during the day and sleep anywhere from 8 to 12 hours at night. Many toddlers are ready to give up the crib in favor of a bed, preferably one with sturdy side rails to prevent falls; however, some toddlers feel safe and sleep best when in a crib. For safety reasons, toddlers should sleep in a bed if they know how to climb out of their cribs. By age 3, children sleep an average of 12.5 hours a day (Iglowstein et al., 2003). Regular and predictable routines (bath, bedtime story, brushing teeth, saying "good night" to family members, a few moments of quiet with a parent, and finally lights out or night-light on) help toddlers to accept the separation and to meet their sleep needs more effectively.

Toddlers are social beings, and resistance to bedtime may well arise. Ages 1 through 3 are marked by an emerging sense of autonomy and a lingering fear of separation. These psychological issues complicate bedtime and naptime rituals. Bedtime difficulties may arise from a low sensory threshold, which causes the young child to be easily distracted by environmental noise, motion, and light; the parent's overconcern or difficulty in separating from the child; inappropriate expectations that a child can separate and fall asleep on demand; ambivalence over regular versus child-initiated routines; and a variety of physiological problems associated with growth (e.g., outgrowing the crib, wakefulness associated with toileting needs), impending illness, fatigue, overstimulation, hunger, and thirst.

Toddlers may sleep on mats on the floor during naptime with a favorite stuffed animal.

Teachers in early care and education programs can work with parents to discuss naptime rituals. Toddlers usually sleep on pads on the floor with their favorite lovee or blanket, and teachers transition toddlers into sleep by reading to them, patting them, and/or creating a calm mood. Toddlers do not all sleep for the same amount of time, so it is helpful to have a separate supervised room where toddlers who wake up can go and possibly have a drink and snack. Children are healthiest when they get an adequate amount of sleep, so it is worth parents' and teachers' time to communicate successes and challenges regarding naptime in a program.

Dental Health. As mentioned earlier in this chapter (see Figure 8.1), all of the child's primary teeth have usually appeared by age 3. Primary teeth usually follow a predictable sequence of eruption, with the lower incisors appearing first. During the second and third years, a total of 20 primary teeth will erupt. The American Academy of Pediatric Dentists recommends a visit to the dentist by the time a child is 1 year old and thereafter every six months. In addition to examining for cavities, the dentist can determine the health of the child's teeth and gums and estimate when new teeth will erupt. The dentist will also counsel parents about nutritional needs, foods to avoid, and the need for fluoride or vitamin supplements to ensure healthy teeth. The dentist will monitor the effects of pacifier use or thumbsucking on the developing oral structures and recommend appropriate handling of these important self-comforting behaviors. Generally, as toddlers get older, begin to talk, and become engaged with a variety of hands-on toys and activities, there is less need or desire for the thumb or pacifier; but during times of boredom, stress, fatigue, or illness, they may rely on these self-comforting behaviors.

Dental health begins in infancy. Regular cleaning of the infant's gums and new teeth after meals with a soft, damp gauze pad begins the process of instilling good oral cleaning habits and avoiding cavities in primary teeth. Avoiding use of the bottle as a pacifier is also necessary to prevent "baby bottle caries," the disease that can lead to cavities in forming teeth. With increasing eye–hand and hand–mouth coordination, the toddler can soon learn to use a brush and a small amount of toothpaste. Encouraging brushing after meals and before bedtime begins an essential self-help habit.

Safety. Toddlers are particularly vulnerable to mishaps. Their impulsive behaviors, lack of experience and judgment, curiosity, and quest for independence place them at risk for accident and injury. Adult expectations also place toddlers at risk for accident and injury when adults assume that toddlers are capable of tasks or judgments that are beyond their years. Table 8.4 outlines important measures for adults to take during the toddler period to prevent accidents and injury.

Table 8.4 Important Accident Prevention Measures for Families to Observe During the Toddler Period

Potential Accident Situations and Environments	Prevention Measures for Health Teaching
Motor vehicles	The AAP reports that motor vehicle crashes are the number one cause of death for children and adolescents ages 1 to 21. The AAP advises parents to keep their infants and toddlers in rear-facing car seats until age 2, or until they reach the maximum height and weight for their seat. "Children should transition from a rear-facing seat to a forward-facing seat with a harness, until they reach the maximum weight or height for that seat. Then a booster will make sure the vehicle's lap-and-shoulder belt fit properly" (American Academy of Pediatrics, 2011) *Never* leave your child in a car alone. "Children who are left in a car can die of heat stroke because temperatures can reach deadly levels in minutes" (Healthychildren.org, 2012).
Garage and Basement Safety	Make sure that the automatic reversing mechanism is properly adjusted on garage doors. Do not allow children to play near the garage. "Keep paints, varnishes, thinners, pesticides, and fertilizers in a locked cabinet or locker" (Healthychildren.org, 2012).
Cribs	Keep a baby's crib away from windows as window blinds and draperies can strangle children.
Falls	Keep house windows closed or keep "child safety" secure screens in place or install window guards (American Academy of Pediatrics, 2010). Place gates at top and bottom of stairs. Do not allow child to walk with sharp objects in hand or mouth. Do not use baby walkers. "Your child may tip it over, fall out of it, or fall down the stairs in it" (Healthychildren.org, 2012).
Aspiration and Strangling	Examine toys for small parts that could be aspirated; remove those that appear dangerous. Do not feed a toddler popcorn, peanuts, etc.; urge children not to eat while running. Keep plastic wrappers and bags away form children as they can form a tight seal if placed over the mouth and nose and may suffocate a child (Healthychildren.org, 2012). Do not use cribs with drop-down sides. Children have suffocated when the side malfunctions. Choose cribs with slats that are no more than 2 3/8 inches apart. Wider spaced slats can trap the infant's head (Healthychildren.org, 2012). Do not leave a toddler alone with a balloon.
Water Safety-Drowning	Do not leave a toddler alone in a bathtub or near water (including buckets of water). Do not leave toddlers alone near a pool or spa—not even for a moment.
Animal bites	Do not allow the toddler to approach strange dogs. Supervise child's play with family pets.

continued

Table 8.4 continued

Potential Accident Situations and Environments	Prevention Measures for Health Teaching
Poisoning and Choking	Never present medication as candy and never take medication in front of a child.
	Keep child-proof caps on medications and dangerous products; put away immediately after use.
	Place all medications and poisons in locked cabinets or overhead shelves where child cannot reach.
	Never leave medication in parents' purse or pocket, where child can reach.
	Always store food or substances in their original containers.
	Learn how to save the life of a choking child.
	Use non–lead-based paint throughout the house.
	Hang plants or set them on high surfaces beyond toddler's grasp.
	Call Poison Help line at 1-800-222-1222 immediately if you think a child has been poisoned.
Burns	Buy flame-retardant clothing.
	Turn handles of pots toward back of stove to prevent toddler from reaching up and pulling them down.
	"NEVER leave cups of hot coffee on tables or counter edges. And NEVER carry hot liquids or food near your child or while holding your child" (Healthychildren.org, 2012).
	Use cool-mist vaporizers.
	Keep screen in front of fireplace or heater.
	Do not leave toddlers unsupervised near lit candles or hot-water faucets.
	Make sure that you have a working smoke alarm on every level of your home and test the alarms every month.
	Do not allow toddlers to blow out matches (teach them that fire is not fun); store matches out of reach.
	Keep electric wires and cords out of toddler's reach; cover electrical outlets with safety plugs.

Issues in Perceptual, Motor, and Physical Development and Health and Nutrition

As infants grow into toddlers and toddlers become preschoolers, their rapid growth and development often suggest greater maturity and capability than are actually present. This can lead to inappropriate expectations. Such expectations place young children at both physical and psychological risk.

Appropriate and Inappropriate Expectations

Knowledge of expected patterns and sequences of physical and motor development helps adults to appreciate each child's unique capabilities and interest and gives direction to the provision of growth-enhancing experiences for children. Further, it is important to acknowledge that young children behave in impulsive and unpredictable ways and are a long way from being able to precede their actions with thoughtful restraint and good judgment. Nor are young children capable of protecting themselves in dangerous situations.

A case in point is the misguided assumption that teaching infants to swim will make them safer in and around swimming pools or other bodies of water. According to health and safety statistics, drowning ranks among the leading causes of unintentional injury and death in children and is highest among children ages 1 through 2 years old (Centers for Disease Control and Prevention, 2007). Although aquatic programs have gained popularity

Toddlers need safe environments and adult protection to enjoy health-promoting, stress-free outdoor play.

in the United States in recent years, their enticements should not suggest to parents that their children can become good swimmers or be able to survive independently in the water—an age-*in*appropriate expectation.

There can be no assurance that infants and toddlers will understand water hazards, use appropriate avoidance and safety strategies, or internalize safety rules. Claims to the contrary mislead parents and give them a false sense of security about their child's safety in the water (American Academy of Pediatrics, 2000). Neither safety skills nor swimming skills are appreciably enhanced when lessons begin in infant or toddler ages. Further, there is no evidence that infant/toddler swimming lessons ensure more rapid mastery of swimming skills. Depth perception, cognizance of risk levels, and judgment are still immature, and it has been noted that the complex motor skills required in swimming can be acquired more readily when fundamental motor skills are coordinated and controlled around age 5 years (American Academy of Pediatrics, 2000). As with all expectations, developmental readiness and individual interest should influence the choice of activities and experiences provided for children.

Examples of inappropriate expectations include expecting small children to use writing tools or scissors, to color within the lines, and to manage complicated clothing before they have the fine motor control to do so; expecting young children to remember safety rules and precautions; and assuming that behaviors demonstrated in one situation (e.g., managing toileting at home) will be manifest routinely in other situations (managing toileting at preschool). The following are important to help adults to gauge expectations and ensure that the opportunities provided for children are in sync with their developmental capabilities and needs: observe toddlers closely; assess where they focus their energies and interests; and note the questions they ask and how they manage various large and small motor tasks, express their needs, and understand, remember, and follow requests.

Sadly, inappropriate expectations have sometimes led to child abuse when parents have become frustrated over a child's "failure" to perform as expected. Indeed, abuse of infants and toddlers has been associated with infant crying, toileting accidents, food spills, inability to verbalize needs or articulate words so as to be understood, sleep/waking

Perceptual, Motor, and Physical Development; Health and Nutrition: Ages One Through Three

Figure 8.4
Healthy Environments
for Young Children

Healthy home and child care environments for young children are characterized by the following:

1. **Adequate space.** Toddlers need sufficient space in which to try out their emerging and uncoordinated motor skills. Tumbles and collisions with furniture are minimized when adequate space is provided.
2. **Clean, sanitary surroundings.** Toddlers put their hands, toys, and other objects into their mouths. All necessary precautions must be taken to protect toddlers from infections and disease.
3. **Safe space and play materials.** Reaching, grasping, and mobility skills tempt toddlers to satisfy their natural curiosity. The toddler's environment must be kept free from obstacles, poisons, sharp edges, small objects, unstable furnishings and play equipment, exposed electrical cords and outlets, and so on.
4. **Developmentally appropriate play items and equipment.** Developmentally appropriate play items help to ensure safety and provide satisfying and engaging experiences that enhance physical, motor, and perceptual development and enrich play activities.
5. **Unrelenting supervision.** Although toddler mobility and curiosity enhance physical, motor, and perceptual growth and cognitive development, constant vigilance is essential. Safety concerns are paramount at this age.
6. **Supervised health care.** To maintain healthy bodies, health care must be supervised by appropriate medical and dental professionals. Proper diet, immunizations, rest and exercise, and specialized medical attention as needed enhance chances for optimal growth and development.

patterns, curiosity and handling of objects in the environment, and many other typical and age-expected behaviors. Inappropriate expectations undermine healthy growth and development and subvert the relationship between children and the adults on whom they depend. The characteristics of healthy environments for young children are listed in Figure 8.4.

Child Abuse and Neglect

Maltreatment is defined as "any act or series of acts of commission or omission by a parent or other caregiver that results in harm, potential for harm, or threat of harm to a child." Child abuse is defined as "words or overt actions that cause harm, potential harm, or threat of harm to a child." Child abuse includes physical abuse, sexual abuse, and psychological abuse. Child neglect is defined as "the failure to provide for a child's basic physical, emotional, or educational needs or to protect a child from harm or potential harm" (Leeb, Paulozzi, Melanson, Simon, & Arias, 2010). For more definitions and information, see the following reference document that is updated continuously: www.cdc.gov/ViolencePrevention/pub/CMP-Surveillance.html and the Web site for the Administration on Children, Youth, and Families in the U.S. Department of Health and Human Services: www.acf.hhs.gov.

Studies have found that infants and children younger than age 3 are particularly susceptible to child abuse (see Box 8.3). As you can see in the table, infants under the age of 1 are at a high risk of maltreatment, just at the age when they need adults the most and learn to trust or not trust adults and others.

> ## Box 8.3   Nonfatal and Fatal Cases of Maltreatment
>
> In 2010, the Centers for Disease Control and Prevention reported the following rates of maltreatment (including abuse and neglect) in 2008:
>
> - 21.7 per 1,000 for 0- to 1 year-olds
> - 12.9 per 1,000 for 1-year-olds
> - 12.4 per 1,000 for 2-year-olds
> - 11.7 per 1,000 for 3-year-olds
>
> In 2008, 80% of the estimated 1,740 children ages 0–17 who died from maltreatment were children under the age of 4.
>
> *Source:* www.cdc.gov/ViolencePrevention/pdf/cm-datasheet-a.pdf

Neglect may take different forms, such as inadequate dietary practices, which impede growth, and failure to provide other necessities such as clothing, shelter, supervision, and protection. Sometimes neglect includes denial of medical attention. Intellectual stimulation and emotional support may also be absent. Some infants are simply abandoned. **Failure to thrive** can be caused by parental withdrawal and hostility, but it is important to remember that there can be multiple causes for failure to thrive including anemia, long-term infections, metabolic disorders, and chromosome abnormalities.

failure to thrive condition in which the infant does not grow as would be expected under usual circumstances

Abuse and neglect occur at all socioeconomic levels, in all ethnic groups, and in all types of families: one-parent, two-parent, extended, large, and small families. The incidence of abuse and neglect in families can be cyclical; however, intervention such as counseling and therapy, education, support groups for families, and subsequent positive life experiences may break the cycle. In some cases, children need to be removed from situations of neglect or abuse. All states have child-abuse-reporting laws under which suspected child abuse must be reported to appropriate authorities.

New technology allows scientists to study the effects of trauma on how the brain develops. Seth Pollak, a scientist who studies how severe trauma affects children's brain function, showed children a series of happy, angry, or fearful faces while researchers measured the children's brain electrical activity. The brain's activity increases when maltreated children see angry faces. They have learned to be hypervigilant to the angry emotional states of adults. This constitutes a change in the brain's "framework of emotions" (Pollak & Kistler, 2002; Pollak & Sinha, 2002; Pollak & Tolley-Schell, 2003). It is an example of how the child's emotional experiences shape brain structure. A review of the literature on the effects of post-traumatic stress disorder (PTSD) concluded that children with PTSD demonstrate smaller medial and posterior portions of the corpus callosum, the structure that facilitates communication between the two hemispheres of the brain (Jackowski, de Araújo, de Lacerda, Mari Jde, & Kaufman, 2009).

Poverty

The extent to which childhood needs for food, clothing, health care, and shelter have been met determines the integrity of overall growth and development. Poverty represents a major impediment to sound growth and development. Children who live in poverty are more likely than other children to die from infections and parasitic diseases, drowning or suffocation, car accidents, or fires. Children who live in poverty are more likely to suffer deleterious outcomes associated with prematurity and low birth weight and to exhibit low weight for their height, which in turn affects brain growth and development and, concurrently, cognitive and social and emotional development. These children are also more likely to live in polluted or toxic environments, drink water that is contaminated with lead or breathe lead-contaminated paint dust, and have parents and other family members who are struggling to meet family survival needs. Families living in these circumstances may be less effective in meeting the unique needs of infants and children. Families living in poverty may have limited resources for safe and stimulating toys, learning materials, and socially and cognitively enriching experiences; are often less able to access high-quality child care; are more likely to live in high-crime neighborhoods; and are less able to access and afford regular, ongoing health care.

Early childhood professionals are sensitive to the needs of children and families living in poverty. This includes helping families to access assistance through various community, state, and federal agencies and early childhood intervention programs, such as home visiting programs, Early Head Start, Head Start, community health care and immunization programs, family counseling services, community child safety initiatives, and other resources. Families living in poverty respond best to assistance from professionals who are nonjudgmental, supportive, and helpful. Physically and psychologically vulnerable children need adults who plan for and support their growth needs, accept and respect them, provide developmentally appropriate programs and expectations, and help to connect them and their families with appropriate intervention and support services.

food security
the ability of the family to meet the nutritional needs of its members

food insecurity
the inability of the family to meet the nutritional needs of all of its members

Food security is a term that refers to the ability of the family to provide for its members' nutritional needs. Studies of **food insecurity** include families in which one or more members have experienced hunger during a specified period of time. Often in food-insecure families, children's food needs take precedence over those of adults, but their nutritional needs may not be adequately met because of poverty, lack of nutritional knowledge, or lack of professional health care guidance.

Nutritional deficiencies exist among families living at all socioeconomic levels. Child hunger in the United States and the effects of malnutrition are topics seldom addressed in the media. However, the prevalence of hunger among children in the United States and around the world represents a serious child development issue. More than 14 million children in the United States were served through Feeding America, a national food bank network, during 2010 (Feeding America, 2011). That is up from 2 million children in 2005 (Second Harvest Food Bank, 2006). As we discuss in later chapters, hunger and malnutrition have immediate and long-term effects on both the physical and mental health of children and are particularly problematic during the very rapid growth of infants and toddlers.

Out-of-home child care settings are generally required by state licensure to provide daily diets that meet one-third or more of a child's daily dietary requirements and to pay particular attention to the special dietary needs of individual children. Where child care takes place in unlicensed child care arrangements, caregivers have a responsibility to provide appropriate formula, foods, and snacks to meet the children's daily nutritional needs. In either setting, caregivers can help to meet these nutritional requirements by becoming knowledgeable about child nutrition and communicating with parents about specific dietary needs, food preferences, or food allergies.

Environmental Toxins

Lead Poisoning. Lead is a toxin that is known to cause brain and nervous system disorders, learning disabilities, behavior problems, kidney damage, and growth retardation. Its prevalence is quite widespread, particularly in large urban areas. Infants and toddlers are more likely than adults to ingest lead because of their inclination to handle and put things in their mouths, and they are more likely to suffer its effects owing to their immature digestive and nervous systems.

Lead is found in certain paints, soil, sometimes food, water from old plumbing, batteries, colored newsprint, toys (particularly imported or antique toys), antique furniture, some ceramic dishes, fishing weights, buckshot, folk remedies, cosmetics, jewelry, workplace dust particles (transported on clothing), petroleum products, and miniblinds manufactured outside the United States before 1996. Children who have elevated lead levels might not exhibit any symptoms for a time. It is possible that high lead levels in the mother's blood can result in placental transmission to the fetus. Prevention of lead poisoning in children requires thorough and careful evaluation of and modifications in the environment, avoiding lead-contaminated objects and places, and screening for blood lead levels through blood tests.

Certain nutrients have been found to aid in the prevention of lead poisoning, especially in young children. A well-balanced diet of grains; fruits; vegetables; dairy products; meat, poultry, or fish; dry beans; and eggs can help decrease the child's susceptibility to lead. It is particularly important for the diet to include adequate amounts of calcium and iron. However, because dietary fat may enhance lead absorption in the body, it should be limited to only recommended amounts. Tap water in older homes and buildings may contain lead from older pipes, and reducing the risk of ingesting lead from this source requires running the cold water faucet for at least one minute before using it for drinking, cooking, or cleaning food. This is a particularly important precaution when infants are bottle-fed formula mixed with water (Pearse & Mitchell, 2003).

Environmental Tobacco Smoke. There are more than 4,000 compounds in environmental tobacco smoke, and it is estimated that more than 50 of them are known to cause cancer. There are two different kinds of tobacco smoke; one (sidestream smoke) is the smoke that is emitted from a burning cigarette, cigar, or pipe between puffs, and the other (mainstream smoke) is smoke that is exhaled by a smoker. Sidestream smoke appears to contain higher concentrations of toxic elements (Canadian Council on Smoking and Health, National Clearinghouse on Tobacco and Health, 1995).

Children who are exposed to environmental tobacco smoke are at greater risk for sudden infant death syndrome (SIDS) and are more prone to respiratory irritations and infections, chronic coughing, bronchitis, pneumonia, asthma, ear infections, and tonsillitis than other children (American Academy of Pediatrics, 2010). Many cities and states have antismoking ads to inform parents of the danger of second-hand smoke for their children.

There are other environmental toxins that affect the health and growth of children. They include carbon monoxide, radon, molds, asbestos, pesticides, and air pollution. Local and regional health officials provide health alerts and information to the public on how to avoid or reduce the effects of these toxins.

Role of the Early Childhood Professional

Promoting Physical and Motor Development in Children Ages 1 Through 3

1. Create and maintain a safe, hygienic, and healthy environment.
2. Provide for proper nutrition and for ongoing health oversight.
3. Know and use developmentally appropriate activities and expectations.
4. Encourage exploration, discovery, and independence.
5. Provide positive, supportive, and protective guidance.
6. Encourage positive body and gender awareness.
7. Provide a variety of materials to encourage both large and small motor development.
8. Provide toys and experiences that facilitate perceptual–motor development.
9. Observe children for signs or symptoms of special needs or illness.
10. Model good health and hygiene behaviors.
11. Ask family members about the nutritious foods they eat and about family rituals around feeding and eating.
12. Share up-to-date safety information with families, for example, that families do not want to use cribs with sides that raise and lower because of the danger of infant death.

Key Terms

adipose
body awareness
cochlear implant
deciduous teeth
developmental possibilities
extensors
failure to thrive

flexors
food insecurity
food security
gender awareness
gender identity
locomotion
nystagmus

perceptual–motor
prehension
self-efficacy
sexuality
standard precautions
strabismus
toilet learning

Review Strategies and Activities

1. Review the key terms individually or with a classmate.
2. Observe two children in a child care setting for approximately one hour during outdoor and indoor activity times. Using the physical and motor milestone lists in this chapter, record all motor behaviors that you observe. Record both large and small motor observations. Compare your lists with those of a classmate. How are the children the same? How do they differ? To what might the differences in motor abilities be attributed?
3. Invite a nutritionist to talk with your class. What dietary plan would she or he recommend for a 1-year-old? A 2-year-old? A 3-year-old? How and why do these diets change as the child gets older?

4. Discuss with a classmate safe ways to encourage toddler exploration, discovery, and independence. List your suggestions. What physical/motor or perceptual development will your suggestions enhance?

5. Visit a child care and education center in which toddlers (ages 1 to 3) are enrolled. How are children's health and physical well-being protected or enhanced? What precautions are taken to prevent the spread of infection or disease?

6. Throughout this course, compile a folder of child health and safety alerts provided through the media, parenting literature, fliers from physicians, reports of the U.S. Product Safety Commission, and other sources. Discuss prevention strategies with your classmates.

7. Given what you now know about physical and motor development in toddlers, what suggestions would you make to parents and caregivers to protect children from unintentional injury and threats to their health or safety? Make a brochure or write a newsletter for parents highlighting important information.

Further Readings

American Public Health Association & American Academy of Pediatrics. (2011). *Caring for our children: National health and safety performance standards: Guidelines for out-of-home child care programs.* Washington, DC, and Elk Grove Village, IL: Authors.

Marian, M. C. (2010). *Guidance of young children* (8th ed.). Upper Saddle River, NJ: Prentice Hall.

Other Resources

Allied Vaccine Group, www.vaccine.org. This web site is dedicated to presenting valid scientific information about vaccines.

American Academy of Pediatrics, www.aap.org. Information on prevention and treatment of poisoning.

American Association of Poison Control Centers (AAPCC). The universal telephone number in the United States is (800) 222–1222. Calls are routed to the local poison control center. The AAPCC supports the nation's 57 poison centers.

American Dental Association, www.ada.org.

Centers for Disease Control and Prevention, Vaccines and Immunizations, www.cdc.gov/vaccines.

Food and Drug Administration, www.fda.gov. This Web site provides the most up-to-date information on foods, drugs, safety, medical devices, vaccines, radiation-emitting products, clinical trials, rare diseases, and preventing SIDS.

Food Research and Action Center (FRAC), www.frac.org. Information is provided on topics such as hunger in America, fighting obesity, and nutrition.

Healthy Child Care America (HCCA), www.healthychildcare.org. "Launched in 1995, HCCA seeks to maximize the health, safety, well-being, and developmental potential of all children so that each child experiences quality child care within a nurturing environment and has a medical home."

National Network for Immunization Information (NNii), www.immunizationinfo.org. "The NNii provides science-based information to healthcare professionals, the media, and the public: everyone who needs to know the facts about vaccines and immunization."

National Safety Council, www.nsc.org. The NSC provides information for safety at home, for employers, and during recreation.

U.S. Consumer Product Safety Commission, www.cpsc.gov. Check regularly for recalls of toys, child furniture, safety seats, clothing, medications, and other items.

chapter 9

Emotional and Social Development: Ages One Through Three

Our words should be like a magic canvas upon which a child cannot help but paint a positive picture of himself.

—Haim G. Ginott

> It is also clear that one of the best ways to enrich an infant or toddler is through unstinting amounts of affection, to build security and self-esteem that will influence all the child's other experiences, and all further enrichments, throughout life.
>
> —Marian Diamond and Janet Hopson

After studying this chapter, you will demonstrate comprehension by:

▶ relating selected theories to the study of social and emotional development during the toddler period;

▶ discussing selected social and emotional experiences associated with brain growth and neurological development during the toddler period;

▶ identifying major social and emotional milestones during the toddler period;

▶ describing factors that influence social and emotional development in toddlers; and

▶ describing the role of adults in facilitating healthy social and emotional development in toddlers.

The toddler period of growth and development presents new challenges for parents and caregivers. The formerly dependent, compliant infant now strives for independence and for ever-widening opportunities to interact, explore, and learn. Increasingly refined motor capabilities and communication skills are emerging, leading to new and unexpected behaviors. These new behaviors can, at the same time, thrill, perplex, frustrate, and intrigue parents and caregivers. The period is also a challenging one for the toddler because the restraints of those who would guide and protect the child present obstacles and frustrations difficult for the child to understand.

The toddler, the child between ages 1 and 3, has many important emotional milestones to achieve. This period is a time of transition from the relative simplicity of the infant's view of self and other to the more mature experience of being an individual person among other people. The growing sense of self is usually referred to as a sense of identity.

Emotional Competence and Development

In the second and third years of life, emotional development goes through dramatic changes. The sense of identity is becoming more complex, with observable behaviors such as self-recognition, fears and anxieties, self-comforting, use of transitional objects, self-control or inhibition, and awareness of abilities. The sense of being an individual within a social context is evidenced by maturing expression of emotions, attachment, and gender awareness. Increasingly, we are able to match those changes to brain activity and development.

The human brain becomes organized and functional from the lower, more primitive parts (brainstem and midbrain) to its higher regions (limbic and cortical regions). (Review Figures 5.1 and 5.2.) As the brain grows and develops in this hierarchical fashion, the limbic, subcortical, and cortical areas begin to influence or control the more primitive behaviors emanating from the lower regions of the brain.

Developing a Sense of Self

Even if an infant knows that she exists as a separate entity from birth, it is at about 18 months that she begins to develop a mental representation of herself as a person. Many of the aspects of this change are described below.

Self-Recognition

An ongoing hypothesis has been that increases in emotional maturity during ages 1 to 3 are related to activation of higher areas of the brain, those involved in executive function. Recently, technology has provided ways for scientists to see which parts of the brain become activated during particular events. It has been extremely helpful in determining when a toddler is developing a self-representation or a mental picture of self.

When recent studies posed self-recognition tasks to toddlers, the parts of the brain that register the self as acting would light up (Lewis & Carmody, 2008). So the image of the brain matches behavior that has been observed for some time, giving us reason to believe that during the second year of life the child creates a mental representation of himself as a separate being. "This is me." According to Rochat (1995), this self-representation includes the awareness "I know that I know" as opposed to the simpler experience of "knowing".

Self-recognition is often identified by infants' ability to recognize themselves in a mirror, photograph, video, or other form of representation (Lewis & Brooks, 1978; Neilsen & Dissanayake, 2004). The classic self-recognition task is surreptitiously putting a dot of rouge on the toddler's nose and then having the toddler look in a mirror. If the toddler touches his own nose, rather than the nose in the mirror, it is taken as evidence that the child understands the image in the mirror is a representation of him. This awareness usually occurs at about 18 months.

Other actions that Lewis and Carmody (2008) feel identify self-representation are pretense and the use of personal pronouns—for example, when the child says "My ball" or "I do it." The use of personal pronouns such as "me" and the ever-popular "mine" also indicates the child's mental representation of self. Pretend play is important because it requires the child to understand, "This is what I pretend to be—not what I am."

Self-Concept and Self-Esteem

The self-concept is the summary definition that one devises of oneself; it represents an awareness of oneself as a separate and unique individual. The self-concept derives from interactions with others, the child's interpretation of those interactions, and the child's ability to accept or negate positive or negative feedback from interactions with others. For the most part, the manner in which others respond to and relate to the child determines the self-concept the child will devise.

The self-concept is dynamic in that it changes over time with additional experiences and increasing physical/motor, social, and cognitive abilities. Generally, the development of the self-concept is composed of four accomplishments: (1) self-awareness, (2) self-recognition, (3) self-definition, and (4) self-esteem.

Self-awareness occurs as infants begin to realize that they are distinct and separate from others and that an object is not an extension of themselves. This ability seems to parallel the cognitive achievement of object permanence, when the child can form and hold mental images. It is usually evident by age 18 months, and most children can

self-awareness
an individual's perceptions of him- or herself as distinct and separate from other people and objects

chapter 9

distinguish their own photograph from someone else's by age 2 (Lewis & Brooks-Gunn, 1979). Self-recognition is described above. **Self-definition** emerges as children begin to use language to describe themselves. The toddler's growing awareness of his or her age, size, gender, and skills assists the child in this definition. This development is observed when young children take pride in telling you how old they are. Holding up two, three, or four fingers and exclaiming "I am 3" is an attempt to define oneself. Also, when children invite attention by saying "Watch me!" they are demonstrating the skills by which they define themselves. "I can reach it," "Watch me jump," and "I am big" are verbal indications of an emerging self-concept. The responses of adults and playmates to these self-identifiers convey acceptance or rejection, respect or disrespect.

Around age 3, children begin to mentally construct an "autobiographical" memory that facilitates a continuous identity carried throughout life (Nelson, 1993). This autobiographical memory is quite dependent on the types of interactions and relationships infants and toddlers have had with their early caregivers and determines the extent to which the child develops positive self-esteem. **Self-esteem** emerges from the feedback young children receive from others and their perceptions of that feedback. Children who perceive themselves as loved, valued, worthy, and competent develop healthy self-esteem.

An interesting aspect of self-definition arises when children begin to self-correct. Rejecting a drawing, coloring over it to "cover it up," throwing an art effort into the trash because "it doesn't look right," starting over on simple tasks, and other similar behaviors indicate that the child is beginning to self-monitor and represent the child's desire to succeed (Cicchetti & Beeghly, 1990). In these events, the emotions of pride, shame, embarrassment, or guilt find expression. Healthy self-esteem ensures that these evaluations weigh more heavily on the positive than on the negative side.

self-definition
the use of criteria to define the self, such as age, size, and physical and mental abilities

self-esteem
the overall sense of worth as a person that the child derives from the qualities that are associated with the self-concept

Fears and Anxieties

As we discussed, separation and stranger anxiety are normal and expected outcomes of increasing cognitive ability and parallel the development of attachments, influencing and being influenced by the quality of the attachment relationships. These anxieties begin to wane around age 2½ to 3. However, around 18 months, additional fears begin to emerge. This is indicative of social/emotional and cognitive development. Because all development is interrelated, a discussion of fears must recognize the interrelated role of cognition. As the child can manipulate mental images and mentally elaborate on past events and experiences, new understandings and concepts—and misunderstandings and misconceptions—can bring about new fears. As the toddler begins to imagine, fantasy and reality are not separated.

Fears are normal. Fears are quite real to the child, can be very disturbing, and can be difficult to allay. In addition to separation and stranger fears, common toddler fears include fear of the dark, the bathtub drain, animals, some storybook or media characters, monsters and ghosts, lightning and thunder, and vacuum cleaners or other noisy equipment.

Toddlers may acquire some of their fears through social referencing and other social interactions. Parents who become fearful during a thunderstorm or who discuss frightening or painful experiences relating to accidents or illnesses, visits to the physician or dentist, or other adult fears may inadvertently instill these fears in their young children. When fear tactics are used to discipline, they create unhealthy and inappropriate fears in the child. For instance, imploring the toddler to "be quiet or Aunt Marti will get you" creates an unfortunate wariness of Aunt Marti and hampers her efforts to establish a positive relationship with the toddler.

Helping the toddler to understand and cope with fears requires sensitivity and patience. Because fears can be quite real to the child, adults should neither laugh at, ridicule, nor minimize them. Very young children will not understand logical explanations; instead, toddlers need adults to help them find ways to deal with their fears. A child who is afraid of the bathtub drain, for instance, can be given "control" over it by being the one who opens or closes the drain or by getting out of the tub before the drain is opened.

Fears are necessary for survival because they signal dangers to be avoided. However, the toddler may not yet have the necessary survival fears for most potentially dangerous situations. The toddler has neither the judgment nor the background of experiences and understanding to avoid such hazards as the street, strangers, fire, poisons, heights, guns, and a host of other potential dangers in their environments. Toddlers lack the space, speed, depth, and other types of perception that are needed to perceive risks accurately. Toddlers need to be protected through close supervision and must be taught in ways that instill knowledge, caution, and skills but do not unduly frighten them. Adults cannot assume that toddlers are aware of dangerous situations. In the event of the child's self-endangerment, adults should not react with physical punishment, but must recognize the child's lack of experience and knowledge. It is the adult's responsibility to monitor and maintain the child's safety and to teach the child about unsafe objects and situations. Adults set limits and rules that both protect and instruct and recognize that with toddlers, frequent and repetitive reminders are required. Box 9.1 lists ideas to help toddlers manage fear.

Box 9.1 Helping Toddlers Manage Fear

Tips from Dr. Ayelet Talmi on helping toddlers manage their fear.

- "Gently expose your child to things that might be scary to him. Coach him and model how to stay calm.

- Explain to your toddler what is real, what is pretend, and how things that might be scary (storms, toilets) actually work.

- Be honest. If you know something scary is going to happen or that something will hurt, tell your toddler the truth. He'll learn to confront fears head-on by following your example and trusting you to tell the truth.

- Manage your own fears, worries, and anxieties without sharing them with your child. In order to develop confidence and a sense of safety, toddlers need to know their caregivers are calm.

- Read books and tell stories about other children who were afraid of similar things and overcame their fears. Young children love to hear about other children overcoming adversity and will likely emulate strong characters."

Source: Adapted from Talmi, A. (2009). Top ten toddler fears. *Parents*. Meredith Corporation. Retrieved from http://www.parents.com/toddlers-preschoolers/development/fear/top-toddler-fears.

Self-Comforting Behaviors

Infants and toddlers employ idiosyncratic self-comforting behaviors when they are feeling lonely, frightened, sad, tired, bored, or overly excited. These behaviors include thumb sucking and attachment to a particular toy, piece of clothing, or blanket. Self-comforting behaviors help children to cope with their own emotional states and to self-regulate their emotions.

Thumb Sucking. Most infants find their fists and thumbs eventually and derive pleasure and solace from sucking on them. Brazelton (1992) suggested that parents should expect their infants to suck their thumbs, fingers, or fists and attributes few consequences to this behavior. Thumb sucking can be the child's source of self-comfort when she or he is tense or frightened or simply trying to relax or fall asleep. Brazelton advises adults to expect a great deal of thumb or finger sucking in the first year, somewhat less in the active second year, and even less in the third and fourth years.

Although infants are sometimes given pacifiers to satisfy the sucking need, pacifiers are most often provided to calm a fussy child. For some infants and toddlers, the pacifier becomes their self-comforting device; other infants reject it or find little pleasure in it. Whether thumb or pacifier has provided the source of self-comfort, either is usually given up at about the same age. Children may fall back on one or the other during periods of illness, stress, or fear.

Transitional Objects. Another self-comforting strategy the toddler uses is the **transitional object,** so named because it assists the child in making the transition from the dependency and protection of infancy to the independence and uncertainty of the toddler period. Attachment to an object such as a teddy bear, special blanket, swatch of soft fabric, doll, or favorite piece of clothing is common and begins in the latter part of the first year, usually around 8 or 9 months. Because these objects have been invested with certain meanings and comforting associations, the child forms an emotional tie to them (Winnicott, 1953, 1971, 1977). The child's attachment to the object can last to age 7 or 8 and sometimes beyond. Some older children take their transitional object to another child's house for a sleep-over and even to college. One young woman took her "blankie" that her grandmother had made her when she was an infant into the delivery room with her to remind her of the generations of women before her who had successfully given birth.

> **transitional object**
> an object, usually a soft, cuddly item, to which a child becomes attached

Adults and children give "soft names" to these objects, such as "stuffies," "cuddlies," "banky," and "bear-bear." These attachments are usually quite strong and extremely important to the child. Children often perceive these objects as extensions of themselves.

Transitional objects serve a variety of comforting roles. Some observers believe that they provide a security link with the home, mother, or other attachment person during times of separation. In this sense, they serve to ease separation anxiety and other fears. The transitional object provides a sense of security in new, strange, frightening, or stressful situations. Children often treat their transitional objects with love and caring, exhibiting their own abilities to express affection. Sometimes, these objects are the child's substitution for the thumb or pacifier and replace these earlier forms of self-comfort. Other children use the transitional object and the thumb or pacifier in combination as a self-comforting strategy. Interference with these attachments is strongly discouraged; rather, adults are encouraged to expect, accept, acknowledge, and appreciate the child's transitional object.

Self-Regulation

Self-regulation is the ability to modulate one's reaction. Myelination of the nerves in the body is completed around the child's second birthday. As you may remember from Chapter 5, myelin is a fatty substance that coats the nerves. It helps the nerves conduct electrical information efficiently. This is part of the physical contribution to the child's increasing ability to regulate his responses.

Morasch and Bell (2011) looked at self-regulation by providing three tasks for children between 24 and 27 months of age while watching brain activity through an MRI. The tasks involved conflict, delay, and compliance. For conflict, the child was shown a ball which was then occluded with a board. When the board was moved, there was either no ball, one ball, or two balls. The child perceived no balls or two balls as a conflict with his expectation. The delay task had the mother reading a magazine and the researcher putting a brand-new box of crayons on the table next to the 2-year-old. The child was told not to touch the crayons until the researcher got back. The third involved the child being compliant while going through the tedious procedure of having an electrode cap put on for the MRI readings. The researchers found that executive function areas of the brain activated if the child inhibited her desire to complete any of the tasks manually.

Self-regulation may be related to socioeconomic status. In a study with 24-month-old children, Johnson (2010) found that children from lower-income homes are less able to regulate their reaction and less able to ignore distractions than those from middle-income homes. Further research is needed to determine the reasons why children of families that live in poverty may find self-regulation more difficult.

An important emotional goal in early childhood is the development of self-control. This is a long-term goal, for self-control develops over a period of many years. For the most part, self-control is learned behavior. It is dependent on external controls at first; then the individual gradually assumes more and more responsibility for his or her own behaviors. In very young children, this process is not a smooth one; self-control emerges haltingly. Marion (2006) listed the following indicators of self-control in children: (1) control of impulses, (2) tolerance of frustration, (3) the ability to postpone immediate gratification, and (4) the initiation of a plan that is carried out over a period of time. As with other areas of emotional development, cognition and social experiences both play a role in the development of self-control. Toddlers can be assisted in their development of self-control if adults use developmentally appropriate teaching and guidance techniques. Suggestions for maximizing self-control in very young children are provided in Box 9.2.

Awareness of Abilities

In the toddler years, children move beyond knowing they can make things happen to taking pride in what they are able to do. New ventures may be accompanied by "Look at me! Look at me!" and then repeated over and over again. Pride is one of the more complex emotions the child is beginning to feel. Just what ability looks like, it turns out, is a fairly highly charged cultural issue. (See Box 9.3.)

Perhaps the biggest lesson an infant or toddler needs to learn is how to be a member of the human race. The toddler learns how people express emotions within her family and culture, how to participate in an attachment relationship, and about gender differences.

As toddlers come to trust their environments, the people within the environments, and themselves, they begin to grow in independence and a sense of autonomy (Erikson, 1963).

Box 9.2   Helping Young Children to Develop Self-Control

(1) Provide an environment in which the child's growing sense of autonomy can flourish; this includes the following:

- Play items and experiences that are engaging and enriching
- Low, open shelves for personal and play items
- Adequate space for use, storage, and retrieval of personal and play items
- Safe and sturdy furnishings and toys
- Placement of dangerous and off-limit items out of sight and reach (or under lock and key as appropriate)

(2) Provide an atmosphere that encourages the toddler to make choices, explore, and discover but that is in keeping with the child's developmental capacities and is free of inappropriate expectations and pressures to perform.

(3) Provide a daily schedule that is predictable so that the toddler can sense the day's rhythms and anticipate and respond appropriately to regular events: mealtime, bathtime, naptime, storytime, and so on.

(4) Set logical, reasonable, and fair limits for behavior, then consistently and predictably expect compliance. Use words and explanation rather than punishment to help toddlers understand the limits that are imposed on them.

(5) Meet the toddler's needs for food, clothing, rest, and attention expeditiously. Adults who impose undue delays on toddlers fail to recognize their inability to delay gratification and tolerate frustration.

(See Figure 9.1 for Erikson's stages of development.) The toddler's efforts to buckle a seat belt, turn a light switch on or off, open a door, and take off socks, shoes, or other clothing are intensely and personally important and can result in tears and tantrums when thwarted by an unsuspecting or impatient adult. Previously dependent behaviors are now being eclipsed by the toddler's efforts to gain competence. Locomotion and emerging fine motor

Box 9.3   Diversity Perspectives: Autonomy

Most American textbooks will describe autonomy as the major achievement of the toddler years. That is because our culture predominantly values independence. We want to raise children who work hard and act in their own behalf. Most other cultures in the world, however, are called collectivist cultures, and they value interdependence. They want their children to grow up acting for the good of the group, even when that conflicts with their own, individual best interest. Autonomy is a culturally based value, somewhat different from wanting our infants and toddlers to be healthy or to learn to walk. Instead of assuming autonomy is the goal for toddlers, let's assume we want toddlers to become more competent at being members of their own family and culture.

Figure 9.1
Erikson's Stages of Psychosocial Development

Development of a healthy sense of trust paves the way for successful resolution of the next stage of psychosocial development: autonomy versus shame and doubt.

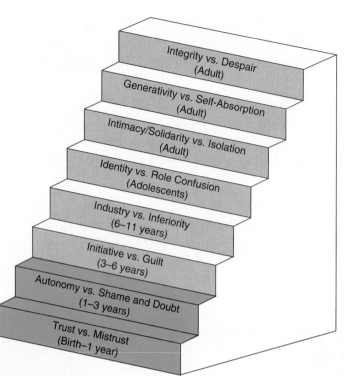

Integrity vs. Despair
(Adult)

Generativity vs. Self-Absorption
(Adult)

Intimacy/Solidarity vs. Isolation
(Adult)

Identity vs. Role Confusion
(Adolescents)

Industry vs. Inferiority
(6–11 years)

Initiative vs. Guilt
(3–6 years)

Autonomy vs. Shame and Doubt
(1–3 years)

Trust vs. Mistrust
(Birth–1 year)

Meeting the toddler's contradictory needs for dependence and independence is often a challenge.

controls encourage this independence as the toddler gains confidence in walking, climbing, running, moving, and manipulating. Language and self-awareness reveal a striving for independence as the toddler asserts, "Me do it!," "No," and "Mine." Although these behaviors can tax adult patience, they are viewed as indications of positive and healthy social and emotional development in our culture, with our emphasis on autonomy.

Being an Individual in a Social Context

The toddler does not develop emotions alone and internally. He must learn how to be a member of his family and his culture. The following emotional achievements of the toddler years are experienced in relationship with others, but they are basically internal, emotional changes. They include emotional expression, attachment, and gender awareness.

Emotional Expression

Toddlers are increasingly engaged in a range of emotional transactions and they are learning a lot about **display rules** of emotions. "Display rules are a social group's informal norms about when, where, and how one should express emotions" (Siegler, 2006). Decoding the display rules of your own culture is an important part of being a member of that culture. In fact, if parents display emotion inappropriately or too subtly to read, it can make understanding them challenging for the child. A study of abusive and unabusive mothers showed that abusive mothers had fewer prototypical angry expressions and less intensity in their happy, sad, and angry vocalizations. This made it very difficult for the children to process these emotional expressions (Shackman, Fatani, Camras, Berkowitz, Bachorowski, & Pollak, 2010).

With help from sensitive adults, toddlers are learning to label and give words to emotions and learn the names of a gradation of feelings such as irritated, annoyed, or angry. By 18 months, toddlers are able to express their emotions clearly—and with intensity. They are beginning to experience more intense emotions such as pride. Over the next 18 months, toddlers develop increasingly complex emotions such as shame, embarassment, and guilt. They often act these feelings out in pretend play (Lagattuta & Thompson, 2007).

Attachment

From about ages 6 months to 3 years, the toddler engages in active **proximity seeking** (Bowlby, 1969/2000). During this phase, the child becomes very aware of and monitors the presence or absence of her attachment person, usually her mother. The child actively seeks to be near and held by her attachment person and cries on separation. When the attachment person is present, the toddler will at first remain quite close, perhaps in the adult's lap, then will

As autonomy emerges, toddlers begin to resist assistance from others.

tenuously venture forth and away, but will return periodically to the attachment person for assurance. As a sense of trust and self-confidence grows, these ventures will be sustained over longer periods of time. As we learned in Chapter 6, the success of these ventures is thought to relate to the quality of infant–caregiver attachments, particularly the mother's sensitivity and responsiveness to infant/toddler cues (Belsky & Fearon, 2002).

As toddlers get older, the ability to visually and auditorally remain attached, even though the attachment person may not be near, emerges. The toddler learns to feel safe from a distance by looking, listening, and vocally communicating. The child becomes more exploratory as feelings of security with the attachment person and with the environment increase. The toddler begins to rely on self-comforting behaviors such as thumb sucking or fondling a soft toy or blanket and may begin to find comfort through interactions with people other than the one with whom he has formed an attachment.

Forming secure attachments and trusting relationships with parents and family members is among the first and most important social and emotional tasks of the infant/toddler period. As the toddler gets older, forming attachments to others beyond the family begins to occur. The success of these extrafamiliar relationships is thought to be an outgrowth of earliest secure attachments and trusting relationships (Sroufe, 1996). Extrafamilial relationships include people outside the immediate or extended family— neighbors, family friends, or babysitters and other caregivers. Infants and toddlers can and do develop strong feelings for and attachments to others outside the family. Positive interactions and successful experiences with extrafamilial relationships enhance the child's social and emotional development (Pianta, 1999).

display rules
social rules determining how and when certain emotions should or should not be expressed

proximity seeking
the child's attempts to maintain nearness and contact with the attachment person

Emotional and Social Development: Ages One Through Three

Children may have a secure relationship with one adult and an insecure relationship with another. Children whose initial attachments have been insecure are more likely to learn to view adults as unresponsive and unreliable. With these disturbing perceptions, the ability to form mutually positive and supportive relationships with others is compromised (Lyons-Ruth & Jacobvitz, 1999). However, securely attached children trust that others, including peers, will be emotionally available to new relationhips (Ziv, Oppenheim, & Sagi-Schwartz, 2004).

In Chapter 6, the section on attachment introduced the idea of a disorganized attachment, classification (D), usually the result of severe maltreatment. There is a lot of interest in this category as researchers hope to find early symptoms with which to identify children lacking a stable attachment partner. One study found that toddlers with a D classification were significantly less likely than children with any other classification to initiate joint attention with a researcher (Claussen, Mundy, Mallik, & Willoughby (2002). Toddlers with a D classification may be more reactive to stress and have fewer coping mechanisms. One study tested the cortisol levels in the saliva of 19-month-old toddlers before putting them through the emotionlly stressful Strange Situation to determine their attachment classification. Toddlers with a D classification had significantly higher cortisol levels than any other group, indicating higher stress levels (Hertsgaard, Gunnar, Erickson, & Nachmias, 1995).

Parents and toddlers with a D classification may be responsive to intervention. Circle of Security, a group treatment using parent education and psychotherapy, was able to help most of the D classified children into one of the other classifications, many of them secure (Hoffman, Martin, Cooper, & Powell, 2006).

Sexual Development

Sexual development is evident in toddlers' awareness of anatomical differences between girls and boys and their curiosity about body parts and their functions. Although they have learned to name many body parts, they may have been taught substitute terms for genitals and their posterior. Such terms convey positive or negative connotations and do or do not facilitate the development of a healthy body image. Additionally, toddlers explore their bodies and may find pleasurable sensations when touching their genitals. Occasional masturbation is not unusual. These behaviors are normal and often occur when the child is tired, stressed, or perhaps trying to self-calm, as when required to sit quietly for an activity such as listening to a story. In these instances, adults use redirection and explanation regarding appropriate time and place (Honig, 2000). Shock and shame confuse children and interfere with learning and developing healthy attitudes toward their bodies and bodily functions.

It is important to understand that early childhood sexuality differs from adult sexuality (Chrisman & Couchenour, 2002). Adults attribute eroticism and value systems associated with modesty, marriage, and procreation to human sexuality, whereas young children are just learning about body parts and functions, learning about the social contexts in which certain topics or behaviors are appropriate or inappropriate, observing the expressions of affection displayed by those around them, and gaining knowledge and experiences associated with gender roles. Adults contribute to this learning in either positive or negative ways, depending on their ability to respond in an unembarrassed manner with age-appropriate, accurate, helpful, nonjudgmental information.

Gender Awareness

Most children are able to proclaim that they are a boy or a girl by age 2½ to 3, having constructed what psychologists call *gender schemata* (Liben & Signorella, 1980). Gender identity has both biological and sociological origins. Biology determines whether the child will be male or female, and the images, hopes, and child-rearing practices of mothers, fathers, and other relatives set the stage for gender identity and gender role expectations. Studies have found that the more sex-stereotyped adult roles are in a society, the more gender specific the child-rearing practices are (Coll & Meyer, 1993).

During the second year, observations of play behaviors begin to reveal differences between boys and girls, much of which are stereotypical and perhaps derived from gender-specific experiences provided by the parents. Parents may tend to be more gentle and cuddling with girls and more rough and tumble with boys; parents may talk more softly and tenderly to girls and more directly to boys. Perhaps these play choices reflect the types of toys and interactions parents have provided for their boys or girls, as well as the children's increasing gender schemata. In a laboratory setting, researchers found that there were differences in how mothers engaged with their 6-, 9-, and 14-month-olds (Clearfield & Nelson, 2006). Mothers of daughters engaged in conversation and interacted with them more than did mothers of boys. The authors of the study concluded that adults may be transmitting, through language and type of interactions, different messages to their male and female infants. Toy preferences are particularly indicative of gender differences. By 1 year of age, boys tend to play with transportation toys, blocks, and manipulatives and girls tend to choose soft toys and dolls (Servin, Bohlin, & Berlin, 1999).

It is not unusual for toddlers to assume that their biological sex can change, that is, that boys can grow up to become mothers and girls can grow up to be fathers. This thinking demonstrates a lack of **gender constancy.** Gender constancy is the realization that one's sex does not change over time or as a result of changes in hairstyle, clothing, or other outward characteristics. Gender constancy is not expected to occur until ages 5 to 7 (Kohlberg, 1966).

gender constancy
the realization that one's gender remains the same, regardless of age or changes in clothing, hairstyles, or other outward characteristics

Toddlers tend to imitate the parent of the same sex, and when gender role behaviors are deemed to be appropriate, parents provide positive feedback. However, when the behavior is deemed to be gender inappropriate, parents tend to intervene. It is not unusual for a parent to express concern about their son's interest in dolls in the nursery school sociodramatic play center. Interestingly, few, if any, inquire about their daughters' play with trucks in the block center. From a developmental perspective, either play choice is sound and in no way threatens the child's gender identity.

Is there a gender difference in the quantity and quality of aggression in toddlers? Recent studies (Coté, 2007; Coté, Vaillancourt, LeBlanc, Nagin, & Tremblay, 2006) of 10,000 Canadian children found that approximately one-third (31.1%) of toddlers used physical aggression infrequently and approximately one-half (52.2%) used moderate levels of physical aggression. However, toddlers who used physical aggression frequently were primarily boys from families who experienced hostile/ineffective parenting. The frequency of aggression for these boys (approximately one-sixth of the children) typically increased as they became older and the gender gap between boys and girls increased. There was also a gender gap in relational aggression (verbal and other indirect ways), with girls exhibiting higher levels as they grew older. The researchers emphasized that physical aggression in boys could be significantly reduced with family-centered intervention.

Psychologists and educators are encouraging less gender stereotyping in the child's early experiences with children's books, toys, entertainment media, and adult expectations (Copple, 2003). Boys can certainly be allowed to show feelings, to nurture and be nurtured, and to participate in a range of activities from gentle to rough. Girls can be encouraged to pursue physical activities and to assert themselves in constructive and positive ways. Neither of these efforts needs be viewed as endangering gender role behaviors at later ages. Congruence, although never absolute between gender identity and gender role expectations, occurs as children experience a broad range of both "feminine" and "masculine" situations and as role models provide healthy and satisfying gender acceptance.

Awareness of Diversity and Individual Differences

> "Race" refers to groups that share visible physical attributes that traditionally are defined as "racial." Although often used as a biological distinction, race is, in fact, a socially constructed label, as is evident in the inconsistent and biased ways in which racial terms are often applied. (Smedley, 1993; Ramsey, 2003, p. 24)

A number of processes are examined in the study of how children become aware of and respond to racial differences. Ramsey (1998) identified these processes as perceptual awareness, valuative concepts, racial identification, racial preferences, behaviors toward other races, and knowledge of racial differences. A primary process, however, is the process called *perceptual narrowing.*

"Can infants distinguish the differences between faces in all ethnic groups, even the ones that they do not see on a regular basis? In a study of babies' ability to distinguish between faces, 3-month-old infants could identify the differences in faces within four ethnic groups, two ethnic groups at 6 months, and only their own ethnic group at 9 months. This ability to distinguish faces in races that are in their own visual environment and not others is called the other race effect (ORE). Authors Kelly et al. (2009) state that the visual system of infants "...becomes 'tuned' in to process the category of faces that are most prevalent in the infant's visual environment" (p. 106), a process called "perceptual narrowing" by Nelson (2001). This range of processes illustrates that the development of racial awareness, understanding, and acceptance is complex. During the toddler period, racial awareness is dominated by perceptions of outward features. Young children attend with interest to facial features, skin and hair color, hairstyle, clothing, and voice and speech patterns. However, racial group–referenced identities do not develop until between ages 3 and 8 (Ramsey, 1998). Mature forms of racial awareness, which do not rely on superficial features but depend on deeper understandings of ethnicity, do not emerge until age 9 or 10 (Aboud, 1988).

The toddler's primary sources of information about race are the family and early care and education providers. Within these settings, racial attitudes are transmitted and racial pride is fostered. Children learn about similarities and differences among people through their experiences with others beyond these settings through their toys, books, and the media. In recent years, there have been improvements in the accuracy with which diverse races and cultural groups are portrayed in children's books, toys, school curricula, and the media, yet there is still a need to monitor these sources of information to ensure accurate, positive, and nonbiased portrayals. The toddler's racial identity and valuative and preferential behaviors depend on accurate information and sensitive guidance.

Moral Development

Moral behavior is most often described as the ability to consider the needs and well-being of others as well as the right and wrong of behavior. People who are thought to be moral exhibit such behaviors as honesty, dependability, helpfulness, and fairness. These individuals do not steal from others or physically hurt or emotionally abuse others. They do not betray trusts and are loyal to their family, friends, and commitments. In short, these people have a personal morality that guides their behaviors. These behaviors represent moral values, reasoning, judgments, and actions.

A series of recent studies suggests that an inclination to prefer fairness and helpfulness may be inherent. Infants as young as 3 months will show a preference for a helpful bunny over a hindering bunny. Karen Wynn, Paul Bloom, and many of their colleagues have been studying infants' reactions to little puppet shows in which one puppet is helpful and one is hindering to the progress of a third puppet. In a variety of scenarios, infants consistently choose helpful characters over neutral or harmful ones and neutral ones over harmful ones (Hamlin & Wynn, 2010; Bloom, 2010; Hamlin, Wynn & Bloom, 2007). They suggest that in every society there is a sense of fairness, a valuing of loyalty and kindness, and a way to judge nice from naughty. There would be an evolutionary benefit for humans to be born with a preference for kindness. Although what is seen as moral in one society may be very different from that of another society, a basic sense of right and wrong may be inborn.

The socialization process must be instructive and timely. Alert adults teach appropriate behaviors when opportunities arise, such as when the toddler grabs a toy from another child, bites to defend himself, and engages in other unacceptable behaviors. Guidance that punishes rather than provides intelligent, logical instruction fails to recognize that moral behaviors take root in cognition (understanding) and prosocial learning (perspective-taking, empathy, altruism, and so on). Embarrassing, demeaning, or power-assertive discipline does little to help the toddler learn and internalize appropriate behaviors. Indeed, many negative and socially unacceptable behaviors accompanied by low self-esteem accrue from inappropriate discipline techniques. Further, moral development is a continuous process throughout life. Social learning experiences in many contexts and involving many others (siblings, babysitters, teachers, family members) accumulate over time to build an internalized sense of morality, or a moral way of behaving governed from within rather than by external rules and constraints.

Earlier chapters describe the backgrounds of experience that the parents of Angela and Jeremy bring to the parent–child relationship. The quality of their childhood experiences, the relationships with their parents and other family members, and the role models that were available to them influence the perceptions they have of themselves and of their roles as parents. Knowledge of child growth and development plays a critical role in this regard. The interplay of all of these factors influences the interactions of parents and children.

Cheryl—young, single, and still an adolescent—is experiencing her own developmental needs, which are typical of most adolescent girls. In addition to her need to obtain and maintain support networks to assist her in nurturing Angela, she has needs relating to learning about and gaining satisfaction in the role of mother and single teen parent, completing her education, participating in the social life of her agemates, and working through Erikson's fifth psychosocial stage, that of developing a sense of identity versus role confusion (Erikson, 1963). Participating in an extended family and projecting a future beyond high school are also tasks before her.

Members of Jeremy's family also have their needs. His parents, now in their 30s, are striving for success in demanding careers. They seek social and economic upward mobility, which is a demanding quest in terms of time, energy, and allocation of family resources. Their needs at this stage relate to maintaining an intellectually, emotionally, and physically satisfying relationship with one another; meshing career, civic, religious, and social desires and responsibilities; relating to extended family members; providing for an economically stable existence; and integrating all of this with their plans for Jeremy and perhaps additional children.

James, low-key and affectionate, enjoys holding Angela on his lap and talking and reading books to her. His manner has an enjoyably calming effect on Angela, and she responds by seeking to be held by him the moment he arrives for his visits. Knowing that he enjoys reading to her, Angela scurries off to obtain a book—any book—to offer to him. Sometimes James greets her with, "Go get a book," whereupon she promptly and happily obliges.

Angela is outgoing, affectionate, observant, and verbal; she names many objects and people in her environment. Although unable to focus her attention for more than a few minutes, she seems to need and enjoy the sustained interactions with James and with the books they share. In anticipating her interest, James encourages Angela to fetch a book. Angela has learned how to seek and hold James's attention. Thus, her developing sense of autonomy, along with her temperament, is becoming enmeshed with the temperament and personality of her father.

Cheryl is more inclined to engage in physically active interactions with Angela. She may chase Angela about the house, play hide and seek, take her on outings, walk around the neighborhood with her, and dance and sing with her. They especially enjoy playing copycat games with each other. Angela has learned when and how to engage her mother in these playful moments, which are quite emotionally satisfying to both of them. James and Cheryl relate to Angela in different ways, each bringing to the interactions their unique personalities and skills. Yet, although quite different in their interactions with Angela, they are complementary.

Angela's high school–based child care center is, by most standards, state of the art. Situated in its own separate building on the high school campus, it is readily accessible to the young mothers whose children are enrolled. Its program and management are guided by a director with skills and knowledge in early childhood care and education. The center exceeds local and state licensing requirements and is accredited by the National Association for the Education of Young Children. Child caregivers are educated in child development and early education and are warm, nurturing, and effective teachers. The setting is aesthetically appealing and rich with developmentally appropriate materials and activities. The daily pace is unhurried, comfortable, yet appropriately stimulating.

Two-year-old Angela is active, alert, and eager to explore and has become reasonably secure in the child care center. She has developed a strong attachment to her primary caregiver, Ms. Ruiz, who has equally strong feelings for Angela.

On arrival today, Angela scans the playroom for the sight and sounds of Ms. Ruiz. Angela's facial expression shows both anticipation and anxiety. Having located Ms. Ruiz, she runs eagerly toward her, reaching up for Ms. Ruiz to acknowledge her presence with a hug. Ms. Ruiz greets Angela with a wide smile and obliges with a hug, then offers to help Angela with her coat. Angela resists, however, wanting to do this herself. Ms. Ruiz reminds Angela to say good-bye to her departing mother, as Cheryl must leave to attend her algebra class. While removing her wraps, Angela stops and watches tentatively as Cheryl leaves. Rushing to the door, she calls to her mother, who returns, kisses her good-bye, tells her to have a good time, and then goes on to class. Perhaps Angela still feels some separation anxiety because her facial expression shows signs of impending tears.

However, Ms. Ruiz, sensitive and reassuring, directs Angela's attention to the large classroom aquarium, points to the fish, and begins to name the items in the aquarium: *gravel, light, water.* She talks with Angela about the fish: "Yes, that is a fish, Angela. This one is an angelfish. Let's put some food in the aquarium for the fish." This interaction has become somewhat routine each morning and, though quite brief, helps Angela to make the transition from home to center and from mother to caregiver.

Once at ease, Angela asserts, "No more fish," and proceeds to another part of the room to play. Very soon, she will approach her friend Leah, and a different interaction will ensue as the girls proceed to the sand table.

The child care center that Jeremy now attends is also judged to be of high quality. Jeremy's parents visited a number of child care centers and preschool programs, asked many questions, and discussed their options before making their final selection.

Jeremy enjoys attending the child care center. However, in recent weeks, separation has become a particular problem for him and for his parents and caregivers. The parents' inquiry to the center director reveals an unusual amount of staff turnover in recent months, and as a consequence, Jeremy has encountered three different primary child caregivers in less than six months.

Unable to comprehend where the caregivers go and why they are not present, Jeremy demonstrates his confusion and anxiety by clinging to his mother and crying.

(continued)

On this day, he has created quite a scene with an angry and fearful tantrum. He vigorously resists Ms. Bell's attempts to comfort him.

Soon, his special friend Josh arrives and, noticing Jeremy crying, makes his way to where Jeremy and Keisha are standing. Josh stares with some concern, as though he sympathizes but isn't sure what to do. Keisha coaxes Jeremy: "Hi, Josh. Jeremy, here is Josh. Josh wants to play with you." Jeremy soon stops crying and, reluctantly and slowly, reaches toward his mother in a quest for a hug. Thus, he signals that he will kiss her good-bye. Mother and child hug and kiss, and Keisha begins to lead Jeremy and Josh toward the block center. Once the two are involved, Jeremy's mother says a reassuring good-bye and departs without further incident.

These examples show that attachments can be formed with individuals, both adults and children, beyond the home and family. These attachments can be quite strong and can provide another source of security for the toddler. It is clear that both Angela and Jeremy have found a sense of security and well-being in their child care center relationships. For Angela, the adult caregiver has become a reliable and trusted source of security in the absence of her mother. For Jeremy, his young friend and playmate Josh has become a trusted friend, a stable presence in the absence of a continuous relationship with a dependable child caregiver.

Wisely selected child care arrangements offer an expanded circle of friends and healthy, supportive relationships for young children. However, as in Jeremy's situation, we can see that staff changes create stress for some children, returning them to earlier and less mature forms of coping and reduced social competence with peers (Howes, 1997; Howes & Hamilton, 1993). Howes cautioned that continuity of caregiving is related to the development of secure attachments in out-of-home settings. This continuity helps the child to make a smooth transition between the home and the child care setting. Howes also asserted that the child who experiences many different caregivers may fail to become attached to any of them.

Competence in Social Development with Peers

parallel play
activities in which two or more children play near one another while engaged in independent activities

Studies of toddler friendships and play behaviors characterize the toddler as engaging in onlooker and/or **parallel play** (Parten, 1933). In parallel play, the toddler enjoys being near and playing beside other children but pursuing her or his own play interest. In parallel play, little if any interaction occurs between children.

Recent research highlights that toddler play can be much more complex than the term "parallel play" implies (Wittmer, 2009). In a study of children attending child care, Howes, Matheson, and Hamilton (1992) found that beginning at approximately 1 year of age, children engaged in complementary and reciprocal play. By 30 to 35 months of age, most toddlers engaged in this type of play and approximately 25% were also capable of cooperative social pretend play. (See Table 9.1.) Toddlers also imitate and learn from each other; for example, 14- to 18-month-olds, in a study conducted by Ryalls, Gul, & Ryalls (2000) could imitate a three-step sequence modeled by a peer (get the ball, throw it, and put it in a basket).

The types and availability of toys also influence the quality of play and the success of toddler interactions. Developmentally appropriate toys ensure reasonably successful toddler play. A truck with a missing wheel cannot be successfully rolled back and forth. A room with one pull toy instead of two creates frustration and tears, whereas pulling toys about the room together can be a joyous social encounter.

Table 9.1 Types of Toddler Play

> 1. *Complementary and reciprocal play*—children demonstrate action-based role reversals in social games such as run and chase or peekaboo displays
> 2. *Cooperative social pretend play*—children enact complementary roles within social pretend play

Although it is true that egocentrism characterizes the toddler's way of thinking, a growing body of evidence suggests that young children may be less egocentric than was once believed. Studies of **prosocial behaviors** in young children, including helping a peer, have begun to modify our thinking about egocentrism.

prosocial behaviors
behavior that benefits others, such as helping, sharing, comforting, and defending

Prosocial Learning and Behaviors

Children younger than age 3 have been observed demonstrating prosocial behaviors through sharing, helping, and cooperating (Eisenberg & Fabes, 1998; Ensor & Hughes, 2005; Howes, 2009; Murphy, 1992; Wittmer, 2009; Zahn-Waxler & Radke-Yarrow, 1990). Studies have led psychologists to believe that very young children are more capable of perceiving the perspectives of others than Piaget's theory suggests.

Kindness, sympathy, generosity, helpfulness, comforting peers, defending, and distress at injustice or cruelty are fairly typical behaviors in young children. Psychologists refer to them as prosocial behaviors because they are intended to benefit or help others without expectation of reward. Growing cognitive abilities contribute to the child's ability to view situations from the perspectives of others. More mature levels of thinking enhance perspective-taking abilities and **empathy.**

empathy
experiencing the feelings or emotions that someone else is experiencing

Prosocial behaviors are influenced by behaviors modeled by others. Parents and caregivers who demonstrate helpfulness, altruism, cooperation, sympathy, and other prosocial attributes provide powerful examples for the toddler. Guidance and discipline strategies with young children also affect the development of prosocial behaviors. Guidance that is empathic, supportive, reasonable, and explained to the child assists toddlers in their understanding of social expectations.

To facilitate the development of prosocial behaviors, toddlers' spontaneous attempts to share, help, or cooperate should be reinforced through positive recognition and responses: "Bobby *feels better* now that you are friends again." "That was *kind* of you to get Tamara a puzzle like yours." "That was very *helpful* of you to put the blocks away with Josh." Such verbal responses, while providing positive feedback and reinforcement, also provide labels for expected prosocial behaviors. With these labels, the child's understanding and appreciation of the views and needs of others increase.

Jeremy's teacher asked him to sit by her and talk about the unfortunate encounter he had just had with a playmate over the use of a puzzle. Both children wanted to work on the puzzle but not together. The teacher asked Jeremy how he thought his friend felt when he hit her. She also asked him to think about what he might do about the situation now that his friend was crying and hurt. His response was not exactly what the teacher sought but was revealing nonetheless: "I think you better watch me, 'cause I think I'm going to hit her again."

Emotional and Social Development: Ages One Through Three

Like Jeremy, toddlers need adults to help them control their impulses (Sims, Hutchin, & Taylor, 1996; Singer & Hannikainen, 2002). An adult who says, "I don't like it when you hit Shannon. Shanon doesn't like it, either. Hitting hurts people," helps the still egocentric toddler to think about the other person. This guidance should be supportive of each child in the encounter. Blaming and punishing only serve to reinforce negative behaviors, and neither provides the child with alternative prosocial options or assists in the development of perspective-taking and empathy.

Toddler Friendships

Young children today spend more time in out-of-home child care situations than did children of past generations. Therefore, many modern-day infants and toddlers have encountered other children from a very early age. Studies have demonstrated that genuine friendships can develop between children in toddler play groups (Greenspan & Greenspan, 1985; Howes, 2009; Rubin, Bukowski, & Parker, 1998). One researcher found that 51% of children ages 16 to 33 months engaged in reciprocal friendships that lasted throughout the year-long study (Howes, 1988, 1996). Researchers Whaley and Rubenstein (1994) identified six dimensions that were present in 2-year-olds' friendships. These dimensions included the following:

- Helping
- Intimacy
- Loyalty
- Sharing
- Similarity
- Ritual activity

Friendships can be a source of pleasure and meaning for toddlers.

Toddler friends imitate one another, laugh with and at one another, follow one another around, and share activities such as looking at books together or filling and dumping objects from a container. These friendships may be short lived or last throughout the toddler years, yet their importance to early social development is an obvious first step in learning to make and maintain friendships. As we saw in an earlier discussion, very young children can become attached to one another, and play is more focused and successful with friends with whom they play on a frequent basis (Howes, 1996).

These friendships are enhanced by teachers when they move a group of children who are familiar with each other to a new room as they age, rather than move one child at a time (Howes, 1988). One study of separation of nursery school infants and toddlers when they were being promoted to new classrooms found that when the children were moved to new classrooms with a close friend, they adapted more readily (Field, Vega-Lahr, & Jagadish, 1984). Don't

Empathic adults help toddlers to learn and accept behavior limits.

worry if these friends "stick together" when they move to a new classroom. This friendship helps children feel secure in the new environment, and after they feel comfortable, they will play with other children, too. Today, many programs have staffing patterns that move the caregiver/teacher to the next age/grade level with a class of children, maintaining continuity and security of relationships as children move to more advanced program needs.

Toddlers can become very good friends.

Conflicts

Conflicts between toddlers provide valuable learning experiences when adults support children's conflict resolution skills (Eckerman & Didow, 1996; Hay & Ross, 1982) and "are natural contexts in which children develop socially, morally, and cognitively" (Chen, Fein, Killen, & Hak-Ping, 2001, p. 523). Conflicts between two toddlers provide an opportunity for the reduction of egocentrism (Shantz, 1987). As toddlers engage in conflicts over toys, space, and control, they learn that others have different perspectives (such as who had the toy first). Piaget's theory predicts that children then experience cognitive disequilibrium that leads to their cognitive and social development. However, certain teacher strategies used during toddler's conflicts are more effective than others.

Teachers who mediate conflicts rather than dictate to children what to do encourage children to express feelings, listen to the other children's perspectives, and identify the problem (Sims, Hutchin, & Taylor, 1996; Singer & Hannikainen, 2002). Teachers who scaffold toddlers' participation in generating and agreeing on solutions promote in young children the ability to learn to solve their own conflicts without teacher support (Bayer, Whaley, & May, 1995).

Aggression

Most importantly, we want to prevent aggressive behavior. Children who are loved and securely attached and receive appropriate physical affection are less likely to exhibit aggressive behaviors. The following quote summarizes recent research concerning the frequency of aggression during the toddler years and the importance of helping young children regulate and channel their aggressive behaviors, while learning prosocial behaviors.

> Most children have initiated the use of physical aggression during infancy, and most will learn to use alternatives in the following years before they enter primary school. Humans seem to learn to regulate the use of physical aggression during the preschool years. Those who do not seem to be at highest risk of serious violent behavior during adolescence and adulthood. (Tremblay et al., 2004, p. 43).

Emotional and Social Development: Ages One Through Three

Issues in Emotional and Social Development

Recognizing the factors that influence social and emotional development during the toddler period helps adults to provide essential and appropriate experiences for toddlers. Optimal social and emotional development depends on these earliest experiences.

Guidance and Discipline Techniques

Guidance and discipline techniques that are consistent, predictable, logical, and supportive help toddlers begin to develop self-control, perspective-taking ability, and increasing competence in social interactions. Toddlers need the security of a guidance system that nurtures their growing independence while recognizing their continuing need for reasonable rules, clear limits, and constant protection. Through positive, instructive, and supportive interactions with adults, toddlers begin to learn to express and perceive emotions.

Opportunities to Learn Through Social Interactions

Interactions with siblings and agemates provide social experiences that lead to social understandings and a grasp of the feelings and intentions of others. Toddler friendships provide experiences for the development of self–other distinctions.

Quality of Play Experiences

Appropriate and satisfying play interactions and developmentally appropriate toys and games enhance social and emotional development in a myriad of ways, overlapping and supporting development in all other domains: physical–motor, cognitive, language, literacy, and social and moral competence. Through play, the toddler tries out a variety of social roles and emerging social skills. The toddler also uses language with increasing facility to communicate needs and play themes and to acquire and understand new concepts and problem-solving strategies. Play enables toddlers to grow in their sense of competence and to resolve a number of fears and anxieties. Through play, toddlers continue to learn emotional display rules. Play introduces toddlers to other social convention rules from which later behaviors may be self-regulated.

Social Learning in Many Contexts

Experiences both within the family and in a variety of sociocultural contexts help children to learn to appreciate their and others' uniqueness. Racial awareness has its origins in these very early years. Self-esteem, family pride, acceptance, and respect for others are fostered in the home and in sensitive, responsive child care settings where nonbiased curriculums are provided.

Toddlers with Special Needs

The National Association for the Education of Young Children (NAEYC) and the Division for Early Childhood (DEC) have written a joint position paper on inclusion of infants, toddlers, and preschoolers in regular early care and education programs.

> ## Box 9.4 The NAEYC and DEC Joint Position Statement on Inclusion
>
> Early childhood inclusion embodies the values, policies, and practices that support the right of every infant and young child and his or her family, regardless of ability, to participate in a broad range of activities and contexts as full members of families, communities, and society. The desired results of inclusive experiences for children with and without disabilities and their families include a sense of belonging and membership, positive social relationships and friendships, and development and learning to reach their full potential. The defining features of inclusion that can be used to identify high quality early childhood programs and services are access, participation, and supports.
>
> NAEYC/DEC. (2009) A joint statement on early childhood inclusion. Retrieved from http://www.naeyc.org/files/naeyc/file/positions/DEC_NAEYC_ECSummary_A.pdf.

See Box 9.4 for the statement. The emphasis in this statement is on *access, participation*, and *supports*.

Access means providing the full array of programs and services to children with special needs as to typically developing children. It also means offering a variety of ways to promote learning and development.

Participation means offering many ways to promote engagement with play and learning and a sense of belonging for every child.

Supports means preparing staff and working with the family and the Early Intervention team to assure high-quality, individualized services.

Children with developmental delays, chronic conditions, or disabilities are especially in need of sound, supportive emotional and social interactions (Diamond & Stacey, 2003). Because these children can be especially vulnerable to prolonged attachment behaviors, fears, anxieties, frustrations, and disappointments, their developing sense of competence, self-concept development, and healthy self-esteem can be at risk. Adults must be particularly sensitive to the child's needs for assistance and encouragement in social situations and for opportunities to develop competence. Adults may need to coach as well as model effective social interaction strategies.

Both children with and without disabilities benefit from participating in inclusive classrooms. Preschool children without disabilities who were in inclusive classrooms gave more helpful ideas for hypothetical classroom dilemmas that included a child with a disability (Diamond & Carpenter, 2000).

Toddlers can feel depressed or act out if they experience hostility from parents.

Toddler Mental Health

Ongoing and rapid developmental processes during the toddler period bring about dramatic changes in physiological, emotional, social, and cognitive characteristics. The interplay of these growth-related changes is evident in the types of behaviors that perplex and frustrate the toddler's caregivers, for example, mood reversals, negativism, oppositional behaviors, tantrums, power struggles, rejection of affection, aggression, and eating and sleeping difficulties. Most of these types of behaviors are perfectly normal; indeed, many of them signal a maturing and healthy child. Concern arises when the primary caregivers' personalities and needs (parents, family members, nonparental caregivers) and the toddler's capabilities and needs are severely at odds and unresponsive to professional efforts to correct them. Difficult behaviors become prolonged and exacerbated; additional behavioral maladaptations (e.g., undue and unresponsive sadness, depression, withdrawal, hostility, and others) may appear (Drotar, 2002). As with all childhood anomalies, early diagnosis, professional intervention, and ongoing professional oversight are required.

Role of the Early Childhood Professional

Enhancing Social and Emotional Development in Children Ages 1 Through 3

1. Recognize the importance of the adult model in directing the course of social and emotional development in young children.
2. Understand both the toddler's egocentric perspective and the capacity for prosocial behavior.
3. Facilitate autonomy by providing safe surroundings, reasonable limits, opportunities to make choices, and judicious assistance as needed.
4. Provide positive, predictable, supportive, and instructive guidance.
5. Understand the toddler's continuing dependency and need for security and protection.
6. Encourage and facilitate play opportunities with other children.
7. Provide labels for emotions and help the toddler to learn about display rules.
8. Promote self-esteem through positive, affirming interactions and sensitive, accurate responses to questions about race and gender.
9. Provide developmentally appropriate and age-appropriate books, toys, and electronic media that enhance the child's understanding of self and others.
10. Learn to observe and respond to the child's cues and clues.

Key Terms

display rules	prosocial behaviors	self-esteem
empathy	proximity seeking	transitional object
gender constancy	self-awareness	
parallel play	self-definition	

Review Strategies and Activities

1. Review the key terms individually or with a classmate.

2. Ask your classmates about the transitional objects they had as young children. How many recall ever having a transitional object? What was the object? For how long did the attachment to the transitional object persist? What does this survey illustrate about transitional objects?

3. Volunteer to assist in a program for toddlers for at least one day. In a journal, describe instances of prosocial behaviors. What preceded the prosocial response? How did the recipient respond? What followed the prosocial encounter?

4. Watch YouTube videos of the morality experiments. Use Karen Wynn or Paul Bloom as search words. Two good ones are:

    Science Nation: Babies and Learning, http://www.youtube.com/watch?v=F-UQkDs9I0I

    Are we born good or evil?, http://www.youtube.com/watch?v=W72vC48kWyo

4. Engage a 3-year-old in conversation. What clues does the child give about his or her self-perceptions regarding age, size, abilities, gender, race, friends, family, and so on? Be careful not to prompt or suggest expected answers.

5. Observe arrival and departure times at a child care center. How do toddlers respond to their parents when the parents drop them off and arrive to take them home? How do parents respond? How do caregivers or teachers respond? Ask the instructor to discuss what these behaviors mean in terms of attachment and separation anxiety.

Further Readings

Adams, E. J. (2011). Teaching children to name their feelings. *Young Children, 66*(3), 66–67.

Lerner, C., & Ciervo, L. (2010). Parenting young children today: What the research tells us. *ZERO TO THREE, 30*(4), 4–9.

Newton, E. K., & Thompson, R. A. (2010). Parents' views of early social and emotional development: More and less than meets the eye. *ZERO TO THREE, 30*(4), 10–17.

Parlakian, R., & Adams, E. (2010). This will be her last day: Supporting infants, toddlers, and their families as they transition out of child care. *ZERO TO THREE, 30*(4), 17–22.

Other Resources

American Academy of Pediatrics brochures:
    Toilet training: Guidelines for parents
    Discipline and your child: Guidelines for parents
    Temper tantrums: A normal part of growing up

National Association for the Education of Young Children brochures:
    Helping children learn self-control: A guide to discipline
    Love and learn: Discipline for young children
    A caring place for your infants
    A caring place for your toddler
    A good preschool for your child
    So many goodbyes: Ways to ease the transition between home and groups for young children

chapter 10

Cognitive, Language, and
Literacy Development:
Ages One Through Three

> Using their sensorimotor capacities and their abilities to master first-order symbol systems, young children develop a vast array of intuitive understandings even before they enter school. Specifically they develop robust and functional theories of matter, life, the minds of other individuals and their own minds and selves. They are aided in this task of theory construction by various constraints, some built into the genome, others a function of the particular circumstances of their culture, and still others a reflection of their own, more idiosyncratic styles and inclinations.
>
> —Howard Gardner

After studying this chapter, you will demonstrate comprehension by:

▶ recognizing theoretical perspectives on cognitive, language, and literacy development in children ages 1 through 3;

▶ describing the cognitive development of children ages 1 through 3;

▶ describing the language development of children ages 1 through 3;

▶ describing the development of literacy of children ages 1 through 3;

▶ identifying issues in cognitive, language, and literacy development of children ages 1 through 3; and

▶ suggesting strategies for promoting cognitive, language, and literacy development in children ages 1 through 3.

Theoretical Perspectives on Cognitive, Language, and Literacy Development

Cognitive development—the aspect of growth and development that involves perception, thinking, attention, memory, problem solving, creativity, language, and literacy—proceeds rapidly during the toddler period. As with other developmental domains, cognitive, language, and literacy development during this age period is explained and described through a variety of contrasting and often complementary theories.

Cognitive Constructionist Theory

You have been introduced to the Piagetian and Neoconstructivist perspectives on cognitive development. Our discussion of theoretical perspectives and descriptions of cognitive, language, and literacy development during ages 1 through 3 years begins with a continuation of the description of Piaget's stages of cognitive development begun in Chapter 7.

Piaget's Theory. As the child moves from infancy into the toddler period, Piaget emphasized that some rather dramatic transitions in cognitive abilities begin to take place as the child moved from sensorimotor activity as the guiding force behind cognitive development to mental representations and verbal interactions. Between the ages of 1 and 2, children are still in the sensorimotor period of cognitive development. Table 10.1 describes Piaget's

Table 10.1 Piaget's Sensorimotor and Preoperational Stages

Stages	Important Concepts	Example
Substage 5: Tertiary Circular Reactions 12–18 Months	Characterized by the toddler's use of **tertiary circular reactions:** • attempts to use novel ways to achieve goals. • is curious and experiments. • uses more systematic imitation. • further development of object permanence. • recognizes cause and effect. • solves problems in his or her mind without the aid of sensorimotor trial and error. • tries new means of acting on objects.	Jeremy tries to place a triangular shape into its corresponding opening in a three-dimensional puzzle. The puzzle slips, and Jeremy misses the opening. He immediately sets the puzzle upright and holds it with one hand while using the other hand to insert the piece into the opening. Jeremy's ability to set the puzzle upright and secure it with one hand indicates that through his actions on objects during the sensorimotor stage, he internalized information about what to do in various situations. He uses this representational intelligence to help him complete his goal of putting the puzzle piece through the opening.
Substage 6: Beginning of Thought 18–24 Months	Substage 6 is characterized by: • person permanence. • representational intelligence. • true object permanence (toddlers can search for objects that they did not see being hidden). According to Piaget, children in this stage of cognitive development realize that objects and people have an identity of their own and continue to exist even when they cannot be seen or heard. • imitation of not just events and behaviors in their immediate experiencing, but also behavior that they have observed at another time. Piaget called this ability **deferred imitation** (Piaget, 1952, 1962).	Jeremy ran from the dining room into the kitchen to look for his mother. Angela uses her mother's hair brush to brush her doll's hair. Jeremy looked for a toy that he hadn't used for a while and found it under a pillow on the floor. Angela, now 18 months old, picks up the remote control for the TV and pretends that she is talking on the phone. She does this when no one has been talking on the phone in her presence for several hours.
Preoperational 2–8 years	Complete	

tertiary circular reactions
an exploratory schema in which children devise new ways of acting on objects in their environment and from which they can derive meaning

deferred imitation
the ability to imitate behaviors that were observed at a prior time or in another place

theory regarding characteristics of toddlers in these stages and also includes examples of Jeremy and Angela demonstrating these skills.

Piaget proposed that by the end of the sensorimotor period, children generally understand that objects, people, and events have certain basic characteristics and can hold complex schemata (or images) of people, objects, and events in their minds. This development sets the stage for learning more advanced concepts about their social and physical world. These abilities, coupled with the increasing use of symbols through gestures, language, and play, facilitate the child's transition into Piaget's next period of cognitive development: preoperational intelligence. The **preoperational stage** of cognitive development extends from age 2 to approximately 8 years of age.

According to Piaget (1952), preoperational children are not capable of operational, or logical, thinking. Logical operational thinking involves the ability to reverse a mental action. For example, the process of addition is reversible through subtraction. Although most older children and adults understand this process, preoperational children do not. However, this inability to reverse thought suggests not that young children are deficient in their thinking, but that their thought processes are simply different.

Through interactions with other children, toddlers are confronted with another's point of view.

Young preoperational children continue to develop the ability to use **mental symbols** in the form of gestures, language, play, and dreams (Piaget, 1962). Notice how Jeremy uses mental imagery, or symbols, in his imitative play:

Jeremy has observed city sanitation workers collecting trash around his neighborhood on his walks with Phyllis. One day, after observing this activity for several weeks, he begins to dump all his toys on his bunk bed. Between loads, he presses the bolts at the end of his bed to "grind up the trash." Through his play, he imitates the adult behaviors of the sanitation workers and uses the bolts on his bed to represent the buttons the sanitation workers use on their truck.

Piaget thought that preoperational thinkers hold idiosyncratic concepts and egocentric perspectives (Piaget, 1952). Maybe you can think of some comments young children have made that illustrate their unique reasoning. Often, these remarks are described as "cute" or "humorous,." Their **transductive reasoning** can be described as thinking with illogical and incomplete concepts (or **preconcepts**). Preconcepts result from the young child's inability to focus attention on any but a few aspects of an object or experience,

preoperational stage the second of Piaget's stages of cognitive development, in which children develop the ability to internally represent sensorimotor actions but do not engage in operational or logical thinking

mental symbols the behaviors that occur at the beginning of the preoperational stage, including speech, imitation, and using one object to represent another

transductive reasoning the reasoning process of very young children, which relies on preconcepts

preconcepts the very young child's disorganized and illogical representations of experience

Cognitive, Language, and Literacy Development: Ages One Through Three sometimes the most inconsequential aspect. Transductive reasoning uses these preconcepts, thus limiting the child's reasoning and problem-solving abilities.

When Angela, age 2½, was asked, "What do you want to be when you grow up?," she answered, "Nothing." "Nothing?" her inquisitor asked. "Why do you say 'nothing'? Isn't there something you have thought you might be when you grow up?" Angela answered, "No, because I can't drive. You have to drive to go to work."

Angela has focused her attention on the fact that grown-ups drive cars to work. Therefore, she cannot imagine what she can be or do when she is grown because her current inability to drive a car would pose insurmountable limitations. Jeremy also demonstrates transductive reasoning through his problem in understanding how gifts are selected and distributed.

Jeremy and his parents visit DeVon's relatives for the holidays. DeVon's brother's family is also there. After dinner, Aunt Sarah gives the children their gifts. Jeremy's 3-year-old cousin Matthew receives several presents, whereas Jeremy is given only one. Aunt Sarah has spent approximately equal amounts of money on both children, thinking that she was being careful to show no partiality to either child. As is typical of the young preoperational child, Jeremy attends to the specifics and the number of presents, because the more general concept of the cost is not within his range of experience or conceptual development. Jeremy becomes upset because cousin Matthew "gots more presents." Aunt Sarah tells DeVon and Keisha that next year she will get the boys the same number of presents and make the presents the same or very similar.

An awareness of young children's thought processes can prevent the travail that accompanies these typical misperceptions. Children's thinking is strongly influenced by their perceptions, which are dominated by how things appear.

Another characteristic of preoperational thinking is that of **idiosyncratic concepts** or personal experiences that are overgeneralized to other situations or experiences.

idiosyncratic concepts ideas of the preoperational child that are based on personal experience and overgeneralized to other situations

Jeremy was awakening at night with dreams of ghosts and monsters. Keisha had learned that young children blend fantasy with reality. She knew that Jeremy's dreams were real to him. For this reason, she did not say, "Jeremy, there are no ghosts or monsters. They are pretend." Instead, she comforted him and reassured him that she and DeVon were there at night to keep him safe. Keisha told Jeremy that they would not let the ghosts and monsters hurt him. After these disturbing dreams continued for several more weeks, Keisha had another idea. She asked Jeremy what he thought could be done to keep the ghosts and monsters out of his room. Jeremy thought for a moment and then said, "Get a sign that says, 'Stop. All ghosts and monsters keep out.'" Keisha got some paper and crayons and drew a sign with that message. She and Jeremy then posted the sign on his door.

Jeremy used his past experience with signs in other contexts and generalized its use to meet his personal experiences. Keisha did not impose adult problem solving and reasoning on Jeremy, but allowed him to solve his problem at his cognitive level. As Jeremy prepares for sleep, DeVon and Keisha remind him that they are there to keep him safe and that there is a sign on his door telling the monsters and ghosts to keep out. During the next few weeks, Jeremy's sleep is more peaceful and less filled with nightmares.

From the Piagetian perspective, the term *egocentrism* is not used to mean that a child is selfish, but rather to indicate that children have difficulty viewing objects or situations from the perspective of others. Their perspectives are based on their own limited experiences. Piaget suggested that through interactions with other children and adults, egocentric thought becomes more socialized. Piaget also believed that childhood conflicts can be beneficial when children are challenged to attend to another child's point of view.

Angela's teacher takes the 3-year-olds outdoors to play. Angela and two other children begin to play in the sand pile. Angela grabs a sifter from one of the children. This child stares at Angela and then leaves the sand area. After several minutes, Angela tries to take a large bucket from another child, Cedrick. He firmly grasps the bucket and refuses to let her have it. Angela then begins hitting Cedrick, who runs crying to the teacher. The teacher calmly asks Cedrick what happened. Cedrick takes her hand and leads her to the sand pile, telling her that Angela took his bucket and hit him. Angela's teacher asks Cedrick to tell Angela why he was crying, and the teacher repeats what Cedrick tells her. Calmly and objectively, the teacher describes the consequences of Angela's behavior. "Angela hit Cedrick. Hitting hurts. Cedrick feels bad and is crying. He said he had the bucket first. Here is another big bucket for you, Angela. We have lots of big buckets in our sand pile."

Angela's teacher does not convey to Angela that she is "a bad girl" for hitting Cedrick. Rather, she repeats what Cedrick said, describing Angela's behavior and the consequences of her actions. The teacher also talks about what Angela could do instead of hitting. The teachers have also organized the environment so that there are duplicate materials, including several big buckets in the sand pile. They know that children at this age can become easily frustrated if they see and want something another child has. Multiple materials can prevent the interruption in children's concrete activity and can promote problem-solving skills. When it is not possible to duplicate materials, teachers can promote more socialized behavior by reinforcing children's concerns. "Cedrick said he had the big bucket first. He still wants to use it. When he is done, Cedrick will give it to you." The teacher then observes carefully to make sure Cedrick eventually shares the bucket with Angela.

Cognitive, Language, and Literacy Development: Ages One Through Three

Beyond Piaget—Neoconstructivism. As discussed above and in Chapter 1, many researchers have questioned Piaget's conclusions about development, especially his concept of egocentrism; his notion of distinct, qualitative stages of development; and his lack of clarification concerning how children vary in their development in different contexts. Neoconstructivists acknowledge the contributions of Piaget and build on Piaget's work. These theorists, however, think further about "the dynamic ways that people's actions differ and change" (Todd & Fischer, 2011; Newcombe, 2010).

Angela is playing in the sociodramatic center of her child care center classroom. She dumps plastic fruit out of a wooden bowl. As she turns the bowl over, its inverted shape suggests that it could become a hat. Angela takes the bowl and, with considerable force, places it on Maria's head, causing Maria to cry. Angela looks very surprised at Maria's reaction. She pats Maria and tries to comfort her. Angela's teacher observes this interaction and tells Maria that Angela did not mean to hurt her. Ms. Ruiz puts Maria on her lap and attempts to calm her. Angela observes Maria and then goes to her cubbyhole, pulls out her "blanky," and gives it to Maria.

Similar behaviors by other young preoperational children have caused observant teachers, parents, and researchers to question Piaget's notion of egocentrism. Angela's behavior appears to indicate that she empathized with Maria. She tried to comfort her through gentle patting and bringing her the blanket. A number of studies have documented that under certain conditions, young children have demonstrated perspective-taking and empathy. One of the earliest studies examining Piaget's notion of egocentrism in very young children was that of Yarrow and Zahn-Waxler (1977). After examining 1,500 incidents, these scholars determined that children as young as 1 year of age demonstrate compassion and other types of prosocial behavior. Other researchers have modified Piaget's well-known mountain experiment (Piaget & Inhelder, 1969) as a basis for demonstrating that young children are not completely egocentric. Piaget's mountain experiment used a three-dimensional model of three mountains. These three mountains differed in appearance. One had snow on it, the second had a house, and the third had a red cross. Children were seated at a table in front of the model. The experimenter then positioned a doll at various locations on the mountains. Children were then asked to select a picture that showed the doll's perspective. Most children usually selected a card that showed their own perspectives rather than the doll's. Piaget reasoned that these behaviors indicated these young children were egocentric because they could not take on the perspective of someone else.

In the 1980s, several experiments (Borke, 1983; Donaldson, 1979, 1983; Hughes & Donaldson, 1983) determined that if tasks are more appropriate and familiar to young children, children are capable of taking the perspectives of other people. Using such familiar props as a toy police officer, Grover from *Sesame Street,* a car, boats, and animals, the children were able to take the viewpoint of another. Eighty-eight percent of 3-year-olds (Hughes & Donaldson, 1983) and 80% of 3- and 4-year-olds (Borke, 1983) were able to see another's point of view.

In a study involving a "magic task," Gelman and Gallistel (1983) explored young children's conservation of number. Piaget's experiments indicated that if two rows contain the same number of objects and one row is lengthened, the preoperational child will say that there are more objects in the longer row. Figure 10.1 illustrates how, according to Piaget, appearances may fool the child's concepts of amount or number In Gelman's and Gallistel's (1983) "magic task," however, children were not asked to distinguish between *more* and *less,* which are abstract concepts and more difficult for young children. Rather, the children were asked to choose a winner or a loser in a number of conservation experiments. Ninety-one percent of the 3-year-olds were able to conserve when presented with various arrays. It appears that if experiments are made more relevant to the real-life experiences of young children, children demonstrate that they are not as egocentric as Piaget believed. In some contexts, if children are given appropriate materials with which they can identify, if the tasks involve basic human purposes to which children can relate, and if the questions asked take into account young children's understanding of language and their motivations in answering questions, they can and do demonstrate somewhat different outcomes than Piaget proposed (Black, 1981; Bowman & Stott, 1994; Flavell, 1985; Sternberg & Berg, 1995; Sugarman, 1987). These findings do not negate Piaget's theory, but refine and focus our observations and subsequent research.

Other Cognitive Theories

Contrary to Piaget's Cognitive Developmental Theory, Multiple Intelligences Theory, Information Processing Theory, and Social Learning/Cognitive Theory do not identify stages of development. Rather, these theorists propose that development is continuous. They emphasize how a child thinks, remembers, processes information, problem solves, and learns.

Multiple Intelligences Theory. A view of intelligence is that proposed by a contemporary scholar, Howard Gardner (1983, 1991a, 1991b, 1993, 1999, 2005), who suggests that intelligence is the ability to solve problems or create a product that is valued by one's culture or community. As the quotation at the beginning of this chapter reveals, Gardner characterizes the learning of very young children as "intuitive." He characterizes early learning as natural, naive, and universal, wherein the young child is "superbly equipped to learn language and other symbolic systems and who evolves serviceable theories of the physical world and of the world of other people during the opening years of life" (Gardner, 1991b, p. 6).

Gardner contrasts the intuitive learner with the "traditional student" (between the ages of 7 and 20), who attempts to master the traditional "literacies, concepts, and disciplinary forms" of the school, and the "disciplinary expert" (at any age), who is able to use the knowledge of one discipline to inform new encounters. These are learners whose knowledge serves them at the application level of thinking and acting.

Gardner proposes that there are many different kinds of minds and that individuals learn, remember, understand, and perform in many different ways. He suggests that human beings are capable of a number of different ways of knowing. His point of view is referred to as a multiple intelligences theory. Gardner proposed that there are at least seven intelligences and in more recent work proposed at least three additional candidate intelligences (Gardner, 1999). These intelligences include the following:

1. *Intrapersonal intelligence:* the ability to "detect and symbolize complex and highly differentiated sets of feelings"
2. *Interpersonal intelligence:* the capacity to recognize distinctions among other people's moods, temperaments, motivations, and intentions
3. *Spatial intelligence:* the ability to accurately perceive the visual–spatial world
4. *Bodily-kinesthetic intelligence:* the capacity to direct one's bodily motions and manipulate objects in a skillful fashion
5. *Musical intelligence:* exceptional awareness of pitch, rhythm, and timbre
6. *Linguistic intelligence:* sensitivity to meaning, order, sounds, rhythms, and inflections of words
7. *Logical–mathematical intelligence:* the ability to attend to patterns, categories, and relationships

The additional candidate intelligences Gardner describes are as follows:

1. *Naturalist intelligence:* the ability to recognize important distinctions in the natural world among plants and animals, natural phenomena, and changes over time
2. *Spiritual intelligence:* the ability to relate to the mysteries of life and death and the "why" questions of human existence, the supernatural, and altered states of consciousness
3. *Existential intelligence:* a strand of spiritual intelligence, which includes the ability to locate oneself within the cosmos—the infinite—while dealing with such intellectual issues as the meaning of life and death and the ultimate fate of the physical and psychological worlds and relating to, and perhaps explaining, the depth and breadth of experiences such as profound love, an absorbing response to a work of art or music, or other mysterious or potent life experiences

Individuals are thought to possess these intelligences in various combinations and to greater or lesser degrees. Rather than pursuing such constructs as the IQ (intelligence quotient), which attempts to define intellectual potential, Gardner's multiple intelligences (MI) theory suggests an approach to studying children that asks not, "How smart are you?" but "How are you smart?" Such an approach emphasizes individual strengths and idiosyncrasies and provides a broader profile of individual capabilities than has been derived historically through traditional intelligence tests.

Information-Processing Perspectives. From the information-processing point of view, young children have a limited capacity to pay attention and to remember. Teachers of toddlers will be quick to affirm that holding their attention for any appreciable length of time is quite a task, and reminders of routines and rules are a constant necessity. As we get older, attention and memory help us to gain and retain information from our experiences. However, young children lack many of the processing skills that older children and adults use. For example, young children are unsystematic in their attentional behaviors, often fail to focus on essentials, and are easily distracted. Inability to engage in focused attention often leads to faulty and incomplete information, as illustrated earlier. Couple this with limited memory functions, and one can see why young children naturally form many incomplete concepts and misperceptions and are unpredictable in their behaviors, sometimes remembering behavioral expectations and at other times not.

Alert, active, and curious, young children confront and are bombarded with far more stimuli and information than they can adequately process. Most information travels through short-term memory storage but is readily lost unless the child has employed some strategy to move it to long-term memory storage. Strategies such as memorization, rehearsal (i.e., repeating something to themselves over and over), or using class and categories or associations to assist memory assist this process, but young children have limited ability to do these things. Young children remember best the activities that they have experienced a number of times: activities that were in some way novel or unusual to them, such as a friend's birthday party last week; or an event that evoked emotion, such as when a sibling got injured; or that they participated in a joyous family occasion, such as a family or holiday celebration. However, some scholars believe that events that evoke overwhelming emotion may alter or inhibit memory processes at the biologi-

Young children remember best what they themselves experience.

cal level, causing certain structures in the brain to inadequately process the information, leading to faulty or no memory of an event (Siegel, 1999). Memory in young children then depends on the child's ability to make meaningful and relevant sense of the event to be remembered. As children get older, they can be helped to use the strategies that move short-term memories into long-term memory storage.

Social Learning/Cognitive Perspective. Recall from previous social learning/cognitive discussions the importance of role models in the lives of young children. Observation of toddlers' imitative behaviors suggests that cognitive, language, and literacy behaviors are often profoundly influenced by the individuals they choose to imitate. Interactions with other toddlers and older children provide additional models of behavior, language, concepts, and misconcepts.

Contextual Theory

Contextual theories, such as sociocultural and bioecological, help us think about how important social interactions are for toddlers and how the quality of early education and care programs affect young children. The research based on these theories informs us of how culture affects how children express emotions and how they interact with other children.

Sociocultural Perspectives. As during infancy, young children continue to learn best and most readily from the social interactions that they experience with important people in their lives. Through these interactions, self-knowledge emerges; curiosity, autonomy, and initiative are encouraged; concepts are imparted; language development is supported and enhanced; and, in the broad sense, cultural values and modes are inculcated. In a major way, cognition, language, and literacy development depend on social contexts to support and enhance them. The toddler is particularly receptive to the learning that occurs in a social context.

Bioecological Perspectives. Many toddlers today participate in brief or extended preschool activities, expanding their spheres of influence beyond the microsystem of the immediate family into a mesosystem of interacting influences that include staff and teachers in part- or whole-day child care arrangements and part- or whole-week preschool programs. The philosophy of the programs, the knowledge and training of the adults who care for the children, and the relationships of parents and other family members to the people and entities in the mesosystem all influence the types of experiences the toddler will have and the learning that will accrue from those experiences. In the best circumstances, cognitive, language, and literacy development are supported through informed, family-centered programs and age-appropriate and developmentally appropriate activities, materials, and expectations for toddlers.

From these many theoretical perspectives on development and learning, it is clear that the thinking of infants and young children differs appreciably from that of older children and adults. A description of the expected cognitive behaviors of young children is provided in Table 10.2.

Table 10.2 The Thinking of Young Children

Early childhood thinking and learning
- is dependent on a meaningful relationship with an adult;
- is perception bound;
- is egocentric but includes beginning perspective-taking ability;
- relies on language and labels for the construction of meaning;
- relies on prior experiences to make meaning of new experiences;
- benefits from repetition;
- is beginning to grasp concepts of cause and effect;
- is beginning to organize and express thoughts;
- is beginning to organize and retell events;
- can be impulsive;
- confuses fantasy and reality;
- is quite literal; and
- appears to be illogical to a more mature thinker, but represents an age-appropriate level of logic and reasoning.

Cognitive Competence and Development

Many changes occur in cognitive competence and development during the toddler years. As a toddler tries different strategies to fit a long chain of large beads into a toy wagon, we see that children have goals, experiment with different strategies, and develop their own theories about how the world works. They are problem-solvers! Innovative research helps us understand how and what toddlers are thinking. In this section we will discuss children's understanding of theory of mind, others' intentions, and imitation as well as toddlers' own goal-oriented behavior.

Theory of Mind

Theory of mind is a term describing how young children begin to understand that others have intentions and thoughts that are different than their own, but that others are also "like me." This concept is critical to our understanding of toddlers' capabilities to be social and to imitate others. Infant researcher Meltzoff (2011) emphasizes that Piaget thought infants and toddlers "have no inkling of the similarity between self and other" (p. 50). Instead, Meltzoff states, modern research has shown that even newborns have powerful ways to discover that others are "like me."

theory of mind description of how young children begin to understand similarities and differences between their own intentions and thoughts and those of others

Understanding Other's Intentions

Early in the second year, many toddlers who have just begun to walk seem to understand if another person is attempting to accomplish a goal, even if the other person can't finish a task. In 1998, Carpenter, Akhtar, and Tomasello created innovative studies to examine whether toddlers would imitate the action of an adult when the adult spun a wheel deliberately and said, "There!" or when an adult accidently touched a lever that set off bright lights and said, "Whoops!" as the adult reached for the wheel. Fourteen to 18-month-olds imitated the adult who spun the wheel but were less likely to imitate the other adult by touching the lever as well. Instead, the toddlers only spun the wheel. They seemed to understand that the researcher who lamented, "Whoops!" was also intending to spin the wheel, even though they didn't see her actually spin it.

Imitation

Infants and toddlers learn by observing others and imitating them. Research in the mid-1980s found that 14-month-olds and 24-month-olds could imitate researchers immediately and after 24 hours. Klein and Meltzoff (1999) even found that 12-month-olds can imitate how to manipulate unusual toys after four weeks and in a different setting. Because these toys were unusual and created by the researcher the toddlers could not have practiced at home.

When toddlers imitate each other, they are communicating. There is a mutuality that occurs as the toddler experiences his or her action and then sees it performed by another. There is also a value to the toddler in being imitated. When a toddler is imitated, the portion of the brain involved with agency—the "I can do it" feeling—is activivated (Deecety, Chaminade, Grezes, & Meltzoff, 2002). This is important for the development of self-identity and self-worth.

Remarkably, toddlers are making decisions about who to imitate. Poulin-Dubois, Brooker, and Polonia (2011) found that toddlers (aged 13 to 16 months) are more likely to imitate a reliable adult than one who played a trick on them by getting excited when looking into an empty container.

Toddlers Are Goal Oriented

Goal-directed behavior becomes more sophisticated during the toddler years. It is interesting to watch a toddler struggle to push a cloth into a small box or figure out what buttons to push on a toy to listen to a song. Jennings (2004) summarized the development of toddlers' goal-directed behavior.

> Between the ages of 1 and 3 years, the ability to organise actions towards achieving goals increases greatly. Furthermore, self-processes, including understanding of agency and evaluation of self, become part of the motivational system that organises goal-directed actions. At 12 months, most actions are carried out with the intention of attaining a goal; however, goals are quite fluid, changing almost moment to moment as attention is drawn to different objects or events in the immediate environment. By the age of 3 years, children are able to maintain a goal over a considerable period of time and to organise a series of disparate actions to accomplish the goal. In addition, children become invested in reaching the goal through their own actions without help, and they show pride when they meet the goal (p. 319).

Language Competence and Development

The toddler period is a particularly important period for the development of language and vocabulary. Talking, singing, and reading to toddlers appear to enhance dendritic growth in the left hemisphere of the brain, the portion of the brain that controls most, though not all, language functions. Although the subsystems of language, sound discrimination, and meaning develop gradually during childhood, with increasing language facility, both **receptive language** (understanding what is heard) and **expressive language** (communicating through language) become tools for the processing of thoughts. The pragmatics of language develop as well, with toddlers using language for a variety of functions, for example, telling, asking, and demanding.

receptive language
language that is comprehended, but not necessarily produced

expressive language
spoken language; oral communication

Angela awakens from her nap at the child care center. She sits up, rubs her eyes, and says, "Waa-waa." Ms. Ruiz fills a cup of water and brings it to her. Angela quickly drinks the water. Ms. Ruiz then allows Angela to play with the empty cup as she changes her diaper and says, "Water all gone, water all gone. Angela drank it all up. Is Angela still thirsty?"

semantics
knowledge of how language carries meaning

This vignette demonstrates that Angela is learning about **semantics** or the way in which language carries meaning. She indicates that she knows language is used to communicate—to mean something. She vocalizes to Ms. Ruiz that she wants "Waa-waa." Ms. Ruiz responds, reinforcing for Angela the notion that Angela is a meaning maker, that she communicates her needs to others through language. Ms. Ruiz facilitates this idea for Angela as she changes her diaper and talks with her about the cup, the water, and being thirsty.

As children attend to the language used in such meaningful interactions, they absorb the speech sounds, or **phonology** of the language system. Jeremy and Angela internalize the basic sounds of the English language system used in the United States, just as French children learn the sounds of the French language. As Jeremy's phonological development continues, he will begin to produce the language sounds that are typical of his socio-cultural context (family, community, and geographic region). Angela will also produce sounds that are typical of her sociocultural context.

As Angela and Jeremy begin to form their first sentences, they demonstrate that they are learning the **syntax,** or structure, of their language system.

phonology
the speech sounds of a particular language system

syntax
the grammar or structure of a particular language system

It is Saturday, and DeVon takes Jeremy with him to run errands. When they return, Keisha asks Jeremy, "Where did you eat lunch?" Jeremy replies, "We eated at McDonald's."

Jeremy's response indicates that he has learned how to put words together in a sentence to convey meaning. In addition, his use of *eated* reflects that he had processed the rule of grammar that past tense words end in *-ed.* This ability to form such gener-alizations is an example of young children's amazing cognitive ability. As Jeremy ma-tures and learns more about the language system, he will come to realize that there are some exceptions to the general patterns of language and will begin to use *ate* instead of *eated.*

Thus, in the first few years of life, young children learn (1) that language conveys meaning, (2) the sound system of the language, and (3) the structure of the language sys-tem. In addition to this linguistic or grammatical competence, they begin to learn a rep-ertoire of behaviors that are often called interactional or **communicative competence,** as illustrated in Figure 10.2. Communicative competence is the ability to adapt language to meet the communicative needs of varying situations. As described in Box 10.1, this idea has a cultural component in addition to a developmental one.

communicative competence
the repertoire of behaviors that help young children to communicate effectively with others

Interaction Between Thought and Language

Piaget believed that young children's thought influences their language. He observed that many children younger than 7 frequently talked to themselves, engaging in monologues and egocentric speech. Piaget viewed this behavior as indicative of young children's egocentric thought. In addition, he viewed this behavior as the child's way of verbalizing random thinking. Piaget thought that as children mature in their cognitive development, egocentric speech eventually disappears and socialized speech develops.

Vygotsky (1962, 1978), by contrast, believed that young children talk to themselves for the purpose of solving problems or guiding behavior. He believed that talking to oneself is communication with the self. It was also his belief that over time and as chil-dren get older, this private speech internalizes as **inner speech,** or thinking in words or sentences.

inner speech
a form of speech associ-ated with the process of internalizing spoken words or sentences

Cognitive, Language, and Literacy Development: Ages One Through Three

Figure 10.2
Linguistic, social/
emotional, and motor
competence interact
to form the child's
communicative
competence.

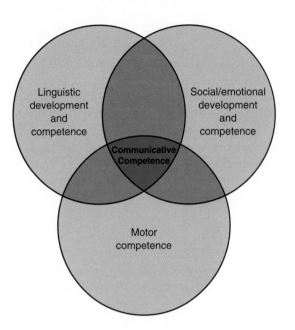

Vygotsky theorized that language and talking to oneself originate in one's early interactions with others. In fact, Vygotsky (1978) thought that all cognitive functioning first evolves in social contexts with others. He believed that adults and more cognitively astute children help less mature children learn by providing verbal suggestions or information, a form

> ## Box 10.1   Diversity Perspectives: Communicative Competence
>
> Young children acquire communicative competence in the same manner in which they acquire linguistic competence: by participating with others in meaningful interactions, conversations, and shared experiences. Nonverbal behaviors and conversational techniques are also acquired through these interactions. These behaviors can vary according to the interactive rule structures of the child's sociolinguistic context. For example, in a number of traditional Native American cultures, children are expected to listen while adults speak. Rather than providing occasions for children to speak, adults create opportunities for children to listen (Shonkoff & Phillips, 2000). Thus, children from some cultural groups view silence as comfortable and expected behavior. Interrupting or speaking too soon after another person has spoken is viewed as rude in some cultural situations (Little Soldier, 1992; Paul, 1992). These interactive behaviors are in contrast to those of other cultural groups in which children and adults engage in simultaneous overlapping conversation and interruption is viewed as acceptable behavior (Au & Kowakami, 1991). In these cultures, adults follow children's lead by adapting their language to the level and interests of the child (Pan, Imbens-Bailey, Winner, & Snow, 1996). A sociocultural perspective on language development takes into account that although grammatical and interactional competence interact to form the child's communicative competence, communicative competence is culturally specific and develops in the context of individual interactions within a cultural context.

of assistance that he termed scaffolding. Vygotsky called the level of concept development at which the child cannot accomplish tasks or understand concepts alone, but can do so with assistance from adults or more cognitively mature children, the zone of proximal development (Vygotsky, 1978).

Piaget viewed cognitive development as a process by which children mentally construct meaning out of their interactions with objects and people, whereas Vygotsky asserted that language and thought were interdependent (Vygotsky, 1986). According to this view, in the beginning, language and thought develop independently, but by around age 2, they begin to mutually influence each other. Language enhances understanding and thought, and the child uses language to interpret information and express understanding. Cultural contexts and social interaction are important contributors to this process.

Research during the past several decades has tended to support Vygotsky's theory about the importance of young children's interactions with both adults and older children in the development of cognition and the relationship between thought and

Scaffolding is a process by which helpful information and suggestions are provided as children explore their own capabilities.

language (Crain-Thoreson, Dahlin, & Powell, 2001; Hart & Risley, 1995). As a result of these findings, what Piaget called *egocentric speech* and Vygotsky called *inner speech* are now referred to as **private speech.** Some scholars suggest that, contrary to Piaget's ideas, very young children who use private speech have higher rates of social participation and are more socially competent than children who do less talking to themselves. In addition, research suggests that cognitively mature children use private speech at earlier ages (Berk & Winsler, 1995). These findings demonstrate the importance of social interaction and communication in the development of language and cognition in young children. This information provides one of the most important implications for promoting the cognitive development of young children: providing opportunities for children and adults to interact and communicate with each other.

private speech
speech to oneself that helps direct one's behavior, thinking, or communication

Receptive Language

Infants and toddlers understand more than most people think they do. If they hear a rich variety of sounds, words, and sentences, they also become very skilled word learners. As you may remember from the chapter on receptive language from birth to age 1, infants are statistical learners, figuring out what sounds are more likely to follow other sounds in words and what words are more likely to follow other words in sentences (Swingley, 2008). It also seems that the more words infants and toddlers hear, and then say, the easier it is to learn more words (Werker, Fennell, Corcoran, & Stager, 2002). This supports the dynamic systems theory. As infants and toddlers learn more vocabulary words, brain development allows them to learn faster. Joint attention is a key concept for language development. By age 1, infants follow the gaze of another person. Older infants and younger toddlers may look at a more interesting object when the adult is talking and attach

Language development is quite rapid during the toddler period.

the word to the object. Later, toddlers use the social cues of the adult, follow the gaze of the adult, and figure out what the adult is talking about, not necessarily what is more interesting to them (Golinkoff & Hirsh-Pasek, 2006). The following quote describes interesting research on the topic.

> Two studies assessed the gaze following of 12-, 14-, and 18-month-old infants. The experimental manipulation was whether an adult could see the targets. In Experiment 1, the adult turned to targets with either open or closed eyes. Infants at all ages looked at the adult's target more in the open- versus closed-eyes condition. In Experiment 2, an inanimate occluder, a blindfold, was compared with a headband control. Infants 14- and 18-months-old looked more at the adult's target in the headband condition, Infants were not simply responding to adult head turning, which was controlled, but were sensitive to the status of the adult's eyes. In the 2nd year, infants interpreted adult looking as object-directed, an act connecting the gazer and the object. (Brooks & Meltzoff, 2002)

Toddlers are learning how to learn.

Expressive Language

Vocabulary Development. Young children's rapid vocabulary development is explained by a process called **fast mapping** (Carey, 1978). Fast mapping refers to the way in which young children learn and remember an average of nine words per day from the onset of speech until age 6 (Clark, 1983). By that time, young children have acquired approximately 14,000 words (Templin, 1957). Opportunities to learn new words with adults and peers result in children's increased fast mapping ability. When Gershkoff-Stowe and Hahn (2007) provided opportunities for children between 16 and 18 months of age to learn the names of unfamiliar objects during 12 weekly sessions, these children more rapidly learned a second set of words than did a control group of children who had only been exposed to the 24 new words at the beginning and the end of the weekly sessions. The authors concluded that, "The data suggest that learning some words primes the system to learn more words. Vocabulary development can thus be conceptualized as a continual process of fine-tuning the lexical system to enable increased accessibility of information" (p. 682). Children need adults who label objects and introduce new words in context.

> First, the fact that infants begin learning words months before their first birthday makes children's rapid progress in language acquisition less mysterious. Children amaze parents and researchers alike when their first spoken words are so quickly followed by many others, and when single words become multiword sentences. Children can do this because of "underground" learning in infancy that is not expressed in day-to-day behavior but that can be detected using laboratory tests. Infants learn the forms of many words and phrases, apparently with substantial phonological accuracy, and they

fast mapping
children's rapid learning of language by relating a word to an internalized concept and remembering it after only one encounter with that word

gather information about the linguistic and situational contexts in which these forms are used. This knowledge provides the foundation of toddlers' vocabularies. Toddlers build upon this foundation when they learn more about what words mean and when they use their phonological knowledge to recognize familiar words and identify novel ones. (Swingley, 2008, p. 311)

Children's initial understanding of a word during the fast-mapping process is often expanded and refined as children continue to learn about the world. The following vignette demonstrates this clarification of vocabulary.

One of Jeremy's favorite early books was Eric Carle's (1979) *The Very Hungry Caterpillar.* Jeremy's first referent for a caterpillar was the tube-shaped animal that crawls. He was somewhat puzzled later on when he had his first encounter with another type of Caterpillar, a toy replica of the earth-moving machine. As children refine and extend their vocabulary, they discover that there are words that sound the same but have different meanings.

As with infants from birth to 1, the language environment influences how effectively toddlers learn new words. Toddlers need to be exposed to a language-rich environment that is responsive but not overstimulating. When an adult is being responsive, toddlers tune in and are engaged. When adults talk without waiting for toddlers to take a turn or when adults aren't responsive to children's attempts to communicate, toddlers turn away, show frustration, or cry.

First Sentences. When children are around 18 to 20 months, they usually have a vocabulary of about 40 to 50 words. At this time, they begin to form their first sentences, consisting of two words. Two-word sentences are often called **telegraphic speech** because only the most necessary words are used (Brown & Fraser, 1963). Prepositions, articles, auxiliary verbs, conjunctions, plurals, possessives, and past endings are usually left out of telegraphic speech. **Rich interpretation** of this sentence structure acknowledges that children know more than they can express. Bloom's (1970) classic example of "Mommy, sock" indicated that these two words could convey a variety of meanings: "Mommy's sock," "Mommy, put on my sock," or "Mommy, give me my sock." Context becomes essential to understanding the child's true meaning in these earliest sentences.

Rich interpretation allows us to recognize that sentences usually entail many elements of communication, questions, descriptions, recurrences, possessions, locations, agent actions, negations, and wishes. Bloom (1970) found that children's first use of *no* conveys nonexistence—for example, "no juice." Next, *no* is used as a negative, as in "no go home." Then *no* is used to convey what the child believes to be not true.

Between ages 2 and 3, simple sentences begin to replace telegraphic expressions, and the structures of these simple sentences reflect the linguistic nuances (e.g., word order) spoken by members of the child's cultural and linguistic community (Maratsos, 1983). Gradually, children between 1½ and 3½ years of age begin to acquire grammatical **morphemes,** which expand the mean length utterance or "sentence." Morphemes are meaningful units of language, including words and grammatical markers such as prefixes and suffixes (e.g., *-ed* for past tense, *-s* for plural). Generally, English-speaking

telegraphic speech
children's early speech, which, like a telegram, includes only the essential words needed to convey meaning

rich interpretation
acknowledging that young children know more than they can verbally express and use nonverbal behaviors to communicate

morpheme
the smallest unit of meaning in oral or written language

Cognitive, Language, and Literacy Development: Ages One Through Three

children in these age groups acquire grammatical morphemes in a fairly predictable order (Shonkoff & Phillips, 2000).

Oral Language Approximations. As children begin to acquire language, their approximations, or attempts to replicate conventional adult language, are replete with overextensions, underextensions, creative vocabulary, and overregularization. Frequently, adults misinterpret young children's developing language as incorrect and believe that it should be corrected. However, these early language approximations represent necessary cognitive processing and evolve into more mature forms of language through maturation and language-rich experiences.

Overextension involves young children's use of a word to refer to a similar but different object, situation, or category. When a child points to an airplane and says, "Truck," the child is overextending the word *truck* to refer to other objects. Young children's efforts at cognitive processing are evident in their use of overextensions. Overextensions always apply to a class of similar referents. Airplanes remind the child of the "bigness" and/or the mobility of trucks.

Overextensions are thought to be a strategy that young children use when they cannot remember the appropriate word or have not had an opportunity to learn it. For example, a child who has never seen an airplane before may attach the label *truck* to it. The child has no knowledge of the word *airplane* or to what it refers. In addition, given the correct names in a comprehension task, children can point out specific objects even though they overextend. This illustrates how comprehension of language precedes production of language.

The opposite of overextension is **underextension** in which the child uses a general term or word to refer to a limited range for its use. For example, the child thinks that the name *Hannah* applies only to her sister Hannah, and no other person can have that name; or the word *dog* applies to collies but not to other types of dogs.

Young children use **creative vocabulary** when they create new words to meet the need for a word that they have not learned or cannot remember, or for which no actual word exists in the language system. For example, one young child referred to a calculator as a "countulator." Another example occurred when several children in an early childhood classroom were playing restaurant. They decided that Justin would be the "cooker."

Overregularization occurs when young children generalize a grammatical rule to apply to all situations. As children begin to unconsciously internalize the general rules for making plurals or past tense, they overgeneralize the rules. For example, the general rule for making past tense is to add -*ed* to a word. In applying this principle, children create *goed, runned, breaked,* and so on. Remember when Jeremy told his mother that they had "eated at McDonald's"? Again, these language behaviors reflect the young child's remarkable cognitive processing of language.

Pragmatics

Once an infant understands that when an adult points (Woodward & Guajardo, 2002), the adult wants the child to look at an object or person, the child begins pointing, too. It is fun to see where and when an infant points. But why does a 1-year-old begin to point? One hypothesis is that he or she is communicating to learn (Southgate, van Maanen, & Csibra, 2007). According to this theory, infants point to encourage the adult to label the object or

---

overextension
the use of a word to refer to a similar but different object, situation, or category

underextension
the use of a general term to refer to a more specific object, situation, or category

creative vocabulary
the creation of new words to meet the need for a word that has not been learned or that has been forgotten, or for which no word exists

overregularization
the tendency to overgeneralize a rule of grammar

to get the adult to do something for the child. Another theory is that infants point to share attention and interest (Liszkowski, Carpenter, Henning, Striano, & Tomasello, 2004).

Sociocultural Aspects of Language: Dialects, Bilingualism, and Multilingualism

When we speak of *cultures* or *cultural diversity,* we are referring to the amalgam of beliefs, value systems, attitudes, traditions, and family practices that are held by different groups of people. Ethnicity refers to a particular group's shared heritage, including the group's common history, language, distinctive traditions and celebrations, and often a common religion. Young children develop language in the context of individual cultural and ethnic group membership and "language is a major medium for transmitting culture across generations" (Katz & Snow, 2000, p. 50).

Gollnick and Chinn (1990) provided a cultural definition of language: "a shared system of vocal sounds and/or nonverbal behavior by which members of a group communicate with one another" (p. 211). Language is expressed differently in different cultural groups and is characterized by both verbal and nonverbal communicative elements. Consequently, the expression of language is unique and often idiosyncratic between and among members of different cultural groups.

Dialects

Linguists say that there are many dialects throughout the United States. Consider the variations in sounds and pronunciations of the New England area, the South, and the Midwest. The state of Texas, for example, is said to have five regional dialects. Linguists define **dialects** as speech differences that are unique to various ethnic populations or geographic regions. Dialects vary in word pronunciation, verb tenses, and sound omissions. According to linguists, dialects are not inferior forms of language but are simply different forms. Dialects are rule governed just as standard English is rule governed. All young children learn the dialect of the home and community in which they live; for example, many young children come from families in which a dialect such as African American Vernacular English (AAVE) is routinely spoken.

dialects
different forms of language used by different ethnic groups or by people who live in different geographic regions

Bilingualism and Multilingualism

From birth, some children learn two languages simultaneously. This is referred to as **simultaneous bilingualism** and these children truly have two first languages. Other children learn a second language after acquiring proficiency in a first language. This process is known as **successive bilingualism,** and these children often encounter the second language in an intensive context, such as when being cared for by an adult who speaks a language different from that of the family or when enrolled in a preschool in which the language is different from that of the home.

simultaneous bilingualism
the process of learning two languages at the same time, beginning at birth

Increasing numbers of children in the United States come from homes in which English is not the first language. Many young children are in home, child care, and preschool environments in which different languages are spoken. Scholars who are interested in the language development of bilingual and multilingual children suggest that second-language acquisition facilitates both cognitive and linguistic skills (Yoshida, 2008). When matched with children who are monolingual, children who are bilingual demonstrate

successive bilingualism
the process of learning a second language after acquiring proficiency in a first language

better attention skills (Poulin-Dubois, Blaye, Coutya, & Bialystok, 2010), and the brains of bilingual children stay open to learning another language longer (Garcia-Sierra et al., 2011). Infant brains are definitely able to learn one or more languages!

The patterns of second-language development parallel those of first-language development. Second-language acquisition, like first-language acquisition as described earlier in this chapter, is creative (deHouwer, 1995). Further, children learning two languages simultaneously do so at a rapid pace, much as if they were learning only one language. Language development in all cultures is a developmentally robust process and is not slowed among young children who are learning more than one language (deHouwer, 1995; National Research Council & National Institute of Medicine, 1997; Petitto, Katerelos, Levy, Gauna, Tétreault, & Ferraro, 2001). Children of all cultures benefit from environments that provide enriching linguistic input.

Input or social interaction with other children and adults is necessary to second-language acquisition just as it is to first-language acquisition.

Literacy Competence and Development

Cheryl has been doing her homework in front of the TV. She takes a break and walks to the kitchen to get something to eat. As she walks back to the living room, she discovers Angela (now 26 months of age) scribbling on her notebook. "Angela, that's my homework!" shouts Cheryl. Angela looks up at Cheryl and says, "Angela, homework."

It is Saturday. Keisha's father has come to visit, and the family decides to go to the mall. As they enter the mall, 2-year-old Jeremy says, "There's Sears." Keisha's father cannot believe his ears. "Jeremy is only 2, and he can read *Sears,*" the proud grandfather remarks.

These vignettes demonstrate that very young children are learning not only about oral language but also about written language. The idea that very young children are aware of and learning about print is relatively recent. Yet we now know that only about half of a population of 2,581 low-income mothers reported reading daily to the children. For English-speaking children in this population, when mothers read more, the children had higher vocabulary and comprehension scores at 14 months and higher vocabulary and cognitive development at 24 months (Raikes et al., 2006).

Interaction Among Thought, Language, and Literacy

Many people believe that children learn to read and write in kindergarten or first grade. But developing literacy skills begins at birth through everyday loving interactions—sharing books, telling stories, singing songs, talking to one another, or pointing out and naming objects. Even painting, drawing or picking things up serves a purpose. These activities help develop hand muscles and coordination—skills necessary for learning how to write (ZERO TO THREE, 2007).

In the past, it was thought that children need to spend approximately the first 5 years of their lives developing a good foundation in oral language before learning to read. When children reached age 6½, they were perceived as generally possessing the maturity and perceptual development required to learn how to read (Morphett & Washburne, 1931). After learning the basic rudiments of reading, children were then ready to begin to learn how to write—to communicate with others via written symbols. This writing for the purpose of communicating with others, as opposed to the perceptual–motor task of handwriting, usually received attention somewhere around the end of the first grade or the beginning of the second. Once introduced to writing, young children were expected to produce interesting stories, with conventional spelling, appropriate grammar, good handwriting, and correct punctuation on their first attempt. If they were not successful, their papers and stories were returned to be corrected.

In the 1960s and 1970s, a number of researchers began to question this sequence of literacy development. Their research provided new information about how young children grow into literacy.

As oral language researchers analyzed tapes of young children's verbalizations, they noticed that many young children talked about and were very much interested in print (Snow, Burns, & Griffin, 1998). The vignettes about Jeremy and Angela illustrate children's awareness of and interest in print.

Toddlers develop an awareness of print as a form of communication when adults read to them.

Reading researchers also recognized that some children entered first grade already knowing how to read. Although some suspected that these children's parents had formally taught them to read, Durkin (1966) undertook a study of early readers and their families to determine exactly how these young children had learned to read. The study found that the parents did not formally teach their young children how to read. However, these parents displayed a number of other behaviors that seemed to facilitate early reading behaviors. Specifically, they (1) read to their children on a consistent and regular basis when the children were quite young, (2) provided their children with access to a wide range of printed materials in the home, (3) read and interacted with printed materials, (4) responded to their children's questions about printed materials, and (5) made writing and drawing tools and paper available to their children.

Further, scholars now recognize that children are sensitive to precise differences in sounds in spoken language. By the age of 6 months, infants recognize sound units in their native language and distinguish between consonants and vowels used in any language, but readily recognize the unique sounds of their own (Kuhl, 2001). The manner in which parents talk with infants (i.e., motherese and fatherese) furthers this development. This capacity is referred to as **phonological sensitivity.** Phonological sensitivity progresses rapidly during the preschool years when children engage in word play and conversations with others and are frequently exposed to rhythm, dance, rhyme, song, and many types of children's literature. Phonological sensitivity is primarily an auditory phenomenon and thus can develop without exposure to print. It must be noted that phonological sensitivity, although it is related to learning to read, is a different concept than

phonological sensitivity
the ability to detect and manipulate the sounds of spoken language

Cognitive, Language, and Literacy Development: Ages One Through Three

"phonics," which refers to a teaching strategy that emphasizes letter/sound correspondence (Whitehurst, 2001).

Much of the literacy research has focused on the process by which young children grow into literacy. Several general ideas describe current thinking about the development of literacy in young children:

- Learning about print begins quite early in life, as early as the first year (Barclay, Benelli, & Curtis, 1995; Rosenkoetter & Barton, 2002; Teale, 1986).
- Young children learn about literacy (reading and writing) by interacting with others in responsive relationships in meaningful situations relating to print material (Neuman, Copple, & Bredekamp, 2000; Teale, 1986).
- Play is an important way that infants and toddlers gain literacy experience (Rosenkoetter & Barton, 2002).
- Young children develop an awareness of oral and written language in a holistic and interrelated way rather than in a sequential stage process. In other words, very young children develop simultaneous notions about oral and written language while they are involved with significant others in meaningful situations (Goodman, 1986; Neuman, Copple, & Bredekamp, 2000).
- There are bridges (Rosenkoetter & Barton, 2002) from infants' and toddlers' early experiences to later reading and writing success. "Language is a strong bridge that connects to later reading and writing because infants and toddlers learn how to communicate—the ultimate purpose of reading and writing. Play is a necessary bridge, playing with sounds, words, and making marks on a page. Learning about symbols is a connecting bridge to literacy as toddlers learn that a picture or an object (a plastic apple) can represent something real that can be seen and touched" (Wittmer & Petersen, 2006, p. 297). Experiences with the tools of literacy—print in books and daily activities, magnetic letters, and writing utensils—are a bridge (Rosenkoetter & Barton, 2002)
- Virtually all children, regardless of socioeconomic background, learn about literacy early in life (Burns, Griffin, & Snow, 1999; Heath, 1983). Only in the few cultural groups that do not use written language do children lack an awareness of print.

The interaction of meaningful experiences with oral and written language is a very important contributor to the development of literacy. Such an awareness suggests it is important that young children have active, meaningful experiences with others involving both oral and written language. These experiences facilitate the child's competence in the development of thought and oral and written communication.

Developing Awareness of Print as a Form of Communication

A major concept that children acquire is that print conveys meaning. Many young children begin to develop this idea as their parents read stories to them (Neuman, Copple, & Bredekamp, 2000) and facilitate language and literacy experiences (Rosenkoetter & Barton, 2002). Indeed, it is believed that reading aloud to children is the single most important activity for building the understanding and skills that are essential for later reading and writing success (Bus, van Ijzendoorn, & Pelligrini, 1995). Other contexts also help children to understand that print conveys messages. Situations that demand attention to environmental printing, such as consulting written directions, writing checks, and using a TV guide to select TV programs, help children to develop the understanding that print communicates. The two primary sources of young children's learning about the communicative nature of print are environmental print and book print.

Environmental Print

In the vignette about Jeremy and Sears, how did Jeremy come to associate the large building at the mall with the letters *S-E-A-R-S* on the facade? The answer is through a variety of meaningful experiences that involved both oral and written language. Jeremy had been in the Sears store on numerous occasions. He was with DeVon and Keisha when they purchased a new washer and dryer. He watched as the Sears truck arrived and the washer and dryer were delivered and installed. Almost every time DeVon and Keisha are in Sears, they take Jeremy to the toy department to look around. Jeremy has also heard and seen advertisements for Sears on TV. Participating in these meaningful experiences with the accompanying oral and written language helped Jeremy to internalize the printed symbols that represent Sears.

As children use and/or observe objects in meaningful contexts, they pay attention to the objects' appearance. Seeing the box of Cheerios every morning on the breakfast table or the tube of Crest toothpaste on the sink, as well as at the grocery store or on TV, helps children to become familiar with and internalize certain features about print encountered in the environment. Studies indicate that although young children around age 2 recognize environmental print such as "Coke," "McDonald's," and "Target," they attend to this print in a very global manner (Goodman, 1980). That is, they pay attention to the whole context and not just the print. For example, very young children attend to the shape of the object, its color, and the design of the print and logo. As their print awareness develops, they begin to focus more directly on the print. Thus, experiences with environmental print are important in facilitating beginning print awareness.

Book Print

For the most part, book print differs from environmental print in that it usually consists of more than just one or two words and is organized into one or more lines. Its purpose differs somewhat from that of environmental print, and it requires a more extended focus. Knowledge of book print and how it works is critical for later success in a school context.

Learning about book print begins at home when parents share books with their children. Many parents introduce their children to books during the first year of life. Often, these experiences involve labeling pictures or talking about pictures. During the second or third year, parents usually begin to read the book text to their children. As children hear these stories, they begin to develop the idea that books can bring them information, pleasure, and comfort. This idea can begin to foster a love of books and independent reading in children. Family book reading provides many opportunities for young children to learn a number of important concepts (Schickedanz, 1999). Specifically, they learn the following:

- New information about the world around them
- New vocabulary
- Conversational turn taking (when parents ask questions and children respond)
- The features of print and how to handle books
- The concept of *story*

The parent plays a critical role in helping young children to develop book print awareness. Parents serve as scaffolders. Recall Vygotsky's zone of proximal development. By responding to their children's interests in pictures and print, engaging in point-and-name activities, asking them questions, and commenting, parents remain in the child's zone of proximal development and thus facilitate young children's understanding and challenge their thinking. Talking with children about stories that have been read encourages reflective thinking.

Finally, intimate encounters with books provide time for parent–child communication. Time spent with books not only facilitates literacy development, but also can promote positive parent–child interactions. Parental behaviors in children's acquisition of literacy have important implications for the role of early childhood professionals in promoting literacy in their classrooms.

Issues In Cognitive, Language, and Literacy Development
Biological Origins of Thinking and Language

Howard Gardner's multiple intelligences theory suggests that there may be genetic predispositions for different intelligences. Nelson (1981) identified differences in young children in the early stages of oral language development that may be a function of brain hemisphere dominance as well as environmental factors. Referential speakers rely mostly on nouns, a few verbs, proper nouns, and adjectives, and they frequently label objects. Expressive speakers use varying forms of speech combinations and frequently use pronouns and compressed one- or two-word sentences. Dyson's (1993) research in the area of young children's writing also documents variation in writing strategies. These differences could be related to individual genetic predisposition as well as to environmental influences.

The interplay of rapid brain growth and neurological development during the first 3 years and the young child's environment influences the extent to which optimal brain growth and neurological development can occur during this period. Enriched environments have been shown to stimulate and fine-tune neurological connections.

All learning is enhanced when the learner is in a state of good health. However, situations in which children are poorly nourished, obtain inadequate amounts of sleep, live with stress and lack of wholesome and protected play time, or endure family discord or other life issues interfere with optimal learning in any context. Further, undiagnosed illnesses, developmental delay, emotional disorders, or disabilities such as vision, hearing, or other sensory impairments interfere with learning and certainly present specific and sometimes profound challenges to the learner.

Again, early diagnosis and intervention is critical particularly during this time when growth, development, and learning are occurring so rapidly. Complementing regular and ongoing professional health care are programs such as the federally funded and comprehensive Early Head Start and Head Start programs for low-income families and children, which provide physical and dental, psychological, and other assessments as well as enriching age-appropriate learning opportunities. Additionally, local and state early intervention and early childhood special education programs provide diagnostic services and care and education programs for children and families. Further, some child care programs and most public schools serving very young children are able to link families to community resources such as the public health department, family services, or other specialized agencies.

Essential to cognitive and language development at all ages is the opportunity to interact in meaningful and engaging ways with others. Interactions that are positive, helpful, affirming, and supportive encourage self-esteem and self-confidence. Interactions that are thoughtful and logical help children gain intellectual clarity about their experiences. Interactions that are playful and appropriately humorous relieve stress and free the child's mind to think creatively. Probably at no other time in life is the nature and quality of one's interactions with others as important as it is during early childhood development. This is particularly true for cognitive, language, and literacy development.

Studies have revealed that the manner in which adults respond to the emerging language of toddlers is associated with the rate at which oral language develops (Hart & Risley, 1995). The importance of talking, singing, storytelling, and reading to and with children has long been associated with positive outcomes in cognitive, language, and literacy development. Further, for children whose early experiences have been less than optimal, shared book reading experiences in which adults or older children engage in dialogue and extend the conversation about a story have been found to increase vocabulary and enhance both receptive and expressive language (Hargrave & Senechal, 2000). When adults encourage the child to continue talking about a story (or conversation) topic, ask questions, interject new information, and substitute new words for familiar ones (e.g., "scamper" for the more familiar word "run"), language development is enhanced and comprehension is strengthened.

Related to this process is the use of extensions and expansions in verbal interactions with children. **Extensions** are responses that include the essence of children's verbalizations and extend the meaning, whereas **expansions** provide children with the opportunity to hear the conventional forms of language. Jeremy said, "Get ball." DeVon replied, "Oh, you need me to help you get your ball. It rolled under the table." Through this extension, DeVon conveys to Jeremy that he understood what Jeremy was verbalizing. DeVon also adds more information about the context through his verbalization. Adults use expansions to provide feedback to young children about their use of overregularizations. Jeremy tells Keisha, "We eated at McDonald's." She replies, "Oh, you ate at McDonald's. What did you have to eat?" She does not directly correct Jeremy's *eated,* but uses the appropriate form in a conversational context and also extends by asking what Jeremy had to eat. Evidence suggests that adults who use these techniques help children to progress more rapidly in their language development and produce more complex sentences than children who are around adults who do not use extensions and expansions (Senechal, LeFevre, Thomas, & Daley, 1998; White, 1985).

There are wide variations in the types and quantity of the language input experiences of children. Most White, middle-class infants and young children in the United States experience child-directed speech during routine and playtime activities (Thiessen, Hill, & Saffran, 2005). However, in some cultures, there is less child-directed speech, and children experience language vicariously from the skilled conversations of the people around them (Floor & Akhtar, 2006). The extent to which cultures influence qualitatively the language outcomes of children within them is not fully understood (Shonkoff & Phillips, 2000). Nevertheless, evidence of the importance of verbal input during infancy and early childhood is mounting. A particularly telling longitudinal study found that the receptive vocabularies of 5-year-old children tested on kindergarten entry ranged from the level of a child 1.9 years old to that of a 10.8-year-old child (Morrison et al., 1998; Morrison,

extensions
responses to children's language that extend the meaning of their language

expansions
responses to young children's use of overregularizations by using the conventional form in the conversational context

Griffith, & Alberts, 1997). These scores appear to be predictive of (1) how teachers perceive and respond to the early learner and (2) how children will fare academically during the early grades.

Variety of Print Contexts

The nature of adult–child interactions in a variety of print contexts influences the child's awareness of various literacy contexts. Children whose parents actively involve them in reading environmental print and book print, provide them with age-appropriate drawing and writing tools so that they can explore print, and respond to the children's questions about print facilitate greater awareness of print than parents who do not respond to children's print interests (Whitehurst, 2001).

Parents as first teachers promote cognitive, language, and literacy development through the many ways that they bring their very young children into awareness of words, concepts, stories, print, and literacy behaviors. Print awareness and literacy development are dependent on the child's experiences, which importantly include adults who do the following:

- Talk and converse in responsive ways with infants and toddlers, sharing everyday events and experiences.
- Verbally label objects, provide names of people familiar to the child, and describe and label events and experiences as they occur.
- Take conversational turns with infants and toddlers.
- Expand what the child says, both semantically and syntactically, while staying on the same topic.
- Look at picture books together, and share stories and print experiences.
- Include sounds, rhythms, rhymes, word play, jingles, and songs in daily interactions.
- Provide opportunities to listen to recorded sounds, voices, and music.
- Model literacy and daily-life print-related experiences (reading books, recipes, news publications; making grocery lists; writing checks and thank-you notes; noticing environmental print; and labeling storage containers).
- Select and read a variety of age-appropriate story and information books.
- Retell in sequence (and encourage the child to retell) "stories" of a recent experience: the trip to the zoo, Daddy washing the car, buying cupcakes for a birthday party, spending the night with grandparents, and so on.
- Label children's drawings and take dictation from them, printing the message(s) the children wish to convey.

readiness
a term that has many different meanings depending on the context in which it is used, but generally refers to a set of prerequisite developmental expectations

Much is written today about children's **readiness** "to learn," for prekindergarten, kindergarten, first grade, or formal instruction. The term *readiness* has many meanings depending on the context in which it is used. This topic is discussed more fully in Chapter 13. However, related to our discussion of literacy development during ages 1 through 3, it is perhaps helpful to identify the types of knowledge and skills that can reasonably be expected to have occurred prior to the actual act of reading, which entails visually, auditorally, and cognitively decoding abstract print symbols and making meaning from the written word. Table 10.3 lists these necessary child development accomplishments during the infant and toddler period. Additional developmental accomplishments during ages 4 through 5 necessarily precede formal reading instruction.

Table 10.3 Early Literacy Development (Birth Through Age 3)

Acquire a beginner's facility with language and nonverbal communication forms

Recognize that words represent the names of objects, people, and events

Listen with interest to the spoken word

Demonstrate facility with both receptive and expressive language

Continue vocabulary development

Demonstrate an interest in and awareness of sounds and rhythms in speech and music

Make subtle distinctions associated with sounds, rhymes, and rhythms in speech and music

Enjoy and experiment with spoken sounds and rhythms

Have an interest in and curiosity about books and book illustrations

Understand that books have both illustrations and print

Understand that print represents spoken language

Understand that print can be used to label, tell a story, and convey a message

Understand the function of books

Demonstrate book handling skills (top/bottom, left/right, front/back orientations, page turning, care, storage, and retrieval)

Demonstrate awareness of, interest in, and curiosity about environmental print

Imitate the literacy behaviors of others: look at books, "read" pictures, retell stories; draw and label, imitate writing, attempt letter/numeral formation, point to print sequences on objects and in books, ask "What does that say?"

Initiate story-reading and book-sharing activities

Demonstrate an interest in making marks on paper with crayons, markers, and paint.

Diversity in Play and Concrete Activity

Most child development experts perceive opportunities for play or concrete, first-hand activity and the quality of play as important factors in facilitating the young child's cognitive, language, and literacy development. Most experts on play suggest that sensorimotor play with or without objects facilitates the young child's beginning cognitive development (Piaget, 1962; Sutton-Smith, 1997). Garvey (1977) noted that object play often involves a four-step sequence: exploration, manipulation, practice, and repetition. Repetitive play with objects facilitates the development of **physical knowledge** and the development of **logicomathematical knowledge** (Piaget, 1969). Children between ages 1 and 3 often play with sounds, syllables, and words. Young children's play with language encourages language development.

During the child's third year, sociodramatic play begins. Three-year-olds' sociodramatic play usually has no organized theme or plot. Their enactments of play roles are often one-dimensional and change frequently, owing to the lack of a general theme. Play at this age often involves collecting, hauling, carrying, and dumping objects. Children tend to repeat play over and over. Jeremy's playing garbage collection is an example. In spite of these characteristics of toddler play, children at this age act out the basics or essentials of certain **scripts**—such as eating a meal, visiting the doctor, or picking up the trash—which support the types of thinking involved in story reading and story creation.

Solitary play and play with others is essential to child development. Play with playthings that are open ended allow the child to mentally construct concepts, meaning, and

physical knowledge
knowledge of physical characteristics of objects and events gained through sensorimotor play

logicomathematical knowledge
knowledge constructed primarily from children's actions on and interpretations of objects and events

scripts
sets of social procedures or events, which include sequences of events and/or roles, often observed in young children's play

ideas that are far more engaging and provide essential supports for early cognitive, language, and literacy development. Unlike toys that have limited use or can be played with in only one way, open-ended toys and playthings can be used in diverse ways and with different levels of proficiency. Blocks, for example, can be used to stack, load in a wagon, build a tower, clap to music, or symbolically represent a person, vehicle, animal, or railroad track. Blocks are enjoyed differently at different ages as play behaviors and capabilities change over time. Blocks have an enduring quality essential to play that supports cognitive and language development at all ages. Think about it: Architects and engineers use blocks to create models of their proposed structures. By contrast, a wind-up mechanical or electronic toy is of little value if all one can do with it is watch it "perform" or if its use requires adult assistance. Older toddlers benefit from opportunities to interact with other children in spontaneous and unstructured pretend play. Through these opportunities, children gain language and social interaction skills. A rich play life in infancy and early childhood builds the bridge to language, learning, literacy, and later academic success.

Media and Young Children

There has been extensive research on the effects of watching TV, DVDs, and computer screens. Box 10.2 describes the pros and cons of young children birth to 3 involved with media.

Box 10.2 Should Infants and Toddlers Watch TV?

Yes, It Makes Sense. Infants and toddlers are watching TV and other media. This prepares them to be a part of a technologically savvy world. In a survey study of 1,000 nationally represented parents, the researchers found that 30% of children ages birth to 3 have televisions in their rooms. The parents of the 1,000 children surveyed reported that on a typical day 71% of their children under the age of 2 are read to, 59% watch TV, 42% watch videos/DVDs, 5% use a computer, and 3% play video games (Rideout, Vandewater, & Wartella, 2003). With so many parents allowing their children to watch TV/videos/DVDs and use a computer, it must be OK.

No, It Doesn't Make Sense. The American Academy of Pediatrics recommends that pediatricians encourage parents to limit children's media time, to discourage television (TV) viewing among children under 2 years of age, and to encourage alternative entertainment for children. Research conducted in 2008 demonstrated those children ages 1, 2, and 3 who played while a TV was playing in the background were more distracted and attended to their play less than when a TV was not present. The very way that infants and toddlers learn is in question with the increase in passive watching of media. We know that children need responsive interactions with adults to learn language. They do not learn how to talk from watching TV or listening to a DVD. They need interactive partners! Infants require adults to talk about the object of the infants' interest. We also know that infants are active learners, manipulating their environment, turning materials upside down to inspect them, hiding objects under blankets, and playing peekaboo with their caregivers and peers. With these experiences, infants and toddlers develop the ability to create, imagine, problem solve, and actively experiment—skills all children will need in a fast changing world.

Role of the Early Childhood Professional

Promoting Cognitive, Language, and Literacy Development in Children Ages 1 Through 3

1. Acknowledge that each child is unique in his or her cognitive, language, and literacy development.

2. Respect sociocultural, linguistic, and socioeconomic differences among young children and their families.

3. Identify cognitive, language, and literacy needs in young children that may require special attention, services, or programs.

4. Understand that young children process information differently than older children and adults.

5. Provide safe and enriched environments so that young children can explore freely and engage in meaningful play.

6. Provide a variety of interesting materials to promote thinking, talking, drawing, reading, and writing.

7. Provide opportunities for young children to interact, talk, read, draw, and write with other children and adults.

8. Demonstrate interest in and curiosity about the world.

9. Use engaging oral language with children and model the uses of writing and print in many meaningful contexts.

10. Respond in a timely manner to children's need for scaffolding to help them grasp a concept or engage in a new skill.

Key Terms

communicative competence
creative vocabulary
deferred imitation
dialects
expansions
expressive language
extensions
fast mapping
idiosyncratic concepts
inner speech
logicomathematical
    knowledge

mental symbols
morpheme
overextension
overregularization
phonological
    sensitivity
phonology
physical knowledge
preconcepts
preoperational stage
private speech
readiness

receptive language
rich interpretation
scripts
semantics
simultaneous bilingualism
successive bilingualism
syntax
telegraphic speech
tertiary circular reactions
theory of mind
transductive reasoning
underextension

Review Strategies and Activities

1. Review the key terms individually or with a classmate.
2. Observe caregivers in an accredited and inclusive classroom for 1-, 2-, and 3-year-olds.
   a. Explain how developmental differences and cultural tendencies and dispositions are addressed.
   b. Describe how the environment is organized to promote cognitive, language, and literacy development.
   c. List the materials available and describe how they promote cognitive, language, and literacy development.
   d. Describe how the day is organized. Is the schedule conducive to cognitive, language, and literacy development?
   e. Observe the role of the teacher. List and describe the specific behaviors that facilitate cognitive, language, and literacy development.
3. Engage in a shared story-reading time with an infant or toddler. What cognitive, language, and/or literacy behaviors does the child demonstrate?

Further Readings

Honig, A. (2007, January/February). Choosing great books for babies: Helping children develop a life-long love of reading. *Early Childhood Today*, *21*(4), 24–26.

Otto, B. (2010). *Language development in early childhood* (3rd ed.). Upper Saddle River, NJ: Merrill.

Other Resources

CELL (Center for Early Literacy Learning), www.earlyliteracylearning.org. This Web site provides a multitude of everyday literacy learning opportunities from the Center for Early Literacy Learning. Orelena Hawks Puckett Institute. Copyright © 2011. Free miniposters for parents and for teachers on a variety of early literacy learning topics are available for downloading.

Individuals with Disabilities Education Act (IDEA), http://idea.ed.gov, U.S. Department of Education, Building the Legacy: IDEA 2004. The Individuals with Disabilities Education Act (IDEA) is a law that governs how states and public agencies provide intervention services for infants and toddlers (Part C of the law) and children and youth ages 3–21 (Part B of the law) with disabilities.

International Society on Early Intervention, www.depts.washington.edu/isei. The Professional Training Resource Library (PTRL) is a searchable, Web-based library with a wide range of free materials to support professional training in the field of early intervention. The types of materials included in the library include: assessment tools, case studies, course syllabuses, internship guidelines, readings, specific curricula, training manuals, Web-based videos, and modules.

National Center for Children in Poverty (NCCP), Mailman School of Public Health, Columbia University, http://nccp.org. The National Center for Children in Poverty (NCCP) is the nation's leading public policy center dedicated to promoting the economic security, health, and well-being of America's low-income families and children. NCCP uses research to inform policy and practice with the goal of ensuring positive outcomes for the next generation. The organization promotes family-oriented solutions at the state and national levels. Its vision includes: family economic security; strong, nurturing families; and healthy child development. Use the young child risk calculator (http://www.nccp.org/tools/risk) to determine the percentage of young children in your state experiencing selected risk factors.

NECTAC (The National Early Childhood Technical Assistance Center), www.nectac.org. NECTAC is the national early childhood technical assistance center supported by the U.S. Department of Education's Office of Special Education Programs (OSEP). The NECTAC Web site provides information for early childhood programs funded under the Individuals with Disabilities Education Act. NECTAC has an early childhood research and reference portal that provides access to a variety of research and reference materials on topics concerning children with special needs.

Talaris Institute, www.talaris.org/our-research. Talaris is committed to supporting parents and caregivers by sharing the latest findings and most current research in early childhood development. Feeds to presentations by researchers are provided. For example, listen to Patricia Kuhl present on "The Linguistic Genius of Babies": www.ted.com/talks/patricia_kuhl_the_linguistic_genius_of_babies.html.

chapter 11

Perceptual, Motor, and
Physical Development;
Health and Nutrition:
Ages Four Through Five

> The first and foremost thing you can expect of a child is that
> he is a child.
>
> —Armin Grams

> A secure, healthful and nourishing environment is a child's basic right.
>
> —Convention on the Rights of the Child

After studying this chapter, you will demonstrate comprehension by:

▶ outlining expected patterns of physical and motor development in children ages 4 through 5;

▶ identifying developmental landmarks in large and small muscle development;

▶ describing perceptual–motor development in children ages 4 through 5;

▶ describing body and gender awareness in children ages 4 through 5;

▶ identifying major factors influencing physical and motor development;

▶ identifying and describing health and well-being issues related to children ages 4 through 5; and

▶ suggesting strategies for enhancing physical and motor and perceptual–motor development in children ages 4 through 5.

Physical and Motor Competence

Physical Characteristics

Physical growth in children seems to follow four stages. From conception to 6 months, growth is dramatically rapid. During the toddler/preschool period, growth rates tend to level off and proceed at a steady pace until puberty. Then growth rates are again strikingly rapid, followed by slower growth into adulthood. In children ages 4 through 5, growth rates are steady, with gains of 2½ to 3½ inches in height and 4 to 5 pounds in weight each year until around age 6. Children grow at individual rates that are influenced by their own genetic makeup and environment. However, sequences of growth are fairly (though not absolutely) predictable among all children. How tall, heavy, or well coordinated a child is (or will become) depends on genetics, health history, nutrition, psychosocial well-being, and opportunities for physical and motor activity.

Body proportions change from the chunky, top-heavy build of the toddler to a leaner, more upright figure. The child's head, which at age 2 was one-fourth of the total body length, at age 5 to 5½ is about one-sixth of the total body length. The brain reaches 90% of its adult weight by age 5, and myelination of axons and dendrites is fairly complete, making more complex motor abilities possible.

Boys and girls during this age period have similar physiques, as baby fat is being replaced with more bone and muscle. However, boys tend to gain more muscle at this age, whereas girls tend to retain more fat. The extent to which this difference is primarily caused by cultural expectations of gender-related activities (e.g., more rough-and-tumble play versus less active pursuits) is not fully known. Changing body proportions result in a larger chest circumference and a flatter stomach, longer arms and legs, and feet that have lost the fatty arch pad characteristic of baby feet.

Health assessments of children during these growing years regularly monitor height and weight gains, providing preliminary information about a child's overall health and nutritional status. Plotting height and weight on growth charts that compare the measurements with standardized norms helps professionals recognize questionable individual growth trends as they arise. In the United States, the CDC (2010a) recommends the use of growth charts developed by the WHO (World Health Organization) for children under 24 months (www.cdc.gov/growthcharts/who_charts.htm) with boys and girls charted separately. The WHO charts identify how children *should grow* when provided optimal conditions, including being breastfed. The CDC (2010a) recommends CDC charts for use with children over 24 months of age. These growth charts also include a body mass index (BMI), which is a calculation used to judge whether a child's weight is appropriate for his or her height. The CDC growth charts allow comparison with norms for age and sex in the general population and identify percentile rankings for each measurement of weight and height for age. Hence, percentiles tell how an individual child's height and weight compare with those of the general population of children of the same age and sex. An 80th percentile ranking means that a child's weight or height is equal to or greater than that of 80% of children of his or her same age and sex. Children whose measurements fall above the 95th percentile or below the 5th or whose measurements show marked change from one measure to the next may have health or nutrition anomalies that require further evaluation. However, in some cases, growth spurts occur. For instance, after a prolonged illness, the body's growth catch-up mechanisms come into play and speed the growth process for a period of time until it reaches where it would have been had the illness not occurred. (This catch-up mechanism is seen in premature and low-birth-weight infants until about age 2, when their measurements begin to follow a more normal growth curve.) Unusual growth patterns can indicate possible health problems: overnutrition or undernutrition, endocrine disorders such as hyperthyroid or hypothyroid functioning, growth hormone imbalance, disease, dehydration, fluid retention, and others.

Large Motor Development

By ages 4 through 5, children are quite motoric. Now that they have mastered walking and running, their movements are expansive and include large muscle coordination that facilitates balancing, hopping, jumping, climbing, sliding, galloping, skipping, and many others. Their large motor skills generally include the following:

Age 4	Age 5
Rides tricycle	Rides bicycle (may need training wheels)
Climbs stairs alternating feet	Descends stairs alternating feet
Balances on one foot for a short period	Balances on one foot to a count of 5 to 10
Climbs playground equipment with agility	Experiments with playground climbing equipment
Enjoys creative responses to music	Enjoys learning simple rhythms and movement routines
Skips on one foot	Skips with both feet
Jumps easily in place	Hops on one foot in place
Throws a ball	Catches a ball
Likes to chase	Enjoys follow-the-leader
Walks a straight taped line on floor	Walks a low, wide kindergarten balance beam
Enjoys noncompetitive games	Enjoys noncompetitive games

Facility in large motor control and coordination enhances the child's development in all other developmental domains. It promotes overall health and vitality, encourages independence and self-sufficiency, and furthers cognitive development by increasing ability to explore an ever-enlarging world. Mastery over body movements enhances self-image and self-confidence. As we will see in later chapters, children with positive self-images and self-confidence enjoy more successful interactions with others.

For growing children, opportunities to use, expand, and refine large motor coordination should make up a significant portion of the day. Regularly engaging in large motor activities leads to physical fitness, which, according to Gallahue and Ozmun (2006), has two very important components: health-related fitness and performance-related fitness. **Health-related fitness** includes muscular strength, muscular endurance, flexibility, cardiovascular endurance, and body composition. **Performance-related fitness** includes balance, coordination, agility, speed, and power. Both health-related fitness and performance-related fitness are essential to healthy, sturdy, well-coordinated bodies, which in turn contribute to perceptual–motor development and learning as sensorimotor mechanisms become increasingly refined.

The importance of health- and performance-related fitness is supported through studies of the effects of physical activity on bone growth in young children. A study of the association between physical activity and bone measures in preschool children ranging in age from 4 to 6 years old examined children's usual physical activity as reported by their parents, including the amount of time engaged in sedentary activities such as daily television viewing, and measured bone mineral content and density. The researchers concluded that physical activity is essential to optimal bone development (Janz et al., 2001).

Yet Brown, McIver, Pfeiffer, Dowda, Addy, and Pate (2009) found when they directly observed 476 children (51% males) in 24 preschools in South Carolina that children were sedentary 94% of the observed time intervals when inside and 56% of the intervals when outside. These researchers conclude that "…day-to-day teacher planning, implementing, and embedding of high-interest activities that promote children's nonsedentary physical activity throughout the preschool day appear to be curricular areas sorely in need of development and evaluation" (p. 55).

A literature review of journals from 1980 to 2007 determined that preschool "boys were more active than girls, that children with active parents tended to be more active, and that children who spent more time outdoors were more active than children who spent less time outdoors." However, age and BMI had no correlation to physical activity (Hinkley, T., Crawford, D., Salmon, J., Okely, A.D. & Hesketh, K., 2008).

Physical activity supports health- and performance-related fitness.

health-related fitness
a physical state in which muscular strength, endurance, flexibility, and the circulatory–respiratory systems are all in optimal condition

performance-related fitness
a physical state in which motor coordination facilitates speed, agility, power, and balance

Small Motor Development

Because motor development generally follows a head-downward direction, small motor development can lag behind large motor controls and coordination. As large motor controls become more refined and coordinated, the muscles of the extremities come under more precise control, and children generally become better equipped to perform a variety of small motor tasks. The ability to perform these small motor tasks becomes possible through the maturation and emergence of prehension and **dexterity.**

dexterity
quick, precise movement and coordination of the hands and fingers

Age 4	Age 5
Exhibits self-help skills in dressing: some difficulty with zippers, small buttons, tying shoes	Dresses with ease Ties shoes
Works a puzzle of several pieces	Enjoys puzzles with many pieces
Exhibits right- or left-handedness; occasional ambidextrous behaviors	Exhibits right- or left-handedness
Enjoys crayons, paint, clay, and other art media	Enjoys drawing, painting, and using a variety of writing tools
Uses beads and strings, snap blocks, and various manipulative toys	Enjoys a variety of manipulative and construction-type toys

Prehension is the ability to grasp or grip an object and to let go of it. By age 5, grasping and prehension abilities are used to handle crayons, paintbrushes, beads and strings, pegs and pegboards, and other small manipulatives and to manage dressing and undressing with efficiency. Prehension follows a fairly predictable pattern of development, beginning in infancy and becoming more refined as the child gets older.

Dexterity refers to quick, precise movement and coordination of the hands and fingers. Although less refined at ages 4 and 5, dexterity is exhibited in the child's ability

Age-appropriate manipulative activities facilitate fine motor coordination.

to maneuver small puzzle pieces into place; manage small buttons, fasteners, and zippers; sort playing cards; and write legible letters and numerals.

Dexterity depends on a neurological process in which certain abilities become localized in the left and right hemispheres of the brain. Handedness is an outgrowth of this developmental process. It is believed to begin prenatally, but is apparent during infancy when a preference for a left- or right-face sleeping position and a preferred reaching hand are observed. Other behaviors, such as foot, eye, and head turning preferences depend on very complex neurological development during the early months and years. Foot preference is fairly well established from ages 3 to 5, but it sometimes takes longer to emerge. Handedness, however, may not be fully dominant until 6, 7, or 8 years of age (Gabbard, Dean, & Haensly, 1991; Hellige, 1993).

Handedness, whether right or left, facilitates the use of small motor abilities, leading to more refined coordination and dexterity. Some children ages 4 and 5 whose handedness is not clearly established use both hands with facility; some use one hand for one activity, such as eating, and the other for another activity, such as throwing or reaching. There is no reason to encourage the use of one hand over the other, as this process is governed by intricate neurological connections in the brain.

Perceptual–Motor Development

Angela has just awakened from her afternoon nap. Hearing the voice of her grandmother chatting with her teacher across the room, she is further aroused. She sits up, rubs her eyes, clumsily retrieves her shoes, and makes her way toward the area from which she heard grandmother's voice. There she is greeted with hugs and questions about her day.

Angela has just demonstrated a simple perceptual–motor sequence, which involved hearing a sound (auditory sensation), recognizing and identifying the sound as that of her grandmother's voice (perception), and making a decision to walk to the source of the sound (locomotion).

We come into the world equipped with sensory abilities: touch, vision, hearing, smell, taste, and kinesthesis (proprioception). The sense organs provide information about what is going on around us and within us. The ability to make sense of these sensations—to interpret them—is called *perception.*

Perception depends on the sense organs and kinesthetic sensitivity (the sensation of body presence, position, and movement), combined with cognitive development and experience. Once a sensation is perceived, one must decide cognitively what to do with that information. Actions that follow are often motoric—for example, turning toward a sound, placing hands over eyes to shield them from a bright light, or reaching for an object. Perceptual–motor skills facilitate cognitive abilities, body awareness, spatial and directional awareness, and time–space orientation.

Perceptual–motor skills are fostered through activities that encourage the child to explore, experiment, and manipulate. Early childhood classrooms, for instance, include a variety of sensory activities: matching fragrance containers (olfactory), mixing and matching fabric patterns (visual) or textures (tactile), and cooking (taste). Musical and rhythmic activities integrate auditory and motor abilities as children respond to such elements as space, tempo, volume, and pitch (kinesthetic).

Children use sensory, perceptual, and motor skills when engaging in sophisticated cognitive tasks in later school years. Perceiving shapes necessary for forming letters and numbers later on, attending to context cues in picture books, responding adequately to tone of voice as a clue to another's message, and interpreting facial and body language cues of others are tasks that rely on sensory, motor, and perceptual abilities.

Most 4- and 5-year-olds enjoy finding out what their bodies can do.

Movement activities and simple games help to coordinate and refine fundamental motor abilities.

Body Awareness, Movement, and Simple Games

During the process of mastering basic locomotor skills, children develop an awareness of their bodies. This awareness includes not just the names and locations of body parts and what they can be willed to do, but also a growing sense that all body parts are interconnected and that their bodies have both abilities and limitations. Body awareness is an outgrowth of the child's visual, auditory, tactile, and kinesthetic perceptions. Body awareness includes the child's positive or negative perceptions and feelings about his or her physical characteristics and capabilities. Particularly important to body awareness are the child's kinesthetic perceptual abilities, that is, the awareness of the body as a whole that occupies space and how one's body fits into space, functions within it, and adjusts to it. The ability to move from place to place without running into people or stumbling over objects depends on vision, hearing, touch, and kinesthetic perception. Kinesthetic perception includes **laterality** (an internal sense of direction), **directionality** (the motoric expression of laterality), **left/right dominance,** and **balance.**

Body awareness is a powerful driving force in all aspects of the child's development: perceptual–motor, psychosocial, and cognitive. Body awareness is incorporated into the child's emerging sense of self and feelings of competence. Body awareness and confidence give the child a sense of control and motivate the child to attempt increasingly complex physical/motor activities.

Movement activities and simple games help to coordinate and refine fundamental body movements; establish laterality, directionality, balance, and left/right orientation; and enhance the development of more complex motor abilities. Most 4- and 5-year-olds especially enjoy movement activities and simple games as they continue to discover what their bodies can do. They enjoy responding to music in spontaneous and creative ways, pantomiming, playing follow-the-leader, and throwing and catching balls and bean bags. Balancing or hopping on one foot, jumping over obstacles, reaching the highest point, and walking a balance beam forward, sideways, and backward become challenging, self-affirming activities.

Jeremy and his friends, Caitlin, DeLisa, Jared, and Mac, have decided to play a racing game to see how fast they can run to the "faraway" tree on their kindergarten playground. They decide that Jeremy will tell them when to go. After he counts to three ("1 . . . 2 . . . 3 . . .") and shouts, "Go!," the five of them take off. DeLisa, who is slightly taller and heavier than her agemates and is quick of mind and movement, is the first off, followed by Caitlin, who has previously demonstrated well-coordinated large muscle control, though she is somewhat shorter than the rest of her agemates. Caitlin is followed by Mac, who is in the 80th percentile for height for boys of his age, though he is in the 40th percentile for weight. Mac is followed in the race by Jared and Jeremy, who are each in the 50th percentile for height and weight and have demonstrated average motor coordination and ability.

The five run with energy and power. However, Jared stumbles and falls, skinning his knees; he leaves the race crying, to find his teacher. Jeremy continues his mighty effort to catch up with the others. DeLisa steps out of the race, panting and out of breath. Caitlin, short and fast, and Mac, tall with his long stride, arrive at the tree at the same time. Each believes that she or he got there first. An argument ensues, unfriendly words are exchanged, and Caitlin announces that she is going to "tell the teacher." Jeremy, in the meantime, fights back his tears. The game was his idea after all, and he fully expected to win the race. Disappointed at losing, he joins DeLisa, and the two determine that they are not going to play with Mac and Caitlin any more.

laterality
an awareness of an ability to use both sides of the body; a recognition of the distinction between left and right

directionality
the application of the internal awareness of right and left to objects and movement

left/right dominance
a neuromaturational preference for one or the other side of the body, as in handedness

balance
a body awareness component in which postural adjustments prevent one from falling

The wide ranges in physical/motor ability, sizes and body builds, and prior experiences place children variously at an advantage and a disadvantage, depending on the required skill. Although physically active games for young children are most enjoyable when they are simple and, at least for the most part, child created, young children generally find competition frustrating, defeating, and unrewarding. Nevertheless, play that entails large motor challenges and activities is growth promoting and should be guided by sensitive adults toward outcomes that are enjoyable for every participant.

Child-created games characteristically entail the spontaneous establishment of rules, an important contribution to social and moral development, as we will see in later chapters. Hence, games serve important psychosocial functions in child development as well as encouraging and enhancing the physical and motor well-being of children.

Children with Special Needs

The reauthorized Individuals with Disabilities Education (IDEA), signed into law in 2004 (U.S. Department of Education, 2008), provides requirements for states to provide assessment and intervention services for children with disabilities. Part B of IDEA provides rules and regulations for states concerning the provision of special education services for children ages 3 to 21. "The term 'special education' means specially designed instruction, at no cost to parents, to meet the unique needs of a child with a disability" (U.S. Department of Education, 2008). States are required to provide free assessments in the child's native language to children to determine eligibility for special education services and to determine the educational needs of children. Some states provide a general category of "preschool child with a disability," whereas other states identify the child's specific category of disability. Many types of delays and disabling conditions affect young children and with varying degrees of severity. The special needs of children generally fall into three categories:

1. *Developmental delay:* delays in one or more of the following developmental domains:
   - Physical/motor: such as growth curves dramatically different from the norm for age; anomalies in gross, fine, and/or oral motor controls
   - Self-help skills: such as difficulties or inabilities to dress, feed, or use a toilet without assistance
   - Social–emotional behaviors: such as attachment problems, difficulty modulating emotions, and social interaction problems
   - Communication: such as limited use of language to communicate and inability to understand or respond to communications with others
   - Cognitive development: such as limited curiosity and interest in learning, lack of focus, difficulty learning, or unusual play behaviors or play themes

2. *Atypical development:* patterns of development are different from expected for the age range, which include the following:
   - Sensorimotor anomalies: such as poor muscle tone, abnormal reflex activity, and sensory impairments
   - Atypical emotional/social patterns: such as atypical attachment behaviors, unusual social responses and expressions of emotions, or inappropriate self-targeted behaviors
   - Atypical cognitive and language development: such as inability to focus and attend (attention span), learning and memory difficulties, difficulties associated with acquisition and use of language, and information-processing difficulties

3. *Medically diagnosed conditions:* any of numerous possible diagnoses, such as aphasia (profound lack of language), cerebral palsy, congenital muscular dystrophy, Down syndrome, drug withdrawal syndrome, failure to thrive, fetal alcohol syndrome, seizure disorders, and spinal cord injury

With laws in place that mandate early screening and identification of children with disabilities, early diagnosis has resulted in timely intervention practices. Intervention services for young children with special needs include access to some or all of the following:

- Early identification
- Screening and assessment
- Assistive technology
- Vision and hearing evaluation and follow-up services
- Family counseling
- Medical and health care services
- Home visits
- Nutrition supervision

- Physical therapy
- Occupational theory
- Psychological services
- Speech and language therapy
- Transportation

As screening for at-risk children has become widespread, the potential for its abuse has become a concern. Professionals in child development and early childhood education stress the importance of standards in the selection of screening instruments and in the qualifications of individuals who screen children and diagnose. If concerns are apparent as a result of the screening test, children have a right to a free multidisciplinary assessment with the family as a part of the team. Assessment for eligibility to special programs and individualized education plans is best achieved from a multifaceted approach that includes the use of medical examinations along with strategies that include focused observation in many contexts over extended periods of time; interviews and consultations with the child and family; and assessment of the *products* of children's work, the manner in which a child engages in work and play (*processes*), and the extent to which the child accomplishes expected goals or outcomes (*performance*). This type of assessment of young children yields comprehensive information about a child that can lead to more accurate diagnoses and can assist adults in planning growth-enhancing experiences for children (Puckett & Black, 2008; Puckett & Diffily, 2004). Programs children attend must meet professional standards of quality and developmental appropriateness and must be judged to serve the best long-term interest of the child (U.S. Department of Education, 2008).

During the assessment and placement process, children must be supported as they enter a new program or begin to receive special education services with a program they already attend. In an inclusive classroom, they, their families, and their teachers (and other resource personnel) need to collaborate in the preparation of the classroom and curricula to support the child's inclusion process.

Research studies on kindergarten children without disabilities accepting children with disabilities show mixed results, but there seems to be a trend toward higher levels of acceptance as the number of inclusive classes increases (Dyson, 2005). A teacher's direct effort to support frequent social interaction between children with disabilities and those without is crucial to the enhancement of children's peer relationships (Dyson, 2005).

Relationship Between Physical/Motor Development and Emotional and Social Development

At ages 4 to 5, the child's self-concept is intimately associated with an awareness of his or her physical characteristics (hair, eye, and skin color; physical abilities; sex; etc.). The young child's physical characteristics and emerging capabilities also influence the child's interactions with others. These interactions provide positive and/or negative feedback, which plays a role in the formation of the self-concept. A child who is viewed as physically (or psychosocially) attractive may receive different feedback than a child who is viewed as unattractive. The child's responses to others vary along positive and negative lines. These interactions influence in both subtle and overt ways subsequent responses and interactions and, ultimately, the child's self-image, self-regard, and self-confidence.

Relationship Between Physical/Motor Development and Cognitive Development

As at earlier ages, children's emerging physical and motor capabilities expand their horizons and afford them new opportunities to learn about the world around them. The 4- to 5-year-old's interest and participation in real-world events that invite the use of motor abilities further cognitive development. A trip to a farm for a pony ride; assisting with selected household chores; responding to music with movement and dance; manipulating books to explore the world of print; performing a broad array of small motor tasks; taking some responsibility for one's own hygiene, health, and safety; and participating in the establishment of safety and health maintenance rules and procedures are some of the events that relate physical and motor development to cognitive development.

Learning to Be Responsible for One's Own Health and Safety

Children at age 4 and 5 years are beginning to understand the importance of such health and safety considerations as eating, sleeping, resting, and exercise and can now be taught to assume some responsibility for themselves. Of course, young children cannot be expected to protect themselves without adult supervision, teaching, and encouragement. Nevertheless, their cooperation can be elicited in these health and safety areas:

- Regular teeth brushing, frequent hand washing, and other hygienic practices
- Predictable naptime and bedtime routines
- Understanding the need for nutritious food rather than junk food
- Appreciating the need for regular medical and dental check-ups and immunizations
- Recognizing potential hazards (e.g., hot items, strangers, electrical items, poisons, unsafe toys, playground and other environmental hazards, streets, driveways, and other traffic hazards)
- Abiding by household and family rules (e.g., television usage and acceptable program content, guided choice of computer activities and electronic games, appropriate time and place for certain behaviors and activities)
- Consistently using transportation safety seats or restraints
- Answering the phone as instructed
- Understanding where to safely play with certain items, such as tricycles or other wheeled toys, and which toys or equipment require adult assistance
- Learning full name, address (with ZIP code), phone numbers (with area code), parent's name(s) and where to find their work phone numbers; how to call for help; and so on

Responsibility for one's own health and safety emerges slowly and sporadically over a course of many years. Children's emerging capabilities and growing sense of responsibility, however, never absolve the adult of responsibility for providing continuing and conscientious supervision and protection. It is easy to assume that young children are more capable in this area than they actually are, but their behaviors are at best inconsistent, owing to their limited long-term memory, limited or inconsistent opportunities to practice, adult inconsistencies in routines and expectations, distraction of more exciting things to do, and eagerness to explore and learn about other things.

The major responsibility to provide safe, hygienic environments and developmentally appropriate experiences and expectations remains with adults. Adults continue to be the child's most powerful role models.

Gender Awareness and Gender Constancy

By age 3, children demonstrate gender awareness and identity by accurately labeling themselves and others as boys or girls. However, gender constancy, the realization that one's gender remains the same regardless of changes in appearance, age, clothing, hairstyles, or individual wishes, begins to emerge between the ages of 5 and 7 (Ruble, D.N. et al, 2007; Kohlberg, 1966). Development of gender constancy seems to follow a pattern, with children attributing gender constancy to themselves before others (Eaton & Von Bargen, 1981). The most frequently observed pattern is (1) gender constancy for self, (2) gender constancy for same-sex others, and (3) gender constancy for individuals of the opposite sex.

The emergence of gender constancy brings with it a growing awareness that boys and girls, and men and women, differ in a number of ways, not the least of which is anatomy. As children begin to realize that anatomy rather than other factors defines gender, they become interested in the human body. Young children are curious about the physiological differences between boys and girls and between men and women. They observe and compare the anatomies and behaviors of each, forming ideas, some stereotypical, about male and female anatomy, roles, and behaviors. They imitate male/female behaviors in their sociodramatic play, experimenting with "being" either male or female. Some of their behaviors evoke chagrin or consternation on the part of adults: asking direct questions about body parts and their functions, giggling about and teasing or ridiculing members of the opposite sex, engaging in "bathroom talk," and playing "doctor." These normal behaviors indicate a growing awareness of the differences between the sexes and are indicative of the earliest stages of sexuality (Chrisman & Couchenour, 2002). Responses to these behaviors should be positive and age-appropriately informing and should guide children toward acceptance and satisfaction in their gender identity.

Adult responses to these behaviors influence the outcomes of positive or negative gender identity and gender role acquisition. A frank, matter-of-fact approach is certainly preferable to shock, embarrassment, or avoidance. Children need adults to help them to learn about the differences between boys and girls and to do so with honest, straightforward answers to their questions. Providing accurate labels, discussing gender roles and behaviors, setting examples, and modeling healthy gender identity and self-acceptance are necessary to building accurate and positive concepts in children. Children must feel comfortable and safe asking questions as they arise. Adults must keep in mind that as children establish gender constancy, they are intensely interested in gender-role behaviors and are particularly interested in and attentive to gender-role models.

Factors Influencing Physical and Motor Development
Genetic Makeup Revisited

Genes control the child's rate of development, dictating when motor abilities will emerge, growth spurts will occur, teeth will erupt, and the outer limits of height range will be achieved. Each individual has inherited a genetic blueprint from his or her parents. This blueprint determines such characteristics as sex, blood type, skin color, hair color and texture, eye color, potential mature height, temperament, sociability, and a host of other characteristics that make each person unique and explain the enormous array of differences among people. Optimal development relies on healthy genetic traits and supportive, healthy environments.

Because each child grows at her or his own pace, comparisons with siblings or agemates can be very misleading. Each child's growth occurs according to the child's biological blueprint and unique sets of experiences and interactions with the environment. Height and weight, for instance, depend on nutrition and other health factors. Motor coordination relies on opportunities to move about, explore, discover, and practice emerging abilities. Adequate health care, proper nutrition, avoidance of accidents and stress, appropriate expectations, and sociocultural factors all contribute to the full realization of a person's genetic potential. So we are reminded that although individuals bring blueprints for development with them, the development that emerges is intertwined with and dependent on environmental influences.

General Health and Freedom from Disease or Injury

Children ages 4 and 5 are more likely to attend prekindergarten and kindergarten programs, and some are enrolled in before- and after-school programs in which they spend a considerable amount of time in the company of other children. Children in groups expose one another to a variety of illnesses—conjunctivitis (pink eye), lice, scabies, impetigo, ear infections, colds, flu, and an assortment of upper respiratory ailments. Children in preschool programs are at greater risk for contracting gastrointestinal infections with diarrhea.

To ensure continuing good health and freedom from diseases, homes, schools, and child care programs must follow a regimen of frequent and thorough cleaning and systematic observation of all children for signs of illness or infection. Providing children with regular, nutritious meals and snacks, predictable rest and sleep schedules, opportunities for vigorous play and exercise, and instruction in hygiene and reducing stress-producing activities in children's lives facilitate the maintenance of good health and growth-enhancing environments.

Healthy Routines

Predictable routines are essential to good health and a psychological sense of well-being. Daily schedules for children are best planned to include regular meal, snack, rest, and activity times and opportunities to self-select what one wants to do. A general rule applied in early childhood programs and certainly applicable in the home is that of alternating quiet and active times throughout the child's day to avoid fatigue and overstimulation. Young children, in spite of their apparent excess energy, do fatigue quickly; they also tend to recover readily when provided brief rest periods. Intermittent rest times (quiet conversation, story reading, short naps, or simply dawdling) ensure a healthier, happier day.

The *overscheduled* child is a phenomenon of modern-day child rearing. It is characterized by a daily schedule loaded with child care, preschool and/or school attendance, academic requirements, homework, school-sponsored events, extracurricular lessons, sports, social activities, family commitments, appointments, parents' employer's requirements, and weekend family and faith-based obligations. Overscheduled children spend an inordinate amount of time in vehicles being transported to many places and activities. The physiological demands of overscheduling are enormous, as are the psychological effects of stress associated with keeping a steady pace of activities and interactions with many different groups of people. The effects of stress on brain growth and neurological development have been studied, and deleterious effects are possible (Gunnar & Quevedo, 2007; Perry, 1996, 1999). Some experts are expressing concern about the cumulative effect of years of this type of feverish activity, noting sleep disturbances, irritability, inattention, moodiness, and inability to "turn down" one's emotions after stressful or exciting events (Dahl, 1998). Many children lose interest and joy in their daily activities and exhibit signs of burnout at very early ages; their self-esteem, when measured against how well they think they are expected to perform in each of the activities, is diminished, and some experts believe that school dropout and teenage depression, substance abuse, and sexual activity are long-term consequences of overscheduling. Both school achievements and social and family interactions are at risk when daily schedules and expectations are excessive.

Nutrition

Children's diets must supply enough nutrients to meet the needs of growing bones and muscles, promote healthy formation and eruption of permanent teeth, and sustain continued growth and development of all body tissues and organs. Much energy is needed to sustain the high activity levels that are typical of 4- and 5-year-old children. More active children may need more food than less active ones of the same age and size.

Because preschool children have decreased their intake of milk, iron-fortified cereals, and nutrients such as calcium, phosphorus, iron, and vitamins A and C from levels consumed during the infant/toddler period and have not developed a taste for a wide variety of foods, particularly vegetables, there may be a need to expand the variety of foods available to them, with particular emphasis on nutrient-dense foods.

Appetites begin to wane as children get older, and food preferences and aversions begin to emerge (see Box 11.1). Parents and adults, anxious to provide adequate and nutritious meals and snacks for preschool children, are often perplexed when children show little interest in, or even distaste for, some foods. There are developmental explanations for these behaviors.

The eating behaviors of young children reflect their changing growth patterns and physiological and psychological needs. Children at ages 4 and 5 are growing less rapidly than they were in previous years and therefore require less nourishment to support their growth needs. At the same time, food preferences are emerging that reflect the child's growing ability to recognize and differentiate tastes, a desire to make choices, and a growing sense of autonomy and initiative, both at home and in other settings. The ability to help oneself to available foods and snacks at ages 4 and 5 fosters a sense of independence and control.

Children ages 4 through 5 are becoming more verbal, conversational, and social and enjoy their interactions with others. For them, mealtimes can be particularly enjoyable, especially when parents and siblings eat together or small groups of children share a meal or snack with one another and an adult in their center or school settings. The social context of eating can improve or impede the nutritional intake of young children, influencing attitudes toward eating and mealtimes and food acceptance patterns. Mealtimes that are hurried, stressful, or coercive or that are marked by negative interactions, threat, or punishment interfere with food intake, digestion, and the development of healthy attitudes

Box 11.1 Childhood Food Preferences

Childhood food preferences reflect the following:

- Cultural practices and preferences
- Peer and sibling influences
- Television and other media advertising
- Naturally occurring fluctuations in the child's interest in certain foods
- Transitory "food jags"
- The child's ability to manage the food—ease in self-feeding, chewing, swallowing
- Food allergy
- A temporary aversion to certain foods associated with an unpleasant experience (e.g., being reprimanded or embarrassed at a time when the food was being consumed; an illness associated with a particular food; same food served too often)
- Associating food with a particularly pleasant memory (e.g., eating at grandparents' or a friend's house; a special occasion; a holiday dinner)
- Appeal of the food based on temperature, texture, color, aroma, size of serving; compatibility with other foods on the plate; cleanliness of eating utensils, dishes, and eating surfaces; aesthetics associated with the table or eating surroundings
- The child's level of cognition and accompanying ability to associate certain foods with good health and feeling good while recognizing food of little nutritional value and learning to reject such foods
- Parental pressure to eat certain foods or "everything on your plate"

toward foods and mealtimes. However, when young children experience mealtimes that are relaxed and conducive to pleasant conversation and free of coercion, their intake of nutritious foods is enhanced. In her extensive research on eating behaviors in young children, Birch and her colleagues demonstrated a number of childhood experiences that influence what and how much children choose to eat and the effect of various approaches to child feeding and nutrition on food acceptance patterns and childhood nutritional status (Birch & Fisher, 1998; Birch, Johnson, Andersen, Peters, & Schulte, 1991; Birch, Johnson, & Fisher, 1995; Johnson & Birch, 1994). Some of the research findings include:

- Food preferences result from responses to a complex combination of stimulation involving taste, smell, appearance, and tactile characteristics, and change over time with increasing experience with foods.
- Learning and experiences within a child's cultural environment shape his or her food acceptance patterns.
- Generally, infants and young children do not readily accept new foods unless they are sweet.
- As exposure to a new food increases, the child's preference for it also increases; however, the child must at some point taste the food and sometimes must be exposed to the food as many as 10 times before acceptance is achieved.

- When foods are given to children in positive social contexts, preferences for those foods are enhanced; however, when children are forced to eat nutritious foods to obtain rewards, liking for the food is reduced.

- Children appear to be innately biased to learn to prefer high-energy foods.

- Children may possess the ability to regulate how much to eat on the basis of the caloric content of the foods they eat over a number of meals, relying more on physiological sensitivity to caloric intake than adults do.

- Although the amount of food consumed at individual meals can be highly variable from meal to meal at ages 2 to 5 years, children's daily overall calorie intake is fairly constant.

- Meager consumption of food at one meal is offset by greater consumption at later meals; these findings suggest that children tend to adjust their calorie needs over a 24-hour period.

- There are wide variations among children in their ability to regulate energy intake.

- Parents who are more controlling in their child-feeding strategies not only negatively affect their children's food acceptance patterns, but also negatively affect their children's ability to self-regulate energy intake, which leads to increases in body fat in these children.

- In the absence of adult coercion, young children meet their satiety needs.

Safety

The primary causes of injury to children ages 4 through 5 are automobile accidents, falls, being struck by or running into an object, being cut or pierced, and poisoning (ChildStats.gov, 2007). Automobile accidents are the leading cause; more children are killed by automobiles as passengers or pedestrians than by any other hazard.

Transportation Safety. Auto accidents are a leading cause of brain damage, spinal cord injury, and cognitive challenges. Many automobile injuries are preventable through proper use of approved car seats and seat restraints for children. Children with disabilities may need special, crashworthy devices and equipment to be safely transported.

Playground Safety. Playground safety is another concern during the early years. Playgrounds are coming under serious scrutiny as the number and seriousness of playground accidents continue to rise. Joe Frost, a nationally recognized expert on playground design and safety, states,

> American public playgrounds are perhaps the worst in the world. They are hazardous. In addition, most playgrounds are designed as though children's play needs are limited to swinging from bars and running across open spaces, as though children cannot think, symbolize, construct, and create. (Frost, 1992, p. 6)

Indeed, safe playgrounds for children can be designed to encourage productive, constructive play that engages physical/motor and cognitive abilities and encourages social interactions (Frost, Pei-San, Sutterby, & Thornton, 2004). However, playground designs have traditionally included equipment that encourages only parallel play and have been characterized by equipment that poses maintenance problems and injury hazards.

Older playgrounds often have equipment designed for older children. Contemporary playground designers are paying closer attention to construction materials and designs that facilitate constructive types of play for different age groups, provide safe surfaces underneath playground equipment, and take into account maintenance and repair considerations and the types of injuries that occur on playgrounds and their frequencies.

Some guidelines offered by experts on playground safety include the following (Frost, Wortham, & Reifel, 2001; Rivkin, 1995; U.S. Consumer Product Safety Commission, 1997):

- Children should always be supervised on playgrounds and encouraged to use the equipment that is most suited to their age and size and should be assisted with the equipment as needed.
- Playgrounds and equipment should be regularly inspected and conscientiously maintained.
- Soft surfaces should be provided underneath playground equipment to reduce the risk of injury from falls (sand, 10 inches deep; wood chips, 12 inches deep; rubber outdoor mats).
- Guardrails at least 38 inches high should surround platforms.
- Platforms should be no higher than 6 feet above the ground.
- There should be no vertical or horizontal spaces less than 3½ inches wide or more than 9 inches wide, which would allow a small child's head to become entrapped.
- Moving parts should be enclosed to protect children or their clothing from entanglement.

Outdoor play is an essential part of the child's day.

- Construction materials should be chosen with regional climate conditions in mind (metal slides, for instance, can become hot enough to burn in warmer climates; painted metal surfaces chip and rust in wet climates).
- Construction materials should be chosen with safety in mind: swing seats, for example, are safer if constructed of rubber or canvas than of wood or metal.
- Placement of equipment should also be considered (a sufficient distance from vehicular and pedestrian traffic areas; a sufficient distance from other equipment to prevent collisions; 6 feet or more from walls or fences).

The National Resource Center for Health and Safety in Child Care and Early Education (http://nrc.uchsc.edu/STATES/states.htm, 2008) reports the specific licensing standards for child care, including requirements for playgrounds, for each state.

Toys, Play Equipment, and Household Safety. In addition to playground design and equipment, reports of injuries from toys, home exercise equipment, children's trampolines, garage doors, and electric garage door openers are on the increase. Box 11.2 describes the wise choice of toys, play equipment, and safety gear.

> ## Box 11.2 Wise Selection of Toys, Play Equipment, and Safety Gear
>
> (1) Know the age, capabilities, and interests of the individual child for whom the item is intended.
>
> (2) Scrutinize the toy, play equipment, or safety gear thoroughly, and read labels and instructions carefully.
> a. For what age child is the item intended?
> b. Are special skills or knowledge needed to use the item?
> c. Is the item appropriate given the child's large and/or small motor abilities, cognitive abilities, and interests?
> d. Is it made of nontoxic materials (avoid items that carry wording such as "harmful if swallowed," "avoid inhalation," "avoid skin contact," and "use with adequate ventilation")?
> e. Is it manufactured by a reputable firm? (Check Consumer Products Safety Commission reports or child health alerts and other publications for recall and safety histories of toys and play equipment.)
> f. Does the item do what the manufacturer claims it will do?
> g. Is the item durable?
>
> (3) Examine the item for hazards such as lead-based paint, sharp or protruding points or edges, weak construction, small parts that can be swallowed or cause choking (watch for eyes, buttons, bells, and other features on dolls and stuffed toys), and flammable materials.
>
> (4) Determine what aspect of development is enhanced through use of the item.
> a. Physical development: large motor; small motor; prehension; pincer movements; eye–hand, hand–mouth, and eye–foot coordination
> b. Cognitive: exploration, curiosity, questions, solving problems, forming concepts, connecting ideas or actions, cause-and-effect understanding, making associations, further inquiry and new ideas
> c. Language and literacy: conversation; labels; new concepts; questions; interest in symbols (signs, letters, numerals); vocabulary and creative use of language through rhymes, storytelling, role playing, songs, and poetry
> d. Psychosocial: pure enjoyment, catharsis and therapy, symbolic play, socio-dramatic play, interactions with others, expression of feelings, sense of self-sufficiency and self-confidence, fantasy, imagination, prosocial understandings
>
> (5) Determine whether the item can be used in a variety of ways and whether it will sustain interest over an extended period of time.

Most common sources of injury from home exercise equipment are entrapment of fingers or toes in stationary bicycle chains or wheel spokes.

There were 109,522 trampoline-related injuries in 2006, prompting the American Academy of Pediatrics to reissue its earlier statement that trampolines should never be used in the home environment (inside or out), in routine gym classes, or on outdoor playgrounds (Bond, 2008). Sixty-five percent of injured children were ages 5 through 14 years old, and 10% were 4 years old or younger (Consumer Product Safety Commission, 2007). In 2001–2002, trampolines sent 104,729 children to the emergency room (Lachner, 2011) with

90% of the injuries occurring at home (DeNoon, 2005). Data from the NEISS (1991–1996) reveal that trampoline injuries occur in spite of warning labels, public education, and adult supervision and occur with the following frequencies: 45% of trampoline injuries involve the lower extremities (legs, feet) in the form of strains or sprains; 30% affect the upper extremities (usually fractures of the arms and hands); and 14% involve head and face injuries, lacerations, concussions, and neck and spinal cord injuries. Deaths from trampoline injuries usually result from cervical spinal cord injury (American Academy of Pediatrics, 1999a; Smith, 1998; U.S. Consumer Product Safety Commission, National Electronic Injury Surveillance System, 1996).

Garage doors are the largest piece of moving equipment in a home and should be treated as a potential hazard to child safety. Most accidents involving garage doors occur when children have access to electronic door openers, activating the door and becoming trapped under it or getting fingers or hands injured by moving door parts. Although many types of garage-door-opening devices are in use, garage doors manufactured since 1991 are required to have a reversing mechanism that causes the door to automatically back up if it touches an object in its path. Doors installed after 1993 are required to have photo eyes connected to the bottom of the track that will cause the door to reverse when its invisible beam is broken. Nothing has to physically touch these photo-beamed doors before they reverse. Guidelines for garage door safety include the following:

- Garage doors and door-opening mechanisms are best installed by professionals who are well acquainted with the product and its installation and use and can advise on proper use and safety precautions.
- The wall control panel for garage doors should be installed out of a child's reach (at least 5 feet above the ground).
- Remote controls should not be handled by young children.
- Children should be instructed not to play underneath the area where garage doors close.
- Users should stay in full view of a moving door until it is completely closed or open.
- Never race to beat the door as it is closing.
- As with all mechanized equipment, adults should model appropriate use and safety precautions.

Another common injury to young children is burns. Many young children are burned by tipped containers of hot food or drink, scalding bath water, microwave-heated foods (which often have hot spots), heating equipment, candles, matches, and cigarette lighters. All of these injuries are preventable. Children generally should not be in a food preparation area unless they are involved in a preparation-related activity that is being very closely supervised. Because serious burns have resulted from undetected hot spots in microwaved foods, both infant formula manufacturers and pediatricians advise against heating foods for infants, toddlers, and young children in the microwave (American Public Health Association & American Academy of Pediatrics, 2002). When a microwave is used, food should be stirred, then tested for hot spots, then cooled to a safe temperature before serving. Bathwater temperatures can be regulated by setting hot water heaters on lower temperatures. Heating equipment should be placed safely behind guards or out of child use areas.

Choking in young children can be prevented by making careful decisions about what food to serve and how to serve it. Infants and toddlers are generally at higher risk for choking because of their tendency to put things into their mouths, their immature chewing and swallowing mechanisms, and their distractibility. However, 4- and 5-year-olds are also prone to choking. The foods and objects that are most often associated with choking in young children are any small item less than half an inch in diameter, nuts, seeds, spherical or cylinder-shaped foods and objects, buttons, small toys, rocks, grapes, pieces of hot dog, round hard candies, and items of unusual or unfamiliar consistencies such as chewing gum, popcorn, corn or potato chips, some uncooked vegetables and fruits, sticky foods (peanut butter, caramel candy, dried fruits, raisins), and hard-to-chew meats. The following suggestions can lower the risk of choking:

- Cook foods to a softness that is pierceable by a fork.
- Substitute thinly sliced meats and well-cooked hamburger for hot dogs.
- Cut foods into manageable, bite-size pieces; avoid slippery round shapes.
- Be sure to remove all packaging from foods, such as bits of clinging cellophane and paper.
- Remove bones in chicken, meats, and fish.
- Remove seeds and pits from fruits.
- Avoid the snacks and foods listed in the preceding paragraph.

In addition to careful selection and preparation of foods, supervision at mealtimes and snack times is a must. Children should be seated when eating, be encouraged to eat slowly, and avoid talking and laughing with food in their mouths. Children should not eat while traveling in a car because sudden jolts and stops can catapult food into the back of the mouth. Moreover, maneuvering a car out of traffic to tend to a choking child compounds the risk. Every adult should become familiar with the American Red Cross first aid procedures for handling a choking incident.

Poisoning is another major safety hazard for young children. Children can breathe toxins from polluted air, ingest some toxins by mouth, or absorb some poisons through the skin. Hazards exist in many forms: medicines, pesticides, aerosol sprays, gases, dusts, paints and solvents, commercial dyes, various art materials (inks, solvent-based glues, chalk dust, tempera paint dust, some crayons, paints, and clay powders). Toxins are also found in building materials (asbestos, formaldehyde, lead-based paint), lead-containing dishes and ceramics, tobacco smoke, and radon gas in soil.

Prevention of childhood poisoning involves both keeping toxic substances away from children and keeping children away from places where environmental toxins pose a hazard. At home, in child care centers, and at school, medicines, cleaning supplies, fertilizers, pesticides, and other toxins must be kept well beyond the child's reach and stored in locked cabinets. Child care center and school licensing and accreditation standards, city ordinances, and state and federal regulations must be followed, and all potentially poisonous products must be used in strict accordance with physicians', pharmacists', or manufacturers' instructions.

Young children and water create an additional safety concern. Beginning quite early in the toddler period, children must be taught to respect water. Infants, toddlers, and young children should never be left unattended in bathtubs, wading pools, or swimming areas. Basic water safety instruction for young children includes precautions such as wearing appropriate water safety devices, proper use of water toys such as floats, going into water only when an adult is present, avoiding breakable toys and dishes around bodies of water, and walking carefully on wet surfaces. Adults must establish, demonstrate, model, and enforce water safety rules with children, know rescue techniques and cardiopulmonary resuscitation, and be especially vigilant around bodies of water. Providing swimming lessons for young children at ages 4 and 5 becomes controversial when adults develop a false sense of confidence in their children's abilities. For young children, the ability to swim is not accompanied by mature judgments about when and where to swim and what to do in an emergency.

Opportunities to Interact, Explore, and Play

Another factor influencing growth and development is the opportunity to interact with others, explore, and play. Children have a natural impulse to be active—to run, climb, jump, hop, skip, shout, and ride wheeled toys. Opportunities to develop and use these abilities occur when children are provided with the space and developmentally appropriate equipment with which to do so. Opportunities to use and coordinate small muscles also occur through experiences with a variety of manipulative materials and self-help activities. Because children need to be physically active, efforts to restrain and keep them quiet for long periods of time not only are difficult, but are actually unhealthy for children. Preschool and kindergarten programs that require children to sit for long periods of time, to work at tables or desks, or to listen to teacher-directed lessons for extended periods of time are developmentally inappropriate because they curtail opportunities for more active and beneficial pursuits. Programs that promote physical and motor development provide activities that meet children's need for movement, for manipulation, and for social interactions and pretend play. For optimal health and physical development, each child's day should include opportunities for movement about the classroom and the learning centers; for singing, creative movement, and dance; and for use of equipment requiring large motor coordination. Outdoor play should be a daily event in every child's life in which running, jumping, skipping, and other large motor activities and games can build the type of physical fitness that includes both health- and performance-related components (Gallahue & Donnely, 2007).

Health and Well-Being Issues

Nutrition Issues

As mentioned earlier, adults are responsible for providing nutritious and adequate diets for children. However, because hunger can be felt only by the child and children can be trusted to regulate their own food intake, the child should exercise control over how much to eat (Birch & Fisher, 1998). Helping children to establish regular eating times, avoiding unnecessary snacks that are high in calories but low in nutrients, and encouraging adequate amounts of exercise and activity assist children in developing sound nutritional habits and food acceptance patterns that will support their growth and ensure long-term healthy outcomes.

A number of nutrition-related issues have surfaced in recent years, including the widely publicized increase in obesity among Americans and its prevalence among younger and younger children; the changing American meal plan characterized by speedily prepared foods that can be eaten on the run; the overabundance and availability of calorie-rich, nutrient-poor snacks; and the increase in nutrition-related illnesses among children, including elevated cholesterol levels, diabetes, high blood pressure, and food-related allergies. Additionally, there are health issues associated with undernutrition, which include compromised growth and development, higher susceptibility to disease, accident proneness, and emotional and learning disabilities (Weinreb et al., 2002).

Obesity could be an issue of concern among 4- and 5-year-old children, and the need for a well-balanced diet rich in protein, vitamins, and minerals and low in fats and sugars is recommended. Because this age is one in which growth is still rapid (but not as rapid as in previous years), immediate professional attention to unusual weight, height, and growth progress is necessary so that intervention, prevention, or corrective measures can be initiated to ensure adequate nutrients to sustain growth while teaching and promoting other behaviors, such as physical activity and exercise to maintain healthy bodies. Learning how to make good food choices and to avoid high-fat, high-sugar, and low-nutrient foods can begin at this age, as can learning to recognize that many foods and snacks advertised in magazines, junk mail, billboards, and television do not make people healthier. Children can be taught about the Choose My Plate initiative and engaged in planning meals and snacks based on it. When young children participate in this manner, they begin to understand the importance of good nutrition and begin to develop more nutritious food preferences. Becoming nutrient savvy at an early age is a powerful defense against risky food behaviors (which often become habitual) and later food-related illnesses. A further discussion of obesity is given in Chapter 14.

Length of Child Care Day and Multiple Caregivers

Some public school programs for young children are half-day (2½ to 3½ hours), some are all day (5½ or 6 to 7½ hours), and some range from 9 to 11 hours. Child care programs (center-based day care and family day homes) range from hourly care to 24 hours. The number of hours per setting per child each day varies. Many children of working parents are enrolled in before- and after-school programs, resulting in as many as three different sets of nonparental caregivers (before, during, and after school). For some of these children, transportation from one setting to another requires additional hours.

The psychosocial effect of these multiple relationships is discussed in later chapters. Concerns for physical and motor development center on stress and fatigue associated with long days, multiple settings, various adult personalities and expectations, changing groups of children, and varying standards and group rules for protecting health and safety. Preventing fatigue and reducing stress entail the following:

- Regularly scheduled and nutritious meals and snacks and ready access to toilet facilities and to fresh drinking water
- Regularly scheduled rest and naptimes, as well as rest periods as needed
- Teachers and staff who have knowledge of and training in child development and understand the effects of multiple settings and caregivers and long days on children
- Provision of outdoor playtimes for children to provide stress-relieving fresh air, sunshine, exercise, and spontaneous play
- Allowing children to make as many choices throughout the day as is reasonable and possible—choices about learning centers, materials and activities, playmates, snacks, and so on
- Opportunities and safe spaces to play alone without pressures to interact with others
- Allowing children to participate in classroom and group rule making to decrease the stress of dealing with multiple sets of rules and standards
- Careful observation of and attention to general health characteristics of individual children and prompt attention to signs of stress, fatigue, and/or impending illness

The complexities involved in providing multiple services through multiple settings and programs create a need for collaboration, coordination, and cooperation among all overlapping programs and services for children and their families.

Meeting the Needs of Children with Disabilities

Including children with disabilities is both an opportunity and a challenge for early childhood programs and professionals. Planning for the safety of all children and preparing to meet the health-supporting requirements of children with special needs is integral to successful inclusion practices. There is always the need for early childhood professionals to establish effective and ongoing communication with parents and other professionals who are involved in the care and education of children with special needs. Classroom layouts and other arrangements may need to be altered to facilitate the use and enjoyment of materials and activities. Special dietary requirements need to be met and considered in classroom food and nutrition lessons, snacks, parties, and other food-related events. Children with visual or hearing difficulties require appropriate adjustments in seating and in the design and placement of classroom visual materials (bulletin boards, charts, art displays, and so on). Toileting areas need to be reassessed, as does shelving and space for personal belongings. Furniture arrangements and pathways need to be configured to accommodate crutches, walkers, wheelchairs, or other assistive equipment.

Special attention must be given to daily health routines—medications, meals and snacks, access to drinking water, toileting, rest and exercise, personal hygiene, and classroom cleanliness and order. The social and intellectual climate of the classroom must be accepting, comfortable, and psychologically safe. The teacher and other adults play an important role in modeling and teaching good health habits, as well as acceptance and respect for all individuals.

Preventing Accidents and Spread of Disease Among Children in Groups

In the quest for higher performance standards at all levels of child care and education, cognitive and academic issues have come to overshadow both the teaching of nutrition, health, and safety and the importance of professional planning to meet the nutrition, health, and safety needs of children in group settings. It is thus quite enlightening that in ordering early childhood professional competency goals, the Child Development Associate (CDA) credentialing program places child health and safety first of six major competency categories (Council for Early Childhood Professional Recognition, 2008): "To establish and maintain a safe, healthy learning environment." This competency is demonstrated by a CDA candidate's ability to

- provide a safe environment to prevent and reduce injury;
- promote good health and nutrition and provide an environment that contributes to the prevention of illness; and
- use space, relationships, materials, and routines as resources for constructing an interesting, secure, and enjoyable environment that encourages play, exploration, and learning (Council for Early Childhood Professional Recognition, 2008).

Standards for safety and health protection of children in group care have existed since the beginning of the 20th century through governmental bodies and professional organizations. Concern over the spread of disease in early childhood settings in recent years has prompted considerable attention and renewed efforts of professional and medical groups to encourage policies and practices that ensure the health and safety of all children in group settings. The National Resource Center for Health and Safety in Child Care and Early Education (nrckids.org) (2008) publishes *Caring for Our Children, National Health and Safety Performance Standards; Guidelines for Early Care and Education Programs, 3rd Edition.* These performance standards are widely used by professionals to evaluate and improve child care and early education settings.

Because children in groups share environmental surfaces, such as tabletops, shelving and other furnishings, toys, sinks, and toileting areas, and are inclined to share food with unwashed hands, the spread of disease is inevitable if precautions are not taken. Further, young children are still inconsistent in health and hygiene habits, such as washing face and hands, using and then discarding facial tissue to contain a sneeze or cough or clear a runny nose, and using toilet tissue. Bandages also present problems because young children love to display this symbol of injury and bravery. Taking the bandage off, examining the wound beneath it, and attempting to replace the bandage or carelessly leaving it about where others might handle it are common occurrences. To prevent the spread of infectious disease, it is necessary to establish routines and behavior habits that include the following:

- Frequent and thorough handwashing with soap and warm water
- Teach children proper handwashing techniques and requiring handwashing after toileting, before and after eating, after coughing or sneezing, and at other appropriate times
- Clean toys, clothing/diaper-changing tables, and play surfaces with a disinfecting solution (commercial or a mixture of one-fourth cup of bleach to a gallon of water)
- Wear barrier gloves when cleaning areas contaminated with blood, vomit, or other bodily fluids
- Observe children for signs or symptoms of illness and isolate an ill child until a parent can be summoned
- Provide nutritious foods, snacks, beverages, and fresh drinking water
- Maintain healthy, predictable schedules of meals, snacks, rest, and play
- Maintain clean and hygienic surroundings

Role of the Early Childhood Professional

Enhancing Physical and Motor Development in Children Ages 4 Through 5

1. Provide safe and healthy surroundings for the child.
2. Provide for the child's nutritional needs.
3. Oversee protection of the child's health through immunizations and other protections from disease.
4. Encourage regular dental examinations.
5. Establish healthy routines for rest, sleep, play, and activity.
6. Control the stress-producing events in the child's life.

(continued)

7. Provide encouragement for emerging large and small motor abilities and body awareness.

8. Provide age-appropriate and developmentally appropriate toys, equipment, and materials for the child.

9. Ensure the child's safety through adequate supervision, monitoring the types and condition of toys, materials, and equipment, and removing environmental hazards.

10. Provide opportunities for satisfying and supportive social and emotional interactions with parents, other adults, and other children.

11. Facilitate the child's awareness of health and safety practices.

12. Encourage a sense of responsibility for one's own health maintenance and safety.

Key Terms

balance
dexterity
directionality

health-related fitness
laterality
left/right dominance

performance-related
fitness

Review Strategies and Activities

1. Review the key terms in this chapter individually or with a classmate.

2. Visit a school playground during recess for kindergarten and for second or third grade. Compare the types of activities and games in each group, including those used by children who are physically challenged. How do the activities differ? How do the children's large motor abilities in the older, younger, and physically challenged groups compare? How might recess be used to enhance physical and motor fitness in all children?

3. Plan a week of nutritious snacks for young children using a calorie and nutrient guide. What nutrients will children derive from these snacks? How many calories will be supplied?

4. Visit a toy store. Using the information in Box 11.2, make a list of acceptable and unacceptable toys or equipment for 4- and 5-year-old children. Consider culture, gender, and challenges faced by children with special needs.

5. With your classmates, develop a home safety checklist. Inspect your home for health and safety hazards for your children or children who may visit in your home. What changes will you need to make?

6. You have interviewed for a teaching position at three different child care centers. What characteristics of each center and its expectations will influence your choice?

7. Invite a pediatrician or pediatric nurse to speak to the class. Ask about his or her perceptions of the health status of today's children. What are this professional's greatest concerns about child health today? How might parents promote optimal growth and development in their children?

Further Readings

Carlson, F. M. (2011). *Big body play: Why boisterous, vigorous, and very physical play is essential to children's development and learning.* Washington, DC: NAEYC.

Early Childhood Learning and Knowledge Center (ECLKC). *I am moving. I am learning. A proactive approach for addressing childhood obesity in Head Start children.* http://eclkc.ohs.acf.hhs.gov/hslc/tta-system/health/Health/Nutrition/Nutrition%20Program%20Staff/IamMovingIam.htm

National Association for Sport and Physical Education. (2010). *101 Tips for increasing physical activity in early childhood.* Reston, VA: Author. www.aahperd.org/naspe

Pica, R. (2011). *Taking movement education outdoors.* http://www.naeyc.org/files/yc/file/201107/LeapsAndBounds_OnlineJuly2011.pdf

Pica, R. (2008). Learning by leaps and bounds: Why motor skills matter. *Young Children, 63*(4), 48–49.

Sorte, J., Daeschel, I., & Amador, C. (2011). *Nutrition, health, and safety for young children: Promoting wellness.* Columbus, OH: Merrill.

Other Resources

American Academy of Pediatrics: Child passenger safety, http://aappolicy.aappublications.org/cgi/content/full/pediatrics;127/4/e1050. This technical report, published online April 1, 2011, describes the best-known recommendations for practices to optimize safety in passenger vehicles for children from birth through adolescence.

Healthy Child Care America, www.healthychildcare.org. The HCCA program is a collaborative effort of health professionals and child care providers working to improve the early education and health and safety of children in out-of-home child care. This includes increasing access to preventive health services, safe physical environments, and a medical home for all children. The program also strives to increase pediatrician participation and effectiveness in providing high-quality care and promoting early education and children's health and well-being.

National Association of Child Care Resource and Referral Agencies (NACCRRA), www.naccrra.org/about. NACCRRA, the National Association of Child Care Resource & Referral Agencies is an active advocacy organization for better chid care policies. It also produces many informational products for families and child care staff.

National Highway Traffic Safety Administration (NHTSA), www.nhtsa.dot.gov. This site provides technical reports on child restraint systems, notices for child restraint systems—Federal Register, and NCAP child safety seat research tests. The NCAP-led child safety seat research tests are also provided.

National Resource Center for Health and Safety in Child Care and Early Education, http://nrckids.org. Provides links to *Caring for Our Children, 3rd Edition,* as well as A–Z child care information links, a nutrition checklist, a physical activity checklist, information on preventing childhood obesity, motion moments, and a licensing toolkit.

U.S. Consumer Product Safety Commission, www.cpsc.gov. Lists recalls of toys and product safety news.

chapter 12

Emotional and Social Development: Ages Four Through Five

And the first step, as you know, is always what matters most, particularly when we are dealing with those who are young and tender. That is the time when they are taking shape and when any impression we choose to make leaves a permanent mark.

—Plato

After studying this chapter, you will demonstrate comprehension by:

▶ relating selected theories to the study of emotional and social development during ages 4 through 5;

▶ describing emotional competence;

▶ discussing selected emotional and social experiences associated with brain growth and neurological development during the preschool years;

▶ describing major emotional and social milestones during this period;

▶ identifying factors that influence earliest emotional and social development; and

▶ describing the role of adults in healthy emotional and social development of 4- and 5-year-old children.

In contrast to children during the turbulent, but terrific, toddler period, 4- and 5-year-olds are more often composed. Refinements in motor abilities have facilitated self-help and autonomy. Advances in cognitive development have sharpened perceptions and enhanced the ability to understand. Language development has opened new and more effective communications, and an increasing ability to delay gratification of needs and desires is evident in more patient and negotiable interactions with others. The desire for and enjoyment of agemates has expanded, and play behaviors are more focused, purposeful, and cooperative. These developments result in a period during which the child is socially more amiable and compliant and emotionally more controlled and predictable.

Theoretical Perspectives on Emotional and Social Development

By the time a child is 4 or 5 years old, he or she has amassed a range of experiences that have influenced the course of development in myriad ways. Most child development theorists place a great deal of importance on the types and quality of experiences children have from birth through the first 3 to 4 years.

As the quotation by Plato suggests, for centuries philosophers and psychologists have hypothesized that events in the earliest years of a child's life influence later development, often in critical ways. Centuries after Plato's admonitions, philosophers, theorists, and scientists continue to study the relationship between early experiences during infancy and childhood and later development and behavior. Sigmund Freud's (1905/1930) psychoanalytic theory, for instance, proposed that experiences and conflicts occurring during early psychosexual stages of development have lasting effects on later personality development and interpersonal relationships. Freud placed considerable importance on the mother–infant relationship in influencing a person's ability to relate to others throughout life.

Building on Freud's work, Erik Erikson's theory of psychosocial development (1963) supported an early experience/later development hypothesis (see Figure 12.1). Successful outcomes at each of Erikson's eight stages of personality development are thought to prepare the child for subsequent stages culminating in a personality that is characterized as having ego integrity, or, as Erikson put it, knowing "how to be a follower of image bearers in religion and in politics, in the economic order and in technology, in aristocratic living and in the arts and sciences. Ego integrity, therefore, implies an emotional integration which permits participation by followership as well as

Figure 12.1
Erikson's Stages
of Psychosocial
Development

Figure 12.1
Erikson's Stages
of Psychosocial
Development

The child whose sense
of initiative is emerging
is eager to master new
skills.

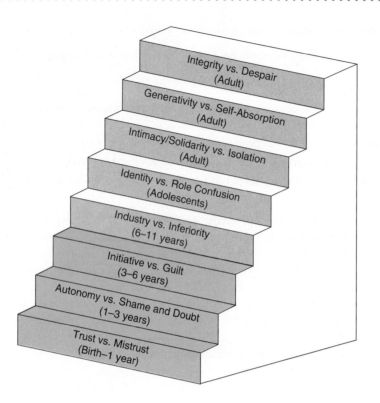

acceptance of the responsibility of leadership" (Erikson, 1963, p. 269). Certainly, a goal of early childhood development is to provide the essential experiences that can lead to a well-integrated personality.

Seligman and Csikszentmihalyi (2000) wrote about the need for Positive Psychology. The following quote summarizes this philosophy that focuses on "... hope, wisdom, creativity, future minedness, courage, spirituality, responsibility, and perseverance..." (p. 5).

> The field of positive psychology at the subjective level is about valued subjective experiences: well-being, contentment, and satisfaction (in the past); hope and optimism (for the future); and flow and happiness (in the present). At the individual level, it is about positive individual traits: the capacity for love and vocation, courage, interpersonal skill, aesthetic sensibility, perseverance, forgiveness, originality, future minedness, spirituality, high talent, and wisdom. At the group level, it is about the civic virtues and the institutions that move individuals toward better citizenship: responsibility, nurturance, altruism, civility, moderation, tolerance, and work ethic. (p. 5)

The authors of positive psychology emphasize that raising children is about "identifying and nurturing their strongest qualities, what they own and are best at, and helping them find niches in which they can best live out these strengths" (Seligman & Csikszentmihalyi, 2000, p. 6).

Transactional theory (Sameroff & MacKenzie, 2003) emphasizes how individuals within relationships influence each other. For example, there are complex interactions between parents and their children. Burgess, Rubin, Cheah, & Nelson (2001) in a summary of research concluded that if a child has an inhibited behavioral style, his or her parents may use more authoritarian behavioral strategies, be more protective, and solve problems for the preschool child when the parents senses the anxiety of the child. The child may then respond with additional anxiety and be more withdrawn socially. Early childhood professionals who understand the complexities of interactions can be more supportive of the family and the child than if they just see a child's concerning behavior as the child's or the parent's fault.

Relationship-based theory (Hinde, 1998, 1992; Hinde & Stevenson-Hinde, 1987) highlights how important relationships are for the optimal development of young children. Children thrive when all of their relationships with parents, family members, teachers, and peers are successful.

In this chapter, we will discuss contexts that contribute to children feeling challenged, and we will also highlight how preschool children demonstrate both emotional and social competence.

Seeking and receiving needed assistance is a form of initiative.

Emotional Competence

Emotional and social competence is important for the preschool child's comfort with himself and enjoyment of others. It is also important because emotional and social skills provide the neural foundation for learning. The National Scientific Council on the Developing Child, Center on the Developing Child (2005) has identified these social and emotional skills as necessary for school success:

- identify and understand one's own feelings,
- accurately read and comprehend emotional states in others,
- manage strong emotions and their expression in a constructive manner,
- regulate one's own behavior,
- develop empathy for others, and
- establish and sustain relationships.

When the years from birth to 3 are filled with loving, ongoing, responsive relationships, the child has the beginnings of all of these skills. The brain develops in a use-dependent fashion. Repeated experiences create strong synapses in the brain, building the very structure of the brain. The preschool child with good experiences will continue to develop the skills that will serve learning and later relationships.

Self-Concept Development and Self-Esteem

According to Erikson (1963), autonomy facilitates new discoveries and the acquisition of new skills and leads to an *activity-based self-concept* that is appropriate to the emergence of a sense of **initiative.** With autonomy in place, the 4- to 5-year-old describes herself or himself according to skills being mastered. At this age, the self-concept has emerged from self-awareness and self-recognition during the infancy and toddler periods to a more attribute-focused self-definition.

At this age, the self-concept is based mostly on the child's perceptions of his or her physical abilities and possessions. It will be a while before the child's self-definition

initiative
the third of Erikson's psychosocial stages, in which the child pursues ideas, individual interests, and activities; when thwarted, the child becomes self-critical and experiences guilt

Emotional and Social Development: Ages Four Through Five

includes inner qualities or character traits (Harter, 2001). A self-description based on perceptions of physical attributes is evident in statements such as "I am bigger," "I can tie my shoes," and "Watch me skip." The child also uses self-descriptions related to age and possessions to affirm the sense of self, for example, "I'm going to be 4 on my birthday" or "I have a new bicycle with training wheels." A positive self-concept provides the sustenance for self-confidence and one's expectations that mastering life's challenges is possible. A well-established sense of one's worth as an individual is protective in that frustrating obstacles and failures are less likely to be followed by the perception of oneself as incapable (Stipek, Recchia, & McClintic, 1992).

Children develop positive self-concepts and self-esteem from their experiences with and the attitudes of people who are important to them: their parents, siblings, other family members, caregivers, and teachers. From the manner in which others respond to them, children form opinions of themselves. Over time, repetition of response behaviors of others reinforces these opinions, and the child begins to build cognitive structures that match important others' attitudes toward her or him. When responses are positive, respectful, and affirming, the self-concept that the child formulates is positive and self-affirming. Conversely, when their interactions with important others are negative, demeaning, humiliating, disengaged, mollifying, or nonsupportive, children construct a concept of self that is distorted and negative. These interactions encourage or impede a critical aspect of healthy social and emotional development, that of self-esteem.

High or low self-esteem is reflected in the child's emotional responses and social interactions. A recursive cycle of feedback occurs when children relate to others according to their positive or negative self-concepts and those with whom they interact respond accordingly in positive or negative ways. Thus, the self-concept (positive or negative) is reinforced in the child, and the behaviors repeat themselves in subsequent interactions. Marsh and Scalas (2010) found a relationship between academic self-concept (ASC) and academic achievement and attributed it to the reciprocal effects model (REM). This model proposes that ASC does not cause academic achievement or vice versa, but rather ASC and academic achievement continually influence each other in children. You have probably seen preschool children who can count 20 objects and who are very proud of their achievement. The ASC then contributes to the children's motivation to learn more (achievement).

Affirming interactions support children's balanced self-concept.

Preschool children's feelings of low self-esteem may result in learned helplessness (Burhans & Dweck, 1995). Children think that they are incapable of accomplishing tasks, so they don't try to start tasks or quickly give up trying to complete them. Obviously, it is critical that this recursive cycle be broken when the child exhibits low self-regard and its accompanying negative interactions with others. This takes sensitive and helpful responses on the part of adults to affirm the child's worth and competence while coaching or facilitating more positive interactions with others and setting logical and fair limits to promote appropriate behaviors.

Children can have difficulty forming positive self-concepts and self-esteem for a variety of reasons, including parenting and child care methods that hinder this development. Developmentally inappropriate expectations, limited opportunities to use and enhance emerging physical and motor abilities, lack of affection and appropriate attention and guidance, harsh or punitive discipline, unstable or insecure relationships with individuals on whom they depend, excessive negative responses to the child, undue teasing or ridicule, insufficient opportunities to play with other children, excessive or demeaning sibling rivalry, and family stress are examples of experiences that hinder healthy development of self-awareness, self-concept, and self-esteem.

However, it is believed that when young children experience supportive bonds with, and unconditional love and acceptance from, those on whom they depend and when parents and teachers use positive authoritative forms of discipline, children develop a more balanced self-concept, more positive self-regard, and higher levels of self-esteem than children who have not experienced these affirming interactions (Lamborn, Mounts, Steinberg, & Dornbusch, 1991; Verschueren, Marcoen, & Schoefs, 1996). Relationships that are marked by unconditional acceptance, genuine interest and concern, and positive guidance techniques should not be confused with permissive discipline that fails to communicate expected behaviors and value systems. Unconditional acceptance is conveyed when adults acknowledge the child's feelings and perspectives and affirm the child's competence and worth when placing limits on inappropriate behaviors.

Regulating One's Own Behavior

> Self-regulation and emotion regulation are clearly defined in the literature, which identifies a self-regulated person as one who can comply with a request, to initiate and cease activities according to situational demands, to modulate the intensity, frequency, and duration of verbal and motor acts in social and educational settings, to postpone acting upon a desired object or goal, and to generate socially approved behavior in the absence of external monitors. (Kopp, 1982, pp. 199–200, cited in Boyer, 2009, p. 175)

At ages 4 and 5, children rely on previously acquired self-comforting strategies to help them cope with uncomfortable or disturbing emotional events. They may regress to thumb sucking, withdraw to a more secure or comfortable place, find comfort in their transitional object, seek the proximity of a trusted playmate or caregiver, or divert their own attention and conversations to other topics. All of these strategies assist children in modulating their emotions, decreasing the intensity and lessening the frequency of emotions. As children get older, they learn, as many adults have, to mask their emotions; some may deny that they are feeling certain emotions. Learning to recognize and acknowledge one's emotions and to handle them in psychologically healthy, socially constructive, and self-affirming ways is a critical part of the socializing process. This process is referred to as *emotional intelligence* (Goleman, 1995), an aspect of human growth and development that has lifelong implications for good mental health and personally satisfying social interactions.

Identifying and Understanding One's Own Feelings

Young children, like adults, experience a range of emotions, from joy and elation to grief and despair. They express feelings of love, acceptance, frustration, anger, hostility, jealousy, shame, embarrassment, guilt, anxiety, fear, distress, depression, pride, humor, astonishment, yearning, and many more emotions. Expressions of emotion are exhibited in numerous ways: talking about emotional events or feelings, crying, shouting, laughing, withdrawing, expressing irritability, pouting, displaying distraction or inattentiveness, engaging in verbal exchanges, being silly, showing aggression toward self and others, making self-deprecating comments, rejecting others and efforts to console, exhibiting destructive behaviors, seeking and offering affection, and many others.

An immensely important developmental task of early childhood is learning about emotions and how to express them. This learning includes *labeling, understanding,* and *modulating* emotions. Aspects of this learning include the child's ability to cognitively grasp the concept of emotion, to take into account the types of situations that cause certain emotional reactions, and to understand how her or his expressions of emotion affect others (Denham, 1998; Saarni, 1999).

Labeling occurs as children are given names for emotions in specific situations or descriptors for emotion-evoking events. ("You are really *angry.*" "Do you feel *unhappy* when your dad and mom are away at work?" "It makes all of us *sad* when someone dies." "When you feel *mad* at someone, let's talk about it." "I can tell that you are very *proud* of yourself." "We are all having such a *joyous* time today.") Such labeling is an important first step in young children's understanding of emotions.

Labels can go only so far, however. Dialogue with children about feelings is important: what feelings mean about our shared humanity; what kinds of situations evoke certain behaviors in all of us; how individuals respond in different contexts; appropriate and inappropriate, effective and ineffective, healthy and unhealthy ways to express and deal with feelings; and how the manner in which we express emotions affects others. These dialogues can explore positive and healthy ways to cope with emotional events and the feelings they create. Helping children to define and cope with their various emotions is essential to their overall mental health and their social development, including their ability to relate to and empathize with others.

By the time children are 4 or 5 years old, they have some understanding of their own emotions and the emotions of others. They have the capacity to reflect on their feelings and some idea that emotions persist for a time after the event that caused them. At this point, although self-control of emotions is far from established, children are learning and beginning to apply display rules, demonstrating knowledge of when and where certain expressions of emotion are acceptable. They are beginning to modulate their expressions of emotion in ways that serve their best interests and are becoming aware of the effects of their expressions of emotion on others.

Anger. Anger is an emotion that ranges in expression and intensity from irritability to aggression to hostility and rage. Lewis and Michalson (1983) identified three components of anger. The first component is the emotional state of anger, the second component is the expression of anger, and the third component is the understanding of anger. In young children, the feeling of anger (the first component) is provoked by frustration in getting needs met or obstacles to goal attainment. Inability to obtain another's attention, a toy that doesn't function as desired, inability to handle clothing (e.g., a zipper that gets stuck or buttonholes that are too small), a playmate who doesn't respond appropriately to play requests, arbitrary or confusing disciplinary restrictions, and an interruption to an enjoyable playtime activity are some examples. Anger is aroused when children experience physical or verbal assault—being hit or pushed, teased, or berated. Feelings of rejection may also arouse anger. Anger arousal thresholds and the manner in which anger is expressed (the second component) differ among individuals, owing to individual differences in temperament, cognitive abilities, and family and cultural expectations and role models. Some scholars have suggested a biological basis for extreme anger responses that readily escalate into violent behaviors, suggesting birth injuries (LeDoux, 1996; Panskepp, 1998; Yager, 1995) and/or prenatal or postnatal abuse or neglect, resulting in abnormal brain growth and neurological development (Perry et al., 1995).

Preschool children need support to express anger in socially acceptable ways.

As children are able to remember past experiences with anger, use language to talk about anger, and regulate their emotions, they develop an understanding of anger (the third component). Preschool children still need adults to help them learn to express anger in productive ways, manage their anger, and understand the emotion (PsychCentral, 2001). A study looking at preschool children's strategies for dealing with sadness and anger, showed that 4-year-olds' ability to develop strategies for coping with anger depended on the mother's ability to structure the situation to help her child out of distress. Children who were left to deal with frustration on their own were less able to develop a successful strategy (Cole, Dennis, Smith-Simon, & Cohen, 2009).

Fear and Anxiety. Early studies of fear attributed its evolution to maturation and increasing cognitive development (Gesell, 1930; Jersild & Holmes, 1935a, 1935b; Jones & Jones, 1928). In one of the earliest studies of childhood fears, Jones and Jones (1928) wrote, "Fear arises when we know enough to recognize the potential danger in the situation but have not advanced to the point of complete comprehension and control of the changing situation" (p. 143).

Maturation and learning contribute to changes in fear behaviors from the infant/ toddler period to ages 4 through 5. The 4- through 5-year-old child experiences a variety of fears caused by insufficient experience, incomplete information or knowledge, and an assortment of misconceptions. For example, after her parents' divorce, Josie feared her own impulses and behaviors lest she "cause" the other parent to leave her.

Some fears are caused by the child's inability to separate fantasy and reality. In role playing the *Three Billy Goats Gruff,* Emma became so immersed in the drama that she began to cry and cling to the teacher in fear that the troll would harm her. Her mother reported that for a time thereafter, Emma had nightmares, feared the dark, and resisted retelling of the fairy tale.

Still other fears are learned through observation of fears modeled by parents, siblings, relatives, and friends. For example, Marisha's mother always referred to rain, regardless of the amount of precipitation or accompanying elements, as a "storm." Her own childhood experience in a tornado had left a lingering fear of storms and a generalization that all rain is a potential deadly storm. Thus, she modeled fear of all rainy weather. Fears are also learned through one's own experience. For example, a child who is bitten by a dog may fear all dogs, or perhaps all small animals, for a time.

The sources of fear and anxiety are numerous. All children experience fear and anxiety from time to time and in varying degrees of intensity. Yet not all childhood fears are the same. Some children fear the dark; others do not. Also, there are individual differences in the way children respond to fear stimuli. One child may quietly withdraw or hover unobtrusively near a trusted adult; another may cry loudly, cling desperately, and resist being consoled. Still others may enter a flight mode and attempt to escape the feared object or event by running away from it.

Many fears or anxieties serve important adaptive or self-preservation functions and, as such, are considered healthy fears. Fears of traffic, strange animals, motorized tools and equipment, fires, dangerous elevations, and firearms are healthy because they prompt appropriate avoidance behaviors. Some children do not develop a healthy fear of danger and require guidance and supervision to protect them from mishaps. Such guidance should be informative without arousing curiosity, which can lead the child into dangerous explorations. A statement such as, "The gun is locked away because guns are very dangerous and can injure and kill," is better than, "Don't you dare touch that gun," which for some children simply arouses their interest and virtually ensures that they will explore the forbidden item. However, explanations should not exaggerate the danger or alarm the child. "Fasten your seat belt, sit still, and tell me about your day at kindergarten" is better than "People get killed in car wrecks every day; if you don't sit still, you're going to make me have a wreck, and we will all be killed."

Helping young children to understand and cope with their fears is a matter of providing appropriate experiences, explanations, and encouragement. Children need age-appropriate dialogue and explanations that provide labels and insights. When adults are calm, encouraging, and knowledgeable, children are reassured. In time, some fears subside and disappear, new fears emerge, and new coping strategies become a part of the child's behavior repertoire.

Effects of Attachment on Later Emotional and Social Development

ethology
the scientific study of behavior

Studies by Bowlby, Ainsworth, and other theorists in **ethology** have examined the effects of early attachments on later social and emotional development (Honig, 2002; Robinson, 2002; Zeanah, 1999). It is apparent that secure attachments can be interrupted by withdrawal of the attachment person from the relationship through such events as maternal or paternal debilitating physical or psychological illness, marital discord, multiple foster care assignments, reversal of adoption decisions, and a host of other disruptive circumstances. Such circumstances are often associated with attachment disorders that interfere with optimal social and emotional development. Contemporary efforts to diagnose and classify attachment disorders have noted various types of behaviors that are associated with disturbed attachment processes during infancy. The following are some of the behaviors outlined by Zeanah, Mammen, and Lieberman (1993, p. 346):

- Atypical expressions of affection in two extremes: lack of warm and affectionate interactions with potential attachment persons and/or promiscuous or nondiscriminate expressions of affection involving unfamiliar people
- Atypical comfort-seeking behaviors when hurt, frightened, or ill, either failing to seek help from a trusted attachment person or doing so in an ambivalent manner
- Excessive dependency behaviors or an inability to seek and use adult support when needed

- Poor compliance behaviors or compulsive compliance
- Failure to ascertain a caregiver's presence and/or support in unfamiliar situations
- Oversolicitous or punitive and controlling responses to caregivers
- Detached behaviors upon reunion following a separation, engaging in avoidant behaviors or anger outbursts, or not showing affection

In studies of healthy attachments, securely attached infants have been shown to be more socially competent on entering preschool (McElwain, Cox, Burchinal, & Macfie, 2003; NICHD Early Child Care Research Network, 2006) and more responsive to their agemates in kindergarten (Sroufe, Carlson, & Schulman, 1993; Thompson, 1999). In other studies, securely attached children were found to be less dependent on adults, to be more ready to explore their environment, and to exhibit fewer behavior problems than were children who had been insecurely attached (NICHD Early Child Care Research Network, 2006; Rubin, 2002). The children who are securely attached also manage stress more competently (Ahnert, Gunnar, Lamb, & Barthel, 2004; Gunnar, Broderson, Nachmias, Buss, & Rigatuso, 1996) and are more competent in problem-solving and memory tasks in preschool (Belsky, Spritz, & Crnic, 1996).

Children who are insecurely attached have been found to experience challenging social interactions with peers. In an analysis of the data from the NICHD, national study researchers (McElwain, Cox, Burchinal, & Macfie, 2003) found that children who were avoidantly attached at 15 months of age were more aggressive with peers at 36 months, whereas those with a resistant attachment history exhibited less self-assertion among peers. Such studies of early attachment successes and failures support the theories that early attachment experiences influence long-term outcomes in social and emotional development.

Again, early therapeutic intervention with at-risk parents and their infants may redirect the interactional dynamics between mother and infant to foster positive outcomes. In nonparental caregiving situations, stable, predictable, supportive relationships with caregivers who are emotionally available are crucial. However, we must not paint a picture that is too bleak. It is important to know that over the long term, the outcomes of both secure and insecure attachments are subject to a number of intervening influences. Children who are insecurely attached to one parent may find security and support through a strong attachment to the other or perhaps to a member of the extended family or some other important adult in their lives (Denham & Weissberg, 2003; Rosen & Rothbaum, 1993). It is also comforting to note that an insecure attachment need not inevitably lead to negative outcomes if an intervening secure attachment takes place.

The extent to which the attachment experience (secure or insecure) has long-term consequences depends on the length of time the child experiences a particular quality of attachment (Lamb, 1987), the nurturing quality of the caregiver (Dozier, Albus, Stovall, & Bates, 2002), or the attachment figure becoming more sensitive (Belsky & Fearon, 2002; NICHD Early Child Care Research Network, 2006). Young children who are securely attached to a parent or caregiver may also become insecurely attached if there is a change in life circumstances, caregiver, or sensitivity of caregivers (Belsky & Fearon, 2002; Howes & Hamilton, 1993; NICHD Early Child Care Research Network, 2006). The research on intervening influences on attachment suggests both optimism for insecurely attached infants and caution against considering a secure attachment in infancy to be a "magic" immunization against later relationship stress.

Secure attachments during the infant and toddler periods pave the way for a smoother transition into Bowlby's phase 4 of the attachment process. Around age 3, according to Bowlby's theory of attachment, children have entered phase 4, which is characterized by *partnership behaviors,* in which they are gaining understanding of others' intentions and can accommodate more cooperatively with the needs and wishes of others. Parent and child interactions can be more mutually goal oriented. Although 4- and 5-year-olds still rely on parents for security and comfort, they are beginning to focus on peers and will often rely on friends for social and emotional support (Bowlby, 1969, 1982, 1988; Furman & Buhrmester, 1992; Strayer & Santos, 1996).

Transitional Objects

Although the importance of transitional objects varies from child to child, transitional objects (a blanket, stuffed animal, or other loved object) continue to represent an important part of the social and emotional development of children ages 4 through 5. The duration of attachments to transitional objects also varies. For some children, the attachment is long-lived; for others, the attachment may be brief, perhaps even being transferred from one object to another for varying periods of time. Affection for the transitional object(s) can be quite deep and openly expressed. At the same time, the object(s) can become the target of aggressive and serious mistreatment as children fantasize or work through emotional and social conflicts.

The need for the transitional object recedes as children shift their energies and attentions from themselves to others and from fantasy to real-life tasks. The child may then choose to carry the object in the car en route to school but leave it there for reunion when the school day is over. Or the child may wish to carry the object into the classroom, where it may be put in a cubbyhole to be visited on occasion during the day. Sometimes, symbolic substitutes signal a more mature approach. A symbolic substitute can take the form of a photograph of the child with the transitional object or a family photograph carried in the child's book bag or lunch box. Classroom teachers often provide bulletin board space for children's photographs of themselves and their families to help children through the transition process.

Children themselves must make the decision as to when to give up the transitional object. Coercion, ridicule, disparaging remarks, or other attempts to separate the child from the transitional object only serve to intensify the child's resolve to cling to it (Jalongo, 1987). Hence, adults should accept the child's right to refuse to share the transitional object with others. Sometimes, the child's maturity in other areas leads adults to believe that the child should have outgrown the need for the transitional object, but this does not necessarily signal a readiness to abandon it. It is

Children must make the decision as to when to give up a transitional object.

always best to take cues from the child in determining when a transitional object will be relinquished or abandoned in favor of a different self-comforting approach.

Jeremy's interest in astronomy has found support in books provided for him by his parents and teachers. Though they are beyond the expected reading abilities for a child his age, Jeremy reads his astronomy books with some facility. Each morning, his backpack is carefully prepared for school with one or two of his current favorite astronomy books *and* his well-worn teddy bear. For the duration of kindergarten, Jeremy carries his teddy bear to school with him, carefully tucked into his backpack. Wisely, neither his parents nor his teachers discourage this practice.

Social Competence

Jeremy has brought to kindergarten a large, multiple-color water painting set that was purchased for him yesterday. He proudly shows it to some of his classmates. Many of them offer to play with him if he will share the water paints. Because the water paints are still new to him, Jeremy emphatically replies, "No, not now! No one can use my paint set." He then retreats to a table to work alone with his paints. One or two persistent classmates follow him to the table and continue to beg and prod. Finally, Jeremy capitulates, "OK, Madeline, you can paint with me, but Joey, you can't paint with us. Maybe tomorrow I will let you paint."

Toys from the sociodramatic center are frequently finding their way into the restroom and remaining there until the teacher retrieves them. In addition to becoming soiled, the toys are "lost" and unavailable to others who want to play with them. Angela's teacher convenes a class meeting to discuss the situation. After explaining her concerns about the availability and cleanliness of the toys, she asks the class to help her find a solution to this problem.

Thomas asserts that whoever is doing that should "get a spanking." Geraldo insists that if the toys are really lost or too dirty to play with, his daddy will buy new toys. Katie suggests that if they get dirty, her mommy can wash them. Rashid implores the teacher to throw the toys away, as they might be "really, really, really dirty!"

Sensing the direction in which the discussion is going, the teacher attempts to bring the children back to the central issue: responsibility for the care of classroom materials. "You have made some interesting suggestions and have been very thoughtful; we all appreciate that. However, I am still wondering if there is something we ourselves can do right here in our classroom and not involve people who are not here with us every day."

(continued)

Emotional and Social Development: Ages Four Through Five

Carson suggests, "We could wash our own toys in the sand–water table."

Then Angela, after moments of musing and listening and with a look of earnest contemplation, suggests, "We can put a sign on the toilet door that says 'No toys allowed' to remind everybody not to take toys in there." Her classmates agree and talk about who will make the sign.

The teacher further enlists the children: "Is there anything else we can do?"

Angela, her problem-solving abilities taxed to the limit, asserts, "They will just have to remember not to do that."

Each of these vignettes illustrates different levels of social competence. How would you characterize a socially competent person? Does that person demonstrate any of these characteristics: positive self-regard, self-confidence, curiosity, spontaneity, humor, warmth, reliability, sense of right and wrong, self-discipline, morally responsible behaviors, awareness of the needs of others, positive interactions with others, genuineness, friendliness, cooperation, problem-solving ability, adaptability, helpfulness, and/or ability to give and receive praise? Which of these or other descriptors did Jeremy display? What characteristics describe Angela's social competence?

Although we can describe social competence and certainly appreciate its value in social interactions, a concrete definition has been difficult for theorists to construct, particularly in terms of measuring social competence achievement (Katz & McClellan, 1997). However, for the most part, experts agree on the antecedents of social competence:

1. Social competence emerges from *social development,* in which the child exhibits a growing awareness of others and chooses to interact or not to interact with them. Social development includes establishing a repertoire of strategies for initiating interactions and ways to sustain them. Feelings and responses evoked by social interactions determine the extent to which the child is motivated to pursue further social interactions.

2. The *socialization processes* and *sociocultural contexts* in which children grow and learn impose values, beliefs, customs, and social skills that have been transmitted from one generation to the next. Through sociocultural contexts, children learn the expectations of their families and cultural groups. Children in various cultural groups develop social perspectives and social abilities that allow them to succeed in a particular sociocultural context (see Box 12.1). Parents are generally the primary socializing agents; other socializing agents include siblings and other extended family members, family friends, and neighbors. The socialization of young children is also influenced by experiences in child care and preschool settings, faith-based affiliations, and other groups. Children also develop social concepts and behaviors through their observations of and interactions with many people in many different places and contexts and through their television and other media experiences. Prosocial development (including perspective-taking ability and a theory of mind), positive self-regard, gender understandings, self-control, moral development, and awareness of diversity and individual differences all influence the development of social competence and the child's emerging abilities to make and sustain friendships and to share mutual benefits from positive interactions with others.

Box 12.1 Diversity Perspectives: Social Inhibition

Toddlers who are shy and wary in new situations show biological differences from more assertive children. They have greater muscle tension and higher levels of cortisol in the saliva. They have elevated resting heart rates (Kagan, Reznick, & Snidman, 1987). When very inhibited children are in social situations, they have few social initiations and poor social assertiveness, as well as visible discomfort and anxiety. This often causes them to be rejected by their peers—in this country (Rubin, Chen, & Hymel, 1993). In China, these children would have the same physiological reactions to being with other children, but they would be seen as well behaved "because group functioning requires behavioral restraint, obedience, and submission" (Rubin, 1998). Shy-inhibited behavior appears to be positively valued and encouraged (Chen, Rubin, & Li, 1997) These children are seen as interactively competent precisely because they don't stand out. They are viewed as achievement oriented, independent, and academically accomplished. They develop positive relationships with their peers (Chen, Rubin, & Li, 1995).

Given these antecedents, we find the summary definition proposed by Katz and McClellan (1997) particularly helpful: "the competent individual is a person who can use environmental and personal resources to achieve a good developmental outcome—an outcome that makes possible satisfying and competent participation in and contributions to the groups, communities, and larger society to which one belongs" (p. 1). According to these scholars, social competence is characterized by several attributes, including the following:

- The ability to regulate emotions
- Social knowledge and understanding sufficient to form friendships
- The ability to recognize and respond appropriately to social cues in others and use language to interact effectively
- Certain social skills such as social approach techniques, giving positive attention to others, contributing to ongoing discussion among peers, and turn taking
- The dispositions or habits of mind that are conducive to effective social relationships, such as cooperativeness, responsibleness, and empathy.

Interaction Patterns and Play Behaviors

Play provides an essential medium for the establishment of friendships and for the development of social knowledge, skills, and competence. According to Parten's (1933) early descriptions of play patterns and similar contemporary descriptions (Creasey, Jarvis, & Berk, 1998; Frost, Wortham, & Reifel, 2001; Howes, 1992, 1996), 4- and 5-year-olds should exhibit increasing skill in *associative* and/or *cooperative* play behaviors (Table 12.1). This play is characterized by greater desire to interact with playmates and participate in collaborative play activities. The onlooker, solitary/independent, and parallel/proximal forms of play that are observed in early stages of play development continue, however, and remain useful and productive play modes throughout life.

Table 12.1 Interaction Patterns in Play

Parten (1933)	Howes (1980, 1992)	Winter (1985)
Onlooker play: Enjoys observing others		
Solitary play: Is content to play alone in same or different activity		*Independent play:* Plays alone or away from others
Parallel play: Plays beside or among others in similar activity without interacting	*Parallel play:* Plays in close proximity in similar activity; no attention to the play of others	*Proximal play:* Plays near others, engaged in own activity with no attempts to interact
Associative play: Plays with others, talking about the activity, but own play goals take precedence	*Mutual regard:* Shows awareness of others but no verbal interaction or attempt to engage in shared activity	*Relational play:* Communicates with others verbally or nonverbally but follows an activity choice without involving others
Cooperative play: Plays in an organized and cooperative way, with assigned roles and mutually agreed-upon play themes or goals	*Simple social play:* Plays in similar activity with social bids such as smiling or offering a toy	*Interactive play:* Is engaged with peers in a common activity
	Complementary play: Plays in same activity with some collaboration but no bids for shared engagement	
	Complementary reciprocal play: Involves social bids for shared engagement and collaborative activities	

associative play
a loosely organized form of social play, characterized by overt social behaviors indicating common activities, shared interests, and interpersonal associations

cooperative play
a well-organized form of social play, characterized by well-defined social roles within play groups, influential peer leaders, and shared materials and equipment used to pursue a well-understood group play goal or theme

In **associative play,** children share and converse about materials and activities, but each player explores and uses the materials in individual ways. Associative play may involve following another child around, imitating or taking cues from other children's play behaviors, and engaging in conversation and nonverbal communication, yet one's own play preferences prevail over those of others. There is little or no bid for shared or focused play activities.

Cooperative play, by contrast, signals the child's growing ability to acknowledge the ideas of others and to incorporate those ideas into his or her play behaviors. This play is characterized by shared planning and organizing of play scenarios around goals or play themes. Who gets to play and who doesn't is decided by certain members of the group and can be inclusive or restrictive. Cooperative play, also referred to as complementary reciprocal play (Howes, 1992, 1996) and interactive play (Winter, 1985), involves higher levels of social interaction skills including interpersonal problem-solving skills and cooperation, acceptance of leadership or followership roles, perspective-taking, flexibility, language, and shared creativity and responsibilities.

Theory of Mind

In addition to understanding the effects of one's behaviors on others, in a complementary development, children around age 4 begin to have a more complex understanding of the existence of mental states in themselves and others. They are growing in their awareness that feelings, desires, intentions, beliefs, and unique perceptions can exist in the mind. Contemporary theorists refer to this development as a child's "theory of mind," also referred to as "mind sight" (Siegel, 1999), or

Both perspective-taking and theory of mind are gained through pretend play.

an understanding of others' minds or mental states (Andrews, Halford, & Bunch, 2003; Astington, 1993). A theory of mind supports perspective-taking ability. A theory of mind proposes that the individual understands that others' thinking is influenced by their perceptions, feelings, desires, and beliefs. The ability to think about and reflect on what others are thinking or feeling is an important part of interpersonal relationships. The study of children's theory of mind includes children's understanding of how the senses provide information to individuals; children's understanding and recognition of emotions in others; and their understanding that others have feelings, desires, and beliefs that are uniquely theirs (Lillard & Curenton, 1999). Researchers believe that as children develop a theory of mind, they begin to enjoy more socially satisfying interactions with others (Eisbach, 2004; Lalonde & Chandler, 1995).

A Social Skill and Attitude: Accurately Read and Comprehend Emotional States in Others

At age 4 to 5, social cognition is becoming evident in the ability to make social judgments on the basis of prior experience, observations of others, and the child's viewpoints and expectations of others. This social cognition is characterized in part by a growing awareness of the effects of one's behaviors on others and increasing (but still imperfect) perspective-taking ability. Thus, aggressive behavior may be self-controlled through an awareness of how aggression hurts others. However, through experience (and perhaps coaching), a child can learn that empathic behaviors evoke warm and friendly responses from others. A study asked preschool children to identify the feelings of faces on cards. Children who had been identified as having secure attachments were more empathic than children with insecure attachments. One conclusion might be that children who have experienced the empathic responses of an adult are better able to feel empathy (Knight, 2010).

In their review of research on social perspective-taking in young children, Rubin and Everett (1982) identified three forms of perspective-taking: (1) cognitive perspective-taking, which includes the ability to consider others' thoughts and intentions; (2) affective perspective-taking, or the ability to take into account the feelings and emotions of others; and (3) spatial perspective-taking, or the ability to consider the other person's physical view of the world. A child who attempts to organize a game may be exhibiting cognitive perspective-taking. A child who attempts to comfort a crying playmate may be exhibiting affective perspective-taking, an awareness of the other child's distress or its cause. A child who removes an obstacle from the path of another, thus preventing an accident, is demonstrating spatial perspective-taking.

During sociodramatic play, pretending promotes perspective-taking (Tan-Niam, 1994). As the child engages in a variety of role-taking experiences ("You be the nurse, and I'll be sick"), awareness of others' roles emerges. In attempting to play out a sociodramatic scenario, the child becomes aware of discrepancies between her or his intentions and those of playmates. In adjusting the sociodrama to the wishes of others, the child's perspective-taking abilities are enlisted.

Adults help children to develop perspective-taking abilities by inviting them to think about the feelings and experiences of others during social encounters: "How do you think Tony felt when you knocked over his block tower?" "Let's let Tony tell us what he thinks about what happened." "Did you notice how Ms. Tamira smiled when you helped open the door for her?" "Did you notice how your baby sister stopped crying and listened when you were singing to her?" "What kinds of things make us happy?... angry?... sad?" "If you will stand over here, you will see what LaToya is describing." "You helped to prevent an accident by moving that tricycle out of the pathway." There are numerous opportunities to help young children develop perspective-taking abilities during their play and interactions with others.

Both perspective-taking and theory of mind are facilitated through pretend play as children assume pretend roles and encounter others' unique ways of interpreting and representing their particular role assignments (Bergen, 2002). The give-and-take required to successfully and cooperatively carry out a sociodrama requires the child's attention to the minds of others (Youngblade & Dunn, 1995). These social cognitions are also facilitated through children's literature, in which dialogue can be used to draw attention to the feelings and experiences of the characters. Parallels can be drawn between characters in stories and individual experiences. The give-and-take of sibling relationships also influences this development, particularly in younger siblings (Lewis, Freeman, Kyriakidou, Maridaki-Kassotaki, & Berridge, 1996).

Friendships

In Miriam Cohen's (1967) sensitive children's book *Will I Have a Friend?,* Jim asks his father on the way to his first day at preschool, "Will I have a friend?" His father answers, "I think you will." This worried question is quite typical for children entering preschool or new play groups. It signals a very important aspect of social and emotional development: establishing and maintaining friendships.

Relating effectively with others is an important aspect of social competence, on which we elaborate later in this chapter. Becoming socially competent with peers involves the development of certain social skills: (1) initiating interactions, (2) maintaining ongoing relations, and (3) resolving interpersonal conflicts (Asher, Renshaw, & Hymel, 1982; Wittmer, 2009).

Some children are more adept than others at initiating interactions, for example, the newcomer who seems to intuitively know how to integrate him- or herself into an unfamiliar group of children or an ongoing play activity. Children who tend to be popular with their peers initiate interactions by suggesting a joint activity or engaging others in talk (Asher, Renshaw, & Hymel, 1982; Hughes, 1999). These children seem to have a better sense of timing, waiting for an opportunity to join in, perhaps during a natural break in an ongoing activity. These children are also less obtrusive and create fewer disruptions in the play in progress. In contrast, unpopular children are more uncertain about how to initiate interactions and use offensive or vague strategies such as smiling or tactics that call attention to themselves rather than integrating themselves into the ongoing activity.

Friendships in 4- and 5-year-old children have their own characteristics, which are indicative of increasing cognitive and social development. As a rule, friendships at this age are dependent on proximity, shared activities or toys, and physical attributes (Epstein, 1989) as well as similar play styles, knowledge, and interests (Dietrich, 2005). These factors are also important for friendships between children with disabilities and those without in inclusive classrooms (Dietrich, 2005).

For friendship maintenance and conflict resolution skills to emerge, young children need to experience peers in a variety of contexts: as visitors in their homes, in preschool settings, in neighborhood play groups, in family gatherings, and so on. There is some evidence that although parents and teachers provide very important guidance for children's developing social skills, children also benefit cognitively and socially from opportunities to interact with peers with minimum adult interaction (Kontos & Wilcox-Herzog, 1997). In the classroom context, these findings imply that activities and materials should be chosen to encourage and facilitate both children's cognitive engagement *and* social interaction.

Becoming Prosocial

An outgrowth of social cognition is the continued development of prosocial behaviors. Prosocial behaviors include empathy and altruism. Empathy is the ability to recognize the feelings of others, such as distress, anxiety, or delight, and to vicariously experience those feelings. **Altruism** is defined as behavior that is intended to help another without expectation of reward. In young children, a number of factors influence prosocial behaviors. Among these factors are age, level of cognitive functioning, perspective-taking abilities, individual personality, family interactions, guidance strategies, and role models.

altruism
intentions to help others without the expectation of reward

Studies have shown that when children observe prosocial models, they generally become more prosocial themselves (Bandura, 1997; Radke-Yarrow, Zahn-Waxler, & Chapman, 1983). This is particularly true when the child and the model have had a warm relationship and the child has experienced nurturing from the model.

Jeremy's friend Shaun has just recovered from an upper respiratory infection and is finally able to visit. Keisha greets Shaun on his arrival and hustles the two children off to Jeremy's room to play. Jeremy's delight in seeing his absent friend is somewhat overshadowed by his observation of his mother's greeting. Nevertheless, he leads Shaun to his room, and the two become involved in a new and rather difficult puzzle. Stumped in putting the puzzle together, Jeremy runs to another room to summon his mother's assistance. As they walk back to his room together, Jeremy engages his mother in his concern: "You didn't tell Shaun you were sorry." Confused, his mother inquires, "Sorry? About what, Jeremy?" "About he's been sick," Jeremy responds.

(continued)

Jeremy's previous experiences with being sick were accompanied by expressions of concern such as "I am so sorry you are not feeling well" and "I am really glad you feel better today." He had also observed his parents convey similar concern with others. Thus, through observation, Jeremy has learned to verbally express concern for others and felt some incongruence when such concern wasn't made evident on this happy occasion with Shaun—an unintentional oversight on his mother's part.

Researchers have asked whether there is consistency in prosocial attitudes and behavior from the preschool years to early adulthood. If there is consistency, then it is important that adults facilitate children's prosocial behavior during their early years. Eisenberg, Guthrie, Murphy, Shepard, Cumberland, and Carlo (1999) followed 32 preschool children from ages 4 to 5 and discovered that *spontaneous* prosocial behaviors observed in the preschool classroom predicted the prosocial behavior of these children as young adults. There are a number of strategies that adults can use to support young children becoming prosocial.

Studies of parenting styles, guidance techniques, and the influence of role models demonstrate that when positive and instructive strategies are employed, prosocial behaviors are more likely to emerge (Baumrind, 1998; Marion, 2006; NICHD Early Child Care Research Network, 2002b). Instructive guidance is characterized by logical limits, reason, respect, warmth, affection, and clear expectations.

In addition to role models and guidance techniques, prosocial development is fostered by the following:

1. Experiences that promote positive self-concepts. There is evidence that positive feelings about oneself are related to higher frequencies of cooperative and positive behaviors among 4- and 5-year-old children (Honig & Wittmer, 1996; Wittmer, 2009).
2. Assignment of age-appropriate responsibilities whereby children come to feel that they are a contributing part of the family, class, or group (DeVries & Zan, 1994).
3. Opportunities to interact with other children and to engage in sociodramatic play that enhance role taking and perspective-taking (Bergen, 2002; Rubin, Bukowski, & Laursen, 2009)
4. Opportunities to participate in noncompetitive, cooperative games and group activities (Orlick, 1981; Slavin, 1990; Schneider, 2006).
5. Opportunities to solve peer social conflicts through problem-solving and cooperation.
6. Exposure to literature, television programs, toys, and computer and video games that project prosocial themes (Rosenkoetter, 1999; Wilson, 2008).

Challenges in Peer Interactions

Some children are challenged by peer interactions. Parents and teachers will observe that some 4- and 5-year-olds withdraw from peer relationships (Bar-Haim, Marshall, Fox, Schorr, & Gordon-Salant, 2003). Children who are withdrawn are likely to be fearful, whereas rejected children may be aggressive. Braza et al. (2007) observed 54 preschool children (15 boys and 39 girls, mean age 5.5) on an open-air playground in Spain.

Children who were rejected demonstrated more person-directed aggression (threatening, smacking, attacking) than did popular children or neglected children. Rejected children also showed the highest level of seizing object aggression, aimed at the retrieval of an object (trying to take an object, taking an object) (p. 199). However, there were no differences in defensive object aggression (a defensive reaction to a perceived threatening seizing object aggression) between popular children and rejected children. (p. 199). The authors conclude that rejected children are caught in a "cycle of failure" (p. 205) with their difficulty in processing social information. They need adult support to learn to understand other children's goals, learn negotiation strategies, and gain socioemotional skills such as empathy (p. 209). The authors in the Braza study conclude that neglected children who withdraw are experiencing high anxiety and also need support to learn sociocognitive skills before they, too, become more aggressive.

Other preschool children may engage in bullying behavior or become victims of bullies. In a study of more than 300 kindergarten children in Switzerland, researchers Perren and Alsaker (2006) found distinct patterns for bullies, children who were victims of bullies, and children who were typically developing. Kindergarten children who were bullies and children who were victims of bullies were generally more aggressive, but bullies had more leadership skills than victims. Aggressive boys preferred bullies as playmates, which unfortunately could lead to further bullying of victims.

Aggression

Aggression is behavior that is directed at another with intentions to threaten, harm, or hurt that person in some manner. Aggression is also directed at animals and objects. Aggression is generally described as *instrumental* or *hostile* (Hartup, 1974) and *accidental* (Feshbach, 1970). Dodge (1994) and his colleagues designated three similar categories: *instrumental, reactive,* and *bullying* aggression. Crick and Grotpeter (1995) discuss *relational* aggression.

Instrumental aggression is provoked through goal blockage that prevents the person from obtaining and retaining something he or she wants (a toy, a privilege, play space). Most aggressive behaviors in young children are of this nature and are seldom accompanied by hostility (Marion, 2006). Often, children's behaviors result in injury or insults to another but are accidental rather than intentional. This, too, is common in young children owing to limitations associated with their young age, such as poor motor control (accidentally running into another block construction, knocking it over), frank and often tactless comments resulting from poor perspective-taking ability or immature theory of mind ("Why is your hair ugly today?"), and taking over a play space or play item presumed abandoned by another whose intentions to return were not apparent or noticed. When a child retaliates for the offense, the aggression is referred to as reactive. Hostile or bullying aggression, however, is generally (though not always) unprovoked and is characterized by intent to threaten, thwart, or hurt. Relational aggression involves psychological cruelty and damages others' opinions of a person through lies, isolation, and rumors (Crick & Grotpeter, 1995; Ross, 1996).

As with anger and other emotions, the frequency, intensity, and character of aggressive behaviors are influenced by the child's individual temperament and level of cognition; the extent to which the child's basic needs for food, clothing, shelter, social interaction, emotional support, and nurturing have been predictably and successfully met; and the teaching and role models to whom the child has been most frequently exposed. In both European and Puerto Rican cultures, mothers' negative affect predicted relational aggression in young school-aged children (Brown, Arnolds, Dobbs, & Doctoroff, 2007). However, in another study both mothers' and fathers' parenting styles influenced young children's aggressive behavior (Casas et al., 2006).

As with other social skills, children learn aggressive behaviors from a variety of role models. Parents and teachers who use discipline techniques that are power assertive, punitive, and/or physically punishing provoke children to be more aggressive. Dodge (1994) and his colleagues discovered a disturbing outcome for children who had been severely punished. These scholars found that such children failed to learn to read intent in the behaviors of others; instead, they were more reactive to other children's accidental aggressions, viewing them as intentional or hostile and thus deserving an aggressive response. These scholars believe that severely punished children acquire chronic patterns of misperceiving the deeds of others in which they interpret any unpleasant interaction with others as hostile and directed at them. If this pattern is allowed to persist, the children enter a recursive cycle in which their hostile manner evokes hostility in others, which in turn confirms their misguided notions about themselves and the intentions of others toward them. The result can be the development of chronic aggression.

Corporal punishment is "the use of physical force with the intention of causing a child to experience pain but not injury for the purposes of correction or control of the child's behavior" (Straus, 1994, p. 4) and can lead to children's and adults' aggressive behavior. In a recent analysis of 88 studies on the effects of corporal punishment, severe punishment of children was found to be related to children's

> decreased moral internalization, increased child aggression, increased child delinquent and antisocial behavior, decreased quality of relationship between parent and child, decreased child mental health, increased risk of being a victim of physical abuse, increased adult aggression, increased adult criminal and antisocial behavior, decreased adult mental health, and increased risk of abusing own child or spouse. (Gershoff, 2002, p. 544)

Other antecedents of aggressive behaviors include some children's television programs, video and computer games, theme toys associated with violent media program characters, advertising, news stories, and the behaviors and expectations of older children and admired adults.

Recognizing the pervasive influence of the media and the toy industry, adults have a responsibility to help children become discerning consumers. Young children can be engaged in evaluative dialogue about what they have seen or heard through the media; how advertising entices to get money for the advertisers; and how what people do in some television programs and media games is dangerous and harmful, unrealistic, and not true for real people. Providing the props for prosocial play and avoiding toys that promote aggressive and violent play are critical if children are to practice and develop prosocial perspectives and constructive interaction patterns. Again, instructive guidance techniques influence how children learn to handle anger and curtail aggression.

The consequences of aggressive behaviors also contribute to its incidence. For instance, when an aggressive child succeeds in hurting, intimidating, or causing another to retreat, the victory increases the likelihood that the aggressive behavior will be repeated. Failure on the part of adults to intervene in aggressive acts can be perceived by the child as condoning the behavior, again increasing the likelihood of repeated occurrences. When adults (parents or teachers) directly or indirectly encourage aggression by praising children who use aggression to get what they want, coaching them to do so, or urging them to

"stand up for themselves," or by laughing at, teasing, or shaming the child who has been victimized by an aggressor, the adults reinforce aggressive attitudes and behaviors.

At this point, it is important to point out that adults in the lives of young children need to be conscientiously proactive in mediating the causes of anger and aggression in children. Identifying the antecedents—family life patterns, sibling relationships, discipline techniques, stress, physical precursors (hunger, fatigue, illness, effects of medications), role models, playmates, play themes, toy preferences, or media influences—is an important first step. Help children to identify and use ways to manage anger (e.g., seeking adult help in resolving conflicts, learning techniques for resolving conflicts in the absence of adult assistance, learning to accept and talk about anger and what makes them and others angry, learning the display rules for anger, learning constructive outlets for anger management). Adults can acknowledge and accept anger in children, recognizing that they, too, get angry from time to time. Adults can be role models for children by exhibiting healthy ways of handling anger, by focusing on prosocial responses rather than simply blaming or venting.

Disruptive Behavior Disorder

Preschoolers are not masters at regulating their emotions, and blocks may get knocked down or names called. Some children are even still having tantrums at this age. But for some children, their behavior is so angry, oppositional, and aggressive that caregivers fear for the safety of the other children, and family members may fear for their own safety. These serious conditions are called disruptive behavior disorders, characterized by aggression, noncompliance, and negative emotionality. The symptoms are pervasive. Emotional and behavioral problems are the largest cause of functional impairment in the pediatric population (Scahill, 2001).

The *DSM-IV-TR* identifies three types of DBDs: (a) oppositional defiant disorder (ODD); (b) conduct disorder (CD); and (c) DBD, not otherwise specified (DBD, NOS) (APA, 2000). Behaviors of ODD include negative emotions, defiance, and disobedience. The features of a CD include physical aggression against people and property. The third category, DBD, NOS, is for people who show serious oppositional or aggresssive behavior but do not meet the criteria for one of the other diagnoses. The key to diagnosis is that the behavior *must* cause significant impairments in the child's functioning with peers, at school or at home. If it's hard to believe that preschool children could have such serious psychological issues, think about the fact that preschool children are expelled from school at three times the rate as children in K–12 (Gilliam, 2005). Most importantly, there are interventions that have proven effective in helping these children when the issues are caught at this young age (Breitenstein, Hill, & Gross, 2009). There may also be a neurobiological basis for some forms of aggression and violent behaviors, as indicated in the discussion earlier in this chapter. These topics and bullying behaviors are discussed further in Chapter 15.

Moral Development

Piaget's (1965) studies of moral development focused on how children develop a respect for rules and a sense of justice. He studied the former by quizzing children about rules as he engaged them in marble play. To assess childhood conceptions of social justice, he used moral dilemma stories with children, followed by questions concerning punishment or appropriateness of certain behaviors. From these studies, Piaget proposed a stage sequence of moral development consisting of (1) a premoral stage, (2) a stage of **moral realism,** and (3) a stage of **moral relativism.**

moral realism
a morality that focuses on rules and the seriousness of the consequences of an act rather than on the intentions behind the act

moral relativism
a morality that focuses on the judgment of situations and intentions underlying individual behavior rather than solely on the consequences of an act

Children younger than age 6 are thought to be in a premoral stage of morality because of an absent or limited concern for rules. For instance, play groups exhibit an assortment of rules and behavior expectations, making up rules as play proceeds and altering them arbitrarily and unilaterally. Awareness of the use of or reasons for rules is minimal.

Toward the end of this stage, around age 6, children begin to exhibit characteristics of Piaget's second stage, moral realism. During this stage, children become quite rule bound, believing that rules are unalterable and set forth by all-knowing authority figures (God, parent, teacher). They believe that one's behavior is judged to be "right" or "wrong" on the basis of having followed the rules or the seriousness of the consequences. This stage is often referred to as a **heteronomous** stage of morality in that the child's behaviors are governed by others rather than by the self, as would be true of autonomous behaviors.

heteronomous morality
a morality that is governed by others rather than by oneself

Because of the characteristic egocentrism of this age, the child believes that others are subject to the same rules and perceive rules in the same way. In addition, the magnitude of the consequences of a deed determines for the child whether the deed is right or wrong. For instance, the child might view breaking a large but very inexpensive item as more serious than breaking a small but expensive one. Moreover, any deed that is punished is deemed wrong.

At this stage of morality, children perceive punishment as it relates to breaking the rule, usually without regard for the rule breaker's intentions. Their suggestions for punishment do not necessarily relate to the misdeed. Some children at this stage may believe that injury or misfortune following their misdeeds is deserved punishment for having broken a rule. Sometimes, unable to control the rule conformity of playmates, older preschoolers seek the assistance of an adult through tattling. One should view this behavior as a natural part of the child's emerging sense of rules and rule infringement and not necessarily as an attempt to be unkind to a playmate. In this regard, tattling might be viewed as a positive aspect of moral development.

Lawrence Kohlberg (1968, 1984) expanded and modified Piaget's theory by proposing an invariant developmental sequence consisting of three levels of moral thinking: premoral (or preconventional), conventional, and postconventional, the outcome of which is a sense of justice. Children are believed to pass through each of the stages, but perhaps at different rates. Each stage incorporates the developments of the preceding stage and builds on them. The preconventional and conventional levels are characteristic of young and school-age children.

Preconventional Level

> *Stage 1: Punishment avoidance and obedience orientation*—At this stage, children are interested in whether they will receive punishments for an action. An action that gets punished is wrong.

> *Stage 2: Exchange of favors and reward orientation*—The child views right actions as those that instrumentally satisfy his or her needs and occasionally the needs of others. Reciprocity is a matter of "you scratch my back and I'll scratch yours."

Conventional Level

> *Stage 3: Morality of conventional role conformity*—At this level, we see a good boy/good girl orientation. Good behavior is that which pleases or helps others and is approved by them. Children (and adults at this stage) follow rules to receive or maintain the respect of others. One seeks approval by being "nice."

> *Stage 4: Law and order*—The child's behaviors are oriented toward authority, fixed rules, and the maintenance of the social order. Right behavior consists of doing what society thinks is right.

Kohlberg's third level, *postconventional moral thinking,* is characterized by "a major thrust toward autonomous moral principles which have validity and application apart from authority of the groups or persons who hold them and apart from the individual's identification with those persons or groups" (Kohlberg, 1968, p. 63). As children are better able to ascertain intentions, take another person's perspective, and understand reciprocity, they make the transition from premoral thinking and behaving to the more mature and reasoned conventional level of morality.

Gender Identity and Gender-Role Development

Children ages 4 through 5 continue to learn gender-role behaviors through the manner in which their masculine or feminine behaviors are encouraged and rewarded or punished. However, they also learn gender-role expectations from their own observations (Bandura, 1986, 1997). Peers, the media, children's literature, and preschool classroom practices all influence a child's gender-role development because they often apply stereotypes about "girl" or "boy" behaviors and capabilities (Alexander & Hines, 1994; Maccoby, 1988).

Kohlberg (1966) proposed a cognitive stage sequence for the development of gender roles:

1. Gender identity, when the child can provide a label for him- or herself as either a boy or a girl. This is usually achieved by age 3.
2. Gender stability, when the child realizes that boys grow up to be men and girls grow up to be women.
3. Gender constancy, when the child realizes that changes in hairstyle or clothing do not alter a person's gender. Gender constancy emerges between ages 5 and 7.

Before achievement of gender stability, children's pretend play is quite androgynous; boys can be mothers, and girls can be fathers. Child development researchers find little cause for concern in these play behaviors of young children, for these behaviors represent opportunities for children to affirm their own gender identities and gender roles. Honig (1983) advises that children need role models who encourage a wide spectrum of expressions of feelings and behaviors. Role models who are comfortable with their own gender assist children in developing healthy gender identities and gender-role behaviors. Marshall, Robeson, and Keefe (2003, p. 111) identify other important opportunities for children to experience gender equity in early childhood education:

- Teacher behaviors that are gender neutral and build children's positive sense of identity as a boy or girl
- Opportunities for children to become involved in activities that may have traditionally been considered gender-typed

Androgynous behaviors are common among young children as they grow in awareness of the various roles each gender might assume.

Emotional and Social Development: Ages Four Through Five

- Opportunities for children to play with both boys and girls
- Knowledge of occupations that both men and women occupy
- Knowledge and awareness of the negative effect of gender-based teasing and exclusion
- Opportunities to play with toys and materials that are not gender labeled

Psychosexual Development. Children ages 4 and 5 continue to have a strong interest in their bodies and are curious about the differences between girls and boys, adults and children. They want to know how babies get here and why girls and boys are anatomically different. When at play, they may imitate the affectional behaviors they have observed within the family and attempt to reenact sexual behaviors observed in other contexts and in the media. "Bathroom talk" ("I see your pee pee." "Your underwear is showing!" "This is my butt.") is used to evoke shock and entertainment.

The developmental goal during this period is to help children to develop healthy attitudes toward their anatomy and the concept of personal privacy; caregivers should provide accurate terms for anatomy, age-appropriate information, and simple but accurate answers to questions. Because these behaviors are typical and represent normal growth and development, it is important that children be given guidance regarding the appropriate time and place for conversations about sexual topics and redirection toward meaningful and constructive play. It is important for adults to respond to each situation in a respectful and matter-of-fact manner. This is not a time for punishment and reprimand, which sends a distorted message about human sexuality. Rather, limits regarding appropriate language, sexual play, nudity, touching, and being touched by others need to be clearly stated and consistently monitored.

It is not uncommon for children who have been sexually abused to act out in provocative ways. They may use explicit language, be more intrusive with playmates, and fondle or attempt penetration or oral contact. Certainly, even these extreme behaviors can represent curiosity, and there are additional symptomatic behaviors associated with child abuse (e.g., visible physical signs, posttraumatic stress disorder, distorted perceptions of self and others, anger, anxiety, depression, avoidance, impaired sense of self, disassociative behaviors, and others) (Briere & Elliott, 1994; Child Abuse Prevention Network, 2007).

If child sexual abuse is suspected, measures must be taken to protect the child from further abuse. It is the law in all states that suspected child abuse be reported to appropriate local and state officials. Child care settings and schools have policies and procedures for child abuse reporting.

Awareness of Diversity and Individual Differences

As noted earlier, self-concept emerges as children become aware of their distinguishing physical characteristics, gender, and abilities. Between ages 3 and 5, children become aware of racial categories but do not always accurately classify themselves. They may believe that their skin color can change by washing, thus changing their racial identity (Quintana, 1998).

Sometimes, when young children discover racial differences, the disturbance in their own tenuous self-identification may cause them to respond with rejection toward others with different racial characteristics. Children at this point are not forming generalized negative attitudes toward other races, but are dealing with their own developing self-concepts and racial identities. There are now discrepancies between self-perceptions and what the child is seeing in others. They are cognitively able to classify and may comment on the differences between others and themselves.

With this discovery, young children behave toward one another in a variety of ways—curious, friendly, unfriendly, apprehensive. They feel one another's hair, compare skin colors, and ask questions. There is some evidence that children from minority groups develop racial awareness earlier than other children (Katz, 1982). Because children's perceptions of others are based on their own experiences with people in limited contexts—pediatrician, dentist, babysitters, teachers, neighbors, playmates, and television and other media personalities—they tend to generalize their experiences with individuals who are members of a particular racial group to new acquaintances of the same group. Their experiences are reinforced or mediated by the attitudes conveyed by members of their family and their caregivers and teachers. Linn and Poussaint (1999) point out the following:

> They may learn denigrating stereotypes from listening to their parents, or others, talking in overtly negative tones about people whose race or ethnicity is different from their own. They may notice that white people, with some exceptions, are dominant in advertisements, book illustrations, stories, and television programs. They observe who is present and who is absent from their schools, churches, or synagogues. Children exposed to television news will note the color of the criminals being arrested in handcuffs and the color of the police officers. All of these images, distorted or not, affect their perceptions of a wide range of people and their place in the world. (p. 50)

The point to be made is that from birth onward, child rearing occurs in a cultural context that instills in the child concepts and attitudes about race, cultural identities, values, and expectations (Derman-Sparks & Ramsey, 2006). Cultural contexts encompass the language spoken in the home, modes of expression, celebrations, holidays, family traditions, family cohesion, disciplinary techniques and authority relationships, food and clothing preferences, family goals and values, achievement orientations, and choices and opportunities in education, work, and recreation and pastime activities. Children's concepts, understandings, and attitudes about race—their own and those of others—derive first from the cultural contexts of home and family.

Early child care, preschool, and kindergarten experiences play a role in supporting or negating children's perceptions of race—their own and that of others. These programs can extend and affirm a child's growing sense of membership in a particular cultural or racial group. Early childhood programs that support positive racial and cultural perspectives:

- Enhance self-concept development and cultural identity
- Help children to develop the social skills of perspective-taking, communicating, cooperating, and conflict resolution
- Broaden children's awareness of varying lifestyles, languages, points of view, and ways of doing things through enriched multicultural curricula (Ramsey, 1998)

In addition, curriculums that are *culturally responsive* acknowledge the racial and cultural representation in a class or group of children and provide experiences and content that respect diverse beliefs and value systems, traditions, family practices, and cultural histories. The provision of antibias curricula and experiences recognizes cultural affiliations and other forms of diversity—language, socioeconomic, gender, and childhood ableness and special needs.

Guidance

Studies of child-rearing practices have provided insights into the kinds of adult–child interactions that are most likely to result in child behaviors that are cooperative, self-controlled, and compliant. Infant attachment studies emphasize the importance of the infant–mother attachment in later development of compliance and social competence (Shonkoff & Phillips, 2000). When infants and toddlers have developed a warm, mutually affectionate relationship with their caregivers, they are more inclined to obey requests. Toddlers whose mothers are affectionate, verbally stimulating, and responsive and use positive methods of control are more compliant (Olson, Bates, & Bayles, 1984; Feldman & Klein, 2003).

Conversely, children whose parents have used arbitrary commands, physical control, or coercive strategies to bring children into compliance are less inclined to cooperate with other adults, regardless of how gentle or friendly those adults are (Londerville & Main, 1981; Main & Weston, 1981). The implications for these children as they enter preschool and kindergarten are clear. Caregivers and early childhood teachers may encounter challenges with such children in establishing rapport and in engendering a spirit of cooperation and compliance within the group.

Guidance techniques are often classified into three types: inductive, power assertive, and permissive. **Inductive discipline** uses a teaching mode in which children are provided reasons and rationales for expectations imposed on them. Inductive discipline sets logical limits for behavior and includes reasonable and logical consequences for noncompliance.

Power-assertive discipline, by contrast, uses coercion in the form of unreasonable and illogical threats (e.g., banishment from the group, withdrawal of love), deprivation of material objects and privileges, belittling remarks, and physical force or punishment. **Permissive discipline** tends to ignore inappropriate behaviors and generally fails to teach appropriate ones.

The consequences of guidance techniques have been the subject of numerous studies since the early research of Diana Baumrind (1967, 1971, 1972), in which parenting behaviors were described and classified as authoritative, authoritarian, permissive, or neglecting, each of which has its corresponding pattern of child behavior.

It is instructive to make a distinction between **authoritative** and **authoritarian** approaches to discipline. Authoritative guidance is inductive in that it provides reasoned and logical limits in a respectful, instructive, consistent, and predictable manner. Baumrind found that children of authoritative parents exhibited greater self-reliance and self-control and friendlier and more cooperative behaviors. They tended to be more curious and optimistic and better able to handle stress than other children. Subsequent studies have also found that inductive forms of discipline result in more cooperative, compliant, and self-controlled behaviors and are associated with more positive relationships and popularity with peers (Hart, DeWolf, Royston, Burts, & Thomasson, 1990; Hart, Ladd, & Burleson, 1990; Kontos & Wilcox-Herzog, 1997). Further, inductive forms of guidance have been associated with advanced moral development (Hoffman, 1988). More recent studies by Baumrind found that children who experienced authoritative parenting engaged in fewer risk-related behaviors during adolescence and were less inclined to experiment with or abuse drugs (Baumrind, 1991a, 1991b).

inductive discipline
a positive, nonpunitive form of discipline that relies on reasons and rationales to help children control their behaviors

power-assertive discipline
a form of discipline in which the power of the adult is used to coerce, deprive of privileges or material goods, or apply physical punishment to modify a child's behavior

permissive discipline
a noncontrolling, non-demanding form of discipline in which the child, for the most part, is allowed to regulate his or her behavior

authoritative discipline
a child-rearing style in which child behavior is directed through rational and reasoned guidance from the adult

authoritarian discipline
a child-rearing style in which parents apply rigid standards of conduct and expect unquestioning obedience from the child

chapter 12

Authoritarian approaches, however, are power-assertive and controlling. This style is often born out of a sensed need to maintain some preconceived order or a set standard of conduct regardless of context or extenuating circumstances. Obedience is expected, usually without benefit of explanation or logical rationale. Authoritarian adults may use coercive, punitive, forceful, or other negative means to maintain their rules or limits. Baumrind's studies found that children who experienced authoritarian guidance exhibited more moodiness, unhappiness, and annoyance; were inclined to show passive aggression or hostility; were less friendly; and were more vulnerable to stress. Studies of children clinically referred for behavior problems find that they have often experienced parenting characterized by low tolerance levels and maturity demands on children that exceed age-related capabilities. These parents often have limited knowledge of development and therefore are insensitive to the guidance and instructional needs appropriate in different behavioral situations (Campbell, 2002).

Where permissive discipline is employed, guidelines, limits, and instruction are for the most part absent. Baumrind's studies found that children who experienced little or no guidance were the least self-controlled and self-reliant. Their behaviors were more inclined to be impulsive, aggressive, and rebellious. They were lower achievers than children who experienced more positive and instructive forms of guidance (Figure 12.2).

However, as we typically do in this text, we look deeper into the complexity of this issue. See Box 12.2 for research on cultural differences in how children respond to guidance approaches.

Clearly, guidance techniques have both short-term and long-term goals and consequences. Meeting short-term goals may require quick thinking and action on the part of an adult to protect the child and others. Conversely, to learn from experiences and guidance, short-term strategies need to cognitively engage the child on topics of prevention, restitution, and limits and why they exist. It is important to realize that short-term "fixes" (e.g., the toy truck put away to stop the possession argument; time-out chair used for one who uttered inappropriate words; chatty friends separated; candy provided for putting toys where they

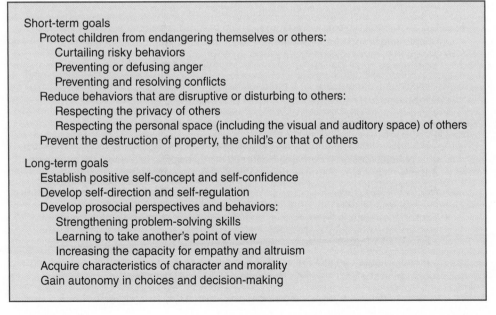

Figure 12.2
Guidance Goals for
Young Children

Short-term goals
    Protect children from endangering themselves or others:
        Curtailing risky behaviors
        Preventing or defusing anger
        Preventing and resolving conflicts
    Reduce behaviors that are disruptive or disturbing to others:
        Respecting the privacy of others
        Respecting the personal space (including the visual and auditory space) of others
    Prevent the destruction of property, the child's or that of others

Long-term goals
    Establish positive self-concept and self-confidence
    Develop self-direction and self-regulation
    Develop prosocial perspectives and behaviors:
        Strengthening problem-solving skills
        Learning to take another's point of view
        Increasing the capacity for empathy and altruism
    Acquire characteristics of character and morality
    Gain autonomy in choices and decision-making

Box 12.2   Diversity: Guidance in Different Cultures

Research studies conclude that harsh, demeaning parenting results in behavioral challenges in several cultures. Authoritarianism, however, doesn't have the same outcomes for children in different cultures.

belong) seldom provide the cognitive or social tools children need in order to self-control. Nor do these events help children acquire the insights needed to interact appropriately with one another or behave as expected in a variety of contexts. Inductive approaches take time and repetition, and better serve long-term social and moral goals (Figure 12.3).

Figure 12.3
Supporting Self-Control in 4- and 5-Year-Old Children

1. Provide an environment in which the child's growing sense of initiative can flourish. Such an environment includes the following:
   - Adequate space for the child to use and pursue toys, equipment, creative materials, and realistic household tools
   - Developmentally appropriate and culturally inclusive play items and activities through which children can experience success and enhanced self-confidence and self-esteem
   - Low, open shelves for personal work and play materials
   - Engaging, enriching play items that encourage decision making, sharing, and cooperating
   - Safe and sturdy furnishing, play items, and surroundings
2. Provide an atmosphere in which it is not only physically but also psychologically safe to explore, experiment, and ask questions. Such an atmosphere includes
   - Rich interactional opportunities that encourage dialogue
   - Answers to questions and encouragement of further curiosities
3. Provide opportunities to interact with other children and to participate in peer groups. This allows children to
   - Share and problem solve with agemates
   - Engage in sustained sociodramatic play with other children
4. Establish a predictable daily schedule to help children develop a sense of time and anticipate and respond appropriately to regular events. Such a schedule
   - Meets the child's physiological needs for food, water, rest, and exercise
   - Adjusts activities and expectations to the child's short but expanding attention span
   - Provides advance notice of a need to change from one event to another
   - Allows time for the completion of tasks once started
   - Avoids long waiting times
5. Involve children in the setting of rules, limits, and standards for behavior:
   - Set simple rules that are few in number, truly necessary, and focused on the most crucial behaviors first. Perhaps the three *D*s of discipline is a good starting point: Set rules that help children recognize things that are Dangerous, Destructive, and/or Disturbing or hurtful to others. However, rules should always be stated in a positive way, telling children *what* to do rather than *what not* to do.
   - Explain the reasons behind rules, and engage children in conversations about logical consequences and the need for reciprocity.
   - Assign age-appropriate chores and responsibilities with adult assistance if needed. Chores can include returning personal items to assigned places, tidying room or toy shelves, watering houseplants, or caring for a pet.

Children with Special Needs

Children with special needs benefit greatly from inclusive classrooms (Odom, 2000). Diamond and Stacey (2003, p. 139) recommend the following strategies for supporting peer interaction among children with disabilities and those without:

- Encourage specialists to support children's social development within the classroom setting
- Encourage children's interest in adaptive equipment
- Ensure that children sit together for social events, eating, and group time
- Emphasize what each child *can* do
- Assign "buddies" for some activities
- Point out shared interests of children with and without disabilities

Children with special needs may benefit from direct instruction in the social behaviors they need to interact successfully with others. Dialogue, role playing, peer mentoring, and role models (both adult and children) can be used to coach and enhance social skills.

Helping other children to accept and interact with children with special needs provides an essential learning experience for them. Because young children are curious and often quite frank, teachers will want to provide reassuring and accurate information about the child and the child's disabilities but should avoid labeling or an otherwise embarrassing discussion. The teacher should provide opportunities for all children to interact and should monitor play and work behaviors for opportunities to assist and to promote prosocial interactions.

Issues in Emotional and Social Development

Sibling Relationships

Siblings influence one another's social and emotional development in reciprocal ways. Although the quality of sibling relationships varies from family to family and depends on a variety of factors, including the number and ages of siblings in the family, children learn from interactions with their siblings. From siblings, children learn family rules and values and how to play with others of different ages. They learn to share family time, space, and resources. They learn about gender and gender-role behaviors. They learn to communicate their needs and to respond to the needs of others. They learn to disagree and to resolve disagreements. They learn about individual differences and individual rights and about loyalty and mutual caring. A study of sibling relationships found that their quality depends on family relationships, especially parental discord and arguments. Interventions were most effective with family-centered approaches that build prosocial skills, address behavior problems, and strengthen parenting skills (Stormshak, Bullock, & Falkenstein, 2009).

Older siblings may be called on to care for younger ones. In this role, the older sibling becomes playmate, teacher, and disciplinarian. Children sometimes form attachment relationships with their older siblings. Although older siblings may focus on the parent as the role model, younger ones focus on the older sibling (Kramer & Conger, 2009). In times of family grief or trauma, siblings may rely on one another for support and comfort (Banks & Kahn, 2003; Chess & Thomas, 1987).

Sibling relationships are generally more positive than negative and are mutually supportive.

It is important to recognize the positive and supportive nature of sibling relationships for children. Four- and 5-year-olds want to talk about their younger and older siblings. They also enjoy having siblings visit their classroom, showing them around, and introducing them to friends. In school and child care settings where siblings may be attending in other classrooms, sensitive adults allow brothers and sisters to visit with one another when possible. It is particularly comforting for younger siblings to locate the older one's classroom to have a mental picture of where a brother or sister is while they are separated. This is often true for the older sibling as well. In times of illness or distress at school, siblings can provide a measure of security until parents can be summoned.

Television and Technology

Today's children enjoy the products of an ever-changing and expanding electronics industry. Although personal computers are running a close second, television remains the most universally accessed electronic medium and has been a topic of concern and research for decades. Currently, most research is concentrating on the relationship of television to obesity. Zimmerman and Bell (2010) found that advertising of unhealthy foods had an effect on obesity but being sedentary or eating while watching television did not. A review of studies done between 1993 and 2005 shows that although watching television is the most sedentary activity of preschool children, time watching television is not related to outdoor play time (Hinkley, Salmon, Okely, & Trost, 2010).

Much of the literature relating to television's influence on children's minds and behaviors has addressed violence and aggression, inadequate and inappropriate gender and cultural role models, and the effects of advertising directed at young consumers. Other studies have attempted to identify the positive influences of television on such aspects of development as language, literacy, knowledge, and prosocial behaviors. The more recent technologies of computers, video equipment, and electronic toys and devices are finding their way into more and more U.S. homes and, like television, are coming under the scrutiny of child development and early education researchers.

The effects of television, video games, assorted electronic toys, and other devices on social and emotional development depend on a number of factors, including the amount of time spent using them, the amount of time spent on alternative healthy and productive activities, the content and quality of the programs and games, and the attitudes and values surrounding the use of these technologies. Time spent watching television precludes physical activities needed to facilitate motor development and physical fitness. The reduction in opportunities to engage in focused interactions with playmates, parents, and others interferes with healthy social and emotional development.

Because it is believed that children learn best through interactive processes, excessive solitary screen time and use of electronic devices can be deleterious to cognitive as well as social development. Because children seek authentic feedback from others to help them make sense of their experiences, excessive screen time and use of electronic devices disrupt human input and interaction. Moreover, the child's limited abilities to separate fantasy from reality and an emerging sense of rules and their applications often make the content of television, video games, and other electronic media confusing and misleading.

Concern over bias, violence, aggression, vulgarity, and explicit sex in media programs and video games has prompted numerous studies on their long-term effects and child advocacy efforts to curtail programming known to result in imitative and desensitized behaviors (Levin, 2003). One study in 1992 estimated that by the time children finish elementary school, they will have seen 8,000 murders and 100,000 other acts of violence (American Psychological Association, 1993), and this trend has not abated (Levin, 2003). Responding to increasing concern over violence in the media, the Governing Board of the National Association for the Education of Young Children (NAEYC) has published a position statement and a teachers' guide (1995) condemning violent television programming, movies, videotapes, computer games, and other forms of media to which young children are exposed.

Bronfenbrenner (1970) expressed concern about the effects of television (and we would add other electronic media) on family interactions when he suggested that "[it is] not so much in the behavior it produces as the behavior it prevents" (p. 170). Family interactions, including talking, arguing, playing games, and taking part in family festivities, are among the forgone opportunities that Bronfrenbrenner (1970, 1986) saw as essential for learning and the formation of character.

Conversely, a number of programs do promote prosocial behaviors and understandings, and child and family viewing can be guided toward them. However, viewing alone does not ensure positive behaviors. Children need adults to help them verbalize their understandings (and misunderstandings) of program topics and role models and to encourage them to role-play and use prosocial behaviors of admired characters in their daily interactions.

Role of the Early Childhood Professional

Enhancing Emotional and Social Development of Children Ages 4 Through 5

1. Support the child's continuing need for nurturance and security.
2. Support the child's emerging sense of self and provide experiences and interactions that promote self-esteem.
3. Model and coach prosocial behaviors.
4. Facilitate initiative while providing safe, reasonable limits.
5. Help children to understand and cope with their fears, anger, and other emotions.
6. Facilitate perspective-taking in children through dialogue and role playing.
7. Provide authoritative and instructive discipline.
8. Facilitate engaged, productive play and interactions with other children.
9. Facilitate positive sibling relationships by minimizing comparisons and competition, and encouraging individuality.
10. Respond respectfully to the child's questions about gender, race, and diversity with focused interest and nonbiased and helpful answers.

Key Terms

altruism	ethology	moral realism
associative play	heteronomous	moral relativism
authoritarian discipline	morality	permissive discipline
authoritative discipline	inductive discipline	power-assertive
cooperative play	initiative	discipline

Review Strategies and Activities

1. Review the key terms in this chapter individually or with a classmate.

2. Visit an exemplary prekindergarten or kindergarten classroom in your local public school.

    a. Observe and record teacher behaviors that model social skills for children, including empathy and altruism, initiating conversations and friendships, accepting and understanding others, perspective-taking, prosocial behaviors, and the cultural perspectives of teachers and parents.

    b. Observe and record attempts to teach or coach social skills.

3. At another time in this same classroom, observe and record anecdotal accounts of associative and cooperative play behaviors among the children. What types of activities promote cooperative play behaviors?

4. Interview several parents of 4- and 5-year-old children. Ask what kinds of limits they set for their children. Which ones do they emphasize most often? Why? How do they enforce these limits at home? How do they support children to become prosocial? What did you learn about the behavior priorities of parents?

5. Interview several prekindergarten or kindergarten teachers. What kinds of limits do they set for children in the classroom? Why? How do they enforce these limits? How do they support children learning how to be prosocial? What did you learn about the behavior priorities of teachers? In what ways are teachers and parents the same or different in this respect?

6. Watch three popular children's television shows several times over a period of three weeks. Record the prosocial and/or aggressive or violent events that take place in each. Compare the different programs. Were there differences in the specific prosocial or aggressive behaviors emphasized by the different programs? How engaging were the role models? How did the commercials communicate with young viewers? What messages do the commercials convey to children?

7. With your classmates, develop a list of television programs and/or video games that might be considered developmentally sound for 4- and 5-year-old children. Make a list of their redeeming features.

8. Discuss with your classmates the role of adults in helping children to use technology in ways that can enhance social and emotional development.

Further Readings

Bruno, H. E. (2011). The neurobiology of emotional intelligence: Using our brain to stay cool under pressure. *Young Children, 66*(1), 22–27.

Florex, I. R. (2011). Developing young children's self-regulation through everyday experiences. *Young Children, 66*(4), 46–51.

Kaiser, B., & Rasminsky, J. S. (2012). *Challenging behavior in young children: Understanding, preventing, and responding effectively* (3rd ed.). Upper Saddle River, NJ: Pearson.

Riley, D., San Juan, R. R., Klinkner, J., & Ramminger, A. (2008). *Social & emotional development. Connecting science and practice in early childhood settings*. St. Paul, MN: Redleaf Press.

Rubin, K. H., Bukowski, W. M., & Laursen, B. (2009). *Handbook of peer interactions, relationships, and groups*. New York, NY: Guilford Press.

Sciaraffa, M., & Randolph, T. (2011). "You want me to talk to children about what?" Responding to the subject of sexuality development in young children. *Young Children, 66*(4), 32–39.

Willis, C. A., & Schiller, P. (2011). Preschoolers' social skills steer life. *Young Children, 66*(1), 42–49.

Other Resources

American Academy of Child and Adolescent Psychiatry Facts for Families (Fact Sheets), http://www.aacap.org/cs/root/facts_for_families/facts_for_families.

Center on the Social and Emotional Foundations for Early Learning, http://csefel.vanderbilt.edu. The Center on the Social and Emotional Foundations for Early Learning (CSEFEL) provides research results and information on evidence-based practices. CSEFEL is a national resource center funded by the Office of Head Start and Child Care Bureau for disseminating research and evidence-based practices to early childhood programs across the country.

National Center for Children in Poverty (NCCP), http://nccp.org/publications/pub_369.html. This site includes publications on the following topics related to social and emotional development in young children:

* *Building Services and Systems to Support the Healthy Emotional Development of Young Children.*
* *Key Findings from Research: Why Policy-Makers Should Invest in Improving Social and Emotional Health in Young Children*

Technical Assistance Center on Social Emotional Intervention for Young Children, www.challengingbehavior.org. The Technical Assistance Center on Social Emotional Intervention for Young Children (TACSEI) provides information and products that improve the social-emotional outcomes for young children with, or at risk for, delays or disabilities.

chapter 13

Cognitive, Language, and Literacy Development: Ages Four Through Five

Was it not then that I acquired all that now sustains me? And I gained so much and so quickly that during the rest of my life I did not acquire a hundredth part of it. From myself as a five-year-old to myself as I now am there is only one step. The distance between myself as an infant and myself at five years is tremendous.

—Leo Tolstoy

After studying this chapter, you will demonstrate comprehension by:

▶ recognizing theoretical perspectives on cognitive, language, and literacy development in children ages 4 through 5;

▶ describing cognitive development in children ages 4 through 5;

▶ describing language development in children ages 4 through 5;

▶ describing literacy development in children ages 4 through 5;

▶ describing the role of play in the enhancement of cognitive, language, and literacy development

▶ identifying major factors influencing cognitive, language, and literacy development in children ages 4 through 5; and

▶ suggesting strategies for promoting cognitive, language, and literacy development in children ages 4 through 5.

From previous chapters, we have learned that cognitive development has both biological and environmental origins, is quite rapid in the years from birth through age 8, is at first dominated by the child's sensory and motor capabilities, and influences and is influenced by growth and development in all other domains—physical, emotional, social, language, and literacy. What are we now learning about the cognitive development of children in the fourth through fifth years? Let's begin by thinking about theoretical perspectives concerning cognitive development.

Theoretical Perspectives on Cognitive, Language, and Literacy Development

Piaget and the 4- Through 5-Year-Old Child

Piaget's research indicated that children younger than age 6 or 7 are not capable of sophisticated mental operations or logical reasoning—hence the term *preoperational*. From Piaget's perspective, this means that young children cannot yet form accurate internal representations of actions because thought is still dependent on perceptions (Piaget & Inhelder, 1969).

Piaget came to his conclusions about the preoperational stage in children's thinking after conducting a number of conservation experiments, such as when an amount of liquid is poured from a tall, slender container into a short, wider one or when a ball of clay is rolled into a long, thin rope. To the preoperational thinker, the original amount changes depending on the size and shape of the container or the shaping of the ball of clay. Such children do not yet apply **conservation** and judge the amount of the liquid and the clay by its appearance (tall is more; long is more), and they do so even when they have seen the liquid poured from one container to the other and back, or the clay rolled from a ball into a rope and back to its original shape. The process of **transformation** eludes them. Children generally do not apply the concept of conservation until they reach the stage of concrete operations.

Piaget's explanation of this lack of ability to conserve was based on young children's behaviors in a number of his experiments. For example, he noted that preoperational children tended to focus on specific events (a thought process that he called **centration**) rather than on the process of transformation, or attending to all states or stages of an event from beginning to end. He proposed that preoperational thought is perception bound; that is, concepts are based on how things are sensed—how they appear, sound, and feel.

conservation
the understanding that physical attributes (e.g., mass and weight) stay the same even if appearance changes

transformation
attending to all the states of an event from the beginning, to in-between, to the final stage

centration
the tendency to attend to a limited number of features of an object or event

In addition to the perception-bound thinking of preoperational children (Table 10.1), Piaget proposed that **irreversibility** is another characteristic of their cognitive processes. Irreversibility refers to the inability of young children to reverse their thinking and return to the beginning point of their thought. This characteristic of preoperational thinking is illustrated by the example provided in Figure 10.1.

irreversibility
the inability of preoperational children to reverse their thinking and to return to their original point of thought

If children ages 2 to 3 are asked to group objects that belong together, they are generally unable to do so. Some time between age 4 and age 6, children begin to group and classify objects on the basis of their attributes, such as color, shape, size, and function. However, their efforts are not systematic, and they often forget the attribute to which they were originally attending. Late in the preoperational period, children can systematically classify objects on the basis of attributes. However, they cannot deal with **class inclusion,** or the hierarchies of classification. This behavior is illustrated by the flower experiment (Flavell, 1985). Children are presented with an array of flowers, most of them red and a few white. The children are asked whether there are "more red flowers or more flowers." The usual response of the preoperational child is that there are more red flowers. This experiment illustrates the preoperational child's inability to focus on the whole class—flowers—and the tendency to center on certain aspects of a situation—color.

class inclusion
understanding the relationship between class and subclass, which occurs during the period of concrete operational thought

A distinguishing feature between the thought of early and later preoperational children is **transivity,** or the ability to seriate (order) according to relational order, such as size, height, and color brightness. Children ages 2 to 3 generally cannot arrange a series of objects from shortest to longest. Older preoperational children can succeed with this task. However, they cannot seriate representationally, that is, mentally place objects or ideas in some relational order, but must use concrete objects to do so (Kamii, 2000, 2003; Piaget & Inhelder, 1956).

transivity
the ability to seriate, or order, according to some attribute, such as height or size

Still another feature of thought processes that develops during the preoperational stage is **identity constancy.** Identity constancy is the understanding that the characteristics of a person or species remain the same even though its appearance can be altered through the use of masks or costumes. Younger preoperational children do not demonstrate identity constancy.

identity constancy
the understanding that a person or species remains the same, even though appearance is changed through masks, costumes, or other transformations

Angela, age 4, visited a toy store with her grandmother, where their friend and neighbor, a salesperson at the store, was dressed as the storybook character Madeline. Angela hid behind her grandmother and peeked out in fear of the costumed person. Even though the voice behind the mask was quite familiar, her fear did not abate until she and her grandmother had left the store to return home.

By the time children are around ages 5 and 6, they begin to understand that identity remains constant even though physical appearance is changed (DeVries, 1969). The development of identity constancy can be observed in Jeremy's behavior in the following vignette:

Shortly after Jeremy turned 3, Keisha's mother came to visit for several weeks. It was close to Halloween, and Grandma wanted to help make Jeremy's costume. Jeremy decided that he wanted to be a ghost. Keisha found an old white sheet, and Grandma began to make Jeremy's costume. At first, Jeremy seemed quite enthusiastic about being a ghost for Halloween. However, as time went on, he seemed increasingly reluctant to be fitted for his costume. When Keisha and her mother picked up Jeremy at school on the day of the Halloween party, they asked Jeremy's teacher whether he had worn his costume during the parade. Ms. Buckley said that he had. Keisha then described the change in Jeremy's behavior while the costume was being made. Jeremy's teacher then explained that at this age, reality and fantasy are not clearly defined in the young child's mind. Jeremy was probably fearful that he might actually become a ghost if he wore the costume. The ghost costume was put in a toy box, but Jeremy did not play with it. Shortly after Jeremy's fourth birthday, he was taking all the toys out of his toy box. He discovered the ghost costume, put it on, and ran around the house shouting, "Boo!" From then on, Jeremy would play "ghost" occasionally. Keisha thought about what Ms. Buckley had said. She also noted that when they were reading, Jeremy was beginning to talk about whether the story could "really happen." These behaviors seemed to indicate that Jeremy was achieving identity constancy and was becoming increasingly able to differentiate between reality and fantasy.

In summary, Piaget wrote that as children move through the preoperational stage, their reliance on perceptual strategies to solve problems decreases. Gradually, they begin to solve conservation problems through manipulation and experimentation with concrete objects, then counting, measuring, and applying other logical strategies. Later in the elementary school years, they do not have to rely as often on concrete experiences to solve conservation problems; however, this process continues to facilitate understanding throughout the schooling years. Indeed, even adults sometimes rely on concrete, firsthand experiences to learn some things.

Neo-Piagetian studies during the past two decades have yielded evidence that young children's thought is more sophisticated and evolving than Piaget indicated. However, Piaget's notion that true understanding of conservation of number, length, liquid, and mass is not possible until age 6 and after is probably accurate (Flavell, 1985).

Information-Processing Theory

While Piaget's theory provides a sense of how a child thinks at different points in growth and development, the information-processing model of child cognition represents a systematic approach to cognitive development that differs from Piaget's invariant stage-sequence theory. As this model suggests, an individual receives information from the environment

As children move through the preoperational stage, their reliance on perception to solve problems decreases.

Cognitive, Language, and Literacy Development: Ages Four Through Five through the senses (vision, hearing, touch, taste, and smell). This information then enters short-term memory storage, the STM file, a place where the mind can work on this information. How does one cognitively "work" on this initial information? According to the information-processing model, certain cognitive events occur that result in either placing this information in long-term memory storage, the LTM, or discarding it. Unlike younger children, as children get older, they begin to employ memory, association, and other strategies to process input information. Such mental strategies include attending, rehearsing (repeating a thought or concept over and over until it can be remembered or understood), retrieving information stored in long-term memory, coding features of a concept to form mental images or representations, making decisions about certain features of the input that make it worth remembering, and employing problem-solving strategies.

In the past, children's cognitive development and thinking processes were explored in terms of their lack of sustained attention. The child's limited ability to store information in long-term and short-term memory and to apply it was viewed as problematic. However, many parents and early childhood professionals have observed that young children can indeed hold information in short-term and long-term memory and, in certain contexts, can demonstrate extended attention spans. Consider the number of 4- and 5-year-olds who show long-term memory and extended attention spans when dealing with a high-interest subject such as dinosaurs. Indeed, investigation has demonstrated that both short- and long-term memory appear to vary more widely than was previously thought (Gauvain, 2001; Siegler, 1998). Consequently, some researchers have modified the memory-store, information-processing approach by proposing a **levels-of-processing theory** (Craig & Lockhart, 1972). This idea suggests that one's attention is not limited by memory constraints but is influenced by the following:

levels-of-processing theory
an information-processing model that focuses on the depth of attention rather than on aspects of memory in explaining levels of cognitive performance

- The child's increasingly effective use of strategies in logical, meaningful circumstances that are easier to process than global or general situations
- The child's interests
- The extent of the child's background knowledge and experience and how new information is associated with previous information
- The amount of freedom and time to mentally combine and consolidate previous ideas or generate new ones
- The manner in which information is presented

Information that is processed meaningfully and linked with other background information is retained and can be demonstrated by the young child. Elaborative talk both during and after an event influenced preschool children's memory of the event, such as a camping experience (Hedrick, Haden, & Ornstein, 2009). Elaborative talk includes asking questions, describing events and observations, and engaging the child in conversational exchanges. In addition, research has shown that preschool children remember threatening or mean behavior of others more accurately than nice behavior (Baltazar, Shutts, & Kinzler, 2012). The authors of this research think that memory of threatening events may be advantageous to children because it allows them to predict threatening behavior in the future. The manner in which the child experiences information does influence their memory.

Early childhood professionals facilitate information processing in young children by engaging them in observing and attending to environmental stimuli and by providing interesting and meaningful experiences and language that develop background information from which children can draw when confronted with new information.

Neoconstructivist Theory

Case (1992) attempted to portray a model of cognitive development that integrates stage-sequence theory with recent research relating to specific tasks, developmental domains, and sociocultural dimensions of cognitive development. His theory is an attempt to unite Piagetian and information-processing theories. Case asserted that research data support the concept of general stages in cognitive development; however, he suggested that this concept does not go far enough. Other groups of neo-Piagetians continue to maintain that differences in cognitive development among and within same-age groups of children are the rule rather than the exception (Kuhn, 1992). It is believed that although children do indeed learn through assimilation and accommodation, there is no global stage for all learning; rather, each learning domain—social conventions, language, mathematics, and so on—has different and distinct stages or sequences of development. Although Piaget's theory has formed the cornerstone for thinking, research, and practice for more than 50 years, more contemporary research identifying weaknesses in Piaget's theory has provided additional ways to view childhood thinking and learning. Information-processing models and information levels-of-processing models continue to be formulated. As with child study in general, this research process is a continuous one and promises further enlightenment with each new revelation.

Sociocultural Perspective

Another explanation for children's differences in cognitive and language development relates the influence of the sociocultural experiences within the family, community, and society to the formation of scripts. Recall from Chapter 10 that as young children repeatedly participate in routine events with adults over a period of time, they develop ideas about the roles people play in certain situations, the objects or materials used, and the order of various events. These ideas are called *scripts*. At first, scripts are sketchy and incomplete and contain misperceptions and mistaken concepts. As children experience similar events and contexts over time, they develop more complete scripts.

Children at 4 and 5 years of age generally demonstrate more knowledge of certain scripts than do most 3-year-olds (Nelson, 1986; Nelson & Gruendel, 1981). When playing restaurant, they take time to decide on the roles: who will be the cook, the server, and the diners. Then children enact these various roles, demonstrating knowledge of behaviors and sequences of events such as entering the restaurant, ordering, eating, paying for the food, and leaving the restaurant. Four- and 5-year-old children often use appropriate materials to facilitate script enactment. They may use real or pretend menus, ordering pads, pencils, dishes, pots and pans, tables, chairs, and cash registers. They may wear aprons and chef's hats. Thus, as children mature, their increased cognitive awareness of the culture is reflected in their scripts.

No one of the various types of theories adequately or singularly explains human cognitive, language, and literacy development. Many theories appear to fill in pieces of a larger puzzle. Nevertheless, we can draw some helpful assumptions from these theories:

- Infants and children are neurologically "wired to learn" and are innately motivated to do so.
- From infancy onward, as brain growth and neurological development proceed, abilities undergo qualitative and quantitative changes and do so in a somewhat predictable fashion.

- Development encompasses many mental processes including perception, attention, thinking, memory, problem solving, creativity, and communicating.
- Cognition is influenced by sensory input and the individual's increasingly more complex communicative and social interactions.
- Development is influenced by the individual's increasingly more complex experiences and interactions with objects and events in the environment.
- Increasing facility with language supports cognition.
- Acquisition of the tools of learning—drawing, writing, spelling, reading, and fundamental math and science thinking—supports cognition as it emerges over time.
- Individuals possess unique cognitive styles and intellectual profiles (e.g., multiple intelligences of different degrees of prowess) that often defy traditional methods of description or measurement. See Box 13.1 for further discussion of the theory of multiple intelligences.
- Later educational and academic outcomes can be traced to the cognitive and social/emotional skills that preschoolers exhibit upon school entry and to the types of early childhood experiences that fostered these capabilities.

Cognitive Competence and Development

Many researchers have focused on the cognitive capacities of 4- and 5-year-olds. Preschool children demonstrate major advancements in executive functioning, using tools (such as drawing and using art materials), imitating others, imagination, and expressing reality through symbols and representational play. These are areas of abilities that develop during these important years. As noted by Veraksa, "Capacities (as opposed to knowledge, skills or habits) have a meaning that lasts for life" (p. 79).

One of the most important capacities is executive functioning. Executive functioning includes planning, regulating attention, mental shifting, and ability to inhibit (Clark, Pritchard, & Woodward, 2010). The connections between neurons increase and the prefrontal cortex continues to develop during this age period (Clark et al., 2010). The game of Simon Says demonstrates many of these skills. When a teacher says, "Simon says, 'touch your head'" does the child touch his head, and when the teacher says simply, "Touch your head" can the child attend, regulate his attention, shift his thinking, and inhibit his behavior in order to avoid touching his head?

One way that teachers can support executive functioning is by planning activities or future events with children. One preschool teacher talked with a small group of 3- to 5-year-olds about a new playground to be built at their school. She asked the children to share what they would like, and she wrote their ideas on a large piece of white paper. She then told the children that they could either draw or build the new playground with blocks. A 4-year-old drew a slide, a ladder to a hide-out, a track for tricycles, swings, and a rock-climbing wall. This type of planning definitely supports children's executive functioning.

Language Competence and Development

In all cultures, language development proceeds at a robust pace throughout the childhood years. Failure or inability to learn language stems from (1) environments that fail to provide adequate quantity and quality of linguistic input, (2) auditory impairments,

Box 13.1 Diversity Perspectives: Multiple Intelligences

Howard Gardner's (1983, 1993, 1999) theory of multiple intelligences (MI) provides another way of looking at cognitive, language, and literacy development in individuals. This multiple intelligences theory is culturally neutral in that Gardner associates differences between and among categories of people (e.g., gender, race, socioeconomic background) with variations in individual experiences and needs and the types of intelligences that are required and/or expected for survival within a particular culture or context. Gardner illustrates how intelligence is closely aligned with cultural contexts, needs, and experience by citing, as an example, findings that women in Western cultures ostensibly perform less successfully on spatial tasks than do men. In an environment where spatial orientation is important for survival, however, such as among the Eskimos, for example, women and men perform equally well on spatial tasks (Gardner, 1999). From this point of view, one must assume that experience, survival needs, gender, and cultural expectations all play roles in the types of intelligences that evolve within an individual and among and between culturally and geographically diverse groups of people.

In the South Sea Islands, the Puluwat culture places a high value on spatial intelligence for the purpose of navigating to and from several hundred islands. Children are taught from an early age to identify the constellations, the islands on the horizon, and textural differences on the surface of the water that pinpoint geographic information. In this society, individuals with major navigational responsibilities have more prestige than the political leaders.

Other cultures prize highly musical intelligence. For example, children of the Anang tribe in Nigeria know hundreds of dances and songs by the time they are 5 years of age. In Hungary, children are expected to learn and read musical notation, owing to the influence of the educator and composer Zoltán Kodály. All cultures have and use combinations of intelligences. Stereotypical references to perceived or alleged racial or ethnic attributes such as athleticism, musical or rhythmic ability, or mathematical or other academic exceptionality fail to acknowledge this fact.

In the United States, the heaviest emphasis in the schooling of children is placed on linguistic intelligence and logical–mathematical intelligence. In many school settings, this has detrimental effects on children whose strengths are found in other types of intelligence(s). The outcomes are better for children whose parents and teachers recognize and facilitate MI development, allowing growth and development to proceed along lines of strength in individual children.

and (3) physiological limits on learning and communicative skills, such as with Down syndrome or autism spectrum disorder (Shonkoff & Phillips, 2000).

The importance of language development and communicative competence to all aspects of child development—social interactions, cognitive development, emotional intelligence, and cultural competence—is worth noting. Facility with language and communicative competence enhances one's relationships with others, facilitates learning, and supports academic performance. As children get older, the ability to remember more information seems to facilitate language development. In addition, as children have more experiences, they internalize more scripts and more language that is appropriate to those scripts. Scripts and the emerging ability to sequence events lead to a more sophisticated level of language development: sustained dialogue between children (Nelson & Gruendel, 1981). This sustained dialogue is often observed as children play out the scripts with which they have become familiar, such as "going to the doctor," "eating out," or "grocery shopping."

Despite this developing competence, young children at 4 and 5 years of age still have a great deal to sort out in terms of language and exactly what it means.

One evening, as Keisha helped Jeremy out of the tub and was drying his feet, she noticed how much his feet were shaped like DeVon's. She said, "Jeremy, you sure have your daddy's feet." Jeremy replied, "I do not have Daddy's feet. These are *my* feet!"

indirect speech
speech that implies more than the actual words uttered

Jeremy did not comprehend Keisha's **indirect speech,** or speech that implies more than the actual utterance. Children begin to understand indirect speech around ages 4 and 5. At first, all young children take others' speech literally. Humor and lying are two indirect speech acts that appear during the early childhood years. Children around 5 years of age begin to be interested in riddles and jokes. They often create "jokes" that have no humorous element to older children and adults. Yet when young children provide the punch line, they laugh uproariously. They have the notion of the form of jokes or riddles, and they know that it is appropriate to laugh. However, most young children around age 5 have yet to internalize the idea that words can have double meanings. Young children also gradually become aware of lying. They are usually not very proficient at lying because they cannot take into account all the attributes of the addressee, the relationship between the addressor and the addressee, and the context (Menyuk, 1988).

Talking about and sharing their experiences with others facilitate both thinking and language development.

Sound Production

Many children become considerably more proficient in the production of various sounds between ages 4 and 5. However, a number of children are still learning to produce some sounds even into the elementary school years. Some children can hear contrasting sounds but cannot produce them (Ingram, 1986). One 4-year-old pronounced "toy" as "tay" and "boy" as "bay" even though she could hear the difference in the words. Awareness of the relative ages for the development of various sounds helps adults to detect delays and provide timely intervention. In addition, this knowledge provides assurance to parents that speech development is proceeding as expected.

chapter 13

Vocabulary Development

From 12 to 18 months of age, children begin to acquire an amazing number of words. Some studies indicate that young children learn and remember an average of nine words a day from the onset of speech until age 6. If this is so, by the time a child is 6 or 7 years old, he or she will have acquired a vocabulary of approximately 14,000 words (Clark, 1983; Templin, 1957).

Although many factors contribute to the child's acquisition and use of words, as the various theoretical perspectives illustrate, perhaps the most important have to do with the interactions children have with their parents and caregivers. One ambitious study of language development in young children determined that language development was overwhelmingly a function of the quantity and quality of the interactions between parents and children. Hart and Risley (1995) studied these interactions in 42 families with young children over a period of 2½ years, spending one hour per month with each family in the home and recording every word spoken between parents and children. From the transcripts of these interactions, these researchers coded and analyzed the words that were used throughout the parent–child interactions. They compared a cross-section of families consisting of professional, working-class, and low-income families. They found an astounding difference of almost 300 words per hour between the professional and low-income parents. By compounding their figures over a year's time, these researchers established that the children in professional families heard approximately 11 million words per year, whereas the children in working-class families heard 6 million words per year and the children in welfare low-income families heard 3 million words per year.

These scholars attributed vocabulary growth not only to the number of words that children hear, but also to certain interactional characteristic (or quality indicators): vocabulary used, sentence structure, providing choices to children, the nature of responsiveness to children's speech, and the emotional quality of the interactions. Hart and Risley found that these indicators were associated with vocabulary development as well as IQ scores measured at age 3 and were better predictors of variation among children than race, gender, or birth order. A critical finding, not only from a cognitive, language point of view, but from a psychosocial one as well, was the finding that children in welfare families more often than others received disproportionate amounts of negative feedback in their language interactions with parents. However, race, income, or gender was not as strong a predictor of children's language as was the amount and quality of the adult language to which children were exposed.

Other contributions to vocabulary growth include:

- the manner and frequency in which adults (parents, teachers, caregivers) label objects, events, and feelings and define words;
- incidental encounters with words, as when hearing the conversations of others;
- watching or hearing the spoken word on television and in movies, videos, and other media;
- listening to stories; and
- interacting with older siblings and playmates.

Preschool children can learn from hearing language spoken to others. One 3-year-old overheard his mother talking with a census worker who came to the family's door. After the census worker left, the 3-year-old asked his mother, "Why that lady say 'population'?"

Cognitive, Language, and Literacy Development: Ages Four Through Five

Hearing rare words during mealtimes and book reading was associated with preschool children's receptive language scores at 5 years of age (Beals & Tabors, 1995). We can't underestimate the importance of adults talking with young children, using a variety of types of words, and reading storybooks for children's language development to thrive.

Development of Syntax

As children enter their fourth year, conjunctions with *and* begin to appear (e.g., "I want cookies *and* milk"). Later connectives such as *then, because, so, if, or,* and *but* appear. Use of *when, then, before,* and *after* develops still later. Embedded sentences, tag questions, indirect object–direct object constructions, and passive sentence forms also begin to appear during ages 4 and 5. Examples of these forms of language are illustrated in Figure 13.1. By the end of the fifth year, most children also have a broader understanding of pronouns. For example, they know that a pronoun does not always refer to the name of another person in the sentence, as in "*She* said Sally was sick." During the fifth year and into the sixth year, children begin to incorporate irregular inflections into their speech. At this time, they may include both the irregular form and the overregularized form within the same sentence (e.g., "We goed/we went/we wented to my grandma's house last night"). These behaviors indicate that children are becoming aware that there are some exceptions to the regularities of inflectional endings and are trying to incorporate these irregularities into their speech (Gleason, 2000).

Figure 13.1
The Emergence of Grammatical Forms and Usage During Ages 4, 5, and 6

1. Conjunctions
  a. Using *and* to connect whole sentences:
    "My daddy picked me up at school *and* we went to the store."
    "We ate breakfast *and* we ate doughnuts, too!"
  b. Later expressing relations between clauses using *because* and *if:*
    "I can't hold my cup *because* I'm just too little."
    "I'll play with my new truck *if* my daddy will bring it."

2. Embedded Sentences
    "I *want to hold* it myself!"
    "I *want to go to sleep* in my big boy bed."
    "My mommy said *she could fix it.*"

3. Tag Questions
    "I can do it myself, can't I?"
    "Caitlin is crying, isn't she, Mommy?"
    "Mommy, this shoe is too small, isn't it, Daddy?"

4. Indirect Object–Direct Object Constructions
    "My Mommy showed Daddy her new briefcase."
    "I gave Nikki my new toy just to share."
    "Mrs. Gray called me on her telephone!"

5. Passive Sentence Forms
    "The car was chased by the dog."
    "My toy was broken by the hammer."
    "The page was ripped by a ghost, Daddy!"

Keisha was concerned about Jeremy's inability to pronounce the *th* sound. Keisha asked about Jeremy's speech at the spring conference with Ms. Buckley. Ms. Buckley showed DeVon and Keisha a chart indicating that the production of *th* is expected to develop in the seventh year. Ms. Buckley reassured DeVon and Keisha that at this stage of Jeremy's language development, there was no need to be concerned.

Communicative Competence

While young children are expanding their vocabularies and learning how to express their thoughts through oral language, they are also gaining interactional and communicative competence. Communicative competence refers to the child's knowledge of the uses of language and appropriate nonverbal behavior, and awareness of conversational conditions and constraints. Grammatical and interactional competence interact to create the child's communicative competence. There are sociocultural considerations in studying communicative competence because there are unique communication styles within various cultures. However, an individual person's communication style cannot be predicted by membership in a particular social group. See Box 13.2 for how communication patterns within and among cultural groups may vary (Elliott, Adams, & Sockalingam, 1999).

Box 13.2 Diversity Perspectives: How Communication Patterns Differ Within and Among Cultural Groups

The communication patterns within and among cultural groups may vary by:

- how much animation and emotion are expressed. There may be a range of expressiveness that is considered appropriate for an individual or culture.

- how direct or indirect a person is when listening or speaking to another person. Some individuals/cultures face the person they are speaking with directly, but not when they are listening. Others face a person when they are listening, but not when they are speaking.

- how much eye contact there is when listening or speaking to another person. In some cultures direct eye contact may be viewed as disrespectful, whereas in other cultures direct eye contact during conversation is expected.

- how frequently and expressively gestures are used.

- how often turns are taken in conversation, including when one person can interrupt another. In some cultures, it may be extremely rude to interrupt an elder.

- the amount of pause time or silence between sentences.

- how much touch occurs or how much space between two people is expected during conversation.

Communication between and among people is facilitated to the extent that different communicative styles are acknowledged and understood. Children acquire unique communicative styles in sociocultural contexts.

Bilingual, Multilingual, and Second Language Learners

Young children who since birth have been learning two languages *simultaneously* follow similar sequences in development as their monolingual agemates but with some variation. The age of appearance of first words is somewhat later. They may also blend parts of words from both languages into the same word. Additionally, they may mix words of the different languages in phrases or sentences. By ages 4 or 5, these characteristics are replaced with language use that distinguishes the separate language systems (Fierro-Cobas & Chan, 2001). The use of the different language systems for distinct purposes also emerges as children learn to associate each language with a person (their teacher), group (classmates), or situation (home or school).

Children who since birth have been learning two languages *sequentially* also follow similar patterns in language development as their monolingual agemates and also exhibit unique language development characteristics. They often make syntactic errors in their first language and apply grammatical rules of the first language to the second language. They may go through a silent period, sometimes referred to as *selective mutism,* for a brief period of time as they mentally process or assimilate one or the other language.

When children experience equal exposure and use of both languages, their development is virtually indistinguishable from that of monolingual language learners. However, most bilingual and monolingual children are more intimately exposed to one language over the other. Most bi- and multilingual children develop a preference for one of their languages, perhaps because they feel more comfortable with it or find its use to be more effective in the contexts in which they find themselves (Fierro-Cobas & Chan, 2001).

Language Delay and Disabilities

Children with language delay or other developmental challenges benefit from early interventions that provide specialized treatments, assistive technology, coaching, and enrichment opportunities. As a case in point, consider that deaf children who experience conventional sign language such as American Sign Language (ASL) since birth acquire that language quite readily and follow the same developmental progression as do children learning spoken language (Malloy, 2003). Exposure to ASL from birth appears to be key because the timing of language inputs, whether signed or spoken, is related to the level of proficiency children will be able to attain. It is also interesting to note that in spite of challenges or disability conditions, most children develop some form of communication system. Children with language-deterring challenges are best served when diagnosis and intervention procedures begin as soon as possible. With all children, a background of enriching experiences and satisfying interactions with others promotes language and communication skills.

Literacy Competence and Development

Reading and writing are tools that can help people (1) achieve goals and meet needs, (2) communicate with others, and (3) increase knowledge and understanding. These tools are essential in a literate society. Literacy is defined as "The ability and the willingness to use reading and writing to construct meaning from printed text, in ways which meet the requirements of a particular social context" (Au, 1993, p. 20).

Unlike language development, which seems to just explode during early childhood and develops naturally without formal instruction, learning to read and write evolves over a longer period of time. It occurs quite easily for some children and is quite elusive for others. For most children, learning to read and write requires some form of instruction, though there is no instructional methodology that works the same with all learners. Learning to read and write is not just a cognitive ability, but involves development in other domains as well: physical (vision, hearing, fine motor development, perceptual motor coordinations), emotional (desire, interest, curiosity, motivation, confidence, enjoyment, perseverance), and social (encouragement, instruction, scaffolding, support, feedback), as Table 13.1 implies.

Adults serve as scaffolders in children's literacy development by engaging them in dialogue about the story.

Individual children come into literacy in unique ways, depending on the quality and quantity of their early language and literacy experiences and their individual methods for attending to and processing information. Indeed, there are wide ranges in literacy-related skills and functioning when children enter education programs at ages 4 and 5. For instance, in a group of 5-year-old children in kindergarten, some may exhibit literacy behaviors that are typical of 3-year-olds, whereas others may exhibit literacy behaviors that are more typical of an 8-year-old (Riley, 1996). As with all other developmental domains, there is considerable variation in rates of literacy development among children of the same age. And as with all other developmental domains, wide variations in rate of literacy development are explained by genetic makeup, infinite variations in experiences, and sociocultural expectations. That having been said, there appear to be some universal patterns in the manner in which children come into literacy.

A home literacy environment (HLE) is crucial to children's success. An HLE includes activities such as "caregivers' joint book reading with children, teaching children the alphabet, familiarizing them with environmental print, guiding them in spelling their names and words, enriching their vocabulary through verbal communicating, supporting their phonological awareness, **graphophonemic mappings,** and more" (Aram & Levin, 2011, p. 189). Teachers and parents can work together to provide children with an assortment of early literacy experiences.

graphophemic
the relationship of letters (symbols) of the alphabet to sounds

Awareness of Print as a Form of Communication

One of the first steps in literacy development is the realization that marks on a page can convey a message (Justice & Piasta, 2011). Children at ages 4 and 5 are very observant of the literacy behaviors of those around them and demonstrate increasing awareness that drawing and writing communicate thought. As 4- and 5-year-olds encounter drawings and print in many forms and contexts, they become increasingly aware that the thoughts they have and share with others can be drawn or written down and read by

Cognitive, Language, and Literacy Development: Ages Four Through Five

Table 13.1 Early Literacy Development (Ages 4 Through 5)

Vocabulary and Comprehension

Increases vocabulary, which facilitates comprehension

Acquires greater proficiency in both receptive and expressive language

Enjoys conversation and dialogue with others

Learns conversational turn-taking skills

Enjoys rhymes, rhythms, chants, songs, and word play

Initiates story-reading and book-sharing activities

Can "fill in" missing words or phrases during shared book-reading activity

Can talk about and retell a story when provided prompts verbally or from storybook illustrations

Role-plays story characters and themes

Incorporates story characters and themes into pretend play

Incorporates story characters and themes into drawings and early writing

Can answer *who, what,* and *where* questions about a story

Print Awareness and Writing Behaviors

Demonstrates interest and increasing prowess in reading environmental print

Recites or sings the alphabet

Combines linear cursive-like scribbles and letter-like marks with drawings

Attempts to draw or copy letters from a prompt

Attempts first pseudo-letters and letters, which occupy various positions in space and may be reversed or upside down

Writes in a way that lacks conventional direction—horizontal and left to right

Recognizes and names most letters

Writes words in a string without spaces between them

Attempts to write letters; letter reversals are common

Attempts to write letters and numerals in order

Pretends to read

Writes familiar letters mixing upper and lower cases

Recognizes that groups of letters can form words

Makes first attempts at writing name, including both upper and lower cases

Starts to make distinctions between upper- and lower-case letters

Learns to write name using appropriate cases

Dictates labels and stories for art and other projects

Writes own labels and stories using developmental (or phonemic) spellings

May not follow left to right/top to bottom progression in early writing

Phonemic Awareness and Alphabetic Principle

Appreciates the fact that information and entertainment can be derived from print experiences

Conveys knowledge and shares information gained from literacy experiences

Develops a disposition to read and self-selects literature of diverse genres others. This realization evolves over a period of time. Concurrently, small motor skills such as eye–hand coordination are developing and facilitating the child's drawing and writing activities, and language development is providing labels and ways of thinking about what she or he wants to draw or write.

Access to paper and drawing or writing tools encourages this process. Young children usually begin to draw about experiences that are meaningful to them. As they think about these experiences and represent them in their drawings, they often talk to themselves or with others who are nearby about their thoughts and drawings (Dyson, 1997). They incorporate these thoughts into their drawings by either dictating to an adult what they want written on or about their drawing or using their own limited knowledge of print to write their ideas. An adult may say, "Tell me about your picture" or "Let me write down what you said." As children observe adults writing what they dictate, they begin to understand that thoughts can be expressed not only through words and pictures, but also through print.

James, Cheryl, and Angela decide to celebrate James's pay raise by going out to eat. Some friends join the celebration. Angela becomes restless while they wait for their food. One of Cheryl's friends gives Angela a pencil, and she begins to write lines imitating adult cursive writing on her paper placemat. Suddenly, she tugs at Cheryl's arm, points to her writing, and says, "This says 'double cheeseburger.' This says 'Coke.' This says 'fries.'" Angela's behavior indicates an awareness of how print is used to make a request. She has observed and has been thinking and deciding what she and others want to eat. These decisions were discussed and then given to the server, who wrote down what they said about the food they wanted to eat. Thought, oral language, and written language were all used in an interactive way to get what they wanted: food.

Keisha and Jeremy are at the greeting card store in the mall. Five-year-old Jeremy knows that it is close to Keisha's birthday and tells her that he wants to get her a card. Keisha asks Jeremy how much money he has in his Mickey Mouse billfold. He tells her, "Four dollars." Keisha shows Jeremy how the price is marked on the back of the card and helps him to decide whether he has enough money. Jeremy begins looking at cards and selects one that has pretty flowers on it. Keisha looks at it and tells him that it is a get-well card. She then directs Jeremy to the birthday cards for mothers. Jeremy finds one he likes and checks with Keisha to see whether he has enough money. Finding that he has enough money, he takes the card to the cash register and pays for it. As soon as they get home, Jeremy goes to a basket on his toy shelf, which holds pencils and felt pens. He selects a red pen and writes "4 U" on the envelope. Inside the card he writes, "I ♥ U JEREMY." Jeremy's behavior indicates that he knows about cards and how thoughts are written on cards to help celebrate birthdays. He uses thought, drawing, and written language to convey his birthday greeting to his mother.

Cognitive, Language, and Literacy Development: Ages Four Through Five

The two vignettes indicate the varied contexts in which young children learn how to talk about and write their thoughts. These examples also demonstrate how adults serve as scaffolders in promoting literacy development. Adults help children to write their thoughts, provide experiences for them to participate in literacy events (e.g., sharing correspondence, making lists, labeling, locating addresses and phone numbers), and provide the tools (paper and writing implements) for them to practice their developing literacy awareness. Thus, there are specific behaviors on the part of adults that ensure the continuation of print awareness in young children.

The first behavior is alertness to opportunities for literacy development in the home, school, and community (Schickedanz, 1999, 2008). Second, appropriate scaffolding and providing answers to children's literacy-related questions help children to become more aware of print. Third, adults provide time and tools for children to engage in the act of writing. Fourth, adults continuously provide opportunities for children to experience many forms of literature through books, storytelling, poetry and rhymes, songs, and drama. Just as children need to hear oral language to learn to talk, they need experiences with spoken and written language to learn to read and write.

The Alphabetic Principle and Phonemic Awareness

alphabetic
a writing system that associates the phonemes of oral language with letters of the alphabet

Through instruction, children learn the **alphabetic** principle, or the fact that there is a relationship between letters and sounds. Children become aware of letters, their unique shapes, and their associated sounds through the use of alphabet books, alphabet songs, alphabet puzzles, and games. They gain experience attending to the sounds of language through rhymes, songs, and storybooks. In this regard, the traditional nursery rhymes and other poetry have been found to relate to phonological sensitivity and later phonological skills (Baker, Serpell, & Sonnenschein, 1995; Gable, 1999).

The ability to think about words as a sequence of sounds (phonemes) is considered an essential aspect of learning to read (Snow, Burns, & Griffin, 1998). The precise role that phonemic awareness plays in the earliest years of literacy development is not fully understood. Although children as young as age 5 have been shown to learn phonics through direct instruction, its value over other literacy experiences for young children is questionable (International Reading Association & National Association for the Education of Young Children, 1998). Nevertheless, children ages 4 and 5 are beginning to hear and respond to letter sounds, and this development is supported through opportunities to listen to and participate in the sharing of predictable texts, rhymes, songs, poetry, and word play. Formal phonetic instruction that takes the form of worksheets and repetitious memorization of isolated concepts is not recommended at this age. Such instruction often precludes more mentally engaging instructional strategies and can interfere with the motivational aspects of learning to read. The nature of the young child's cognitive processes makes this type of abstract learning very difficult and potentially discouraging.

Relationship Between Reading and Writing

In the past, reading was thought to develop first, followed by learning to write. It is now widely accepted that children can learn about reading and writing at the same time and at earlier stages than was previously thought. However, this does not suggest that children at ages 4 and 5 should be expected to read and write like older children and adults. Even though it is now recognized that children learn about reading and writing earlier than was previously believed, this process takes time. Furthermore, early reading and writing behaviors differ in many ways from those of older children and adults. Invented spelling and the use of fingers to match the text with verbal language are two such examples.

An awareness of the apparent interrelationship between reading and writing is important in facilitating literacy development. The importance of books and reading to young children is evident when we see young children becoming aware that words, not letters, match with the oral text of the story. If young children are also provided with opportunities to write or to have their thoughts written down, they can also begin to develop concepts about what a word is. Learning to write their names, developing their own vocabulary cards, and having adults who talk about what letters are in words, the letter sounds, and what words say all help children to learn to read as well as to write. In addition, if children have thoughts that they want to write about, this motivates them to read what they have written. Thus, experiences in writing help to provide the young child with information about reading and vice versa.

Early Writing Behavior

At some point during the fourth or fifth year, most children begin to realize that drawings represent objects and people and that writing represents words for objects, people, or thoughts. However, some young children in the primary grades continue to incorporate drawings into their writing to help them convey meaning (Davis, 1990; Dyson, 1993, 1997). Jeremy's "I ♥ U" is such an example. Occasionally, letters and numerals are also combined to express thought, as in "I 8 ic krem" ("I ate ice cream").

Children's first attempts at writing may include imitation of adult cursive writing as they attempt to write their names or various configurations of the letters in their names and other letters of the alphabet that they recognize and can reproduce (Clay, 1993). Just as young children experiment with blocks and paint, they play and experiment with letters, as is illustrated in Figure 13.2. Through this experimentation and opportunities to explore writing, children begin to learn about the characteristics of written language. This, too, is a complex process that takes time and adult support.

Another characteristic of early writing is its lack of conventional direction. It is not always horizontal, nor does it always follow a left-to-right sequence. Gradually, young writers learn that print proceeds from left to right; over time, through reading and writing experiences, they will come to internalize this aspect of reading and writing (Clay, 1993). At times, letters are inverted, sideways, or in some other nonconventional position. An important concept that the child learns about print is **constancy of position in space.** For example, a shoe is a shoe regardless of what position it is in. The same is true for a hamburger, a glass, a towel, and most other objects in the environment. This is not so for letters of our alphabet. Change the orientation of *b,* and it is no longer a *b.* It can become a *d,* a *p,* or a *q.*

constancy of position in space
the notion that letters of the alphabet must have fixed positions to maintain their identity

In addition, young children may reverse certain letters, words, or phrases. These **reversals** are normal developmental behavior. Only if the behavior is still frequent by the end of first grade should concern arise. As children cognitively and physiologically internalize left/right and top/bottom orientations, their ability to perceive the differences between similar letters such as *p, d, b,* and *q* is enhanced. Physical activities such as rhythms and dance that promote left/right concepts and games that entail the use of top/bottom, in front/behind, over/under, and other positional orientations help children

reversals
printing letters or words in reverse

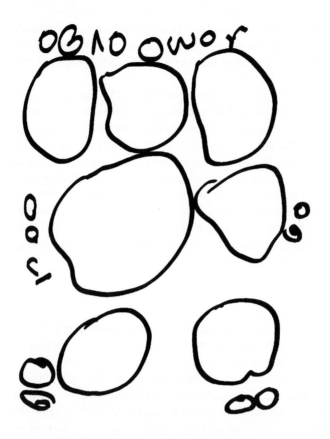

Figure 13.2
Four-year-old Jon has labeled the rocks in his drawing. He has used various letter-like shapes and configurations of the letters in his name, such as Os and inverted or partial Js and Ns.

to internalize these directional concepts on a physiological level as well as a cognitive one. When they are faced with confusingly similar letters, talking about the placement of the curved lines on the straight lines—for instance, on the *p, b, d*—clears up the confusion.

Another explanation for reversals, or mirror writing, is found in the nature of various letters of the alphabet. Certain letters—for example, *J* and *S*—end in a right-to-left orientation. Occasionally, children who have names beginning with these letters continue writing from right to left rather than left to right. As children use these letters in their writing and begin to understand the principles of directionality, reversals of these letters also appear. Jeremy signed his name on Keisha's card by reversing the *J*. This behavior suggests that he is working on the left-to-right principle of print but has not yet sorted out letters that end in the opposite direction. Sorting out these irregularities of written language can be compared to young children's sorting out irregularities in oral language ("We goed to Grandma's" rather than "We went to Grandma's").

Another common writing behavior in young children is the omission of spaces between words. They may run out of space and finish part of a word by starting another line of print below the first. Or a picture may take up most of the space, and the word is written in a vertical or other unconventional position, illustrating that the child does not yet have the concept that a word is a group of letters printed in close proximity. Children may not yet realize that there are supposed to be spaces between words. (At least this is true for English. However, some language systems use no spacing between words. Laotian print, for example, has spacing between sentences but not between words.)

A third explanation is that children may not think about the needs of their reader, that is, that using spaces between words is a convention that makes it easier for others to read what we write. Finally, because writing is a complex task, it is difficult for young children to think about what they want to write, how to make the letters represent the sounds in the words, and at the same time remember to leave spaces between words. Some children may use their own markers, such as a dash between words, when they realize a need to separate words.

Early Spelling

As children begin to realize that each letter represents a sound or phoneme in the language system, their writing becomes more communicative. Early writing is characterized by phonemic spelling, often referred to as **invented spelling** or **developmental spelling** (e.g., *bs* for *bus, mi* for *my, snac* for *snake*). Usually, young children's invented spelling first contains consonant sounds, perhaps only the initial consonant sound, such a *b* for *bus*. Later, final and medial sounds may appear with long vowel sounds, such as *bs* for *bus* and *lik* for *like*. Short vowel sounds usually appear later and are often substituted for one another, for example, *git* for get.

These early attempts to convey meaning through print provide teachers and parents an opportunity to observe and better understand the systematic thinking behind children's early spelling. By attending to the nature of the misspelling, and resisting the urge to correct the spelling, teachers can find clues to individual phonemic awareness, cognitive understandings, language facility, and other developmental indicators. Encouraging children to use their private spelling facilitates their active involvement in the writing process. Young children can be told that there is **public spelling,** the spelling that everyone learns over a long time. There is also **private spelling,** which is their own way of spelling words. Adults can remind children that learning to spell conventionally takes time, just like learning to walk, talk, or play soccer, and they can provide the tools and assistance as appropriate to help children make distinctions between their private spelling and conventional spelling.

A print-rich environment based on usefulness and meaning in young children's lives helps them to gradually become aware of conventional spellings. Interaction with the print in favorite books, environmental print, print in the classroom such as signs, labels, charts, stories, and accompanying artwork, and the placing of relevant print in various learning centers all encourage young children's growing awareness of conventional spelling (Fields & Spangler, 2000). In addition, as children begin to make comparisons between their private spelling and public spelling, opportunities for direct instruction occur. This instruction can be quite meaningful

invented/developmental spelling
spelling that young children create based on their perceptions of sound–symbol relationships

public spelling
conventional spelling that children learn through both experience with writing and direct instruction

private spelling
phonemic spelling or invented spelling that young children create when they first begin to write their ideas and thoughts

Young children are naturally motivated to read what they have written.

to the child, for it addresses words and spellings of immediate import to the learner and motivates interest in learning to spell other words.

Table 13.1 provides examples of developmental sequences.

The Importance of Reading and How to Read to Children

As with infants and toddlers, reading to and with young children on a consistent basis is the most reliable factor in successful literacy development (Bus, van Ijendoorn, & Pellegrini, 1995; Justice & Piasta, 2011; Raikes et al., 2006; Whitehurst, Epstein, Angell, Smith, & Fischel, 1994). Reading to children ages 4 and 5 promotes oral language development by introducing new vocabulary words (Hart & Risley, 1995). Reading to young children also promotes other important behaviors that facilitate literacy development.

Young children who have many story-reading experiences learn how to use a book. They learn that a book has a front and a back and that the story does not begin on the title page. They learn about reading one page and then going to the next, page turning, and the general left-to-right progression of pages. Although young children often indicate that the illustrations tell the story, the scaffolding behavior of adults can help them realize that the print actually tells the story. Discussions about the title of the book and the names of the author and illustrator, telling and showing the child, "This is where the words are that tell me what to read to you," and pointing to the words can help young children to get the notion that print conveys information about the book, the title, and the author as well as the story.

predictable books
books that have repeating patterns and predictable text

Using **predictable books,** books with repeated patterns and predictable text, facilitates print awareness. Repeated readings of these books encourage children to internalize the story lines. Because the illustrations in a good predictable book support the text on that page, young children often become aware of the text and how it works. Early on, many children think that each letter represents a word. Attempts to match the predictable text with the letters in a word may not work. Children eventually figure out that each cluster of letters represents a word. Adults can help young children to grasp the relationship of words to story line. Pointing to the text with a finger or a pointer in reading a predictable book also helps children to understand the relationship between speech and print. In this early stage of literacy development, pointing is helpful in establishing the one-to-one relationship between speech and text.

Just as young children need to hear oral language to learn to talk, they need to see and hear written language to develop ideas about how to read and write. Oral language differs from written language. Spoken language often relies on the immediate context of the situation to provide needed meaning, whereas written language must be more formal and complete so that the reader can comprehend the meaning. In addition, as children interact with books, they see the meanings that stories can have for them in their lives. They can see that, in one book, Alexander has "terrible, horrible, no good, very bad days" just as they do. They also can find it interesting to learn that a triceratops had three horns. They discover that books can provide information, comfort, and joy.

Studies indicate that participation in the form of interruptions, questions, and comments between adults and children while stories are being read facilitates children's comprehension of the stories and also of school dialogue patterns. For example, the questions that adults ask very young children about a story are similar to the kinds of questions teachers ask children in the more formal environment of the elementary school.

The Role of Play in Promoting Cognitive, Language, and Literacy Development

Piaget (1962) suggested that children follow a developmental pattern that depends on a unique interplay between innate human characteristics and the environment. Typically, 4- and 5-year-old children's play activities correspond to their level of cognitive development. The years from age 3 to 6 are peak years for fantasy and sociodramatic play (Hughes, 1999). Sociodramatic play activities are characterized by a group of children assuming roles and engaging in loosely coordinated performances. These sociodramatic plays represent common events in children's lives, such as going to the store, playing house, or going to the hospital. The play scripts are based on reality, and as children engage in social play more frequently, they expect their peers to be knowledgeable about the details of particular roles or social contexts. Early in the preoperational stage, these enactments are one dimensional, easily understood, and generally simplistic by adult standards. However, these early attempts to integrate a body of social knowledge and to allow these ideas to dictate their role playing are rather remarkable for an egocentric, preoperational child. As children's cognitive abilities develop, their sociodramatic play incorporates more detailed information and more peer participants. However, children are less reliant on play objects to facilitate their activities. During the preoperational stage, children engage in fantasy play activities. Fantasy play is characterized by multifaceted characterizations and dynamic, enthusiastic physical activity. Surprisingly, with more abstract social information, more peer participants, and a heightened level of activity, older preschool children effectively perform the task of coordinating all the elements of their fantasy play. Concrete objects continue to be used to represent needed props to support the play theme. Character roles are constantly shifting and changing focus, and new characteristics are added at the whim of the participants. Fantasy play activities incorporate new themes and new participants to suit the desires of the entire play group or the play group leader.

Fantasy and sociodramatic play contribute to cognitive, language, and literacy development in a variety of ways:

Contributions to Social and Emotional Development

Through pretend play, children are able to reenact joyful events in their lives and confront troubling ones, often playing them out in ways that give the children a sense of power and mastery over people and situations in which they have little power. They can reconstruct these scripts to achieve the goals or endings that they prefer.

Social pretend play also contributes to the development of the ability to comprehend a peer's point of view in social situations. There is then a close relationship between group sociodramatic play and perspective-taking (Johnson & Yawkey, 1988). During the initiation and development of group play activities, an understanding of others' perspectives among participants is essential. Further, during dramatic play, two styles of communication occur. First, pretend communication takes place and is acted out in character in a way that is generally consistent with the social parameters of the dramatic activity. Second, **metacommunication** (communicating about their talk and scripts) occurs as children reconstruct, plan, and talk about their play scripts.

metacommunication
the cognitive ability to reflect on and talk about verbal interactions

As play contributes to social and emotional development, it has been shown to promote academic success in later years. A review of studies of social–emotional and cognitive development found direct links between successful and enriching early childhood social interaction opportunities and later school performance (Kauffman Foundation, 2002). The findings support historical studies of the importance of early social and emotional development to optimal outcomes in many domains including cognitive development and school achievement.

Contributions to Cognitive Development

As children create alternative worlds through their play scripts, they engage in hypothetical activity, manipulating reality to fit their play script goals. This activity engages what-if types of thinking that form the basis for more mature hypothetical reasoning and problem solving (Bretherton, 1986). In addition, play has been found to contribute to the development of divergent problem-solving ability and creative thinking and has been associated with later creativity (Dansky, 1980). Through sociodramatic play, decentration is evidenced by the child's ability to attend simultaneously to different features of events or objects in the environment. This ability improves children's conceptual abilities by providing more complete information than is evident to them when they can focus on only one feature.

Contributions to Language Development

Through social play interactions, children engage in planning, dialogue, debate, and many other verbal and gestural forms of communication. They gain communicative competence as they experience the give-and-take of social interaction. Through pretend play, children can experiment with and practice a variety of forms of communication: word use, phrasing, gestures and body language, inflections, listening, and so on. In bilingual and multilingual groups, they hear and learn words and sentences in other languages, learning to accept and respond to a variety of language and communicative styles.

Contributions to Literacy Development

Using a variety of literacy-related props, children engage their emerging knowledge of print, writing, book reading, and other literacy behaviors. For example, the classroom sociodramatic center may have a number of literacy-related props: telephone with phone book and individual address books, storybooks, recipe cards, grocery list pads, note cards and stationery, mailbox, toy catalogs, TV guide, notebook, message board, and so on. Literacy-related materials can be incorporated into all of the learning centers to be used in both conventional and pretend ways (Neuman, Copple, & Bredekamp, 2000; Puckett, 2002). These experiences provide concrete opportunities to learn about reading, writing, and spelling in engaging and meaningful ways.

Bodrova and Leong (1998), who are scholars in the Vygotskian tradition, sum up well the importance of play:

> Play provides the optimal context for the emergence and continued growth of the most important cognitive and social processes of young children or their "developmental accomplishments" [Elkonin, 1977]…play prepares the foundation for the processes yet to emerge—that will appear at a later time in the context of academic activities of the school age. For Vygotskians, play influences the most essential aspects of the development of a child as a whole. Play does not simply affect discrete skills. It promotes the restructuring of the child's psychological processes and is the source of systemic change in mental development. (p. 116)

Issues in Cognitive, Language, and Literacy Development

Neurological Integrity

As we saw in previous chapters, the brain grows in response to the individual's experiences and is particularly vulnerable to certain types of experiences during certain periods of rapid growth. As noted before, but worth mentioning again here in the context of thinking about 4- and 5-year-old children, motor development, first and second language development, math, logic, and musical learning are particularly important during the early childhood years. This is a time for adults to be especially cognizant of sensory integrity, motor skills, and speech production as indicators of development or a need for assessment and intervention. Providing rich opportunities for children to experience music and movement, thought games involving numbers, and assistance in learning a second language when that is required or desired is an important way to contribute to the growth of the brain and the neurological system.

Nutrition, Health, and Well-Being

As with infants and toddlers, 4- and 5-year-old children have continuing yet varying needs for sleep, rest, exercise, and nourishment. Even though many 4- and 5-year-old children are enrolled in prekindergarten and kindergarten, their need for predictable routines and adequate diets remains paramount. They continue to need vigorous exercise and unstructured play time. To realize this, it helps to put their age in perspective by converting years into months: Four- and 5-year-olds are 48 and 60 months old, respectively. It is important to remember that 4- and 5-year-old children, in spite of their increasing sophistication with language and learning, are still quite young.

Types of Preschool and K Programs

There are many different types of preschool and K programs provided in the United States and in other countries. Young children attend state-funded or school district–funded preschool and K programs, Head Start, private child care centers, and family child care home programs. The combination of increased enrollment, expansion of publicly funded preschool programs, and recognition of the unique role of early education experiences in the establishment of education success has led to a current state in which children's entry into the system of formal education, for all intents and purposes, starts for the majority of children in the United States at age 4 (Pianta, 2005) (Mashburn et al., 2008, p. 732).

Quality in Prekindergarten and Kindergarten Programs: What Characteristics are Related to Present and Later Child Outcomes?

Early childhood programs that are sensitive to the unique characteristics and physical and psychological needs of young children play a critical and essential role in their overall growth and development. These programs strategically plan for enrichment and support of growth, development, and learning in all developmental domains and work with families to ensure optimal outcomes for each child. Such programs provide linkages to professional services to meet the needs of children with special developmental or learning challenges. Assessment of growth and progress is ongoing without subjecting young children to testing situations that yield limited information while imposing undue expectations on individual children.

Quality programs for young children meet accreditation standards set by professional organizations such as the National Association for the Education of Young Children (2004). Accreditation standards address teacher training and qualifications as well as educational routines, nutrition, safety requirements, curricular expectations, and family involvement issues. NAEYC (2008) has revised a position paper on "Developmentally Appropriate Practice in Early Childhood Programs Serving Children Birth to Age 8." This document promotes a framework for best practice in ECE. The reader is encouraged to review this position statement that is grounded in research on child development, learning, and educational effectiveness.

In their review of research on the effects of developmentally appropriate programs for young children, Dunn and Kontos (1997) noted that studies reveal the following:

- Children in child-initiated classrooms scored higher on measures of creativity and divergent thinking than did children in academically oriented classrooms.
- In child-initiated classrooms, children demonstrated better outcomes in language development, showing better verbal skills than children in academically oriented programs.
- Where literacy environments were of high quality, children's receptive language was better.
- Children in developmentally appropriate programs demonstrated greater confidence in their cognitive abilities and described their abilities in more positive terms.
- Most studies indicate that a didactic approach to instruction with young children is less successful.
- Findings regarding reading and mathematics achievement were mixed; some found better scores among children attending developmentally appropriate programs in kindergarten through second grade, others found more achievement in academically oriented classrooms, and still others found no difference between the two models.
- Children of low socioeconomic status attending developmentally appropriate kindergarten classrooms tend to have better reading achievement scores in first grade than children attending inappropriate kindergarten programs.
- Differences between children in more or less appropriate classrooms often do not appear until a year or more later.
- There are emotional costs associated with academically oriented classrooms, particularly for children from low-socioeconomic-status and minority groups.

The conclusion of more recent research is that the quality of teacher–child interactions is a key factor for emotional, academic, and language outcomes for children (Mashburn et al., 2008). Based on observations of 2,439 children enrolled in 671 pre-K classrooms in 11 states, the emotional and instructional interactions (process variables) with the children made more difference for children's development than did structural variables that include child-to-teacher ratios and smaller class sizes. Teachers' use of instructional practices that included elaboration on children's language, feedback on their ideas, and frequent discussions to promote complex higher-order thinking skills and creativity predicted children's academic and language skills. Teachers' emotional interactions with children that included providing a positive climate (teachers' demonstration of enthusiasm, enjoyment, and respect), comfort, reassurance, and encouragement predicted the teachers' ratings of children's higher social competence and lower problem behaviors. As summarized by Mashburn et al., "For a variety of reasons, it is not surprising that young children in pre-K classrooms learn more when teachers interact with them in stimulating and emotionally supportive ways" (2008, p. 743).

When children grow up in low-income families experiencing stress, rich preschool environments are required. One study concluded that children from low-income families who attended a *high*-quality early care and development program in their first five years have better math and reading scores in middle childhood than did low-income children who attended lower-quality programs (Dearing, McCartney, & Taylor, 2009). The authors of the study (Dearing et al., 2009, p. 1329) identify the four factors that characterize high quality as the following:

(a) high levels of language stimulation,

(b) access to developmentally appropriate learning materials,

(c) a positive emotional climate with sensitive and responsive caregivers, and

(d) opportunities for children to explore their environments (e.g., McCartney, 1984; NICHD Early Child Care Research Network, 2000).

Many longitudinal studies conclude that when children from low-income families attend *quality* early childhood, they:

- are less likely to repeat grades;
- have higher average levels of mathematics and reading achievement;
- have higher earning in adulthood; and
- are less likely to be in special education programs (Early et al., 2007; Lally, Mangione, & Honig, 1988; Schweinhart et al., 2005).

Quality programs involve families in their child's language and literacy development, achievement, readiness, and self-regulation. It is essential to work with families, involve them in programs, and understand their cultural orientations concerning school success (Ryan, Casas, Kelly-Vance, Ryalls, & Nero, 2010). The U.S. Department of Education (2011) provides a framework for promoting family engagement and school readiness from prenatally to age 8.

School Readiness and Transitions

Many children enter prekindergarten and kindergarten programs at between ages 4 and 5. The demands on them are changing as public policy attempts to respond to the combined growing awareness of the importance of the early years coupled with political efforts to exact school accountability and define "school readiness" (see Box 13.3). Some demands are misguided, requiring very young children to behave and perform as though they were participants in a later grade. Expectations that fail to acknowledge the actual ages and widely held knowledge of age-related characteristics and capabilities place many children at risk during their very first schooling experiences. This trend must be closely monitored by parents and professionals for its potential for both physical and psychological harm. Some school schedules logistically planned to accommodate the scheduling needs of other grades can fail to provide for timely exercise, rest, refreshment, and nourishment. The fatigue and stress associated with rigorous schedules and performance expectations often lead to somatic and psycho-somatic illnesses and behavioral problems. Where children are further scheduled into out-of-school time activities that leave little time for rest, refreshment, nourishment, and unstructured play, their health and psychological well-being is jeopardized.

Box 13.3   What Is *Readiness*?

Readiness is a term that holds different meanings for different situations depending on the context in which it is used. The term first came into use in the 1930s, when the physician and psychologist Arnold Gesell, who established the Clinic of Child Development at Yale University, conducted research on the "ages and stages" of early growth and development. These studies led to norms for motor skills, adaptive behaviors, language, and personal–social behavior. Gesell's studies demonstrated that each child develops at an individual pace but according to predictable patterns that are similar for all children (Gesell, 1925; Gesell & Amatruda, 1941). His research led to the theory that development is determined primarily by genetic makeup, with environment playing a lesser role. Based on his findings, Gesell argued that children should begin school on the basis of their behavioral characteristics rather than their chronological age.

Today, the interpretation of the term *readiness* depends on what the interpreter intends to do *with* or *for* children. For some, readiness means that a child has attained a certain level of proficiency with certain knowledge or skills, for example, has mastered toilet learning prior to enrollment in preschool; can talk and communicate sufficiently to be understood by caregivers; has mastered a certain set of "prereading" skills; demonstrates certain behavioral attributes of compliance and self-control; and meets an assortment of other "readiness" criteria. Often these expectations are arbitrary and lack empirical evidence that they matter in terms of the child's ability to benefit from the experiences offered.

In the public policy–oriented context, readiness means that the child enters formal schooling with certain knowledge, skills, and abilities sufficient to ostensibly benefit from the curriculum provided; and, from a rather self-serving point of view, that the child can do so without jeopardizing the school's ranking on state or local accountability measures. Certainly, there are capabilities that facilitate a child's successful participation in a school setting. Delineating those capabilities in such a way that they can be generalized to every child upon school entry is difficult, if not impossible. Because early growth and development are rapid and dynamic, evidence of the absence of certain knowledge or skills or the presence of problematic behaviors at some given point in time does not necessarily foretell how a child will fare, nor does prowess necessarily foretell a successful schooling experience.

Still another point of view is one that assumes that if a child can score at an acceptable level on a selected standardized test, then the child is considered "ready" for admission to a particular program or school. This practice continues to

continued

Box 13.3 continued

be widespread in spite of mounting evidence of the limits of standardized tests for providing a complete and accurate profile of a child's abilities (NAEYC, 2008).

A thorough understanding of child growth and development, and acknowledgment of the wide variations in children's experiences and accomplishments during the early years, renders the term "ready" problematic. Children are born learning; that is what their brains do. The responsibility for providing opportunities to learn rests with their families and caregivers. Throughout childhood, children grow, develop, and learn; their successes are celebrated; their challenges are mediated. When measures of supposed readiness assume a deficit perspective on childhood accomplishments, the expectations and the outcomes for individual children are less than optimal.

As has been implicit throughout this text, readiness should not be defined by what a child can or cannot do, but by the goodness of fit between individual children and the expectations imposed upon them.

Role of the Early Childhood Professional

Promoting Cognitive, Language, and Literacy Development in Children Ages 4 Through 5

1. Provide opportunities for individual and social construction of knowledge that takes into account children's intelligences, sociocultural backgrounds, and special learning needs.

2. Provide opportunities for language development that accommodate children with special language needs and diverse sociolinguistic backgrounds:
   - Be aware of children's attitudes and responses to physical touch and personal space preferences.
   - Show appreciation for all languages and dialects.
   - Avoid criticizing or correcting children's language.
   - Encourage cross-linguistic conversation.
   - Facilitate second language acquisition.

3. Provide rich and varied firsthand experiences from which children can draw experiential information and inspiration for language, writing, and reading.

4. Provide a cognitively engaging classroom that challenges but does not overwhelm children. Provide developmentally sound curriculums and materials, routines, and activities. Gauge expectations to the age and individuality of children.

5. Provide a language-rich environment in which children have opportunities to talk with one another and with the adults in the environment and where storytelling, book reading, dialogue, and discussion are valued and written communication is encouraged and supported.

(continued)

6. Provide a print-rich environment in which books, writing materials, visuals, and other items encourage beginning readers.

7. Provide centers and appropriate props and play materials to promote rich pretend play.

8. Make parental participation essential, and ensure that parents play an active role in their children's learning experiences.

9. Provide support and resource information for families experiencing poverty, stress, children with behavioral challenges, and other challenging situations.

Key Terms

alphabetic	identity constancy	metacommunication
centration	indirect speech	predictable books
class inclusion	invented/developmental	private spelling
conservation	spelling	public spelling
constancy of position	irreversibility	reversals
in space	levels-of-processing	transformation
graphophemic	theory	transivity

Review Strategies and Activities

1. Review the key terms in this chapter individually or with a classmate.

2. Observe children in the sociodramatic area of the classroom or in other learning areas. Provide anecdotal examples of the following:

   a. Children's knowledge of scripts

   b. Communicative competence

   c. Literacy-related behaviors

3. Collect samples of young children's writing. Analyze them for children's concepts about print, including the following:

   a. Meaning

   b. Use of space

   c. Knowledge of directionality

   d. Concept of word

   e. Invented spelling

4. Interview early childhood professionals in inclusive classroom settings. Ask them to describe how they provide cognitive, language, and literacy experiences for children with diverse developmental needs.

Further Readings

Copple, C., & Bredekamp, S. (2008). Getting clear about developmentally appropriate practice. *Young Children, 63*(1), 54–55.

Genishi, C., & Dyson, A.H. (2009). *Children language and literacy. Diverse learners in diverse times.* New York, NY: Teachers College Press.

Otto, B. (2010). *Language development in early childhood* (3rd ed.). Upper Saddle River, NJ: Merrill.

Tabor, P. O. (2008). *One child, two languages: A guide for preschool educators of children learning English as a second language* (2nd ed.). Baltimore, MD: Brookes.

Other Resources

American Academy of Pediatrics Reach Out and Read Program, www.reachoutandread.org. Reach Out and Read is an evidence-based nonprofit organization that promotes early language and literacy development in partnership with the medical profession.

American Speech-Language-Hearing Association, www.asha.org. Provides monographs, reports, and newsletters to help professionals and parents promote children's effective communication.

Association for Childhood Education International, www.acei.org. This is an association that promotes the inherent rights, education, and well-being of all children. The website provides global resources, news and publications, and advocacy information for early childhood education and care professionals and families.

National Institute for Early Education Research (NIEER), http://nieer.org. NIEER both conducts research and communicates the results of research to support high-quality, effective early childhood education for all young children. Research results, publications, facts and figures, state yearbooks, and videos highlight quality, exemplary practices and policies, and public opinion. You can request a complimentary copy of the video *Growing and Learning in Preschool, Part One,* which focuses on how to integrate play into learning.

chapter 14

Perceptual, Motor, and
Physical Development;
Health and Nutrition:
Ages Six Through Eight

Children are, after all, growing organisms whose development
shows an organization, pattern, and direction that is characteristic
of the species.

—David Elkind

> Health is a state of complete physical, mental, and social well-being
> and not merely the absence of disease or infirmity.
>
> —World Health Organization

After studying this chapter, you will demonstrate comprehension by:

▶ describing perceptual–motor development in children;

▶ identifying landmarks in large and small motor development in children;

▶ outlining expected patterns of physical development in children;

▶ explaining the relationship between physical/motor and social/emotional and cognitive development;

▶ identifying major issues in physical and motor development in children;

▶ describing children with special needs; and

▶ suggesting strategies for enhancing physical and motor and perceptual–motor development in children.

Perceptual Competence and Development

At ages 6, 7, and 8, children have fairly well-organized perceptual abilities. These abilities continue to be refined as children combine sensory and motor activities with cognitively challenging endeavors. Perceptual–motor development is dependent on maturation and experience.

Recall that the components of perceptual–motor development include both sensory abilities and kinesthetic sensitivity. The sensory components of perceptual–motor abilities include visual (depth, form, and figure perception), auditory (discrimination and memory), and tactile (discrimination and memory) perception. Kinesthetic abilities include body, spatial, and directional awareness and temporal awareness relating to rhythm, sequence, and synchrony.

Some important perceptual abilities during this period include recognizing and adjusting to one's and others' personal space and spatial and directional awareness needed for effective participation in games. Following directions in school (e.g., "Please walk in a single line on the right side of the hallway") requires perceptual abilities, as does the ability to focus on the dominant figure in a picture without being distracted by elements in the background, **figure–ground discrimination.** Figure–ground discrimination is dependent on size, shape, and form perceptions, which are helpful in forming letters and numbers. Visual memory assists the child in following written instructions, and auditory memory facilitates carrying out verbal instructions.

figure–ground discrimination
the ability to focus on the dominant figure in a picture without being distracted by elements in the background

Perceptual–motor abilities at this age are fostered through both large and small motor activities. Games and activities that require visual–motor coordinations, such as playing tag (large motor) and manipulating puzzle pieces (small motor), foster visual–perceptual development. Auditory–motor coordinations are fostered through rhythm and dance activities (large motor) and listening to match pairs of tone bells (small motor). Tactile discriminations occur when children attempt to tear (rather than cut) shapes from art paper. Kinesthetic awareness is fostered by such activities as rhythm and dance, pantomime, and active outdoor play.

The relationship between these abilities and school success is worth noting. Refined perceptual motor abilities enhance the child's ability to meet the expectations of the school experience. Visual, auditory, tactile, and kinesthetic perceptions, integrated with refined motor coordinations, enhance all learning.

Vision and Hearing

Jeremy's third-grade teacher has noticed that Jeremy's interest in reading has diminished. He appears stressed when called upon to read, makes mistakes, and acts silly to distract his classmates during reading times. He has also begun to make many mistakes in his math work, particularly in paper-and-pencil tasks. Upon closer observation, his teacher, Mr. Frederick, notices that Jeremy rubs his eyes frequently and holds books and papers rather close to his face. He decides that a parent conference might alert his parents to the possibility that Jeremy should have his vision checked. Indeed, an ophthalmological examination reveals that Jeremy needs corrective lenses.

When children seem to be doing poorly in school, early childhood professionals consider the possibility that vision or hearing problems exist. Although profound vision or hearing impairments have typically been diagnosed by the time children enter school, the more subtle impairments often go undetected until children must attend to the visual and auditory tasks associated with early schooling. Tasks such as focusing on print in books and other media, copying from charts or the chalkboard, following directional signs in the school building, discriminating phonemic sounds, learning words to songs, and following verbal directions can pose challenges for children who have vision or hearing difficulties. Review Tables 14.1 and 14.2, which list signs and behaviors

Table 14.1 Behaviors Associated with Visual Impairment

Red or swollen eyelids
Tearing or drainage from one or both eyes
Unusual sensitivity to light
Squinting
Excessive blinking or grimacing
Misaligned eyes (as with strabismus)
Frequent rubbing of the eyes
Complaints of headaches, difficulty seeing, or blurred vision
Holding face unusually close to reading or table work
Unusual twisting or tilting the head to see
Closing or covering one eye to look at something
Awkward and uneven drawing and writing
Limited visual curiosity
Avoidance of tasks requiring tedious visual work
Frequent bumping into objects or people

Table 14.2 Behaviors Associated with Hearing Impairment

Complaints of ear pain or itching
Complaints of ringing or popping noises in the ear
Drainage from one or both ears
Frequent ear infections
Mouth breathing
Unusual speech patterns: faulty pitch, volume, tone, inflection
Poor articulation
Difficulty producing certain speech sounds
Lack of inflections in speech (monotone)
Tendency to rely on gestures to communicate
Tendency to focus attention on speaker's mouth
Frequent requests for speaker to repeat
Failure to respond when spoken to in a normal voice
Inappropriate responses to questions, directions, or requests
Turning or tilting the head toward a sound
Need for more than usual volume on audio equipment
Complaints of dizziness
Inattentiveness or daydreaming
Difficulty hearing or being understood by playmates
Social withdrawal or preference for solitary activities

suggestive of vision and hearing problems. Where treatment or intervention has not oc-curred at an earlier age, the appearance of these behaviors at ages 6 to 8 suggests a need for professional assessment.

Motor Competence and Development

If you've ever seen 6- to 8-year-olds on a playground, you know that many of them are busy climbing, swinging, and running from one place to another. Their fine motor skills are becoming more refined as well.

Large Motor Development

The importance of coordinated large motor abilities was stressed in earlier chapters. Such coordination facilitates the **fundamental movements** of walking, running, reach-ing, climbing, jumping, and kicking. Facility with fundamental movements paves the way for the acquisition of more complex coordination and movements that are involved in typical activities and sports of the 6- through 8-year-old—baseball, soccer, and dance, for example—and for small motor controls. Motor skills advance with increasing age and are enhanced by opportunities to use emerging abilities in active, unstructured play and child-initiated games.

fundamental movements coordination basic to all other movement abilities

Perceptual, Motor, and Physical Development; Health and Nutrition: Ages Six Through Eight

Organized Games and Sports

Should young children be given formal instruction in specific skill areas, such as dance, gymnastics, or swimming? Should young children participate in organized team sports? Is there a particular point in growth and development when beginning instruction and participation is advisable?

There may be optimal periods for instruction in specific skill areas. Gallahue and Ozmun (2006) maintained that fundamental movement abilities must not only be present, but also be refined before the introduction of specific skill training. Gallahue identified three main categories of fundamental movement skills (Gallahue & Donnely, 2007):

1. *Stability movement* skills, which include bending, stretching, twisting, turning, swinging, balancing, inverted balancing (e.g., handstand), body rolling, starting, stopping, and dodging

2. *Locomotor movement* skills, which include walking, running, jumping, hopping, skipping, sliding, leaping, climbing, and galloping

3. *Manipulative movement* skills, which include throwing, catching, kicking, punting, trapping, striking, volleying, bouncing, and ball rolling

According to Gallahue, these skills do not automatically emerge with maturation but also rely on encouragement, instruction, and practice. The goal of early motor development is that of becoming a skillful mover. "Skillful movers are individuals who move with control, efficiency, and coordination in the performance of fundamental or specialized movement tasks" (Gallahue & Donnely, 2007, p. 51).

Today, middle class and affluent children are likely to become involved in organized sports and dance classes as young as preschool age. It is important, if these are the activities chosen by the family, that they be conducted in playful, non-competitive circumstances. Creative dance can be imaginative as well as good exercise. Skill training exercises for most sports can be practiced as cooperative games. The games can be played without keeping score. Of greater concern are the children living in or near poverty in our country who have no access to challenging and engaging outdoor play spaces. Many children can't even use outdoor play spaces because their neighborhoods are so dangerous.

There is growing concern over the disproportionate amount of time children spend

Creative outdoor equipment and activities encourage creative and physically active play.

in sedentary pursuits as opposed to physically active ones. Computers and electronic games, television, latch key time, school days without recess, limited physical education in schools, unsafe neighborhoods, homework, and family lifestyles characterized by low physical activity all contribute to daily schedules devoid of vigorous and growth-promoting physical activity. A lifestyle with limited physical activity is associated with a number of health-related issues, including obesity, diabetes, heart disease, and others. Physical activity, particularly running, has been associated with **neurogenesis,** the continuous creation of neurons. Vigorous exercise such as running increases heart rate and blood flow, leading to the transport of more growth factors into the brain and stimulation of neurogenesis (Gage & Jacob, 2001). It is speculated that vigorous exercise also increases levels of serotonin, a chemical neurotransmitter that influences many brain functions including mood and simple movements. Low levels of serotonin are associated with depression. Sedentary lifestyles contribute to poor physical and mental health, which in turn interferes with normal growth and learning. A study of slightly older, obese children (8–10 years old) demonstrated the significant importance of strenuous exercise by linking it to improved executive function of the brain in mathematics. "Besides its importance for maintaining weight and reducing health risks during a childhood obesity epidemic, physical activity may prove to be a simple, important method of enhancing aspects of children's mental functioning that are central to cognitive development (Davis, Bennett, Befort, & Nollen, 2011).

> **neurogenesis**
> the continuous production
> of neurons

Concerns such as these have led a number of state legislatures to establish laws requiring public schools to provide daily physical education from the early childhood grades through high school. The National Association for Sport and Physical Education (2011) provides physical education national standards as well as topical position statements such as *Physical Education Is Critical to Educating the Whole Child* and *Code of Conduct for Physical Educators 2011.*

Small Motor Development

Facility in small motor development also affects many facets of a child's life, not the least of which are self-help tasks that lead to independence and self-confidence. By ages 6, 7, and 8, prehension is exhibited in the ability to hold a pencil or other writing implement, select and pick up the small pieces of a jigsaw puzzle, squeeze glue from a plastic bottle, and cut with scissors. Dexterity is revealed in assembling models and other small constructions, dressing dolls and action figures, shuffling and sorting playing cards, and using household tools such as a hammer or screwdriver with reasonable efficiency. Managing clothes and food packaging, unlocking a door with a key, turning the pages of a book, and folding paper along straight lines all require dexterity and are skills generally exhibited by the early primary grades.

Children benefit from curriculum materials that help to coordinate and refine small motor skills.

As children enter the primary grades, handwriting becomes an important skill. Because small motor coordination depends on fairly well-established large motor coordination, most first-graders do not exhibit well-coordinated drawing and handwriting skills until they have mastered most fundamental movement coordination. Skilled handwriting, drawing, painting, and cutting with scissors depend on the following:

- Facility with fundamental large motor movements
- Facility with small motor controls
- Prehension and dexterity
- Eye–hand coordination
- Ability to manage a variety of tools for writing and drawing (e.g., crayons, pencils, markers, paper, paintbrushes, objects and templates for tracing)
- Ability to make basic strokes—large and sweeping, small and refined
- Perception of space, shape, and symbol (letters, numerals, and other symbols)
- Ability to draw basic shapes and intentionally make straight or curved lines
- Awareness that print conveys meaning
- Desire to communicate through drawing and writing

In addition to ongoing large motor activities and a variety of manipulative games and activities, opportunities to use the tools of reading and writing assist children in eye–hand coordination and visual/perceptual refinements. An assortment of writing implements such as felt markers, pencils, and pens and paper in a variety of sizes, shapes, and textures encourage children to use their emerging drawing and handwriting skills. Experiences with print, such as story reading and environmental print, and opportunities to copy or replicate environmental print and drawings, write notes, make lists, dictate, and watch others write enhance the visual and perceptual abilities children need for later skilled drawing and handwriting.

General Physical Development and Characteristics

Childhood height is closely related to the heights of a child's parents, but children today seem to top out at an average of 1 to 2 inches taller than their parents. This has been attributed to improved nutrition and health care for children over the past 50 years. It is generally believed that physical growth in school-age children proceeds at a slow but steady pace, with a slight decline in rate of growth during ages 6 to 10, followed by a growth spurt during *puberty* and early adolescence. The expected height of a 6-year-old is about 45 inches. Over the next 2 or 3 years, increases in height average 2 to 3 inches each year. Individual heights, however, can range from 2 to 2½ inches on either side of the average of 45 inches.

In school-age children, individual variations in height and growth rates are attributed to genes; health history, including prior or present illness, thyroid or pituitary gland function, injury, or trauma; nutrition history, which may be characterized by overnutrition or undernutrition; and the extent to which the environment has facilitated and supported growth. Through regular physical examinations, growth patterns are evaluated and growth problems are diagnosed.

Graphs of boys' and girls' weights reveal similar trends. Although boys are usually heavier than girls at birth, girls catch up with them, and by age 8, boys and girls weigh about the same. The weight of 6-year-old boys at the 50th percentile on the National Center for Health Statistics (NCHS) growth chart is around 45.5 pounds. Boys gain an average of about 5 pounds per year over the next three years. The weight of girls at the 50th percentile position on the NCHS growth chart is slightly less than that of boys at 6 years old (42.9 pounds), but by age 8, there is little difference in girls' and boys' weights, with girls weighing around 54.6 pounds and surpassing boys in weight by age 10 to 12 (Centers for Disease Control and Prevention, 2010).

Variations in weight are caused by many of the same factors as those associated with variations in height. Differences may be attributed simply to differences in genetically predetermined body build but may also be caused by overnutrition and undernutrition and, as discussed in Chapter 11, inappropriate feeding practices and examples set by role models. Activity levels play a critical role in weight characteristics of children. Metabolic disorders can also alter growth trajectories for some children.

Body proportions change with increases in height as slender legs and arms continue to grow longer in proportion to the trunk. Muscles of the arms and legs are small and thin; the hands and feet continue to grow more slowly than the arms and legs. The abdomen becomes flatter, the shoulders more square, and the chest broader and flatter. The trunk is slimmer and more elongated, and posture is more erect. The head is still proportionally large, but the top-heavy look of younger bodies is diminishing. Facial features are also changing. The forehead is more proportionate to the rest of the face, and the nose is growing larger. The most dramatic changes to facial features during this period are those brought on by the shedding of deciduous (baby) teeth and the eruption of permanent teeth. Figure 14.1 shows the approximate ages at which the permanent teeth erupt.

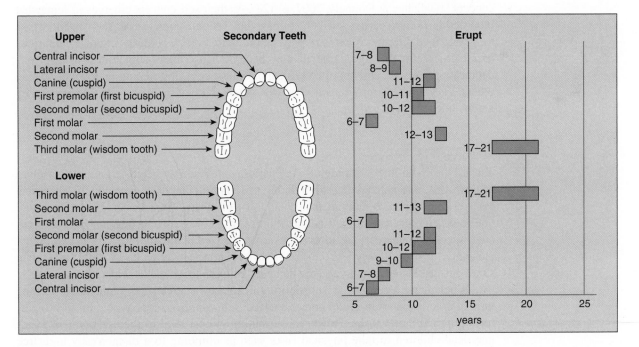

Figure 14.1 Eruption of Permanent Teeth

Facial features change dramatically during the period from ages 6 to 8 with the shedding of deciduous teeth and the eruption of permanent teeth.

Studies of growth trends in children provide interesting new perspectives on how and when growth occurs. Growth researcher Michelle Lampl and her colleagues suggested that rather than growing at a gradual, regular pace, as is generally assumed, children may grow in short, dramatic spurts, with starts and stops (Lampl, Veldhuis, & Johnson, 1992). Lampl found that some children in the population she studied grew as much as half an inch in a day, followed by a period of no growth at all for several days and sometimes weeks and even months. She also noted that children exhibited distinct behaviors before and during growth pulses, including being irritable, sleeping more, and having greater hunger than usual. On the basis of her findings, Lampl suggested a need for studies relating to hormonal influences on growth and the biochemical processes that trigger growth spurts. Her research, along with continuing studies of the growth hormone, which is released by the pituitary gland, may enable more accurate future treatments for children with growth disorders.

Relationship Between Physical/Motor Development and Emotional and Social Development

Self-Concept

Whereas the younger child's self-concept is based on general physical characteristics, a more abstract, less physically based concept emerges during the early school years. Children ages 6 through 8 have the ability to compare themselves with others and are gaining a more accurate awareness of their own unique abilities and traits. "Recognizing, respecting, and celebrating one's personal uniqueness are hallmarks of a positive self-concept" (Gallahue & Donnely, 2007, p. 128). As their self-concept emerges in somewhat modified form from earlier self-perceptions, they become cognizant of their relationships to others, including the roles they play within their family, culture, school, and various social groups. At this age, children may become self-critical, sometimes making self-deprecating remarks, and are often critical of others, engaging in putting down or teasing others. They are becoming sensitive to what others think of them and whether or not they are included in social groupings.

Self-Imposed Expectations

Toward the end of the 6- through 8-year period, children may begin to assess themselves against some internalized measure relating to some self-imposed expectation. They may exaggerate or diminish their attributes and those of others. Their levels of aspiration may not be synchronized with their actual abilities or their age. Their internalized measures are expressed in interests and efforts and are verbalized in remarks such as, "I can't draw pictures." "I'm so clumsy." "You should have seen me at my recital; I didn't make one single mistake!" and "Next year, my daddy is going to teach me to ride a motorcycle!"

When these attempts at self-definition are self-critical, the child may become unwilling to take part in group games and feel self-consciousness about abilities to perform physical/motor tasks. However, attributing greater skill to themselves than exists may lead children to take physical risks such as climbing to a dangerously high tree branch, riding a bicycle at breakneck speed, attempting to lift something quite heavy, or other risky behaviors. When aspirations exceed abilities, children often experience failure, resulting in embarrassment or negative self-regard and less motivation to try new tasks. One of the goals in early childhood education is to help children accurately assess their abilities and accept their uniqueness as well as that of others. On this point, the appropriateness of competitive classroom games and sports is again called into question. Imaginative play provides better opportunities to be a hero or a sports star, roles that can be set aside when the game is over without damage to the child's self-esteem.

Relationships with Others

Positive and affirming interactions with others, particularly parents and teachers, assist young children in developing reasonable expectations for themselves and positive regard for their physical characteristics and abilities. Providing opportunities to enhance motor skills that are appropriate to age and capabilities facilitates individual physical and motor competence and the formulation of positive self-concepts and self-esteem (Strauss, Rodzilsky, Burack, & Cole, 2001). Further, studies have found that children with high physical competence have more opportunities to develop social knowledge, which enhances their peer relationships.

In a British study linking physical competence and social status, "physical activity was perceived as a positive attribute and linked to social status among boys. Among girls the association between physical activity ability and social status was more complex, appearing to differ by the norms of the group to which participants belonged" (Jago et al., 2009).

From her study of the effect of physical competence on the peer relations of eight second-grade children with high and low motor skills, Barbour (1995) was able to draw these implications:

- Motor skill proficiency provides an avenue for improving social competence. Children with low physical competence who improve their physical skills relative to their peers have a better chance of group inclusion and improved social status and self-image.

- Physical education and free play programs that are developmental with a focus on increasing the physical competence of every child (as opposed to an unstructured, nonsequential activities approach or emphasis on large group competitive games) give low physically competent children opportunities to increase motor skill development, increase social knowledge, and improve peer relations.

- Participation in organized sports and games is a vehicle for popularity among boys in second grade, an age at which lack of participation can be detrimental to peer relationships among boys.

- Physical competence influences play behaviors of children. For example, low physically competent boys may choose quieter, less competitive forms of play (such as dramatic play with a domestic theme); high physically competent girls may choose more active games and sports.

- Physical competence influences cross-gender play behaviors and cross-grade and age groupings. Girls with high physical competence and boys with low physical competence may be more likely to play with peers of the opposite sex, whereas their same-sex counterparts may prefer same-sex groupings. When boys respond negatively to other boys who choose to play with girls, the low physically competent boys are further placed at a social disadvantage.

- Compensatory strategies may need to be taught to low physically competent children to help them to be more successful in the peer relations. Such strategies might include learning more about prosocial behaviors (cooperating, sharing, helping, having empathy, and so on), organizing play around sociodramatic scripts, and learning to use humor. Compensatory strategies may also help children to understand the effects of inappropriate behaviors, such as bossiness or withdrawal, on others (Barbour, 1995, pp. 44–45).

Gender-Related Play Behaviors

Unlike one's sex, which is biologically determined, gender is psychologically and socially constructed. Different cultures label various behaviors or expectations as *feminine* or *masculine* and may vary these labels and expectations over time relative to context- and age-expected behaviors (Wood, 1994). In most cultures in the United States, young children know their sex by ages 6 to 8 and have some understanding of society's gender expectations. This sense of gender is acquired through interactions with others: parents, siblings, peers, teachers, and other individuals. The media also play an influencing role in gender role identities. Hamlin and Ruble (2010) describe young children as "gender detectives" who are constantly looking for clues in their environment to help them understand the look and behavior of their gender. From infancy onward, children watch and imitate the behaviors of those who are important to them and eventually internalize many of those behaviors, particularly ones that result in positive feedback and affirmation.

For preadolescent children, gender identity is seen by Egan and Perry (2001) as having five major components:

(a) membership knowledge (knowledge of membership in a gender category);

(b) gender typicality (the degree to which one feels one is a typical member of one's gender category);

(c) gender contentedness (the degree to which one is happy with one's gender assignment);

(d) felt pressure for gender conformity (the degree to which one feels pressure from parents, peers, and self for conformity to gender stereotypes); and

(e) intergroup bias (the extent to which one believes one's own sex is superior to the other) (Carver, Yunger, & Perry, 2003, p. 95).

Carver, Yunger, and Perry (2003) reported that both (b) and (c) in the list above were positively related to children's adjustment while (d) and (e) were negatively associated with adjustment.

From a very early age, environmental cues and parental behaviors influence the play behaviors of children through role models, expectations, and the selection and provision of gender-typed toys (e.g., dolls for girls, trains for boys) (Serbin, Powlishta, & Gulko, 1993). Toddlers and preschoolers have been found to prefer gender-typed toys (Levy, 1999; Ruble & Martin, 1998). Preschool children's toy collections in Sweden, a country that emphasizes gender equality, were found to be gender-typed as well (Nelson, 2005). Identity is influenced through the kinds of behaviors that are condoned or expected. For instance, in our culture, boys are more likely to be encouraged to be independent, aggressive, and exploratory, while girls may be protected, cuddled, and hugged (Fagot, 1988). These early gender-typed experiences influence the perceptions children form about themselves and their gender and about the gender-role expectations held by persons important to them. In turn, a child's play themes, physical activities, and choice of friends generally reflect these perceptions.

Sexuality Delvelopment

Another development in gender identity and gender-role behaviors is the child's emerging interests in topics related to sex and procreation. This interest usually begins with curiosity about the differences between boys' and girls' genitals. Discovery of genital differences usually occurs between 16 and 19 months of age (Galenson, 1993), a time when giving appropriate names to body parts is occurring ("Where is your nose?" "Where are your knees? your toes?"). Common in our culture, however, are substitute names for genitals such as "pecker" or "wee-wee." To avoid misperceptions and distorted concepts and feelings about anatomy, it is better to teach the correct anatomical names of "penis" and "vagina." Think about it: Seldom is a child

Environmental cues and parental behaviors influence the gendered play behaviors of children.

taught to call the eyes "peepers"; perhaps it would be cute, but it is hardly cognitively or developmentally helpful. Children who, beginning at this early stage, have experienced unembarrassed, frank, and accurate information about their bodies and bodily functions and the anatomical differences between boys and girls can be more forthcoming as they get older with their questions about sex-related topics. School-age children whose earlier questions about where babies come from have been answered frankly are more likely to continue such dialogue with their parents. However, television, books, and peers will augment the child's knowledge. Sometimes, the information derived from these other sources is accurate and helpful. Often, however, the information the child obtains is inaccurate and sometimes distorted. Television and other electronic media, comic books, and other print material may depict human sexuality and reproduction in sensational and perhaps sordid and frightening ways. Information shared among friends also can be misleading.

As children get older, their sexual curiosity becomes more disguised. The frank questions and unrestrained curiosity of an earlier age are less evident. Interests tend to focus on pregnancies and babies: how long the baby will be inside the mother, how the baby will get out, and the role father plays in reproduction. The 6- to 8-year-old does not, however, seek as much information as one might think. Children need simple, accurate information from adults who understand what the child is really asking and are sensitive to the child's developmental abilities to understand. At times, asking the child what she or he thinks about a question asked can provide the adults with background information about what the child is really asking, reveal possible misinformation, and give clues as to how to respond to the child's questions.

During this age period, self-consciousness associated with modesty begins to emerge. Dressing, undressing, and toileting in the presence of others are fiercely avoided. The "bathroom" talk of earlier ages decreases, though it is occasionally used to shock or insult others. Adults who provide an atmosphere of rapport and respect for children assist children in becoming comfortable with their own sexuality and accepting of their own anatomies (Chrisman & Couchenour, 2002; Honig, 2000).

Relationship Between Physical/Motor Development and Cognitive Development

Many researchers are now engaged in looking at the contribution of physical activity to cognitive development. A large-scale, longitudinal, randomized trial found that physical activity in the classroom increased academic performance for elementary school children. The actual classroom instruction had active physical components. "Physically active academic lessons of moderate intensity improved overall performance on a standardized test of academic achievement by 6% compared to a decrease of 1% for controls" (Donnelly & Lambourne, 2011). A similar study integrating physical activity into classroom work using pedometers showed children in the experimental group performed significantly better on a fluid intelligence test. Fluid intelligence is the ability to reason quickly and think abstractly. Children in the experimental group performed significantly better on the state-mandated social studies academic achievement test. Experimental group children also received higher scores in English/language arts, math, and science (Reed, 2010), This promising area of research may change and improve classroom practices in both physical activity and academics.

Children with Special Needs

Children with special needs, developmental delay, or chronic illness may not grow and acquire physical skills at the same pace as their agemates. This, of course, depends on the nature and severity of their challenges. Although early diagnosis is essential to provide timely and appropriate interventions, continuing assessment and ongoing monitoring of growth and development progress are particularly important as children enter formal schooling and face more rigorous performance expectations.

Monitoring the physical well-being of children with special needs includes observing and assessing growth rates with attention to height-for-age and weight-for-height, sensory integrity, food intake and nutrition status, energy and activity levels, alertness, mental engagement, emotionality, sleep/resting behaviors, self-help skills, apparent effectiveness of medicines and other treatments, and competence with adaptive equipment. Movement and motor skills, fine motor proficiency, strength, stamina, and tenacity are additional indicators of well-being. Further, skilled observation includes paying close attention to the capability, attitudinal, and/or environmental obstacles to full participation in planned activities.

The Division for Early Childhood (www.dec-sped.org) of the Council for Exceptional Children places considerable emphasis on the appropriateness of both formal and informal assessment practices. Included in its extensive set of recommended practices in early intervention/early childhood special education is the recommendation that assessments employ materials and procedures that "accommodate a child's sensory, response, affective, and cultural characteristics" (Sandall, McLean, & Smith, 2000, p. 21).

Home and classroom physical activities can be adapted to increase or maintain the physical and performance fitness of individual children according to their physical, mental, and emotional challenges. Physical education programs for children with special needs are classified as adapted, remedial, and developmental (Gallahue & Donnely, 2007). *Adapted* programs permit the child to function within his or her range of abilities. Modifications in activities are recommended by the child's IEP to ensure maximum participation. *Remedial* physical education programs provide corrective exercises and physical activities designed to improve body mechanics and perceptual motor development. Remedial physical education programs require specialized training and equipment as well as the oversight and guidance of

Children with special needs benefit from materials and activities that accommodate their individual interests and capabilities.

a health care professional. *Developmental* physical education programs serve all children (with or without special challenges) and are concerned with individual improvement in movement, skill acquisition, fitness, cognitive, and social and emotional development.

Regardless of how the program is classified, all children should be assessed for skill and fitness levels before a specific program is implemented, provided many and varied opportunities to participate in physical/motor activities in inclusive settings, and monitored for enjoyment and progress over time.

Issues in Physical and Motor Development

A major goal of early childhood development is the promotion and protection of the general health and well-being of children. A number of factors influence this goal. Certainly, the child's genetic makeup sets limits on growth and development and determines the presence or absence of certain disabilities. In addition, environmental factors influence the extent to which optimal growth and development can be achieved. Proper nutrition; dental and medical care (including timely immunizations and other protections from disease); adequate rest, sleep, and physical/motor activity (Figure 14.2); protection from accidents and injury; and emotional and social support are necessary for optimal growth and development. *Help Your Child Grow Healthy and Strong* (2011) is a useful document produced by the U.S. Departments of Health, Agriculture, and Education.

Nutrition

Though the school years are often referred to as the "latent growth period," children ages 6 through 8 continue to need a well-balanced diet, as depicted in the MyPlate graphic from the United States Department of Agriculture (www.choosemyplate.gov). Their

Figure 14.2
A Child's Physical
Activity Pyramid

growing bodies need adequate supplies of protein, carbohydrates, minerals, vitamins, and some fat to maintain growth, energy, and good health. A child who, during the toddler and preschool years, has experienced a wide variety of foods and has learned to enjoy a range of foods in all of the food groups is likely to continue to make good food choices in school and other out-of-home contexts.

Growth patterns and appetite generally parallel one another; that is, appetite generally waxes and wanes with periods of fast and slow growth. During the period of ages 6 through 8, growth has decelerated but proceeds on a relatively steady course. Food intake in school-age children depends on amount of physical activity, **basal metabolic rate,** and state of wellness or illness. Food preferences of earlier years can change as children are repeatedly exposed to additional new foods—as well as to previously rejected foods—and as food is experienced in a wider variety of settings (e.g., school, camp, or the homes of friends). Learning about food and nutrition through school and other activities may also change and improve food preferences and intake patterns.

Though food patterns and habits that are modeled in the home influence a child's initial food preferences, which often persist into adulthood, peers, the media, and the

basal metabolic rate
the amount of energy required to keep the heart beating, sustain breathing, repair tissues, and keep the brain and nerves functioning

child's body image can also modify (for better or for worse) a child's food preferences. Daily routines such as meeting a school bus, attending a school-age child care program, participating in organized sports activities, or taking lessons in music, dance, or another activity create unique schedules in which meals and snacks may occur irregularly. Unpredictable meal and snack times can change the eating patterns and food preferences of children and interfere with adequate intake of necessary nutrients. As with younger children, to the extent that the adult provides nutritious snacks and meals, the child has an opportunity to consume appropriate foods as hunger dictates. Skipping meals (as sometimes happens with early morning bus schedules) should not be an option for children, and parental control of the type and amount of between-meal snacks is necessary at this age. Also, as children and families take many of their meals at fast-food restaurants, the opportunity arises to help children learn about high-fat, high-calorie foods and how to make wise selections when eating away from home.

Malnutrition

The term malnutrition encompasses undernutrition and overnutrition. Undernutrition (consuming insufficient calories to maintain energy, growth, and health) can have serious consequences for children ages 6 through 8. Children who are undernourished have difficulty in school because they tire readily, have difficulty sustaining physical and mental attention, and are more susceptible to infection, which may cause more frequent absences from school. Overnutrition means taking in more calories than are needed by the body, especially calories from foods that do not provide nutrients. Overnutrition can lead to obesity, Type II diabetes, and heart attacks.

One common example of poor nutrition is skipping breakfast, which affects a student's performance in school. Research on the link between children's nutrition and academic performance and behaviors indicates the following effects related to starting the day with a nutritious breakfast:

- 6- to 8-year-old boys and girls who ate oatmeal instead of ready-to-eat cereals or no breakfast had better spatial memory and better auditory attention, and the girls exhibited better short-term memory as well (Mahoney, Taylor, Kanarek, & Samuel, 2005).
- Children who skip breakfast have lower math scores and are more likely to repeat grades (Alaimo, Olson, & Frongillo, 2001).
- Children who are hungry exhibit more behavioral, emotional, and academic problems (Kleinman et al., 1998; Pollitt & Matthews, 1998).
- Children who have breakfast at the start of the school day show increased math and reading scores (Murphy, Pagano, & Bishop, 2001).
- The timing of breakfast closer to class or test-taking times enhances performance and improves standardized test scores (Vaisman, Voet, Akivis, & Vakil, 1996).
- Children who have breakfast show improved speed and memory in cognitive tests (Grantham-McGregor, Chang, & Walker, 1998).
- Children who participate in school breakfast programs have lower rates of absenteeism and tardiness (Cook, Ohri-Vachaspati, & Kelly, 1996).
- Children who eat breakfast exhibit fewer discipline problems and visit the school nurse less often (Minnesota Department of Children, Families and Learning, 1998).

Healthy Eating Index (HEI)
a U.S. Department of Agriculture measure of diet quality, which assesses the degree to which a person's diet conforms to the Food Guide Pyramid; limits saturated fat, cholesterol, and sodium; and includes a variety of foods

An important study that relates to all meals, not only breakfast, found that children who consume breakfast have higher overall **Healthy Eating Index (HEI)** scores than children who do not (Basiotis, Linn, & Anand, 1999). Healthy eating habits include eating well-balanced meals in line with the recommendations of MyPlate; limiting fats, cholesterol, and sodium (salt) in the diet; and consuming a variety of foods from all of the food groups. These healthy eating habits begin in childhood.

Many children living in poverty are also living with food insecurity, which is defined by the United States Department of Agriculture as the following:

- Running out of food and not having money to buy more
- Reduced quality, variety, or desirability of diet
- Missing meals for lack of food. (USDA, 2012)

According to the organization Feeding America, "In 2010, 48.8 million Americans lived in food insecure households, 32.6 million adults and 16.2 million children" (2012).

Because adequate nutrition during the growing years is essential to growth and development, health and well-being, and overall integrity of the human organism, programs serving children must be prepared to meet childhood nutritional needs. To this end, free and reduced-price meals are provided in schools and child care programs.

School Meal Programs. Begun in 1946 and expanded and modified over the years, Congress created the National School Lunch Program (NSLP) as a "measure of national security, to safeguard the health and well-being of the nation's children." Its creation was a response to a concern that arose when many young men attempting to enter the armed forces during World War II had to be rejected because of physical conditions associated with malnutrition. Today, the federal government provides additional food and nutrition programs, including the Supplemental Food Program for Women, Infants, and Children mentioned in Chapter 5, the School Breakfast Program, the Child and Adult Care Food Program, and the Summer Food Program. These supplemental food programs are made available to public and some nonprofit schools, child care programs, and residential care programs for children through the U.S. Department of Agriculture (USDA). The Food and Nutrition Service, an agency within the USDA, administers the programs, which provide cash assistance and supplemental foods to states to provide free and reduced-price meals for eligible children. State education agencies in conjunction with local school districts administer the NSLP and the School Breakfast Program at the local level. More than 97,000 schools and residential child care institutions participate in the NSLP. In addition, 75,000 schools nationwide participate in the School Breakfast Program (Food Research and Action Center, 2007).

The increase in families with both parents in the work force and the high number of single-parent families have resulted in more children attending before- and after-school programs. In addition to school lunch and breakfast programs, the Child and Adult Care Food Program subsidizes the cost of nutritious meals in licensed or registered child and adult day care facilities and allows schools to use the NSLP as a means to serve snacks in school-sponsored and other after-school programs such as those provided by nonprofit organizations, for example, YMCAs, YWCAs, Boys and Girls Clubs, and park and recreation department programs. The USDA Summer Food Service Program provides meals for children from low-income families during the summer months, when school is not in session. Recreation programs, schools, tutoring services, and other summer programs for children living in poverty can take advantage of this program.

Parents must apply to their child's school or school district for their child to receive free or reduced-price lunch and breakfast. Household income is used to determine whether a child will pay the full price for meals or will receive a reduced-price or free meal.

Schools receiving funds from the National School Lunch or School Breakfast Programs must provide meals that meet the USDA Dietary Guidelines for Americans. These guidelines specify menu composition and serving sizes that are commensurate with the Food Guide Pyramid (Figure 8.3). Whereas school lunches in the past tended to be high in carbohydrates and fats, when

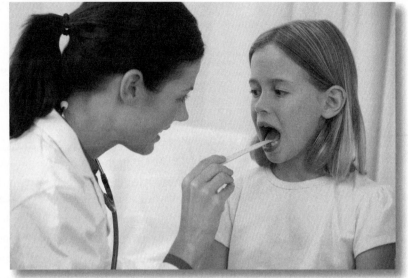

School-age children need regular health check-ups.

meal planners follow the Food Guide Pyramid, sugars and fats are reduced and grains, fruits, and vegetables are increased. In addition to modifying menus for children, attention is being given to food service strategies that promote interest in nutritious meals, appealing presentation of foods, and educational programs that enhance knowledge of the importance of good nutrition.

Obesity

As with undernutrition, obesity has debilitating outcomes, and, in a study presented at the Centers for Disease Control and Prevention's "Weight of the Nation" meeting (*Des Moines Register,* May 7, 2012) it was reported that one third of American chidren are fat or obese. Researchers want to see less advertising of unhealthy foods aimed at children, easier access to healthy foods, and better physical education programs in our schools.

The health risks associated with obesity reported by the Institute of Medicine include a much higher incidence of cardiovascular disease, diabetes, several cancers, hypertension, high cholesterol, asthma, osteoarthritis, and liver disease (Hammond, 2012).

Obesity is the most common cause of abnormal growth acceleration during childhood. In females, obesity has been associated with early onset of puberty and the menarche. In boys, obesity has been found to relate to both early and delayed puberty. Diabetes and glucose intolerance have been noted in obese children whose family has a history of diabetes. Hypertension and elevated cholesterol levels are also found in obese children. Obese children are more likely to experience sleep disorders such as snoring, difficulty breathing, restlessness, night waking, sweating, bed wetting, and daytime sleepiness. Overweight children are at higher risk of becoming overweight adults with accompanying high risk of debilitating chronic diseases and overall poor health (which includes diabetes, gallbladder disease, cardiovascular disease, hypertension, and breast and colon cancer).

The obese child faces both physiological and psychological penalties. School-age obesity has many possible causes, including the following:

1. Inactivity and inadequate amounts of physical exercise
2. Electronic entertainment (television, computers, and other electronic devices), which interferes with more active pursuits and may also encourage snacking
3. Food and drink advertising in the media, often for high-calorie/low-nutrient foods
4. Overeating, associated with boredom and psychological needs for self-comfort or self-reward
5. Availability of high-calorie/low-nutrient foods in the home
6. Parenting styles that use food to reward children or to relieve parental anxiety or guilt, as when adults judge their success as parents on how well their children are fed
7. Adult insistence on a "clean plate" after a meal
8. Failure to recognize and respond to one's feelings of satiety
9. Excessive daily homework requirements following a mostly sedentary school day
10. Inherited body types that predispose some children toward obesity

School-age children who are prone to obesity should be under professional health care supervision. With professional guidance, parents and teachers will need to monitor growth rates, nutrient and calorie intake, exercise and other physical activity, and social and emotional health. The family may need nutrition counseling and to modify eating and exercise habits. Responses of those who care for the child must be sensible and sensitive. Only medically approved diets should be implemented because the child's nutritional needs remain basically the same as those for all children the same age. Failure to adequately meet the child's nutritional needs places the child at risk for complications associated with malnutrition, decreased resistance to disease, and failure to grow in height.

Sensitivity to the child's emotional and social needs is particularly important. Care must be taken to affirm the child's dignity and worth. The child may need help in finding acceptance within the peer group and realizing her or his special attributes. The child's need for acceptance and belonging, self-esteem, initiative, and industry must be supported and encouraged.

Oral Health

Around age 5 or 6 years, children begin to lose their primary teeth, and permanent teeth begin to erupt. When the primary teeth have been well cared for through professional dental supervision that includes regular checkups and cleaning, attention to caries, fluoride treatment, and monitoring for any preventive or corrective oral or dental treatments, the permanent teeth arrive in healthy form. To maintain dental and oral health, children need to consume a well-balanced diet; avoid sugary foods, which lead to tooth decay; habitually brush their teeth at least twice a day; avoid (or seek immediate dental treatment for) mouth or tooth injury; and have regular dental check-ups.

There is some evidence that untreated childhood caries can slow a child's growth (American Academy of Pediatrics, 1999b). Ostensibly, the pain and infection accompanying dental caries change a child's eating and sleeping patterns, leading to slowed growth. Findings such as this point out the importance of dental health supervision and prevention of or early attention to dental caries or gum disease.

Safety

Children ages 6 through 8 are subject to many of the same hazards that younger children are, and some of these risks increase as they begin to expand their activities beyond the home and classroom. Their ability to explore the neighborhood, visit with friends, and play in groups or on playgrounds; their interest in physically active games and sports and spontaneous rough-and-tumble play; and their beginning use of bicycles and other sports equipment all subject them to potential hazards.

As children get older, they may be away from home more frequently and have less direct adult supervision. They are eager to do things for themselves and are often willing to go along with their friends. Common hazards for this age group are organized team sports, particularly in organizations or settings in which performance expectations are developmentally inappropriate and rules about wearing appropriate gear and using age-appropriate equipment are not enforced; inappropriate use of toys and playground equipment and inadequate supervision of children using them; traffic and pedestrian accidents; swimming pools and other bodies of water; flammable agents; tools and home appliances; toxic substances; and firearms.

Some popular recreational items are particularly dangerous. The time-honored bicycle poses very serious safety concerns. The annual number of bicycle-related deaths exceeds the number of deaths from accidental poisonings, falls, and firearm accidents combined. The use of bicycle safety helmets can reduce the risk of head trauma and brain injury by as much as 88% (Storo, 1993). Children must be taught the importance of bicycle helmet use and safe bicycling practices. Safety helmets should have a sticker indicating that they meet the safety standards of the American National Standards Institute or the Snell Memorial Foundation. Helmets should fit the wearer snugly and be free of dents.

Skateboarding and in-line skating are other popular recreational activities that pose hazards to children. Children using in-line skates, skateboards, and similar equipment must also wear helmets to prevent head injury. The U.S. Consumer Product Safety Commission recommends that children not be allowed to skate at night, when visibility is reduced, or on rough surfaces, which can cause loss of control, and not wear anything that can obstruct vision or hearing. A number of states and communities now have laws restricting in-line skating in areas near traffic and in certain other potentially dangerous locations. Most injuries associated with skating are to the wrists, elbows, and knees. Appropriate gear for this sport must include helmets, wrist guards with palm protection, elbow and knee pads, and skates that are properly fitted to the user. Participants should be given lessons on proper use and safety, including how to react to road debris and defects and how to stop quickly and fall safely. "Truck-surfing" or "skitching" (skating behind or alongside a vehicle while the skater holds onto the vehicle) must be prohibited (American Academy of Pediatrics, Committee on Injury and Poison Prevention and Committee on Sports Medicine and Fitness, 1998).

Accident and injury prevention includes both setting rules and boundaries for and with children and teaching children about hazards and how to protect themselves. Adult surveillance and supervision of play, sports activities, and sports areas are a must if children are to be protected from preventable injuries. Table 14.3 lists typical hazards at this age and suggests topics to discuss with children. In addition to the safety issues addressed in Table 14.3, adults who are aware of children's play themes and cognizant of the influences of television, movies, the Internet, video games, and advertising on these themes are in a better position to intervene and guide the focus and quality of children's play. Some childhood aggressive

Table 14.3 Preventing Accidents in the School-Age Child

Prevent Burns and Fire-Related Accidents

Older children experience more flame burns than younger children.

- Prevent steam burns—don't allow microwave use until child is both tall enough to reach in safely and able to understand that steam can cause burns.
- Set your water heater to 120 degrees or lower.
- Teach your children not to play with matches.
- Develop a fire escape route.

Prevent Head Injuries and Falls.

- Install safety guards on windows that are not emergency exits and keep furniture away from windows.
- Watch children when they are on decks or balconies.

Prevent Poisoning

- Keep cleaning products, vitamins, medicine, and alcohol in the original containers, and keep them locked or safely out of the reach of children.
- Install carbon monoxide (CO) detectors.

Promote Bike and Wheels Safety

- Require children to wear helmets when riding a bike or scooter or riding a skateboard.
- Install reflectors on bikes.
- Do not allow children to ride bikes or other wheeled objects around cars.
- Check the brakes, gears, and other equipment often.

Prevent Drowning

- Never leave children unattended in public or home swimming pools, spas, and bathtubs.
- Teach children to swim, but don't let this lull you into thinking your child is safe in the water.
- Install fences according to code around a home pool or spa.
- Learn CPR.
- Install an alarm to alert you if anybody wanders into a pool area.

Promote Playground Safety

- Check playground equipment to ensure safety.
- Remove hood and neck drawstrings from sweatshirts, coats, etc. to prevent strangulation.
- Teach children to behave appropriately on playgrounds.

Promote Car and Pedestrian Safety

- Never allow children to play in a car alone.
- Always buckle your children up for safety. (Check the American Academy of Pediatrics [AAP] website for up-to-date information on the latest recommendations for car seats and safety in cars.)
- Children are still impulsive at this age, so do not allow children to walk alone on sidewalks and roads.

Note: This list does not cover all safety hazards for children and families. Please see the AAP Web site and Safe Kids Web site for more information.

Source: Adapted from Safe Kids U.S.A. (2009). Retrieved from http://www.safekids.org/safety-basics/big-kids/at-home.

and violent behaviors have been associated with specific media events and the behaviors of individuals children admire both at home and in the media. Mediating these impressions is an important responsibility of parents and adults who work with young children.

Exposure to Violence and Asocial Models

Violence is sadly a part of the landscape of childhood today. Children are exposed to it on many fronts, vicariously through the electronic and print media, tangentially as witnesses, directly as victims, and sometimes as perpetrators. Violence in the lives of children has become so pervasive in recent years that education and health care professionals, legislative and law enforcement agencies, and numerous faith-based and civic organizations have launched various campaigns, education programs, and research studies in an attempt to understand and curtail it. Studies reveal that having witnessed or having been victimized by violence during childhood is strongly correlated with violence and weapon carrying in adolescents (Browne & Hamilton-Giachristis, 2005; Huesmann, Moise-Titus, Podolski, & Eron, 2003). Further, children who have been victims of physical or emotional abuse are more prone to aggressive behaviors than children who have not had these experiences (Garbarino, 1999). Excessive viewing of violent content on television has been linked to depression and violence in children (Singer, Slovak, Frierson, & York, 1998). A study of parents' beliefs about how children would react to finding guns revealed that most believed that their children would not touch guns that they found, often reasoning that children were "too smart" or "knew better" (Connor & Wesolowski, 2003). Yet gun accident statistics render these parental assumptions dangerously inaccurate. American children under age 15 are 12 times more likely to die from gunfire than children in 25 other industrialized countries combined (Children's Defense Fund, 2005). In 1998, 3,761 children and teens lost their lives to gunfire. This computes to one child every 2½ hours, 10 children and teens every day, more than 70 young lives every week.

These and other studies of the prevalence and effects of violence in the lives of children have been widely researched and reported. The findings are disquieting. Parents and professionals can play a role in its prevention in the following ways:

1. Establish healthy routines that not only support growth and development, but build attitudes of respect and caring for one's health and well-being and that of others.

2. Promote and facilitate the development of positive attitudes toward oneself and others.

3. Provide constructive, health-promoting, enjoyable outlets for energy, interests, and talents, and encourage best efforts without undue pressure to succeed or "win."

4. Select toys, books, video games, music, movies, and other recreational activities for their prosocial qualities, avoiding those that encourage or glamorize aggressive, violent, or provocative behaviors.

5. Teach children to resist pressure from friends and the media to buy inappropriate toys or games; help them to become discerning consumers, able to resist cleverly advertised but unacceptable products or activities.

6. Set limits on television viewing (and other entertainment media: videos, video games, music), and provide substitute activities when content is inappropriate. Monitor and set limits and guidelines on the use of the computer and the Internet.

7. Provide many opportunities for children to interact and play with other children in wholesome contexts.

8. Teach children how to respond to angry, aggressive, bullying, or threatening behaviors of others.

9. Teach children how to safely care for themselves when adults are not present, including how to handle emergencies and contact parents or other supervising adults.

10. Plan for supervision, and monitor safe and productive after-school activities.

11. Model and teach anger management, conflict resolution, and negotiating skills.

12. Be available to children to engage in dialogue; answer questions; respond to concerns, fears, or anxieties; buffer daily challenges; and celebrate successes.

13. Encourage relationships with good citizen role models among peers and adults.

14. Help children to set personal goals and to prioritize the use of their time and money.

15. Encourage, facilitate, and acknowledge academic effort and success, and advocate for acceptance of individual differences and the uniqueness of each child.

Position statements and guidelines for parents have been published by various professional and civic organizations in an effort to provide information and safety precautions on subjects associated with violence: handguns and other dangerous weapons, television, video games, the Internet, music, advertising, toys and games, the need for street-smart behaviors, dealing with aggression, handling stress and frustration, learning to resolve conflicts, and many other topics. In addition, efforts to provide support and education for families who are at risk for violence and abuse also have been widespread. Protecting the often fragile and vulnerable mental health of children, particularly during the years when neurological development is profound, is of critical importance. Numerous studies have documented a relationship between exposure to violence and childhood social and emotional development—a warning that cannot be dismissed.

Child Maltreatment, Abuse, and Neglect

Four types of child abuse have been identified—physical, sexual, emotional abuse, and neglect (Lowenthal, 2001). All of these can have a profound effect on children's physical and motor development as well as their social, emotional, and cognitive development. Physical abuse is defined differently based on the society and cultural norms and laws, but in many countries, the definition requires that a physical mark be apparent on the child or that the abusive act is witnessed. Child neglect can include a deficient diet, inadequate medical care, lack of supervision, and inadequate housing and educational opportunities.

Physical growth can be a significant problem among children who have experienced long-term physical abuse. One study (Oliva'n, 2003) reported that children who had suffered both long-term (more than six months) physical neglect and emotional abuse were significantly shorter than children who had not been abused when they entered a residential facility between 24 and 48 months of age. Within one year, however, these children were able show a significant catch-up for growth in height and weight, while still remaining below their typical peers. This study shows the beneficial effect of identifying physical neglect early in a child's life and providing appropriate interventions.

Teachers and other school professionals have an opportunity to observe children and identify abuse on a daily basis (Horton & Cruise, 2001). Dentists and physicians also have the responsibility to report suspected cases of abuse and neglect. The American Academy of Pediatrics (2010), discussing the oral and dental aspects of child abuse and neglect, reports that injuries of the head, face, and neck occur in more than half of the cases of child abuse and that because the oral cavity is so central to communication and nutrition, it may often be the central focus of child abuse and neglect. One type of abuse involving the oral cavity includes dental neglect (dental caries, periodontal diseases, and other oral conditions) that can lead to pain and infection and can adversely affect children's learning and normal growth and development. It is important that teachers and those in the medical profession know the symptoms of all types of abuse including physical abuse and neglect.

Risky Behaviors

Children who are healthy are not just free of disease, but, importantly, are learning to make choices that promote health and well-being. They understand concepts of risk and danger and are learning to avoid situations that place their health and safety in jeopardy or jeopardize the health and safety of others. This developmental goal takes time, guidance, and education to achieve.

Children of elementary school age do not have complete self-control, often act on impulse, are seldom good judges of character or situational potential, and have had limited life experiences. Hence, risky behaviors such as failing to follow safety precautions, testing boundaries and the limits of authority, exploring the enticements of risky friends, and succumbing to curiosities that lead them into danger are not uncommon. In the absence of guidance and education, the origins of risky behaviors such as experimentation with medicines, illicit drugs, tobacco, and alcohol and early sexual activity seen in some older children can rest in these early explorations.

Few data exist on the prevalence of these latter risky behaviors among children younger than age 12, but studies of the age of initiation reveal that some children engage in these behaviors at or before age 10. The 1996 Youth Risk Behavior Survey found that 11% of children age 16 who smoked began smoking at or before age 10 (Everett et al., 1999). Studies of other risky behaviors found that initiation of the use of alcohol occurred by fifth grade or earlier in 14% of the children studied, inhalants in 6.9%, smokeless tobacco in 4.5%, and marijuana in 3.2% (Johnson, O'Malley, & Bachman, 2001). The National Center for Health Statistics (2002) reported that, though it is rare, some girls under age 13 have given birth. In 1998, 202 girls age 12 gave birth, 23 girls age 11 gave birth, and 5 girls age 10 gave birth. Sexual activity is more prevalent among young boys than young girls, with 12.2% compared with 4.4%, respectively, reporting first intercourse before age 13 (Centers for Disease Control and Prevention [CDC], 2000). Both the short- and the long-term health and social consequences of these behaviors in children (and adolescents) have been widely publicized, are of serious concern, and include short- and long-term health problems, brain damage, early death from illness and accidents, learning disabilities, emotional problems, delinquent and criminal behaviors, social rejection, and dropping out of school.

Many factors contribute to the initiation of risky behaviors, and there are few guarantees of a "risk-free" child. However, prevention begins in early childhood and entails many of the same precautions as those listed in the discussion of violence in children's lives. Additionally, parents and other adults (teachers, caregivers, counselors, group leaders) should conscientiously monitor the risky behaviors and attitudes of young and elementary-age children. Without overresponding to typical age-related behaviors, it is important to note the frequency and tenacity with which children engage in risky behaviors, while setting age-appropriate expectations for behaviors (discussed in the chapters dealing with social and emotional development) and providing logical, reasonable, predictable, and consistent limits and guidelines. Teaching children, both at home and at school, the importance of good health and safety habits, the consequences of poor health, and the risks involved in certain behaviors is needed if they are to learn to protect themselves and make wise choices in the face of curiosity and temptations.

The young child who is in self-care has been referred to as the "latchkey child," so named for the house key worn on a string around the child's neck or pinned to clothing to allow entry into the home upon return from school or other activities. There is good reason to be concerned about this practice. Children in self-care, or cared for by a sibling, are at risk for accidents and injuries, social and behavior problems, and academic achievement and school adjustment problems (Vandivere, Tout, Capizzano, & Zaslow, 2003). Children in self-care are vulnerable to a host of in-home risks including exploitation, physical and sexual abuse, household accidents and exposure to toxic substances, and experimentation with unsecured medicines, drugs, alcohol, tobacco, and firearms. Telephone, television, and computer use are unsupervised. Children in self-care often experience isolation and loneliness and miss desired opportunities to participate in nonschool-related activities and interactions with friends.

Few 6- to 9-year-old children are mature enough to care for themselves on a regular basis, and they lack the experience and judgment to make quick and appropriate decisions in emergency situations. Vandivere et al. (2003) drew data from the 1999 National Survey of America's Families to determine the circumstances under which children are left in self-care. The studies determined that two groups of children may be particularly vulnerable: the youngest latch-key children and low-income children. Younger school-age children are at risk for the reasons stated previously; low-income children's risks are increased with the likelihood of living in unsafe neighborhoods (Vandivere et al., 2003). Both groups of children lose opportunities to benefit from adult guidance, social interaction, and enrichment opportunities provided through high-quality child care or after-school programs. School and community planners and policy makers can assist families by encouraging and providing other options such as high-quality child care after school and also during nontraditional hours (e.g., for parents who are employed evenings or weekends), publicizing resource and referral systems where parents can locate high-quality programs and activities or qualified, trained adults, and offering specialized training for babysitters.

The benefits of high-quality out-of-school time have been documented in a number of studies. Some have found that children who attend high-quality after-school programs have better peer relations, emotional adjustment, grades, and conduct in school than their peers who do not participate in after-school programs. In high-quality programs, children spend less time watching television and enjoy more opportunities to learn and participate in enrichment activities (Baker & Witt, 1996; Posner & Vandell, 1994). Another study found that children who are supervised by adults during out-of-school time have better social skills and higher self-esteem than their peers who spend a greater deal of time unsupervised after school (Witt, 1997). In still another study, teachers and principals reported more cooperative behaviors and greater ability to handle conflicts among children who attended high-quality after-school programs. They also reported these children as having more interest in recreational reading and achieving higher grades.

Safe and healthy settings provide nutritious snacks, opportunities to rest, enriching play activities, satisfying and enjoyable interactions with other children, guidance from nurturing and supportive adults, and help with homework. Such programs can provide a wide range of opportunities and experiences for children, including library times; field trips; participation in organizations such as Cub Scouts, Boy Scouts, Girl Scouts, Camp Fire Girls and Boys, and similar groups; arts and crafts activities using community volunteers; guided music and dance opportunities; instruction in specific games and sports and many others. Such efforts to enrich out-of-school time for children provide positive experiences through which children can build social relationships and self-confidence. Remember, all children need down time during the day, particularly after a day of school. Unstructured, unencumbered time may be more important than well-intentioned planned activities.

Rather than being unsupervised, children can benefit from after-school programs in many ways.

Role of the Early Childhood Professional

Enhancing Physical and Motor Development in Children Ages 6 Through 8

1. Provide safe, hygienic, and healthy surroundings for children.
2. Provide for the child's nutritional needs.
3. Prevent the spread of childhood diseases through immunization requirements for group participation, and take all appropriate precautions to protect children from disease.
4. Insist on regular dental checkups and appropriate vision and hearing examinations.
5. Establish healthy routines for food, drink, rest, sleep, play, and physical fitness activities.
6. Maintain a reasonably stress-free physical, emotional, social, and academic environment.
7. Provide opportunities to refine perceptual–motor abilities.
8. Provide age-appropriate and developmentally appropriate games, play equipment, and sports activities and protective sports attire.
9. Ensure the child's safety through adequate planning, rules, supervision, and education.
10. Facilitate satisfying and supportive social and emotional interactions with peers, family, and others.
11. Encourage a sense of responsibility for one's health maintenance and safety.
12. Promote high-quality, enriching out-of-school time opportunities.

Perceptual, Motor, and Physical Development; Health and Nutrition: Ages Six Through Eight

Key Terms

basal metabolic rate
figure–ground
  discrimination

fundamental movements
Healthy Eating Index (HEI)
neurogenesis

Review Strategies and Activities

1. Review the key terms individually or with a classmate.

2. Select several children ages 6 to 8. Ask them what three gifts they would like to receive for their birthdays. Compare the boys' and the girls' preferences. How many of the items are gender stereotypical? How many are not gender specific? How many are opposite-gender items? Compare your survey with that of a classmate. What trends do you see in gender-related toys or gift preferences of boys and girls in this age range?

3. Visit a physical education class in which physically challenged children participate. What kinds of activities are planned for these children? What types of other-mediated activities take place? What physical and motor benefits can be realized from physical education activities? How do these activities differ from traditional physical education requirements?

4. Attend an organized sports event for children in the 6- to 8-year age range. What fundamental movement abilities are required for the sport? Are the expectations developmentally appropriate? Does each child have an opportunity to participate? Is the coach sensitive to age and individual differences? Are children's needs for rest and refreshments met? Are children required to wear and use appropriate safety gear and equipment? What appears to be the emphasis expressed by adults: winning or opportunities to learn, participation, and fun?

5. Collect a month's supply of public school breakfast and lunch menus. Compare them for child appeal, adherence to MyPlate, variety, and estimated calorie content.

6. Interview several families where both the mother and father are employed outside the home or a single mother or father is employed outside the home. What challenges do they have for finding after-school care? What after-school programs are available in their community? What is the cost for the family?

7. Interview several children in this age group concerning how much time they spend outdoors. How much of this time is playing organized games and sports? Conversely, how much of their time is watching TV or playing/working on the computer? Ask the children what they wish they could do after school.

Further Readings

Carlson, F. (2011). *Big body play: Why boisterous, vigorous, and very physical play is essential to children's development and learning.* Washington, DC: NAEYC.

Trawick-Smith, J. (2010). *From playpen to playground—The importance of physical play for the motor development of young children: Annotated bibliography.* Retrieved from National Center for Physical Development and Outdoor Play (2010), www.aahperd.org/headstartbodystart/activityresources/upload/BenefitsOfPlay_AnnoBib.pdf.

Other Resources

American Dietetic Association, www.eatright.org/Public/. Provides information concerning childhood obesity, healthy weight loss, nutrition for life, and food and nutrition topics including a document titled *Making Fitness Fun for the Whole Family.*

American Academy of Pediatrics, www.aap.org. American Academy of Pediatrics TIPP (The Injury Prevention Program) provides age-related health and safety sheets on topics such as water safety, safety tips for the holidays, and sports safety.

Child Trends, www.childtrends.org. An independent research and policy center that focuses on research concerning poverty, child welfare, early childhood development, education, fatherhood and parenting, health, evaluation, and indicators of child well-being.

National Resource Center for Health and Safety in Child Care and Early Education, http://nrckids.org. Includes documents on preventing childhood obesity in early care and education programs.

Safe Kids, USA: Preventing Injuries: At home, at Play, and on the Way, www.safekids.org. Provides top tips every parent needs to keep kids safe.

United States Department of Agriculture (USDA), Center for Nutrition Policy and Promotion, ChooseMyPlate, www.choosemyplate.gov. Guidelines from the USDA for nutritional needs of children as well as activities to teach children about nutrition.

chapter 15

Emotional and Social Development: Ages Six Through Eight

If you see a child without a smile, give him yours.

—Talmud

After studying this chapter, you will demonstrate comprehension by:

▶ relating selected theories to the study of emotional and social development during ages 6 through 8;

▶ discussing selected emotional and social experiences associated with brain growth and neurological development during ages 6 through 8;

▶ identifying major emotional and social milestones in development during this period;

▶ describing factors that influence emotional and social development in young school-age children; and

▶ describing the role of adults in facilitating healthy emotional and social development of 6- through 8-year-olds.

In a popular U.S. Children's Bureau booklet from the 1960s, the 6- to 8-year-old is described as a "commuter to the wonderful outside world of middle childhood," traveling "back and forth between the outside world and the smaller more personal one of [the] family." The child's travels are said to start with short trips at age 6, becoming longer trips away from the family's "home station" with increasing age (Chilman, 1966, p. 5).

As this description implies, the social and emotional experiences of the 6- through 8-year-old are beginning to expand rapidly beyond the home and family. By age 6, children are growing less dependent on their parents and are now encountering widening circles of influence. Curiosity and a desire to know more about the world beyond home and school spur more outward-bound interests. This includes a growing interest in the adult world, which is characterized by listening more intently to adult conversations and seeking to be included in more adult-like activities.

During this age period, some children are highly active, boisterous, sometimes verbally aggressive, and teasing, while others are more sedentary, quiet, or withdrawn. Children can usually play games with rules, although at times they may still want to change the rules in their favor. Most children this age enjoy playful interactions that employ humor, jokes, and riddles. Giggling and teasing are also typical. Helpfulness and consideration of others are more evident, and friendships are assuming prominent roles in the child's life. Many children are becoming more self-critical and self-conscious while struggling to gain greater self-confidence. Children may react with both interest and hostility toward the opposite sex. What do these descriptions tell us about the 6- through 8-year-old's social and emotional development? Let us begin the discussion by revisiting several of the theories that attempt to explain social and emotional development as they apply to the development of school-age children.

Theoretical Perspectives on Emotional and Social Development

Erikson's Psychosocial Theory: Industry Versus Inferiority

As depicted in Figure 15.1, between ages 6 and 11, the child is in Erikson's fourth stage of psychosocial development, in which the development of a sense of industry versus inferiority is the psychosocial conflict to be resolved. The fantasy and make-believe of earlier years begin to defer to more reality-based thinking and play themes. Children at this stage are eager to learn how things work and want to master "real" tasks. Process characterized the efforts of previous stages, whereas products are now important, as

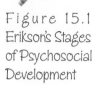

Figure 15.1
Erikson's Stages of Psychosocial Development

Supported by a healthy sense of trust, autonomy, and initiative, a sense of industry facilitates learning and enhances self-confidence.

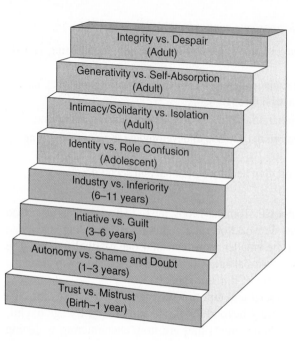

- Integrity vs. Despair (Adult)
- Generativity vs. Self-Absorption (Adult)
- Intimacy/Solidarity vs. Isolation (Adult)
- Identity vs. Role Confusion (Adolescent)
- Industry vs. Inferiority (6–11 years)
- Intiative vs. Guilt (3–6 years)
- Autonomy vs. Shame and Doubt (1–3 years)
- Trust vs. Mistrust (Birth–1 year)

children begin to take pride in their abilities to create and to produce. Art projects, blocks and other constructions, cooking, and participating in household chores become sources of pride and accomplishment. The child's activities are, in a word, *industrious*.

At this time, formal schooling takes on new importance to the child, setting goals and expectations, imposing limits on behaviors and activities, and multiplying social interactions. The child is eager to learn the real skills that school can teach, and the child's sense of competence becomes vulnerable to the influences of classmates, teachers, curriculums, grades, and comparative test scores. Success with school tasks fosters a sense of competence, self-worth, and **industry.** However, for the child who experiences too many failures in school, either academic or social, the sense of industry can be intruded on or even overridden by a sense of inferiority. Confidence and feelings of self-worth begin to suffer, as do social interactions, when children develop negative self-regard.

As children begin to develop a sense of industry (or inferiority), their individual skills and personal interests become more evident. Aspirations emerge, though levels of aspirations often outpace capabilities. Participation in a broad array of age-appropriate activities helps children to recognize and appreciate their skill areas and the products of their labors. The fifth stage of psychosocial development, developing a sense of identity (versus role confusion), has its origins in these early discoveries of skills/interests and their subsequent development.

industry
the sense of mastery of social and academic skills necessary to feel self-assured

Development of Self-Theory

Fully Functioning Person. Through his work in counseling and psychotherapy, Carl Rogers (1961; Rogers & Freiberg, 1994) became interested in how the unique self evolves and what it means to be a fully functioning person. He believed that each individual is striving to become a fully functioning person. Rogers's self-theory proposes that each individual's perceptions of his or her countless experiences are subjective and private and hold special meanings for the individual. Self-concept emerges from these subjective perceptions.

In Rogers's theory, a fully functioning person is self-accepting, governed by his or her expectations rather than the expectations of others, and open to new experiences. She or he has no need to mask or repress unpleasant thoughts, feelings, or memories. The fully functioning person accepts others as separate and different individuals and can tolerate behaviors in others that he or she would not exhibit.

Adults help a child in this process of becoming a fully functioning individual when they do the following:

1. Recognize and accept their feelings and recognize the role their own feelings and attitudes play in their interactions and relationships with the child
2. Establish relationships with the child that are characterized by acceptance, rapport, mutual support, and recognition
3. Recognize and accept the child's feelings (both positive and negative) and help the child to find constructive outlets for the expression of feelings
4. Assume a helping role in which genuine understanding and empathy are effectively communicated to the child
5. Support the child's growing sense of self by helping the child to recognize and build on his or her strengths and capabilities

Self-actualization. As discussed briefly in Chapter 1, Maslow (1968, 1970) described a hierarchy of human needs leading to self-esteem and self-actualization. Individuals are said to progress from lower needs to higher needs on the way to becoming self-actualized. Lower and higher needs differ in the degree to which they are species specific; that is, the lower physiological needs for food and water are common to all living things, and the need for love might be shared with the higher apes, but the needs for self-esteem and self-actualization are uniquely human and shared with no other animals. The first and lowest, but most potent, level of the five in Maslow's hierarchy of needs is the need for physiological well-being, which includes most basically the need for food and drink. Classroom teachers are well aware that children who come to school hungry and thirsty are mentally and physically sluggish and not very interested in learning. According to Maslow, their energies and innermost thoughts are directed toward satisfying this physiological need. That is one reason why the United States Department of Agriculture's Healthy Hunger-Free Kids Act of 2010 requires that schools participating in the National School Lunch Program provide healthy breakfasts and lunches as well as make free water accessible to children throughout the day (2012).

Level two, safety needs, includes security, stability, and dependency needs; the need for freedom from fear, anxiety, and chaos; and the need for structure, order, law, limits, protection, and strength in a protector (Maslow, 1970). As mentioned frequently throughout this text, predictable routines help children to feel safe. Unpredictable adults and routines are unsettling to children. Chaotic and uncontrolled home life or classrooms elicit anxiety and fear and the child's felt need for the adult protector (parent or teacher) to be in greater control.

At level three, belonging and love needs are evident when the person feels the need for others. Hungering for love, affection, and acceptance, the child seeks a place in the family, play or school group, or other social entity. Parents and teachers who provide assurance to children of their place within the family or school and their value to the group help to fulfill this need.

At level four, esteem needs emerge. According to Maslow, a need for a stable and firmly based positive self-evaluation is prevalent in all individuals. The need for self-respect and the esteem of others is central to healthy personality development. Self-esteem includes feelings of self-confidence, self-worth, and efficacy and feelings of being wanted and needed. Individuals who lack self-esteem feel helpless, weak, discouraged, and unneeded. These feelings can lead to compensatory behaviors such as the **defense mechanisms** described in Table 15.1.

defense mechanism
a psychological response to ego threat, frustration, or failure

Table 15.1 Common Defense Mechanisms

Defense Mechanism	Description	Example
Regression	Returning to earlier, less mature behaviors	Bed wetting; thumb sucking; wanting to be carried in a caregiver's arms
Repression	Inhibiting uncomfortable, frightening memories and storing them in the unconscious	Child abuse victim's inability to name abuser
Projection	Attributing to others one's thoughts, motives, and traits	Seeking a cookie for oneself while asserting that a playmate needs it
Reaction formation	Behavior opposite from true feelings	Jealous sibling's exaggerated show of affection for newborn brother or sister
Displacement	Shifting feelings or emotions from something that is threatening to a substitute	Premature weaning and adult disapproval of thumb sucking lead to nail biting or chewing on a toy
Rationalizing	Attempting to provide a logical excuse for one's disappointments, failures, or shortcomings	Person who was not invited to a party saying, "I didn't want to go to her birthday party anyway—parties are boring."
Denial	Refusing to accept or acknowledge the reality of a situation	Clinging to Santa Claus myth after learning the truth
Fixation	Serious conflict or trauma at one age or stage that arrests further development	Prolonged separation anxiety resulting from traumatic event associated with an earlier separation
Sublimation	Channeling of psychological energies (e.g., aggression) into other outlets	Overachieving in school, sports, or hobby
Escape/withdrawal	Avoiding a situation by physically or psychologically removing oneself from it	Nonparticipation in classroom discussions; avoiding eye contact with others
Compensation	Finding a satisfying substitute for inadequate abilities	Pursuing hobbies or collections when social interactions are difficult

Maslow cautioned that true self-esteem derives from authentic accomplishments or deserved respect, not from contrived or trivial praise, popularity, or fame. An individual must come to base his or her self-esteem on real competence rather than on the opinions of others. This raises the question about the often overused classroom management technique in which the teacher praises inconsequential behaviors with statements such as, "That's great," "Wonderful," or "You are awesome" rather than commenting on the child's effort and eliciting the child's evaluation of his or her work.

Moral Development Theory

Recall that Piaget's stage-sequence theory of moral development cites three stages: premoral, moral realism, and moral relativism. Earlier chapters discussed stage 1 in describing the moral behaviors of children younger than 6. Children in the 6 through 8 age group exhibit characteristics of Piaget's stage 2 level of moral development, that of moral realism. Moral realism is characterized by rule-bound thinking and behaving. The term *heteronomy* describes this stage, for it implies that individuals are other-governed rather than autonomous, or self-governed.

Piaget thought that children at this stage of moral development believe the following:

1. Rules are rules, regardless of intentions.
2. Rules are unalterable.
3. Rules have been set by an all-knowing and powerful authority figure (God, parent, teacher).
4. The importance of a rule is in direct proportion to the severity of the punishment.
5. Obedience to rules means one is good; disobedience means one is bad.
6. Punishment is a necessary result of breaking a rule.

However, research on the social and cognitive abilities of children demonstrates that children distinguish between different kinds of rules at a young age. Turiel in 1980 identified different kinds of rules: social conventional rules and moral rules. *Social conventional* rules are social regulations such as those governing the modes of dress that fit the occasion, which side of the street to drive on, and how to address the classroom teacher. Such rules are arbitrary in that they do not generalize to all situations, places, cultures; they are not universal. However, *moral* rules are rules relating to generalized values such as honesty, fairness, and justice. According to Turiel, children as young as 6 years are able to distinguish between conventional rules and rules of morality and justice. We know now that even younger children are autonomous in their thinking about rules (Killen & Smetana, 2008).

Lagattuta, Nucci, and Bosacki (2010) studied judgments made by 4-, 5-, and 7-year–olds about moral rules and rules that pertained more to the personal domain—friends, activities, and clothing choices. There were significant increases as children became older in their judgments that a character in a vignette would comply with moral rules but disobey rules that pertained to the personal domain. In addition, many children said that they would feel good about obeying moral rules. Many 6- to 8-year-olds do not follow adult authority blindly but rather judge rules based on whether they are social conventional or moral.

Schools, however, may not punish children based on whether a rule is social conventional or moral. Goodman (2006) wrote that school discipline is in moral disarray. In her studies of schools she found that schools were likely to punish moral rules (violence, lying, etc.), derivatively moral rules (rules that are not by themselves immoral but become moral under particular situations e.g. eating in class), and conventional rules with similar punishments. Schools were not distinguishing between moral rules and conventional rules, although as we saw in Lagattuta, et al. (2010) that children from 4 to 7 years distinguish between them. We can ask, "Should there be differences in punishments, reasons given for rules, and school community emphasis based on the type of rules?"

Children imitate the social conventions and moral values of adults who are important to them. Through these imitations during their social interactions, children become increasingly aware of moral rules and values. However, adults can be misled by some of these behaviors, believing that verbalized values and imitated social conventions indicate mature understanding and **internalization** of behaviors. Actually, children are in the process of understanding, and such behaviors must be practiced and the consequences observed or experienced before internalized moral behavior can occur.

At this age, sociodramatic play continues to be a powerful contributor to moral understanding. Imitations of adult moral and social conventions and transgressions can be explored in the safe context of pretend play. Moreover, role-taking abilities increase through sociodramatic play, as does experiencing competing points of view. These experiences are necessary precursors to solving moral dilemmas later on.

internalization
a process in which behavior standards are adopted as one's own and acted upon without explicit instruction from others

During recess, Angela and several of her playmates get into an argument over how to manage their turn taking, which is supposed to proceed in an orderly fashion as they recite a jump-rope chant, each player jumping in on cue as the other exits. Angela is certain that her friends are not following the instructions that they learned from their student teacher and has become angry with her friends. She leaves the group to tell the teacher. She reports to her teacher, "They are not playing jump rope the right way." When Ms. Quinonez intervenes, she observes that each child has a different interpretation of the rules of the game. Rather than correcting Angela for tattling or reproving Angela's friends, Ms. Quinonez engages the participants in a discussion of how the game can be played so that each player has an equal opportunity to participate. In so doing, she helps the children come to a common perspective on the rules.

Development of Conscience

The conscience is said to be a facet of the personality that comes into play when children are able to internalize adult standards and know what is expected of them. It elicits judgments of right and wrong, inhibition of behaviors that have been learned to be inappropriate, feelings of discomfort, and promotion of behaviors that are deemed right or acceptable. It facilitates to some extent the development of self-control in the absence of external restraints.

Suppose Kia, who is 6, decides to move a chair over to the cookie jar and eat five cookies when her mother is out of the room, even though she knows that her mother would disapprove. After eating the cookies, she very carefully and quietly wipes off her face and moves the chair back to the table. Will she feel guilty about her transgression?

Whether she does or not may depend on the type of discipline she has received in the home. Discipline strategies used by parents in the home that maintain supportive and affectionate relationships are associated with the development of a conscience more than are other forms of discipline. Inductive discipline techniques that elicit reflection, perspective taking, empathy, altruism, and other prosocial attitudes and behaviors are closely associated with the development of conscience (Hoffman, 2000). A mother using inductive strategies could say, "I need to be able to trust you" or "I feel so sad. Now Daddy won't have any cookies to take to work tomorrow." However, love-withdraw techniques—including statements of disappointment in the child (Patrick & Gibbs, 2007) and power-assertive strategies, e.g. saying, "Go to your room" without explanation—provide little impetus for the development of conscience (Hoffman. 2000).

Culture plays an important role in the development of conscience by setting the parameters of behavior communicated between children and authority figures, a premise advanced by Vygotsky (1978). Children who have internalized standards of right and wrong from their earlier family experiences fall back on these standards when confronted with discrepancies and temptations outside the family. Although self-control might not always be present in these situations, the conscience is. The conscience becomes a stand-in for the parent and attempts to guide behaviors along internalized family expectations.

Emotional Competence and Development

It is important to keep in mind that while there are windows of opportunity for certain types of development, most of which occur during the early years, the brain continues to grow neurological connections and prune and refine those connections throughout life. In short, the windows do not close at age 3, 5, 8, or even 10. Child developmentalists assert that learning new ways of behaving, although perhaps becoming more difficult as we get older, does continue except in cases of extreme neglect, abuse, and trauma, particularly when the effects of these affronts to development are persistent.

Expression and Understanding of Emotions

School-age children grow in their ability to perceive and label different emotions in themselves and others (Vicari, Reily, Pasqualetti, Vizzotto, & Caltagirone, 2000). They are able to name the emotions they experience, and their ability to regulate their emotions is increasing and continues to be an important aspect of their psychological and social health. Emotion regulation entails moving beyond initial (heat of the moment) responses, which can interfere with the capacity to think clearly and act responsibly, to mentally organizing the perceptions and understandings of the provocation, then regulating the behaviors that respond to the provocation (Denham, 1998). Children who succeed in this development enjoy more positive social feedback. Further, there is some evidence that children who are skilled at identifying emotions and their provocations show more empathic moral thinking and behaviors (Arsenio & Lover, 1995). Again, both experience and empathic guidance help children to reflect and learn. Anticipating and role-playing appropriate responses to emotion-provoking situations helps children to develop understanding and skills.

Effects of Earlier Attachments

Decades of research document that what children learn, how they react to the events and people in their lives, and what they expect from themselves and others are significantly affected by the relationships they have with their primary caregivers and the nature of their home environments (Shonkoff & Phillips, 2000). Moreover, the quality of the relationship between infants and young children and their primary caregivers is considered of paramount importance to an individual's mental health throughout the life span (National Scientific Council on the Developing Child, Center on the Developing Child, 2004b). Quality parent or caregiver relationships originate in the bonding and attachment success of the infancy and toddler periods. All aspects of childhood social and emotional development are affected by the nature of these caring and nurturing relationships over time. Positive, protecting, and nurturing relationships support self-concept, self-esteem, self-efficacy, and resiliency and assist the child in acquiring social, emotional, and moral competence.

In school-age children, the nature of their earliest attachment experiences influences the manner in which they later relate to teachers. The child's senses of trust or mistrust, reciprocity in relationships, and empathy toward others derive from early attachment relationships. Children who have experienced secure attachments and have developed a sturdy sense of trust are more successful in their relationships with caregivers and teachers in their child care and schooling situations (Berlin, Cassidy, & Appleyard, 2008; Howes & Ritchie, 2002). Indeed, many children form healthy attachments to their nonparental caregivers and teachers. However, children whose earliest experiences (e.g., maltreatment, prenatal exposure to drugs, parental mental disorders, extreme poverty) resulted in insecure attachments distrust their teachers and have greater difficulty forming positive relationships with them (Carlson, Sroufe, & Egeland, 2004; Sroufe, Egeland, Carlson, & Collins, 2005). According to Howes and Ritchie (2002), children with avoidant, ambivalent/resistant, and disorganized attachment patterns display a number of challenging behaviors such as making "preemptive strikes" in their interactions with teachers, acting out in inappropriate, even hostile ways before the teacher has an opportunity to be rejecting. Or they may avoid the adult out of fear of being rejected. They presume rejection from those on whom they depend based on their real or perceived experiences of rejection within the family. Children who experienced inconsistent care and nurturing display insecure, ambivalent/resistant patterns and exhibit confusion over whether adults will meet their needs for protection and emotional support. Needful of comfort and security, these children may appear to seek them but then reject the teacher's attempts to provide them. They may exhibit dependency behaviors such as proximity seeking but use inappropriate means, such as interpersonal conflict, to engage the teacher's attention.

Attachment histories also influence the child's ability to make and maintain friendships in much the same manner as just described. Children who have experienced secure attachments are more trusting of others and therefore more successful in their peer interactions. Children who have experienced continuous insecure attachment relationships at home and at school have difficulty in their peer relationships (Howes & Ritchie, 2002; Lyons-Ruth, Alpern, & Repacholi, 1993). The development of important social skills, such as establishing rapport, trusting, cooperating, perspective-taking, sharing, negotiating, caring, and communicating effectively, is often delayed, and these skills are often difficult to acquire. Ziv, Oppenheim, and Sagi-Schwartz (2004) studied the quality of attachment of a group of children at 12 months of age and the same children's social information processing skills in middle childhood (7.5 years old). These researchers found that the major difference between securely and insecurely attached children was that in middle childhood secure children (measured at 12 months of age) expected both peers and adults to be emotionally and instrumentally available to them, whereas insecurely attached children did not expect others to be available to them. However, securely attached children did not expect peers whose behavior was socially unacceptable to be available to them. Although generally trusting and communicating well with many of their peers, securely attached children could discern which children would be unlikely to reciprocate or to be emotionally available to them.

Self-Concept, Self-Esteem, and Self-Regulation

Self-concept is more stable at ages 6 to 8, owing at least in part to gender constancy and to realizations about the permanence of racial and cultural group memberships. Self-concept during this period begins to include not only what children think about themselves, but also what they believe others think about them. This period is marked by self-criticism and comparisons of themselves with others. Self-appraisal arises from experiences in the home and school and with peers and organized groups. Self-appraisals can be self-affirming or self-defeating.

Research on self-concept development consistently reports a relationship between a person's self-concept and his or her achievements. Because the development of a sense of industry is a major social and emotional task of this age period and feelings of competence and self-confidence are necessary for the development of a sense of industry, school plays a critical role in the child's developing sense of competence or incompetence. Academic self-concept and academic achievement influence each other in a reciprocal effects model (REM) (Marsh & Scalas, 2010). Conversely, children who feel that they are incapable often experience reduced success in new tasks. Successes at this stage, then, are paramount; failures are damaging and can lead the child to a self-perception of inadequacy and inferiority, the polar opposite of Erikson's sense of industry.

When children feel inadequate, they often employ coping strategies known to psychologists as defense mechanisms (see Table 15.1). Defense mechanisms begin to emerge during the school years. Freud was among the first to suggest that during these years, defense mechanisms emerge to protect the ego from frustration and failure. Defense mechanisms serve to relieve anxiety when a person anticipates or experiences failures, mistakes, or mishaps. If there is anything positive to say about defense mechanisms, it is that they serve to relieve distress or embarrassment, at least temporarily.

However, when defense mechanisms are relied on excessively, the individual

School plays a critical role in the child's developing sense of competence or incompetence.

Emotional and Social Development: Ages Six Through Eight

escapes reality. When children begin to employ defense mechanisms to excess, parents and teachers must assess the expectations and stresses being placed on them. Perhaps the child is experiencing excessive teasing or ridicule from a classmate or sibling; experiences in school may be threatening in some way, as is often true when competition is used to motivate or when expectations exceed the child's capabilities; perhaps the child fears peer or parental disappointment or disapproval over his or her inadequacies or failures. Harsh, punitive, or demeaning discipline may elicit defense mechanisms. There are many possible provocations for the employment of defense mechanisms. In any case, for the most part, the behaviors are potentially damaging to the self-concept and to interpersonal relationships.

Individual Temperament and Personality

From previous chapters, we have seen that children have distinctive temperamental characteristics, which are genetically derived but are also influenced in a variety of ways by their environment. The manner and contexts in which temperament is expressed influence the types of reciprocal interactions the child will experience. For example, a child with a very high activity level could be viewed in positive terms ("energetic," "lively") or negative terms ("jumpy," "restless"). Such views influence the person's responses to and interactions with the child. The child, then, is subjected to a variety of responses that are based on how others perceive his or her temperament. (The frequently overused "diagnosis" of attention deficit hyperactivity disorder may actually represent adults' failure to recognize their reaction to individual temperament types.)

Differences in personality at ages 6 through 8 have their roots in these early and continuing perceptions and interactions. Recent studies have attempted to ascertain the relationship between early personality traits and later social and emotional adjustment. Some traits have been found to persist. For instance, highly aggressive children have been found to remain relatively more aggressive than others as they get older (Alink, et al. AlA). Other studies have suggested that negative emotional behaviors such as aggressiveness, being hard to please, undercompliance, and difficulties with peers are fairly stable over the course of childhood and affect later adjustment. Children who have been socially rejected during their earliest elementary school years are at greater risk for social difficulties in adolescence and early adulthood (Ladd, 2006). Sturaro, Pol, van Lier, Cuijpers, & Koot (2011) in a study of 740 children followed from kindergarten to first grade found that peer rejection led to children's externalizing behavior and vice-versus. Teachers must intervene to try to change the pattern of peer rejection in a classroom.

Fears and Anxieties

The close relationship between fears and cognitive development is evidenced by the changes in causes of and responses to fears as children get older. Cognitive development results in increasing abilities to perceive meanings not previously perceived and to relate those meanings to oneself. With increasing experiences and understandings during the 6- to 8-year period, fear becomes less specific (e.g., fear of dogs, fear of the dark) and more general (e.g., fear of not being liked at school). The ability to imagine, empathize, and take the perspectives of others changes the nature of children's fears. Table 15.2 summarizes the way in which children's fears change as they get older.

Unlike the toddler, whose fear responses are often vociferous, the older child responds in less intense or overt ways when frightened. Older children may repress or mask their

Table 15.2 Changes in Children's Fears from Infancy Through Age 8

Infants	Toddlers	Children Ages 4 to 5	Children Ages 6 to 8
Loud noises	Heights	Unfamiliar/sudden noises	Dark
Loss of support	Separation	Imaginary creatures/events	Being left alone
	Strangers	Punishment	Scoldings
	Sudden surprise (e.g., jack-in-the-box toy)	Dogs, small animals	Physical injury, sickness
	Loud noises	Storms	Ridicule, embarrassment
		Supernatural figures (ghosts, witches)	Being different in physical appearance and abilities (e.g., clothes, hairstyles, etc.)
			Worries (what could be): school failure/retention, family safety, death of a family member, storms, gun violence
			Parental or teacher rejection

fears. Their behaviors bespeak their discomfort: nail biting, inattention or distractibility, change in eating or sleeping patterns, heightened emotionality, increased dependency, or feigned illness. They may deny that they are afraid, or they may boast of their bravery.

Previous experiences and life circumstances influence what children fear and how they respond: family life trauma, accidents and illnesses, loss of a parent to divorce or death, severe punishments, frightening movies or television programs, adult conversations not fully comprehended, and violence. School-age children typically fear being different from their peers, and in school, they fear teacher rejection and grade retention. Physical and psychological well-being also influences fear responses. As with adults, discomfort such as hunger, fatigue, illness, and stress cause children to exaggerate events, real or imagined, and respond in disproportionate ways.

As with fears of earlier years, older children need adults to talk with them about their fears and help them to find ways to cope with and control feared situations. Children learn about their fears and gain mastery over them when adults respond to childhood fears in respectful, frank, and instructive ways. Allowing children to talk about their fears as they arise gives adults clues about particular topics and misconceptions that need to be addressed. Helping children to both *feel* safe and *be* safe is how adults help children with their fears. Adults are helpful when they do the following:

- Allow children to bring up subjects that concern them
- Assure children that parents and teachers are there to protect them
- Never use fear to coerce or discipline
- Explore children's topics of concern in an authoritative and unemotional way
- Provide accurate information about topics of concern, and clarify misconceptions
- Help children to learn to obtain factual information about that which they fear
- Involve children in developing a plan for seeking help and protecting themselves in specific types of situations that they may fear

- Develop together, role play, and practice family plans to meet emergencies such as a house fire, separation in a crowd, and a medical emergency
- Help children to learn important contact phone numbers (mother, father, grandparent, or other relative or neighbor) and addresses (including area phone codes and ZIP codes)
- Assess and be prepared, should they arise, to offer appropriate advice and guidance on contemporary catastrophic subjects or events to which children are vicariously (via friends, neighbors, and news media) or directly exposed, such as gun violence, terrorism, war, child abduction, and extraordinary weather events

Transitional Objects

Attachment to transitional objects of earlier years may well persist into the period from ages 6 through 8 and possibly beyond. By age 7, a child who still clings to a transitional object may do so in more private and subtle ways, perhaps preferring its comfort only at bedtime or during times of stress or illness. Soon other sentimental objects will compete for the child's attentions, and the need for the original transitional object may wane. For some children, however, discarding the transitional object altogether is out of the question. The teddy bear may remain on the shelf well into adolescence; the worn special blanket may be safely tucked away in a drawer to remain there indefinitely. No attempt should be made to dispose of transitional objects because they represent the child's continuing need to find self-comforting strategies. The affection for the transitional object continues, and only the child should decide what to do with it when it is no longer in use. Because adults now demonstrate more acceptance of children's transitional objects, many children take their transitional objects with them to college or into a birthing room. These objects provide a link to the past and continue providing comfort to the children as they move into adulthood.

Social Competence and Development

Peer Relationships

As children get older, an expanding social circle, from parents and family to individuals and groups outside of the family, brings additional influences on the child's social and emotional development. Social interactions include incidental encounters (sharing the sights of the toy aisle at the supermarket with an acquaintance), informal interactions with individuals (riding bicycles with a special friend) and with loosely formed groups (neighborhood play groups), and formal or organized activities (Pee-Wee and Little League).

The peer group emerges as a powerful socializing force in the child's life during the early school years. The child has shifted from seeking interactions with adults more than with children to seeking interactions with children more than with adults. Peer group acceptance becomes paramount to the child.

Friendships

Friendships among school-age children should be taken seriously (Healy, 2011) as they are a critically important aspect of children's social experience. Friendship choices are becoming more and more based on attributes ("She is real nice") rather than possessions or situational factors, as with younger children ("I like him because he has a Lego set to play with") (Boggiano, Klinger, & Main, 1986). The social competence skills of initiating and maintaining friendships and resolving conflicts become important skills to have mastered by early school age.

Cooperation emerges through these early friendships and sustains them (Hartup, 1989). Through friendships, children derive companionship, emotional security and support, enhanced feelings of self-worth, interpersonal relationship skills, and knowledge about cultures and social conventions.

At this age, children establish and maintain close friendships with one or more agemates and enjoy visiting in one another's homes, sometimes overnight.

The peer group emerges as a powerful socializing force during the 6- through 8-year period.

Such friendships help children to grow in independence and social interaction skills. Through these friendships, children learn the importance of give-and-take and gain a sense of loyalty.

Children enlarge their friendship circles through loosely formed social groups. As a rule, these groups simply play around with one another. However, their organization may take on the elements of a club or gang, with leaders and followers, membership preferences, rules, and sometimes a name. Adults can harness the energy and enthusiasm that emerges from these friendship groups.

Jeremy, age 6, is a member of the Walla Street Club. This group includes the 7-year-old boy next door, the two brothers (ages 8 and 9) who live across the street, a 7-year-old from several houses down the street, and another 6-year-old from a block away. Girls are not admitted to the club, though two of the members have younger sisters who are allowed to participate in their games on rare occasions. The boys spend as much time together after school or on weekends as they can. They seem to have an insatiable desire to be together and boundless energy when engaged in play.

Jeremy's dad has initiated a weekend project for the boys: building a clubhouse in the backyard. The design, collection of building materials and tools (some borrowed from other members' parents), and construction of the house have been going on for about two months. The boys plan each step with energy and enthusiasm. Their wills occasionally clash: which board should go where, where the door will be, who is going to bring more nails? At home, the boys draw pictures of their clubhouse, gather items to furnish it, and brag to their siblings about their private place. They talk about the fun or complain about the conflicts with their parents. Together, they anticipate their meetings and what they will do, who will come, and who can never come into the clubhouse. It is a dynamic and ongoing avocation in their lives.

What do children gain from experiences like these? In these loosely formed groups, children experience leading and following, negotiating and compromising, rule setting, rule changing, and rule constraints. They become aware of the needs and wishes of others, and they practice perspective-taking and diplomacy. They experience loyalty and disloyalty, democracy, and autocracy. Their sense of industry is tapped, and their sense of belonging is reinforced. Their confidence and self-esteem are enhanced.

Despite all the positive influences of these social groupings, there can be difficulties associated with membership. Children ages 6 through 8 measure themselves against their perceptions of others and, in so doing, are self-critical and critical of others. When group expectations are at odds with the child's abilities and desires, conflicts occur, and group membership may become detrimental. Treating others unkindly, expecting members to engage in mischief or forbidden activities, setting standards for dress, imposing undesired rivalry and competition, excluding a valued friend, and devaluing one's contribution or other activities (e.g., piano lessons, participation in scouting or a family picnic) are influences that can strain the child's abilities to negotiate. Adults need to be aware of these problems and sensitive to the child's dilemma. Guidance and support are needed, and in some instances so are intervention and coaching (Howes & Ritchie, 2002; Kim, 2003).

Peer Rejection and Peer Neglect

Approximately 10% to 20% of children in early childhood classrooms are classified as popular, 10% to 22% as rejected, and 12% to 20% as neglected by peers. The remaining children are classified as having an average status of popularity (Kim, 2003). Concern arises as psychologists are learning disturbing facts about the outcomes of persistent peer rejection, some of which are associated with (though not independently causative of) later dire behaviors that make headlines. Obviously, not all children who experience peer rejection or neglect respond in dangerous or destructive ways; many, however, suffer privately (to lesser or greater degrees) often well into their adult lives. Many forms of maladaptive emotional and social behaviors arise from continuous failure to find peer acceptance.

Peers can be both rejecting and neglecting. Rejected children can fail to learn friendship-building behaviors of approach and integration skills, prosocial attitudes, and other interpersonal relationship requirements. As stated earlier in this chapter rejected children often employ behaviors that cause their peers to reject them, such as aggressive, hostile, and physically assertive behaviors (e.g., grabbing, pushing, and struggling), and they may tease, bully, or be verbally abusive (Ladd, 2006).

Children who are neglected by their peers often display withdrawn behaviors in group situations. They may persistently play alone without demonstrating a desire to interact with others or that they can do so competently when they want to. They may exhibit shyness, anxiety, and fearfulness and convey to others more negative than positive expressions (Cassidy & Asher, 1992; Provost & LaFreniere, 1991).

Because the types of behaviors that elicit peer rejection or neglect may be indicative of serious underlying social and emotional developmental risks, early and consistent efforts to intervene are necessary. Shy, withdrawn children can be helped by providing opportunities for them to interact with one or two children with whom they can feel comfortable; coaching and scaffolding may be necessary to assist the friendship development process. It has been suggested that pairing the shy child with a younger playmate may assist him or her in gaining confidence in his or her interaction abilities (Kemple, 1992). Coaching children on approach, entry, and integration skills to help them gain acceptance into peer groups may be necessary. Teaching children to respond to the overtures of others in positive ways and helping children learn to express their enjoyments and discontents in assertive and nonaggressive ways also provide them with the tools for more satisfying peer interactions.

These informal groups, which are often based on proximity and accessibility, may also define their memberships arbitrarily along age, gender, socioeconomic, cultural, or religious lines. Children who are excluded are subjected to feelings of rejection and lowered self-esteem. Sensitive adults need to provide positive guidance for handling these situations when they arise. Adult intervention is needed to guide the group toward more prosocial goals and inclusive and antibiased behaviors. Here again, adults serve as social role models and coaches for children.

Bullying

Bullying is a pervasive problem in schools in the United States and other countries. Bullying can be physical, verbal, or relational, and there can be long-lasting negative effects for both the bully and the victim (Berger, 2006). Relational bullying has also been called psychological bullying and includes intimidation, exclusion, and spreading rumors. A new type of bullying called cyber bullying includes sending mean text, e-mail, or instant messages. In the United States, more than 16% of school children say that they have been victims of bullies (Erikson, 2001).

We must be careful not to label children as bullies, but rather identify physical and emotional abuse of others as bullying behavior. Identifying specific behaviors that hurt or intimidate others is more likely to result in changes in children's behavior because often children who use bullying behavior at times may not consider themselves to be bullies (Indiana University, 2009). We must also delve into why children may bully each other. A study of 500 Dutch elementary-school children ages 9 to 12 found that children who use bullying behavior are trying to gain status, affection, and attention among children of their own gender by choosing victims that are not liked by others (Veenstra, Lindenberg, Munniksma, & Dijkstra, 2010). Teachers and parents will want to support a child to gain attention and status in other more productive ways.

A recent study of 373 second-graders and their teachers studied victims of bullying behavior such as teasing, gossip, physical intimidation, or aggressive behavior (Rudolph, Abaied, Flynn, Sugimura, & Agoston, 2012). These researchers found that those children whose social goals were to prevent attracting attention to themselves and to avoid negative judgments from peers were more likely to become victims of bullying behavior. These children were less likely to use the problem-solving strategies that children who were interested in developing relationships with peers used when they were harassed. More of this type of research will help us understand children's goals and problem-solving strategies and result in more effective bullying prevention programs.

Schools must develop a comprehensive approach that includes the following:

- A school district policy
- An assessment of how much and the types of bullying occurring in the school
- A focus on social and emotional development and the social environment for children

- Discipline codes
- Involving parents, professionals, and training staff
- Immediate intervention in bullying situations
- Focusing class time on bullying prevention (U.S. Department of Health and Human Services, 2008)

Gender Identity and Gender Role Development

As children reach ages 6 through 8, gender identity and gender-role behaviors are evident in their mannerisms, language, play choices, and friendships. Having formed gender-role stereotypes, children in the United States now have rather inflexible ideas about girl/boy expectations, attributing to gender certain behaviors, clothing, hairstyles, play and school activities, home chores, and adult occupations. Children who play in gender-integrated partnerships and groups have greater opportunity to learn about and from each other. Indeed, studies have found that integrated play and work groups result in greater social competence (Feiring & Lewis, 1991).

Friendships begin to segregate along gender lines as early as the toddler years, a process that increases dramatically during the 6- through 8-year period (Powlishta, 1995). In another year or so, same-sex peer group preference will reach its peak. Many scholars believe that gender segregation and its accompanying stereotyping can result in stereotypical thinking and social patterns that persist into adult social behaviors.

Children's stereotypes are learned from those around them and are sometimes imposed on them by their families and cultures. School experiences particularly influence gender identity and gender-role development. There is some evidence of gender bias on the part of classroom teachers. The research of Myra Sadker and David Sadker (1985, 1994) demonstrated that teachers engage in more conversations, assistance, and praise with boys than they do with girls. They also respond to boys' questions with more precision and often answer girls' questions with bland or diffused responses.

How schools are organized makes a difference in how strongly peer cultures are segregated according to gender. Corsaro (2006) studied Italian children from preschool through elementary school. Preschool children stay with the same peer group and teacher during the three years of preschool. When they enter elementary school, they stay with the same peer group with two teachers during the five elementary years. Because this model creates

Children who play and work in gender-integrated partnerships and groups have more opportunity to learn about and from each other.

chapter 15

a "highly integrated community" (Corsaro, p. 106), and because there is an emphasis in the Italian schools on discussion and negotiation, there is less gender segregation than in the United States.

The differences between play behaviors of girls and boys may explain the gender segregation that occurs beginning among toddlers and continuing in early childhood and the primary grades. Boys generally engage in rough-and-tumble play and enjoy play themes and electronic games that are action oriented, whereas girls typically show a preference for sociodramatic play centering on themes such as family, school, stage performing, and dressing up (Goodman, 2001; Honig, 2000; Maccoby, 2000). Girls tend to play in closer proximity to adults than do boys and display more cooperative and negotiable play behaviors. Boys tend to play in larger groups than do girls and engage in more competition (Maccoby, 1990). Boys avoid feminine toys more than girls avoid masculine toys (Etaugh & Liss, 1992). All of these gender-related behaviors can become more intense in the primary grades as children sometimes find it difficult to play and work in mixed-gender groups.

Grogan and Bechtel (2003) provided suggestions for improving gender relationships in elementary school classrooms, including the following:

- Address the class as a whole: Rather than "Good morning, boys and girls," use greetings such as, "Good morning, everyone, . . . class, . . . children."
- Refrain from grouping or lining up children by boy/girl classifications; instead, use other classifications, such as birthdays, favorite foods, and similar interests.
- Integrate boys and girls in seating arrangements.
- Partner boys and girls for class projects and tasks.
- Select bias-free literature and visual materials.
- Engage in dialogue on gender issues with children as they arise.

Stereotyping is often unconscious and subtle, but its potential for perpetuating stereotypes in children is great. Stereotypes imposed on girls and boys—such as attributing aggression, independence, and mathematical skills to boys and verbal, dependent, and passive behaviors to girls—can influence their self-perceptions well into adult life.

Studies of gender-role development emphasize gender schemata in which young children organize and internalize information about what is typical or appropriate for male and female individuals in their particular sociocultural contexts (Levy & Carter, 1989; Maccoby, 1990). According to these studies, such schemata do not necessarily depend on the emergence of gender constancy, but derive from a variety of developmental and experiential sources from infancy onward. Although Kohlberg's stage descriptions emphasize the importance of the child's notion of gender constancy as a point at which the child becomes more aware of gender-related attributes, these recent theories emphasize an information-processing perspective. This point of view proposes that each person may possess internal motivations (schemata) to conform to sociocultural gender-role expectations and stereotypes.

Sexuality Development

Emerging sexuality development is evidenced, in part, by the typical gender segregation of school-age children. As they begin to find that play and work groups can include both boys and girls and friendships can be forged, their comfort level is being challenged.

The gender-related play behaviors to which they have become accustomed during earlier years often interfere with their ability to relate, negotiate, and cooperate. This difficulty is often exhibited in defensive types of behaviors in which boys and girls refer to one another in derogatory terms and ridicule or tease one another. Some of this teasing may refer to "boyfriends" and "girlfriends," who is going to "marry" whom, and chasing and teasing on the playground.

Curiosity continues, as does using inappropriate words or provocative body language, now often accompanied with giggling and a sense of daring and enjoyment of shock effect. Children may giggle at television, magazine, or billboard images of children or adults depicted in revealing clothing and provide their own names for body parts and their interpretations of the depicted poses or behaviors. Questions about sex continue to arise and often become more specific. Children may have acquired inaccurate or distorted information from siblings, playmates, the media, or other extrafamilial sources and may have drawn conclusions that confuse or frighten them.

Although most acting-out behaviors are inconsequential, some behaviors are clearly inappropriate. Responding appropriately to these behaviors requires that adults help children to learn to respect themselves and to interact with others in positive and respectful ways. Intervention is necessary when behaviors occur that tease, demean, intimidate, or make others uncomfortable. Failure to curtail and respond in instructive ways to this behavior teaches children, both boys and girls, to accept hostility and victimization (Chrisman & Couchenour, 2002).

Children's questions often perplex adults, who are not sure what or how much should be discussed with children. Responding appropriately to a child's questions requires that adults determine exactly what it is that the child is actually asking and engage in dialogue with the child to ascertain what he or she already knows to determine if there are distortions and misinformation that need to be clarified. Age-appropriate discussion needs to be simple, frank, and unembarrassed and should provide accurate information and terminology. There is no need for great detail, but there is need to determine whether the child has understood the information provided to avoid further confusion or distorted concepts.

Issues in Emotional and Social Development
Need for Support for a Sense of Industry Versus Inferiority

Again, the extent to which the child's resolution of the industry versus inferiority psychosocial conflict (Erikson, 1963) is supported through experiences in the home, school, and extracurricular activities determines the extent to which a child will develop the subsequent healthy sense of identity that is so important during adolescence. (Important aspects of this identity development process are understanding group membership, including race/ethnicity, and fostering an appreciation for diversity; see Boxes 15.1 and 15.2 for more on these topics.) Hence, 6- through 8-year-olds need the types of opportunities that engage their unique interests and abilities; that enlist them in mutual caring and support for the family, class, or other group to which they belong; and that provide opportunities to succeed and experience an authentic sense of accomplishment.

Box 15.1   Diversity Perspectives: Children's Awareness of Diversity and Individual Differences

Development moves from preoperational thinking to concrete operational thinking, and differences emerge in the way children view diversity. As children begin to decenter and become less egocentric, their awareness of groups emerges. Around age 5, they begin to use categories to define these groups. Children at this age are said to be **sociocentric,** that is, while they have formed a repertoire of group categories, they nevertheless are unable to take or accept the perspectives of other groups as valid. This declines after age 7, when children can focus more on individuality than on group categories and characteristics. Children's feelings about their own racial or cultural group identity are tested when they experience diverse groups of people, some of whom may exhibit stereotypes and bias.

In Aboud's (1988) theory, children at step 3 should be most susceptible to information and interventions that build positive relationships with others. At this point, children can appreciate the fact that ethnicity doesn't change, that there are individual internal qualities to be appreciated, and that differences among groups are reconcilable. Aboud called this development the *focus of attentions sequence* and noted the following progression:

sociocentric
the inability to take or accept as valid the perspectives of another group

Step 1:

- Egocentrism

Step 2:

- Preoccupation with groups and the differences between one's own and other groups
- Exaggeration of contrasts between groups, which can lead to pro- or antiperspectives
- Later increasing awareness of similarities as well as differences between one's own and other groups

Step 3:

- Focus on individuals and unique personalities
- Liking or disliking people on the basis of personal rather than ethnic group qualities
- Continuing to hold some ethnic group stereotypes

As in the development of self-concept and gender identity, the child's growing acceptance and appreciation of his or her ethnicity pave the way for acceptance of the uniqueness of others. Individuals who are comfortable with their ethnicity have little difficulty building relationships with members of other groups and do so without feelings of conflict or insecurity (Aboud, 1988).

Parents and early childhood professionals take an active role in fostering an appreciation for diversity in children. If antibias attitudes and feelings are to develop, young children need informative, positive, self-affirming, and perspective-taking experiences.

Box 15.2   Diversity Perspectives: Sociocultural Experiences

The racial and ethnic composition of groups to which children belong (child care, school, out-of-school groups, and family affiliations) is increasingly more diverse and will continue to be so in the years to come (Federal Interagency Forum on Child and Family Statistics, 2007). Unlike generations of the past, today's children experience opportunities to interact with and gain knowledge of cultures beyond their own, hear and learn other languages, and practice accepting and nonbiased social interactions. Children today will experience more cross-cultural friendships and shared cultural experiences than their parents experienced as children. In addition, the number of biracial families is also increasing in the United States (Chiong, 1998). The extent to which children are comfortable with and proud of their ethnicity and cultural heritage determines the extent to which all of these experiences can contribute to healthy social and emotional development.

Essential in this process is the child's growing sense of identity and family and cultural affiliation. A person's sense of identity includes perceptions of his or her physical characteristics and gender, innate and acquired abilities, socioeconomic status, and ethnic or racial group membership. Self-perceptions originate in the relationships and interactions that children persistently have with parents, family members, caregivers, teachers, and peers. Within families, children first learn racial pride and acquire attitudes of acceptance or rejection of others. Having positive and self-affirming feelings about one's race or ethnicity is a critical aspect of social and emotional development. However, equally important to successful social and emotional development is the acquisition of knowledge and attitudes conducive to nonbiased relationships with others.

Nature of Adult–Child Relationships

Qualities of early experiences such as attachment, parenting styles, nonparental child care, and reactions to individual temperament are associated with social and emotional outcomes. Certain aspects of the relationship between the parent and the child have also been related to the child's social and emotional development. One study observed playful mother–child and father–child interactions and correlated them with the child's adaptation to peers (MacDonald & Parke, 1984). The findings suggest that boys who were competent with their peers had fathers who were physically playful and affectionate. The fathers of competent girls engaged their daughters in stimulating verbal exchanges. Certain maternal behaviors have been found to influence social acceptance with peers. Children whose mothers used positive verbal interactions, such as polite requests and suggestions, and were less demanding of and disagreeable with their children were found to be less abrasive and more positive in their peer interactions (Putallaz, 1987).

It is generally believed that the social skills that are necessary for later successful peer group interactions are learned through early experiences in the family (Howes & Ritchie, 2002). The quality of parent–child interactions is not the only influence on social and emotional development. By providing opportunities for peer group interaction, encouraging and facilitating friendships, and monitoring children's relationships for positive outcomes, parents provide the scaffolding that is essential to the development of social competence.

Out-of-School Time

For some school-age children, the out-of-home day may be as long as 10 to 13 hours. Long days are tiring and stressful. The daily before-school/school/after-school routine may involve two or more different settings, perhaps in two or more locations; different sets of adult authorities with different levels of education and training; different teaching and discipline styles; different behavior and performance expectations; and different modes of interacting with individual children. There may also be different peer groups with different group configurations and interactional dynamics. Clearly, children in these situations are called on to be flexible, resilient, and adaptable, not to mention physically hearty!

For some children, these demands present no problems. For others, adapting to multiple authority figures and different peer groups can be stressful and difficult. Parents, caregivers, and classroom teachers need to be sensitive to the physical and psychological demands of these routines. When a balanced schedule that includes rest, relaxation, play, self-directed activities, outdoor and indoor activities, and group and solitary moments, along with structured and adult-directed activities, is provided, the child's day can be productive and enjoyable. However, emphasis on group participation, schoolwork, and academic endeavors before, during, and after school would tax any child.

Teachers and caregivers need to provide space (both physical and psychological) for children to distance themselves from the group from time to time. Schedules in both the school and the child care program need to be sensitive to the physiological needs for nourishment, physical exercise, rest, spontaneous play, and informal interactions with friends and siblings. After-school programs need to resist the urge to "help" with schooling by insisting on additional schoolwork activities. Likewise, schools and teachers must resist the temptation to defer practice and reinforcement activities to after-school times. This, of course, opens the debate on whether homework should be regularly assigned. This topic, while critical, is beyond the intent of this discussion. The points here are as follows:

1. Long days with repeated structured activities impede school learning by causing fatigue, frustration, and burnout.
2. Children's physical and motor needs (addressed in Chapters 11 and 14) must be met for children to be physically and neurologically healthy.
3. Sound social and emotional development relies on warm, nurturing, supportive, and meaningful adult–child relationships.
4. Social competence, which includes making and maintaining friendships, social problem-solving skills, perspective-taking abilities, and prosocial abilities, depends on opportunities to interact with others in meaningful ways and be reasonably free from adult interference.

Before- and after-school child care can play a positive and supportive role in social and emotional development. When children are allowed to experience autonomy and control in the use of their time and energies and are provided with activities over which they can have a sense of mastery, adaptability to the routines of child care and school is facilitated.

Programs that provide for the safety and nurturing needs of children offer a valuable support system for families (Halpern, 2003). When parents feel secure and confident about the experiences their children are having while they are at work, family relationships are enhanced. Relieved of the worry and stress associated with unpredictable or

Emotional and Social Development: Ages Six Through Eight

self-care arrangements, parents can pursue their own work in a more productive manner. Emerging prescriptions for child care will include greater coordination among family, school, and child care programs and more efforts to meet a variety of family support service needs.

Sibling Relationships

The sense of self derives in part from the relationships a child has with siblings. Siblings face a variety of self-concept issues relating to their close or distant relationships, their feelings of acceptance or rejection of one another, and their feelings of being similar to or different from one another (Banks & Kahn, 2003). These relationships and the perceptions that accompany them play a complex role in the child's developing sense of self as a unique and separate individual and also as part of a broader identity that includes brothers and sisters.

Rivalrous behavior at ages 6 through 8 is often an indication of the child's emerging sense of identity. Children at this age compare themselves with others in an attempt to affirm their self-worth. In families, brothers and sisters become objects for comparison as children seek to distinguish similarities and differences between themselves and others. At the same time, children begin to identify with one or more of their siblings, who are often powerful role models.

Stress, Depression, and Mental Health

Children, like adults, experience stress from time to time. Unlike adults, young children lack sufficient knowledge and experience to understand their stressors and a repertoire of strategies for dealing with stress.

The causes of stress in young children are many and varied. Honig (1986) categorized stressor variables as follows:

1. *Personal,* including prematurity, sex, temperament, neurological sturdiness, age of child, and intellectual capacity
2. *Ecological,* including characteristics of living environments such as neighborhood crime, antisocial role models, unaesthetic surroundings, household density, individual privacy requirements, and inadequate play space
3. *Socioeconomic status*
4. *Catastrophes and terrors,* including hospitalization, societal disasters, threat of nuclear war, and terrorism
5. *Family events,* including birth of siblings, death of parent or sibling, separation and divorce, and blended families

Obviously, a great number of potential stressors exist for young children. Pressures to perform tasks or to achieve beyond one's years and developmental capacities, changes in school or child care arrangements, and childhood social events such as birthday parties and school field trips may also be stressful. Certainly, not all of these events cause anxiety or stress in all children. Responses to stress are as varied as the stressors themselves and may be physiological (headache, stomachache, loss of appetite, sleep disturbances) or psychological (crying, nightmares, regression, irritability, increased dependency) (Stanford & Yamamoto, 2001). See Table 15.3.

Table 15.3 Stress-Related Behaviors

Physical reactions

    Physical or psychosomatic symptoms: stomach or abdominal pain, headache, sweaty palms, biting nails, hyperalertness, eating and sleep disturbances

    Regression to earlier forms of behaving: thumb sucking, toileting accidents

Emotional and social reactions

    Heightened sensitivity, irritability, low tolerance for frustration, crying

    Aggressive or oppositional behaviors, defensive outbursts

    Whining, or proximity seeking, reluctance to be alone

    Worrying, excessive concerns about what "might" or "could" happen

    Excessive shyness, avoiding interactions or challenges, fear of embarrassment

Cognitive reactions

    Inability to focus, sustain attention, think creatively

    Rationalizing undue fears and anxieties

    Poor problem-solving perspectives

    Worry about failures and consequences

    Learning difficulties

Stress can be described as either positive or negative; each type alerts us to respond or adapt in some particular way. Both types bring about physiological and psychological changes and physical and emotional responses. The effect of stress and the ability to cope with or adapt to stressful situations or demands depends on many interrelated factors: age, temperament, prior experience, knowledge, cognitive and metacognitive abilities, emotional intelligence, and support networks. Stressor characteristics of intensity, persistence, and duration also influence its effect.

Characteristics that are often associated with stress-related personalities, such as competitiveness, impatience, aggressiveness, low tolerance for frustration, hostility, and high achievement orientation, have been found in very young children. The child's ability to appraise a stressful situation influences the extent to which the child will cope. Children need adults to help them to identify their stressors and to evaluate them with a goal toward eliminating the stressors when possible or finding constructive ways to deal with stress.

Jeremy's second-grade teacher invited his parents to a conference. His usual classroom performance had deteriorated since the beginning of the school year, and she was concerned. Jeremy's behaviors in school were off-task and disruptive. He teased his classmates, antagonized his project partners, and resorted to name calling when they protested. When the teacher intervened, he withdrew, became sullen, and often cried.

In conference, Keisha and DeVon revealed that similar behaviors were occurring at home, and they did not know what to do. Their individual work commitments, church work, and social life were consuming larger and larger amounts of their time

(continued)

Emotional and Social Development: Ages Six Through Eight

and energies. In addition, Keisha's mother had recently undergone surgery and needed Keisha's assistance during her recovery.

The teacher asked them to focus on Jeremy's routines. What did he do before and after school and on the weekends? Jeremy's schedule included regular before- and after-school care at a child care center near the school. In addition, he was taking piano lessons early each Monday morning, had karate lessons on Wednesday afternoons, and played Pee-Wee League baseball on Saturday mornings.

Clearly, all members of the family had become overcommitted and overscheduled. The stress of such scheduling, the logistics of transportation and attendance, and the reduced opportunities for family interaction and mutual support were beginning to take their toll on each member. Jeremy's behavior in school was a clue to the stress he was encountering.

A reassessment of their commitments, goals, and priorities led DeVon and Keisha to conclude that each member of the family would benefit from a change. Jeremy was encouraged to talk about the extracurricular activities in which he was enrolled and was allowed to decide which one or ones were most important to him and most enjoyable. Keisha and DeVon did the same assessment of their own activities. From this exercise, each family member eliminated all but the most pressing and important activities. Jeremy chose to drop the piano and karate lessons. Maybe he will want to pursue those lessons later; for now, he feels relieved. With commitments and extracurricular activities returned to a manageable level, Jeremy and his parents have more time and energy to respond to one another and to interact with focused attention.

Television and Other Media Influences

The following research statements summarized by scholars at the Nemours Foundation (2008) from studies by the American Academy of Pediatrics (AAP), the American Psychological Association, and others are enlightening:

- Children in the United States watch about four hours of TV a day.
- 70% of child care centers use TV during the day with young children even though AAP has advised against any screen time for children during the first 2 years.
- Too much screen time contributes to childhood overweight, obesity, and diminished physical fitness.
- Children who watch violent television and other media programs believe that the world is scary and that something bad will happen to them. This is particularly true for children ages 2 to 7.
- Children learn various forms of aggression and believe these forms are acceptable ways of getting what one wants.
- Children learn distorted gender and racial stereotypes from popular media.
- By age 18, the American child will have witnessed 200,000 violent acts on television.
- In the United States, child viewers will be confronted with 40,000 commercials each year.
- A preponderance of toys advertised and sold are linked to movies and TV programs that are characterized by aggression and violence.

Clearly, television and other electronic media play a major role in the socialization and culturalization of children. Children learn from these electronic sources, and their behaviors are influenced by what they learn. Studies of violence and aggression on television have overwhelmingly concluded that television has a measurable effect on behavior. Concern over this issue continues. Studies of gender and of racial and cultural groups on television have pointed out misrepresentations in television programming and the potentially deleterious effects of stereotyping. Studies of commercials have likewise suggested that childhood values and attitudes may be distorted and that commercials exploit children for financial gains.

Programs with prosocial themes and role models have also been shown to influence behavior, but the effect of these programs is thought to be less potent than that of programs that feature violence and aggression (Radke-Yarrow, Zahn-Waxler, & Chapman, 1983).

Contemporary studies of the effect of television on children's lives are attempting to determine the extent to which children actually attend to television when the set is on, what types of program events or program attributes attract and hold the child's attention (e.g., other children, puppets, unusual voices, animation, rhyming, laughing, and repetition), and the extent to which children comprehend what they view. Studies of the effect of other media are also emerging. Large amounts of screen time interfere with social and emotional development in the following ways:

1. Physical activity and outdoor play are curtailed. Lack of exercise impedes physical motor development and sound physical and mental health.

2. Interaction with other children is reduced. As we have seen, children need the social experiences that peer group interaction affords. Without these experiences, they are deprived of opportunities to gain social knowledge and social competence.

3. Children who are unskilled in social interaction with peers or are unpopular and rejected by playmates find escape in screen time, further reducing their interactions with others and further impeding their social and emotional development.

4. Parent–child conversations and interactions are interrupted. Both children and parents forgo dialogue and in-depth conversations when television viewing dominates their free time. Opportunities to address issues of concern to the child and to provide needed emotional and social guidance are often irretrievably lost.

5. Opportunities for children to discover their interests and unique capabilities or talents are reduced. Children who are developing initiative, industry, self-concept, and self-esteem need to explore and experience a variety of endeavors and interests on the way to self-discovery.

Adults can help children become discerning viewers of television by watching television with children and engaging them in dialogue about the programs and advertisements that they see. Family values and concepts of character, ethics, and integrity can be brought into these discussions. As with nutrition, adults control the content of children's media diets and set standards for the amount of time that can be devoted to television viewing. It is important to remember that when the television set is on, children are receiving visual and auditory input whether they are seated in front of the set or moving about, engaged in other activities. The content of adult programs and the news may not be appropriate for them. These programs contributed to fear of fantasy characters, transformations, and interpersonal violence in a study of 3- to 7-year-olds (Custers & Van den Buick, 2012).

Efforts to help children to become critical consumers of television and computer fare, whether formal (preprogrammed lessons or structured discussions) or informal (incidental and spontaneous) in the home or school, should be focused on the following:

- Decrease the belief that TV programs are real.
- Increase the child's tendency to compare what is seen on TV with other sources of information.
- Decrease television's credibility by teaching children about the economic and production aspects of television.
- Teach children to evaluate the content of television programming.

Parents and teachers have important roles to play in facilitating the positive effects of television for children (Table 15.4). The amount of time children spend viewing television can be curtailed in favor of more physically and mentally challenging activities and increased social interactions with others. Parents can make the children's use of TV and other media equipment contingent on physical activity. One study of overweight or obese children ages 8–12 found that the children's enjoyment of physical activity increased

Table 15.4 Critical Screen Time Skills Instructional Tips

Point out how television and computers can provide both worthwhile and objectionable programs.
Compare programs for redeeming versus objectionable characteristics.
Role-play characters and scripts viewed on screen to convey the concept of acting and actors playing a role, as opposed to portraying real events in real time.
Compare the roles of screen characters with those of individuals the child knows personally.
Teach children to watch and listen for special effects such as laugh tracks, sounds, lighting, and rapidly sequenced photos.
Listen to background and theme music, identifying familiar tunes or specific musical or sound instruments.
Talk about a story just viewed; employ creative ways of thinking about the story: a better ending, a change in character roles, or whether another person or actor played a certain role.
Answer questions children pose following their viewing while the subject is fresh in their minds.
Point out how commercials use loud, fast talk, flashy colors, unusual design elements, and sound or music to capture attention.
Together, make a list of famous people who make commercials, pointing out how these people are used to promote products.
Compare products advertised with ones the family prefers, and, when shopping, make price and quality comparisons.
Help children draw conclusions about the feasibility of purchasing advertised products.

when they were required to engage in physical activity for a certain period of time to earn an hour of watching TV (Goldfield, 2012).

Wise program choices can result when children are taught to evaluate the offerings. In addition, children need adults to talk with them about the content of programs they see and to help them become discerning viewers.

Computers, the Internet, and Social Media

Computers are marvelous sources of information, entertainment, and communicative expediency. They are an essential tool for learners, from preschool to senior citizens. Online services give children an endless supply of resources—encyclopedias, libraries, search capabilities, and current events coverage. However, children may access sites that have content that is inappropriate or overwhelming; promote prejudice, violence, hate, or pornography; bombard children with advertising, which may be misleading; offer children prizes; or invite them to join a "club" and attempt to arrange a meeting.

Just as children are taught not to talk with people they do not know, open the door to their home when they are alone and do not know who is there, or give personal information on the phone, they must also be taught the concept that "strangers" exist online. Just as they monitor children's choice of friends, where they play, and what television, music, books, and magazines they read, parents (and teachers) must supervise the appropriate use of online capabilities. Children particularly need to be taught not to provide personal information (their name, family names, addresses, phone numbers, work places, schools, credit card information, computer passwords, and so on) to any online site. Certainly, children need to be taught *never* to agree to actually meet someone they meet online. Parents and teachers can take advantage of commercially available software programs that restrict access to certain sites. They need to teach children how to communicate with parents at their work sites and coach children on the etiquette of computer communications, which is the same as for face-to-face communications.

Collections and Hobbies

During the early school years, children find enjoyment in objects to collect: popular theme cards, baseball and football cards, rocks, seashells, miniature toys or figures, insects, postcards, jewelry, doll clothes and accessories, stuffed toys, candy wrappers, comic books, and so on. Sometimes trading and bartering go along with these collections, and some children become avid collectors through this process. Children also enjoy perusing toy and electronics catalogs and thumbing through junk mail for hidden treasures. Making lists is another form of collecting: "what I want for Christmas," telephone numbers, addresses, birthdays, and other topics of interest.

Collections and hobbies enhance children's sense of self and their abilities, interests, and aspirations and expand their knowledge of certain objects or topics. Collections and hobbies engage the child in identifying, sorting, ordering, classifying, and researching tasks; they expand the child's knowledge and awareness and enhance cognitive development. They provide focus and entertainment during moments of self-imposed privacy as well as a medium for initiating contacts with others. To adults, some childhood collections may seem valueless and trivial. However, these collections and others yet to come may spark an interest that will endure and grow into other, related interests. Some represent the origins of what may someday become an occupation or a career.

Children with Special Needs

Children with special needs face greater social and emotional challenges as they move through the elementary grades. They share needs for acceptance, belonging, and self-esteem with their agemates. The extent to which they have had opportunities to develop the social skills of initiating and maintaining friendships and resolving conflicts through inclusive programs and activities will influence their successes with interpersonal relationships and peer acceptance. By the same token, the extent to which other children have learned to understand and relate to their peers with disabilities also influences the climate for acceptance and participation.

A common challenge for children with special needs, regardless of type of disability, is the feeling of being different from other children. The self-concepts of many children with disabilities may center too heavily on their disabilities. Teachers who seek positive and successful social and emotional experiences for children with special needs will find effective ways to promote group understandings and acceptance. Teachers will structure both the physical and social and emotional environments to encourage social interactions among all children (Sandall, McLean, & Smith, 2000).

Teachers should be aware that any emphasis on competition among children can be particularly detrimental to the social and emotional development of children with special needs. Instead, arranging for more cooperative group endeavors assists all children in the development of social skills and social competence (Baloche, 1998; Jacobs, Power, & Loh, 2002; Slavin, 1995).

Role of the Early Childhood Professional

Enhancing Emotional and Social Development in Children Ages 6 Through 8

1. Support the child's continuing need for nurturing and security.
2. Enhance the child's self-esteem through positive and supportive interactions.
3. Model prosocial and moral behaviors; help children to understand the need and rationales for rules.
4. Support the child's sense of industry through opportunities to participate in meaningful activities and to experience authentic accomplishments.
5. Understand the child's increasing needs for social interactions, and encourage and facilitate a variety of social interactions.
6. Recognize the child's continuing need for boundaries and guidance.
7. Provide positive, inductive, authoritative discipline.
8. Respond to the child's changing interests in gender with acceptance and respect while guiding the child toward antibias perspectives.
9. Provide appropriate media experiences, and help the child to become a critical evaluator of media programs.
10. Monitor and guide children's use of the Internet

Key Terms

defense mechanism   internalization
industry   sociocentric

Review Strategies and Activities

1. Review the key terms individually or with a classmate.
2. Develop an annotated bibliography of children's books that addresses the issues children confront in making and maintaining friendships.
3. Observe an exemplary third-grade classroom. How is social interaction encouraged? Are informal social groups evident? Observe these friendship groups on the play-ground at recess. What are the compositions of the groups? How do they interact with one another? Is there a leader? What rules seem to be evident? How do the children respond to nongroup members?
4. Engage in a dialogue with a member of a different ethnic background. Discuss similarities and differences in your child rearing with regard to school achievement, authority, independence, responsibilities, choice of friends, and gender and racial group membership.
5. With a partner, brainstorm ways to promote and facilitate the developing sense of industry in young school-age children.
6. Discuss with your classmates the social challenges for children with disabilities.

Further Reading

Rubin, K. H., Bukowsky, W. M., & Laursen, B. (2011). *Handbook of peer interactions, relationships, and groups (social, emotional, and personality development in context)*. New York: Guilford Press.

Other Resources

American Psychological Association, www.apahelpcenter.org/articles. Downloadable brochures for many topics, including the following:
> *Anxiety and sadness may increase on anniversary of a traumatic event*
> *Making step-families work*
> *Painful shyness*
> *Understanding depression and effective treatment*
> *What makes kids care? Teaching gentleness in a violent world*

American School Counselor Association, www.schoolcounselor.org. Resources on many topics including character education, test anxiety, bullying, cyber-safety, grief, anger, gender, and others.

Stop Bullying, www.stopbullying.gov. This site has excellent webisodes for kids, video clips, tip sheets, and many excellent resources to help stop bullying now.

chapter 16

Cognitive, Language, and Literacy Development: Ages Six Through Eight

Virtually no one argues that a given child's life course is set by the time of school entry. People are not like rockets whose trajectory is established at the moment they are launched. Indeed, it is the lifelong capacity for change and reorganization that renders human beings capable of dramatic recovery from early harm and incapable of being inoculated against later adversity. This lifelong plasticity renders us both adaptive and vulnerable.

—Jack Shonkoff and Deborah Phillips

Many a child's development is disrupted when family life failed
to prepare him for school life, or when school life fails to sustain
the promises of earlier stages.

—Erik Erikson

After studying this chapter, you will demonstrate comprehension by:

▶ knowing current ways of using technology to understand executive function; recognizing theoretical perspectives on cognitive, language, and literacy development in children ages 6 through 8;

▶ describing the cognitive development of children ages 6 through 8;

▶ describing the language development of children ages 6 through 8;

▶ describing the literacy development of children ages 6 through 8;

▶ relating cognitive, language, and literacy development to other developmental domains;

▶ identifying major factors influencing cognitive, language, and literacy development in children ages 6 through 8; and

▶ suggesting strategies for promoting cognitive, language, and literacy development in children ages 6 through 8.

Cognitive development—the aspect of growth and development that deals with thinking, problem solving, intelligence, and language—is about to undergo a major shift, altering the way children perceive, respond to new information, and interact with objects and people. Perhaps it is no accident that formal schooling begins during ages 5 to 6 or 7. This "5 to 7 shift," as it is often called, is best described by looking at current science.

Cognitive Competence and Development

The brain is developing facility with executive function in these years, which enables the child to learn in greater depth and complexity. Executive function is the term for the frontal cortex's work in organizing other mental processes, allowing learning to become more integrated and allowing the brain to respond to new information and events. Catale et al (2011) simplified the definition by reducing it to "inhibition *(regulation),* working memory, and mental flexibility." There is now an enormous collection of research using brain imagery to demonstrate the brain processing executive functions such as working memory, attention maintenance, organization, and integration of information. The following is a brief desciption of the kind of research being done on EF with children from ages 6–8.

Because maintaining attention is a foundational aspect of learning, it is of concern that the ability to attend without being easily distracted appears to be highly associated with social economic status. A study by Stevens, Lauinger, & Nelville (2009) specifically looked at the level of the mother's education (no college or some college) related to the ability to maintain attention. The 16 children ages 3–8 each wore a plastic cap embedded with electrodes that recorded brain activity through an electroencephologram. The children listened to a stereo recording that played one story on the right side and a different one on the left. They were directed to listen to a certain side and were provided with small visual clues to help them remember—a 2 1/2 inch screen with an arrow pointing to the target side and showing illustrations of the target story. The children were asked to listen for a certain sound within the target story, either a sylla-ble or a sort of buzz. If they attended to the sound, the EEG would record the response. The children whose mothers had less education were significanty less able to ignore the distracting story.

Moreno et al (2009) looked at the use of training to improve brain skills. Children with musical training have significantly more grey matter in their brains. Using functional Magnetic Resonance Imagery (fMIR) researchers found that after six months of musical training, children had increased grey matter, steadily improved in reading and writing skills and understanding, and better grasped the use of pitch in language. So, while a strong argument is made for the importance of the first two years of life for brain develop-ment, the brain continues to show plasticity throughout life.

In a review of the literature on working memory in the classroom (Alloway & Gathercole, 2006), working memory is defined as the ability "to store information while other material is being mentally manipulated during the classroom learning activities that form the foundations for the acquisition of complex skills and knowl-edge" (p. 134). Examples include the need to hold basic math skills in memory while solving more complex problems. On the other hand, "Reading disabilities can be characterized by marked difficulties in mastering skills including word recognition, spelling, and reading comprehension" (p. 135). In a very different approach from the musical training mentioned previously, these authors suggest that classroom structure increased support for children with low memories: provide shorter directions more frequently, give directions only for that phase of the work, provide spelling of key words at the child's desk, and encourage the child to ask for information and not abandon a project (p. 138).

From the literature on how the brain becomes neurologically "wired" during the early years, we have learned that the brain functions most efficiently in relatively stress-free environments and in situations in which the learner is in a relaxed–alert state of mind (as opposed to fearful, anxious, or relaxed–bored, for example). Relaxed alertness is characterized by a sense of low threat and high challenge. When learning events be-come overwhelming (as when expectations repeatedly exceed the learner's capabilities) or monotonous and boring or when the classroom social and emotional tone creates a psychologically unsafe environment, a phenomenon known as perceptual narrowing occurs. This perceptual narrowing has been aptly referred to as **downshifting** (Hart, 1983). As described by Caine and Caine (1997), downshifting is a psychophysiologi-cal response that affects the brain's ability to function at high levels of engagement and thwarts creative thinking and problem solving. It is provoked by perceived threat and fatigue. In downshifting, the individual's responses are limited, and he or she is less able to consider all aspects of a situation. The learner is less able to engage in com-plex intellectual tasks, particularly those requiring creativity and the ability to engage in open-ended thinking and questioning. Downshifting appears to affect higher-order cognitive functions of the brain. In the developing brain, situations that persistently pro-voke downshifting interfere with optimal brain growth and neurological development. Psychologically unsafe environments include threat of physical harm, failure, embar-rassment, infringement on privacy, ridicule, retribution, and other stressors.

Attention Deficit Hyperactivity Disorder (ADHD) is another topic within the field of childhood cognitive and biological development that has received major attention in recent years. See Box 16.1 for more information about this condition.

downshifting
a psychophysiological response to perceived threat that is accompanied by a sense of helplessness or lack of self-efficacy, which affects the brain's ability to function at optimal levels

Box 16.1   What Is Attention Deficit Hyperactivity Disorder?

The American Academy of Pediatrics (AAP) describes ADHD as a disorder, characterized by chronic neurological conditions, that results from persistent dysfunction within the central nervous system. ADHD is not related to gender, level of intelligence, or cultural environment. It is not a result of inappropriate parenting. The actual cause or causes of ADHD are not fully understood. A defining characteristic is that the symptoms persist over time without improvement under conditions of typical guidance and education procedures. It is estimated that 6% to 9% of school-age children are referred for evaluation (Reiff & Tippins, 2004).

Parents, caregivers, and teachers may notice behaviors or difficulties such as the following:

- Understanding and following through on directions and procedures as well as relating to descriptions and other instructional information.

- Sequencing tasks, such as ordering or grouping items by an attribute such as height, color brightness, weight, or use

- Following procedures in a required sequence of steps

- Awkward, ungraceful large motor movement

- Difficulty with fine motor tasks

- Motoric restlessness

- Hyper- or hypoalertness (i.e., over- or underresponding to sensory stimuli)

- Difficulty bringing emotions into control

- Emotional responses that are out of proportion to the provocation or persistent failure to exhibit expected proportionate emotions

- Uncontrolled talking, speaking out of turn, excitable communications, inappropriate voice volume

- Low tolerance for frustration

- Social interaction difficulties including failure to behave appropriately in specific contexts

- Failure to read the social cues of others

Because ADHD is often suspected in children who are outgoing, loquacious, and energetic and its symptoms are common to those of other potential problems, there are risks of misdiagnosis, which can have long-term deleterious consequences for the child. Any potential neurological disorder requires comprehensive professional evaluation for accurate diagnosis (Haber, 2000). A child with ADHD needs accurate assessment and helpful medical, psychological, and/or educational intervention. Assessment and diagnosis of ADHD require professional evaluation of the *presence* or *absence* and the *combination* of symptoms. ADHD symptoms can range from mild (almost unnoticeable) to severe (significantly interfering with daily functioning).

continued

> ## Box 16.1 continued
>
> Treatment is determined by an evaluation team that includes the child's primary care physician, parents, licensed (certified) diagnostician or psychologist, and the child's classroom teacher. Medication may or may not be prescribed. Because ADHD represents a combination of symptoms that are found in different configurations and to greater or lesser degrees in different children, treatment programs are highly individualized. Some symptoms respond to medication, whereas others respond more readily to changes in the child's environment, such as developing a specialized and individualized education and behavioral guidance plan. All evaluations of children are legally private information and can only be shared with individuals who have a legitimate reason to have the information. Discussing or labeling the child with fellow workers, friends, or other children or parents is unethical and in some cases illegal. Professionals have a responsibility to protect the dignity of every child while ensuring she or he receives timely and appropriately designed treatment and education services.

Constructivist Theory

Jerome Bruner is a major leader in American education, believing that children are active learners who construct meaning from the world and learn through discovery. He called his theory *constructivism*. At a time when education was driven by behaviorism, Bruner turned interest back to internal processes of learning—always developing through the culture and context of the learning experience. Beginning in the 1940s, he started examining how needs, motivations, and expectations affect perception. In other words, we do not see or understand objectively but through our own personal lens. However, he turned from that intrapersonal approach to understanding the enormous impact of culture and social relationships in learning. In 1960 he published a highly influential book called the *Process of Education*. From that book came his major themes on learning and instruction.

The Role of Structure in Learning and Teaching. Bruner proposed that as knowledge accumulates "The teaching and learning of structure, rather than simply the mastery of facts and techniques, is at the center of the classic problem of transfer… If earlier learning is to render later learning easier, it must do so by providing a general picture in terms of which the relations between things encountered earlier and later are made as clear as possible" (Bruner, 1960, p. 12).

spiral curriculum
educational method in which new concepts build on previous experience and knowledge as the student progresses so that he or she is learning increasingly complex facets of the already-introduced subject

Readiness for Learning. Bruner believed that schools wasted time by waiting to teach subjects they believed were too difficult. On the contrary, he wrote, "We begin with the hypothesis that any subject can be taught effectively in some intellectually honest form to any child at any stage of development (ibid., 33). He also expounded upon the idea of the **spiral curriculum:** "A curriculum as it develops should revisit the basic ideas repeatedly, building upon them until the student has grasped the full formal apparatus that goes with them" (ibid., 13).

Intuitive and Analytical Thinking. Bruner valued intuitive thinking as a way experts in a field often came to a conclusion that was later proved or disproved by analytical thinking. He believed that schools should create an atmosphere that promoted creativity and intuition.

Motives for Learning. Bruner believed that the best motivation for learning was interest in the topic. He was concerned that "in an age of spectatorship" motivations for learning must not be allowed to become passive.

Thirty-three years later, in 1996 (at the age of 82) he wrote *The Culture of Education*, a series of nine essays in which he summarized his ever-evolving understanding of learning and instruction. He wrote of the importance of learning the values, beliefs, and behaviors of your culture and of the way the mind makes meaning of the world, including the importance of catagorization. Bruner believed that people make hierarchical levels of catagories from which they are able to create cognitive maps of knowledge. (See Table 16.1.)

Later in his career (he is still working at age 96), he delved into the importance of narrative in learning. He also became involved in an ongoing partnership with the infant, toddler, and preschool programs of Reggio Emilia.

Other Learning Theories

Many of the learning theories of the twentieth century are built on Bruner's work. They mark the importance of the individual learner making sense of his or her world; the central role of culture and social relationships; the need for a structured curriculum that meets the learner where he or she is; and the idea of cognitive mapping. Other theories of importance include multiple intelligences, information-processing, social learning, and bioecological theory.

Table 16.1

Catagories are rules that specify four things about objects:
- What the critical attributes (characteristics that define a category) are; for example, an animal with four legs who eats grass, has a double stomach, and gives milk would be included in the "cow" category.
- How critical attributes are combined.
- What weights are assigned to various characteristics; for example, if a cow had lost a leg, it would still be a cow.
- What limits are set on attributes; for example, if an animal didn't have a double stomach, it wouldn't be a cow.

Three types of categories include the following:
- *Identity categories* are based on attributes or features of objects.
- *Equivalence categories* are determined by affective criteria, which make objects equivalent by emotional reactions, functional criteria, based on related functions or by formal criteria such as law, science, or cultural agreement.
- *Coding systems* create related categories from sensory input.

Cognitive, Language, and Literacy Development: Ages Six Through Eight

Counting experiences with concrete objects, including their fingers, help children ages 6–8.

What Are Children Learning?

In addition to learning language and literacy in the first through third grades, children are expected to learn about many topics. With a natural interest in everything around them and new abilities for learning, children cover many subjects in school.

In science curricula, they learn about weather, earth's materials, air, seasons, and the sun. They learn about living things and life cycles, how fossils tell us of our history, and how one's habitat provides for the needs of living things. Young children learn about the use of tools from scissors to pulleys to computers.

In mathematics, children are expected to learn to count, use counting to tell the number of objects, learn the basic ideas of addition and subtraction, perform addition and subtraction within 1000, classify objects, use money, and create and compare shapes. By third grade students can understand fractions as numbers, represent and solve problems using multiplication and division, and use visual displays to represent data.

In social studies, children are expected to understand how people learn about and interpret history and that people in the past affect our current families and communities. Students learn about the United States as a country made up of people from all over the world and a place where all races and religions are equal citizens. By third grade children are learning about their own, local history.

Every state has created a set of expected child outcomes for K–12. In addition to the topics listed previously, there are standards in physical health and education as well as the arts. Some states continue to carry outcomes for social and emotional development into the elementary grades.

Language Competence and Development

Children at 6, 7, and 8 years of age demonstrate sophisticated language competencies. They have developed an awareness of the *phonemes* of their language and can pronounce them and hear them in the speech of others. They have acquired the knowledge that words stand for, or symbolize, things, and their knowledge of *semantics* has begun to facilitate the acquisition of words and word meanings. Using the *morphemes* of their language, they can construct and speak in meaningful phrases and sentences. Using their knowledge of *syntax,* they are able to combine words into meaningful and appropriately constructed sentences. Moreover, they have learned a great deal about the *pragmatics* of language, which is the knowledge of how language is used in different contexts—or, more simply stated, the rules of conversation. With increasing mastery of these elements of language, by the time children enter school, their language (both receptive and expressive) appears rather adultlike. However, studies indicate that there are some aspects of language development that children continue to acquire through the elementary school years, into adolescence, and throughout adult life.

Typically, figures of speech such as metaphors and similes are used to amplify meaning and are common in adult language. However, young children, including 6- to 8-year-olds, have difficulty with them. Their understanding of figures of speech is a gradual process that depends on cognitive development and the reduction of the constraints of literal thinking. For example, the expression "She eats like a bird" is no longer interpreted literally as a girl eating worms or pecking at food in a birdlike manner. Rather, this simile is understood as meaning that a person eats sparingly. As children are exposed to figures of speech, they begin to understand them (Pamling & Samuelsson, 2007).

Understanding of figures of speech is accompanied by the awareness of puns and jokes. Children during the early school years demonstrate increasing awareness of puns and jokes because of their ability to think about the multiple meanings of words, the relationships among words, and the structure of narratives. They also become more proficient liars (should they be motivated to do so), both because they can now think about events simultaneously and because of their broader knowledge base. The use of white lies and of lying to prevent hurting another's feelings emerges as a result of children's increased social and cognitive awareness (Menyuk, 1988).

Another area of increased understanding of language is reflected in the comprehension and use of sarcasm. Adults rely on the nonverbal cues of context and tone of voice when interpreting sarcasm. Young children often miss these cues. However, Ackerman (1982) found that first graders were able to interpret sarcasm if the context was evident before the sarcastic remark was made. By third grade, children were increasingly better able to detect sarcastic remarks, using context and facial and intonation cues. A research team from Israel found that damage to any of three areas of the brain (left hemisphere, frontal lobes, and right hemisphere) makes it difficult for people to understand sarcasm. "Reading between the lines" requires interpreting the other person's state of mind, emotional tone, and complex interactions among the three parts of the brain (Shamay-Tsoory, Tomer, & Aharon-Peretz, 2005).

Metalinguistic awareness, or the ability to think about the meanings and forms of language, becomes more evident as children mature. Metalinguistic abilities do not develop suddenly (Menyuk, 1988). Rather, the awareness of various aspects of language develops at different times for different categories and relationships in language. However, the process by which metalinguistic awareness develops appears to have a definite pattern. First, children incorporate new structures on an unconscious level. Then they develop the ability to recognize appropriate or inappropriate uses of the structure. Finally, children become able to talk about the structures of language (deVilliers & deVilliers, 1992).

The understanding of pronominal references appears to increase with age. By second grade, children use pronouns more frequently than they did when they were younger. In addition, children during the primary grades begin to talk more about topics and ideas that are not in their immediate context.

Development of Syntax

Development of syntax continues through the primary-grade years. One grammatical development that occurs during this period is the ability to understand infinitive phrases. At age 5, children do not relate the grammatical subject with the agent role. For example, when they are presented with a blindfolded doll and asked, "Is the doll easy or hard to see," their response is "Hard to see." By age 10, the response changes to "Easy to see" (Chomsky, 1969). Understanding the passive voice ("The ball was hit by Joe" rather than "Joe hit the ball") also takes place over an extended period of time and is not achieved until the end of the elementary school years. Virtually all morphological indicators of plurals, possessives, and past tense are acquired between ages 6 and 8.

Vocabulary Development

Vocabulary development continues to expand, spurred onward by the child's cumulative background of experiences and social interactions, more sophisticated cognitive processes, and formal instruction. As vocabulary increases, children begin to use words in more conventional and accurate ways. Overextensions begin to disappear, and new words are used to describe existing and new concepts. For example, a child might no longer just use the word *doggie*, but might talk about *poodles, German shepherds, mutts,* and *puppies,* indicating increased cognitive awareness of the various categorical labels under the general class *dogs.*

Communicative Competence

Children at ages 6, 7, and 8 are subject to an increasing number of experiences in new environments and with diverse groups of people. Upon entering first grade, children learn not only about their own teacher and classroom, but also about other teachers and classrooms; about expected behaviors in the lunchroom, in the library, and on the playground; and about special classes such as art, physical education, and music. In addition, many school-age children visit friends' homes, join sports and civics organizations such as Brownies and Cub Scouts, take lessons, and participate in faith-based activities. These experiences and interactions add to the child's repertoire of scripts, or behaviors and language appropriate to each context.

Opportunities to interact with others in various contexts help children gain knowledge of and competence in the conventions of conversational language, such as focused and respectful listening, turn taking, and other verbal courtesies. The conversational technique of **shading** is used to change the topic of a conversation. Shading requires a level of tact and finesse generally uncommon in young children, but it is beginning to appear during the 6-to 8-year age period.

Primary-grade children also demonstrate an increasing awareness of the intent of many utterances and take cues from inflections. A second-grader knows that when mother says, "This room is a disaster area," the child had better get the room cleaned up right away. In addition, children ages 6, 7, and 8 indicate an increasing awareness of **registers,** or the speech variations needed in different social situations.

There is great "variability in language development" depending on their "linguistic experience" (Vasilyeva & Waterfall, 2011, pp. 36–37). A number of research studies have

shading
gradually changing the topic of conversation

registers
variations in the style of speech according to the particular social setting

Opportunities for children to talk with one another during their activities promote communicative competence.

shown that children need models, adults who are contingently responsive to their language. Exposure to a rich and varied vocabulary, non-negative talk, and cognitive challenging language are related to children's language growth (Vasilyeva & Waterfall, 2011). As you will see, children's language development is related to their literacy development.

Literacy Competence and Development

By the time children enter first grade, they have had many and varied experiences with print in their preschool, kindergarten, and child care settings and in their homes. Obviously, there are wide variations in the quantity and quality of these experiences among children and in the child's responses and developmental outcomes. Nevertheless, by age 6, most children have mastered most of the concepts and skills listed in Table 13.1.

Literacy Learning in the Primary Grades: Reading

During the primary grades, children are introduced more formally to reading, writing, and spelling through both direct instruction and hands-on, concrete experiences. In first grade, children begin to read orally; by the end of first grade, they do so with some fluency; use letter–sound correspondence, word parts, and context cues to identify new words; identify an increasing number of sight words; write coherent stories on topics that are of particular interest to them; include more letters (sounds) in their private spellings; and learn about punctuation and capitalization.

During second grade, children begin to apply more sophisticated learning strategies (e.g., asking questions, rereading, observing others) to comprehend the written word. They use phonemic strategies more efficiently to identify unfamiliar words, can rely on an ever-increasing number of familiar **sight words,** begin to write with a specific audience in mind, demonstrate more conventional spelling in both their private and public writing, use punctuation and capitalization more often and more accurately, and can use reading for both enjoyment and to obtain information about specific topics.

sight words
words in print that young children recognize immediately

By third grade, children who have become fairly fluent readers tend to enjoy reading and seek opportunities to do so. Their vocabularies, now quite large, facilitate greater comprehension. They can now use many different strategies for deriving meaning from text, can use phonics cues quite readily (if not automatically) to read unfamiliar words, and use writing in many different contexts: to correspond with others, write reports, make lists, create a story or poem, and so on.

These developments follow a rather predictable flow from book awareness and exploration experiences in infancy to relatively fluent reading by third and fourth grade. They cannot be hurried because learning to read is one of the most challenging perceptual and cognitive tasks of early childhood. Learning to competently read, write, and spell requires a rich background of literacy-related experiences.

Literacy Instruction in the Primary Grades: Reading. Because literacy is so important to all other school learning, our society expects its schools to provide successful reading instruction. When and how formal instruction should begin and what types of instructional strategies are thought to be the most successful are issues on which there are wide disagreements among scholars and professionals.

Generally the debates fall within two camps: Those who believe that children learn best when introduced first to parts and then to wholes, and those who believe that children learn best when introduced first to wholes and then to parts. Differences in instructional strategies look something like this:

Part-to-Whole Approach	Whole-to-Part Approach
Learn letters' names, sounds	Learn familiar words in a context of specific, meaningful experiences
Use letter sounds to sound out an unfamiliar word	Identify new words using context cues
Segment words and sentences into parts	Create labels, phrases, and sentences using familiar words in writing
Use basal readers with decodable words	Use familiar children's books and literature
Encourage conventional spelling through preselected word lists and conventional spelling rules	Accept phonemic spelling as part of a learning-to-spell continuum
Use worksheets and pencil-and-paper tasks	Use first-hand experiences and concrete materials

In efforts to bring empirical data to guide the understanding of how (and when) children most successfully come into literacy and to find common points of agreement among opposing views, contemporary researchers have begun to examine research from decades of studies from many different disciplines. Collections of reviews of research have attempted to be helpful.

A summary of research on reading instruction published in 1990 found that there was no definitely superior method for teaching reading. Neither a whole-word approach nor a **phonics**-based (sound–letter correspondence) approach was found to be better than the other (Adams, 1990). The researcher commented,

> Much of the controversy in beginning reading centers on phonics. But like beauty, what people mean by phonics is often in the eye of the beholder. To some, phonics is irrelevant. To others, it is essential. To some, phonics instruction is a mind-numbing collection of worksheets that are assigned to keep students busy and that seem to be divorced from any real practice in reading. To others, phonics instruction is a teacher working with a group of children to initiate them directly into written language by revealing its code. Phonics can be all of these things, and even in instructional programs that claim not to teach phonics, phonics instruction can take place. It may be possible to teach reading without paying some attention to the forms of written words. On the other hand, it is possible, but not desirable, to teach only phonics and ignore the meaning of written words. (Adams, 1990, p. iii)

A full summary of the findings of this review is beyond the scope of this text, but following are some examples of Adams's (1990) review of research findings:

- Basic familiarity with letters and letter names is a strong predictor of reading success.
- Awareness that spoken language is composed of phonemes is also a predictor of success in learning to read.
- A child's general awareness of the nature and functions of print is a strong index of readiness to learn to read.
- The single most important activity for building the knowledge and skills required for learning to read appears to be reading aloud to children regularly and interactively.

An important document came with the convening of a representative committee of professionals in child development, early childhood education, elementary education, reading, psychology, and other related fields to examine the prevention of reading difficulties. The report of this committee was published by the National Academy of Sciences, which had been commissioned by the U.S. Department of Education and the U.S. Department of Health and Human Services to study the issue. The report was published under the title *Preventing Reading Difficulties in Young Children* (Snow, Burns, & Griffin, 1998). This document took a very strong (though not absolute) position in favor of part-to-whole instruction, with heavy emphasis beginning in kindergarten on a phonics-based, direct instruction approach.

The report emphasized the importance of the understanding of how sounds are represented alphabetically and encouraged more direct instruction than is commonly viewed as appropriate for young children. A few of their recommendations include practices that early childhood professionals have traditionally used, though many are at odds with widely held views of early childhood development and learning. Again, a review of all of the recommendations of this report is beyond the scope of this text. However, some of their recommendations are explicit instruction and practice that lead to phonemic awareness and letter–sound correspondence, learning to sound out words, the use of meaningful texts, the recognition and use of phonemic spelling as a beginning writing process, focused instruction on conventional spelling, curricula that build rich linguistic and conceptual knowledge, direct instruction, and providing early intervention and support for children who show signs of having difficulties acquiring early language and literacy skills.

Soon after the publication of the National Research Council's report, the National Association for the Education of Young Children (NAEYC) and the International Reading Association (IRA) published a joint statement, *Learning to Read and Write: Developmentally Appropriate Practices for Young Children* (Neuman, Copple, & Bredekamp, 2000). Although asserting that it is essential to teach children to read and write competently, the authors of this statement expressed concern about inappropriate practices: "Recognizing the early beginnings of literacy acquisition too often has resulted in use of inappropriate teaching practices suited to older children or adults perhaps but ineffective with children in preschool, kindergarten and the early grades" (Neuman et al., 1999, p. 5). Further, this statement advised, "The roots of phonemic awareness, which is related to later reading success, are found in traditional rhyming, skipping, and word games" (p. 9); and, "In the primary grades, approaches that favor some type of systematic code instruction along with meaningful connected reading promote children's superior progress in reading" (p. 12).

More recently, the discussion concerning the most appropriate way for children to learn to read focuses on evidence that "…has been accumulating that the effect of literacy instruction strategies does indeed appear to depend on student characteristics" (Connor, 2011, p. 256). These instructional strategies that focus on literacy instruction as related to child characteristics is called "child characteristic-by-instruction (C-I) interactions" (Connor, 2011, p. 256). Teachers who are well grounded in knowledge of child growth and development soon learn the unique characteristics and needs of individual children and find that important goodness of fit between instructional strategies and the learner.

The following vignette demonstrates that the responsiveness of the teacher to literacy experiences is also crucial to children's learning:

Six-year-old Angela was playing with several neighborhood children in her garage. One of the children discovered a tarantula crawling across the cement floor. The children discussed what they should do and whether tarantulas were really dangerous. Finally, one of the children suggested killing the tarantula with bug spray. The tarantula was sprayed and sprayed with insecticide. Finally, it died. The children used a garden tool to turn the tarantula over and then examined it closely. Next, they scooped it up, put it in a plastic container, and went on a tour of the neighborhood, showing the tarantula to other children. The tarantula episode was the main topic at the family dinner table that evening.

The next day, Angela went to her classroom. She painted a picture and then dictated the story of the tarantula to one of the teachers in her classroom (see Figure 16.1). The spelling of *tarantula* was checked by using the dictionary. Angela's picture and story (consisting of 23 words) were hung on the classroom wall at the children's eye level. One of the teachers found some books about tarantulas to read to interested children. They discovered, among other things, that tarantulas are really not all that dangerous. Several days later, Angela and a teacher were looking at her picture and story and talking about her experience with the tarantula. The teacher asked Angela whether she could find the word *tarantula*. Without any hesitation and jumping in with pride, Joanie, a classmate, pointed accurately to the word.

This vignette demonstrates the powerful relationships among thought, experience, language, and literacy. Angela had a very meaningful experience. It was talked and read about with others in several contexts: in the neighborhood, at the family dinner table, and at school. The experience was shared symbolically through Angela's painting and through oral language. It was translated into written language, which was read by Angela, her teacher, and other children. The interaction among thought, oral language, and written language in this vignette demonstrates how the wholeness of language can promote the development of literacy. Angela knew where the long word *tarantula* was located among 23 words, as did a classmate with whom she shared her story.

Figure 16.1

Long words with a specific meaning, such as *tarantula,* are easier for young children to identify than shorter words without a simple meaning, such as *the* and *what*.

We had a big tarantula
We killed it by bug-spray
We had a black wasp in
our house.
We were scared to death.

Cognitive, Language, and Literacy Development: Ages Six Through Eight

Holistic approaches to language and literacy development are characterized by the following:

- Systematic planning around the assessed capabilities, prior experiences, cultural backgrounds, and special interests and needs of individual children
- The integration of language and literacy experiences in all aspects of the curriculum and daily routines
- The use of firsthand experiences to initiate learning opportunities
- The use of concrete materials to enhance concept development
- The use of children's literature to heighten interest and engage the learner
- The use of immediately available print in the learner's surroundings
- Social interaction that engages children in language, metalanguage, and broadened perspectives
- Ongoing teacher–student interactions that provide assessment, scaffolding, immediate feedback, clarification of concepts and processes, and opportunities to encourage metacognitive and metalanguage thinking
- Both structured and spontaneous literacy activities
- Encouragement of writing and reading for meaning
- Contextualized skill lessons (phonics, word order, word spacing, letter formations, spelling, and so on)

Shared learning experiences enhance cognitive, social, and emotional development.

Relationship Between Reading and Writing

As the vignette about Angela and the tarantula indicates, reading and writing appear to be interrelated and to facilitate the development of literacy. Children learn to read by reading what they write and by reading print that is important to them. They learn to write if they believe that they have thoughts and messages that are important enough to be shared with others in a written context (Dyson, 1993, 1997).

Both Jeremy's and Angela's first-grade teachers see the teaching of reading and writing as inseparable. They do not relegate reading and writing to separate time slots during the day; rather, both reading and writing are taught throughout the day in many contexts and in interrelated ways. Both teachers continue many of the literacy experiences that Angela and Jeremy encountered in their preprimary classrooms.

Jeremy's and Angela's primary-grade classrooms are organized to promote interaction with materials and with other children. Abundant print materials are located throughout the classroom and in learning centers. These materials include calendars, several kinds of charts (helper charts, charts with pen pal names, charts written by the children with spelling strategies, charts for figuring out words, charts listing the steps in the writing process, and charts of science experiment results), recipes for applesauce and pancakes, the Pledge of Allegiance, the weekly schedule, a story about the author of the week, children's artwork and written reports, learning center signs describing the learning that takes place in the center, books, and magazines. Paper and writing tools are located in each center. The class library is stocked with a wide variety of books: class-made books, individually made books, big books, and many patterned or predictable books, information books, first dictionaries, and a child's thesaurus. There are various centers in the classrooms: art, publishing/writing, computer, math, science, listening, and a display area. There are animals and plants to observe and to draw and write about. Both teachers attractively display children's writing on bulletin boards. Desks are clustered in groups of four to promote interaction, or children may work around small tables strategically placed near needed materials. Children are encouraged to talk as they engage in their learning activities. Recognizing that learning to read requires many instructional strategies, selected basal readers and other direct instruction strategies are used when they are appropriate or particularly helpful to individual students.

Literacy Instruction in the Primary Grades: Writing

The ability to write varies greatly among the children in Ms. Wood's class. The children want to write and have others read their writing. Mailboxes, pen pals, and message boards facilitate this communication process. Through writing that is meaningful to the children, they gradually learn about the forms of writing, including spelling and punctuation. They discover that the spelling of some words makes sense, but a number of words are spelled in ways that do not. Jeremy says that *egg* should have an *a* in it, not an *e*. First graders struggle with the silent *e* and try to understand how the same letter can be used for different sounds, such as the *g* in *giant* and the *g* in *gate*.

By the end of the first-grade year, the children in Ms. Wood's room have learned much about writing. The environment has been supportive, meaningful, and rich with print experiences. Jeremy's story about dinosaurs reveals that he is confident in himself as a writer (see Figure 16.2). He organizes and presents his thoughts in a logical manner. He demonstrates no hesitancy in spelling long dinosaur names. He indicates that he has learned much about handwriting, spacing, and punctuation, and he gives evidence of moving into conventional spelling.

Both Jeremy's and Angela's first-grade teachers know that if children in their classes are to become truly literate, comprehension or understanding of the text is essential. Fields and Spangler (2000) suggested that literacy development is "a process in which reading involves *interacting* with the thoughts someone else has expressed in writing, in which writing is perceived as recording one's own thoughts, and in which thinking is basic" (p. 133). Reading aloud both high-quality fiction and nonfiction books encourages the development of critical thinking and problem solving, as well as flexibility in reading for young children (Doiron, 1994).

As children continue to develop their reading abilities in second and third grades, it is important to continue to help them to use various strategies to identify unfamiliar

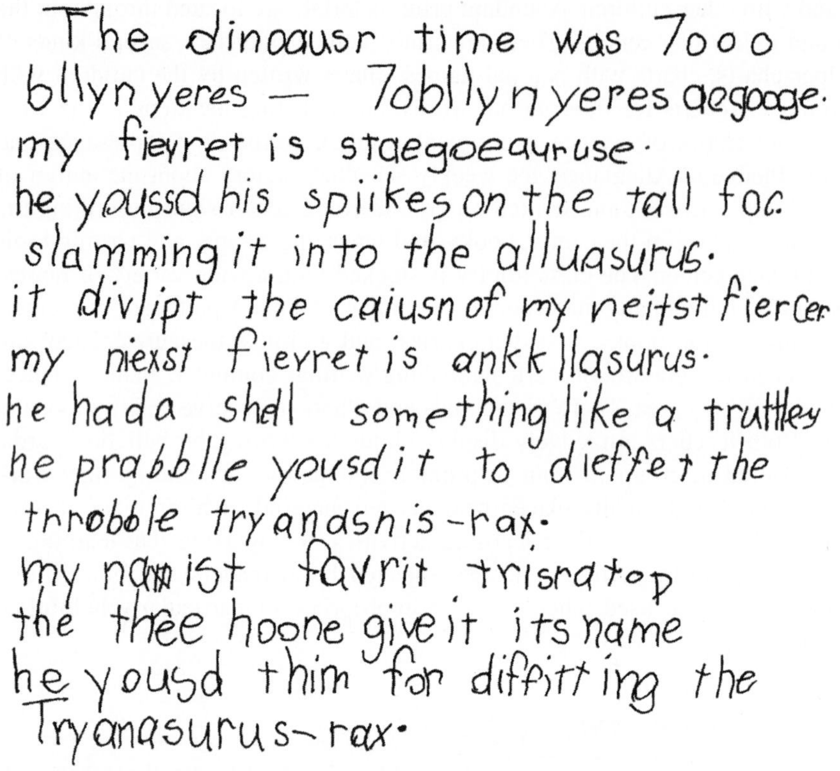

Figure 16.2

Jeremy's story about dinosaurs, written in first grade, reveals that he is most confident in himself as a writer.

The dinoausr time was 7000
bllyn yeres — 7obllyn yeres aegooge.
my fievret is staegoeayruse.
he youssd his spiikes on the tall foc.
slamming it into the alluasurus.
it divlipt the caiusn of my neitst fiercer
my niexst fievret is ankkllasurus.
he had a shal something like a truttley
he prabblle yousd it to dieffet the
throbble tryanasnis-rax.
my namist favrit trisratop
the thee hoone give it its name
he yousd thim for diffitting the
Tryanasurus-rax.

words (sounding out, context cues) while keeping the primary focus on the meaning of print. Third grade is usually the year in which children are expected to deal with more content knowledge in the areas of science, health, and social studies. Specific textbooks are often introduced at this grade level, and children are expected to read for meaning and be accountable for the material through tests. If literacy experiences during the first and second grades have facilitated the development of decoding skills in ways that enhance the child's desire to read and helped children to learn that there is meaning in print, children will have the critical mindset that print has a message for them. This concept will help them as they continue to learn throughout their school years. Conversely, if young children view reading as a skill/drill activity that is focused primarily on isolated performance, comprehending content material and reading independently may be a problem as they progress through the elementary school grades.

Literacy Learning in the Primary Grades: Writing

Ms. Wood continues many of the writing and print experiences of Jeremy's kindergarten in her first-grade classroom. She models writing for the children and facilitates purposeful opportunities for them to write in a variety of situations, from thank-you notes to stories to lists of needed classroom supplies. Ms. Wood allows children to freely explore their writing. She provides ample time for the rehearsal stage of writing, in which the children can draw or talk about their writing. This talking and drawing help to organize children's thoughts so that they can write.

Ms. Wood also continues to read to the children. She also uses a strategy called "print referencing" to promote children's "print knowledge" (Justice & Piasta, 2011, p. 200). As she reads with an individual or small group, she explicitly will "(1) draw children's attention toward the print within the text and (2) provide children with information about specific aspects of print forms and functions" (Justice & Piasta, 2011, p. 205). Hearing and seeing the written language help children to learn about reading and writing. Ms. Wood also carefully observes children and acts as an instructor, facilitator, and scaffolder to move them into new awareness of the processes of reading and writing.

Early in the school year, the principal at Jeremy's school invites a children's book author to visit for a day. Through this experience, children learn about the editing process and what it means to be an author. Approximately once a month, Jeremy's class publishes a class book. Ms. Wood serves as the editor and helps the children with revisions. Suggested revisions are made in pencil, and then the children recopy their stories for the published book. The final edition is read to other classes and is then placed in the school library for a period of time before becoming part of the classroom library. This experience introduces Jeremy and the other first-grade children to the editing process. Ms. Wood does little correcting of children's expressive and creative writing until (and unless) she sees a need to teach the conventional spelling of a word, as perhaps in some editing activities when children are learning the difference between their private and public writing. At this point she principally wants the children to feel competent about their writing, and she knows that invented spellings, reversals, inattention to spacing, and lack of punctuation are prevalent and developmentally appropriate behaviors at age 6. She uses her assessments of these behaviors to plan meaningful instructional strategies for individual children. Figure 16.3 illustrates a typical first grader's attempt at writing.

Ms. Wood shares her strategies for helping children grow into conventional spellers and writers at parent orientation sessions and conferences. Showing examples (such as the ones illustrated in Figures 16.3 and 16.4) of how writing develops throughout the first-grade year also enables parents to see that children will make progress in their written language without those traditional red corrections. If parents want further information, Ms. Wood willingly shares articles from professional journals and books about the development of young children's writing. She also helps parents to understand that they can help their children to write at home by providing writing materials, taking advantage of opportunities to write, and being supportive of children's efforts to write at home.

Given supportive environments, children in the primary years can develop positive attitudes about writing and spelling as well as knowledge about the functions of writing. These experiences facilitate competence in reading.

If primary-grade teachers have students who do not seem to be comprehending or thinking about what they are reading, they may want to do an analysis of children's concepts about reading (Strommen & Mates, 1997). If the results indicate that these children

Figure 16.3

A 6-year-old wrote this letter to his grandparents during holiday time.

HLo Hv iyou Ben d!
thing icsixiing P?. gbl gblgbl.
git samnys Pegnt gbl.
I em giting a bowt you
ckaming dring san
niesqesnts and for
ds Love Jon xoxox

have distorted concepts about the reading act and limited strategies for reading, teachers need to help them to learn that (1) reading is getting meaning from print; (2) good readers sometimes read quickly and sometimes read slowly, depending on the purpose for reading; and (3) good readers make mistakes in reading, but they can use a number of strategies to help them identify and correct their mistakes.

Figure 16.4
"The Wndrfl Fgi A dat Burds"

Children ages 6 to 8 are still developing their physiological ability to hear and reproduce sounds.

THO WNDRFL FGI
A d AT BURDS

Issues in Cognitive, Language, and Literacy Development

Nutrition, Health, and Well-Being

A theme that runs throughout this text is the importance of nutrition, health, exercise, and psychological well-being. As children get older, they are confronted with larger circles of influence and greater expectations for appropriate behaviors and achievement. Because the school day can be quite long, particularly for children who attend before- and after-school programs and those engaged in extracurricular activities, the role of proper nutrition, rest, and exercise routines is quite important. The importance of breakfast in preparing the body for a day of work and learning has long been noted. A report in the *American Academy of Pediatric News* (Sears, 1998) revealed that because the biochemical messengers known as neurotransmitters help the brain to make the right connections and because the food we eat influences how neurotransmitters operate, the more balanced a person's breakfast is, the more balanced the brain's neurotransmitters function.

Highly publicized findings of increasing obesity rates among the nation's school-age children point out the responsibilities of parents, caregivers, and educators to ensure that daily schedules allocate time for physical activity. Weight control is only one reason for increasing children's opportunities for physical activity. It is easy to give classroom academic activities a high priority. However, limited attention to physiological needs for vigorous and active play, movement, and physical education negates the perceived advantages of more time on subject matter tasks. Indeed, exercise contributes to the learning process by relaxing mind and body; relieving stress; bathing the brain and its neurological structures in nature's mood- and attention-enhancing hormones; increasing physical strength, endurance, and agility; coordinating large and small motor controls; increasing cardiovascular efficiency; and improving the body's rest, thirst, and hunger rhythms.

The Nature of Prior Experiences

Studies have revealed that the effects of early child care experiences linger into the elementary school years. Children who attended child care centers with high-quality classroom practices were shown to have better language and math skills through the second grade than children who attended lower-quality programs. Quite compelling is the fact that children who had closer relationships with their child care teachers had fewer problem behaviors and better thinking skills in school. Also, it appears that warm teacher–child relationships influence children's language and math skills (NICHD Early Child Care Research Network, 2000; Peisner-Feinberg et al., 1999). Clearly, the types of nonparental experiences that children have with other adults influence not only their social and emotional development, but their cognitive, language, and literacy development as well, and these relationships appear to have long-lasting implications.

The Nature of Instructional Strategies and Performance Expectations

As the discussions of literacy development and strategies for teaching reading and writing reveal, instructional strategies cannot be framed around a one-size-fits-all paradigm. The uniqueness of development in each child reflects multiple influences, including family and cultural backgrounds, biologically determined individual rates of growth and development, individual cognitive styles and strengths, language diversity, differences in types and quality of out-of-home child care and preschool experiences, the nature of prekindergarten and kindergarten experiences, and many, many others. The mistake that pedagogues often make is attempting to apply one teaching/learning model to all children in a particular grade or group. The decision to teach from a part-to-whole perspective, a whole-to-part perspective, or some weighted combination of the two perspectives can be based only on intimate knowledge of how best an individual learner can respond.

Because in today's society considerable attention is directed toward the "outcomes" of children's education, schools are being required to meet stated goals and standards for student achievement and to demonstrate this achievement through accountability measures that include subjecting children to a variety of tests and measurements. The more rigorous and public the accountability measures are for a school or a school district, the less likely it is that child performance expectations will be individualized and developmentally appropriate.

Optimal learning and positive behaviors are promoted when the learner experiences the following:

- A mutually respecting, warm, and supportive relationship with teachers
- A sense of physical and psychological protection and well-being
- Recognition of his or her individuality and strengths
- Expectations that are challenging and hold the learner responsible while providing the supports necessary to accomplish assigned tasks
- Relationships that instill a sense of self-respect, self-efficacy, and shared respect for others
- A sense of belonging in this time and place with other members of the learning community

Before- and After-School Child Care

Studies have found that children ages 5 to 9 who have experienced quality after-school child care exhibit more positive behaviors with peers and adults, have fewer emotional and behavioral problems, develop better work habits, and perform better in school than do children in less formal child care settings, self-care, or baby-sitting situations (Vandell & Shumow, 1999). Quality before- and after-school programs provide children safe, supervised settings with opportunities to play and interact with other children and nurturing caregivers. Well-conceptualized school-age child care provides for "down time" that includes unstructured blocks of time for children to rest and renew, and private spaces where a child can distance herself or himself from the group for brief periods of time. This is necessary both from a psychological perspective and a physiological one, not unlike the adult's need for a "coffee break." Nutritious snacks (or meals) and beverages should be available, as should opportunities for vigorous physical activity (music and movement, dance, games, and outdoor play and sports). There should be time for homework and an undisturbed place for reading and study. Tutoring and special activities should be available to tap individual interests such as dance or singing; soccer, basketball, T-ball, or other sports; art; gardening; rock collecting; and singing. Props should be available for pretend play. Considering the number of hours of out-of-home time many children experience, such programs can contribute significantly to child and family well-being. The issue for consumers is the great need in contemporary society for well-designed and well-regulated school-age child care programs that are affordable and accessible to the increasing numbers of families who need them. Unfortunately, many programs fall short of these qualities. Parents need to be informed consumers who choose wisely and who diligently monitor their children's daily care and experiences in school-age child care.

Media Literacy

Both in-school and out-of-school time for most children includes time spent working at a computer, watching television or video programs, and, for some, accessing the Internet. These activities present both opportunities and challenges for children and families.

Some scholars propose that children need to develop **media literacy,** or the "ability to encode and decode the symbols transmitted via media and the ability to synthesize, analyze, and produce mediated messages' (Alliance for a Media Literate America, 2008). Although this understanding is dependent on the active participation of an adult, the nature of television programs, advertising, and other media makes it a worthwhile endeavor (Levin, 2003; Troseth & DeLoache, 1998).

media literacy
ability to understand the symbols transmitted via media

Television. To become television literate, young children need to be able to make distinctions between reality and fantasy and between fact, opinion, and hyperbole. Parents and teachers can help children to become TV literate by employing a number of strategies:

- Place children on a reduced TV diet, allowing them to watch a favorite unfavorable show only once or twice a week but with assignments such as the following:
  a. Count the number of violent acts against another person during a specified number of minutes (e.g., 10 minutes).
  b. Describe what the "good" characters did when violence occurred.
  c. Imagine a character who could prevent or settle conflicts through nonviolent means.
- Watch and discuss the program with the children, pointing out its unrealistic and inappropriate features that do not (or should never) occur in real-life situations.
- Have children imagine how the story might be changed to have a different, more positive outcome (Boyatzis, 1997; Levine, 1994).
- Discuss how advertisers use television to sell products to their viewers. Have children count the number of times a program is interrupted to sell a product.
- Talk about the difference between fact, opinion, and hyperbole. Point out these elements when coviewing a program with children.

Violence is not the only aspect of television that influences the social, emotional, and cognitive development of children. In addition, watching television consumes time, interfering with physical activity, exercise, sleep, homework, and other worthwhile activities; it contributes to snacking, preferences for advertised foods that are often less nutritious than desirable, and obesity; it exposes children to adult behaviors such as sex and abrasive and obscene language and questionable role models; and it entices them with tantalizing commercials for toys, clothes, foods, drinks, sporting gear, and other items pitched to children.

Cognitive, Language, and Literacy Development: Ages Six Through Eight

However, high-quality, nonviolent children's shows can have positive effects on their social, emotional, and cognitive development. Television can promote young children's cognitive, language, and literacy development if (1) programming is appropriate to young children's age and cognitive development, (2) adults are involved in the viewing process and discuss the program with children, and (3) children have opportunities to engage in other, more socially interactive and physically challenging activities that promote cognitive, language, and literacy development.

Computers, Video Games, and Other Media. The explosion of computer technologies, video games, innumerable types of software, digital technologies, the expanding Internet, and other technologies are dramatically transforming our personal lives and education. All types of activities can take place on one's personal computer and other electronic devices, and computers in the classroom are opening its curricula to wider and wider vistas. Today's children are growing up in a technological world in which the possibilities are astounding. Children are exposed to computer technology every place they go: home, school, child care programs, recreational programs, shopping malls, toy stores, sporting events, libraries, and museums. Electronic toys and video games abound. Today's children are at ease with all manner of electronic devices and equipment, and have experienced software that teaches them to draw, write, read, compute, research and do homework, communicate with friends and relatives through e-mail, and play all manner of games.

Experiences in the classroom with computers and other electronics can be highly sociable, promoting language and interaction with both adults and other children. Teachers appear to facilitate this interaction by encouraging group participation rather than individual activity and through their availability to children. In addition, teachers can encourage children to use one another as resources for learning to use computers and software, as well as other electronic devices. Knowledge of developmentally appropriate software programs can help teachers to determine how much independence children can assume and when the teacher's assistance is needed.

Computer experiences also seem to facilitate divergent and creative thinking. Software is now available that can be used to interface with differences in interests and intelligences. Computer experiences allow young children to make all manner of discoveries about an almost unlimited number of topics. Software exists to teach and tutor in school skills and school subjects, and programs exist to assist in learning English and other languages as a second language. Electronic portfolios can document children's learning and achievements.

Computers and other electronic devices can help children to develop reading, writing, spelling, and mathematics skills. Word processing can assist children in more in-depth composing by freeing them from the small motor task of handwriting. The process of revision is also facilitated because word processing makes it easier for children to edit their compositions (Hoot & Silvern, 1989).

Yet, like television, computers and other electronic devices offer both promise and peril. Educators are confronted with scores of catalogs of computer software and classroom computer-based technologies. The selection process can be overwhelming. Wise selection is vital to how beneficial computer use will be for learners. Just because a program is fun does not always mean that it is a developmentally appropriate or worthwhile learning activity. Drill should not be confused with thinking and learning. Teachers must evaluate software for ineffective approaches to instruction for young children, such as isolated drills and activities that resemble workbooks, which, when used at all, should be used quite sparingly.

The use of computers and other electronic devices in the classroom is now commonplace. Yet the electronics business is extremely competitive. Educators are cautioned against high-pressure sales techniques that encourage schools to spend large amounts of money on inappropriate programs. Teachers and school technology resource personnel should carefully evaluate all software programs and devices for their developmental appropriateness for young children.

Further, because not all children have access to computers and other electronic devices in their homes, many children will be less computer competent than others. For this reason, electronic equipment that is readily accessible within the classroom facilitates equity in technology learning. All children benefit when a computer and other electronic devices are located where they can coordinate use with other classroom activities. Both at home and in the classroom, the use of the Internet should be closely monitored.

Role of the Early Childhood Professional

Enhancing Cognitive, Language, and Literacy Development in Children Ages 6 Through 8

1. Provide for continuity of learning experiences from kindergarten to first grade and through the primary grades. Include families in planning for a smooth transition.
2. Acknowledge and plan for wide variations in rate of development in cognitive, language, and literacy development among children.
3. Provide learning experiences that are concrete, whole, and integrated rather than experiences that are abstract, are isolated, or overemphasize skill/drill learning strategies.
4. Provide learning experiences that allow children to interact with materials, other children, and adults.
5. Provide opportunities for child-initiated learning.
6. Spend time in one-on-one conversation and scaffolding activities with individual learners
7. Demonstrate curiosity and interest in learning.
8. Model appropriate oral and written language and enjoyment of good literature. Read frequently to and with children, sharing engaging and stimulating literature.
9. Engage parents as partners and collaborators in the cognitive, language, and literacy development process.
10. Provide appropriate and meaningful technological and media experiences.
11. Continue to encourage and support sociodramatic play and incorporate literacy activities into it.
12. Maintain a stress-free atmosphere around literacy that encourages interest and involvement in a relaxed–alert frame of mind.
13. Control or reduce stress-provoking situations in the schooling process.

Key Terms

downshifting	registers	sight words
media literacy	shading	spiral curriculum
phonics		

Review Strategies and Activities

1. Review the key terms individually or with a classmate.
2. Interview principals and kindergarten and primary-grade teachers in several school districts to determine how transitions from prekindergarten and kindergarten to the primary grades are managed.
3. Collect samples of children's writing from first, second, and third grades. Analyze them according to (a) content, (b) form, and (c) developmental progression.
4. Make a list of the many ways in which computers and other electronic devices affect children's lives. Discuss your list with your classmates. Reflect on how children can benefit from computer technology and ways in which their development may be negatively affected by this technology.
5. Examine the teachers' manuals for several different reading programs used in the primary grades. Compare the programs for part-to-whole and whole-to-part orientations to literacy development.

Further Readings

Berson, I. R., & Berson, M. J. (Eds.). (2010). *High-tech tots: Childhood in a digital world*. A Volume in I. R. Berson & M. J. Berson (Series Eds.), *Research in global child advocacy*. Charlotte, NC: Information Age Publishing.

Brenner, S. M. (2010). *Promising practices for elementary teachers: Make no excuses*. Thousand Oaks, CA: Corwin Press.

Fields, M. V., Groth, L. A., & Spangler, K. L. (2008). *Let's begin reading right: A developmental approach to emergent literacy* (6th ed.). Upper Saddle River, NJ: Merrill/Prentice Hall.

Other Resources

American Academy of Child and Adolescent Psychiatry, www.aacap.org. Resource centers provide definitions, answers to frequently asked questions, clinical resources, and expert videos on the following topics:
  - Anxiety disorders
  - Attention Deficit/Hyperactivity Disorder (ADHD)
  - Autism
  - Disaster

Brain Explorer, www.brainexplorer.org. This Website provides written and visual information on the brain.

National Association of Elementary School Principals, www.naesp.org. This Web site provides extensive information for principals and professionals interested in school leadership.

National Institute for Early Education Research, www.nieer.org. Here you will find media, research findings, publications, facts on the cost and efficacy of early childhood programs, and the *State Preschool Yearbook*. A collection of papers edited by Ron Haskins and Steve Barnett focuses on promising ideas for new directions in federal preschool and early childhood policy.

Epilogue

The universe of knowledge in the field of child growth and development is growing by leaps and bounds. Each textbook can touch on only a tiny segment of the scholarship on the many topics relating to how children grow and learn. Once begun, the study of child growth, development, and learning evokes a multitude of interests to explore further. The authors hope that this introductory text has drawn you in and its content and questions have captivated your curiosity, motivating you to explore further its topics or questions that are yet unanswered for you.

We were all children once, and what we learn about child growth and development makes us reflect on our own experiences, feelings, and behaviors. A measure of self-understanding prepares us to interact more effectively with others, and knowledge of the resilience and plasticity of childhood assures us that not all childhood experiences determine our destiny. The understanding of oneself is not the purpose of child study, however, but is only an interesting by-product of it.

The purpose of child study is to gain a level of knowledge and understanding that leads to good, enjoyable, and successful parenting; supportive and nurturing child care and education programs and experiences; enriching and challenging teaching; practical and helpful public policies; and, for every child, a protected and satisfying childhood— a childhood with every hope for the child of reaching his or her potential.

Appendix

Acronyms Associated with Childhood-Related Terms, Agencies, and Associations

AACAP	American Academy of Child and Adolescent Psychiatry
AAP	American Academy of Pediatrics
ACEI	Association for Childhood Education International
ACOG	American College of Obstetricians and Gynecologists
ACYF	Administration for Children, Youth, and Families (U.S. DHHS)
ADA	Americans with Disabilities Act
ADD	attention deficit disorder
ADHD	attention deficit hyperactivity disorder
AFP	alphafetoprotein test
AIDS	acquired immunodeficiency syndrome
APGAR	appearance, pulse, grimace, activity, and respiration assessment of the newborn
BMI	body mass index
BMR	basal metabolic rate
CA	chronological age
CACFP	Child and Adult Care Food Program
CAPTA	Child Abuse Prevention and Treatment Act (changed in 2003 to the Keeping Children and Families Safe Act of 2003 [P. L. 108-36])
CCDBG	Child Care and Development Block Grant
CCDF	Child Care and Development Fund (federal)
CCDP	comprehensive child development program
CDA	Child Development Associate
CDF	Children's Defense Fund
CDC	Centers for Disease Control and Prevention
CEC	Council for Exceptional Children
CECPR	Council for Early Childhood Professional Recognition
CHIP	Children's Health Insurance Program
CNS	central nervous system
CPS	Child Protective Services
CPSC	Consumer Product Safety Commission
CSE	Child Support Enforcement
CVT	chorionic villus test
CWLA	Child Welfare League of America
DAP	developmentally appropriate practices
DB	deaf/blindness
DCTC	Dependent Care Tax Credit
DEC/CEC	Division for Early Childhood of the Council for Exceptional Children
DNA	deoxyribonucleic acid
ECCE	early childhood care and education
ECI	Early Childhood Intervention
ECLKC	Early Childhood Learning and Knowledge Center
ECS	Education Commission of the States
ECSE	Early Childhood Special Education
ED	emotional disturbance or emotionally disturbed

EHS	Early Head Start
EHS NRC	Early Head Start National Resource Center
EI	early intervention
EIIT	Early Intervention for Infants and Toddlers (Part C of IDEA)
EITC	earned income tax credit
EPA	Environmental Protection Agency
EPSDT	Early and Periodic Screening, Diagnosis and Treatment (Medicaid)
ERIC/ECE	Education Research and Information Clearinghouse/Early Childhood Education
ES	Even Start
ESEA	Elementary and Secondary Education Act
ESL	English as a Second Language
FAPE	Free Appropriate Public Education (IDEA)
FAS	fetal alcohol syndrome
FDA	U.S. Food and Drug Administration
FHCC	family home child care
FMLA	Family and Medical Leave Act of 1993
FRAC	Food Research and Action Council
GAO	U.S. Government Accountability Office
HEI	Healthy Eating Index
HHS	U.S. Department of Health and Human Services
HI	hearing impaired
HIPPY	Home Instruction Program for Preschool Youngsters
HMBANA	Human Milk Banking Association of North America
HUD	U.S. Department of Housing and Urban Development
IDEA	Individuals with Disabilities Act
IDRA	Intercultural Development Research Association
IEP	Individual Education Plan (IDEA)
IFSP	Individualized Family Services Plan (IDEA)
IOM	(National) Institute of Medicine
IQ	intelligence quotient
IRA	International Reading Association
LAD	language acquisition device
LBW	low birth weight
LEP	limited English proficiency
LGA	large for gestational age
L1	native or first language
L2	second language
MD	multiple disabilities
ML	multilingual
MMWR	*Morbidity and Mortality Weekly Report*
MR	mental retardation
NAA	National AfterSchool Association
NAESP	National Association of Elementary School Principals
NAEYC	National Association for the Education of Young Children
NACCP	National Association of Child Care Professionals
NACCRRA	National Association of Child Care Resource and Referral Agencies
NAEYC	National Association for the Education of Young Children

NAFCC	National Association for Family Child Care
NBCDI	National Black Child Development Institute
NCATE	National Council for Accreditation of Teacher Education
NCCIC	National Child Care Information Center
NCCP	National Center for Children in Poverty
NCES	National Center for Educational Statistics
NCLB	No Child Left Behind Education Act of 2001
NEISS	National Electronic Injury Survey System
NICHD	National Institute of Child Health and Human Development
NIDCD	National Institute on Deafness and Other Communication Disorders
NIECPD	National Institute for Early Childhood Professional Development
NIH	National Institutes of Health
NIMH	National Institute of Mental Health
NRC	National Research Council
NTI	ZERO TO THREE's National Training Institute
NTSB	National Transportation Safety Board
OHI	other health impairments
OI	orthopedic impaired
OMEP	World Organization for Early Childhood Education
PAFT	Parents as First Teachers
PCR	polymerase chain reaction test
PKU	phenylketonuria
SCHIP	State Child Health Insurance Program
SECA	Southern Early Childhood Association
SGA	small for gestational age
SIDS	sudden infant death syndrome
SLI	speech or language impairment
SRCD	Society for Research in Child Development
SSA	Social Security Administration
SSI	Social Security Supplemental Security Income program
STD	sexually transmitted disease
TANF	Temporary Assistance to Needy Families
TBI	traumatic brain injury
UNCRC	United Nations Convention of the Rights of the Child
UNICEF	United Nations Children's Fund
USDA	U.S. Department of Agriculture
USDE	U.S. Department of Education
US HHS	U.S. Department of Health and Human Services
VAERS	Vaccine Adverse Event Reporting System
VI	visual impairment
VLBW	very low birth weight
WHO	World Health Organization
WIC	U.S. Special Supplemental Nutrition Program for Women, Infants, and Children
ZPD	zone of proximal development

Glossary

abortion   the ending of a pregnancy

accommodation   the cognitive process by which patterns of thought (schemata) and related behaviors are modified to conform to new information or experience

achievement test   a test that measures what children have learned as a result of instruction

acquired immunodeficiency syndrome (AIDS)   a disease that attacks the immune system, causing death from illnesses that the immune system cannot ward off

adaptation   the process by which one adjusts to changes in the environment

adipose   tissue in which there is an accumulation of connective tissue cells, each containing a relatively large deposit of fat

alphabetic   a writing system that associates the phonemes of oral language with letters of the alphabet

alphafetoprotein test (AFP)   a blood test that can identify disorders in the brain or spinal column in the fetus

altruism   intentions to help others without the expectation of reward

amniocentesis   a technique that involves extracting amniotic fluid for the purpose of detecting all chromosomal and more than 100 biomedical disorders

anecdotal record   a type of narrative observation that describes an incident in detail

anemia   a condition caused by a lack of red blood cells

anorexia   a severe disorder, usually seen in adolescent girls, characterized by self-starvation

Apgar score   a score that rates the physical condition of newborns in the areas of appearance, pulse, grimace, activity, and respiration

apnea   absence of breathing for a period of up to 20 seconds

assimilation   the process of incorporating new motor or conceptual learning into existing schemata

associative play   a loosely organized form of social play, characterized by overt social behaviors indicating common activities, shared interests, and interpersonal associations

at-risk   infants and children who are subject to any of a number of risk factors (such as poverty, drug exposure, genetic and/or developmental anomalies, and family dynamics) that make them vulnerable to compromised growth and development

atrophy   waste away, diminish in size and/or function

attachment   a strong emotional relationship between two people, characterized by mutual affection and a desire to maintain proximity

authentic assessment   the ongoing, continuous, context-based observation and documentation of children's learning behaviors

authoritarian discipline   a child-rearing style in which parents apply rigid standards of conduct and expect unquestioning obedience from the child

authoritative discipline   a child-rearing style in which child behavior is directed through rational and reasoned guidance from the adult

axon   a branchlike projection from the neuron that carries information away from the cell body

balance   a body awareness component in which postural adjustments prevent one from falling

basal metabolic rate   the amount of energy required to keep the heart beating, sustain breathing, repair tissues, and keep the brain and nerves functioning

behavior modification   a system of techniques employing positive and/or negative reinforcers to change behavior

behavioral theory   a theory that emphasizes that learning is the acquisition of specific responses provoked by specific stimuli

bilabial trills   the production of sounds such as m, b, and p that are formed in the front of the mouth with the lips closed and move from the lips toward the back of the mouth (other structures for the articulation of sounds include the lips, teeth, roof of the mouth, and tongue)

bioecological systems theory   a theory that argues that a variety of social systems influence the development of children

body awareness   cognizance of one's body, its parts, its functions, and what it can be willed to do

bonding   a complex psychobiological connection between parent and infant

botulism   a potentially fatal form of food poisoning

Brazelton Neonatal Behavioral Assessment Scale   an assessment of 16 reflexes, responsiveness, state changes, and ability to self-calm in the newborn

breech position delivery   a birth in which a body part other than the head presents itself for delivery first, usually the buttocks, feet, or in some cases the umbilical cord

bulimia   a severe disorder, usually seen in adolescent girls, characterized by binging and then self-induced vomiting

centration   the tendency to attend to a limited number of features of an object or event

cerebral cortex   the outer layer of the cerebral hemisphere, which is mostly responsible for higher mental functions, sensory processing, and motor control

cervix   the opening of the uterus

cesarean delivery   a surgical procedure during which an incision is made through the abdominal and uterine walls of the mother to deliver the baby

493

checklist a list of developmental behaviors that the observer identifies as being present or absent

child-directed speech speech that has qualities of elevated pitch, conspicuous inflections, long pauses, and exaggerated stress on syllables

chorionic villus test (CVT) a test that analyzes samples of the hairlike projections (chorionic villi) of tissue in the placenta to determine chromosomal disorders (can be done earlier than amniocentesis)

chromosomes ordered groups of genes within the nucleus of a cell

class inclusion understanding the relationship between class and subclass, which occurs during the period of concrete operational thought

classical conditioning theory a theory according to which, when an unconditioned neutral stimulus and an uncon-ditioned response are paired repeatedly, a conditioned response is the result

Clostridium botulinum the bacterium that causes botulism

cochlear implant an electronic device placed in the skull, which, with help from an external hearing aid, enhances the detection of sound

cognitive development the aspect of development that involves thinking, problem solving, intelligence, and language

cognitive developmental theory a theory that explains the development of learning in terms of how children think and process information

cognitive flexibility the ability to be mentally flexible and adjust to new situations

colostrum the first fluid secreted by the mammary glands soon after childbirth, before true milk is formed

communicative competence the repertoire of behaviors that help young children to communicate effectively with others

congenital anomalies skeletal or body system abnormalities caused by defective genes within the chromosomes, which usually affect the developing embryo during the first eight weeks of pregnancy

conservation the understanding that physical attributes (e.g., mass and weight) stay the same even if appearance changes

constancy of position in space the notion that letters of the alphabet must have fixed positions to maintain their identity

constructivism a term used to describe learning as an active process of creating meaning

contraction the movement of the muscles of the uterus that pushes the baby through the cervical opening and into the birth canal

cooperative play a well-organized form of social play, characterized by well-defined social roles within play groups, influential peer leaders, and shared materials and equipment used to pursue a well-understood group play goal or theme

correlational study research that attempts to determine a relationship between two or more sets of measurements

cortisol a steroid hormone produced by the adrenal gland and released in response to stress

creative vocabulary the creation of new words to meet the need for a word that has not been learned or that has been forgotten, or for which no word exists

critical period a time of physiological and/or psychological sensitivity during which the normal development of a major organ or structural system is vulnerable to insult or injury

cross-sectional study research that studies subjects of different ages at the same time

deciduous teeth the first set of teeth, which erupts during infancy; also called temporary or baby teeth; later replaced by a set of 36 permanent teeth

defense mechanism a psychological response to ego threat, frustration, or failure

deferred imitation the ability to imitate behaviors that were observed at a prior time or in another place

dendrites branches from the neuron that carry information toward the cell body; a neuron can have several dendrites

descriptive study research collected by observing and recording behavior and providing a description of the observed behavior

developmental possibilities significant events during the course of growth and development

developmental screening test an initial procedure for identi-fying individuals who may need formal diagnostic tests

developmentally appropriate pertains to (1) age appropriate-ness, the universal and predictable patterns of growth and development that occur in children from birth through age 8, and (2) individual appropriateness, the individual rates and patterns of physical/motor, social, emotional, cognitive, language and literacy development, personality and learning style, and family and cultural background of each child

developmentally inappropriate expectations or practices that fail to acknowledge age and individual characteristics and needs

dexterity quick, precise movement and coordination of the hands and fingers

diagnostic test a process of compiling and assessing charac-teristics and symptoms (physiological, emotional, or social) to identify needs and establish treatment and/or intervention strategies

dialects different forms of language used by different ethnic groups or by people who live in different geographic regions

dilation the gradual opening of the cervix, which occurs in the first stage of labor

directionality the application of the internal awareness of right and left to objects and movement

disequilibrium an imbalance in thinking that leads the thinker to assimilate or accommodate

display rules social rules determining how and when certain emotions should or should not be expressed

DNA deoxyribonucleic acid, the molecule containing the information that causes the formation of proteins that stimulate the development of tissues and organs and affect other genes and physiological functions

doula a Greek word for a female who provides assistance and support during childbirth

downshifting a psychophysiological response to perceived threat that is accompanied by a sense of helplessness or lack of self-efficacy, which affects the brain's ability to function at optimal levels

echolalia replication in repetitive fashion of the sounds of another speaker in an infant–other turn-taking "conversation"

eclampsia convulsions due to high blood pressure in the mother—a serious condition for the health of the baby and the mother

electronic fetal monitor a device used during labor, which is attached to the abdomen of the pregnant woman or the scalp of the fetus to determine the fetal heart rate

embryonic cell mass the developing fertilized ovum during the first three months of pregnancy when cells are dividing rapidly to form the fetus

embryonic stage weeks three through eight of pregnancy, during which the major organ systems are formed

empathy experiencing the feelings or emotions that someone else is experiencing

environment the experiences, conditions, objects, and people that directly or indirectly influence the development and behavior of a child

episiotomy an incision made in the opening of the vulva to prevent it from tearing during delivery

equilibration the attempt to restore cognitive balance by modifying existing cognitive structures when confronted with new information

essential experiences experiences deemed critical at certain times during early growth and development, which have growth-inducing influence on the brain's neurological structures

ethology the scientific study of behavior

event sampling a procedure in which the researcher notes the occurrences of particular behaviors or events

executive function the brain's ability to plan, stay focused, process information, and filter out distractions

expansions responses to young children's use of overregularizations by using the conventional form in the conversational context

experimental study research that involves treating each of two or more groups in different ways to determine cause-and-effect relationships

expressive language spoken language; oral communication

extensions responses to children's language that extend the meaning of their language

extensors muscles that act to stretch or extend a limb

extinguish stopping a behavior or response by not reinforcing it over a period of time

extrafamilial actions and behaviors occurring outside the immediate family

extrauterine the environment outside of the uterus

failure to thrive condition in which the infant does not grow as would be expected under usual circumstances

fast mapping children's rapid learning of language by relating a word to an internalized concept and remembering it after only one encounter with that word

fatherese modifications in the father's speech when talking with infants and young children; can differ from motherese

fertility the capability of conceiving a child

fertility rate the number of births per 1,000 women ages 15 to 44

fetal stage the stage that begins after the first eight weeks of pregnancy and continues until birth

fetus the developing human from nine weeks after conception to birth

figure–ground discrimination the ability to focus on the dominant figure in a picture without being distracted by elements in the background

fixation in psychoanalytic theory, a point in development that becomes fixed, failing to move forward to more mature forms

flexors muscles that act to bend a joint

fontanelles membranous spaces between the cranial bones of the fetus and infant

food insecurity the inability of the family to meet the nutritional needs of all of its members

food security the ability of the family to meet the nutritional needs of its members

forceps a surgical instrument, similar to tongs, that is applied to the head of the fetus to facilitate delivery

formal assessment information gathered about young children, usually through standardized tests

fraternal twins twins whose development began by the fertilization of two ova (eggs) by two sperm, causing each twin to have a different genetic code

fundamental movements coordination basic to all other movement abilities

gavage feeding introducing fluids or foods through a tube passed orally or through a nasal passage into the stomach

gender awareness the realization that men and women, girls and boys, are different

gender constancy the realization that one's gender remains the same, regardless of age or changes in clothing, hairstyles, or other outward characteristics

gender identity the cognizance of being male or female

gender the maleness or femaleness of the zygote as determined by the kind of sperm fertilizing the ovum (Y sperm: genetically male; X sperm: genetically female)

genes   molecules of DNA that encode and transmit the characteristics of past generations

genetic counseling   information provided to parents or prospective parents about the possibility and nature of genetic disorders in their offspring

genome   the sum total of gene types possessed by a particular species

genotype   the combination of genes inherited from both parents and their ancestors

gestation   the length of an average pregnancy of 280 days, or 40 weeks, from the first day of the last menstrual period; can range from 37 to 42 weeks

gestational diabetes   diabetes that develops after a woman becomes pregnant

glial cells   supporting cells, which serve to protect and insulate (as in myelin) cells in the nervous system

graphophemic   the relationship of letters (symbols) of the alphabet to sounds

grey matter   neuronal cell bodies involved in muscle control, sensory perception, memory, emotions, and speech

health-related fitness   a physical state in which muscular strength, endurance, flexibility, and the circulatory–respiratory systems are all in optimal condition

Healthy Eating Index (HEI)   a U.S. Department of Agriculture measure of diet quality, which assesses the degree to which a person's diet conforms to the Food Guide Pyramid; limits saturated fat, cholesterol, and sodium; and includes a variety of foods

heredity   the inherited characteristics of humans encoded by genes

heteronomous morality   a morality that is governed by others rather than by oneself

holophrase   the use of one word to convey a phrase or a sentence

home visitor   a trained nurse or paraprofessional who provides in-home education and support services to pregnant women and families with young children

human immunodeficiency virus (HIV)   the virus that causes AIDS; it can be transmitted from an infected mother to the fetus or embryo via the placenta or delivery fluids

humanistic   a theory that believes in the fundamental goodness of human beings

hypertension   high blood pressure

hyperthermia   a very high body temperature

hypothermia   a below-normal body temperature

hypothesis   a hunch or supposition that one wants to verify or prove

identical twins   twins whose development began when the zygote split into two identical halves, thus ensuring that both twins have the identical genetic code

identity constancy   the understanding that a person or species remains the same, even though appearance is changed through masks, costumes, or other transformations

idiosyncratic concepts   ideas of the preoperational child that are based on personal experience and overgeneralized to other situations

in utero   the environment in which the fetus grows within the uterus

inclusion   the education model that includes children with developmental challenges in general education settings

indirect speech   speech that implies more than the actual words uttered

inductive discipline   a positive, nonpunitive form of discipline that relies on reasons and rationales to help children control their behaviors

industry   the sense of mastery of social and academic skills necessary to feel self-assured

informal assessment   information gathered about young children through approaches other than standardized tests

inhibitory control   the skills of paying attention, filtering out distractions, and regulating thoughts and actions

initiative   the third of Erikson's psychosocial stages, in which the child pursues ideas, individual interests, and activities; when thwarted, the child becomes self-critical and experiences guilt

inner speech   a form of speech associated with the process of internalizing spoken words or sentences

inservice   individuals who have completed professional training programs and are employed in the early childhood profession

intelligence test   a standardized measure used to establish an intelligence level rating (e.g., intelligence quotient [IQ]) by measuring a child's ability to perform various selected mental tasks

internalization   a process in which behavior standards are adopted as one's own and acted upon without explicit instruction from others

interview   engaging in a dialogue with a child that is either free-flowing or with predetermined questions to assess understandings and feelings

intrafamilial   actions and behaviors occurring within the immediate family

invented/developmental spelling   spelling that young children create based on their perceptions of sound–symbol relationships

irreversibility   the inability of preoperational children to reverse their thinking and to return to their original point of thought

isolette   a small crib, which provides a controlled environment for newborns

labor   the three stages of the birth process: dilation, birth of the baby, and discharge of the placenta

Lamaze method   a method developed by Fernand Lamaze, which involves training the prospective mother and a partner/coach in breathing and relaxation techniques to be used during labor

Glossary

language acquisition device (LAD) an innate mental mechanism some theorists believe makes language development possible

laterality an awareness of an ability to use both sides of the body; a recognition of the distinction between left and right

left/right dominance a neuromaturational preference for one or the other side of the body, as in handedness

levels-of-processing theory an information-processing model that focuses on the depth of attention rather than on aspects of memory in explaining levels of cognitive performance

locomotion the ability to move independently from place to place

logicomathematical knowledge knowledge constructed primarily from children's actions on and interpretations of objects and events

longitudinal study research that collects information about the same subjects at different ages over a period of time

low birth weight a newborn weight of less than 2,500 grams, or 5½ pounds

low-risk infants and children whose risk factors are minimal or absent

maturational theory a theory that holds that growth and development are predetermined by inheritance and largely unaffected by the environment

media literacy ability to understand the symbols transmitted via media

mental symbols the behaviors that occur at the beginning of the preoperational stage, including speech, imitation, and using one object to represent another

metabolic pertains to the body's complex chemical conversion of food into substances and energy necessary for maintenance of life

metacommunication the cognitive ability to reflect on and talk about verbal interactions

moral realism a morality that focuses on rules and the seriousness of the consequences of an act rather than on the intentions behind the act

moral relativism a morality that focuses on the judgment of situations and intentions underlying individual behavior rather than solely on the consequences of an act

morpheme the smallest unit of meaning in oral or written language

motherese modifications in the mother's speech when talking with infants and young children

myelin a fatty substance surrounding the axons and dendrites of some neurons, which speeds the conduction of nerve impulses

narrative observation a written observation of behavior

neonate the newborn from birth to 4 weeks

neonatologist a physician who specializes in the care and treatment of the neonate, or newborn infant, during the first 4 to 6 weeks

neural connectivity the organized connections that occur between neurons (nerve cells) in the brain

neural network circuits created by connections of neurons

neural tube the rudimentary beginning of the brain and spinal cord

neurobiological agents hormones and chemicals that facilitate the transmission of information throughout the nervous system

neurogenesis the continuous production of neurons

neuron a type of cell that conveys information; a nerve cell

neurotransmitter a chemical that facilitates the transmission of information through the synapse

norms the average ages of the emergence of certain behaviors or average scores on tests that are based on large representative samples of a population

nystagmus involuntary and jerky repetitive movement of the eyeballs

object permanence the realization that objects and people continue to exist even though they may not be visible or detected through other senses

objectivity the ability to observe and draw inferences about child development that are free of observer bias

operant conditioning theory a theory in which behavior is changed or modified through the positive or negative consequences that follow the behavior

ossification the conversion of the softer cartilage of the skeletal system into bone

overextension the use of a word to refer to a similar but different object, situation, or category

overregularization the tendency to overgeneralize a rule of grammar

parallel play activities in which two or more children play near one another while engaged in independent activities

parentese modifications in the parent's speech when talking with infants and young children

participant–observer a researcher who participates in the daily lives of the subjects of the study

peers other children who are the same age as a particular child

perception the physiological process by which sensory input is interpreted

perceptual–motor interrelationship between sensory information and motor responses

performance-related fitness a physical state in which motor coordination facilitates speed, agility, power, and balance

perinatal the period encompassing the weeks before a birth, the birth, and the few weeks thereafter

permissive discipline a noncontrolling, non-demanding form of discipline in which the child, for the most part, is allowed to regulate his or her behavior

Glossary

perspective-taking   the ability to understand one's own or another's viewpoint and be aware of the coordinated and inter-related sets of ideas and actions that are reflected in behavior

phonics   the sound–symbol relationship of a language system

phonological sensitivity   the ability to detect and manipulate the sounds of spoken language

phonology   the speech sounds of a particular language system

physical knowledge   knowledge of physical characteristics of objects and events gained through sensorimotor play

placenta   an organ attached to the wall of the uterus, which transmits nutrients from the mother to the embryo/fetus and filters wastes from the embryo/fetus to the mother

plasticity   the ability of some parts of the nervous system to alter their functional characteristics

polymerase chain reaction (PCR)   a procedure used to identify disease-causing genes in an eight-cell embryo

portfolio   an assemblage of information derived from various assessment strategies, including representative samples of the child's play creations and academic products

postpartum depression   a period of depression that affects most mothers for a few days and in some cases for weeks and months after childbirth

postpartum psychosis   a psychological condition associated with severe depression following childbirth in which there is a loss of insight, good judgment, and coping strength; sometimes there is a loss of touch with reality

postterm   infants born after 40 weeks of gestation

power-assertive discipline   a form of discipline in which the power of the adult is used to coerce, deprive of privileges or material goods, or apply physical punishment to modify a child's behavior

preconcepts   the very young child's disorganized and illogical representations of experience

predictable books   books that have repeating patterns and predictable text

prehension   the coordination of fingers and thumb to permit grasping

prematurity   a preterm delivery that occurs prior to 37 completed weeks of gestation

prenatal   the time from conception until birth, an average of 266 days, or 38 weeks

preoperational stage   the second of Piaget's stages of cognitive development, in which children develop the ability to internally represent sensorimotor actions but do not engage in operational or logical thinking

preprimary   the time in young children's lives before they enter the primary (first, second, and third) grades

preservice   individuals who are in training to teach or serve young children

preterm   infants born several weeks before the full term (38 weeks) of pregnancy

primary caregiver   the person primarily responsible for the care and nurturing of a child

primitive reflexes   reflexes controlled by subcortical structures in the brain, which gradually disappear during the first year

private speech   speech to oneself that helps direct one's behavior, thinking, or communication

private spelling   phonemic spelling or invented spelling that young children create when they first begin to write their ideas and thoughts

professionals   individuals who have internalized the evolving knowledge base of their particular fields and use this knowledge to improve practices that affect the lives of children and families

proprioceptive system   stimuli that are connected with the position and movement of the body

prosocial behaviors   behavior that benefits others, such as helping, sharing, comforting, and defending

proximity seeking   the child's attempts to maintain nearness and contact with the attachment person

pruning   the reduction of neurons and synapses in the brain which leaves a more efficient system

psychoanalytic theory   a theory that attempts to explain the inner thoughts and feelings, at both the conscious and subconscious levels, that influence behavior

psychosexual theory   a theory that suggests that sexual drives play an important role in personality development

psychosocial theory   a theory that proposes that social interactions are more important than sexual drives in personality development

public spelling   conventional spelling that children learn through both experience with writing and direct instruction

random selection   a procedure for assigning subjects to an experimental or control group so that each person has the same chance of being selected for either group

rating scale   a scale with various traits or categories that allows the observer to indicate the importance of the observed behaviors

readiness   a term that has many different meanings depending on the context in which it is used, but generally refers to a set of prerequisite developmental expectations

readiness test   a test that measures capabilities needed for certain new experiences or types of curriculum

receptive language   language that is comprehended, but not necessarily produced

recessive gene   a gene that carries a trait that may not appear unless a gene for the same trait is inherited from both parents

reciprocal determinism   a socialization process through which the individual both influences and is influenced by the environment

reflecting-in-action   an ongoing process in which educators think about and critically analyze their own and their students' performance to review, assess, and modify interactions, expectations, and instructional strategies

registers   variations in the style of speech according to the particular social setting

reliability   the consistency with which various research methods produce the same or similar results for each individual from one assessment to the next

replicability   the likelihood that a research procedure can be followed by another person with the same or similar results

representative sample   a sample of subjects who are representative of the larger population of individuals about whom the researcher wants to draw conclusions

resource persons   people outside the educational setting, usually from health-related fields, who can provide information about young children's development and learning

reversals   printing letters or words in reverse

Rh factor   a condition in the mother that produces antibodies that destroy the red blood cells of her second baby and subsequent babies

rich interpretation   acknowledging that young children know more than they can verbally express and use nonverbal behaviors to communicate

rubella   a viral disease that can cause birth disorders if the mother contracts it during the first three months of pregnancy (also known as German measles)

running record   a type of narrative observation that records all behaviors in sequential order as they occur

satiety   the feeling of having consumed sufficient food to satisfy hunger

scaffolding   a process by which adults or more skilled children facilitate the acquisition of knowledge or skills in the learner through coaching or supplying needed information

schemata   mental concepts or categories; plural for schema

scripts   sets of social procedures or events, which include sequences of events and/or roles, often observed in young children's play

self-actualization   the process of having basic physical and social/emotional needs met so that the individual develops positive self-regard and becomes a creative, contributing member of society

self-awareness   an individual's perceptions of him- or herself as distinct and separate from other people and objects

self-definition   the use of criteria to define the self, such as age, size, and physical and mental abilities

self-efficacy   the feeling that one's efforts are effective; the perception that one can succeed

self-esteem   the overall sense of worth as a person that the child derives from the qualities that are associated with the self-concept

semantics   knowledge of how language carries meaning

separation anxiety   fear of being separated from the attachment person

sexuality   the relational, biological, and procreational aspects of gender

shading   gradually changing the topic of conversation

shaken baby syndrome   head (intracranial) or long bone injury caused by forceful shaking or jerking of an infant; may result in serious injuries (including blindness) and often death

sight words   words in print that young children recognize immediately

simultaneous bilingualism   the process of learning two languages at the same time, beginning at birth

skeletal age   a measure of physical development based on examination of skeletal X-rays

social cognition   the ability to understand the thoughts, intentions, and behaviors of oneself and others

social learning theory   a theory that proposes that learning occurs through observing others, and emphasizes the influencing role of behavioral models

socialization   the process by which individuals acquire the accepted behaviors and values of their families and society

sociocentric   the inability to take or accept as valid the perspectives of another group

specimen record   a type of narrative observation that provides detailed information about a particular event, child, or time of day

spiral curriculum   educational method in which new concepts build on previous experience and knowledge as the student progresses so that he or she is learning increasingly complex facets of the already-introduced subject

standard precautions   procedures involving the use of protective barriers such as nonporous gloves, aprons, disposable diapers and diaper table paper, disposable towels, and surfaces that can be sanitized to reduce the risk of exposure to pathogens

standardized test   a test that is administered and scored according to set procedures and whose scores can be interpreted according to predetermined statistical measures

strabismus   a condition referred to as crossed eyes, in which one or both eyes turn in, out, up, or down

stranger anxiety   fear of strangers, characterized by avoidance, crying, or other distress signals

subcortical   refers to the portion of the brain just below the cerebral cortex, which is responsible for controlling unlearned and reflexive behavior

subcutaneous tissue   tissue that forms beneath the skin

successive bilingualism   the process of learning a second language after acquiring proficiency in a first language

support staff   other people within the educational setting who support the learning and development of young children, such as nurses, social workers, diagnosticians, psychologists, secretaries, and food service and housekeeping personnel

survival reflexes   reflexes essential to sustaining life

synapses   the point of contact between nerve fibers

syndrome   a group of combined symptoms that characterizes a physiological or psychological disorder

syntax   the grammar or structure of a particular language system

teacher-as-learner the process by which educators continue to learn from children, parents, other professionals, and the changing professional research and literature throughout their careers

teacher-as-researcher the process by which early childhood professionals, through their perspective-taking and reflecting-in-action, acquire and demonstrate the behaviors of a researcher

telegraphic speech children's early speech, which, like a telegram, includes only the essential words needed to convey meaning

teratogens environmental factors, such as viruses and chemical substances, that can cause abnormalities in the developing embryo or fetus

tertiary circular reactions an exploratory schema in which children devise new ways of acting on objects in their environment and from which they can derive meaning

theories bodies of principles used to interpret a set of circumstances or facts

theory of mind description of how young children begin to understand similarities and differences between their own intentions and thoughts and those of others

time sampling a procedure for recording selected observations on a predetermined schedule

toilet learning a gradual maturational process in which the child gains control over elimination

toxemia a disease of unknown cause that occurs in the last trimester and can cause death to both mother and child

toxoplasmosis a viral infection that can be transmitted from cat droppings or raw meat to the mother and from her to the fetus or embryo via the placenta, causing birth disorders

transductive reasoning the reasoning process of very young children, which relies on preconcepts

transformation attending to all the states of an event from the beginning, to in-between, to the final stage

transitional object an object, usually a soft, cuddly item, to which a child becomes attached

transivity the ability to seriate, or order, according to some attribute, such as height or size

trimester the first, second, or third three months of pregnancy

ultrasound a technique using sound frequencies that can detect structural characteristics of the fetus and the approximate week of pregnancy

underextension the use of a general term to refer to a more specific object, situation, or category

validity the degree to which an instrument or a procedure measures what it is intended to measure

viability the capability of sustaining extrauterine survival

vocables early sound patterns used by infants that approximate words

water intoxication a dangerous, potentially life-threatening physiological condition caused by overconsumption of water apart from or in overdiluted formula or juices

well-being a state of feeling that all is well physically, mentally, and socially

working memory aspect of memory that refers to the capacity to remember and manipulate information

zone of proximal development the level of concept development that is too difficult for the child to accomplish alone but can be achieved with the help of adults or more skilled children through scaffolding

zygote the first cell resulting from the fertilization of the ovum by the sperm

References

Abelman, R. (1984). Children and TV: The ABC's of TV literacy. *Childhood Education, 60*, 200–205.

Aboud, F. (1988). *Children and prejudice.* Cambridge, MA: Blackwell.

Abramovitch, R., Corter, C., Pepler, D. J., & Stanhope, L. (1986). Sibling and peer interaction: A final follow-up and a comparison. *Child Development, 57*, 217–229.

Abramson, R., Altfeld, S., & Tiebloom-Mishkin, J. (2000). The community-based doula: An emerging role in family support. *Zero to Three, 21*(2), 11–16.

Abramson, R., Breedlove, G., & Isaacs, B. (2006). *The community based doula: Supporting families before, during and after childbirth.* Washington, DC: ZERO TO THREE Press.

Ackerman, B. (1982). Contextual integration and utterance interpretation: The ability of children and adults to interpret sarcastic utterances. *Child Development, 53*, 1075–1083.

Adair, R., Baucher, H., Philipp, B., Levenson, S., & Zuckerman, B. (1991). Night waking during infancy: Role of parental presence at bedtime. *Pediatrics, 87*(4), 500–504.

Adams, M. J. (1990). *Beginning to read: Thinking and learning about print: A summary.* Urbana-Champaign, IL: Center for the Study of Reading, University of Illinois at Urbana-Champaign.

Adams, R. J., Mauer, D., & Davis, M. (1986). Newborns' discrimination of chromatic from achromatic stimuli. *Journal of Experimental Child Psychology, 41*, 267–281.

Administration for Children & Families. National Child Care Information and Technical Assistance Program (NCCIC). (2010). *National profile.* Retrieved from http://nccic.acf.hhs.gov/

Adolph, K. E. (2009). Learning to move. *Current Directions in Psychological Science, 17*, 213–218.

Adolph, K. E., & Berger, S. A. (2006). Motor development. In W. Damon & R. Lerner (Series Eds.) & D. Kuhn & R. S. Siegler (Vol. Eds.), *Handbook of child psychology: Vol. 2: Cognitive, perception and language* (6th ed., pp. 161–213). New York, NY: John Wiley.

Adolph, K. E., Berger, S., & Leo, A. J. (2011). Developmental continuity? Crawling, cruising, and walking. *Developmental Science, 14*(2), 306–318.

Adolph, K. E., Eppler, M. A., & Joh, A. S. (2010). Infants' perception of affordances of slopes under low and high friction conditions. *Journal of Experimental Psychology: Human Perception & Performance, 36*, 797–811.

Adolph, K. E., Karasik, L. B. & Tamis-LeMonda, C. S. (2009). Moving between cultures: Cross-cultural research on motor development. In M. Bornstein (Ed.), *Handbook of cross-cultural developmental science, Vol. 1, Domains of development across cultures* (pp. 61–88). Mahwah, NJ: Erlbaum.

Ahnert, L., Gunnar, M. R., Lamb, M. E., & Barthel, M. (2004). Transition to child care: Associations with infant-mother attachment, infant negative emotions, and cortisol elevations. *Child Development, 75*(3), 639–650.

Ainsworth, M. D. S. (1967). *Infancy in Uganda: Infant care and the growth of love.* Baltimore: Johns Hopkins University Press.

Ainsworth, M. D. S. (1973). The development of infant–mother attachment. In B. M. Caldwell & H. N. Ricciuti (Eds.), *Review of child development research* (Vol. 3, pp. 1–94). Chicago, IL: University of Chicago Press.

Ainsworth, M. D. S., Bell, S. M., & Stayton, D. J. (1974). Infant–mother attachment and social development: Socialization as a product of reciprocal responsiveness to signals. In M. P. M. Richards (Ed.), *The integration of the child into a social world* (pp. 99–135). London, England: Cambridge University Press.

Ainsworth, M. D. S., & Wittig, B. A. (1969). Attachment and the exploratory behavior of one-year-olds in a strange situation. In B. M. Foss (Ed.), *Determinants of infant behavior* (Vol. 4, pp. 113–136). London, England: Methuen.

Alaimo, K., Olson, C. M., & Frongillo, E. A., Jr. (2001). Food insufficiency and American school-aged children's cognitive, academic, and psychosocial development. *Pediatrics, 108*, 44–53.

Alan Guttmacher Institute. (2002). *Family planning can reduce high infant mortality levels* (Issues in Brief, 2002 Series, No. 2). New York, NY: Author.

Alan Guttmacher Institute. (2003). *In their own right: Addressing the sexual and reproductive health needs of men worldwide.* New York, NY: AGI.

Alexander, G. M., & Hines, M. (1994). Gender labels and play styles: Their relative contribution to children's selection of playmates. *Child Development, 65*, 869–879.

Algarin, C., Peirano, P., Garrido, M., Pizarro, F., & Lozoff, B. (2003). Iron deficiency anemia in infancy: Long-lasting effects on auditory and visual system functioning. *Pediatric Research, 53*(2), 217–223.

Alink, L. A., Mesman, J., Van Zeijl, J., Stolk, M. N., Juffer, F., Koot, H. M., & Van IJzendoorn, M. H. (2006). The early childhood aggression curve: Development of physical aggression in 10- to 50-month-old children. *Child Development, 77*(4), 954–966.

Alliance for a Media Literate America. (2008). Retrieved from http://www.amlainfo.org

Als, H., & Gilkerson, L. (1995). Developmentally supportive care in the neonatal intensive care unit. *Zero to Three, 15*(6), 1, 3–10.

American Academy of Family Physicians. (1996). *Recommended core educational guidelines for family practice residents.* Kansas City, MO: Author.

American Academy of Pediatric Dentistry. (2010a.). *Guidelines on oral and dental aspects of child abuse and neglect.* Retrieved from http://www.aapd.org/media/policies_guidelines/g_childabuse.pdf

American Academy of Pediatrics. (1998a). *Pediatric nutrition handbook* (4th ed.). Elk Grove Village, IL: Author.

American Academy of Pediatrics. (1998b). *A woman's guide to breastfeeding.* Elk Grove Village, IL: Author.

American Academy of Pediatrics. (1999a). Health Alert: Avoid using home trampolines, Academy says. *AAP News, 15*(5), 31.

American Academy of Pediatrics. (2000, April). *Swimming programs for infants and toddlers: Policy statement.* Retrieved from http://www.aap.org/policy/re9940.html

American Academy of Pediatrics. (2005). AAP policy. Breastfeeding and the use of human milk. *Pediatrics, 115*(2), 496–506. Retrieved from http://pediatrics.aappublications.org/content/115/2/496.full

American Academy of Pediatrics. (2007). *Year 2007 position statement: Principles and guidelines for early hearing detection and intervention programs.* Retrieved from http://aappolicy.aappublications .org/cgi/content/full/pediatrics;120/4/898

American Academy of Pediatrics. (2010a). *Hospital stay for healthy term newborns.* Retrieved from http://aappolicy.aappublications.org/cgi/content/full/pediatrics;113/5/1434

American Academy of Pediatrics. (2010b). *Maternal and paternal smoking associated with mental health conditions and obesity.* Retrieved July 10, 2011, from http://www.healthychildren.org/

American Academy of Pediatrics. (2011). SIDS and Other Sleep-Related Infant Deaths: Expansion of Recommendations for a Safe Infant Sleeping Environment. *Pediatrics, 128*(5), e1341–e1367. Retrieved from: http://pediatrics.aappublications.org/content/128/5/e1341.full

American Academy of Pediatrics. (2012). Asthma. Healthy Children.Org, Retrieved from http://www .healthychildren.org/English/health-issues/conditions/allergies-asthma/Pages/Asthma.aspx

American Academy of Pediatrics. (n.d.). *Effects of tobacco on children.* Retrieved from http://www .aap.org/richmondcenter/EffectsOfTobaccoOnChildren.html

American Academy of Pediatrics & American Congress of Obstetricians and Gynecologists. (1992). *Guidelines for prenatal care.* Elk Grove Village, IL: Author.

American Academy of Pediatrics, Committee on Injury and Poison Prevention and Committee on Sports Medicine and Fitness. (1998). In-line skating injuries in children and adolescents. *Pediatrics, 101*(4), 720–722.

American Academy of Pediatrics, Read, J. S., & the Committee on Pediatric AIDS. (2010). *Diagnosis of HIV-1 infection in children younger than 18 months in the United States.* Retrieved from http://aappolicy.aappublications.org

American Academy of Pediatrics, Task Force on Sudden Infant Death Syndrome. (2005). The changing concept of sudden infant death syndrome: diagnostic coding shifts, controversies regarding the sleeping environment, and new variables to consider in reducing risk. *Pediatrics, 116*(5), 1245–1255.

American Congress of Obstetricians and Gynecologists. (2008). ACOG recommends routine HIV testing for women ages 19–64. Retrieved from http://www.acog.org/~/media/ACOG%20Today/acogToday0808.pdf?dmc=1&ts=20120519T1749568441

American Congress of Obstetricians and Gynecologists. (2011a). FAQ: HIV and pregnancy. Retrieved from http://www.acog.org/~/media/For%20Patients/faq113.pdf?dmc=1&ts=20120417T1940119581

American Congress of Obstetricians and Gynecologists. (2011b). *HIV and pregnancy.* Retrieved from http://www.acog.org/~/media/For%20Patients/faq113.pdf?dmc=1&ts=20120413T2158320838

American Dental Association. (2011). *Tooth eruption charts.* Retrieved from http://www.ada.org/2930.aspx

American Psychological Association. (1993). *Violence and youth: Psychology's response. Vol. 1: Summary report.* Washington, DC: Author.

American Psychological Association. (2002). *Ethical principles of psychologists and code of conduct.* Washington, DC: Author.

American Psychological Association, Committee on Ethical Standards in Psychological Research. (1972, May). Ethical standards for research with human subjects. *APA Monitor,* I–XIX.

American Psychiatric Association. (2000) *Diagnostic and statistical manual of mental disorders* (4th ed.). Washington, DC: American Psychiatric Association,

American Public Health Association & American Academy of Pediatrics. (2011). *Caring for our children: National health and safety performance standards: Guidelines for early education programs* (3rd ed.). Washington, DC, and Elk Grove Village, IL: Author.

Anderson, D., & Collins, P. (1988). *The impact on children's education: Television's influence on cognitive development.* Washington, DC: U.S. Department of Education, Office of Educational Research and Improvement.

Andrews, G., Halford, G., & Bunch, K. (2003). Theory of mind and relational complexity. *Child Development, 74,* 1476–1499.

Annie E. Casey Foundation. (2010). *2010 KIDS COUNT Data Book: State Profiles of Child Well-being.* Retrieved from http://www.aecf.org/

Anselmo, S. (1987). *Early childhood development: Prenatal through age eight.* Upper Saddle River, NJ: Merrill/Prentice Hall.

Apgar, V. A. (1953). A proposal for a new method of evaluation in the newborn infant. *Current Research in Anesthesia and Analgesia, 32,* 260–267.

Aram, D., & Levin, I. (2011). Home support of children in the writing process: Contributions to early literacy. In S. B. Neuman & D. K. Dickinson (Eds.), *Handbook of early literacy research* (3rd ed., pp. 189–200). New York, NY: Guilford Press.

Armitage R., Flynn H., Hoffmann R.,Vazquez, D., Lopez, J., & Marcus S. (2009). Early developmental changes in sleep in infants: The impact of maternal depression. *Sleep, 32*(5), 693–696.

Arsenio, W. F., & Lover, A. (1995). Children's conceptions of sociomoral affect: Happy victimizers, mixed emotions, and other expressions. In M. Killen & D. Hart (Eds.), *Morality in everyday life: Developmental perspectives* (pp. 87–128). New York, NY: Cambridge University Press.

Asher, S. R., Renshaw, P. D., & Hymel, S. (1982). Peer relations and the development of social skills. In S. G. Moore & C. R. Cooper (Eds.), *The young child: Reviews of research* (Vol. 3, pp. 137–158). Washington, DC: National Association for the Education of Young Children.

Astington, J. W. (1993). *The child's discovery of the mind.* Cambridge, MA: Harvard University Press.

Au, K. H. (1993). *Literacy instruction in multicultural settings.* Fort Worth, TX: Harcourt Brace.

Au, K. H., & Kowakami, A. J. (1991). Culture and ownership: Schooling minority students. *Childhood Education, 67*(5), 280–284.

Autism Society. (2012). Retrieved from http://www.autism-society.org/

Baillargeon, R. (1987). Object permanence in 3½- and 4½-month-old infants. *Developmental Psychology, 23*(5), 655–664.

Baker, D., & Witt, P. A. (1996). Evaluation of the impact of two after-school recreation programs. *Journal of Park and Recreation Administration, 14*(3), 23–44.

Baker, L., Serpell, R., & Sonnenschein, S. (1995). Opportunities for literacy learning in the homes of urban preschoolers. In L. M. Morrow (Ed.), *Family literacy: Connections in schools and communities.* Newark, DE: International Reading Association.

Baldwin, D., Baird, J., Saylor, M., & Clark, A. (2001). Infants parse dynamic human action. *Child Development, 72,* 708–717.

Ball, M. A., & Wolfe, C. D. (2004). Emotion and cognition: An intricately bound developmental process. *Child Development, 75*(2), 366–370.

Baloche, L. (1998). *The cooperative classroom: Empowering learning.* Upper Saddle River, NJ: Prentice Hall.

Baltazar, N. C., Shutts, K., & Kinzler, K. D. (2012). Children show heightened memory for threatening social actions. *Journal Of Experimental Child Psychology, 112*(1), 102–110.

Baltes, P. B., Dittman-Kohli, F., & Dixon, R. A. (1984). New perspectives on the development of intelligence in adulthood: Toward a dual-process conception and a model of selective optimization with compensation. In P. B. Baltes & O. G. Brim, Jr. (Eds.), *Life-span development and behavior* (Vol. 6, pp. 33–76). New York, NY: Academic.

Bandura, A. (1962). *Social Learning through Imitation.* University of Nebraska Press: Lincoln, NE.

Bandura, A. (1977). *Social learning theory.* Upper Saddle River, NJ: Prentice Hall.

Bandura, A. (1986). *Social foundation of thoughts and actions: A social cognitive theory.* Upper Saddle River, NJ: Prentice Hall.

Bandura, A. (1989). Social cognitive theory. In R. Vasta (Ed.), *Annals of child development, Vol. 6: Theories of child development: Revised formulations and current issues* (pp. 1–60). Greenwich, CT: JAI.

Bandura, A. (1997). *Self-efficacy: The exercise of control.* New York, NY: Freeman.

Bandura, A. (2001). Social cognitive theory: An agentive perspective. *Annual review of psychology, 52,* 1–26.

Bandura, A., & Walters, R. (1963). *Social learning and personality development.* New York, NY: Holt, Rinehart & Winston.

Banks, S. P., & Kahn, M. D. (2003). *The sibling bond.* New York, NY: Basic Books.

Barbour, A. C. (1995). Physical competence and peer relations in 2nd graders: Qualitative case studies from recess play. *Journal of Research in Childhood Education, 11*(1), 35–46.

Barclay, K., Benelli, C., & Curtis, A. (1995). Literacy begins at birth: What caregivers can learn from parents of children who read early. *Young Children, 50*(4), 24–28.

Bar-Haim, Y., Marshall, P. J., Fox, N. A., Schorr, E., & Gordon-Salant, S. (2003). Mismatch negativity in socially withdrawn children. *Biological Psychiatry, 54,* 17–24.

Barnett, W. S. (1995). Long-term effects of early childhood programs on cognitive and school outcomes. In R. E. Behrman (Ed.), *The future of children, 5*(3), 25–50. Los Altos, CA: The Center for the Future of Children/The David and Lucile Packard Foundation.

Baron, A. S., & Banaji, M. R. (2006). The development of implicit attitudes: Evidence of race evaluations from ages 6, 10 & adulthood. *Psychological Science, 17,* 53–58.

Basiotis, P. P., Linn, M., & Anand, R. S. (1999, December). *Eating breakfast greatly improves school-children's diet quality* (Nutrition Insights #15, Fact Sheet). Washington, DC: USDA Center for Nutrition Policy and Promotion.

Baskett, L. M., & Johnson, S. M. (1982). The young child's interaction with parents versus siblings: A behavioral analysis. *Child Development, 53,* 643–650.

Baumrind, D. (1967). Child care practices anteceding three patterns of preschool behavior. *Genetic Psychology Monographs, 75,* 43–88.

Baumrind, D. (1971). Current patterns of parental authority. *Developmental Psychology Monographs, 4* (No. 1, Pt. 2).

Baumrind, D. (1972). Socialization and instrumental competence in young children. In W. W. Hartrup (Ed.), *The young child: Reviews of research* (Vol. 2, pp. 202–224). Washington, DC: National Association for the Education of Young Children.

Baumrind, D. (1991a). Parenting styles and adolescent development. In R. Lerner, A. C. Petersen, & J. Brooks-Gunn (Eds.). *The encyclopedia of adolescence* (pp. 746–758). New York, NY: Garland.

Baumrind, D. (1991b). The influence of parenting style on adolescent competence and substance use. *Journal of Early Adolescence 1,* 56–95.

Baumrind, D. (1998). Reflections on character and competence. In A. Colby, J. James, & D. Hart (Eds.), *Competence and character through life* (pp. 1–28). Chicago, IL: University of Chicago Press.

Bayer, C., Whaley, K., & May, S. (1995). Strategic assistance in toddler disputes II. Sequences and patterns of teachers' message strategies. *Early Education and Development, 6*(4), 406–432.

References

Beals, D. E., & Tabors, P. O. (1995). Arboretum, bureaucratic, and carbohydrates: Preschoolers' exposure to rare vocabulary at home. *First Language, 15*, 57–76.

Beauchamp, G. K., & Mennella, J. A. (2009). Early flavor learning and its impact on later feeding behavior. *Journal of Pediatric Gastroenterology & Nutrition, 48*, 25–30.

Bebko, J. M., Burke, L., Craven, J., & Sarlo, N. (1992). The importance of motor activity in sensorimotor development: A perspective from children with physical handicaps. *Human Development, 35*(4), 226–240.

Becker, J. (1994). Pragmatic socialization: Parental input to preschoolers. *Discourse Processes, 17*, 131–148.

Beddard, J. R., & Chi, M. T. H. (1992). Expertise. *Current Directions in Psychological Science, 1*, 135–139.

Belsky, J. (1988). The effects of infant day care reconsidered. *Early Childhood Research Quarterly, 3*, 235–272.

Belsky, J. (2006a). Early child care and early child development: Major findings of the NICHD Study of Early Child Care. *European Journal of Developmental Psychology, 3*, 95–110.

Belsky, J. (2006b). Quality, quantity and type of child care: Effects on child development in the USA. In G. Bentley & R. Mace, *Alloparenting in human societies*. London, England: Berghahn Books.

Belsky, J., & Fearon, R. M. P. (2002). Early attachment security, subsequent maternal sensitivity, and later child development: Does continuity in development depend upon continuity of caregiving? *Attachment and Human Development, 4*(3), 361–387.

Belsky, J., Hsieh, K., & Crnic, K. (1998). Mothering, fathering and infant negativity as antecedents of boys' externalizing problems and inhibition at age 3: Differential susceptibility to rearing influence? *Development and Psychopathology, 10*, 301–319.

Belsky, J., & Rovine, M. (1988). Non-maternal care in the first year of life and the security of infant–parent attachment. *Child Development, 59*(1), 157–167.

Belsky, J., Spritz, B., & Crnic, K. (1996). Infant attachment security and affective cognitive information processing at age three. *Psychological Science, 7*, 111–114.

Bergen, D. (2002). The role of pretend play in children's cognitive development. *ECRP, 4*(10). Retrieved from http://ecrp.uiuc.edu/v4n1/bergen.html

Berger, K. S. (2006). Update on bullying at school: Science forgotten. *Developmental Review, 27*(1), 90–126.

Berk, L. E., & Winsler, A. (1995). *Scaffolding children's learning: Vygotsky and early childhood education*. Washington, DC: National Association for the Education of Young Children.

Berkowitz, G. S., Wolff, M. S., Janevic, T. M., Holzman, I. R., Yehuda, R., & Landrigan, P. J. (2003). The World Trade Center disaster and intrauterine growth restriction. *Journal of the American Medical Association, 290*, 595–596.

Berreuta-Clement, J. R., Schweinhart, L. J., Barnett, W. S., Epstein, A. S., & Weikart, D. P. (1984). *Changed lives: The effects of the Perry Preschool Program on youths through age 19* [Monographs of the High/Scope Educational Research Foundation, 8]. Ypsilanti, MI: High/Scope Press.

Bettegowda V. R., Dias, T., Davidoff, M. J., Damus, K., Callaghan, W. M., & Petrini, J. R. (2008). The relationship between cesarean delivery and gestational age among U.S. singleton births. *Clinics in Perinatology, 35*, 309–323.

Bierman, K. L. (2003). *Peer rejection: Developmental processes and intervention strategies*. New York, NY: Guilford.

Bigelow, B. J., Tesson, G., & Lewko, J. H. (1996). *Learning the rules: The anatomy of children's relationships*. New York, NY: Guilford.

Birch, L. L., & Fisher, J. O. (1998). Development of eating behaviors among children and adolescents. *Pediatrics, 101*(3, Supplement), 539–549.

Birch, L. L., Johnson, S. L., Andersen, G., Peters, J. C., & Schulte, M. C. (1991). The variability of young children's energy intake. *New England Journal of Medicine, 324*, 232–235.

Birch, L. L., Johnson, S. L., & Fisher, J. A. (1995). Research in review: Children's eating: The development of food-acceptance patterns. *Young Children 50*(2), 71–78.

Black, J. K. (1981). Are young children really egocentric? *Young Children, 36*(6), 51–55.

Blass, E. M., & Shah, A. (1995). Pain-reducing properties of sucrose in human newborns. *Chemical Senses, 20*(1), 29–35.

Bloom, B. (1964). *Stability and change in human characteristics.* New York, NY: Wiley.

Bloom, L. (1970). *Form and function in emerging grammars.* Cambridge, MA: MIT Press.

Bloom, P. (2010). The moral life of babies. *The New York Times Magazine,* May 9, 2010, MM44.

Blosch, N., Tabachnick, B. R., & Espinosa-Dulanto, D. (1994). Teacher perspectives on the strengths and achievements of young children: Relationship to ethnicity, language, gender and class. In B. L. Mallory & R. S. New (Eds.), *Diversity and developmentally appropriate practices* (pp. 223–249). New York, NY: Teachers College Press.

Bodrova, E., & Leong, D. J. (1998). Development of dramatic play in young children and its effects on self-regulation: The Vygotskian approach. *Journal of Early Childhood Teacher Education, 19*(2), 115–124.

Boggiano, A. K., Klinger, C. A., & Main, D. S. (1986). Enhancing interest in peer interaction: A developmental analysis. *Child Development, 57*, 852–861.

Bond, A. (2008). Trampolines unsafe for children at any age. AAP News: American Academy of Pediatrics. Retrieved from http://aapnews.aappublications.org/content/29/4/29.6.full

Bonds, J. (2010). Recommendations for improving research, practice, and policy on paternal involvement in pregnancy outcomes. Retrieved from http://www.gcyf.org/usr_doc/CPIPO_ Recommendations_by_Jermane_Bond.pdf

Booth-LaForce, C., & Oxford, M. L. (2008). Trajectories of social withdrawal from grades 1 to 6: Prediction from early parenting, attachment, and temperament. *Developmental Psychology, 44*(5), 1298–1313.

Boothe, R. G., Dobson, V., & Teller, D. Y. (1985). Postnatal development of vision in human and nonhuman primates. *Annual Review of Neuroscience, 8*, 495–545.

Borke, H. (1983). Piaget's mountains revisited: Changes in the egocentric landscape. In M. Donaldson, R. Grieve, & C. Pratt (Eds.), *Early childhood development and education: Readings in psychology* (pp. 254–259). New York, NY: Guilford.

Bornstein, M. H. (1984). A descriptive taxonomy of psychological categories used by infants. In C. Sophian (Ed.), *Origins of cognitive skills. The eighteenth annual Carnegie symposium on cognition* (pp. 313–338). Hillsdale, NJ: Erlbaum.

Bornstein, M. H. (1985). Human infant color vision and color perception. *Infant Behavior and Development, 8*, 109–113.

Bower, T. G. R. (1982). *Development in infancy* (2nd ed.). New York, NY: Freeman.

Bowlby, J. (1969/2000). *Attachment and loss: Vol. 1. Attachment* (2nd ed.). New York, NY: Basic Books.

Bowlby, J. (1973). *Attachment and loss: Vol. 2. Separation: Anxiety and anger.* New York, NY: Basic Books.

Bowlby, J. (1982). *Attachment.* New York: Basic Books.

Bowlby, J. (1988). *A secure base: Parent-child attachment and healthy human development.* New York, NY: Basic Books.

Bowlby, J. (1999). *Attachment and loss.* New York, NY: Basic Books.

Bowman, B. T., & Stott, F. M. (1994). Understanding development in a cultural context: The challenge for teachers. In B. L. Mallory & R. S. New (Eds.), *Diversity and developmentally appropriate practices* (pp. 119–133). New York, NY: Teachers College Press.

Boyatzis, C. J. (1997). Of power rangers and v-chips. *Young Children, 52*(7), 74–79.

Boyd, J., Barnett, W. S., Bodrova, E., Leong, D. J., & Gomby, D. (2005). *Promoting children's social and emotional development through preschool education.* National Institute for Early Education Research.

Boyer, W. (2009). Crossing the glass wall: Using preschool educators' knowledge to enhance parental understanding of children's self-regulation and emotion regulation. *Early Childhood Education Journal, 37*, 175–182.

Braza, F., Braza, P., Carreras, M. R., Muñoz, J. M., Sánchez-Martín, J. R., Azurmendi, A., et al. (2007). Behavioral profiles of different types of social status in preschool children: An observational approach. *Social Behavior and Personality, 35*(2), 195–212.

Brazelton, T. B. (1973). *Neonatal Behavioral Assessment Scale* (Clinics in Developmental Medicine No. 50, Spastics International Medical Publication). Philadelphia: Lippincott.

References

Brazelton, T. B. (1992). *Touchpoints: The essential reference: Your child's emotional and behavioral development.* Reading, MA: Perseus Books.

Brazelton Institute. (2007) The newborn behavioral observations system: What is it? Retrieved from http://www.brazelton-institute.com/clnbas.html

Brecht, M. C. (1989). The tragedy of infant mortality. *Nursing Outlook, 37,* 18.

Breitenstein, S. M., Hill, C., & Gross, D. (2009). Understanding disruptive behavior problems in preschool children. *Journal of Pediatric Nursing, 24*(1), 3–12.

Bretherton, I. (1986). Representing the social world in symbolic play: Reality and fantasy. In A. S. Gottfried & C. C. Brown (Eds.), *Play interactions: The contributions of play materials and parental involvement to children's development* (pp. 119–148). Lexington, MA: Lexington.

Bretherton, I. (2010). Fathers in attachment theory and research: A review. *Early Child Development and Care, 180*(1/2), 9–23.

Bretherton, I., & Walters, E. (Eds.). (1985). *Growing points in attachment theory and research.* Monographs of the Society for Research in Child Development, Vol. 50, No. 1–2, serial no. 209. Chicago, IL: University of Chicago Press.

Briere, J. N., & Elliott, D. M. (1994). Immediate and long-term impacts of child sexual abuse. *The Future of Children, 4*(2), 54–69.

Bronfenbrenner, U. (1970, November). *Who cares for America's children?* Keynote address delivered at the Annual Conference of the National Association for the Education of Young Children, Boston, MA.

Bronfenbrenner, U. (1977). Toward an experimental ecology of human development. *American Psychologist, 32,* 513–531.

Bronfenbrenner, U. (1979). *The ecology of human development.* Cambridge, MA: Harvard University Press.

Bronfenbrenner, U. (1986). Ecology of the family as a context for human development: Research perspectives. *Developmental Psychology, 22,* 723–742.

Bronfenbrenner, U. (2004). *Making human beings human: Bioecological perspectives on human development.* Thousand Oaks, CA: Sage Publications.

Bronfenbrenner, U. (2005). *Making human beings human: Bioecological perspectives on human development.* Thousand Oaks, CA: Sage Publications [Paperback].

Bronfenbrenner, U., & Ceci, S. J. (1994). Nature–nurture reconceptualized in developmental perspective: A bioecological model. *Psychological Review, 101*(4), 568–586.

Bronfenbrenner, U., & Morris, P. A. (2006). The bioecological model of human development. In R. M. Lerner (Ed.), *Handbook of child development: Vol. 1. Theoretical models of human development* (6th ed., pp. 793–828). Hoboken, NJ: Wiley.

Brooks, R., & Meltzoff, A. N. (2002). The importance of eyes: How infants interpret adult looking behavior. *Developmental Psychology, 38*(6), 958–966.

Brooks, R., & Meltzoff, A. N. (2005). The development of gaze following and its relation to language. *Developmental Science 8,* 535–543.

Brooks-Gunn, J., & Lewis, M. (1982). The development of self-knowledge. In C. Kropp & J. Krakow (Eds.), *The child: Development in a social context* (pp. 333–387). Reading, MA: Addison-Wesley.

Brown, R., & Fraser, C. (1963). The acquisition of syntax. In C. N. Cofer & B. S. Musgrave (Eds.), *Verbal behavior and learning: Problems and processes* (pp. 158–209). New York, NY: McGraw-Hill.

Brown, S. L. (2010). Marriage and child well-being: Research and policy perspectives. *Journal of Marriage and Family, 72*(5), 1059–1077.

Brown, S. A., Arnolds, D. H., Dobbs, J., & Doctoroff, G. (2007). Parenting predictors of relational aggression among Puerto Rican and European American school-age children. *Early Childhood Research Quarterly, 221,* 147–159.

Browne, K. D., & Hamilton-Giachristis, C. (2005). The influence of violent media on children and adolescents: A public health approach. *Lancet, 365,* 702–710.

Brown, W. H., McIver, K. L., Pfeiffer, K. A., Dowda, M., Addy, C. L., & Pate, R. R. (2009). Social and environmental factors associated with preschoolers' non-sedentary physical activity. *Child Development, 80*(1), 45–58.

Bruner, J. (1960). *The process of education.* Cambridge, MA: Harvard University Press.

Bruner, J. (1966). *Toward a theory of instruction.* Cambridge, MA: Harvard University Press.

Bruner, J. (1983). *Child's talk.* New York, NY: W. W. Norton & Company.

Bruner, J. (1990). *Acts of meaning.* Cambridge, MA: Harvard University Press.

Bruner, J. (1996). *The culture of education.* Cambridge, MA: Harvard University Press.

Bryant, G. A., & Barrett, H. C. (2007). Recognizing intentions in infant-directed speech: Evidence for universals. *Psychological Science, 18*(8), 746–751.

Buchsbaum, D., Griffiths, T. L., Gopnik, A., & Baldwin, D. (2009). Learning from actions and their consequences: Inferring causal variables from continuous sequences of human action. 31st Annual Meeting of the Cognitive Science Society. *Cognitive Science Journal Archive.* Retrieved from http://csjarchive.cogsci.rpi.edu/Proceedings/2009

Bull, M., & Engle, W. (2009). Safe transportation of preterm and low birth weight infants at hospital discharge. *Pediatrics, 123*, 1424–1429.

Burgess, K. B., Rubin, K. H., Cheah, C. S. L., & Nelson, L. J. (2001). Behavioral inhibition, social withdrawal, and parenting. In W. R. Crozier & L. E. Alden (Eds.), *International Handbook of Social Anxiety: Concepts, Research, and Interventions Relating to the Self and Shyness* (pp. 137–158). Sussex, UK: John Wiley & Sons.

Burhans, K. K., & Dweck, C. S. (1995). Helplessness in early childhood: The role of contingent worth. *Child Development, 66*(6), 1719–1738.

Burns, M. S., Griffin, P., & Snow, C. (Eds.). (1999). *Starting out right: A guide to promoting children reading success.* Washington, DC: National Academy Press.

Bus, A., van Ijzendoorn, M., & Pellegrini, A. D. (1995). Mothers reading to their 3-year-olds: The role of mother–child attachment security in becoming literate. *Reading Research Quarterly, 30*, 998–1015.

Busco, M., & Barclay, L. (2007). Sibling studies, response-to name research show promise in early detection of autism. *Archives of Pediatric Adolescent Medicine, 161.*

Buss, A. H., & Plomin, R. (1984). *Temperament: Early developing personality traits.* Hillsdale, NJ: Erlbaum.

Cabrera, N., Hofferth, S., & Chae, S. (2011). Patterns and predictors of father-infant engagement across race/ethnic groups, *Early Childhood Research Quarterly, 26*, 365–375.

Caine, R. N., & Caine, G. (1997). *Education on the edge of possibility.* Alexandria, VA: Association for Supervision and Curriculum Development.

Camilli, G., Vargas, S., Ryan, S., & Barnett, S. (2010). Meta-analysis of the effects of early education interventions on cognitive and social development. *Teachers College Record, 112*(3), 579–620. Retrieved from http://www.tcrecord.org/Content.asp?ContentId=15440

Campbell, S. B. (2002). *Behavior problems in preschool children: Clinical and developmental issues* (2nd ed.). New York, NY: Guilford.

Campos, J. J., & Stenberg, C. R. (1981). Perception appraisal and emotion: The onset of social referencing. In M. E. Lamb & L. R. Sherrod (Eds.), *Infant social cognition: Empirical and theoretical considerations* (pp. 273–314). Hillsdale, NJ: Erlbaum.

Camras, L. A., & Witherington, D. C. (2005). Dynamical systems approaches to emotional development. *Developmental Review, 25*, 328–350.

Canadian Council on Smoking and Health, National Clearinghouse on Tobacco and Health. (1995). *Environmental tobacco smoke (ETS) in home environments.* Toronto, Canada: Author.

Cardone, I. (2002). Maternal mental health: Early identification in a hospital-based multidisciplinary setting. *Zero to Three, 22*(6), 35–36.

Cannon, M. (2009). Contrasting effects of maternal and paternal age on offspring intelligence. *PLoS Med 6*(3).

Carey, S. (1978). The child as word learner. In M. Halle, J. Bresnan, & G. Miller (Eds.), *Linguistic theory and psychological reality* (pp. 264–293). Cambridge, MA: MIT Press.

Carle, E. (1979). *The very hungry caterpillar.* New York, NY: Collins.

Carver, P. R., Yunger, J. L., & Perry, D. G. (2003). Gender identity and adjustment in middle childhood. *Sex Roles, 49*(3/4), 95–109.

Case, R. (1992). *The mind's staircase: Exploring the conceptual underpinnings of children's thought and knowledge.* Hillsdale, NJ: Erlbaum.

References

Casas, J. F., Weigel, S. M., Crick, N. R., Ostrov, J. M., Woods, K. E., Yeh, E. A. J., & Huddleston-Casas, C. A. (2006). Early parenting and children's relational and physical aggression in the preschool and home contexts. *Journal of Applied Developmental Psychology, 27*(3), 209–227.

Casper, V., Cooper, R. M., Finn, C. D., & Stott, R. (2003). Caregiver goals and societal expectations. *Zero to Three, 23*(5), 4–6.

Cassidy, J., & Asher, S. R. (1992). Loneliness and peer relations in young children. *Child Development, 63*, 350–365.

Cassidy, J., & Shaver, P. R. (Eds.). (2008). *Handbook of attachment: Theory, research and clinical applications* (2nd ed.). New York, NY: Guilford Publications.

Centers for Disease Control and Prevention (CDC). (2001). CDC identifies nutritional deficiencies among young children. *Morbidity and Mortality Weekly Report.* Retrieved from http://www.cdc.gov

Centers for Disease Control and Prevention (CDC). (2007). Injury center. Retrieved from http://www .cdc.gov

Centers for Disease Control and Prevention (CDC). (2010a). Growth charts. Retrieved from http://www .cdc.gov/growthcharts/who_charts.htm

Centers for Disease Control and Prevention (CDC). (2010b). Identifying infants with hearing loss— United States, 1999–2007. Retrieved from http://www.cdc.gov/mmwr/preview/mmwrhtml/ mm5908a2.htm

Centers for Disease Control and Prevention (CDC). (2010c.). *Tuberculosis (TB). Basic TB Facts.* Retrieved from http://www.cdc.gov/tb/topic/basics/default.htm

Centers for Disease Control and Prevention (CDC). (2011a). Autism spectrum disorders (ASDs). Retrieved from http://www.cdc.gov/ncbddd/autism/index.html

Centers for Disease Control and Prevention (CDC). (2011b). *Injury prevention & control: Traumatic brain injury.* Retrieved from http://www.cdc.gov/TraumaticBrainInjury/infants_toddlers.html

Centers for Disease Control and Prevention (CDC). (2011c). Obesity rates among low-income preschool children. Retrieved from http://www.cdc.gov/obesity/childhood/data.html

Chambers, B., Cheung, A., Slavin, R. E., Smith, D., & Laurenzano, M. (2010). Effective early child-hood education programs: A systematic review. Retrieved from http://www.bestevidence.org/word/ early_child_ed_Sep_22_2010.pdf

Charpak, N., Ruiz-Pelaz, J., & Figueroa, Z. (2005). Influence of feeding patterns and other factors on early somatic growth of healthy, preterm infants in home-based kangaroo mother care: A cohort study. *Journal of Pediatric Gastroenterol Nutrition, 41*(4), 430–437.

Chen, D. W., Fein, G. G., Killen, M., & Tam, H. (2001). Peer conflicts of preschool children: Issues, resolution, incidence, and age-related patterns. *Early Education & Development, 12*(4), 523–544.

Chen, X., Rubin, K. H., & Li, B. (1995). Social and school adjustment of shy and aggressive children in China. *Developmental and Psychopathology, 7*, 337–349.

Chen, X., Rubin, K. H., & Li, D. (1997). Maternal acceptance and social and school adjustment: A four-year longitudinal study. *Merrill-Palmer Quarterly, 43*, 663–681.

Chess, S., & Thomas, A. (1987). *Origins and evolution of behavior disorders from infancy to early adult life.* Cambridge, MA: Harvard University Press.

Chess, S., & Thomas, A. (1996). *Temperament: Theory and practice.* New York, NY: Brunner/Mazel.

Child Abuse Prevention Network. (2007). Retrieved from http://child-abuse.com

Children's Defense Fund. (2002). *The state of children in America's union, 2002.* Washington, DC: Author.

Children's Defense Fund. (2005). *The state of America's children, 2005.* Washington, DC: Author.

Children's Defense Fund. (2011). State of America's Children ® 2011 Report. Retrieved from http:// www.childrensdefense.org/child-research-data-publications/data/state-of-americas-children-2011- report.html

Childs, C. P., & Greenfield, P. M. (1980). Informal modes of learning and teaching: The case of Zinacanteco learning. In N. Warren (Ed.), *Studies in cross-cultural psychology* (Vol. 2). New York, NY: Academic.

ChildStats.gov. (2007). America's children: key national indicators of well being, 2007. Retrieved from http://www.childstats.gov/index.asp

ChildStats.gov. (2010). *Forum on child and family statistics. America's children in brief: Key national indicators of well-being, 2010.* Retrieved from http://www.childstats.gov/

ChildStats.gov. (2011a) America's children in brief: Key national indicators of well-being, 2011. Retrieved from http://www.childstats.gov/americaschildren/index.asp

ChildStats.gov. (2011b). *Forum on child and family statistics. America's children: Key national indicators of well-being, 2011. Infant mortality.* Retrieved from http://www.childstats.gov/americaschildren/health2.asp

Chilman, C. S. (1966). *Your child from 6 to 12.* Washington, DC: Children's Bureau, U.S. Department of Health, Education, and Welfare.

Chiong, J. (1998). *Racial categorization of multiracial children in schools.* Westport, CT: Bergin and Garvey.

Chomsky, N. (1968). *Language and mind.* San Diego, CA: Harcourt Brace Jovanovich.

Chomsky, N. (1969). *The acquisition of syntax in children from five to ten.* Cambridge, MA: MIT Press.

Chomsky, N. (1980). *Rules and representations.* New York, NY: Columbia University Press.

Chomsky, N. (1993). *Language and thought.* Kingston, RI: Moyer Bell.

Chrisman, K., & Couchenour, D. (2002). *Healthy sexuality development: A guide for early childhood educators and families.* Washington, DC: National Association for the Education of Young Children.

Christakis, D. A., Zimmerman, F. J., DiGuiseppe, D. L., & McCarty, C. A. (2004). Early television exposure and subsequent attentional problems in children. *Pediatrics, 113*(4), 708–713.

Chugani, H. T. (1997). Neuroimaging of developmental non-linearity and developmental pathologies. In R. W. Thatcher, G. R. Lyon, J. Rumsey, & N. Krasnegor (Eds.), *Developmental neuroimaging: Mapping the development of brain and behavior* (pp. 187–195). San Diego, CA: Academic Press.

Chugani, H. T., Behen, M. E., Muzik, O., Juhasz, C., Nagy, F., Chugani, D. C. (2001). Local brain functional activity following early deprivation: A study of postinstitutionalized Romanian orphans. *NeuroImage, 14*(6), 1290–1301.

Cicchetti, D., & Beeghly, M. (Eds.). (1990). *The self in transition: Infancy to childhood.* Chicago, IL: University of Chicago Press.

Clark, C. A., Pritchard, V. E., & Woodard, L. J. (2010). Preschool executive functioning abilities predict early mathematics achievement. *Developmental Psychology, 46*(5), 1176–1191.

Clark, E. V. (1983). Meanings and concepts. In J. H. Flavel & E. M. Markman (Eds.), *Handbook of child psychology. Vol. 3: Cognitive development* (4th ed., pp. 787–840). New York, NY: Wiley.

Claussen, A. H., Mundy, P. C., Mallik S. A., & Willoughby J. C. (2002). Joint attention and disorganized attachment status in infants at risk. *Developmental Psychopathology, 14*(2), 279–291.

Clay, M. M. (1993). *An observation survey of early literacy achievement.* Auckland, New Zealand: Heinemann.

Clearfield, M. W., & Nelson, N. M. (2006). Sex differences in mothers' speech and play behaviors with 6-, 9-, and 14-Month-Old Infants. *Sex Roles, 54*(1/2), 127–137.

Cleary-Goldman J., Bettes B., Robinson J. N., Norwitz E., D'Alton M. E., Schulkin J. (2006). Postterm pregnancy: practice patterns of contemporary obstetricians and gynecologists. *American Journal of Perinatology, 23*(1),15–20.

Cohen, M. (1967). *Will I have a friend?* New York, NY: Macmillan.

Cole, R. (1997). *The moral intelligence of children: How to raise a moral child.* New York, NY: Plume.

Cole, P. M., Dennis, T. A., Smith-Simon, K. E. & Cohen, L. H. (2009). Preschoolers' emotion regulation strategy understanding: Relations with emotion socialization and child self-regulation. *Social Development, 18*(2), 324–352.

Coll, C. G., & Meyer, E. C. (1993). The sociocultural context of infant development. In C. H. Zeanah, Jr. (Ed.), *Handbook of infant mental health* (pp. 56–69). New York, NY: Guilford.

Connor, C. M. (2011). Child characteristics: Instruction interactions: Implications for students' literacy skills development in the early grades. In S. B. Neuman & D. K. Dickinson (Eds.), *Handbook of Early Literacy Research* (pp. 256–275). New York, NY: Guilford Press.

Connor, S. M., & Wesolowski, K. L. (2003). "They're too smart for that": Predicting what children would do in the presence of guns. *Pediatrics, 111*, e109–e114.

Consumer Product Safety Commission. (2007). Consumer product safety review, 11(4). Retrieved from http://www.cpsc.gov/CPSCPUB/PUBS/cpsr_nws44.pdf

Cook, J. T., Ohri-Vachaspati, P., & Kelly, G. L. (1996). *Evaluation of a universally-free school breakfast program demonstration project, Central Falls, Rhode Island.* Medford, MA: Tufts University, Center on Hunger, Poverty, and Nutrition Policy.

Copple, C. (Ed.). (2003). *A world of difference. Readings on teaching young children in a diverse society.* Washington, DC: NAEYC.

Copple, C., & Bredekamp, S. (Eds.) (2009). *Developmentally appropriate practice in Early Childhood programs serving children from birth through age 8* (3rd Ed.). Washington, DC: NAEYC.

Corsaro, W. A. (2003). *We're friends right?: Inside kids' culture.* Washington, DC: Joseph Henry Press.

Coté, S. M. (2007). Sex differences in physical and indirect aggression: A developmental perspective. *European Journal on Criminality and Research, 13*(3–4), 183–200.

Coté, S. M., Vaillancourt, T., LeBlanc, J. C., Nagin, D. S., & Tremblay, R. E. (2006). The development of physical aggression from toddlerhood to pre-adolescence: A nationwide longitudinal study of Canadian children (clinical report). *Journal of Abnormal Child Psychology, 34*(1), 71–86.

Council for Early Childhood Professional Recognition. (2008). About us. Retrieved January 2008 from http://www.cdacouncil.org/about.htm

Courchesne, E., Pierce, K., Schumann, C. M., Redcay, E., Buckwalter, J. A., Kennedy, D. P. & Morgan, J. (2007) Mapping early brain development in autism. *Neuron, 56*(2), 399–413.

Cozolino, L. (2006). *The neuroscience of human relationships: attachment and the developing social brain.* W. W. Norton & Company.

Craik, F. I. M., & Lockhart, R. S. (1972). Levels of processing: A framework for memory research. *Journal of Verbal Learning and Verbal Behavior, 11*, 671–684.

Crain-Thoreson, C., Dahlin, M. P., & Powell. T. A. (2001). Parent-child interaction in three conversational contexts: Variations in style and strategy. In P. R. Britto & J. Brooks-Gunn (Eds.), *The role of family literacy environments in promoting young children's emerging literacy skills* (pp. 23–38). San Francisco, CA: Jossey-Bass.

Crais, E. R. (2009). *Early infant/toddler behaviors that may lead to a diagnosis of autism.* Presented at the annual Ohio Speech-Language-Hearing Association, March 7, 2009, at Columbus, Ohio. Retrieved from http://www.ohioslha.org/pdf/Convention/2009%20Handouts/Elizabeth%20Crais-Early%20Infant%20Toddler-Reduced.pdf

Creasy, G., Jarvis, P., & Berk, L. (1998). Play and social competence. In O. Saracho & B. Spodek (Eds.), *Multiple perspectives on play in early childhood* (pp. 116–143). Albany, NY: State University of New York Press.

Creswell, J. W. (2008). *Educational research: Planning, conducting, and evaluating quantitative and qualitative research* (3rd ed.). Upper Saddle River, NJ: Merrill/Prentice Hall.

Crick, N., & Grotpeter, J. (1995). Relational aggression, gender, and social-psychological adjustment. *Child Development, 66*, 710–722.

Crockenberg, S., Leerkes, E., & Lekka, S. K. (2007). Pathways from marital aggression to infant emotion regulation: The development of withdrawal in infancy. *Infant Behavior and Development, 30*(1), 97–113.

Crockenberg, S., & Litman, C. (1990). Autonomy as competence in two-year-olds: Maternal correlates of child compliance, defiance, and self-assertion. *Development Psychology, 26*, 961–971.

Dahl, R. (1998). Life's gracefulness lost on overstimulated, overtired children. *American Academy of Pediatrics News, 14*(5), 28.

Dansky, J. L. (1980). Make-believe: A mediator of the relationship between play and associative fluency. *Child Development, 51*, 576–579.

Darwin, C. (1859). *On the origin of species.* London, England: Murray.

Dasanayake, A. P., Gennaro, S. Hendricks-Munoz, K.D., & Chhun, N. (2008) Maternal periodontal disease, pregnancy, and neonatal outcomes. *American Journal of Maternal and Child Nursing, 33*(1), 45–49.

Davis, C., Tomporowski, P. D., McDowell, J. E., Austin, B. P., Miller, P. H., Yanasak, N. E., Allison, J. D., & Naglieri, J. A. (2011). Exercise improves executive function and achievement and alters brain activation in overweight children: A randomized, controlled trial. *Health Psychology, 30*(1), 91–98.

Davis, R. (1990). *A comparison of the reading and writing performance of children in a whole language pre-first grade class and a modified traditional first grade class.* Unpublished doctoral dissertation, University of North Texas, Denton.

Dearing, E., McCartney, K., & Taylor, B. (2009). Does higher quality early child care promote low-income children's math and reading achievement in middle childhood? *Child Development, 80*(5), 1329–1349.

DeCasper, A. J., & Fifer, W. P. (1980). Of human bonding: Newborns prefer their mothers' voices. *Science, 208*, 1174–1176.

DeCasper, A. J., & Spence, M. J. (1986). Prenatal maternal speech influences newborn's perception of speech sounds. *Infant Behavior and Development, 9*, 133–150.

Decety, J., Chaminade, T., Grezes, J., & Meltzoff, A. N. (2002). A PET exploration of the neural mechanisms involved in reciprocal imitation. *NeuroImage, 15*, 265–272.

DeFranco, E. A., Lian, M., Muglia, L. J., & Schootman, M. (2008). Area-level poverty and preterm birth risk: A population-based multilevel analysis. *BMC Public Health*. Retrieved from http://www.biomedcentral.com/1471-2458/8/316

deHouwer, A. (1995). Bilingual language acquisition. In P. Fletcher & B. MacWhinney (Eds.), *The handbook of child language* (pp. 219–250). Oxford, England: Blackwell.

de Zubicaray, G. I. (2006). Cognitive neuroimaging: Cognitive science out of the armchair. *Brain and Cognition, 60*(3), 272–281.

Deiner, P. L. (1997). *Infant and toddlers: Development and program planning.* Fort Worth, TX: Harcourt Brace.

Delcomyn, F. (1998). *Foundations of neurobiology.* New York, NY: Freeman.

Denham, S. A. (1998). *Emotional development in young children.* New York, NY: Guilford.

Denham, S., & Weissberg, R. (2004). Social–emotional learning in early childhood: What we know and where to go from here. In E. Chesebrough, P. King, T. P. Gullotta, & M. Bloom (Eds.), *A blueprint for the promotion of prosocial behavior in early childhood* (pp. 13–34). New York, NY: Kluwer/Academic.

DeNoon, D. (2005). Trampoline injuries jump. WebMD. Retrieved from http://www.webmd.com/parenting/news/20050516/trampoline-injuries-jump

Derman-Sparks, L., & Ramsey, P. G. (2006). *What if all the kids are white? Anti-bias multicultural education with young children and families.* New York, NY: Teachers College Press.

Dettling, A., Gunnar, M. R., & Donzella, B. (1999). Cortisol levels of young children in full-day childcare centers: Relations with age and temperament. *Psychoneuroendocrinology, 24*, 505–518.

Dettling, A. C., Parker, S., Lane, S. K., Sebanc, A. N. M., & Gunnar, M. R. (2000). Quality of care and temperament determine whether cortisol levels rise over the day for children in full-day childcare. *Psychneuroendocrinology, 25, 819–518.*

deVilliers, P. A., & deVilliers, J. G. (1992). Language development. In M. E. Lamb & M. H. Bornstein (Eds.), *Developmental psychology: An advanced textbook* (3rd ed.). Hillsdale, NJ: Erlbaum.

DeVries, R. (1969). *Constancy of generic identity in the years three to six.* Monographs of the Society for Research in Child Development, Vol. 34, No. 3, serial no. 127. Chicago, IL: University of Chicago Press.

DeVries, R., & Zan, B. (1994). *Moral classrooms, moral children: Creating a constructivist atmosphere in early education.* New York, NY: Teachers College Press.

Diamond, J. (1990). War babies. *Discover, 11*(12), 70–75.

Diamond, K. E., & Stacey, S. (2003). The other children at preschool: Experiences of typically developing children in inclusive programs. In C. Copple (Ed.), *A world of difference: Readings on teaching young children in a diverse society.* (pp. 135–139). Washington, DC: NAEYC.

Diego, M. A., Field, T., Hernandez-Reif, M., Deeds, O., Ascencio, A., Begert, G. (2007). Preterm infant massage elicits consistent increases in vagal activity and gastric motility that are associated with greater weight gain. *Acta Paediatrica, 96*, 1588–1591.

Dietrich, S. L. (2005). A look at friendships between preschool children with and without disabilities in two inclusive classrooms. *Journal of Early Childhood Research, 3*(2), 193–215.

Dodd, V. (2005). Implications of kangaroo care for growth and development in preterm infants. *Journal of Obstetrics, Gynecologic, and Neonatal Nursing, 34*(2), 218–232.

References

Dodge, K. A. (1994). Studying mechanism in the cycle of violence. In C. Thompson & P. Cowas (Eds.), *Violence: Basic and clinical science.* Oxford, England: Butterworth-Hernemas.

Doiron, R. (1994). Using nonfiction in a read-aloud program: Letting the facts speak for themselves, *Reading Teacher, 47*(8), 616–624.

Donaldson, M. (1979). *Children's minds.* New York, NY: Norton.

Donaldson, M. (1983). Children's reasoning. In M. Donaldson, R. Grieve, & C. Pratt (Eds.), *Early childhood development and education: Readings in psychology* (pp. 231–236). New York, NY: Guilford.

Dorr, A. (1983). No shortcuts to judging reality. In P. E. Bryant & S. Anderson (Eds.), *Watching and understanding TV: Research on children's attention and comprehension.* New York, NY: Academic Press.

Dozier, M., Albus, K. E., Stovall, K. C., & Bates, B. (2002). Attachment for infants in foster care: The role of caregiver state of mind. *Child Development, 72,* 1467–1477.

Dunn, L., & Kontos, S. (1997). Research in review: What have we learned about developmentally appropriate practice? *Young Children, 52*(5), 4–13.

Durkin, D. (1966). *Children who read early.* New York, NY: Teachers College Press.

Dyson, A. H. (1993). *Social worlds of children learning to write in an urban primary school.* New York, NY: Teachers College Press.

Dyson, A. H. (1997). *Writing superheroes: Contemporary childhood, popular culture, and classroom literacy.* New York, NY: Teachers College Press.

Dyson, L. L. (2005). Kindergarten children's understanding of and attitudes toward people with disabilities. *TECSE, 25*(2), 95–101.

Early, D. M., et al. (2007). Teachers' education, classroom quality, and young children's academic skills: Results from seven studies of preschool programs. *Child Development, 78*(2), 558–580.

Early Head Start. (2010). Tip sheet, no. 2 – revised. Teacher qualification & EHS. Retrieved from http://www.ehsnrc.org/Publications/English%20Tip%20Sheets/TIP_SHEET_2.pdf

Eaton, W. O., & Von Bargen, D. (1981). Asynchronous development of gender understanding in preschool children. *Child Development, 52,* 1020–1027.

Eckerman, C. O., & Didow, S. M. (1996). Nonverbal imitation and toddlers' mastery of verbal means of achieving coordinated action. *Developmental Psychology, 32,* 141–152.

Egan, S. K., & Perry, D. G. (2001). Gender identity: A multidimensional analysis with implications for psychosocial adjustment. *Developmental Psychology, 37,* 451–463.

Eisbach, A. O. (2004). Children's developing awareness of diversity in people's trains of thought. *Child Development, 75,* 1694–1707.

Eisenberg, N., & Fabes, R. A. (1998). Prosocial development. In W. Damon (Ed.), *Handbook of child psychology* (5th ed., Vol. 3, pp. 701–778). New York, NY: Wiley and Sons.

Eisenberg, N., Guthrie, I. K., Murphy, B. C., Shepard, S. A., Cumberland, A., & Carlo, G. (1999). Personality and social development consistently and development of prosocial dispositions: A longitudinal study. *Child Development, 70*(6), 1360–1372.

Elliott, C., Adams, J. R., & Sockalingam, S. (1999). Multicultural toolkit. Executive summary. Retrieved from http://www.awesomelibrary.org/multiculturaltoolkit-patterns.html

Emde, R. N., & Buchsbaum, H. K. (1990). "Didn't you hear my mommy?": Autonomy with connectedness in moral self-emergence. In D. Cicchetti & M. Beeghly (Eds.), *Infancy to Childhood* (pp. 35–60). Chicago, IL: University of Chicago Press.

Emde, R. N., & Harmon, R. J. (1972). Endogenous and exogenous smiling systems in early infancy. *Journal of the American Academy of Child Psychiatry, 11,* 177–200.

Emory, E. K., Schlackman, L. J., & Fiano, K. (1996). Drug–hormone interactions on neurobehavioral responses in human neonates. *Infant Behavior and Development, 19*(2), 213–220.

Engle, W. A., Tomashek, K. M., Wallman, C., & the Committee on Fetus and Newborn. (2007). Late-preterm infants: A population at risk. Retrieved from http://aappolicy.aappublications.org/cgi/content/full/pediatrics;120/6/1390

Engstrand, O., Williams, K., & Lacerda, F. (2003). Listener responses to vocalizations produced by Swedish and American 12- and 18-month-olds. *Phonetica, 60,* 17–44.

Ensor, R., & Hughes, C. (2005). More than talk: Relations between emotion understanding and positive behaviour in toddlers. *British Journal of Developmental Psychology, 23,* 343–363.

Epperson, N. (2002). Postpartum mood changes: Are hormones to blame? *Zero to Three, 22*(6), 17–23.

Epstein, J. L. (1989). The selection of friends: Changes across the grades and in different school environments. In T. J. Berndt & G. W. Ladd (Eds.), *Peer relations in child development* (pp. 158–187). New York, NY: Wiley.

Erikson, E. (1963). *Childhood and society* (2nd ed.). New York, NY: Norton.

Erikson, E. (1959, 1980, Reissued 1994). *Identity and the life cycle.* New York, NY: W. W. Norton & Company.

Ericson, N. (2001, June). Addressing the problem of juvenile bullying. *Fact Sheet #200127.* Washington, DC: Office of Juvenile Justice and Delinquency Prevention.

Eron, L. D. (1992, June 18). The impact of televised violence. Testimony on behalf of the American Psychological Association before the Senate Committee on Governmental Affairs, *Congressional Record, 1992.*

Essex, M. J., Klein, M. H., Cho, E., & Kalin, N. H. (2002). Maternal stress beginning in infancy may sensitize children to later stress exposure: Effects on cortisol and behavior. *Biological Psychiatry, 52,* 776–784

Etaugh, C., & Liss, M. B. (1992). Home, school, and playroom: Training grounds for adult gender roles. *Sex Roles, 26,* 639–648.

Everett, S. A., Warren, C. W., Sharp, D., Kann, L., Husten, C. G., & Crossett, L. S. (1999). Initiation of cigarette smoking and subsequent smoking behavior among U.S. high school students. *Preventive Medicine, 29,* 337–333.

Fagot, B. I. (1988). Toddlers, play and sex stereotyping. In D. Bergen (Ed.), *Play as a medium for learning and development: A handbook of theory and practice* (pp. 133–135). Portsmouth, NH: Heinemann.

Fagot, B. I. (1997). Attachment, parenting, and peer interactions of toddler children. *Developmental Psychology, 33*(3), 489–499.

Fantz, R. L. (1961). The origin of form perception. *Scientific American, 204,* 66–72.

Federal Interagency Forum on Child and Family Statistics. (2007). *America's children: Key national indicators of well-being 2002.* Washington, DC: U.S. Government Printing Office.

Feeding America. (2011). How we fight hunger. Retrieved from http://feedingamerica.org/how-we-fight-hunger.aspx

Feinberg, M. E., Jones, D.E., Kan, M. L., & Goslin, M. C. (2010). Effects of family foundations on parents and children: 3.5 years after baseline. *Journal of Family Psychology, 24*(5), 532–542.

Feiring, C., & Lewis, M. (1991). The development of social networks from early to middle childhood: Gender differences and the relation to school competence. *Sex Roles, 25,* 527–253.

Feldman, R. S. (2007). *Child development* (4th ed.). Upper Saddle River, NJ: Pearson Prentice Hall.

Feldman, R. S., & Klein, P. S. (2003). Toddler's self-regulated compliance to mothers, caregivers, and fathers: Implications for theories of socialization. *Developmental Psychology, 39*(4), 680–692.

Feldman, R., Eidelman, A. I., Sirota, L., & Weller, A. (2002). Comparison of skin-to-skin (kangaroo) and traditional care: Parenting outcomes and preterm infant development. *Pediatrics, 110,* 16–26.

Ferguson, C. A. (1977). Learning to pronounce: The earliest stages of phonological development in the child. In F. D. Minifie & L. L. Lloyd (Eds.), *Communicative and cognitive abilities: Early behavioral assessment* (pp. 141–155). Baltimore: University Park Press.

Feshbach, S. (1970). Aggression. In P. Mussen (Ed.), *Carmichael's manual of child psychology* (Vol. 2). New York, NY: Wiley.

Field, T. M., Schanberg, S. M., Scafidi, F., Bauer, C. R., Vega-Lahr, N., Garcia, R., ...Kuhn, C. M. (1986). Tactile/kinesthetic stimulation effects on preform neonates. *Pediatrics, 77,* 654–658.

Field, T. M., Vega-Lahr, N., & Jagadish, S. (1984). Separation stress of nursery school infants and toddlers graduating to new classes. *Infant Behavior and Development, 7,* 277–284.

Fields, M. V., & Spangler, K. L. (2000). *Let's begin reading right: A developmental approach to emergent literacy* (4th ed.). Upper Saddle River, NJ: Merrill/Prentice Hall.

Feinberg, M. E., Jones, D. E., Kan, M. L., & Goslin, M. C. (2010). Effects of family foundations on parents and children: 3.5 years after baseline. *Journal of Family Psychology, 24*(5), 532–542.

Fierro-Cobas, V., & Chan, E. (2001). Language development in bilingual children: A primer for pediatricians. *Contemporary Pediatrics, 7,* 79.

References

Fifer, W. P., & Moon, C. M. (1995). The effects of fetal experience with sound. In J. P. Lecanuet, W. E. Fifer, N. A. Krasnegor, & W. P. Smotherman (Eds.), *Fetal development: A psychobiological perspective.* Hillsdale, NJ: Erlbaum.

Fike, R. D. (1993). Personal relationship-building between fathers and infants. *Childhood Education, 5*(4), 1–2.

Fisch, H., Hyun, G., Golden, R., Hensle, T. W., Olsson, C. A., & Liberson, G. L. (2003). The influence of paternal age on Down syndrome. *Journal of Urology, 169*(6), 2275–2278.

Fitzgerald, M., & Walker, S. M. (2009). Infant pain management: A developmental neurobiological approach. *Nature Reviews Neurology, 5*, 35–50.

Fivush, R. (1984). Learning about school: The development of kindergartners' school scripts. *Child Development, 55*, 1697–1709.

Fivush, R., Hudson, J., & Lucariello, J. M. (2002). Introduction: Katherine Nelson's theoretical vision. *Journal of Cognition and Development, 3*(1), 1–3.

Flavell, J. H. (1963). *The developmental psychology of Jean Piaget.* New York, NY: Van Nostrand.

Flavell, J. H. (1985). *Cognitive development* (2nd ed.). Upper Saddle River, NJ: Prentice Hall.

Fleege, P. O., Charlesworth, R., Burts, D. C., & Hart, C. H. (1992). Stress begins in kindergarten: A look at behavior during standardized testing. *Journal of Research in Childhood Education, 7*(1), 20–26.

Fleer, M. (2006a). A sociocultural perspective on Early Childhood Education: Rethinking, reconceptualising and re-inventing. In M. Fleer, S. Edwards, M. Hammer, A. Kennedy, A. Ridgway, J. Robbins, & L. Surman. *Early childhood learning communities.* Upper Saddle River, NJ: Pearson Australian Co.

Fleer, M. (2006b). The cultural construction of child development: creating cultural intersubjectivy. *Journal of Early Years Education, 14*(2), 127–140.

Floor, P., & Akhtar, N. (2006). Can 18-month-old infants learn words by listening in on conversations? *Infancy, 9*(13), 327–339.

FNS-USDA. (2010). Women, infants, and children. Retrieved from http://www.fns.usda.gov/wic/

Food Research and Action Center. (2007). *Current news and analyses.* Retrieved from http://www.frac.org

Frank, M. G., Issa, N. P., & Stryker, M. P. (2001) Sleep enhances plasticity in the developing visual cortex. *Neuron, 30*, 275–287.

Freel, K. S. (1996). Finding complexities and balancing perspectives: Using an ethnographic viewpoint to understand children and families. *Zero to Three, 16*(3), 3–7.

Freeman, J. B., Rule, N. O., Adams, Jr., R. B., & Ambady, N. (2009). Culture shapes a mesolimbic response to signals of dominance and subordination that associates with behavior. *NeuroImage, 47*(1), 353–359.

Freud, S. (1905/1930). *Three contributions to the theory of sex.* New York, NY: Nervous and Mental Disease Publishing.

Freud, S. (1933). *New introductory lectures on psychoanalysis.* New York, NY: Norton.

Freud, S. (1938). The history of the psychoanalytic movement. In A. A. Brill (Ed. and Trans.), *The basic writings of Sigmund Freud* (pp. 931–977). New York, NY: Modern Library.

Frost, J. L. (1992). Reflections on research and practice in outdoor play environments. *Dimensions, 20*(4), 6–10.

Frost, J. L., Pei-San, B., Sutterby, J. A., & Thornton, C. D. (2004). *The developmental benefits of play.* Olney, Maryland: Association for Childhood Education International.

Frost, J. L., Wortham, S. L., & Reifel, S. (2001). *Play and child development.* Upper Saddle River, NJ: Merrill/Prentice Hall.

Furman, W., & Buhrmester, D. (1992). Age and sex difference in perceptions of networks of personal relationships. *Child Development, 63*, 103–115.

Furth, H. G. (1992a). The developmental origin of human societies. In H. Beilin and P. B. Pufall (Eds.), *Piaget's theory: Prospects and possibilities.* Hillsdale, NJ: Erlbaum.

Furth, H. G. (1992b). Life's essential—The story of mind over body: A review of "I raise my eyes to say yes": A memoir by Ruth Sienkiewicz-Mercer & S. B. Kaplan. *Human Development, 35*(2), 254–261.

Furth, H. G. (1992c). Commentary on Bebko, Burke, Craven & Sarlo (1992): The importance of sensorimotor development: A perspective from children with physical handicaps. *Human Development, 36*(4), 226–240.

Gabbard, C., Dean, M., & Haensly, P. (1991). Foot preference behavior during early childhood. *Journal of Applied Developmental Psychology, 12*(1), 131–137.

Gable, S. (1999). Promoting children's literacy with poetry. *Young Children, 54*(5), 12–15.

Gage, F. H., & Jacob, B. (2001, July 15). Exercise and adult neurogenesis. *London News, Financial Times,* p. 11.

Gallahue, D. L., & Ozmun, J. C. (2006). *Understanding motor development: Infants, children, adolescents, adults* (5th ed.). New York, NY: McGraw-Hill.

Gallahue, D. L., & Donnely, F. C. (2007). *Developmental physical education for all children.* Champaign, IL: Human Kinetics.

Galenson, E. (1993). Sexual development in preoedipal females: Arrest versus intrapsychic conflict. In T. B. Cohen & M. Etezady (Eds.), *The vulnerable child* (Vol. 1). Madison, CT: International Universities Press.

Garbarino, J. (1999). *Rasing children in a socially toxic environment.* San Francisco, CA: Jossey-Bass.

Garcia-Sierra, A., et al. (2011). Bilingual language learning: An ERP study relating early brain responses to speech, language input, and later word production. *Journal of Phonetics, 39*(4), 546–557.

Gardner, H. (1983). *Frames of mind: Theory of multiple intelligences.* New York, NY: Basic Books.

Gardner, H. (1991a). Assessment in context: The alternative to standardized testing. In B. R. Gifford & M. C. O'Connor (Eds.), *Changing assessments: Alternative views of attitude, achievement and instruction.* Boston, MA: Kluwer.

Gardner, H. (1991b). *The unschooled mind: How children think and how schools should teach.* New York, NY: Basic Books.

Gardner, H. (1993). *Multiple intelligences: The theory in practice.* New York, NY: Basic Books.

Gardner, H. (1999). *Intelligence reframed: Multiple intelligences for the 21st century.* New York, NY: Basic Books.

Gardner, H. (2005). *The development and education of the mind: The collected works of Howard Gardner.* London, England: Taylor and Francis.

Garrett, P., Ferron, J., Ng'Andu, N., Bryant, D., & Harbin, G. (1994). A structural model for the developmental status of young children. *Journal of Marriage and the Family, 56*(1), 147–163.

Garvey, C. (1977). *Play.* Cambridge, MA: Harvard University Press.

Gauthier, Y. (2003). Infant mental health as we enter the third millennium: Can we prevent aggression? *Infant Mental Health Journal, 24*(3), 296–308.

Gelman, R., & Gallistel, C. R. (1983). The child's understanding of number. In M. Donaldson, R. Grieve, & C. Pratt (Eds.), *Early childhood development and education: Readings in psychology* (pp. 185–203). New York, NY: Guilford.

Gershoff, E. T. (2002). Corporal punishment by parents and assoicated child behaviors and experiences: A meta-analytic and theoretical review. *Psychological Bulletin, 128*(4), 539–579.

Gershkoff-Stowe, L., & Hahn, E. R. (2007). Fast mapping skills in the developing lexicon. *Journal of Speech, Language, and Hearing Research, 50,* 682–697.

Gesell, A. (1925). *The mental growth of the preschool child: A psychological outline of normal development from birth to the sixth year.* New York, NY: Macmillan.

Gesell, A. (1928). *Infancy and human growth.* New York, NY: Macmillan.

Gesell, A. (1930). *Guidance of mental growth in infant and child.* New York, NY: Macmillan.

Gesell, A., & Amatruda, C. S. (1941). *Developmental diagnosis: Normal and abnormal child development.* New York, NY: Hoeber.

Gibson, J. J. & Gibson, E. J. (1955). Perceptual learning: Differentiation or enrichment? *Psychological Review, 62,* 32–41.

Gilgun, J. (2001). Protective factors, resilience and child abuse and neglect. *Healthy Generations, 2*(1), 4–5. Retrieved from http://www.epi.umn.edu/MCH/resources/hg/hg_abuse.pdf

Gilliam, W. S. (2005). *Prekindergarteners left behind: Explusion rates in state prekindergarten systems.* Yale University Child Study Center. Retrieved from http://www.med.yale.edu/chldstdy/faculty/pdf/Gilliam05.pdf

Gilligan, C. (1982). *In a different voice.* Cambridge, MA: Harvard University Press.

Glaser, D. (2000), Child abuse and neglect and the brain—A review. *Journal of Child Psychology and Psychiatry,* 41, 97–116.

Gleason, J. B. (2000). *The development of language* (5th ed.). Boston, MA: Allyn & Bacon.

Goleman, D. (1995). *Emotional intelligence.* New York, NY: Bantam.

Golinkoff, R. M., & Hirsh-Pasek, K. (2006). Baby wordsmith. *Association for Psychological Science, 15*(1), 30–33.

Gollnick, D. M., & Chinn, P. C. (1990). *Multicultural education in a pluralistic society* (3rd ed.). Upper Saddle River, NJ: Merrill/Prentice Hall.

Goodman, J. F. (2006). School discipline in moral disarray. *Journal of Moral Education, 35*(2), 213–230.

Goodman, K. (1986). *What's whole in whole language?* Portsmouth, NH: Heinemann.

Goodman, R. F. (2001). *A view from the middle: Life through the eyes of middle childhood: A critique of research conducted by Sesame Workshop.* New York University Child Study Center. Retrieved from http://www.aboutourkids.org

Goodman, Y. (1980). *The Roots of Literacy.* Claremont Reading Conference Yearbook 44, 1–32.

Goodsell, T. L., & Meldrum, J. T. (2010). Nurturing fathers: A qualitative examination of child-father attachment. *Early Child Development & Care, 180*(1/2), 249–262.

Gopnik, A. (July, 2010). How babies think. *Scientific American,* 76–81.

Gopnik, A., Meltzoff, A. N., & Kuhl, P. K. (1999). *The scientist in the crib: Minds, brains, and how children learn.* New York, NY: Morrow.

Gordon-Salant, W. (2003). The role of chronic peer difficulties in the development of children's psychological adjustment problems. *Child Development, 74*, 1344–1367.

Gottfried, A. (1984). Touch as an organizer of human development. In C. Brown (Ed.), *The many facets of touch* (pp. 114–120). Skillman, NJ: Johnson & Johnson.

Grantham-McGregor, S., Chang, S., & Walker, S. (1998). Evaluation of school feeding programs: Some Jamaican examples. *American Journal of Clinical Nutrition, 67*, 785S–789S.

Greenough, W., Gunnar, M., Emde, R. N., Massinga, R., & Shonkoff, J. P. (2001). The impact of the caregiving environment on young children's development: Different ways of knowing. *Zero to Three, 21*(5), 16–23.

Greenspan, S., & Greenspan, N. T. (1985). *First feelings.* New York, NY: Penguin.

Grisham-Brown, J. (n.d.). Influences on early childhood development. Retrieved from www.education .com/reference/article/early-childhood-development

Grogan, T., & Bechtel, L. (2003). Boys and girls together: Improving gender relationships in school. *Responsive Classroom, 15*(1), 1–2.

Grossmann, K., Grossmann, K. E., Fremmer-Bombik, E., Kindler, H., Scheuerer-Englisch, H., & Zimmermann, P. (2002). The uniqueness of the child-father attachment relationships: Fathers' sensitive and challenging play as a pivotal variable in a 16-year longitudinal study. *Social Development, 11*(3), 301–337.

Gun-Mette, B. R., Slinning, K., Eberhard-Gran, M., Røysamb, E., & Tambs, K. (2011). Partner relationship satisfaction and maternal emotional distress in early pregnancy. *BMC Public Health, 11*(161). Retrieved from http://www.biomedcentral.com/content/pdf/1471-2458-11-161.pdf

Gunnar, M. R. (1996). *Quality of care and the buffering of stress physiology: Its potential in protecting the developing human brain.* Minneapolis: University of Minnesota Institute of Child Development.

Gunnar, M. R. (1998). Quality of early care and buffering of neuroendocrine stress reactions: Potential effects on the developing human brain. *Preventive Medicine, 27*, 208–211.

Gunnar, M. R., Broderson, L., Nachmias, M., Buss, K., & Rigatuso, J. (1996). Stress reactivity and attachment security. *Developmental Psychology, 29*(3), 191–204.

Gunnar, M. R., & Cheatham, C. L. (2003). Brain and behavior interface: Stress and the developing brain. *Infant Mental Health Journal, 24*(3), 195–211.

Gunnar, M. R., & Quevedo, K. (2007). The neurobiology of stress and development. In S. Fiske (Ed.) *Annual Review of Psychology, 58*, 145–174.

Guttmacher Institute (2010). Following decade-long decline, U.S. teen pregnancy rate increases as both births and abortions rise. Retrieved from http://www.guttmacher.org/media/nr/2010/01/26/index.html

Guttmacher Institute. (2012). U.S. teenage pregnancies, births and abortions: National and state trends and trends by race and ethnicity. Retrieved from http://www.guttmacher.org/pubs/USTPtrends.pdf

Haber, J. S. (2000). *The great misdiagnosis: ADHD.* Dallas, TX: Taylor.

Hack, M., Schluchter, M., Cartar, L., Rahman, M., Cuttler, L., & Borawski, E. (2003). *Pediatrics, 112*(1), e30–e38. Retrieved from http://www.pediatrics.aappublications.org

Haith, M. M. (1966). The response of human newborns to visual movement. *Journal of Experimental Child Psychology, 3,* 235–243.

Halbreich, U., & Karkun, S. (2005). Cross-cultural and social diversity of prevalence of postpartum depression and depressive symptoms. *Journal of Affective Disorders, 91*(2–3), 97–111.

Halim, M. L., & Ruble, D. (2010). Gender identity and stereotyping in early and middle childhood. *Handbook of Gender Research in Psychology, 7,* 495–525.

Hall, G. S. (1893). *The contents of children's minds.* New York, NY: Kellogg.

Halpern, R. (2003). *Making play work: The promise of after-school programs for low-income children.* New York, NY: Teachers College Press.

Hamilton, B. E., Martin, J. A., & Ventura, S. J. (2010). Births: Preliminary data for 2010. National Vital Statistics Reports, 60(2), 1–26. Retrieved from http:///www.cdc.gov/nchs/data/nvsr/nvsr60/nvsr60_02.pdf

Hamlin, J. K., Wynn, K., & Bloom, P. (2007) Social evaluation by preverbal infants. *Nature, 450*(7169), 557–559.

Hamlin, J. K. & Wynn, K. (2011). Young infants prefer prosocial to antisocial others. *Cognitive Development, 26*(1), 30–39.

Hamre, B. K., & Pianta, R. C. (2005). Can instructional and emotional support in the first grade classroom make a difference for children at risk of school failure? *Child Development, 76*(5), 949–967.

Hargrave, A. C., & Senechal, M. (2000). A book reading intervention with preschool children who have limited vocabularies: The benefits of regular reading and dialogic reading. *Early Childhood Research Quarterly, 15*(1), 78–90.

Hari, R., & Kujala, M. V. (2009). Brain basis of human social interaction: From concepts to brain imaging. *Physiological Review, 89,* 453–479.

Hart, B., & Risley, T. R. (1995). *Meaningful differences in the everyday experience of young American children.* Baltimore, MD: Brookes.

Hart, C. H., DeWolf, D. M., Royston, K. E., Burts, D. C., & Thomasson, R. H. (1990). *Maternal and paternal disciplinary styles: Relationships to behavioral orientations and sociometric status.* Paper presented at the annual conference of the American Educational Research Association, Boston, MA.

Hart, C. H., Ladd, G. W., & Burleson, B. R. (1990). Children's expectations of the outcomes of social strategies: Relations with sociometric status and maternal disciplinary styles. *Child Development, 61,* 127–137.

Hart, L. (1983). *Human brain, human learning.* New York, NY: Longman.

Harter, S. (2001). *The construction of self: A developmental perspective.* New York, NY: Guilford.

Hartup, W. W. (1974). Aggression in childhood: Developmental perspectives. *American Psychologist, 29,* 336–341.

Hartup, W. W. (1989). Behavioral manifestations of children's friendships. In T. J. Berndt & G. W. Ladd (Eds.), *Peer relationships in child development* (pp. 46–70). New York, NY: Wiley.

Hauch, F. R., Thompson, J. M., Tanabe, K. O., Moon, R. Y., & Vennemann, M. M. (2011). Breastfeeding and reduced risk of sudden infant death syndrome: A meta-analysis. *Pediatrics, 128*(1), 103–110.

Hay, W. W., Levin, M. J., Sondheimer, J. M., & Deterding, R. R. (Eds.). (2011). Current diagnosis and treatment. *Pediatrics* (20th ed.). New York, NY: McGraw Hill LANGE.

Healthychildren.org. (2012). Retrieved from Healthychildren.org.

Healy, M. (2011). Should we take the friendships of children seriously? *Journal of Moral Education, 40*(4), 441–456.

Heath, D. C. (1977). *Maturity and competence: A transcultural view.* New York, NY: Gardner.

Heath, S. B. (1983). *Ways with words: Language life and work in communities and classrooms.* Cambridge, England: Cambridge University Press.

Helburn, S., & Bergmann, B. (2002). *America's child care problem: The way out.* New York, NY: Palgrave for St. Martin's Press.

Hellige, J. B. (1993). *Hemispheric asymmetry: What's right and what's left.* Cambridge, MA: Harvard University Press.

Henshaw, S. K. (2003). *U.S. teenage pregnancy statistics with comparative statistics for women aged 20–24.* Alan Guttmacher Institute. Retrieved from http://www.guttmacher.org

Hertsgaard, L., Gunnar, M., Erickson, M. F., & Nachmias, M. (1995). Adrenocortical responses to the strange situation in infants with disorganized/disoriented attachment relationships. *Child Development, 66*(4), 1100–1106.

High/Scope. (2007). Perry preschool study. Lifetime effects: The High/Scope Perry Preschool Study. Retrieved from http://www.highscope.org/Content.asp?ContentId=219

Higley, A. M., & Morin, K. H. (2004). Behavioral responses of substance-exposed newborns: a retrospective study. *Applied Nursing Research, 17*(1), 32–40.

Hinde, R. (1992). Ethological and relationship approaches. In R. Vasta (Ed.), *Six theories of child development: Revised formulations and current issues* (pp. 251–285). London, England: JKP Press.

Hinkley, T., Salmon, J., Okely, A. D., & Trost, S. G. (2010). Correlates of sedentary behaviours in preschool children: a review. *International Journal of Behavioral Nutrition and Physical Activity, 7*, 66. Retrieved from: http://www.ijbnpa.org/content/7/1/66

Hiscock, H., & Wake, M. (2001). Infant sleep problems and postnatal depression: A community-based study. *Pediatrics, 107*(6), 1317–1322.

HMBANA. (2011). Human milk banking association of North America. Retrieved from http://www.hmbana.org/

Hoffman, K. T., Marvin, R. S., Cooper, G., & Powell, B. (2006). Changing toddlers' and preschoolers' attachment classifications: The Circle of Security intervention. *Journal of Consultation in Clinical Psychology. 74*(6), 1017–1026.

Hoffman, M. L. (1988). Moral development. In M. H. Bornstein & M. E. Lamb (Eds.), *Developmental psychology: An advanced textbook* (2nd ed., pp. 497–548). Hillsdale, NJ: Erlbaum.

Hoffman, M. L. (2000). Empathy and moral development: Implications for caring and justice. Cambridge, England: Cambridge University Press.

Hohmann, C. (1990). *Young children and computers.* Ypsilanti, MI: High/Scope Press.

Honig, A.S. (1973) Toilet Learning. *Early Childhood Education Journal, 21*(1), 6–9.

Honig, A. S. (1983). Research in review: Sex role socialization in early childhood. *Young Children, 38*(6), 57–70.

Honig, A. S. (1986). Research in review: Stress and coping in children (Part I). *Young Children, 41*(4), 50–63.

Honig, A. S. (2000). Psychosexual development in infants and young children: Implications for care-givers. *Young Children, 55*(5), 70–77.

Honig, A. S. (2002). *Secure relationships: Nurturing infant/toddler attachment in early care settings.* Washington, DC: NAEYC.

Honig, A., & Wittmer, D. (1996). Helping children become more prosocial: Ideas for classrooms, families, school, and communities (Part 2). *Young Children, 51*(2), 62–70.

Hoot, J. L., & Silvern, S. (Eds.). (1989). *Writing with computers in the early grades.* New York, NY: Teachers College Press.

Horton, C. B., & Cruise, T. K. (2001). *Child abuse and neglect: The school's response.* New York, NY: Guilford Press.

Houston, A. C., Donnerstein, E., Fairchild, H., Feshbach, N. D., Katz, P. A., Murray, J. P., et al. (1992). *Big world, small screen.* Lincoln, NE: University of Nebraska Press.

Howes, C. (1980). Peer play scale as an index of complexity of peer interaction. *Developmental Psychology, 16*, 371–372.

Howes, C. (1988). *Peer interaction in young children.* [Monographs of the Society for Research in Child Development, Vol. 53, No, 1, serial no. 217.

Howes, C. (1992). *The collaborative construction of pretend: Social pretend play functions.* Albany, NY: State University of New York Press.

Howes, C. (1996). The earliest friendships. In W. M. Berkowski, A. F. Newcomb, & W. W. Hartup (Eds.), *The company they keep: Friendships in childhood and adolescence.* Cambridge, MA: Cambridge University Press.

Howes, C. (1997). Children's experiences in center-based child care as a function of teacher background and adult: child ratio. *Merrill-Palmer Quarterly, 43,* 404–425.

Howes, C. (2009). Friendship in early childhood. In K. H. Rubin, W. Bukowski, & B. Laursen (Eds.), *Peer interactions, relationships, and groups* (pp. 180–192). New York: Guilford.

Howes, C., & Hamilton, C. E. (1993). The changing experience of child care: Changes in teachers and in teacher–child relationships and children's social competence with peers. *Early Childhood Research Quarterly, 8*(1), 15–32.

Howes, C., Matheson, C., & Hamilton, C. E. (1992). Sequences in the development of competent play with peers: Social and social-pretend play. *Developmental Psychology, 28,* 961–974.

Howes, C., & Ritchie, S. (2002). *A matter of trust: Connecting teachers and learners in the early childhood classroom.* New York, NY: Teachers College Press.

Huang, S., Chen, H., Haiso, Y., & Tsai, M. (2006). *Infants' endogenous smiles, social smiles and open-mouth smiles in the first year.* Paper presented at the annual meeting of the XVth Biennial International Conference on Infant Studies, Westin Miyako, Kyoto, Japan, June 19, 2006.

Huesmann, L. R., Eron, L. D., Lefkowitz, M. M., & Walder, L. O. (1984). Stability over time and generations. *Developmental Psychology, 20,* 1120–1134.

Huesmann, L. R., Moise-Titus, J., Podolski, C., & Eron, L. (2003). Longitudinal relations between children's exposure to TV violence and their aggressive and violent behavior in young adulthood: 1977–1992. *Developmental Psychology, 39*(2), 201–210.

Hughes, F. P. (1999). *Children, play and development* (3rd ed.). Boston, MA: Allyn & Bacon.

Hughes, M., & Donaldson, M. (1983). The use of hiding games for studying coordination of points. In M. Donaldson, R. Grieve, & C. Pratt (Eds.), *Early childhood development and education: Readings in psychology* (pp. 245–253). New York, NY: Guilford.

Hughes, M., & Grieve, R. (1983). On asking children bizarre questions. In M. Donaldson, R. Grieve, & C. Pratt (Eds.), *Early childhood development and education: Readings in psychology* (pp. 104–114). New York, NY: Guilford.

Hunt, J. M. (1961). *Intelligence and experience.* New York, NY: Ronald.

Hupp, J. M., Smith, J. L., Coleman, J. M. & Brunell, A. B. (2010). That's a boy's toy: Gender-typed knowledge in toddlers as a function of mother's marital status. *The Journal of Genetic Psychology: Research and Theory on Human Development, 171*(4), 389–401.

Hymel, S., Rubin, K., Rowden, L., & LeMare, L. (1990). Children's peer relationships: Longitudinal prediction of internalizing and externalizing problems from middle to late childhood. *Child Development, 61,* 2004–2021.

IDEA. (2004). Retrieved from http://idea.ed.gov/

Iglowstein, I., Jenni, O. G., Molinari, L., & Largo, R. H. (2003). Sleep duration from infancy to adolescence: Reference values and generational trends. *Pediatrics, 111,* 302–307.

Indiana University. (2009, August 10). No bullies here: student labels of 'Bullying' can be misleading. *ScienceDaily.* Retrieved May 9, 2012 from http://www.sciencedaily.com/releases/2009/08/090810030056.htm

Ingram, D. (1986). Phonological development: Production. In P. Fletcher & M. Garman (Eds.), *Language acquisition* (2nd ed., pp. 223–239). Cambridge, England: Cambridge University Press.

International Reading Association & National Association for the Education of Young Children. (1998). *Learning to read and write: A joint position statement.* Newark, DE: Author.

Izard, C. E. (1991). *The psychology of emotions.* New York, NY: Plenum.

Jacobs, G. M., Power, M. A., & Loh, W. I. (2002). *The teacher's sourcebook for cooperative learning: Practical techniques, basic principles, and frequently asked questions.* Thousand Oaks, CA: Corwin Press.

Jago, R., Brockman, R., Fox, K. R., Cartwright, K., Page, A. S., & Thompson, J. L. (2009). Friendship groups and physical activity: qualitative findings on how physical activity is initiated and maintained among 10–11 year old children. *International Journal of Behavioral Nutrition and Physical Activity, 6*(4). 1–9.

Jalongo, M. R. (1987). Do security blankets belong in preschool? *Young Children, 42*(3), 3–8.

Janz, K. F., Burns, T. L., Torner, J. C., Levy, S. M., Paulos, R., Willing, M. C., et al. (2001). Physical activity and bone measure in young children: The Iowa bone development study. *Pediatrics, 107*, 1387–1393.

Jeffer, F., Bakermans-Kranenburg, M. J., & van Ijzendoorn, M. H. (2005). The importance of parenting in the development of disorganized attachment: evidence from a preventive intervention study in adoptive families. *Journal Child Psychology and Psychiatry, 46*(3), 263–274.

Jenni, O. G., & O'Connor, B. B. (2005). Children's sleep: An interplay between culture and biology. *Pediatricss, 114*, 204–216.

Jennings, K. D. (2004). Development of goal-directed behaviour and related self-processes in toddlers. *International Journal of Behavioral Development, 28*(4), 319–327.

Jersild, A. T., & Holmes, F. B. (1935a). *Children's fears.* New York, NY: Teachers College Press.

Jersild, A. T., & Holmes, F. B. (1935b). Methods of overcoming children's fears. *Journal of Psychology, 1*, 75–104.

Johnson, J. E., & Yawkey, T. D. (1988). Play and integration. In T. D. Yawkey & J. E. Johnson (Eds.), *Integrative processes and socialization: Early to middle childhood* (pp. 97–117). Hillsdale, NJ: Erlbaum.

Johnson, E. M. (2010). *Reflections on the weird evolution of human psychology.* Retrieved from http://blogs.plos.org/blog/2010/09/23/reflections-on-the-weird-evolution-of-human-psychology

Johnson, L. D., O'Malley, P. M., & Bachman, J. G. (2001). *Monitoring the future. National survey results on drug use, 1975–2000. Vol. I: Secondary school students.* [National Institute of Health Publication #01–4924]. Bethesda, MD: National Institute on Drug Abuse.

Johnson, S. L., & Birch, L. L. (1994). Parents' and children's adiposity and eating style. *Pediatrics, 94*(5), 653–661.

Jones, H. E., & Jones, M. C. (1928). A study of fear. *Childhood Education, 5*, 136–143.

Justice, L. M., & Piasta, S. B. (2011). Developing children's print knowledge through adult-child storybook reading interactions: Print referencing as an instructional practice. In S. B. Neuman & D. K. Dickinson (Eds.), *Handbook of early literacy research* (3rd ed., pp. 200–213). New York , NY: Guilford Press.

Kagan, J. (1997). *Galen's prophecy: Temperament in human nature.* New York, NY: Perseus.

Kagan, J., Reznick, J. S., & Snidman, N. (1987). The physiology and psychology of behavioral inhibition in children. *Child Development, 58*, 1459–1473.

Kagan, J., Snidman, N., & Arcus, D. M. (1992). Initial reactions to unfamiliarity. *Current Directions in Psychological Science, 1*, 171–174.

Kaley, F., Reid, V., & Flynn, E. (2011), The psychology of infant colic: A review of current research. *Infant Mental Health Journal, 32*, 526–541.

Kamii, C. K. (2000). *Young children reinvent arithmetic: Implications of Piaget's theory* (2nd ed.). New York, NY: Teachers College Press.

Kamii, C. K. (2003). *Young children reinvent arithmetic (2nd grade): Implications of Piaget's theory* (2nd ed.). New York, NY: Teachers College Press.

Karasik, L., Adolph, K., Tamis, C., Tamis-LeMonda, C. S., & Bornstein, M. H. (2010). WEIRD walking: Cross-cultural research on motor development. *Behavioral And Brain Sciences, 33*(2/3), 35–36.

Karmel, M. (1959). *Thank you, Dr. Lamaze: Painless childbirth.* Philadelphia: Lippincott.

Katz, J. R., & Snow, C. (2000). Language development in early childhood: The role of social interaction. In D. H. Cryer (Ed.), *Infants and toddlers in out-of-home care* (pp. 49–86). Baltimore, MD: Paul H. Brookes.

Katz, L. G., & McClellan, D. E. (1997). *Fostering children's social competence: The teacher's role.* Washington, DC: National Association for the Education of Young Children.

Katz, P. A. (1982). Development of children's awareness and intergroup attitudes. In L. G. Katz (Ed.), *Current topics in early childhood education* (Vol. 4, pp. 17–54). Norwood, NJ: Ablex.

Kauffman Foundation. (2002). *New report links school success to early childhood social, emotional development.* Retrieved from http://www.kauffman.org

Kelly, D. J., Liu, S., Lee, K., Quinn, P. C., Pascalis, O., Slater, A. M., & Ge, L. (2009). Development of the other-race effect during infancy: Evidence toward universality. *Journal of Experimental Child Psychology, 104*(1), 105–114.

Kemp, C. (1999). Early life social–emotional experiences affect brain development. *American Academy of Pediatric News, 15*(6), 18.

Kemple, K. M. (1992). *Understanding and facilitating preschool children's peer acceptance* (Report No. EDO-PS-92–5; ERIC Document Reproduction Service No. ED 345866). East Lansing, MI: National Center for Research on Teacher Learning.

Kim, Y. A. (2003). Review of research: Necessary social skills related to peer acceptance. *Childhood Education, 79*, 234–238.

Kinzler, K. D., & Spelke, E. S. (2005). *The effect of language on infants' preference for faces.* Poster presented at the Biennial Meeting of the Society for Research in Child Development, Atlanta, GA.

Kinzler, K. D., & Spelke, E. S. (2007). Core systems in human development. In C. von Hofsten & K. Rosander (Eds.), *Progress in brain research, 164*, 257–264.

Kisilevsky, B. S., et al. (2003). Effects of experience on fetal voice recognition. *Psychological Science, 14*, 220–224.

Kisilevsky, B. S., et al. (2009). Fetal sensitivity to properties of maternal speech and language. *Infant Behavior and Development, 32*, 59–71.

Klahr, D., & Wallace, J. G. (1976). *Cognitive development: An information processing view.* Hillsdale, NJ: Erlbaum.

Klaus, M. H., & Kennell, J. H. (1982). *Parent–infant bonding* (2nd ed.). St. Louis, MO: Mosby.

Klaus, M. H., Kennell, J. H., & Klaus, P. H. (1993). *Mothering the mother.* Reading, MA: Addison-Wesley.

Klaus, M. H., Klaus, P. H., & Kennell, J. H. (2002). *The doula book: How a trained labor companion can help you have a shorter, easier, and healthier birth.* New York, NY: Perseus.

Kleinman, R. E., Murphy, J. M., Little, M., Pagano, M. E., Wehler, C. A., Regal, K., et al. (1998). Hunger in children in the United States: Potential behavioral and emotional correlates. *Pediatrics, 101*, E3.

Knickmeyer, R. C., Gouttard, S., Kang, C., Evans, D., Wilber, K., Smith, K., ... Gilmore, J. H. (2008). A structural MRI study of human brain development from birth to 2 years. *The Journal of Neuroscience, 28*(47), 12176–12182.

Knight, R. (2010). Attachment theory: In search of a relationship between attachment security and preschool children's level of empathy. *The Plymouth Student Scientist, 4*(1), 240–258.

Knitzer, J., Theberge, S., & Johnson, K. (2008). *Project thrive issue brief no. 2: Reducing maternal depression and its impact on young children: toward a responsive early childhood policy framework.* New York, NY: National Center for Children in Poverty.

Kohlberg, L. (1966). A cognitive-developmental analysis of children's sex-role concepts and attitudes. In E. E. Maccoby (Ed.), *The development of sex differences* (pp. 82–173). Stanford, CA: Stanford University Press.

Kohlberg, L. (September, 1968). The child as a moral philosopher. *Psychology Today, 2*(4), 24–30.

Kohlberg, L. (1984). *Essays on moral development. Vol. 2: The psychology of moral development.* San Francisco: Harper & Row.

Kohn, A. (2001). Five reasons to stop saying "good job." *Young Children, 56*(5), 24–28.

Kontos, S., & Wilcox-Herzog, A. (1997). Research in review: Teachers' interactions with children: Why are they so important? *Young Children, 52*(2), 4–12.

Kopp, C. (1982). Antecedents of self-regulation: A developmental perspective. *Developmental Psychology, 18*, 199–214.

Kramer, L., & Conger, K. J. (2009). What we learn from our sisters and brothers: for better or for worse. *New Directions for Child and Adolescent Development, 126*, 1–12.

Kuhl, P. K. (2000). A new view of language acquisition. Proceedings of the National Academy of Sciences, 97, 11850–11857.

Kuhl, P. K. (2001, July 27). *Born to learn: Language, reading, and the brain of the child.* Paper presented at the White House summit: Early childhood cognitive development: Ready to read; Ready to learn. Washington, DC.

References

Kuhl, P. K. (2007). Is speech learning 'gated' by the social brain? *Developmental Science, 10*, 110–120.

Kuhl, P. K., & Meltzoff, A. N. (1984). The bimodal representation of speech in infants. *Infant Behavior and Development, 7*, 361–381.

Kuhl, P. K., & Meltzoff, A. N. (1988). Speech as an intermodal object of perception. In A. Yonas (Ed.), *Perceptual development in infancy: The Minnesota Symposia on Child Psychology* (Vol. 20, pp. 235–266). Hillsdale, NJ: Erlbaum.

Kuhl, P., & Rivera-Gaxiola, M. (2008). Neural substrates of language acquisition. *Annual Review Neuroscience, 31*, 511–534.

Kuhl, P. K., Stevens, E., Hayashi, A., Deguchi, T., Kiritani, S., & Iverson, P. (2006). Infants show a facilitation effect for native language phonetic perception between 6 and 12 months. *Developmental Science, 9*, F13–F21.

Kuhl, P. K., Tsao, F. M., & Liu, H. M. (2003). Foreign-language experience in infancy: effects of short-term exposure and social interaction on phonetic learning. *Proceedings of the National Academy of Sciences, 100*, 9096–9101.

Kuhn, D. (1992). Cognitive development. In M. H. Bornstein & M. E. Lamb. (Eds.), *Developmental psychology: An advanced textbook*. Hillsdale, NJ: Erlbaum.

Kumpulainen, K., Rasanen, E., Henttonen, I., Almqvist, F., Kresanov, K., Sirkka-Liisa, L., et al. (1998). Bullying and psychiatric symptoms among elementary school-age children. *Child Abuse and Neglect, 7*, 705–717.

Lachner, D. (2011). Statistics on trampoline injuries. Retrieved from LiveStrong: http://www.livestrong.com/article/347980-statistics-on-trampoline-injuries/

Lagattuta, K. H., Nucci, L., & Bosacki, S. L. (2010). Theory of mind and the personal domain: Children's reasoning about resistance to parental control. *Child Development, 81*(2), 616–635.

Lagattuta, K. H., & Thompson, R. A. (2007). The development of self-conscious emotions: Cognitive processes and social influences. In J. L. Tracy, R. W. Robins, & J. P. Tangney (Eds.), *The self-conscious emotions: Theory and research.* New York, NY: Guilford Press.

Lally, J. R., Mangione, P. L., & Honig, A. S. (1988). The Syracuse University Family Development Research Program: Long-range impact of an early intervention with low-income children and their families. In D. Powell (Ed.), *Parent education as early childhood intervention: Emerging directions in theory, research, and practice* (pp. 79–104). Norwood, NJ: Ablex.

Lalonde, C. E., & Chandler, M. J. (1995). False belief understanding goes to school: On the social–emotional consequences of coming early or late to a first theory of mind. *Cognition and Emotion, 9*, 167–185.

Lamb, M. E. (1978). The development of sibling relationships in infancy: A short-term longitudinal study. *Child Development, 49*, 1189–1196.

Lamb, M. E. (1987). Predictive implications of individual differences in attachment. *Journal of Consulting and Clinical Psychology, 55*, 817–824.

Lamb, M. E. (2005). Attachments, social networks, and developmental contexts. *Human Development, 48*(1/2), 108–112.

Lamb, M. E., Morrison, D. C., & Malkin, C. M. (1987). The development of infant social expectations in face-to-face interaction: A longitudinal study. *Merrill-Palmer Quarterly, 33*, 241–254.

Lamborn, S. D., Mounts, N. S., Steinberg, L., & Dornbusch, S. M. (1991). Patterns of competence and adjustment among adolescents from authoritative, authoritarian, indulgent and neglectful families. *Child Development 62*, 1049–1065.

Lampl, M., Veldhuis, J. D., & Johnson, M. L. (1992). Saltation and stasis: A model of human growth. *Science, 258*, 801–803.

Landa, R. J. (2008). Diagnosis of autism spectrum disorders in the first 3 years of life. *Nature Clinical Practice Neurology, 4*, 138–147.

Lazar, I., & Darlington, R. (1982). *Lasting effects of early education: A report from the Consortium for Longitudinal Studies* [Monographs of the Society for Research in Child Development, Vol. 47, No. 2–3, serial no. 195]. Chicago, IL: University of Chicago Press.

Leckman, J. F., & Mayes, L. C. (1999). Preoccupations and behaviors associated with romantic and parental love—The origin of obsessive-compulsive disorder? *Child and Adolescent Psychiatry Clinics of North America, 8*, 635–665.

LeDoux, J. (1996). *The emotional brain.* New York, NY: Touchstone.

Leeb, R. T., Paulozzi, L., Melanson, C., Simon, T., & Arias, I. (2010). *Child Maltreatment Surveillance: Uniform Definitions for Public Health and Recommended Data Elements* (2010). Available from: http://www.cdc.gov/ViolencePrevention/pub/CMP-Surveillance.html

Lever, J. (1976). Sex differences in games children play. *Social Problems, 23,* 478–487.

Levin, D. E. (1998). *Remote control childhood? Combating the hazards of media culture.* Washington, DC: National Association for the Education of Young Children.

Levin, D. E. (2003). *Teaching young children in violent times* (2nd ed.). Washington, DC: National Association for the Education of Young Children.

Levine, S. B. (1994). Caution: Children watching. *Ms. 1994* (July/August), 23–25.

Levy, G. D. (1999). Gender-typed and non-gender-typed category awareness in toddlers. *Sex Roles, 41*(11–12), 851–873.

Levy, G. D., & Carter, D. B. (1989). Gender schema, gender constancy, and gender role knowledge: The roles of cognitive factors in preschoolers' gender-role stereotype attributions. *Developmental Psychology, 25,* 444–449.

Lewin, T. (2010). Census finds single mothers and live-in partners. Retrieved from http://www.nytimes.com/2010/11/06/us/06moms.html

Lewis, M. (1987). Social development in infancy and early childhood. In J. D. Osofsky (Ed.), *Handbook of infant development* (2nd ed., pp. 419–493). New York, NY: Wiley.

Lewis, M. (2005). The child and its family: The social network model. *Human Development, 48,* 8–27.

Lewis, M., & Brooks-Gunn, J. (1979). *Social cognition and the acquisition of self.* New York, NY: Plenum.

Lewis, M., & Brooks, J. (1978). Self-knowledge and emotional development. In M. Lewis & L. Rosenblum (Eds.), *The development of affect* (pp. 205–226). New York, NY: Plenum.

Lewis, M., & Carmody, D. P. (2008). Self-representation and brain development. *Developmental Psychology 44*(5), 1329–1334.

Lewis, C., Freeman, N., Kyriakidou, C., Maridaki-Kassotaki, K., & Berridge, D. (1996). Social influences on false belief access: Specific sibling influences or general apprenticeship? *Child Development, 67,* 2930–2947.

Lewis, M., & Haviland-Jones, J. M. (2000). *Handbook of emotions.* New York, NY: Guilford Press.

Lewis, M., & Michalson, L. (1983). *Children's emotions and moods.* New York, NY: Plenum.

Liben, L. S., & Signorella, M. L. (1980). Gender-related schemata and constructive memory in children. *Child Development, 51*(1), 11–18.

Lieberman, A. F., & Pawl, J. H. (1988). Clinical applications of attachment theory. In J. Belsky, & T. Nezworski (Eds), *Clinical implications of attachment.* Hillsdale, NJ: Eribaum.

Lieberman, A. F., & Van Horn, P. (2008). *Psychotherapy with infants and young children: Repairing the effects of stress and trauma on early attachment.* New York, NY: Guilford Press.

Lieberman, A. F., & Zeanah, C. Y. (1995). Disorders of attachment in infancy. *Infant Psychiatry 4*(3), 571–587.

Lillard, A., & Curenton, S. M. (1999). Research in review: Do young children understand what others feel, want, and know? *Young Children, 54*(5), 52–57.

Linn, S., & Poussaint, A. F. (1999). Watching television: What are children learning about race and ethnicity? *Child Care Information Exchange, 128,* 50–52.

Lino, M. (2011). *Expenditures on children by families, 2010.* USDA, Center for Nutrition Policy and Promotion. Miscellaneous Publication Number 1528-2010. Retrieved from http://www.cnpp.usda.gov/publications/crc/crc2010.pdf

Liszkowski, U., Carpenter, M., Henning, A., Striano, T., & Tomasello, M. (2004). Twelve-month-olds point to share attention and interest. *Developmental Science, 7,* 297–307.

Little Soldier, L. (1992). Working with Native American children. *Young Children, 47*(6), 15–21.

Livingston, G., & Cohn, D. (2010). *The new demography of American motherhood.* Retrieved from http://pewresearch.org

Londerville, S., & Main, M. (1981). Security attachment, compliance, and maternal training methods in the second year of life. *Developmental Psychology, 17,* 289–299.

Lowenthal, B. (2001). *Abuse and neglect. The educator's guide to the identification and prevention of child maltreatment.* Baltimore, MD: Paul H. Brookes.

Lubell, K. M., Lofton, T., & Singer, H. H. (2008). *Promoting healthy parenting practices across cultural groups: A CDC research brief.* Atlanta, GA: Centers for Disease Control and Prevention, National Center for Injury Prevention and Control. Retrieved from http://www.cdc.gov/ncipc/images/dvp/healthy_parenting_rib_a.pdf

Lucariello, J., & Nelson, K. (1985). Slot-filler categories as memory organizers for young children. *Developmental Psychology, 21*, 272–282.

Lucas, A., Morley, R., & Coles, T. J. (1998). Randomized trial of early diet in preterm babies and later intelligence quotient. *British Medical Journal, 317*, 1481–1487.

Ludington-Hoe, S., Hosseini, R., & Torowicz, D. (2005). Skin-to-skin contact (kangaroo care) analgesia for preterm infant heel stick. *AACN Clinical Issues, 16*(3), 373–387.

Lyons-Ruth, K. (1996). Attachment relationships among children with aggressive behavior problems: The role of disorganized early attachment patterns. *Journal of Counseling and Clinical Psychology, 64*, 64–73.

Lyons-Ruth, K., Alpern, L., & Repacholi, B. (1993). Disorganized infant attachment classification and maternal psychosocial problems as predictors of hostile aggressive behavior in the preschool classroom. *Child Development, 64*, 572–585.

Lyons-Ruth, K., & Jacobvitz, D. (1999). Attachment disorganization: Unresolved loss, relational violence, and lapses in behavioral and attentional strategies. In J. Cassidy & P. R. Shaver (Eds.), *Handbook of attachment theory, research, and clinical applications* (pp. 520–554). New York, NY: Guilford.

Maccoby, E. (1988). Gender as a social category. *Developmental Psychology, 24*, 755–765.

Maccoby, E. E. (1990). Gender and relationships: A developmental account. *American Psychologist, 45*, 513–520.

Maccoby, E. E. (2000). Parenting and its effects on children: On reading and misreading behavior genetics. *Annual Review of Psychology, 51*(1), 1–27.

Maccoby, E. E., & Jacklin, C. N. (1974/1980). Sex differences in aggression: A rejoinder and a reprise. *Child Development, 51*, 964–980.

MacDonald, K., & Parke, R. D. (1984). Bridging the gap. Parent–child play interaction and peer interactive competence. *Child Development, 55*, 1265–1277.

MacDorman, M. F., & Kirmeyer, S. (2009). *Fetal and perinatal mortality, United States, 2005. National Vital Statistics Reports (NVSS), 57*(8). Retrieved from http://www.cdc.gov/nchs/data/nvsr/nvsr57/nvsr57_08.pdf

MacNeilage, P. F., & Davis, B. L. (2000). On the origin of internal structure of words. *Science, 21*(5465), 527–531.

Mahoney, C. R., Taylor, H. A., Kanarek, R. B., & Samuel, P. (2005). Effect of breakfast composition on cognitive processes in elementary school children. *Physiology & Behavior, 85*, 635–645.

Mahoney, G., Robinson, C., & Perales, F. (2004). Early motor intervention: The need for new treatment paradigms. *Infants and Young Children, 17*(4), 291–300.

Main, M., & Solomon, J. (1990). Procedures for identifying infants as disorganized/disoriented during the Ainsworth strange situation. In M. Greenberg, D. Cicchetti, & E. M. Cummings (Eds.), *Attachment in the preschool years: Theory, research, and intervention* (pp. 121–160). Chicago, IL: University of Chicago Press.

Main, M., & Weston, D. R. (1981). The quality of the toddler's relationship to mother and father: Related to conflict behavior and the readiness to establish new relationships. *Child Development, 52*, 932–940.

Malloy, T. V. (2003). Sign language use for deaf, hard of hearing and hearing babies: The evidence supports it. American Society for Deaf Children. Retrieved from http://www.deafchildren.org/resources/49_Sign%20Language%20Use.pdf

Mandler, J. M. (1990). A new perspective on cognitive development in infancy. *American Scientist, 78*(3), 236–243.

Mandler, J. M. (1992). Commentary on Bebko, Burke, Craven and Sarlo: The importance of sensorimotor development: A perspective from children with physical handicaps. *Human Development, 36*(4), 226–240.

Maratsos, M. (1983). Some current issues in the study of the acquisition of grammar. In J. H. Flavell & E. M. Markman (Eds.), *Handbook of child psychology. Vol. 3: Cognitive development* (4th ed., pp. 707–786). New York, NY: Wiley.

March of Dimes. (2008a). Low birthweight. Retrieved from http://www.marchofdimes.com/professionals/medicalresources_lowbirthweight.html

March of Dimes. (2008b). Sexually transmitted infections. Retrieved from http://www.marchofdimes.com/pregnancy/complications_stis.html

March of Dimes. (2009). Down syndrome. Retrieved from http://www.marchofdimes.com/baby/birthdefects_downsyndrome.html

March of Dimes. (2010). Premature labor. Retrieved from http://www.marchofdimes.com/pregnancy/preterm_indepth.html

March of Dimes. (2011a). Amniocentesis. Retrieved from http://www.marchofdimes.com/professionals/14332_1164.asp#head5

March of Dimes. (2011b). Trying to get pregnant. Retrieved from http://www.marchofdimes.com/pregnancy/trying_after35.html

Mareschal, D. (2011). From *NEO*constructivism to *NEURO*constructivism. *Child Development Perspectives, 5*, 169–170.

Marion, M. (2006). *Guidance of young children* (7th ed.). Upper Saddle River, NJ: Merrill/Prentice Hall.

Marsh, H. W., & Scalas, L. F. (2010). Self-concept in learning: Reciprocal effects model between academic self-concept and academic achievement. *International Encyclopedia of Education,* 660–667.

Marshall, N. L., Robeson, W. W., & Keefe, N. (2003). Gender equity in early childhood education. In C. Copple (Ed.), *A world of difference: Readings on teaching young children in a diverse society.* Washington, DC: NAEYC.

Marshall, P. J., Fox, N. A., Schorr, E., & Gordon-Salant, S. (2003). Mismatch negativity in socially withdrawn children. *Biological Psychiatry, 54*, 17–24.

Mashburn, et al. (2008). Measures of classroom quality in prekindergarten and children's development of academic, language, and social skills. *Child Development, 79*(3), 732–749.

Maslow, A. H. (1962). Some basic propositions of a growth and self-actualization psychology. In A. W. Combs (Ed.), *Perceiving, behaving, becoming: Association for Supervision and Curriculum Development 1962 Yearbook* (pp. 34–49). Alexandria, VA: Association for Supervision and Curriculum Development.

Maslow, A. (1968). *Toward a psychology of being* (2nd ed.). Princeton, NJ: Van Nostrand.

Maslow, A. (1970). *Motivation and personality* (2nd ed.). New York, NY: Harper & Row.

Matsuda, Y., Ueno, K., Waggoner, R. A., Erickson, S., Shimura, Y., Tanaka, K., et al. (2007). Processing of infant-directed speech in parents: An fMRI study. *Neuroscience Research, 58I(1)*, S45.

Mayes, L. C. (2002). Parental preoccupation and perinatal mental health. *Zero to Three, 22*(6), 4–9.

Mayo Clinic. (2009). Whooping cough. Definition. Retrieved July 10, 2011, from http://www.mayoclinic.com/health/whooping-cough/DS00445

Mayo Clinic. (2010). *Rh factor blood test.* Retrieved from http://www.mayoclinic.com/health/rh-factor/MY01163

Mayo Clinic. (2011a). *Ear tubes.* Retrieved from http://www.mayoclinic.com/health/ear-tubes/MY00601

Mayo Clinic. (2011b). *Tuberculosis.* Retrieved from http://www.mayoclinic.com/health/tuberculosis/DS00372

McElwain, N. L., Cox, M. J., Burchinal, M. R., & Macfie, J. (2003). Differentiating among insecure mother-infant attachment classifications: A focus on child-friend interaction and exploration during solitary play at 36 months. *Attachment and Human Development, 5*(2), 136–164.

McGaha, C. (2003). The importance of the senses for infants. Retrieved from http://www.acei.org/it.vol.16.1%20infantsenses.htm

McKee, C. (2006). The effect of social information on infants' food preferences. Unpublished honors thesis, Harvard University, April 2006.

Melmed, M. (1997). Public policy report: Parents speak: Zero to Three's findings from research on parents' views of early childhood development. *Young Children, 52*(5), 46–49.

Meltzoff, A. N. (1989). Imitation in newborn infants: Exploring the range of gestures initiated and the underlying mechanisms. *Developmental Psychology, 25*, 954–962.

Meltzoff, A. N. (1995). Understanding the intentions of others: Re-enactment of intended acts by 18-month-old children. *Developmental Psychology 3*, 838–850.

Meltzoff, A. N., Kuhl, P. K., Movellan, J., & Sejnowski, T. J. (2009). Foundations for a new science of learning. *Science, 325*, 284–288.

Meltzoff, A. N., & Moore, M. K. (1977). Imitation of facial and manual gestures by human neonates. *Science, 198*, 75–78.

Meltzoff, A. N., & Williamson, R. A. (2010). The importance of imitation for theories of social-cognitive development. In G. Bremner & T. Wachs (Eds.), *Handbook of infant development* (2nd ed., pp. 345–364). Oxford: Wiley-Blackwell.

Mennella, J. A., Jagnow, C. P., & Beauchamp, G. K. (2001). Prenatal and postnatal flavor learning by human infants. *Pediatrics, 107*, e88. Retrieved from http://pediatrics.aappublications.org/content/107/6/e88.full

Menting, B., van Lier, P. C., & Koot, H. M. (2011). Language skills, peer rejection, and the development of externalizing behavior from kindergarten to fourth grade. *Journal Of Child Psychology & Psychiatry, 52*(1), 72–79.

Menyuk, P. (1988). *Language development: Knowledge and use.* Glenview, IL: Scott Foresman.

Meyerhoff, M. K. (1994, March). Perspectives on parenting: Crawling around. *Pediatrics for Parents,* 8–9.

Miller, G. A. (1956). The magical number seven, plus or minus two: Some limits on our capacity for processing information. *Psychological Review, 63*, 81–97.

Miller, N. E., & Dollard, J. (1941). *Social learning and imitation.* New Haven, CT: Yale University Press.

Miller, P. M., Danaher, D. L., & Forbes, D. (1986). Sex- related strategies for coping with interpersonal conflict in children aged five and seven. *Developmental Psychology, 22*, 543–548.

Minnesota Department of Children, Families and Learning. (1998). *School breakfast programs energizing the classroom.* Roseville, MN: Author.

Mohrbacher, N., & Stock, J. (2003). The breastfeeding answer book. Schaumburg, IL: LaLeche League International.

Monk, C. F., Fifer, W. P., Myers, M. M., Sloan, R. P., Trein, L., & Hurtado, A. (2000). Maternal stress responses and anxiety during pregnancy: Effects on fetal heart rate. *Developmental Psychology, 36*(1), 67–77.

Moore, K. A., Redd, Z., Burkhauser, M., Mbwana, K., & Collins, A. (2009). Child trends research briefs. Children in poverty: Trends, consequences, and policy options. Retrieved from http://www.childtrends.org/Files//Child_Trends-2009_04_07_RB_ChildreninPoverty.pdf

Moore, M. K., & Meltzoff, A. N. (2010). Numerical identity and the development of object permanence. In S. P. Johnson (Ed.), *Neoconstructivism: The new science of cognitive development* (pp. 61–86). London, England: Oxford University Press.

Moreno, S., Marques, C., Santos, A., Santos, M., Castro. S. L., & Besson, M. (2009). Musical training influences linguistic abilities in 8-year-old children: More evidence for brain plasticity. *Cerebral Cortex, 19*(3), 712–723.

Morphett, M. V., & Washburne, C. (1931). When should children begin to read? *Elementary School Journal, 31*, 496–503.

Morrison, F. J., Frazier, J. A., Hardway, C. L., Griffith, E. M., Williamson, G. I., & Miyazaki, Y. (1998). *Early literacy: The nature and sources of individual differences.* New York, NY: MTA Cooperative Group.

Morrison, F. J., Griffith, E. M., & Alberts, D. M. (1997). Nature–nurture in the classroom: Entrance age, school readiness, and learning in children. *Developmental Psychology, 33*(2), 254–262.

Mossman, M., Heaman, M., Dennis, C., & Morris, M. (2008). The influence of adolescent mothers' breastfeeding confidence and attitudes on breastfeeding initiation and duration. *Journal of Human Lactation, 24*(3), 268–277.

Murphy, L. B. (1992). Sympathetic behavior in very young children. *Zero to Three, XII*(4), 1–5.

Murphy, J. M., Pagano, M., & Bishop, S. J. (2001). *Impact of a universally free, in-classroom school breakfast program on achievement: Results of the ABELL Foundation Baltimore Breakfast Challenge Program.* Boston, MA: Massachusetts General Hospital.

Myers, B. J. (1982). Early intervention using Brazelton training with middle-class mothers and fathers of newborns. *Child Development, 53*, 462–471.

Nadig, A., Ozonoff, S., Young, G., Rozga, A., Sigman, M., & Rogers, S. J. (2007). A prospective study of response-to-name in infants at risk for autism. *Archives of Pediatrics and Adolescent Medicine, Theme Issue on Autism, 161(4)*, 378–383.

National Association for Sport and Physical Education. (2011). Retrieved from http://www.aahperd.org/naspe/

National Association for the Education of Young Children. (1988). *Position statement on standardized testing of young children 3 through 8 years of age.* Washington, DC: Author.

National Association for the Education of Young Children. (1995). *Media violence and children: A guide for parents.* Washington, DC: Author.

National Association for the Education of Young Children. (1996). *NAEYC guidelines for preparation of early childhood professionals.* Washington, DC: Author.

National Association for the Education of Young Children. (2004). *Early childhood program standards and accreditation criteria.* Washington, DC: Author.

National Association for the Education of Young Children. (2008). *Developmentally appropriate practices in early childhood programs serving children from birth through age 8.* Retrieved from http://www.naeyc.org

National Association for the Education of Young Children. (2011). 2010 NAEYC standards for initial & advanced early childhood professional preparation programs. For use by associate, baccalaureate and graduate degree programs. Retrieved from http://www.naeyc.org/ncate/files/ncate/NAEYC%20Initial%20and%20Advanced%20Standards%206_2011-final_2.pdf

National Association for the Education of Young Children. (n.d.). NCATE: NAEYC recognition of baccalaureate and graduate degree programs. Retrieved from http://www.naeyc.org/ncate/

National Center for Health Statistics. (1994, July). *Vital and health statistics* [Series 20, No. 24; DHHS Pub. No. (PHS) (94–1852)]. Hyattsville, MD: U.S. Department of Health and Human Services.

National Center for Health Statistics. (2002). *Vital statistics of the United States, 1998. Vol. I: Natality.* Atlanta, GA: Centers for Disease Control and Prevention, National Center for Health Statistics.

National Center for Health Statistics. (2010). NCHS data brief recent trends in cesarean delivery in the United States. Retrieved from: http://www.cdc.gov/nchs/data/databriefs/db35.htm#summary

National Center on Sleep Disorders Research. (2003). Sleep and early brain development and plasticity. *National Sleep Disorders Research Plan.* Washington, DC: Author. Retrieved from http://www.nhlbi.nih.gov/health/prof/sleep/res_plan/index.html

National Infant & Toddler Child Care Initiative and ZERO TO THREE Policy Center. (2010).

National Institute of Child Health and Human Development. (2006). SIDS infants show abnormalities in brain area controlling breathing, heart rate serotonin-using brain cells implicated in abnormalities. Retrieved from http://www.nichd.nih.gov/news/releases/sids_serotonin.cfm

National Institute of Child Health and Human Development. (2010). *Study overview.* Retrieved from http://www.nichd.nih.gov/research/supported/seccyd/overview.cfm#publications

National Institute of Mental Health. (2008). Attention Deficit Hyperactivity Disorder. Retrieved from http://www.nimh.nih.gov/health/publications/adhd/complete-publication.shtml

National Research Council & National Institute of Medicine. (1997). *Improving schooling for language-minority children: A research agenda.* Washington, DC: National Academy Press.

National Resource Center for Health and Safety in Child Care and Early Education. (2008). Retrieved from http://nrckids.org/

National Safety Council. (2011). NHTSA issues new child seat guidelines. Retrieved from http://www.nsc.org/safetyhealth/Pages/NHTSAissuesnewchildseatguidelines_3.23.11.aspx

National Scientific Council on the Developing Child, Center on the Developing Child. (2004a). *Children's emotional development is built into the architecture of their brains: Working paper No. 2.* Retrieved from http://www.developingchild.harvard.edu

National Scientific Council on the Developing Child, Center on the Developing Child. (2004b). *Young children develop in an environment of relationships: Working paer No. 1.* Retrieved from http://www.developingchild.harvard.edu

National Scientific Council on the Developing Child, Center on the Developing Child. (2005). *Excessive stress disrupts the architecture of the developing brain: Working paper #3.* Retrieved from http://www.developingchild.net

National Scientific Council on the Developing Child (2006). *Excessive stress disrupts the architecture of the developing brain: Working Paper No. 3.* Retrieved from http://www.developingchild.harvard.edu

NCTSN (National Child Traumatic Stress Network). (2011). Treatments that work. Retrieved from http://www.nctsn.org

Neilsen, E., & Dissanayake, C. (2004). Pretend play, mirror self-recognition and imitation: A longitudinal investigation through the second year. *Infant behavior and development, 27*(3), 342–365.

Nelson, A. (2005). Children's toy collections in Sweden—A less gender-typed country? *Sex Roles, 52*(1–2), 93–102.

Nelson, K. (1981). Individual differences in language development: Implications for development and language. *Developmental Psychology, 17,* 170–187.

Nelson, K. (1986). *Event knowledge.* Hillsdale, NJ: Erlbaum.

Nelson, K. (1993). The psychological and social origins of autobiographical memory. *Psychological Science, 4,* 7–14.

Nelson, K. (1996). *Language in cognitive development: Emergence of the mediated mind.* Cambridge, England: Cambridge University Press.

Nelson, K., & Gruendel, J. (1981). Generalized event representations: Basic building blocks of cognitive development. In M. Lamb & A. Brown (Eds.), *Advances in development psychology* (Vol. 1, pp. 131–158). Hillsdale, NJ: Erlbaum.

Nelson, K., & Gruendel, J. M. (1986). Children's scripts. In K. Nelson (Ed.), *Event knowledge: Structure and function in development.* Hillsdale, NJ: Erlbaum.

Nelson, K., & Lucariello, J. (1985). The development of meaning in first words. In M. Barrett (Ed.), *Children's single word speech.* New York, NY: Wiley.

Nemours Foundation. (2008). Kids health: How TV affects your child. Retrieved from http://www.kidshealth.org

Neuman, S. B., Copple, C., & Bredekamp, S. (2000). *Learning to read and write: Developmentally appropriate practices for young children.* Washington, DC: National Association for the Education of Young Children.

Newcombe, N. S. (2010). What is neoconstructivism? In Johnson, S.P. (Ed.), *Neoconstructivism: The new science of cognitive development* (pp. v–viii). New York, NY: Oxford University Press.

Newcombe, N. S. (2011a). What Is Neoconstructivism? *Child Development Perspectives, 5,* 157–160.

Newcombe, N. S. (2011b). Three families of Isms. *Child Development Perspectives, 5,* 171–172.

NICHD Early Child Care Research Network. (2000). Characteristics and quality of child care for toddlers and preschoolers. *Applied Developmental Science, 4*(3), 116–135.

NICHD Early Child Care Research Network. (2002a). Child-care structure, process, outcome: Direct and indirect effects of child-care quality on young children's development. *Psychological Science, 13.*

NICHD Early Child Care Research Network. (2002b). The interaction of child care and family risk in relation to child development at 24 and 36 months. *Applied Developmental Science, 6*(3), 144–157.

NICHD Early Child Care Research Network. (2004). Affect dysregulation in the mother-child relationship in the toddler years: Antecedents and consequences. *Development and Psychopathology, 16,* 43–68.

NICHD Early Child Care Research Network. (2006). Infant-mother attachment classification: Risk and protection to changing maternal caregiving quality. *Developmental Psychology, 42*(1), 38–58.

NICHD Early Child Care Research Network. (2009). Family–peer linkages: The mediational role of attentional processes. *Social Development, 18*(4), 875–895.

Odom, S. L. (2000). Preschool inclusion: What we know and where we go from here. *Topics in Early Childhood Special Education, 20*(1), 20–27.

Ogbu, J. U. (1981). Origins of human competence: A cultural ecological perspective. *Child Development, 52*(2), 413–429.

Ohgi, S., Arisawa, K., Takahashi, T., Kusumoto, T., Goto, Y, Akiyama, T., & Saito, H. (2003). Neonatal behavioral assessment scale as a predictor of later developmental disabilities of low birth-weight and/or premature infants. *Brain Development, 25*(5), 313–321.

Oliva'n, G. (2003). Catch-up growth assessment in long-term physically neglected and emotionally abused preschool age male children. *Child Abuse and Neglect, 27*(1), 103–108.

Olson, S. L., Bates, J. E., & Bayles, K. (1984). Mother–infant interaction and the development of individual differences in children's cognitive competence. *Developmental Psychology, 20,* 166–179.

Orlick, T. D. (1981). Positive socialization via cooperative games. *Developmental Psychology, 17,* 426–429.

Pamling, N., & Samuelsson, I. P. (2007). The prosaics of figurative language in preschool: Some observations and suggestions for research. *Early Child Development and Care, 177*(6 & 7), 707–717.

Pan, B. A., Imbens-Bailey, A., Winner, K., & Snow, C. (1996). Communicative intents expressed by parents in interaction with young children. *Merrill-Palmer Quarterly, 42,* 248–266.

Panskepp, J. (1998). *Affective neuroscience: The foundations of human and animal emotions.* New York, NY: Oxford University Press.

Parten, M. B. (1933). Social participation among preschool children. *Journal of Abnormal Psychology, 27,* 243–269.

Paul, A. S. (1992). American Indian (Native American) influences. In L. R. Williams & D. P. Fromberg (Eds.), *Encyclopedia of early education* (pp. 11–13). New York, NY: Garland.

Paul, R., & Roth, F. P. (2011). Characterizing and predicting outcomes of communication delays in infants and toddlers: Implications for clinical practice. *Language, Speech & Hearing Services in Schools, 42*(3), 331–340.

Pearse, A. J., & Mitchell, M. D. (2003). *Nutrition and childhood lead poisoning* (Ohio State University Extension Fact Sheet). Retrieved from http://ohioline.osu.edu/hyg-fact/5000/5536.html

Peisner-Feinberg, E. S., Burchinal, M. R., Clifford, R. M., Yazejian, N., Culkin, M. L., Zelazo, J., et al. (1999). *The children of the Cost, Quality, and Outcomes Study go to school (executive summary).* Chapel Hill, NC: University of North Carolina.

Perren, S., & Alsaker, F. D. (2006). Social behavior and peer relationships of victims, bully-victims, and bullies in kindergarten. *Journal of Child Psychology and Psychiatry, 47*(1), 45–57.

Perry, B. D. (1993a). Neurodevelopmental and the neurophysiology of trauma I: Conceptional considerations for clinical work with maltreated children. *The Advisor 6*(1, Spring), 1–2, 14–17.

Perry, B. D. (1993b). Neurodevelopmental and the neurophysiology of trauma II: Clinical work along the alarm-fear-terror continuum. *The Advisor 6*(1, Summer), 1–2, 14–18.

Perry, B. D. (1996). Incubated in terror: Neurodevelopmental factors in the "cycle of violence." In J. Osofsky (Ed.), *Children, youth, and violence: The search for solutions* (pp. 2–20). New York, NY: Guilford Press.

Perry, B. D. (1998). *Brain growth and neurological development in infants.* Keynote presentation at the annual conference of the Texas Association for the Education of Young Children, Fort Worth, Texas, October 9, 1998.

Perry, B. D. (1999). Early life social–emotional experiences affect brain development. *American Academy of Pediatric News 15*(6), 18–19.

Perry, B. D. (2006). Applying principles of neurodevelopment to clinical work with maltreated and traumatized children: The neurosequential model of therapeutics. In N. B. Webb (Ed.), *Working with traumatized youth in child welfare* (pp. 27–52). New York, NY: Guilford Press.

Perry, B. D., Pollard, R. A., Blakley, T. L., Baker, W. L., & Vigilante, D. (1995). Childhood trauma, the neurobiology of adaptation, and 'use-dependent' development of the brain: How "states" become "traits." *Infant Mental Health Journal, 16*(4), 271–291.

Petitto, L. A., Holowka, S., Sergio, L. E., Levy, B., & Ostry, D. J. (2004). Baby hands that move to the rhythm of language: hearing babies acquiring sign languages babble silently on the hands. *Cognition, 93,* 43–73.

References

Petitto, L. A., Katerelos, M., Levy, B. G., Gauna, K., Tétreault, K., & Ferraro, V. (2001). Bilingual signed and spoken language acquisition from birth: Implications for the mechanisms underlying early bilingual language acquisition. *Journal of Child Language, 28*(2), 453–496.

Piaget, J. (1952). *The origins of intelligence in children.* New York, NY: Norton.

Piaget, J. (1954). *The construction of reality in the child.* New York, NY: Basic Books.

Piaget, J. (1962). *Play, dreams and imitation in childhood.* New York, NY: Norton.

Piaget, J. (1965). *The moral judgment of the child.* New York, NY: Norton.

Piaget, J. (1969). *Six psychological studies.* New York, NY: Vintage.

Piaget, J., & Inhelder, B. (1956). *The child's conception of space.* London, England: Routledge.

Piaget, J., & Inhelder, B. (1969). *The psychology of the child.* New York, NY: Basic Books.

Pianta, R. C. (1999). *Enhancing relationships between children and teachers.* Washington, DC: American Psychological Association.

Plomin, R. (1987). Developmental behavioral genetics and infancy. In J. Osofsky (Ed.), *Handbook of infant development* (pp. 363–414). New York, NY: Wiley.

Pollak, S. D., & Kistler, D. J. (2002). Early experience is associated with the development of categorical representations for facial expressions of emotion. *Proceedings of the National Academy of Sciences USA, 99*(13), 9072–9076. (Epub 2002 Jun 18.) Washington, DC: National Academy of Sciences.

Pollak, S. D., & Sinha, P. (2002). Effects of early experience on children's recognition of facial displays of emotion. *Developmental Psychology, 38*, 784–791.

Pollak, S. D. & Tolley-Schell, S. A. (2003). Selective attention to facial emotion in physically abused children. *Journal of Abnormal Psychology, 112*(3), 323–328.

Pollitt, E., & Matthews, R. (1998). Breakfast and cognition: An integrative summary. *American Journal of Clinical Nutrition, 67*, 804S–813S.

Porter, F. L., Miller, R. H., & Marshall, R. E. (1986). Neonatal pain cries: Effect of circumcision on acoustic features and perceived urgency. *Child Development, 57*, 790–802.

Posner, J. K., & Vandell, D. L. (1994). Low-income children's after-school care: Are there beneficial effects of after-school programs? *Child Development, 65*, 440–456.

Poulin-Dubois, D., Blaye, A., Coutya, J., & Bialystok, E. (2010). The effects of bilingualism on toddlers' executive functioning. *Journal of Experimental Child Psychology, 108*(3), 567–579.

Poulin-Dubois, D., Brooker, I., Polonia, A. (2011). Infants prefer to imitate a reliable person. *Infant Behavior and Development, 34*(2), 303–309.

Powlishta, K. K. (1995). Research in review: Gender segregation among children: Understanding the "cootie phenomenon." *Young Children, 50*(4), 61–69.

Provost, M. A., & LaFreniere, P. J. (1991). Social participation and peer competence in preschool children. Evidence for discriminant and convergent validity. *Child Study Journal, 21*, 57–71.

PsychCentral. (2001). Helping children deal with anger. U.S. Department of Education. Retrieved from http://psychcentral.com/library/child_anger.htm

Puckett, M. B. (Ed.). (2002). *Room to grow: How to create quality early childhood environments* (3rd ed.). Austin, TX: Texas Association for the Education of Young Children.

Puckett, M. B., & Black, J. K. (2008). *Meaningful assessments of the young child: Celebrating development and learning* (3rd ed.). Upper Saddle River, NJ: Merrill/Prentice Hall.

Puckett, M. B., & Diffily, D. (2004). *Teaching young children: An introduction to the early childhood profession* (2nd ed.). Clifton Park, NY: Delmar Learning.

Putallaz, M. (1987). Maternal behavior and children's sociometric status. *Child Development, 58*, 324–340.

Quinn, P. C., Yahr, J., Kuhn, A., Slater, A. M., & Pascalis, O. (2002). Representation of the gender of human faces by infants: A preference for female. *Perception, 31*, 1109–1121.

Quintana, S. M. (1998). Development of children's understanding of ethnicity and race. *Applied & Preventive Psychology: Current Scientific Perspectives, 7*, 27–45.

Radke-Yarrow, M., Zahn-Waxler, C., & Chapman, M. (1983). Children's prosocial dispositions and behavior. In E. M. Hetherington (Ed.), *Handbook of child psychology. Vol. 4: Socialization, personality and social development* (4th ed., pp. 469–545). New York, NY: Wiley.

Raikes, H. (1993). Relationship duration in infant care: Time with a high ability teacher and infant–teacher attachment. *Early Childhood Research Quarterly, 8*(3), 309–325.

Raikes, H. H., Pan, B., Luze, G., Tamis-LeMonda, C., Brooks-Gunn, J., Tarullo, L., Raikes, H. A., & Rodriguez, E. (2006). Mother-child bookreading in low-income families: Predictors and outcomes during the first three years of life. *Child Development, 77*, 921–953.

Ramsey, P. G. (1998). *Teaching and learning in a diverse world* (2nd ed.). New York, NY: Teachers College Press.

Ramsey, P. G. (2003). Growing up with the contradictions of race and class. In C. Copple (Ed.), *A world of difference: Readings on teaching young children in a diverse society* (pp. 24–28). Washington, DC: NAEYC.

Rantanen, E., Pöntinen, S., Nippert, I., Sequeiros, J., & Kääriäinen, H. (2009). Expertise, empathy and ethical awareness: ideals of genetic counseling based on framing of genetic information in international guidelines. *New Genetics & Society, 28*(4), 301–316.

Reiff, M. I., & Tippins, S. (Eds.). (2004). *The American Academy of Pediatrics: ADHD: A complete and authoritative guide.* New York, NY: HarperCollins.

Reilly, J., Armstrong, J., Dorosty, A., Emmett, P., Ness, A., Rogers, I.,…Sherriff, A. (2005). Early life risk factors for obesity in childhood: Cohort study. *British Medical Journal, 330*(7504), 1357.

Rhodes, W., & Hennessy, E. (2001). The effects of specialized training on caregivers and children in early-years settings: As evaluation of the foundation course in playgroup practice. *Early Childhood Research Quarterly, 15*, 559–576.

Riley, J. (1996). *The teaching of reading.* London, England: Chapman.

Rivkin, M. (1995). *The great outdoors: Restoring children's right to play outside.* Washington, DC: National Association for the Education of Young Children.

Robinson, J. (2002). Attachment problems and disorders in infants and young children: Identification, assessment, and intervention. *Infants and Young Children, 14*(2), 6–18.

Rochlen, A. B., McKelley, R. A., & Whittaker, T. W. (2010). Stay-at-home fathers' reasons for entering the role and stigma experiences: A preliminary report. *Psychology of Men and Masculinity, 11*(4), 7–14.

Rogers, C. R. (1961). *On becoming a person.* Boston, MA: Houghton Mifflin.

Rogers, C. (1962). Toward becoming a fully functioning person. In A. W. Combs (Ed.), *Perceiving, behaving, becoming: Association for Supervision and Curriculum Development 1962 Yearbook.* Alexandria, VA: Association for Supervision and Curriculum Development.

Rogers, C. R. (1969). *Freedom to learn: A view of what education might become.* Columbus, OH: Charles E. Merrill Publishing Company.

Rogers, C. R. (1983). *Freedom to learn for the 80s.* Columbus, OH: Charles E. Merrill Publishing Company.

Rogers, C., & Freiberg, H. J. (1994). *Freedom to learn* (3rd. ed.). New York, NY: Merrill/Macmillan.

Rogoff, B. (1990). *Apprenticeship in thinking: Cognitive development in social context.* New York, NY: Oxford University Press.

Rogoff, B. (2003). *The cultural nature of human development.* New York, NY: Oxford University Press.

Rogoff, B. (2011). *Developing destinies: A Mayan midwife and town.* New York, NY: Oxford University Press.

Romberg, A. R., & Saffran, J. R. (2010). Statistical learning and language acquisition. *Cognitive Science, 1*(6), 906–914.

Roncagliolo, M., Garrido, M., Walter, T., Peirano, P., & Lozoff, B. (1998). Evidence of altered central nervous system development in infants with iron deficiency anemia at 6 mo: Delayed maturation of auditory brainstem responses. *American Journal Clinical Nutrition, 68*(3), 683–690.

Røsand, G. M. B., Slinning, K., Eberhard-Gran, M., Røysamb, E., & Tambs, K. (2011). Partner relationship satisfaction and maternal emotional distress in early pregnancy. *BMC Public Health, 11*, 161. Retrieved from http://www.biomedcentral.com/content/pdf/1471-2458-11-161.pdf

Rosen, K. S., & Rothbaum, F. (1993). Quality of parental caregiving and security of attachment. *Developmental Psychology, 29*, 358–367.

Rosenkoetter, L. (1999). The television situation comedy and children's prosocial behavior. *Journal of Applied Social Psychology, 29*(5), 979–993.

Rosenkoetter, S., & Barton, L. R. (2002). Bridges to literacy: Early routines that promote later school success. *Zero to Three, 22*(4), 33–38.

Röska-Hardy, L., & Neumann-Held, E. M. (2010). *Learning from animals?: Examining the nature of human uniqueness.* Taylor & Francis.

Ross, D. M. (1996). *Childhood bullying and teasing: What school personnel, other professionals, and parents can do.* Alexandria, VA: American Counseling Association.

Rothbart, M. K., Ahadi, S. A., & Evans, D. E. (2000). Temperament and personality: Origins and outcomes. *Journal of Personality and Social Psychology, 78*, 122–135.

Rothbaum, F., Grauer, A., & Rubin, D. J. (1997). Becoming sexual: Differences between child and adult sexuality. *Young Children, 52*(6), 22–28.

Rousseau, J. J. (1762). *Émile.* Amsterdam: Néaulme.

Ruble, D. N., & Martin, C. (1998). Gender development. In N. Eisenberg (Ed.), *Handbook of Child Psychology: Vol. 3, Personality and Social Development.* New York, NY: John Wiley & Sons.

Rubin, K. H. (1998). Social and emotional development from a cultural perspective. *Developmental Psychology, 34*(4), 611–615.

Rubin, K. H. (2002). *The friendship factor.* New York, NY: Penguin Books.

Rubin, K. H., Bukowski, W., & Parker, J. G. (1998). Peer interactions, relationships and groups. In W. Damon (Ed.), *Handbook of child psychology. Vol. 3: Social, emotional, and personality development* (5th ed.). New York, NY: Wiley.

Rubin, K. H., Cben, X., & Hymel, S. (1993). Socio-emotional characteristics of aggressive and withdrawn children. *Merrill-Palmer Quarterly, 49*, 518–534.

Rubin, K. H., & Clark, M. L. (1983). Preschool teachers' ratings of behavioral problems: Observational, sociometric, and social-cognitive correlates. *Journal of Abnormal Child Psychology, 11*, 273–286.

Rubin, K. H., & Everett, B. (1982). Social perspective-taking in young children. In S. G. Moore & C. R. Cooper (Eds.), *The young child: Reviews of research* (Vol. 3, pp. 97–113). Washington, DC: National Association for the Education of Young Children.

Rudolph, K. D., Abaied, J. L., Flynn, M., Sugimura, N., Agoston, A. M. (2011). Developing relationships, being cool, and not looking like a loser: Social goal orientation predicts children's responses to peer aggression. *Child Development, 82*(5), 1518–1530.

Russell, S. L. & Mayberry, L. J. (2008). Pregnancy and oral health: A review and recommendations to reduce gaps in practice and research. *American Journal of Maternal and Child Nursing, 33*(1), 32–37.

Rutstein, S. O. (2008). Further evidence of the effects of preceding birth intervals on neonatal, infant, and under-five-years mortality and nutritional status in developing countries: Evidence from the demographic and health surveys. *USAID from the American People.* Retrieved from http://www.measuredhs.com/pubs/pdf/WP41/WP41.pdf

Ryalls, B. O., Gul, R. E., & Ryalls, K. R. (2000). Infant imitation of peer and adult models: Evidence for a peer model advantage. *Merrill-Palmer Quarterly, 46*(1), 188–202.

Ryan, C. A., & Finer, N. N. (1994). Changing attitudes and practices regarding local analgesia for newborn circumcision. *Pediatrics, 94*(2), 230–233.

Ryan, C. S., Casas, J. F., Kelly-Vance, L., Ryalls, B. O., & Nero, C. (2010). Parent involvement and views of school success: The role of parents' Latino and White American cultural orientations. *Psychology in the Schools, 47*(4), 391–405.

Saarni, C. (1999). *The development of emotional competence.* New York, NY: Guilford.

Sadker, M., & Sadker, D. (1985). Sexism in the schoolroom of the '80s. *Psychology Today, 1985*(March), 54–57.

Sadker, M., & Sadker, D. (1994). *Failing at fairness: How our schools cheat girls.* New York, NY: Simon & Schuster.

Sameroff, A. J. (1995). General systems theories and developmental psychopathology. In D. Cicchetti & D. J. Cohen (Eds.), *Developmental psychopathology. Vol. 1: Theory and methods.* New York, NY: Wiley.

Sameroff, A. J. (1999). Models of development and developmental risk. In C. H. Zeanah, Jr. (Ed.), *Handbook of infant mental health* (2nd ed., pp. 3–19). New York, NY: Guilford Press.

Sameroff, A. (2010). A unified theory of development: A dialectic integration of nature and nurture. *Child Development, 81*, 6–22.

Sameroff, A. J., & Fiese, B. H. (2000). Transactional regulation: The development ecology of early intervention. In J. P. Shonkoff & S. J. Meisels (Eds.), *Handbook of early childhood intervention* (2nd ed., 135–159). New York, NY: Cambridge University Press.

Samuels, C. A. (1985). Attention to eye contact opportunity and facial motion by three-month-old infants. *Journal of Experimental Child Psychology, 40*, 105–114.

Sandall, S., McLean, M. E., & Smith, B. J. (2000). *Division for Early Childhood recommended practice in early intervention/early childhood special education.* Denver, CO: Division for Early Childhood of the Council for Exceptional Children.

Sadah, A., Tikotzky, L., & Scher, A. (2010). Parenting and infant sleep. *Sleep Medicine Reviews, 14*(2), 89–96.

Sanefuji, W., Ohgami, H., & Hashiya, K. (2006). Preference for peers in infancy. *Infant Behavior and Development, 29*(4), 584–593.

Santelli J. S., Lindberg, L. D., Finer, L. B., & Singh, S. (2007). Explaining recent declines in adolescent pregnancy in the United States: The contribution of abstinence and improved contraceptive use. *American Journal of Public Health, 97*(1), 150–156.

Saracho, O.N., & Spodek, B. (2007). Early childhood teachers' preparation and the quality of program outcomes. *Early Child Development and Care, 177*(1), 71–91.

Scahill, L. (2001). Surgeon general's conference on children's mental health: Developing a national action agenda. *Journal of the American Psychiatric Nurses Association, 7*, 51–56.

Schickedanz, J. A. (1999). *Much more than ABCs: The early stages of reading and writing.* Washington, DC: National Association for the Education of Young Children.

Schickedanz, J. A. (2008). *Increasing the power of instruction: Integration of language, literacy, and math across the preschool day.* Washington, DC: NAEYC.

Schiller, P. (2010). Early brain development research review and update. *EXCHANGE, 32*(6), 26–32.

Schmidt, M. E., Pempek, T., Kirkorian, H. L., Lund, A. F., & Anderson, D. R. (2008). The effects of background television on the toy play behavior of very young children. *Child Development, 79*(4), 1137–1151.

Schneider, B., Atkinson, L., & Tardif, C. (2001). Child-parent attachment and children's peer relations: A quantitative review. *Developmental Psychology, 37*(1), 86–100.

Schore, A. N. (2001). Effects of a secure attachment relationship on right brain development, affect regulation, and infant mental health. *Infant Mental Health Journal, 22*(1–2), 7–66.

Schubiner, H. H., & Robin, A. L. (1998, July). Attention-deficit/hyperactivity disorder in adolescence. *Adolescent Health Update, 10*(3), 1–8.

Schuder, M. R., & Lyons-Ruth, K. (2004). "Hidden trauma" in infancy: Attachment, fearful arousal, and early dysfunction of the stress response system. In J. Osofsky (Ed.), *Young children and trauma: Intervention and treatment* (pp. 69–104). New York, NY: Guilford Press.

Schunk, D. H. (1981). Modeling and attributional effects on children's achievement: A self-efficacy analysis. *Journal of Educational Psychology, 73*, 93–105.

Schweinhart, L. J., Barnes, A. V., & Weikart, D. P. (1993). *Significant benefits: The High/Scope Perry Preschool Study through age 27* [Monographs of the High/Scope Educational Research Foundation, 10]. Ypsilanti, MI: High/Scope Press.

Schweinhart, L. J., Montie, J., Xiang, Z., Barnett, W. S., Belfield, C. R., & Nores, M. (2005). *Lifetime effects: The High/Scope Perry Preschool study through age 40.* [Monographs of the High/Scope Educational Research Foundation, 14]. Ypsilanti, MI: High/Scope Press.

Schweinhart, L. J., & Weikart, D. P. (1997). The High/Scope Preschool Curriculum Comparison Study through age 23. *Early Childhood Research Quarterly, 12*, 117–143.

Sears, W. P. (1998). Parents, patients need to know about breakfast–brain connection. *American Academy Pediatric News, 14*(9), 30.

Seidl, A. (2007). Infants' use and weighting of prosodic cues in clause segmentation. *Journal of Memory and Language, 57*, 24–48.

Senechal, M., LeFevre, J., Thomas, E., & Daley, K. (1998). Different effects of home literacy experiences on the development of oral and written language. *Reading Research Quarterly, 32*, 96–114.

Sepkowski, C. (1985). Maternal obstetric medication and newborn behavior. In J. W. Scanlon (Ed.), *Prenatal anesthesia.* London, England: Blackwell.

Serbin, L. A., Powlishta, K. K., & Gulko, J. (1993). *The development of sex typing in middle childhood.* Monographs of the Society for Research in Child Development, *58.* Chicago, IL: University of Chicago Press.

Servin, A., Bohlin, G., & Berlin, L. (1999). Sex differences in 1-, 3-, and 5-year-olds' toy-choice in a structured play-session. *Scandinavian Journal of Psychology, 40*(1), 43–48.

Sexton, D. (1990). Quality integrated programs for infants and toddlers with special needs. In E. Surbeck & M. F. Kelley (Eds.), *Personalizing care of infants, toddlers and families* (pp. 41–50). Olney, MD: Association for Childhood Education International.

Shackman, J. E., Fatani, S., Camras, L. A., Berkowitz, M. J., Bachorowski, J., & Pollak, S. D. (2010). Emotion expression among abusive mothers is associated with their children's emotion processing and problem behaviours. *Cognition & Emotion, 24*(8), 1421–1430. Retrieved from http://www.tandfonline.com/doi/full/10.1080/02699930903399376#tabModule

Shamay-Tsoory, S. G., Tomer, R., & Aharon-Peretz, J. (2005). The neuroanatomical bases of understanding sarcasm and its relationship to social cognition. *Neuropsychology, 19*(3), 288–300.

Shaver, P. R., & Fraley, R. C. (2008). Attachment, loss, and grief: Bowlby's views and current controversies. In J. Cassidy & P. R. Shaver (Eds.), *Handbook of attachment: Theory, research, and clinical applications* (2nd ed.) (pp. 48–77). New York, NY: Guilford Press.

Shaw, P., Noor J., Kabani, JaLerch, J. P., Eckstrand, K., Lenroot, R., ... Wise, S. P. (2008) Neurodevelopmental trajectories of the human cerebral cortex. *The Journal of Neuroscience, 28*(14), 3586–3594.

Shaw, D. S., & Vondra, J. I. (1995). Infant attachment security and maternal predictors of early behavior problems: a longitudinal study of low-income famlies. *Journal of Abnormal Child Psychology, 23*(3), 335–357.

Shea, K. M. (2003). Antibiotic resistance: What is the impact of agricultural uses of antibiotics on children's health? *Pediatrics, 112,* 253–258.

Shi, R., & Werker, J. F. (2001). Six-month-old infants' preferences for lexical words. *Psychological Science, 12*(1), 70–75.

Shin, Y., Bozzette, M., Kenner, C., & Kim, T. I. (2004). Evaluation of Korean newborns with the Brazelton Neonatal Behavioral Assessment Scale. *Journal of Obstetric, Gynecologic, and Neonatal Nursing, 33*(5), 589–596.

Shonkoff, J. P., & Phillips, D. A. (2000). *From neurons to neighborhoods: The science of early childhood development.* Washington, DC: National Academy Press.

Shonkoff, J. P., Phillips, D. A., & Keilty, B. (Ed.). (2000). *Early childhood intervention: Views from the field.* Washington, DC: National Academy Press.

Shore, R. (1997/2003). *Rethinking the brain: New insights into early development.* New York, NY: Families and Work Institute.

Shumway, S., & Wetherby, A. M. (2009). Communicative acts of children with autism spectrum disorders in the second year of life. *Journal of Speech, Language, and Hearing Research, 52*(5), 1139–1156.

Siegel, D. J. (1999). *The developing mind: Toward a neurobiology of interpersonal experience.* New York, NY: Guilford.

Siegler, R. S. (1998). *Children's thinking* (3rd ed.). Upper Saddle River, NJ: Prentice Hall.

Siegler, R. (2006). *How children develop: Exploring child development student media tool kit & Scientific American Reader to accompany how children develop.* New York, NY: Worth Publishers.

Simons, R. (2002). *Odd girl out: The hidden culture of aggression in girls.* New York, NY: Harcourt.

Sims, M., Hutchin, T., & Taylor, M. (1996). Young children in child care: The role adults play in managing their conflict. *Early Child Development and Care, 124,* 1–9.

Singer, D. G., & Singer, J. L. (Eds.). (2001). *Handbook of children and the media.* Thousand Oaks, CA: Sage.

Singer, E., & Hannikainen, M. (2002). The teacher's role in territorial conflicts of 2- to 3-year-old children. *Journal of Research in Childhood Education, 17*(1), 5–18.

Singer, M. I., Slovak, K., Frierson, T., & York, P. (1998). Viewing preferences, symptoms of psychological trauma, and violent behaviors among children who watch television. *Journal of the American Academy of Child and Adolescent Psychiatry, 37,* 1041–1048.

Singh, L., Morgan, J. L., & White, K. S. (2004). Preference and processing: The role of speech affect in early spoken word recognition. *Journal of Memory and Language, 51*, 173–189.

Skinner, B. F. (1948). *Walden two.* New York, NY: Macmillan.

Skinner, B. F. (1979). *The shaping of a behaviorist.* New York, NY: Knopf.

Slade, A. (2002). Keeping the baby in mind: A critical factor in perinatal mental health. *Zero to Three, 22*(6), 10–11.

Slavin, R. E. (1990). *Cooperative learning: Theory, research and practice.* Upper Saddle River, NJ: Prentice Hall.

Slavin, R. E. (1995). *Cooperative learning: Theory, research, and practice* (2nd ed.). Englewood Cliffs, NJ: Prentice Hall.

Smedley, A. (1993). *Race in North America: Origin and evolution of a worldview.* San Francisco, CA: Westview Press, Inc.

Smith, G. A. (1998). Injuries to children in the United States related to trampolines, 1990–1995: A national epidemic. *Pediatrics, 101*(3), 406–412.

Snow, C. E., Burns, S., & Griffin, P. (Eds.). (1998). *Preventing reading difficulties in young children.* Washington, DC: National Academy Press.

Snyder, M., Snyder, R., & Snyder, R., Jr. (1980). *The young child as person: Toward the development of healthy conscience.* New York, NY: Human Sciences.

Sobolewski, J. M. & King, V. (2005). The importance of the coparental relationship for nonresident fathers' ties to children. *Journal of Marriage and Family, 67*, 1196–1212.

Society for Research in Child Development, Committee on Ethical Standards for Research with Children. (1990–1991). *Ethical standards for research with children.* Ann Arbor, MI: Author.

Society for Research in Child Development. (2007). Ethical standards for research with children. Retrieved from http://www.srcd.org/ethicalstandards.html

Solomon, J. (2003). The caregiving system in separated and divorcing parents. *Zero to Three, 23*(3), 33–37.

Solomon, J., & George, C. (1996). Defining the caregiving system: Toward a theory of caregiving. *Infant Mental Health Journal, 17*, 182–197.

Sommerville, J. A., Hildebrand, E. A., & Crane, C. C. (2008). Experience matters: The impact of doing versus watching on infants' subsequent perception of tool-use events. *Developmental Psychology, 44*(5), 1249–1256.

Sommerville, J. A., Woodward, A. L., & Needham, A. (2005). Action experience alters 3-month-old infants' perception of others actions. *Cognition, 96*, B1–B11.

Southgate, V., van Maanen, C., & Csibra, G. (2007). Infant pointing: Communication to cooperate or communication to learn, *Child Development, 78*(3), 735–740.

Spelke, E. S. (2000). Core knowledge. *American Psychology, 55*, 1233–1243.

Spelke, E. S. (2003). Core knowledge. In N. Kanwisher & J. Duncan (Eds.), *Attention and performance, Vol. 20: Functional neuroimaging of visual cognition.* Cambridge, MA: MIT Press.

Spelke, E., Ah Lee, S., & Izard, V. (2010). Beyond core knowledge: Natural geometry. *Cognitive Science, 34*, 863–884.

Spierer, A., Royzman, Z., & Kuint, J. (2004). Visual acuity in pre-term and full-term infants. *Ophthalmologics, 218*(6), 397–401.

Sroufe, L. A. (1996). *Emotional development: The organization of emotional life in the early years.* New York, NY: Cambridge University Press.

Sroufe, L. A., Carlson, E., & Schulman, S. (1993). Individuals in relationships: Development from infancy through adolescence. In D. C. Funder, R. D. Parke, C. Tomlinson-Keasey, & K. Widaman, (Eds.), *Studying lives through time: Personality and development.* Washington, DC: American Psychological Association.

Stanford, B. H., & Yamamoto, K. (Eds.). (2001). *Children and stress: Understanding and helping.* Olney, MD: Association for Childhood Education International.

Stebbins, H., & Langford, B. H. (2006). Guide to *Calculating the cost and quality of early care and education.* Retrieved from http://www.financeproject.org/publications/costguide.pdf

Steiner, J. E. (1979). Human facial expressions in response to taste and smell stimulation. In H. Reese & L. Lipsitt (Eds.), *Advances in child development and behavior* (Vol. 13, pp. 257–295). New York, NY: Academic.

References

Stern, D. (2008). The clinical relevance of infancy: A progress report. *Infant Mental Health Journal, 29*(3), 177–188,

Sternberg, R. J. (1985). *Beyond IQ: A triarchic theory of human intelligence.* New York, NY: Cambridge University Press.

Sternberg, R. J., & Berg, C. A. (Eds.). (1995). *Intellectual development.* New York, NY: Cambridge University Press.

Stewart, R. B., Mobley, L. A., Van Tuyl, S. S., & Salvador, M. A. (1987). The firstborn's adjustment to the birth of a sibling: A longitudinal assessment. *Child Development, 58,* 341.

Stewart, P. W., Reihman, J., Lonky, E., Darvill, T. & Pagano, J. (2000). Prenatal PCB exposure and Neonatal Behavioral Assessment Scale (NBAS) performance. *Neurotoxicology & Teratology, 22* 21–29.

Stipek, D., Recchia, S., & McClintic, S. (1992). *Self-evaluation in young children.* Monographs of the Society for Research in Child Development, Vol. 57, No. 1, serial no. 226. Chicago, IL: University of Chicago Press.

Stormshak, E. A., Bullock, B. M., & Falkenstein, C. A. (2009). Harnessing the power of sibling relationships as a tool for optimizing social–emotional development. Special issue: Siblings as agents of socialization. *New Directions for Child and Adolescent Development, 126,* 61–77.

Storo, W. (1993). Role of bicycle helmet in bicycle related injury prevention. *Clinical Digest Series, 4*(3), 23. [Reprinted from *Clinical Pediatrics* (1992), *31,* 421–427.]

Strathearn, L., Li, J., Fonagy, P., Read, M. P. (2008). What's in a smile? Maternal brain responses to *infant* facial cues. *Pediatrics, 122*(1), 40–51.

Straus, M. A. (1994). *Beating the devil out of them: Corporal punishment in American families.* New York, NY: Lexington Books.

Strauss, R. S., Rodzilsky, D., Burack, G., & Cole, M. (2001). Psychosocial correlates of physical activity in healthy children. *Archives of Pediatric and Adolescent Medicine, 155,* 897–902.

Strayer, F. F., & Santos, A. J. (1996). Affiliative structures in preschool peer groups. *Social Development, 5*(2), 117–130.

Strid, K., Tjus, T., Smith, L., Meltzoff, A. N., & Heimann, M. (2006). Infant recall memory and communication predicts later cognitive development. *Infant Behavior and Development, 29*(4), 545–553.

Stringer, E. T. (2007). *This way: Action research* (3rd ed.). Thousand Oaks, CA: Sage Publications.

Strommen, L. T., & Mates, B. F. (1997). What readers do: Young children's ideas about the nature of reading. *Reading Teacher, 51*(2), 98–107.

Sugarman, S. (1987). *Piaget's construction of the child's reality.* Cambridge, England: Cambridge University Press.

Susman-Stillman, A., Appleyard, K., & Siebenbruner, J. (2003). For better or for worse: An ecological perspective on parents' relationships and parent–infant interaction. *Zero to Three, 23*(3), 4–12.

Susman-Stillman, A., & Banghart, P. (2008). Demographics of family, friend, and neighbor child care in the United States. National Center for Children in Poverty (NCCP). Retrieved from http://www.nccp.org/about/publications_banghart.html

Sutton-Smith, B. (1997). *The ambiguity of play.* Cambridge, MA: Harvard University Press.

Swingley, D. (2008). The roots of the early vocabulary in infants' learning from speech. *Current Directions in Psychological Science, 17,* 308–312.

Sylwester, R. (1995). *A celebration of neurons: An educator's guide to the human brain.* Alexandria, VA: Association for Supervision and Curriculum Development.

Taguchi, H. L. (2007). Deconstructing and transgressing the theory—Practice dichotomy in early education. *Educational Philosophy and Theory, 39*(3), 275–290.

Tanner, J. M. (1989). *Fetus into man: Physical growth from conception to maturity* (Rev. ed.). Cambridge, MA: Harvard University Press.

Tan-Niam, C. (1994). Thematic fantasy play: Effects on the perspective-taking ability of preschool children. *International Journal of Early Years Education, 2*(1), 5–16.

Taveras, E. M., Rifas-Shiman, S. L., Oken, E, Gunderson, E. P., & Gillman, M. W. (2008). Short sleep duration in infancy and risk of childhood overweight. *Archives of Pediatric & Adolescent Medicine, 162*(4), 305–311.

Teale, W. H. (1986). Home background and young children's literacy development. In W. H. Teale & E. Sulzby (Eds.), *Emergent literacy: Writing and reading* (pp. 173–206). Norwood, NJ: Ablex.

Teicher, M. H. (2000). Wounds that time won't heal: The neurobiology of child abuse. *Cerebrum, 4*(2), 50–67.

Teicher, M. H. (2002). Scars that won't heal: The neurobiology of child abuse. *Scientific American, 286*(3), 68–75.

Teitler, J. O. (2001). Father involvement, child health and maternal health behavior. *Children and Youth Services Review, 23*(4/5), 403–425.

Templin, M. C. (1957). *Certain skills in children: Their development and interrelationships.* Minneapolis, MN: University of Minnesota Institute of Child Welfare.

Teti, D. M., & Towe-Goodman, N. (2008). Post-partum depression, effects on child. In M. Haith & J. Benson (Eds.), *Encyclopedia of infant & early child development.* Oxford, UK: Elsevier.

Thelen, E., & Bates, E. (2003) Connectionism and dynamic systems: are they really different? *Developmental Science, 6*(4), 378–391.

Thelen, E., & Smith, L. B. (1996). *A dynamic systems approach to the development of cognition and action.* Cambridge: MIT Press.

Thiessen, E. D., Hill, E. A., & Saffran, J. R. (2005). Infant-directed speech facilitates word segmentation. *Infancy, 7*(1), 53–71.

Thomas, A., & Chess, S. (1977). *Temperament and development.* New York, NY: Brunner/Mazel.

Thompson, R. A. (1999). Early attachment and later development. In J. Cassidy & P. R. Shaver (Eds.), *Handbook of attachment: Theory, research, and clinical application* (pp. 265–286). New York, NY: Guilford.

Thompson, R. A., & Meyer, S. (2006). Understanding values in relationship: The development of conscience. In M. Killen & J. G. Smetana (Eds.), *Handbook of moral development* (pp. 269–298). Mahwah, N.J: Lawrence Erlbaum Associates.

Thompson, R. S. (2009). Doing what doesn't come naturally: The development of self-regulation. *ZERO TO THREE, 30*(2), 33–39.

Thompson, R. A., Lewis, M. C., & Calkins, S. (2008). Reassessing emotion regulation. *Child Development, 2*(3), 124–131.

Todd, R. L., & Fischer, K. W. (2009). Dynamic development: A Neo-Piagetian approach. In U. Muller, J. I. Carpendale, & L. Smith (Eds.), *The Cambridge companion to Piaget.* Cambridge University Press. Cambridge Collections Online.

Trautmann-Villalba, P., Gschwendt, M., Schmidt, M.H., & Laucht, M. (2005). Father-infant interaction patterns as precursors of children's later externalizing behavior problems. A longitudinal study over 11 years. *European Archives of Psychiatry and Clinical Neuroscience, 256*(6), 344–349.

Trepanier-Street, M., Hong, S. B., & Donegan, M. M. (2001). Constructing the image of the teacher in a Reggio-inspired teacher preparation program. *Journal of Early Childhood Teacher Education, 22*(1), 47–52.

Tronick, E. (2007). *The neurobehavioral and social-emotional development of infants and children.* New York, NY: W.W. Norton & Company, Inc.

Troseth, G. L., & DeLoache, J. S. (1998). The medium can obscure the message: Young children's understanding of video. *Child Development, 69*(4), 950–965.

Turati, C., Cassia, V., Simion, F., & Leo, I. (2006). Newborns' Face Recognition: Role of Inner and Outer Facial Features. *Child Development, 77*(2), 297–311. Retrieved from: http://www.ii.metu .edu.tr/~hohenberger/development/literature/Turati_etal_2006_Face_ChDev.pdf

Turiel, E. (1980). The development of social-conventional and moral concepts. In M. Windmiller, N. Lambert, & E. Turiel (Eds.), *Moral development and socialization* (pp. 69–106). Boston, MA: Allyn & Bacon.

U.S. Census Bureau. (2011). *Poverty thresholds.* Retrieved from http://www.census.gov/hhes/www/ poverty/data/threshld/index.html

U.S. Consumer Product Safety Commission. (1997). *Handbook for public playground safety.* Washington, DC: Author.

References

U.S. Consumer Product Safety Commission, National Electronic Injury Surveillance System. (1996). *Consumer Product Safety Review, 2*(4).

U.S. Department of Education. (2008). *Building the legacy: IDEA 2004.* Retrieved from http://idea.ed.gov

U.S. Departments of Health, Agriculture, and Education. (2011). Grow healthy and strong. Retrieved from www2.ed.gov/parents/academic/health/growhealthy/growhealthy.pdf

U.S. Department of Health and Human Services. (2008). Stop bullying now. Retrieved from http://stopbullyingnow.hrsa.gov

U.S. Department of Health and Human Services, Administration for Children & Families, National Child Care Information and Technical Assistance Program (NCCIC). (2010). *National profile.* Retrieved from http://nccic.acf.hhs.gov

U.S. Department of Health and Human Services, Administration for Children and Families, Office of Head Start. (2011). Parent, family, and community engagement framework: Promoting family engagement and school readiness from prenatal to age 8. Retrieved from http://www.hfrp.org/publications-resources/browse-our-publications/parent-family-and-community-engagement-framework-promoting-family-engagement-and-school-readiness-from-prenatal-to-age-8

U.S. Department of Health and Human Services National Institutes of Health. (2011). Sickle cell anemia. Retrieved from http://www.nhlbi.nih.gov/health/dci/Diseases/Sca/SCA_WhatIs.html

U.S. General Accounting Office. (2003, March). *Newborn screening: Characteristics of state programs.* Washington, DC: Author.

U.S. Preventive Services Task Force. (2011). Vision screening for children 1 to 5 years of age: U.S. Preventive Services Task Force recommendation statement. *Pediatrics, 127*(2), 340–346.

U.S. Surgeon General. (2000). *United States Public Health Service report of the Surgeon General's conference on children's mental health: A national action agenda.* Washington, DC: Department of Health and Human Services.

Usta, I. M., and Nassar, A. H. (2008). Advanced maternal age. Part I: Obstetric complications. *American Journal of Perinatology, 25*(8), 521–534.

Vaisman, N., Voet, H., Akivis, A., & Vakil, E. (1996). Effects of breakfast timing on the cognitive functions of elementary school students. *Archives of Pediatric and Adolescent Medicine, 150*, 1089–1092.

Vandell, D., Belsky, J., Burchinal, M., Steinberg, L., Vandergrift, N., & the NICHD Early Child Care Research Network. (2010). Do effects of early child care extend to age 15 years? Results from the NICHD Study of Early Child Care and Youth Development. *Child Development, 81*(3), 737–756.

Vandell, D. L., & Shumow, L. (1999). After-school child care programs. *The Future of Children, 9*(2), 64–80.

Vandivere, M. P., Tout, K., Capizzano, J., & Zaslow, M. (2003, April). *Left unsupervised: A look at the most vulnerable children.* Washington, DC: Child Trends.

Varendi, H. & Porter, R. H. (2001). Breast odour as the only maternal stimulus elicits crawling towards the odour source. *Acta Paediatrica, 90*(4), 372–375.

Vasilyeva, M., & Waterfall, H. (in press). Beyond syntactic priming: Evidence for activation of alternative syntactic structures. *Journal of Child Language.*

Ventura, S. J. (2009). *Changing patterns of nonmarital childbearing.* Centers for Disease Control and Prevention. Retrieved from http://www.cdc.gov/nchs/data/databriefs/db18.htm

Verschueren, K., Marcoen, A., & Schoefs, V. (1996). The internal working model of the self, attachment and competence in five year olds. *Child Development, 67*, 2493–2511.

Vicari, S., Reilly, J., Pasqualetti, P., Vizzotto, A., & Caltagirone, C. (2000). Recognition of facial expressions of emotions in school-age children: the intersection of perceptual and semantic categories. *Acta Paediatrica, 89*(7), 836–845.

Vincent, S. (2011). Skin-to-skin contact. Part two: The evidence. *Practising Midwife, 14*(6), 44–46.

von Hapsburg, D., & Davis, B. L. (2006). Auditory sensitivity and the prelinguistic vocalizations of early-amplified infants. *Journal of Speech, Language, and Hearing Research, 49*, 809–822.

Vygotsky, L. S. (1962). *Thought and language.* Cambridge, MA: MIT Press.

Vygotsky, L. S. (1978). *Mind in society: The development of higher mental processes.* Cambridge, MA: Harvard University Press.

Vygotsky, L. S. (1986). *Thought and language.* Cambridge: MIT Press.

Vygotsky, L. S. (1987). Thinking and speech. In N. Minick (Transl.), *The collected works of L. S. Vygotsky. Vol. 1: Problems in general psychology.* New York, NY: Plenum.

Wagner, C. L., Greer, F. R., and the Section on Breastfeeding and Committee on Nutrition. (2008). Prevention of rickets and vitamin D deficiency in infants, children, and adolescents. http://aappolicy .aappublications.org/cgi/content/full/pediatrics;122/5/1142.

Warren, S. L., & Simmens, S. J. (2005). Predicting toddler anxiety/depressive symptoms: Effects of caregiver sensitivity on temperamentally vulnerable children. *Infant Mental Health Journal, 26*(1), 40–55.

Washington, V., & Andrews, J. D. (Eds). (2010). *Children of 2020: Creating a better tomorrow.* Washington, DC: Council for Professional Recognition and National Association for the Education of Young Children.

Watson, J. B. (1930). *Behaviorism* (revised edition). Chicago, IL: University of Chicago Press.

Watson, J. B. (1928). *Psychological care of infant and child.* New York, NY: Norton.

Watson, J. B., & Rayner, R. (1920). Conditioned emotional reactions. *Journal of Experimental Psychology, 3*, 1–14.

Waxler, E., Thelen, K., & Muzik, M. (2011). Maternal perinatal depression: Impact on infant and child development. *European Psychiatric Review, 4*, 41–47.

Weinreb, L., Wehler, C., Perloff, J., Scott, R., Hosmer, D., Sagor, L., et al. (2002). Hunger: Its impact on children's health and mental health. *Pediatrics 110*, ep41. Retrieved October from http://www .pediatrics.org/cgi/content/full/110/4/e41

Weismer, S. E., Lord, C., & Esler, A. (2010). Early language patterns of toddlers on the autism spectrum compared to toddlers with developmental delay. *Journal of Autism Developmental Disorders, 40.* 1259–1273.

Wellhousen, K. (1996). Girls can be bull riders, too! Supporting children's understanding of gender roles through children's literature. *Young Children 51*(5), 79–83.

Werker, J. F., Fennell, C. T., Corcoran, K. M., & Stager, C. L. (2002). Infant's ability to learn phonetically similar words: Effects of age and vocabulary size. *Infancy, 3*(1), 1–30.

Werner, E. E. (1989). Children of the garden island. *Scientific American, 260*, 107–111.

Werner, E. E., & Smith, R. S. (1982). *Vulnerable but invincible: A longitudinal study of resilient children and youth.* New York, NY: McGraw-Hill.

Werner, E., & Smith, R. (1992). *Overcoming the odds: High-risk children from birth to adulthood.* New York, NY: Cornell University Press.

Whaley, K., & Rubenstein, T. (1994). How toddlers "do" friendship: A descriptive analysis of naturally occurring friendships in a group childcare setting. *Journal of Social and Personal Relationships, 11*, 383–400.

White, B. (1985). *The first three years of life.* Upper Saddle River, NJ: Prentice Hall.

Whitehurst, G. J. (2001, July 26). White House summit: Early childhood cognitive development: Ready to read; ready to learn. (Untitled presentation on pre-reading skills.) Washington, DC.

Whitehurst, G. J., Epstein, A. J., Angell, A., Smith, M., & Fischel, J. (1994). A picture book reading intervention in day care and home for children from low income families. *Developmental Psychology, 30*, 679–689.

Wilson, B. J. (2008). Media and children's aggression, fear, and altruism. *Children and Electronic Media, 18*(1). Retrieved from http://www.princeton.edu/futureofchildren/publications/journals/ article/index.xml?journalid=32&articleid=58&sectionid=275

Winnicott, D. W. (1953). Transitional objects and transitional phenomena. *International Journal of Psycho-Analysis, 34*, 1–9.

Winnicott, D. W. (1971). *Playing and reality.* London, England: Tavistock.

Winnicott, D. W. (1977). *The piggle: An account of the psychoanalytic treatment of a little girl.* New York, NY: International Universities Press.

References

Winter, W. M. (1985). Toddler play behaviors and equipment choices in an outdoor play environment. In J. L. Frost & S. Sunderlin (Eds.), *When children play.* Olney, MD: Association for Childhood Education International.

Wishart, J. G., & Bower, T. G. R. (1985). A longitudinal study of the development of the object concept. *British Journal of Developmental Psychology, 3*, 243–258.

Witt, P. A. (1997). *Evaluation of the impact of three after-school recreation programs sponsored by the Dallas Park and Recreation Department.* Retreived from http://wwwrpts.tamu.edu/rpts/faculty/pubs/wittpub2.htm

Wittmer, D. S., & Petersen, S. H. (2012). *Infant and toddler development and responsive program plannng. A relationship-based approach* (3rd ed.). Upper Saddle River, NJ: Pearson.

Wood, J. T. (1994). *Gendered lives.* Belmont, CA: Wadsworth.

Woodward, A. L., & Guajardo, J. J. (2002). Infants' understanding of the point gesture as an object-directed action. *Cognitive Development, 17*, 1061–1084.

Wright, J. C., Huston, A. C., Ross, R. P., Calvert, S. L., Rolandelli, D., Weeks, L. A., Raeissi, P., & Potts, R. (1984). Pace and continuity of television programs: Effects on children's attentions and comprehension. *Developmental Psychology, 20*, 653–666.

Wynn, K. (1992). Addition and subtraction by human infants. *Nature, 358*, 749–750.

Yager, J. (1995). Clinical manifestations of psychiatric disorders. In H. I. Kaplan & B. J. Sadock (Eds.), *Comprehensive textbook of psychiatry* (Vol. 1, 5th ed., Chapter 10). Baltimore: Williams & Wilkins.

Yarrow, M. R., & Zahn-Waxler, C. Z. (1977). The emergence and functions of prosocial behaviors in young children. In R. C. Smart & M. S. Smart (Eds.), *Readings in child development and relationships* (2nd ed., pp. 77–81). New York, NY: Macmillan.

Yoshida, H. (2008). The cognitive consequences of early bilingualism. *ZERO TO THREE, 29*(2), 26–30.

Yoshinaga-Itano, C. (1999). Benefits of early intervention for infants with hearing loss. *Otolaryngologic Clinics of North America.* Philadelphia: W.B. Saunders Company.

Yoshinaga-Itano, C. (2000). Development of audition and speech: Implications for early intervention with infants who are deaf or hard of hearing. In C. Yoshinaga-Itano & A. L. Sedey (Eds.), *Language, speech and social-emotional development of children who are deaf and hard-of-hearing: The early years, The Volta Review,* 100, 213–234.

Yoshinaga-Itano, C. (2001). *From screening to early identification and intervention: Discovering predictors to successful outcomes for children with significant hearing loss.* Proceedings from the International Congress of the Deaf. Deaf Studies and Deaf Education.

Youngblade, L. M., & Dunn, J. (1995). Individual differences in young children's pretend play with mother and sibling: Links to relationships and understanding of other people's feeling and beliefs. *Child Development, 66*, 1472–1492.

Zahn-Waxler, C., & Radke-Yarrow, M. (1990). The origins of empathic concern. *Motivation and Emotion, 14*, 107–130.

Zakin, A. (2007). Metacognition and the use of inner speech in children's thinking: A tool teachers can use. *Journal of Education and Human Development, 1*(2).

Zeanah, C. H., Jr., Mammen, O. K., & Lieberman, A. F. (1993). Disorders of attachment. In C. H. Zeanah, Jr. (Ed.), *Handbook of infant mental health* (pp. 332–349). New York, NY: Guilford.

Zeanah, C. H., Scheeringa, M., Boris, N., Heller, S., Smyke, A., & Trapani, J. (2004). Reactive attachment disorder in maltreated toddlers. *Child Abuse and Neglect, 28*(8), 877–888.

Zeanah, C. H., & Smyke, A. T. (2008). Attachment disorders and severe deprivation. In M. Rutter, D. Bishop, D. Pine, S. Scott, J. Stevenson, E. Taylor, & A. Thapar (Eds.), *Rutter's child and adolescent psychiatry,* pp. 906–915. London, England: Blackwell.

ZERO TO THREE. (2007). *Early language & literacy.* Retrieved from http://www.zerotothree.org/site/PageServer?pagename=key_language

ZERO TO THREE. (2009). *Data driven.* Informing family choices about infants and toddlers. Retrieved from http://www.zerotothree.org/public-policy/policy-toolkit/datamar5singles.pdf

ZERO TO THREE. (2011). *Early experiences matter. Strong families.* Retrieved from http://www.zerotothree.org/public-policy/policy-toolkit/strong-families-policy-toolkit.html

ZERO TO THREE. (2012). *Early experiences matter. Child care.* Retrieved from http://www.zerotothree .org/early-care-education/child-care/

Ziv, Y., Oppenheim, D., & Sagi-Schwartz, A. (2004). Children's social information processing in middle childhood related to the quality of attachment with mother at 12 months. *Attachment & Human Development, 6*(3), 327–329.

Zhu, Y., Zhang, L., Fan, J., & Han, S. (2007). Neural basis of cultural influence on self-representation. *NeuroImage, 34*(3), 1310–1316.

Zimmerman, F. J. & Bell, J. F. (2010). Associations of television content type and obesity in children. *American Journal of Public Health, 100*(2), 334–340.

Name Index

Subject Index

552

V

W

Z